The Ashdown Diaries

VOLUME I: 1988–1997

A SHOT ACROSS THE BOWS

PADDY ASHDOWN

The Ashdown Diaries

VOLUME I: 1988–1997

ALLEN LANE
THE PENGUIN PRESS

ALLEN LANE
THE PENGUIN PRESS

Published by the Penguin Group
Penguin Books Ltd, 27 Wrights Lane, London w8 5tz, England
Penguin Putnam Inc., 375 Hudson Street, New York, New York 10014, USA
Penguin Books Australia Ltd, Ringwood, Victoria, Australia
Penguin Books Canada Ltd, 10 Alcorn Avenue, Toronto, Ontario, Canada m4v 3b2
Penguin Books India (P) Ltd, 11 Community Centre, Panchsheel Park, New Delhi – 110 017, India
Penguin Books (NZ) Ltd, Private Bag 102902, NSMC, Auckland, New Zealand
Penguin Books (South Africa) (Pty) Ltd, 5 Watkins Street, Denver Ext 4, Johannesburg 2094, South Africa

Penguin Books Ltd, Registered Offices: Harmondsworth, Middlesex, England

First published 2000
1

Set in 10.25/13.75 pt Linotype Sabon
Typeset by Rowland Phototypesetting Ltd, Bury St Edmunds, Suffolk
Printed and bound in Great Britain by Clays Ltd, St Ives plc
Cover repro by Concise Cover Printers

A CIP catalogue record for this book is available from the British Library

ISBN 0-713-99510-6

To our neighbours and friends in Norton-sub-Hamdon in Somerset, Methley Street in London and Irancy in Burgundy, who gave Jane and me the priceless gifts of peace, friendship and privacy over these years.

Contents

List of Illustrations ix
List of Plates xi
Preface xiii
Acknowledgements xvi
Map of the Balkans xix

1988 3
1989 21
1990 75
1991 103
1992 127
1993 213
1994 247
1995 299
1996 377
1997 493

Appendices 563
A Extracts from Position Papers 565
B The Chard Speech 590
C Letter Abandoning Equidistance 595
D Emma Nicholson's Letter to the Prime Minister 598
E The Lib Dems and Partnership Politics 599
F Peter Thurnham's Letter to the Prime Minister 603
G Partnership for Britain's Future (First Draft) 605

H Partnership for Britain's Future (Second Draft) 609
I Memorandum Prepared by Tom McNally 613
J Liberal Democrat Seats after the May 1997 General Election 619

Index 621

List of Illustrations

(Every effort has been made to contact all copyright holders. The publishers will be glad to make good in future editions any errors or omissions brought to their attention.)

Frontispiece. Nick Garland, *Daily Telegraph*, 4 May 1991
p. 14. Les Gibbard, *Guardian*, 29 September 1988
p. 68. Les Gibbard, *Guardian*, 16 September 1989
p. 87. Dave Gaskill, *Today*, 2 May 1990
p. 124. Nick Garland, *Daily Telegraph*, 7 November 1991
p. 154. Les Gibbard, *Guardian*, 3 April 1992
p. 201. Richard Wilson, *The Times*, 4 November 1992
p. 226. Peter Brookes, *The Times*, 8 May 1993
p. 260. Richard Wilson, *The Times*, 12 May 1994
p. 281. Colin Wheeler, *Independent*, 19 September 1994
p. 316. Franjo Tudjman, 6 May 1995
p. 339. Dave Gaskill, *Today*, 20 August 1995
p. 342. Nick Garland, *Daily Telegraph*, 19 September 1995
p. 391. Nick Newman, *Sunday Times*, 2 February 1996
p. 463. Nick Garland, *Daily Telegraph*, 1 October 1996
p. 503. Wally Fawkes, *Daily Telegraph*, 6 January 1997
p. 538. Peter Schrank, *Independent*, 17 March 1997

List of Plates

(Photographic acknowledgements are given in parentheses)

1. Thursday, 28 July 1988, Cowley Street (Press Association/Topham)
2. Thursday, 29 September 1988, Blackpool First Conference (*Guardian*)
3. Monday, 29 August 1988, Irancy
4. Sunday, 18 June 1989, Somerset (Jane Ashdown)
5. Thursday, 4 May 1989, Somerset
6. Monday, 14 September 1992, Harrogate (*Liberal Democrat News*)
7. Thursday, 9 April 1992, Somerset (*Daily Mail*/David Crump)
8. Thursday, 2 April 1992, Sutton (*The Times*)
9. Monday, 10 August 1992, Manjaca, Yugoslavia (Camera Press/Lord Russell-Johnston)
10. Monday, 10 August 1992, Manjaca, Yugoslavia (Camera Press/Lord Russell-Johnston)
11. Saturday, 12 December 1992, to Yugoslavia (Nick South)
12. Sunday, 9 August 1992, Pale, Yugoslavia (Lord Russell-Johnston)
13. Sunday, 13 December 1992, Dinaric Alps, Yugoslavia (Nick South)
14. Sunday, 13 December 1992, Vitez, Yugoslavia (Nick South)
15. Tuesday, 15 December 1992, Sarajevo (Nick South)
16. Tuesday, 15 December 1992, Sarajevo (Nick South)
17. Sunday, 12 December 1993, Sarajevo (Nick South)
18. Tuesday, 19 January 1993, Monktonhall (Paul Reas)
19. Thursday, 11 July 1996, London (Associated Press/Alistair Grant)
20. Tuesday, 21 February 1995, New York (UNN/DPI/E. Schneider)
21. Sunday, 20 August 1995, London VJ Day Parade (Press Association/Neil Munns)
22. Friday, 28 July 1995, Littleborough & Saddleworth (*Independent*/Glynn Griffiths)
23. Saturday, 31 August 1996, Burgundy (Stephanie Bailey)

24. Saturday, 19 April 1997 (*L'Yonne Républicaine*)

25. Thursday, 7 September 1995, Irancy (Jane Ashdown)

26. Saturday, 30 December 1995, London (*Independent*/David Rose)

27. Friday, 19 October 1990, Eastbourne (*Guardian*)

28. Sunday, 17 September 1995, Glasgow (Press Association/Topham/ David Giles)

29. Friday, 12 July 1996, Oxford (*Guardian*)

30. Wednesday, 30 April 1997 (Popperfoto/Reuters/Paul Hackett)

31. Thursday, 1 May 1997, Somerset (Popperfoto/Reuters/Dennis Owen)

32. Friday, 2 May 1997, London (Lord Rennard)

Preface

On the morning of 28 July 1988, the day I was elected Leader of the Liberal Democrats, I was walking through the Members' Lobby of the House of Commons and was stopped by Tam Dalyell. He said, 'Paddy, you will be elected today. Here is a piece of advice. Keep a diary. You will find in a few years' time it will be invaluable to you.' I followed his advice, starting that night, and have continued ever since.

I decided from the beginning that the best way to write a diary was to have someone in mind to whom the entries were addressed. So I dictated these records for the grandchildren I hoped to have and of whom I am now so proud. My intention was to paint a picture for them of what my life had been like over my years in politics. Only near the end of my time as Party Leader did a friend suggest they might also be of wider interest.

One of the things I have since discovered is that people are intensely curious about exactly how diaries are recorded. No doubt everyone does it differently. I dictate my diaries a day at a time. The rule I set myself (sometimes broken, I confess) is to dictate the day's events that evening, or, at worst, on the following day. In some cases, for instance my meetings with John Major and Tony Blair, I dictated immediately after the event. The recordings were then typed up and stored securely in my Yeovil bank. I did not, for obvious reasons, tape the conversations that are recounted here, but I have tried to ensure that the records which I made of them while my memory was still fresh were as faithful and accurate as possible.

Inevitably, diaries recorded in this way, often when I was tired and late at night, do not necessarily emerge as perfect prose. In preparing for publication, I have excised some passages and tidied up others to make them more reader-friendly. But under the stern gaze of my wonderful editor Sally Holloway, the original sense has, I hope, remained unaltered. The original texts, together with my other papers, will be placed in the archive of the London School of Economics.

A further word of warning. I discover from assembling these entries that diaries can be the most seductive form of historical inaccuracy. They appear accurate because they are contemporaneous but, being wholly subjective, they can, in fact, be quite the opposite. What follows, therefore, is *my* view of events – no more and no less. So temper all harsh opinions of others as the judgements of an impatient personality, too easily given to frustration and often too tired to be conscious of being unfair.

As for the substance, I leave that to the reader to judge. Inevitably, however, what has been assembled here is not the humdrum norm, but the highs and lows – with probably more than a fair share of the latter, since they make more interesting reading.

Under the scrutiny of the modern media, with its twenty-four-hour, seven-day-a-week demands, politics is an accelerated life – one which puts great strain on family and friends. This makes it at times exhausting and at others painful. These pages contain plenty of examples of both. But whatever the price one pays for a life in politics, it is small in comparison with the rewards.

I have enjoyed myself enormously. My eleven years as Leader of the Liberal Democrats turn out to have been the thing for which the rest of my life was a preparation.

And they were also great fun.

I have visited places I would never otherwise have seen; been moved by events I would otherwise have observed only from a distance; made many new friends; and been saved from innumerable disasters by the courage, wisdom and loyalty of many old ones. I owe an incalculable debt to them and to the countless ordinary Liberal Democrats whose refusal to give in and determination to win were the real ingredients of our successes.

Life in politics is, by its nature, a jumble of mostly disconnected events – that is one of the things which make it so enjoyable. Nevertheless, there are some strong currents which flow through the years these diaries record: the early struggle for the survival of the Party; the battle to elbow our way back into mainstream politics; the Balkans, which came unbidden into my life and swiftly became almost an obsession; and, in the later years, my partnership with Tony Blair, and our attempt to reshape the centre-left in Britain and make better sense of our politics in the face of its ingrained traditions of tribal warfare – something, I rediscover from these pages, which was a dream almost from the very first day of my Leadership.

This first volume begins with the Liberal Democrats' journey back from oblivion and finishes with the doubling of our number of MPs in the 1997

General Election, the election of Prime Minister Blair and the fateful decision of 2 May 1997 that it would somehow be an affront to the landslide verdict of the British electorate if we went ahead with the coalition Government that he and I had considered for so long. You will see just how close we came to realizing that dream. And perhaps you will think, as I now do, that if we had grasped that moment we would have been able to carry our reluctant parties with us, begin the process of reshaping our politics and give Britain a different kind of Government.

The second volume, which I shall not publish until after the next General Election, covers our attempts to recover the opportunity we lost that day. I remain convinced that this opportunity is still there to be realized – and perhaps will be, after the next election.

Re-reading these pages, I often ask myself if I would have done things differently. Though doubtless I could have done many things more wisely, I think the honest answer to that question is mostly no. Over these years, the Liberal Democrats became the second party of government in Britain at the local level; we elected our first European MEPs; doubled our MPs in Westminster; helped to bring devolved government to Scotland and Wales; participated in the government of Scotland; and can, I think, claim credit for the introduction of Britain's first-ever nationwide election using proportional representation. My only regret is that, ultimately, I failed in my greatest ambition, which was to see the Liberal Democrats participating in the national government of our country.

For the rest, I am happy to leave these pages as a record of the first half of a journey which I am proud to have undertaken, and which, more than anything else I have ever done, has left me with a deep sense of contentment.

Paddy Ashdown
Yeovil
August 2000

Acknowledgements

There are so many people to whom I owe a debt of gratitude for helping me with this book that to name some will be to commit the sin of omitting others. To those I have inadvertently left out, I apologize.

To all included below I owe my thanks for help and advice which, in every case, has improved what would otherwise have been in these pages; but none is responsible for the errors and infelicities, which are all my own.

Cathy Bakewell, Clare Conway, Becks Darling, Lisa Dorse, Sarah Frapple and Becky Vye have all had, over the years, the unenviable task of working with me as my Personal Assistants. Apart from all the other burdens of this job, they also had to cope with my late-night dictation. In this they showed an ability which would make a code breaker envious in the conversion of tired gibberish into the prose I would have wanted to dictate, with the meaning I had originally intended. Pat Gibbs and Sarah have borne most of the endless burden of typing and retyping the manuscript. Sarah and Cathy also had the task of collating the original diaries and keeping them secure in the vaults of Lloyds Bank in Yeovil, whose staff have been, over eleven years, unfailingly helpful and courteous, even though extracting the heavy deposit boxes at short notice and carrying them up from the vaults must have put a severe strain on both their backs and their patience.

I am especially grateful to Julian Astle, who painstakingly accomplished the Herculean task of trimming 800,000 words of confusion down to 300,000 which made some kind of sense; to Ian Patrick, for his careful diligent work in correcting my mistakes, compiling the footnotes and holding the whole operation together; and to Ben Wiseman, for his research skills and uncomplaining assistance.

I inflicted an early version of this text, or extracts from it, on a number of friends, family and colleagues, all of whom gave me invaluable advice and suggestions. These included Max Atkinson, Jane and Simon Ashdown,

Steph Bailey, Martin Bell, Ming and Elspeth Campbell, Alex Carlile, Les Farris, Miranda Green, Richard Holme, Roy Jenkins, Greg and Lesley Jefferies, David Laws, Andrew Phillips, Archy Kirkwood, Alan Leaman, Tom McNally, Mark Payne, Steve Radley, Neil Sherlock, Nick South, Kate and Sebastien Theurel, Paul Tyler and Ian Wright.

I am indebted to Steph Bailey, Russell Johnston, Chris Rennard, Paul Reas and Nick South for the use of their photos and to Debbie Johnson for helping me choose them. I especially thank Gemma Levine for her kind permission to let me use by far the most flattering photo of me ever taken for the front cover. Thanks also to Richard Holme, Tom McNally, Nick Harvey, Archy Kirkwood, Chris Rennard, Emma Nicholson, Peter Thurnham and John Major for their permission to use various letters and memos.

To Chryss and Tony O'Reilly and Tom Flood and his colleagues I owe an invaluable few days of peace at a crucial moment in Castlemartin, Co. Kildare. To my agent Michael Sissons, the confidence and encouragement to start this in the first place. To my publisher Stuart Proffitt, to Dan Hind and the staff at Penguin, the advice and support to carry it through. And to my editor Sally Holloway, who was so completely unreasonable about getting rid of the things I wanted to keep, so annoyingly unyielding about my mistakes, so outrageously demanding about footnotes, so inflexibly uncompromising about the standards she expected me to observe that I almost certainly owe to her the fact that this book was produced at all.

The Balkans

- - - - - Yugoslav provincial boundaries
───── Yugoslav republican boundaries
– – – Frontlines, 1 January 1995

0   100 km

HUNGARY

Sava

■ Zagreb

CROATIA

Sava

Slavonski
Brod

• Prijedor

Banja
Luka   Posavena
Corridor   • Brcko   Belgrade ■

Manjaca •

Sava

BOSNIA–
HERZEGOVINA   • Maglaj

Vlasic Mountain   • Vitez   Srbrenica
Turbe •   • Srbrenica

YUGOSLAVIA

Gornji
Vakuf •   Kisseljak •   Sarajevo ■
Prozor •   Mount Igman   • Pale
          Mount Bjelasnica   Zvornik •

• Tomislavgrad
          • Jablanica   • Gorazde

• Split

ADRIATIC

SEA

MONTENEGRO

ALBANIA

N

Background Note

Having had a highly successful election in 1983, at which they very nearly beat the Labour Party into third place, the Liberal/SDP Alliance fought the 1987 election with high hopes. The result was a disappointment, with the Alliance losing a fifth of its seats. There was an immediate call for a merger of the two parties, led by David Steel and me for the Liberals and Bob Maclennan and Charles Kennedy for the SDP. After an all-member ballot, the new party, the Social and Liberal Democrats, was born. The new party faced grave challenges. A minority of members on both sides refused to accept the merger and subsequently formed breakaway groups, using the old party names, under David Owen (SDP) and Michael Meadcroft (Liberals). The new party's difficulties were compounded by having a period of joint leadership between David Steel and Bob Maclennan and a disastrous policy launch (which became known as the Dead Parrot, after the *Monty Python* sketch). The Social and Liberal Democrats sank disastrously in the polls and became the subject of ridicule. In the subsequent Leadership election, David Steel and Bob Maclennan announced they would not stand. Alan Beith and I fought a campaign over some three months. This ran in parallel with the election for the new party's President. Every Party member had a vote for the new Leader and new President. The count and announcement of results was fixed for 28 July 1988.

1988

Thursday, 28 July, Westminster

I have decided to keep a confidential diary from today, the day I was elected as Leader of the Social and Liberal Democrats.

I went to the count at the Electoral Reform Society in Chancery Street and walked in to find that they had already finished it. Alan Beith[1] and Monro Palmer,[2] his agent, were there. Alan said, 'Welcome to the new Leader.' The result was 72 per cent for me and 28 per cent for Alan.

I took Alan to one side in the rather tumbledown office of the Electoral Reform Society, where we had a good, if much interrupted, conversation. I impressed on him his importance to me and the Party. I told him that I would be delighted if he would put his name forward as Deputy Leader, but would understand if he declined. I suggested that we should save any decision until after we had both had a holiday.

We then returned to the steps at Cowley Street,[3] where I gave my acceptance speech. Alan was gracious in defeat but put down one or two markers which, I confess, worry me: he did not alter his 'values' line from the campaign.[4] Des Wilson[5] refused to attend, which was churlish. I spoke to him on his mobile phone and, while he would not discuss his own position, he said he was delighted about mine.

Immediately after the count, the press conference. It went better than

1 Member of Parliament (Liberal, then Liberal Democrat) for Berwick-upon-Tweed since 1973. My competitor for the Leadership in 1988. Subsequently Alan became Treasury Spokesman, Deputy Leader of the Liberal Democrats and our Home Affairs spokesman.
2 Subsequently our candidate in Hastings & Rye.
3 Party Headquarters. Unbeknownst to me, half an hour before I arrived for the declaration, two men from the Inland Revenue had preceded me to close the place down because of our persistent failure to pay National Insurance contributions for our staff. They were persuaded to come back later and were hurried off the premises before we and the press arrived.
4 During his campaign, Alan had stressed that he would preserve and protect the values of the old Liberal Party (by inference contrasting this with those of the SDP) in the new party.
5 Des Wilson stood in the elections for Party President, held on the same day, which he lost to Ian Wrigglesworth. He went on to run a superb General Election campaign in 1992 for us, although our relationship has often had difficult moments.

I feared, though my nervousness showed in too much aggression with one or two of the journalists, notably Tony Bevins of the *Independent*.

The rest of the day was wall-to-wall interviews. The highlight, the celebration party at Pizza on the Park. We got to bed at about 2.00am and I slept fitfully, too worried about what would happen next.

Saturday, 30 July, Somerset

Up early for a busy constituency surgery at Chard. I am constantly being stopped and congratulated in the street. Many more people now seem to recognize me. I am not sure I welcome this.

Then to Yeovil to present a cheque to a local charity and home to dictate replies to the many thank-you letters, cards and telexes. Alisoun [my sister] called from Australia. She seems delighted. I am still frightened.

Jane has been wonderful, coping with the houseful of friends who are staying with us.

Wednesday, 3 August, London

Saw Charles Kennedy[1] briefly at 11.30, who wanted to know what I had planned for him ('something important', he hoped) and to tell me the importance of Bob Maclennan[2] in the new Parliamentary team.

Jim Wallace[3] at 11.30 to discuss spokesmanships. We drew up an outline plan of our approach and who would fill which posts. Jim is being both supportive and helpful.

---

1 Member of Parliament (SDP then Liberal Democrat) for Ross, Skye & Inverness West since 1983 (formerly Ross, Cromarty & Skye). Charles was successively our spokesman for Trade and Industry, Health and Europe. He was elected Party President in 1990, and succeeded me as Leader of the Liberal Democrats.

2 Robert Maclennan, Member of Parliament (Labour 1966–81, SDP 1981–8, Liberal Democrat since 1988) for Caithness since 1966. Ex-Leader of the SDP. Our Home Affairs, then Constitutional Affairs spokesman. He followed Charles as President of the Party in 1994.

3 Member of Parliament (Liberal then Liberal Democrat) for Orkney & Shetland since 1983. Jim was my first Chief Whip, later became the leader of the Scottish Party and is now Deputy First Minister of Scotland.

At 2 o'clock a meeting with the Party Officers and Executives from the state and regional parties[1] etc., in Cowley Street. I described the position as I saw it – that we were an organizational shambles, financially bankrupt, electorally irrelevant and inherently split between the two old parent parties, the Liberals and the SDP. Our first task was to stabilize and unify the Party internally – only then could we begin to make ourselves relevant again.

At 6.30 a meeting with Tessa Blackstone[2] and John Eatwell[3] to discuss, entirely off the record, the formation of the Labour Party's 'think tank'. We have a number of options if, as I hope, we establish a think tank as well. The first is organic merger with Labour, the second is for us to commission work from the IPPR (they claim to be independent) and the third is to set up a parallel organization with good operational liaison. The third option seems best. My own view is that any kind of formal relationship with Labour before the next election is unthinkable. But there could be a real chance for realignment if the conservatives win for a fourth time. We could pave the way by drawing together various opposition MPs around a set of ideas, rather than a formal relationship. Tessa Blackstone's mind seems to be going along the same lines.

Monday, 29 August, Somerset and London

[*Having spent a glorious and much-needed two weeks at a semi-derelict cottage in Irancy, northern Burgundy, which we have bought with our friends Greg and Lesley Jefferies, it was back to the business of being Party Leader again.*]

1 The Liberal Democrats are organized on a federal basis with separate parties in Scotland and Wales, and 12 regional parties in each of the regions of Britain. Each of these has an elected Regional Chairman.
2 At the time an academic involved in the newly formed Labour think tank, the Institute for Public Policy Research (IPPR). Later a Labour peer and a Government Minister in the Lords for Education.
3 John Eatwell worked with Tessa Blackstone on the IPPR. He also became a Labour peer. He was one of Neil Kinnock's advisers until he entered the Lords.

A run in the morning and then up to London with Jane and [our son] Simon. We spent two hours in the evening arranging my new office (complete with Asquith's desk!).

Tuesday, 6 September, Westminster

At 4 o'clock a meeting in Cowley Street about the Party's finances. We are in a desperate situation. A potential deficit of a quarter of a million and an immediate cash-flow problem which means that we cannot pay any bills except for salaries, and even those are precarious. We agreed to tackle this straight after the Party Conference. Far too much is riding on the Conference being a success.

At 6 o'clock a meeting with the Policy Committee. I am worried about Edmund Dell,[1] who seems on the verge of resigning. We got through a good deal of business, but not with the despatch that I had hoped. Chairing this Committee is going to be a major task. I am certain that my decision to do so is right, however – tight control of policy will be essential for our recovery. But I will need a good Vice-Chairman.

Monday, 19 September, London and Watford

Interviewing all morning for the Chief Executive's post. Finished by 1.00, then a *World At One* interview, commenting on the speech by David Owen[2] at the rump SDP Conference. This went quite well, though I am worried about sounding too aggressive. Owen seems to be having a depressingly good Conference.

Then a train to Watford Junction to film the Party Political Broadcast. We seem to get through it remarkably quickly. I am not sure that the format will work.

Then back for an hour or so's work and some more interviews

1 Edmund Dell (1921–99), Member of Parliament (Labour) for Birkenhead 1964–79. Former member of the Labour Cabinet, founding member of the SDP and distinguished author.
2 Member of Parliament (Labour 1966–81, SDP 1981–92) for Plymouth Sutton 1966–74, Plymouth Devonport 1974–92. He was the Leader of the SDP from 1983 until its break-up.

between 5.00 and 6.00 and out to dinner with Harriett Smith,[1] Tom McNally,[2] William Wallace[3] and Juliet Hutchinson.[4] We discussed the speech and press lines for the Conference at some length. I also had a very difficult conversation with Alan Beith, who seems in an unhelpful mood. He refuses to talk about how we might resolve the problem of his potential spokesmanship, but wants to spend the time crawling over the past. We may have to do without him in the end, but I will try a little more patience. I offered him Defence but he expressed an interest in Treasury and will let me know tomorrow night. Meanwhile, Ming Campbell[5] (bless him) has indicated that if getting Alan on board means offering him Treasury, he would be prepared to stand down. If only all my colleagues were so good!

Back home to complete the mail and bed at about midnight.

Tuesday, 20 September, London and Somerset

A working breakfast with Tom McNally, Ian Wrigglesworth[6] and Harriett to discuss the forthcoming Conference – press lines, management of debates, etc. Then interviews throughout the morning for the Policy job in my office. I decided to give this to Alan Leaman.[7]

1 Harriett Smith had handled the press operation in my Leadership campaign.

2 Friend and adviser. I had first met him in 1974 at the Cyprus Peace Conference in Geneva when he was PPS to Jim Callaghan (then Foreign Secretary) and I was a First Secretary to the UK Mission there. Member of Parliament (Labour 1979–81, SDP 1981–3) for Stockport South 1979–83. A founder member of the SDP, and in 1995 made a Liberal Democrat peer.

3 A close adviser and an expert on foreign affairs and Europe. For many years he was a Director at the Royal Institute for International Affairs. He now sits in the House of Lords and is a Professor at the LSE.

4 Juliet Hutchinson worked briefly in my office and later married Tom McNally.

5 Menzies 'Ming' Campbell CBE QC has been my close friend and adviser ever since he entered Parliament. Member of Parliament (Liberal, then Liberal Democrat) for North East Fife since 1987. Party spokesman for Defence and Foreign Affairs. I had previously suggested he should take the Treasury spokesmanship.

6 Member of Parliament (Labour Co-op 1974–81, SDP 1981–7) for Thornaby Teeside 1974–83, Stockton South 1983–7. Founding member of the SDP. Elected the first President of the Liberal Democrats on the same day I was elected Leader. He was a rock in the difficult early days of the Party and remains a close friend.

7 A close friend and adviser over many years who ran my Westminster Office for the first five years of my Leadership. Later became the Party's Director of Planning and Strategy. Awarded OBE.

Caught the 3.10 train back to Yeovil. A meeting with Chard Town Council in the evening, and an interview for *Newsnight*. The pace of life is beginning to quicken.

I am still concerned that Owen has had far too good a Conference and that the SDP are in reasonable heart. I await the first opinion polls with trepidation.

Before leaving London I had a session with David Alton.[1] I tried to be as gentle as possible. I am very worried that he will, if pushed, join the Owenites. Indeed, he hinted as much. He is insisting on inviting John Cartwright[2] to our Conference, which is an extremely unhelpful thing to do. I sense something of a wish for martyrdom and told him that he would have an uncomfortable Conference. He seems to be resigned to this, even to welcome it. My concern is to keep open some kind of a life-line to him.

At home for the *Newsnight* interview, and to meet John Carvel,[3] who stayed overnight and is writing a piece for the *Guardian*.

Rang Ming in the evening, anticipating that Alan Beith would choose the Treasury spokesmanship. Ming has agreed to accept Defence, if necessary.

No more than an hour later I heard from Jim Wallace that Alan had rung to say he does indeed want the Treasury spokesmanship. Glad I prepared the ground. I passed the word back that I agreed.

Wednesday, 21 September, London

I tried to spend all day working on my Conference speech. But the morning was taken up by

1. a photo session with *The Times*,

2. an extended piece for *Newsnight*, and

3. further discussions with John Carvel and others.

---

1 Member of Parliament (Liberal then Liberal Democrat) for Liverpool Edge Hill 1978–83, Liverpool Mossley Hill 1983–97. Now sits in the House of Lords. David and I often had differences of opinion.

2 Member of Parliament (Labour 1974–81, SDP 1981–90, Social Democrat 1990–92) for Greenwich and Woolwich East 1974–83, Woolwich 1983–92. John was the President of the continuing SDP, but left national politics after they disbanded.

3 Political Correspondent for the *Guardian*. Carvel went on to hold other positions at the *Guardian* and is currently the Education Editor.

The speech is proving difficult and muddled. It will take a lot of work. In the evening a visit to the Diabetic Society, then phone conversations with Jim Wallace. Bob Maclennan has agreed to serve (hooray!). The full team of spokesmen is now assembled.

Friday, 23 September, Yeovil, London and Blackpool

Up on the 6.36 (15 minutes late) to London. I had a prickly half hour with Alan Beith in the office. He is not going to make life easy, but at least he is on board.

We left at around 1.30 for Blackpool. The M1 was very crowded and it took us a full six hours to get there. I immediately had a sauna and did some exercises, which made me feel much better. People seem in a reasonable mood – though everyone very nervous about the name debate.[1]

Saturday, 24 September, Blackpool

A photo call early in the morning, then the *Today* programme. Various interviews throughout the day. I practised my speech for the evening with Max[2] and Liz[3] (both immensely helpful).

A brief meeting with the Federal Executive,[4] where I took a strong line on the name and made myself, I think, rather unpopular. I told them that

1 The party had been formed under the title 'The Social and Liberal Democrats'. This immediately proved too much of a mouthful and was quickly shortened by the Press to SLD, or, more usually and disdainfully, 'The SLIDS' or 'The Salads'. We all agreed we needed a single, short name. I had a very clear idea that I wanted the Party to be different from both the old Liberals and the SDP and proposed 'The Democrats'. But I underestimated people's sense of insecurity about losing their old parties, and especially the importance of the 'Liberal' name and tradition. This debate, which on the surface was about the name, was, in reality, about our identity and both dominated and disrupted the first year of the new Party.
2 Max Atkinson, one of my oldest friends. Author of the ground-breaking work on political speeches *Our Masters Voices* and probably Britain's foremost authority on speech techniques. The Atkinsons and the Ashdowns go skiing every year. Max had been an adviser since before I became Leader.
3 Liz Lynne, who helped me with speech-writing. Later elected Member of Parliament for Rochdale 1992–7 and our spokeswoman for Health, then Social Security. Now sits as a Liberal Democrat in the European Parliament.
4 The Federal Executive, or FE, is an elected body responsible for the day-to-day running of the national Party.

they had to take a decision (many were in favour of saying nothing) and also why I thought we ought to be called the Democrats. I think I shocked some of my supporters, including TCJ[1] and co.

Then a splendid fringe meeting with Jo Grimond[2] on the new agenda. Jo was in terrific form. After this dinner with Jane, Jo and others. Then a speech at the Agents and Organizers' Dinner. They seemed to react to a fairly tough message very well.

Finally, a meeting with Tom McNally, Richard Holme[3] and Harriett to discuss the following day's speech.

I announced my spokesmanship team today. The press conference went well enough.

Sunday, 25 September, Blackpool

EVE OF THE PARTY CONFERENCE

TV AM with David Frost, immediately followed by *The World This Weekend* with Gordon Clough. It's blowing a gale now . . .

At 4 o'clock we had the opening Party press conference, then on to my first major speech at a rally in the Empress Ballroom. David Steel[4] made a very fine speech. Altogether a good rally with spirits high and people lifted. I fear the name debate tomorrow will cause a different kind of reaction. I felt nervous about my speech and was, I think, rather stilted. But the reception was warm and I got a loyal standing ovation.

---

1 Tim Clement-Jones, a close friend and adviser. Tim ran my Leadership campaign and the 1994 European Elections campaign. He went on to be the Deputy Chairman of the 1997 General Election campaign. He took his seat in the House of Lords in 1998.

2 Lord Grimond (1913–93) was a previous Leader of the Liberal Party, and the person who had brought me to liberalism. I regarded him as my model for Leader of the Party. Member of Parliament (Liberal) for Orkney and Shetland 1950–83.

3 One of my closest friends and advisers, previously adviser to David Steel. Richard was subsequently made a peer and ran the very successful 1997 General Election campaign.

4 Leader of the Liberal Party until 1988. Member of Parliament (Liberal then Liberal Democrat) Tweeddale, Etterick and Lauderdale until 1997. David continued to have a keen interest in foreign affairs, being our senior spokesman and then becoming President of Liberal International. David is now the Presiding Officer of the Scottish Parliament. Later to become Sir David, then Lord Steel, he is currently Presiding Officer (Speaker) of the Scottish Parliament.

At 11.15 the Parliamentary Party Meeting.[1] Tempers frayed and everyone in a foul mood. Especially Alan Beith, who never stopped making sharp comments whenever he got the opportunity. I persuaded the MPs that, whatever the outcome of the name debate, they should refrain from saying anything about their future intentions until after the PPM tomorrow evening.

Monday, 26 September, Blackpool

FIRST DAY OF THE PARTY CONFERENCE

Breakfast, then a number of interviews and the start of the Conference proper. The debate on the name was tense and difficult. The speeches were extremely good, with Shirley[2] making a two-minute intervention which swung the day. I was surprised when 'The Democrats' won by a clear margin – 650 to 500. But people remain very cross. Nevertheless my Parliamentary colleagues have stuck to the agreement of the previous night to keep silent until after this evening's PPM.

The PPM itself, at 11.15, was tense, but we reached an agreement after some arm twisting. The worst aspect was the press outside, who simply refused to believe that we would not break up over the issue – largely because that's what some colleagues had threatened earlier. More trouble to come on this.

Thursday, 29 September, Blackpool

THE DAY OF MY FIRST LEADER'S SPEECH

TV AM, the *Today* programme and then most of the morning working on the speech. I was extremely nervous. But I like the Autocue. It gives me much more freedom.

I was surprised at how well the speech [very strong on environmentalism] was received. A five-and-a-half-minute standing ovation, then a myriad of

---

1 The Parliamentary Party Meeting, or PPM, is a meeting of all Liberal Democrat MPs – usually held weekly on Wednesdays, but held daily at Party Conference.
2 Shirley Williams. Ex-Labour Member of Parliament for Hitchin, then SDP MP for Crosby. Shirley held various positions within the Labour Government and was one of the founding members of the SDP and a member of the Gang of Four. She later became a peer and is now Deputy Leader of the Liberal Democrats in the House of Lords.

interviews. Morale has been lifted and I hear that a number of people who were intending to leave will now stay on.

At 6.10 a thirty-minute television interview on *Conference Day*, then on to *Question Time* and finally *Newsnight*. I was shattered by the end of it. However, the interviews over, I joined the Glee Club,[1] where spirits were very high. Altogether it's been a successful Conference.

Wednesday, 12 October, London

Up to London on the 6.35am. At least it arrived on time. A full day's meetings, starting with discussions on the press and the forthcoming Party Political Broadcast.

Then at 11.30am our meeting in Cowley Street. Some very tough decisions to take on what looks like a £500,000 deficit at the end of 1989. We will be technically bankrupt by November. We have had to put together an emergency package to give us cover by borrowing against Party buildings and to wrestle

1 The traditional end-of-Conference sing-song.

through a rearrangement of our staff. This will result in six redundancies.

I warned that we could not get through this crisis without some heads rolling at the top, 'including some of those who sit in this room'. This produced a shocked silence. However, it is important that people realize that the buck stops with them. We cannot dodge our responsibilities.

I also said we should restructure at Cowley Street but retain our campaigning strength in the country. There is a long way to go before we are out of the woods on this.

Tuesday, 18 October, London

Into the office very early for a meeting with Party Officers on the financial situation, which shows no signs of improvement. Then over to Cowley Street for the dreaded meeting with the staff. They were furious and not prepared to listen. We must establish better communications with them. At present we only speak to the staff to tell them they are going to be sacked. This has created an atmosphere of deep mistrust between Party Officers and staff.

Then an equally difficult meeting with the Chairs of the Regional Parties. They, however, understood the importance of the action we were taking. We are caught between two extremes, with the staff saying we are being too pessimistic about our budget and could afford to keep more people on, whilst the Chairs insist that we were far too optimistic and ought to be getting rid of more. Probably got it about right, then. Altogether a very demanding two and a half hours.

Back to the office and a student magazine interview. Then, at 4 o'clock, an interview with the *Belfast Telegraph* and at 5 o'clock three-quarters of an hour with Alan Leaman over a glass of whisky. Only then did I get down to trying to deal with the day's mail.

I had to get a takeaway curry, which I ate at Methley Street[1] (Simon had friends in). I ended the day extremely tired and rather dispirited. It seems there is no end to the bottomless pit of crises we are facing. Perhaps tomorrow things will look better.

At 11.30 I was woken to be told that the Government would be making a statement banning Sinn Fein from access to the BBC. Running largely on instinct, I said we were opposed.

1 Our London flat.

Wednesday, 9 November, Westminster

At 12.40 to lunch at 10 Downing Street with the Prime Minister, in honour of the President of Senegal. About 100 people. Mrs Thatcher was rather engaging, though she has a very odd handshake. She grabs your hand and then passes you across her body and on to the next person, as if to get rid of you as quickly as possible. Very off-putting.

I thought Downing Street rather tatty. Jane remarked on the dead chrysanthemums and I noticed the worn carpets and 1960s style convector heaters in the corners of the rooms.

At 7.15 straight on to the Federal Executive. A long, tricky and tiring meeting which will, I hope, put the final full stop to the whole financial crisis (it needs to – it has taken up far, far too much of my time and energy).[1]

Then home to bed at 3.30. Things are still getting worse.

Thursday, 10 November, London and Oxford

Into the office early. At 10.00 I met with Lords Bonham-Carter[2] and Harris[3] to discuss Northern Ireland. We seemed to agree on most key

1 This was, however, far from the end of our financial problems. Over the course of the next few months, the crisis deepened. I eventually decided that we had to cut very severely in order to prevent us going under completely and to preserve a basic structure we could sustain. This meant sacking our entire staff of agents in the field and losing our Chief Executive. I had to move Archy Kirkwood (Liberal Democrat MP for Roxburgh and Berwickshire and a key and constant supporter) in to run Cowley Street until our affairs stabilized. We were forced to take out further overdrafts from the bank, secured with commitments from senior members of the Party against their personal finances. It was as a result of this very painful experience that I decided that we couldn't continue, as we had for so many years, getting ourselves hopelessly into debt at elections and then sacking our hard-working and dedicated staff afterwards. I was determined to fund the Party on a proper basis; to insist on fighting future elections within our means, and to create a framework of stability which would enable us to build up a core of professional career staff to serve the Party.

2 Mark Bonham-Carter (1922–94). A Liberal peer and Asquith's grandson. Member of Parliament (Liberal) for Torrington (1958–9). First Chairman of the Race Relations Board.

3 John Harris, Lord Harris of Greenwich. Peer (Labour then Liberal Democrat) 1974. John was Roy Jenkins' special assistant whilst a Labour Cabinet Minister. A founding member of the SDP, he is our current Chief Whip in the Lords.

items, including the need to support Tom King[1] (with reservations).

A fast dash to Oxford. We arrived at 6.25 and had to go through a group of left-wingers and students demonstrating against cuts in the NHS. Since I was speaking in favour of the NHS in the forthcoming debate [at the Oxford Union], I was rather surprised to have eggs and tomatoes thrown at me as well. I cannot imagine why I should be a target, I expect they got fed up waiting for Kenneth Clarke[2] and decided to throw things at me on general principle.

It was a very long debate in a very hot room. I had not prepared much of a speech, scribbling it as I waited to speak. It seemed to be a success, however, and I was cheered at the end.

To the bar for a drink and back to London around 3.00am.

Sunday, 13 November, London

REMEMBRANCE SUNDAY

Up at 8 o'clock to prepare for the Cenotaph. Jane and I walked through the crowds in Parliament Square and into the Foreign Office buildings. A magnificent cloudless day.

The Cenotaph party included the entire Cabinet, sundry prelates, senior Service Chiefs, a Chief Constable or two, other notables of state, Kinnock[3] and myself. We all met for a cup of coffee in a crowded room while Jane went off to observe the ceremony from a balcony near by. Owen gave me a rather cold look and went off to talk to people he clearly thought were more important. I had an engaging chat with Kinnock, however. He is an ebullient fellow but I find him curiously unimpressive. Difficult to imagine him as a future Prime Minister.

I also spoke to a tall lady with a clerical collar. She turned out to be last year's President of the Methodist Church and asked me, 'In what capacity

1 Member of Parliament (Conservative) for Bridgwater since 1970. Member of the Conservative Government notably, at this point, Secretary of State for Northern Ireland, and later for Defence.

2 Member of Parliament (Conservative) for Rushcliffe since 1970. Senior member of the Conservative Cabinet, most notably Chancellor of the Exchequer, but at this point Secretary of State for Health.

3 Neil Kinnock, at the time Leader of the Labour Party. Member of Parliament (Labour) Bedwellty 1970–83, Islwyn 1983–95. A European Commissioner since 1995 and now a Vice-President of the European Commission.

are you attending the Cenotaph?' She was deeply embarrassed when I gave her the answer. I felt for her. It wasn't an unreasonable question.

Maggie fussed around, bossing us all into two lines and telling us where to stand. She then proceeded to go down the lined-up Cabinet like a sergeant-major inspecting new recruits, adjusting the Foreign Secretary's tie, flicking specks of dust off the Chancellor's coat, etc.

Then we marched down the highly polished Foreign Office corridors towards the front door. I was presented with our wreath and walked out with Neil Kinnock on to the sunlit parade behind Maggie. I kept on worrying during the two minutes' silence whether I would trip over my shoe laces as I put down my wreath on the Cenotaph steps, but it all went off without mishap.

We then went back inside and were received by the Queen. This was a very informal and rather jolly occasion. Prince Philip said that my training on the parade ground had clearly not left me. Prince Charles and I talked about the environment. I thought Diana looked rather less pretty than she is supposed to be and the Queen looked tired. Then upstairs to a reception at which a good deal of gin was drunk on the Foreign Office expense account. Jane turned up, having spent her time on the balcony making friends with Mary Wilson and Audrey Callaghan. It turns out that Mary Wilson is an old girl of Jane's former school.

Thursday, 17 November, London

A meeting with Tim Razzall[1] at 10 o'clock to discuss fund raising for the Richmond by-election.[2] I am determined that we should really make an effort. I also spoke to Jim Wallace about the possibility of adopting a more aggressive stance in the House of Commons. We agreed that he should get together a small 'War Committee' consisting of George Cunningham,[3] John Roper[4] and himself to plan more disruptive tactics in the House.

1 Party Treasurer throughout the years of my Leadership and close friend and adviser. Created Liberal Democrat peer 1997.
2 Called because sitting MP Leon Brittan had become a European Commissioner in Brussels.
3 Member of Parliament (Labour 1970–81, Independent 1981–2, SDP 1982–3) for Islington South (and Finsbury). Founding member of the SDP.
4 Member of Parliament (Labour 1970–81, SDP 1981–3) for Farnworth. Founding member of the SDP.

At 12.30 lunch with Lord Gladwyn.[1] He is a remarkable old man but, though still very lucid on paper, his speech is now not always intelligible. I picked up about one word in fifteen, which made lunch rather difficult. I ended up nodding sagely and eating as fast as I could so that I could get away. On the basis of our discussion I dictated a note to Ming Campbell about the need to speed up our review of defence policy.

This evening Jane and I were invited to my first event as a Party Leader, to Buckingham Palace. Jane asked me why we had to go. I said I supposed there were certain events which we would now have to attend as representatives of the British body politic – our role was just to be there. We were part of 'the wallpaper of State'. Tonight's event was the annual Diplomatic Reception for all foreign Ambassadors and their senior Embassy staff at Buckingham Palace.

Jane immediately saw this as an opportunity for a new dress. But I despaired about where I could get the white tie and tails I apparently have to wear. Myles Raikes[2] came to my rescue, offering to lend me his. I tried on the jacket and trousers back in Yeovil and they seemed to fit, so I took them up to London for the occasion. Just before we were due to leave for Buckingham Palace, with Jane looking a million dollars in her new dress and the taxi ticking over outside, I got to the stage in dressing where I had to put on the waistcoat which Myles had lent me as part of his outfit. To my horror, I discovered that, though Myles's trousers and jacket fitted me perfectly, my body is much longer than his with the result that his waistcoat ended halfway up my stomach.

This threw me into a complete panic. But Jane, cool as a cucumber and in full regalia, got up on one of our kitchen chairs, cut the waistcoat halter at the back of my neck, fetched a ball of green gardening string out of a kitchen drawer and lowered the waistcoat on two bits of twine to its proper level, instructing me to move very carefully during the evening if I didn't want disaster.

And so to Buckingham Palace.

It turned out to be an amazing affair. About 600 present and full of the most extraordinary pomp. Buckingham Palace inside is ludicrously ornate, but with some wonderful pictures, and tonight the place was stuffed full

---

1 Hubert Gladwyn (1900–96). Secretary-General of the United Nations, February 1946. Permanent Representative of the UK to the United Nations 1950–54. Ambassador to France 1954–60. Liberal peer 1960. Member of the European Parliament (Liberal) 1973–6.
2 Canon Myles Raikes, then Chair of the Yeovil Constituency Party.

of strange people in strange garb – none stranger than the Gentlemen at Arms, who, dressed in Ruritanian uniforms of red with lashings of gold braid, have to wear half a dead chicken on their heads and, apparently, to walk backwards in front of the Queen at all times.

I enjoyed myself making gentle fun of it all to a Lady-in-Waiting – Susan Hussey, the wife of Marmaduke Hussey,[1] who turned out to have gone to school with Jane, too. (Is there nowhere I am safe from these people?) I spoke Chinese to the Chinese and about Royal Marines to a few Royal Marines present.

We left at around midnight through the porch at the Grand Entrance of Buckingham Palace, to which were being called Ambassadors' cars and important people's chauffeur-driven limousines. I asked how I called for a taxi, to be firmly informed by the staff that no such conveyance had ever entered the Palace grounds, and certainly not on the night of the Diplomatic Reception. So Jane and I, in full tails and evening dress, walked resolutely through the Courtyard and out of the iron gates, to the considerable amusement of the policemen on duty. We headed towards Victoria Station, where I knew we could get a taxi. Most passers-by ignored us, but some revellers cheered ironically.

We joined the taxi queue at Victoria, where we swiftly became the object of attention of a group of well-oiled Scottish rugby-supporters. 'I know you,' said one. 'You're that snooker player, Steve Davis.' Another disagreed. 'No you're not. You're the Leader of that political party no one knows the name of.'

Home at about 12.30. Altogether an amusing evening, provided one was an observer, not a participant. But not something I shall be keen to repeat in a hurry.

Wednesday, 21 December, Somerset

Horrific news of an air crash in Scotland. A Boeing 747 seems to have fallen out of the air. Sounds like a bomb. All lives lost on the plane and it seems certain many will have been lost on the ground as well, a village called Lockerbie. I rang the House and fixed that David Steel should make the statement tomorrow. It would have been better if I had been in London.

---

1 Chairman of the Board of Governors of the BBC.

1989

Wednesday, 11 January, London

Despite our success at Epping[1] and my hopes that we would finally establish ourselves as a credible party and dissuade the Doctor, we are still getting a pretty miserable reception. When we will break out of this? It looks as though the next couple of months will require my full reserves of willpower and energy to get people going.

The Richmond by-election seems to be going quite well. But Andy Ellis's[2] private opinion is that we are unlikely to win.

At the 5.30 Parliamentary Party Meeting we chiefly discussed relations with Labour. I am under a good deal of pressure from editorials in the *Guardian* and elsewhere to make some kind of a response to the various overtures from Labour.[3] But it simply doesn't make sense yet. Simon Hughes,[4] it turns out, has been approached by no fewer than six Labour spokesmen to discuss pacts and there are indications that Kinnock is passing a message, through him to me, that he would like to meet for further discussions. I told my colleagues I would take a slightly softer line on joint discussions on ideas, but we all agreed to hold hard to the 'no pacts' line and review the situation after Richmond.

Rather depressed today. I seem to be going round in circles.

Friday, 13 January, Norwich

Depart from Liverpool Street at 9.30 for campaigning in Norwich. An excellent programme of events which included interviews with every local newspaper and television service as well as local radio. I went over the top on the polluted water in the Anglian area and will doubtless get some

1 The Epping by-election was held on 15 December 1988: Conservative 13,183; Lib Dem 8,679; Labour 6,261.
2 Andy Ellis was the Secretary General of the Liberal Party and the Chief Executive of the new Party after merger.
3 Editorials were discussing the possibility of a pact between us and the Labour Party.
4 Member of Parliament (Liberal then Liberal Democrat) for Southwark and Bermondsey since 1982. Simon has held many senior positions within the Parliamentary Party.

reactions from the water companies on this. But I will, at least, have established our lead on the green agenda.

Then *Cross Questions*, a sort of regional *Question Time* on Anglia TV. I was on with Tony Newton[1] and Michael Meacher.[2]

Back to London in an Anglia TV car (a huge BMW) with Mark Payne[3] and Michael Meacher. Meacher was extraordinarily frank about just how demoralized they are in the highest reaches of the Labour Party. He admitted that they could not win the next election, that Kinnock was considered useless and that they were all in the depths of despair.

Wednesday, 1 February, London and Richmond

A Parliamentary Party meeting at 5.00pm. Alan Beith is still in a very destructive mood and sees everything as a conspiracy. More problems to come from him, I fear. However, we got through the meeting quickly, ending by 7.00.

Then a dash to King's Cross for the 8 o'clock train to Richmond. I arrived at 10.00 for a council of war in the car with Paul Jacobs[4] and Barbara Pearce.[5] They seem optimistic. I am nervous, however, about the effect of the Owenite campaign on the national press. Much will depend on our ability to establish ourselves in second position as early as possible. Stayed the night in Richmond with some Party members, who were extraordinarily hospitable.

I am getting over-tired and my future programme does not look any easier. The writ for the Richmond by-election was formally moved today, together with that for Pontypridd. Polling day for both is 23 February. This is the crucial day which will mark whether we are on the way up and the Owenites on the way out or vice versa.

1 Tony Newton was soon to become the Secretary of State for Social Security. Member of Parliament (Conservative) for Braintree 1974–97. After serving as the Leader of the House of Commons in the 1992 Parliament, he moved to the House of Lords.

2 At the time, Opposition spokesman for Employment. Member of Parliament (Labour) for Oldham West since 1970. He is now a member of the Labour Government.

3 Mark Payne OBE was a close adviser during the Leadership contest and ran my office until the 1992 General Election. He organized my tour schedule for both the 1992 and 1997 elections and accompanied me throughout these two campaigns.

4 Our Party Agent for the Richmond by-election.

5 Our candidate in Richmond.

Tuesday, 7 February, London and Richmond

A bright sunny day. Up early again for breakfast with Des Wilson in the Horseguards Hotel. Des was in rather good form. I expected a whole breakfast moaning. I explained to him my plans for the General Election (that we should set up an immediate sub-committee, consisting of himself, Alec McGivan,[1] Tim Clement-Jones and Tom McNally). He was quite vitriolic about Ian Wrigglesworth, whom he regards as hopeless and inefficient. But Des always has to have it in for somebody.

Mark drove me to the Cabinet Office, where we rehearsed the procedure for being sworn in to the Privy Council.[2] A performance straight out of Gilbert and Sullivan! The Privy Council Secretary is a very pleasant but rather pompous man who made us rehearse the routine beforehand in minute detail. I found it faintly irksome. I was to be sworn in with Ian Stewart,[3] Peter Frazer (the new Lord Advocate for Scotland) and Lord Trefgarne.[4]

Straight to the inner courtyard of Buckingham Palace, then into the main reception room, where we joined John Wakeham,[5] Ken Clarke and Norman Lamont.[6] The Queen was delayed with an ambassador, so we spent twenty minutes or so chatting in the sunshine.

Ken Clarke told me, in a rather sorry way, that he felt that the whole effect of the National Health Service review (which is keeping him very busy at the moment) would not be felt until about April 1991. Just nicely

1 National Organizer of the SDP before the merger, and key adviser to David Steel in the formation of the new Party. He now works in public relations and headed Britain's bid for the 2006 World Cup.

2 There are about three hundred Privy Councillors. The Privy Council is made up of senior politicians, senior members of the judiciary and senior members of the Royal Household. Cabinet members and senior members of the opposition parties are normally made Privy Councillors when assuming their positions.

3 Minister of State in the Northern Ireland Office. Member of Parliament (Conservative) for Hitchin, 1974–83, North Hertfordshire 1983–92. He now sits in the House of Lords.

4 Minister of State at the Ministry of Defence. Went on to hold various other positions in the Conservative Government.

5 Lord President of the Council. Member of Parliament (Conservative) for Maldon 1974–92. Later went on to lead the House of Lords.

6 At the time Norman was Chief Secretary to the Treasury, later to become the Chancellor of the Exchequer. MP (Conservative) Kingston-upon-Thames, 1972–97. He now sits in the House of Lords.

placed to help us (the Opposition) with the General Election, I said. He pulled a long face and agreed that this was probably so.

We were then called in to see the Queen. The routine is as follows:

We all gather outside one of the reception rooms on the ground floor. A bell is then rung for the start of the Privy Council meeting and the great mirrored doors open. Present Privy Council members go in first. Then those to be sworn in.

We bow, shake hands with the Queen and move in line to the right of the established Privy Council members. The President of the Council then reads out the business for the Privy Council, which includes our swearing in. We then move forward and kneel (on the right knee, we were firmly instructed) on funny little red footstools in front of the Queen (who now reminded me of an impatient housewife in a shopping queue, sort of hopping from one foot to the other). A gilt table stands near by.

The oath of loyalty is read out and we hold up a Bible in our right hands. (I felt, frankly, rather silly.)

After this, and with no further words, we move forward in turn to another red stool in front of the Queen. We then kiss her hand (unlike other people, Privy Councillors are actually allowed to touch her hand with their lips – a detail which was carefully explained to us beforehand). Then back to the line that we started from and the Privy Councillors' oath is read out (long one, this) with us holding our Bibles,[1] silent throughout, except at the end when we say 'I do'. Like getting married.

John Wakeham then ran through a series of Bills etc, after each of which the Queen said 'Approved' or 'Defer'. The whole thing took about ten minutes, after which Wakeham said, 'That ends the business of the Privy Council, Ma'am.'

At this, the Queen put down her pen and came forward and we all had an engaging little chat. She talked about murders in Jamaica (she had to approve a court sentence there), insider trading – 'Isn't the Privy Council dealing with very modern things these days?' – etc. Then out into the sunshine again and back to reality . . .

After a couple of meetings, the evening train to Richmond. I found our Richmond team rather depressed. The SDP have done a very good job getting posters up on farm fields. After the adoption meeting for Barbara Pearce, dinner with them all.

---

1 On election to the Privy Council, each Privy Councillor is given a personal copy of the New Testament, suitably inscribed.

Thursday, 23 February, London

DAY OF THE RICHMOND AND PONTYPRIDD BY-ELECTIONS

Into the office by 8.15. A Leader's Briefing Meeting in which we discussed the Conference in some detail. Then a meeting with Roy Jenkins,[1] David Steel and Richard Holme to discuss the arrangements for the post-Richmond by-election press conference tomorrow. Our general strategy will be (a) to make sure the Party appears united behind me, and (b) to make Owen look the intransigent one, rather than us.

We also decided to draft a letter along these lines in Matthew Taylor's[2] name, co-signed by Charles Kennedy, Shirley Williams and many others for publication in tomorrow's *Independent*.

Before Prime Minister's Questions I sat down alongside Alan Beith, who had been taking Treasury Questions. He immediately told me that he had seen Matthew Taylor's letter and that if it was published he would break the rule of silence and make it clear that he disagreed with the general strategy. He doesn't seem to realize he will be eaten alive by the Party for this.

I had a meeting with David Steel afterwards and we agreed to beard Alan in my office. He came along at 4.15 and was deeply ambivalent. He refused to identify exactly what he believed. I had already had sight of a letter he had written to the *Guardian* complaining bitterly about the name issue. Apparently he said to Jim Wallace that his situation is untenable and he will resign the Whip if he has to. When Jim asked him what he wanted to do, he refused to answer, saying, 'That's Paddy's problem'. I also had wind of the fact that Russell Johnston[3] is wobbling as well.

1 Lord Jenkins of Hillhead, Member of Parliament for Southwark (Labour) 1948–50, Birmingham Stechford (Labour) 1950–76, Glasgow Hillhead (SDP) 1982–7. Roy held very senior positions within the Labour Government, most notably Home Secretary and Chancellor of the Exchequer. He was one of the 'Gang of Four'. Roy later became an indispensable link between Tony Blair and myself and a constant source of advice and support during my Leadership. He also later chaired the Electoral Reform Commission.
2 Member of Parliament (Liberal then Liberal Democrat) for Truro & St Austell, where he was elected after David Penhaligon's tragic death, in 1987. Matthew has held various senior positions within the Parliamentary Party.
3 Russell was our Senior Spokesman on Foreign and Commonwealth Affairs. Member of Parliament (Liberal then Liberal Democrat) for Inverness 1964–83, Inverness Nairn & Lochaber 1983–97. He later became the Deputy Leader of the Liberal Democrats. He is now a member of the House of Lords and is currently President of the Parliamentary Assembly of the Council of Europe.

David promised to play a part (he is being very helpful and supportive) in trying to get Alan and Russell on board as soon as possible. I understand that Alan is also meeting with Jim tonight. Altogether a very bad omen for tomorrow.

We must grit our teeth and be very careful if we are to get through the next two weeks. Dinner with Charles Kennedy, who is splendid support.

Then back to my office to do the outstanding three days' mail. Home at 11.00 to watch the by-election results. Richmond will not be counted until tomorrow morning. The programme on the Pontypridd result didn't start until 1.10 and the result was not announced until about 2.30. We beat the SDP, who lost their deposit! Tomorrow looks as though it will be a very tricky day. To bed at about 3.00.

Friday, 24 February, London

Into the office early for extended discussions on my speech. Then, at 12.30pm, with word coming in of the Richmond count, we started to watch the results programme on BBC with growing nervousness. Early signs were promising. The boxes of voting papers showed us a good 4 or 5 per cent ahead of the SDP.

But then we received a bombshell report from the count to say that Potter, the SDP candidate, might win. It immediately became apparent that the line we had mapped out [that is, saying to the SDP 'come and join'] simply would not hold. The result finally came through at about 2.30. The Tory candidate, William Hague, squeaked in by about 1,500 and the SDP beat us into third place by about 5,000.

In the interviews which followed, I tried to be magnanimous and congratulate the SDP. When I got back to the office, I was told that the Richmond people had seen the interviews and were apoplectic. I became extremely depressed that I had let the Party down, taken the wrong line and that the whole thing was going to descend into a disaster. I needed desperately to find a way to ride the punch.

Then the press lobby. They were baying for blood, having just had Owen, triumphant. I tried to appear dignified and said that the obvious thing, if we wanted to beat the Tories, was for the two parties to put aside their differences and come together. They appeared a little taken aback by this fast footwork. But at least it gave me something to say.

Mark bossed me around, piling me into the car for our journey north for tomorrow's engagements as quickly as possible so as to get me out of the way.

We left the House around 4.30, heading for *Newsnight* in Manchester, after which we would spend the night in Mark's house. I was in the blackest of black depressions. I turned on the 5 o'clock news to hear an extraordinary interview with Owen. He was asked for his reaction to my proposal to form a single party. There was about a minute's silence. The interviewer queried if he was still there. Pressed to answer the question, Owen refused, then stalked out of the studio. My spirits immediately started to lift. My line at the press conference had wrongfooted him.

I suddenly had a brainwave. We ought to put pressure on the Doctor[1] by offering him joint open selection (JOS)[2] – something we knew very well he wouldn't accept, but which would keep the initiative with us.

It would require careful briefing, but if we could get the Party to keep calm, we could turn the focus back on Owen and change the story from our failure in Richmond to his refusal to respond to a sensible proposal to heal the split. I became more and more convinced of the idea and was unable to sleep much, planning it.

Saturday, 25 February, Manchester

Up at 9.00 to have a look at the papers. The pops gave me a very rough time, but the heavies are beginning to turn against Owen and, in particular, his refusal to join together in a single party. Excellent! We may have an opportunity, after all, to salvage something of real advantage out of a bad defeat.

1 David Owen. His nickname during the Alliance days.
2 A means by which both parties' membership would come together at constituency level to elect a single local candidate – something Owen had always resolutely opposed.

Sunday, 26 February, Oxford

At 8.30 a meeting at Willy Goodhart's[1] house with Tom McNally, Richard Holme, Tim Clement-Jones, Alan Leaman, Richard Livsey[2] and representatives from the Association of Social and Liberal Democrat Councillors (ASLDC)[3] to discuss my plan for using JOS as a means of dealing with the SDP post-Richmond. We did about an hour and a half's work on the plan and came to the conclusion that it was worth a run. Most were enthusiastic, though the Councillors were very apprehensive.

The rest of the day was spent putting the thing together, drafting the letter carrying my proposals to Owen and making sure we had the widest possible consultation in the Party. It was a mad rush and required a great deal of telephoning. I am very apprehensive about this initiative, as much could go wrong with it. But otherwise I can see only protracted trench warfare which will destroy both our parties and give Labour the chance it needs.

At 12 o'clock I did *The World This Weekend*, followed by *On The Record* with Jonathan Dimbleby.

Left Oxford around 5 o'clock for Roy Jenkins' house at East Hendred. When I arrived he poured me a glass of claret and we sat in front of his raging fire. He cheered me up enormously by declaring the idea 'an absolute masterstroke'. I left much encouraged and drove through blinding snow and rain to Yeovil.

Outside Hungerford I received a call on my mobile from Ian Wrigglesworth to say he had been contacted by Patrick Wintour of the *Guardian*, who had got the whole story (apparently by 3 o'clock!). I asked Ian to put Patrick straight on to me. I immediately decided to let Patrick see the letter I had written to Owen, so that the real story would come out, rather than a distorted version of it. I worried that the press would know the details before Owen got his letter. So I asked Richard Holme what he thought about giving Owen a call. He strongly advised against, as did Ian.

Home around 9.30 for a supper in front of the fire and a stream of phone

1 A friend and close adviser. Willy was a founding member of the SDP. He now sits in the House of Lords.
2 Member of Parliament (Liberal then Liberal Democrat) for Brecon and Radnor 1985–92 and since 1997. Richard was Leader of the Welsh Party and has always spoken on Welsh issues for us.
3 The Official Councillors organization of the Party.

calls. I had previously asked Alan Leaman to release the text to the Press Association. I contemplate tomorrow with trepidation.

Monday, 27 February, Somerset

My birthday.

The phone started ringing very early. I did the *Today* programme. Owen is expressing outrage at the fact that the letter was 'leaked' before he received it. I knew he would. But we seem to be dominating the news, which is what I hoped.

After surgery in Yeovil, straight up to London. The whole journey was peppered with telephone calls. At 6.45pm into the Federal Executive. I was expecting a fairly easy ride but didn't get it. Almost everybody expressed concern about what I had done – though Dick Taverne,[1] Tom McNally and Tim Clement-Jones spoke up for me. Des Wilson called the weekend's events muddle-headed, silly and 'Toy Town politics'. Nevertheless, I eventually got the support I needed.

If we hadn't found a way to get back into the story, the Owenites' success would have dominated the weekend's news. This way we had turned it to make it look as though we, not they, were behaving sensibly. Risky, but we are off the back foot and have put Owen there instead.

Then back down to the office for half an hour and home to Jane and Kate [my daughter] for a birthday dinner. I worry greatly about tomorrow's press. To bed pretty late, but not much sleep.

Wednesday, 1 March, London

Into the office early to deal with the mail. No slackening in the volume – 200 plus letters today, mostly supportive.

At 12.30 off to do a piece in the Conference Centre studio on our forthcoming Spring Conference. Then a very engaging lunch with Peter Preston and Dave McKie of the *Guardian*. They seemed to think that we

1 Member of Parliament (Labour 1962–72, Democratic Labour 1973–4) for Lincoln 1962–1974. Dick held various positions within the Treasury during the Labour Government. Founding member of the SDP. Later became a peer.

had done well post-Richmond – though no sign of it in their columns, of course.

At 5.30 the Parliamentary Party Meeting, which I was dreading. We covered the routine business and then got on to the main topic, the Richmond by-election. Alex[1] was first to go and mounted a strenuous attack on what I had done. To my great surprise, however, Nancy Seear[2] waded in to support me, saying that our position would have been much much worse if I hadn't acted. I was then supported in succession by all the rest of my colleagues, leaving Alex somewhat isolated. There were strong reverberations of the name debate in all this, however. Ming Campbell suggested it should not be raised today and most people accepted this.

I am *very* nervous of the Conference. Things can spin apart in all number of ways. Nevertheless, I was heartened by the support of my colleagues today.

Saturday, 4 March, Bournemouth

FIRST DAY OF THE SPRING PARTY CONFERENCE

The dreaded day. A Parliamentary Party Meeting, then into the debate, centring on my moves with the SDP after Richmond. You could see the seething discontent in many sections of the Party. However, Charles Kennedy picked up the speeches criticizing what I had done, and in the first few lines of summing up simply destroyed the arguments. It was an excellent example of his skill as a debater.

We came out at the end with a vote of 850 to 216 or so. Everybody else was jubilant – but not me. In these kinds of things it is nearly always the case that the issue itself is confused with a vote of confidence in the Leader. I am well aware that I have strained people's loyalty. I felt rather bad during the debate and even worse afterwards. However, I am still convinced that what I did was right. This is certainly the overwhelming view now of the press, my Parliamentary colleagues and other senior members of the Party.

It's difficult, however, for some of our ordinary members to see the bigger picture.

1 Alex Carlile QC, Member of Parliament (Liberal then Liberal Democrat) for Montgomery 1983–97. Alex held various positions within the Liberal Democrats, most notably as the Leader of the Welsh Party. He now sits in the House of Lords.
2 The late Baroness Seear (1913–97). Liberal peer created 1971. For most of my Leadership Nancy was the Deputy Leader of the Party in the House of Lords. She was also a good friend.

Tuesday, 7 March, London

At 8 o'clock a private dinner with Peter Boizot[1] and David Sainsbury[2] to discuss the Owenites. I find Sainsbury extremely engaging and highly intelligent. He told me that he had strongly advised the Doctor not to set up a separate party by himself and was still advising him that the only way forward was to join us. However, he made it clear that if Owen, whom he clearly regards as a 'great man', decides to continue on his own, he will stick with him.

We ended the evening at around 10.00, with Sainsbury agreeing to set up a dinner with me, Owen and himself on neutral territory in the near future.

Back home extremely tired. I slept badly. I fear we are coming into round four of the post-Richmond situation. I am worried about Party morale and how this will affect our staffing situation, finances and membership renewal rates.

Wednesday, 8 March, Westminster

At 5.30 the Parliamentary Party Meeting. This was a long one in which we discussed the Vale of Glamorgan by-election (should we stand or not?),[3] the name (I asked them not to make public statements until we had a chance to discuss the thing in private) and various other prickly topics.

A meeting at 8 o'clock to discuss what we might do with Owen's reaction when it comes. Afterwards, dinner with colleagues. Very useful – I got an agreement from Geraint Howell[4] not to raise the name issue until after the county elections [on 4 May]. Geraint gave this freely and told me that he

1 Long-term supporter of the Party, and of the Liberal Party before it. He is also a famous restaurateur and president of Peterborough FC.
2 Trustee of the SDP, before and after merger. Now a member of the Labour Government in the House of Lords.
3 A by-election was pending in the Vale of Glamorgan following the death of the Conservative MP Sir Herbert Gower. He had had a 6221 majority over Labour at the 1987 General Election.
4 Member of Parliament (Liberal then Liberal Democrat) for Cardigan 1974–83 Ceredigion and Pembroke North 1983–92. He was our spokesman for Agriculture and Welsh matters. Geraint is now in the House of Lords.

would persuade others to the same point of view. He recognizes that it's very important to hold everything together at the moment.

Later on that evening I met with David Steel and Archy Kirkwood[1] to discuss the name again. I persuaded them to similar conclusions to those I had reached with Geraint. The matter must be held over as long as possible to let it cool down, then handled with great care.

To bed around 1.00, very tired.

Thursday, 16 March, London

At 8.15 to David Sainsbury's for dinner with David Owen. All done under the greatest secrecy.

The Sainsburys live in a beautiful 1840s house which they have restored with evident pride. It was previously Tony Crosland's[2] home.

I was greeted at the door by David Sainsbury's wife and two children, who are both very bright and charming.

A drink before dinner. Owen was clearly ill at ease. I had decided previously to play Sainsbury as the audience. Owen was trying to do the same thing. In the early part of our conversation, which was wholly pleasantries, he refused to look at me. But eventually he came out of his shell. After a long explanation of each other's positions, I got on to Owen's strategy of assisting Labour. I pointed out why I didn't think it would work at this stage. Until Labour was electable, too close an association with them would undermine our position as the main opponents to the Tories in the South.

We then got on to the nitty-gritty. I said that most of the suggestions in the letters he wrote responding formally to my post-Richmond proposals were acceptable (though not without causing some difficulty with the Party), apart from three specific points:

Firstly, we could not accept any kind of dialogue between the parties which did not include the local constituency level; secondly, any arrangement had to be on a by-election case-by-case basis. However, if things

---

1 Close friend and constant source of support and wise advice during my leadership. Member of Parliament (Liberal then Liberal Democrat) for Roxburgh since 1983. He later became our Chief Whip 1992–7. He is now Chair of the House of Commons Social Security Select Committee and a member of the House of Commons Commission.

2 Foreign Secretary in Callaghan's Government who died prematurely in 1977. An intellectual, he wrote *The Future of Socialism* and many articles about the Labour Party and social democracy.

worked on the by-election front, it could develop further. Thirdly, there could be no question of wider deals encompassing other seats beyond by-elections.

We had quite a discussion about this. Sainsbury explained to me that joint open selection (JOS) was unacceptable to them. In their view, JOS was simply shorthand for merger. I admitted that this could be the case, but, if JOS meant merger to them, any discussion with the Owenites meant, to my party, 'giving in'. I was prepared to take the risk. Why wasn't he prepared to do the same?

I went on to suggest that we might find a mechanism which didn't involve JOS. For instance, it might be possible to get the two parties to agree who should fight a seat and then let that party choose, under its own mechanisms, its own candidate.

The hardest task came when Owen and Sainsbury combined forces to try and persuade me to state publicly that I would support local parties coming to local agreements. I said I could do no such thing as it ran totally contrary to the resolution passed at our Bournemouth Conference. I did, however, explain that our constitution allowed for local parties not to field candidates in favour of other parties, and if they chose to do so there was no way I could stand in the way.

I went on to complain to Owen about his insistence on calling us the Liberal Party, since we weren't. He agreed that he was being deliberately contentious and that he would stop doing so, if it helped improve relations.

Owen then suggested a European election deal, particularly in the South-West. I told him that there could be no question of this. However, again, if local parties came to their own decisions, I would not seek to stop them. I also agreed that it would be best if we were to conduct any further exchanges, as far as possible, outside the press.

We finally agreed that we should keep an amicable dialogue open, though it was clear that the bottom lines for both parties had not changed and would not change. I reiterated the point that the by-election deal should be seen very much as a first step. According to how successful it was, we could decide how and when to go further, if we wished.

I was picked up by Mark at 10.30pm and driven home. Altogether, a pretty good evening:

1. I have managed to open up a gap between Sainsbury and Owen on what the long-term strategy was – with Sainsbury agreeing rather more with me than with him.

2. It was a reasonable discussion and at least Sainsbury does not see me as inflexible.

3. Further dialogue will be conducted in private, which means that the possibility of us getting the wrong side of the argument is diminished.

4. Owen clearly understands the limits of my position. He repeatedly said that he did not want a national pact but wished to see things sorted out on 'a local level'.

Friday, 7 April, London

At 9.30pm, to the Guildhall to a reception for Gorbachev.[1] All the top-table guests gathered beforehand for a cup of coffee, etc. Gorbachev came into the room and spoke to most of us.

George Younger[2] told me a very funny story about his opposite number in the Soviet Government who had just been through an election and had come out of it feeling very bruised. He 'only' got 70 per cent of the vote. He was standing against a young journalist who, he complained, 'used some very misleading statements and slogans'. What an extraordinary experience it must have been for those senior Communist Party apparatchiks to stand in democratic elections!

Then into the Guildhall to hear Gorbachev's speech. About 300 present and all the full pageantry of the Guildhall. Gorbachev is smaller than I thought, but possesses an extraordinary sense of calm and power. He has an almost permanent enigmatic smile playing about his face. A man who appears totally in control of himself and of events. His speech was startling in only one aspect – it had been heavily touted as proposing new initiatives, but it didn't. In fact it was a consolidating speech, quite hard in places and clearly designed to put Mrs Thatcher on the spot. He summed up the position on *perestroika* in the Soviet Union and then listed the kind of things they had done to cut the arms race. The implication was, 'We've gone this far, now it's up to you.' He was hardest of all on the question of modernization of nuclear weapons, linking it to other advances in disarmament.

1 Mikhail Gorbachev, General Secretary of the Central Committee of the Communist Party of the Soviet Union 1985–91, was on his first official trip to Britain since taking office.
2 Sir George Younger, at the time Secretary of State for Defence. Member of Parliament (Conservative) for Ayr 1964–92.

Mrs Thatcher gave a speech in which her voice was much better modulated than I had heard previously. But it was clearly out of kilter with what Gorbachev said. She commented on things which he was expected to say but didn't. Gorbachev probably changed his speech at the last moment. For the first time I sensed some menace in what Gorbachev said. He may well be worried that he cannot keep his own internal problems in check unless the West gives him more in recognition of how far he has moved.

Tuesday, 25 April, Westminster

Dinner with Jim Wallace and Archy Kirkwood. Afterwards a long session with them in my office. We agreed that we must now confront the Parliamentary Party and try to bring out all the complaints in one go on the Wednesday after the County Council elections. Morale in the Party is terribly low. If we do not hold our own in the County elections, we are heading for a very difficult time. For my part I am fed up to the back teeth with people who are not prepared to play their part or are still weeping into their beer. We will, therefore, tackle (a) the name, (b) the question of strategy, and (c) Parliamentary collective responsibility.

Wednesday, 26 April, Vale of Glamorgan

Arrived the Vale of Glamorgan at 7.30 to address about twenty people in the Leisure Centre at Cowbridge. I walked in to hear that Geraint Howells had made a statement in the Welsh Grand Committee[1] which said that we couldn't win Glamorgan. Really we are a pathetic bunch of idiots sometimes! I had to dispose of the story by being rude about Geraint. They are fighting magnificently here but will, of course, do dreadfully next week.

---

1 A standing committee of the House of Commons, made up of Members of Parliament representing Welsh constituencies.

Sunday, 30 April, Somerset

I have, this week, reached some important private conclusions about how politics on the left should develop in the future. I am beginning to clarify my mind on positioning.[1] I think the best thing to do is to set up some kind of external organization (i.e. external to ourselves and Labour) and suggested to Richard Holme that he might stimulate a group of people in Charter 88[2] into writing 'A Programme for Britain'. This would cover much of the agenda about which I have been making speeches.

My proposal is that we might have two people from each party who are non-representative but senior, one politician and one thinker (e.g. Denis Healey[3] and Ben Pimlott,[4] David Steel and David Marquand[5] – we could even widen membership to include John Cartwright and Professor Skidelsky[6] from the SDP, Jonathon Porritt[7] plus one other Green) who would write up their programme for Britain. Others could then attach themselves to it. I would, of course, give the whole thing a rather cool welcome to start with but would then be dragged in later, 'against my will'.

1 Since my secret meeting with David Owen in March, it had become clear, following a number of crucial mistakes made by the Owenites, that we were now going to win the battle for the centre ground and that the rump SDP was disintegrating. Throughout this period, however, I was painfully aware that the real battle was not with the SDP, but with the Tories; that the splits on the left had given the Conservatives more chances in Government over the century than they should have had, and that these were now making it much more difficult to defeat Thatcherism, which was doing such damage to the country.

2 An organization lobbying for democratic reform, including a change to the electoral system.

3 Member of Parliament (Labour) for South East Leeds 1952–5, Leeds East 1955–92. Member of the Labour Government, most notably as Chancellor of the Exchequer. Since 1992 Denis has sat in the House of Lords.

4 Professor of Politics and Contemporary History, Birkbeck College, London, 1987–98. Warden of Goldsmith's College, London, since 1998. Distinguished biographer.

5 Professor David Marquand, Member of Parliament (Labour) for Ashfield 1966–77. Founding member of the SDP; joined the Liberal Democrats then defected back to Labour. Professor of Politics at Sheffield University 1991–6. Principal of Mansfield College, Oxford, since 1996.

6 Professor Robert Skidelsky, now Lord Skidelsky, Professor of Political Economy at Warwick University since 1990. Historian and biographer of J. M. Keynes. A member of the SDP who then joined the Conservatives and now sits on their benches in the House of Lords.

7 Stood as an Ecology Party candidate in various elections between 1977 and 1983. He then became Director of Friends of the Earth and has held various senior positions with the Ecology/Green Party, most notably Party Chairman.

It seemed to me that this might provide a framework for the programme for a new government, around which we could bring together the next stage of the realignment. If it failed to bring Labour in formally during the pre-election period, it could still serve to put more pressure on them after they have lost the next election.

Tuesday, 2 May, Westminster and the Vale of Glamorgan

Into the office early to deal with the mail and then, at 10 o'clock, a meeting with Ian Wrigglesworth. I have decided that Andy Ellis cannot stay on as our Secretary General. I am very worried about deep divisions in the Party, low morale among our activists and disillusion with Cowley Street. We must move fast to tackle these before they get worse and I will have to take a number of risks. I have also decided to take on the Parliamentary Party. The time for mucking about has stopped. I have fixed a meeting with a few key colleagues for next Tuesday to discuss the issue.

After PMQs, a brief interview with ITN's Michael Brunson on the forthcoming local elections and straight off to Barry.[1] We arrived there a little early at around 7.00. Charles Kennedy[2] and co. are doing a brilliant job, making bricks without straw. Off to the public meeting at 8.00. About sixty present (David Owen and Denis Healey are in town as well). Quite a lively meeting, then dinner and off to spend the night with Sir Brian Hopkins, a professor at the University of Cardiff.

Thursday, 4 May, Somerset and Cowley Street

COUNTY COUNCIL ELECTIONS AND GLAMORGAN BY-ELECTION DAY

Up at 6.30 for final preparations and phone calls. A photo-op outside Vane Cottage, then off to vote at the village hall, with TV cameras in attendance.

The rest of the day spent going round the constituency committee rooms. We have let our organization in the Constituency go to rack and ruin. If we get through these elections, it will be by the skin of our teeth.

At 6.30pm, we left for Cowley Street to watch the national results programmes. In the event, we ended the night with only 105 losses. I put

1 For more campaigning in the Vale of Glamorgan by-election.
2 I had sent Charles down to the Vale of Glamorgan to act as 'godfather' to the campaign.

out press releases saying that 'the fortress of the centre ground has held and it's in our hands. The period of retreat and retrenchment is over and it's time to move forward.'

The Party has come through a test of fire in these local elections. Our mettle lies more in our campaigning strength on the ground than in our leadership strata. We have been in retreat for nearly two years, but, given that we are a new party, we have managed to hold together quite well. I know that there are criticisms of my performance, in particular lack of press coverage – though people do not realize how little attention the media pay you when you are at 10 per cent or less in the opinion polls.

Friday, 5 May, Cowley Street

Up at 6.30 and into Cowley Street. We have lost no more seats, so the position has held overnight.

Then off to the *Today* programme and *Breakfast Time*. I also did ITN and most of the other news broadcasts. Early word from Glamorgan is that we will get about 6 per cent and will save our deposit. However, the result, which I heard on the 1.10 train going back to Yeovil, gave us under 5 per cent. An excellent win for Labour (though not as good as they had expected) with a 6,000 majority. All other parties except the Tories lost their deposits.[1]

My comment was 'disappointing but expected'. There will be some pressure on me. But the full weight of criticism ought to fall on the SDP, who have been virtually wiped out – just over 2 per cent in Glamorgan and fewer than ten councillors elected across Britain.

Sunday, 7 May, Somerset

The press is becoming a little better for us. Nevertheless, Labour is on a strong surge, following their Glamorgan by-election success. Kinnock is being talked about as a possible future Prime Minister. Meanwhile, Owen has suggested that he would work under Kinnock and Cartwright has said

---

1 Labour got 48.9%, Conservatives 36.3%, we got 4.2%, Plaid Cymru 3.5% and the SDP 2.3%. All of those under 5% lost their deposits.

that he might join Labour. Rosie Barnes[1] on the radio today saying she disagrees with both of them! The SDP must be in wonderful disarray. I think this marks the end of the SDP as a credible force.

Tuesday, 9 May, Westminster

At 10 o'clock a meeting with Matthew Taylor, Archy Kirkwood, Jim Wallace and Richard Livsey to discuss Wednesday's Parliamentary Party Meeting. There is stronger and more widespread hostility on the name issue than I had thought. However, I agreed to have a story planted in *The Times* along the lines of 'Ashdown gets a grip etc.'

Wednesday, 10 May, Westminster

At 11.30 a press conference in which I tried to undermine the Labour Party's current policy review. This is going all too well. A lot of questions on Owen, who has said he is going to join Labour. Owen is now being treated as something of a joke. News is coming in of a number of his councillors resigning, particularly in Plymouth. Meanwhile, the General Secretary of the SDP left in a huff on Monday. Are we at last through the Owen problem?

At 5.30 the Parliamentary Party Meeting. We were to discuss the name on this occasion, but Alan, Geraint and Russell were all away. However, Nancy made one or two comments, together with Richard Livsey and Ming, which make me believe I have a bigger problem here than I thought. I can see their grumbles, but what practical action do we take? I will have to hold the line very firmly on this.

We also had a general discussion on strategy. People are in a supportive frame and seem to understand that this is the moment when we must get our act together and start doing some proper work in the House of Commons. The Party at large is getting very resentful of the Parliamentarians not pulling together.

1 Member of Parliament (SDP 1987–90, Social Democrat 1990–92) for Greenwich 1987–92. Stayed with the continuing SDP after merger. Rosie left national politics after the collapse of the SDP.

Thursday, 11 May, Santiago de Compostela, Spain

BILDERBERG CONFERENCE

At 2 o'clock to Heathrow to catch a flight to Santiago de Compostela for the Bilderberg Conference – described to me as 'fifty people who run the world and twenty hangers on'. No doubt which category I am in!

I discovered that the people here include Henry Kissinger, Lord Carrington,[1] the King and Queen of Spain, the Queen of Holland, Felipe Gonzalez the Prime Minister of Spain, Wilfried Martens the Prime Minister of Belgium, Dr Franz Vranitzky the Chancellor of Austria, John Smith[2] and too many Tory Government Ministers to name.

Dinner was excellent. I ate a dozen oysters and a load of shellfish. This could be fun.

Afterwards, Cecil Parkinson,[3] John Smith and I sat in armchairs drinking brandy. Cecil turned out to be rather engaging and astonishingly frank about the Government's position. He left for bed early and John and I continued for another hour or so, accompanied by considerably more brandy.

Smith believes that the Labour Party can do it by themselves and are well on their way to just this. He rejects the idea of pacts. I got the impression of somebody who has a very quick but rather narrow mind. I am not sure whether this is his natural way or comes from belonging to the Labour Party since birth. He is an engaging talker, but there seems to be something missing. Everything seems to be politics.

Friday, 12 May, Santiago de Compostela

BILDERBERG CONFERENCE

A bit of a thick head following John Smith and the brandy last night. A brief breakfast then into the meeting. We sat in a glass-panelled room

---

1 Lord Carrington had just finished his appointment as Secretary General of NATO. Before this he held various Cabinet positions in Conservative Governments.
2 Rt Hon. John Smith MP (1938–94). At the time the Shadow Chancellor of the Exchequer. He subsequently became Leader of the Labour Party until his sudden and unexpected death. Member of Parliament (Labour) for Lanarkshire North 1970–83, Monklands East 1983–94.
3 Secretary of State for Energy. Member of Parliament (Conservative) for Enfield West November 1970–74, Hertfordshire South 1974–83, Hertsmere 1983–92. He now sits in the House of Lords.

overlooking the sea, slightly crowded together. Nevertheless very congenial. The first discussion was on recent developments in Eastern Europe. Tim Garton Ash[1] gave an exceptionally good talk.

In the afternoon a discussion on arms control, chaired by Carrington, in which Henry Kissinger and Teo Sommer (the editor of *Die Zeit*) gave an inside view. Fascinating stuff. Kissinger was a bit hesitant to start with but his summing-up was brilliant.

In the afternoon we talked about Europe, Giovanni Agnelli[2] and Lloyd Bentsen[3] giving their versions. The show was stolen, however, by Peter Sutherland,[4] who is very, very bright. The general view is that the Soviet Union's economy is in the most wretched state and bound to fail, along with those of most of the Eastern Bloc countries. The West should not encourage the break-up of the Warsaw Pact, but should help the process of *rapprochement* as far as it can.

Saturday, 13 May, Santiago de Compostela

BILDERBERG CONFERENCE

US/Soviet relations in the morning. This was by far and away our best session, with Rosanne Ridgeway, the Chief of the Disarmament Staff in the White House, giving us her view. She is a remarkable lady with seemingly a firm grip on everything around her. However, I found her attitude to modernization quite chilling. Apparently the Soviets are about to offer deep cuts in conventional forces down to parity. She didn't think this made any difference to the question of stationing modernized nuclear weapons in Germany. She must be mad!

In the afternoon a long discussion on monetary union in Europe. Nearly everybody attacked Mrs Thatcher, even her closest admirers. The only exception was Cecil Parkinson, who put up a spirited loyal defence, but didn't make any sense and had his leg pulled by everyone else.

---

1 Fellow of St Antony's College, Oxford. Author of many books and articles on international affairs, especially Eastern Europe.
2 International industrialist.
3 The 1988 Democratic Party nominee for US Vice-President. He served in Clinton's first Administration as Secretary to the Treasury.
4 Formerly a European Commissioner, now an international businessman.

Sunday, 14 May, Santiago de Compostela

BILDERBERG CONFERENCE

Contacted by ITN at 11.00am, who told me that Owen had held a meeting the night before and the SDP had decided they were no longer a national party. To put a brave face on it, Owen has apparently indicated that he will continue with 'guerrilla tactics', whatever that means. ITN asked me for a comment and I tried not to sound triumphalist. I deliberately left the door open to the possibility of a merger, though, of course, this is not in reality a practical option. But we must look as welcoming as possible.

At last! This long wretched period – at least in so far as Owen is concerned – appears over. I have not felt so cheered in years.

A brilliant cloudless day. I spent the afternoon by the swimming pool, reading through the proofs of *Citizens' Britain*,[1] and making further amendments. The trick will be to ensure that reviewers see it not just as a motley collection of ideas, but as a framework for the new shape of progressive politics in Britain.

Monday, 15 May, Cowley Street

Into the office early to deal with the mail which had piled up over the last three or four days. Then a series of meetings discussing impending staff cuts, first with the Party Officers, then with my close advisers and finally the Federal Executive in the evening. The staff are threatening industrial action and there is a considerable amount of anger about.

At 5 o'clock into the FFAC[2] meeting. We are now facing a bigger deficit than we originally planned (about £147,000). However, membership and income appear to be up.

Then at 6 o'clock into the Federal Executive. A long and tortuous discussion on the financial situation. Tom McNally did one of his exploding

1 At the beginning of 1989, I had decided to write a book as a part of my plan to reverse the decline of the Party and start building for the future. The aim was to mark out a core of ideas which would articulate what we stood for and explain why we still had a role. The book was completed in the summer and published for our Autumn Conference.
2 The Federal Finance and Administration Committee (FFAC) is charged with the day-to-day management of the Party's finance, administration and staff.

acts which was intended to be supportive but was, in fact, deeply unhelpful. It will also damage his own image in the Party. I will have some smoothing of feathers to do tomorrow.

Then off to dinner in a little Italian restaurant with Dick Newby,[1] Tim Clement-Jones, Archy Kirkwood, Jim Wallace, Clive Lindley[2] and Ian Wrigglesworth. We are developing into a good team who can work together and enjoy each other's company.

Probably the most successful thing I did today was to raise, right at the end of a tiring and fraught Federal Executive, two matters I want to get through. I bumped them into agreeing to both of them. The first was that Archy should take over as Chairman of the Campaigns and Communications Committee[3] (passed unanimously), and the second (also passed unanimously, to my greater surprise) that I should establish a sub-committee to consider General Election structure. It gives me control over the General Election team, which is vital.

Saturday, 3 June, London

After a day's campaigning in Newcastle,[4] I finally got back to the London flat and turned on the TV to receive the horrifying news of a massacre in progress in Tiananmen Square. Dozens reported killed. But, by the sound of heavy machine-guns firing into massed crowds and the swirl of armour through pedestrian-filled streets, I think the figure is more likely to be in the thousands.

Sunday, 4 June, London

Up early to hear of even more atrocities overnight in Beijing. At 10.30 we met for a briefing for *On The Record*. They now plan to devote the whole

---

1 Dick was the National Secretary of the SDP until merger, and in 1997 was a Deputy Chairman of the General Election campaign. Dick is now Chief of Staff to Charles Kennedy and sits in the House of Lords.
2 International businessman. Since the formation of the Party, Clive has worked for and sat on many of its internal bodies and provided crucial support in our difficult early days.
3 The Party's Committee charged with managing all campaigning and media communications.
4 For the European Elections, to be held on 15 June.

programme to the developing situation in China. Then down to join a demonstration outside the Chinese Embassy. A very moving affair during which I gave a speech in Mandarin. I am glad that I expressed such reservations about the Anglo-Chinese Agreement on Hong Kong when it went through the House four years ago. Time to resuscitate the proposals I made then that we should honour our moral obligations to all those who hold British passports in Hong Kong by giving them right of abode[1] in Britain. This will be a key issue over the next few days.

To bed late and very tired.

Tuesday, 6 June, Westminster

PMQs. I was amazed that neither Thatcher nor Kinnock seem to have picked up on what has happened in China. So I got up and asked a very rude Question ('Does [the Prime Minister] realize that, in comparison with the words of President Bush, her muted response immediately following the massacre in Peking will be regarded by many as a matter of shame? Is she aware that, in comparison to the attitude of the Portuguese Government to their citizens in Macau, her complete denial of moral responsibility after 1997 for those in Hong Kong who hold British passports will be regarded by many as a matter of dishonour?') She was furious but gave, I thought, rather a poor reply. As soon as I came out of the chamber, I was descended on by the press.

Then back into the chamber to take the Foreign Secretary's statement on China. I made a mistake here, trying to be too 'decent'. I said that, after the initial response, it was probably time to wait and see how things developed for a couple of days. I was immediately accused, not unreasonably, of being inconsistent. However, the point was made.

Before I left for a meeting in Maidstone, Bob Maclennan came to see me, suggesting that he should go to Hong Kong. I agreed, but said that we should both go, and set about making urgent arrangements.

1 We subsequently adopted this highly contentious policy, which was rejected by both the other parties and which caused us some difficulty internally and a good deal of unpopularity externally. It was one of the defining points of the creation of the new Party, giving it heart and showing others that we were prepared to stand up for our principles as an internationalist party.

Wednesday, 7 June, London

Up early to go on *Breakfast Time* at 7.30. Rather a good session, this. Apparently, the Government had briefed the press to the effect that they were prepared to be flexible about the application of the British Nationality Act to Hong Kong passport holders, provided that the people who applied had more than £150,000. I immediately wrote a letter to the Prime Minister, kicking up a merry fuss about a chequebook immigration policy.

Then back to the office and a brief chat with Mark and Bob. They had spoken to the Party branch in Hong Kong, who agreed that a useful programme could be arranged. So we decided to go for 6 o'clock that evening. The timing appears excellent, since we have beaten the Labour Party to it by two days, and Geoffrey Howe[1] is still havering about whether to go or not.

A quick dash back to the House and, at 3.30, to Heathrow. As soon as I checked in, there were calls from TV AM and Sky Television for further interviews. An opportunity we cannot afford to miss. So I went back out through Customs to do the pieces.

We boarded late, but the weather looked good. Slept only fitfully. Bob talked about the Party and constitutional reform for most of the journey. Brilliant views of the Himalayas at dawn.

Friday, 9 June, Hong Kong

A day full of meetings and visits, perhaps the most moving of which was to the New China News Agency building in Happy Valley, which is regarded as the unofficial Beijing Embassy in the colony.

Here, huge crowds of protesting Chinese, mounds of flowers and thousands of messages of condolence and anger for the Beijing Chinese from the Chinese of Hong Kong. They have created a small replica of the Statue of Liberty. I spoke to a girl there who had been in Tiananmen Square and told me terrible stories about what had happened. The sense of anger from

---

1 Member of Parliament (Conservative) for Bebington 1964–6, Reigate 1970–74, Surrey East 1974–92. Member of the Conservative Government, most notably as Deputy Prime Minister, Chancellor of the Exchequer and, at this point, Foreign Secretary.

the Chinese here is extraordinary. They told me a million people had turned up at Happy Valley and not a bottle was broken. I did a brief interview in Mandarin and signed the book of condolence in Chinese.

Saturday, 10 June, Hong Kong

Down to see David Ford,[1] who was his usual charming self. He told me that he thought the administration's credibility in Hong Kong would now be undermined and our capacity to rule the colony diminished unless the British Government moved on the right of abode issue.

Then at 9.30 down to the General Chamber of Commerce. Here I met representatives of all the major British firms – and of most of the other powerful companies in the colony. From top to bottom there was a sense of anger and concern. Again the feeling of solidarity was immense.

Then back home to Heidi and Mark's[2] house, where I packed. Three American students who had just got out of Beijing spent the evening with us. We went to Chieu Chow Restaurant in Causeway Bay. Fantastic food – Chieu Chow crab, giblets, duck soup, hot Chieu Chow red wine, etc.

Then, at 9.30, to the airport, where I met Bob. On the flight I again couldn't sleep, so I sat in the dark typing up an article. Bob snored loudly beside me from Kowloon to Gatwick.

Tuesday, 13 June, Westminster

THE LAST WEEK'S CAMPAIGNING IN THE EUROPEAN ELECTIONS

At the end of our morning's campaigning I began to receive reports of the Greens doing well. The word on the ground is that they may well beat us on Thursday.

This is devastating news. This year seems to have been like doing battle with the multi-headed Gorgon. As soon as you cut one head off, another one sprouts in its place. First of all we had to beat the Doctor, which we did. Then we had to cope with a Labour hype, which we are just getting

---

1 Chief Secretary of the Hong Kong Government. David and I had previously studied Chinese together in Hong Kong.
2 Heidi and Mark Tang. Friends from my days studying Chinese in the Colony.

to grips with. And now, it seems, yet another challenger for the 'centre ground' rises to confront us. How I long for this to be over!

Into PMQs at 3.15. I asked her about Hong Kong ('What would she do if the scenes in Beijing were repeated in Hong Kong in eight years' time [i.e., when Britain hands Hong Kong back to the Chinese] and she had refused to give refuge to passport holders?'). She gave a long rambling reply in the middle of which I shouted 'Dishonourable'.[1] The house broke into complete disorder. The Speaker demanded I withdraw. I attempted to do so on three occasions. But before I could get the sentence out I was howled down from all sides. In the end, I said that I wasn't claiming that she was dishonourable. Just her policies.

Wednesday, 14 June, London

The opinion polls this morning show the Greens will get around 10 per cent, with us at around 6. I am beginning to fear Thursday greatly.

At our last Press Conference of the Campaign at 11.30 I tried to put a brave face on the outcome.

At 5.30 off to the Parliamentary Party Meeting. This was brief, but full of ominous rumblings. Precursors of the kinds of problems we will have if we do badly on Thursday. We discussed doing Hong Kong for our 'supply day'[2] on Monday. I am enthusiastic. It will help raise our profile.

Then at 6.30 to the Coliseum where I met Jane and Kate to see *Don*

---

1 The precise exchange, from Hansard, was as follows:

MR ASHDOWN: Will the Prime Minister give a few moments today to consider the plight of young Chinese students who, because of their faith in democracy, are hiding for their lives in Peking and are waiting for the knock on the door that will take them to gaol or before the firing squad? Will she now tell the House what she will say if, in eight years' time, those scenes are re-enacted in Hong Kong and involved British passport holders to whom she and the Labour party have refused to give refuge?

THE PRIME MINISTER: The right hon. Gentleman does not have a monopoly of strong feeling on this matter. I think that throughout the House we feel equally as shocked and appalled as he does. That applies to both sides of the House. Just because he has been to Hong Kong and finds it easy to say things, because he has no responsibility.

MR ASHDOWN: Dishonourable.

2 A certain number of days are set aside in the Parliamentary programme as 'Opposition Supply Days', when the opposition parties can choose the subject of debate. Most go to the 'Official Opposition' (Labour at that time), but we also get a few, and this was one of ours.

Giovanni for Kate's birthday. An excellent production and Kate was enthralled. I was slightly put off by the lady next to me who, in the last act, kept on nudging me and squeezing my arm. Clearly she was somewhat turned on by the Don's descent into Hell.

Thursday, 15 June, London and Somerset

EUROPEAN ELECTION DAY

After appearing on Robin Day's penultimate *Question Time*, I drove down to Somerset, arriving just in time to turn on the television and receive the bad news.

The exit poll has the Greens at 15 per cent, with Labour a full 12 per cent ahead, and us at 6 per cent. The full results won't be known until Sunday when the Euro votes are counted. But this looks set to be a real disaster. The Vauxhall by-election result came through early and we were only a blip behind the Tories. Some comfort there. But we got wiped out in Glasgow Central, with the Greens polling more votes than ourselves and the SDP put together.

I am now very worried about the Green phenomenon.

All the programmes are talking about our demise and the Greens' rise. It will be very difficult to hold our nerve. The problem is not what will happen in the polls (I think as soon as people know what the Greens actually stand for they will stop voting for them very quickly), but how to maintain Party morale – which will now be rock bottom, with implications for membership, finance, the wretched name and everything else.

I am plagued by the nightmare that the party that started with Gladstone will end with Ashdown.

Saturday, 17 June, Somerset

Very, very depressed still. A nasty piece in the *Independent* today saying that it is all down to my leadership.

Into Yeovil for a reasonably busy surgery, starting at 9.30. Then home to work on *Citizens' Britain*.

I can't snap out of the depression. We seem on the edge of oblivion. I don't think I have ever felt so miserable in my entire life. Looking back, however, I am certain I could not have done anything differently. We need just one lucky break to turn things round.

I conceived *Citizens' Britain* as a means of starting afresh after seeing off Owen. Now it is an essential part of our strategy for survival after this disaster. Our greatest danger is of being squeezed out by the Labour Party moving into the centre ground and by the Greens capturing the radical agenda from us. If we blink in the face of this, we are dead.

There seems to be a general realization of our situation and at last a pulling together of the Parliamentary team. I spoke to Alex Carlile, who was depressed but grimly determined.

Sunday, 18 June, Somerset and London

Another glorious day. Sat out in the courtyard at home, did some work and read the papers in the morning. They have largely ignored us, but there are signs of some sort of attack developing on the Greens. A good thing.

We arrived in London at around 8.30pm. There followed a progression of truly terrible results. We even managed to come fourth to the Greens in Somerset. The Greens, meanwhile, have done stunningly well – about 16 per cent of the vote, while we will come out with about 6 per cent. I put a brave face on it for television and radio, but it was very difficult.

To bed about 3.00. I couldn't sleep a wink. We are in a very black position indeed.

Monday, 19 June, London

Up very early feeling extremely tired. My brain would not stop thinking about the results of the European Elections, which are going to have a devastating effect on Party morale and will also heighten the moves to change the name.[1]

To the office, where people are in a catatonic mood of depression. I told

1 By now it was clear that, despite the decision taken by the Party Conference last year to adopt the short title 'Democrats', the issue of the name was still an open sore. I had privately come to accept that we would probably adopt the name 'Liberal Democrats', but this had to be done through the Party's proper procedures. It could not be imposed on the Party unilaterally by the MPs, if more splits were not to be opened up. It was this question of process that now became the main issue of contention among MPs.

them that if we are to get through this crisis, we must sound cheerful and optimistic. Then across to Cowley Street for a chat with our equally shell-shocked staff. A word or two with Archy, who is, thank goodness, getting to grips with things in Cowley Street. Jim tells me that, as expected, open rebellion is growing in the Parliamentary Party over the name.

At 6 o'clock an Asian TV interview on Hong Kong. Then dinner with colleagues. Alex was in a particularly obstreperous mood and kept on pressing about the name, etc. Despite the valiant attempts of others to save our dinner-table conversation, it all became a bit disjointed and unpleasant with Alex, Alan and co. not losing the opportunity to place the blame on me. Archy was, as usual, brilliant at trying to defuse the situation. After the ten o'clock vote, a meeting with Russell, Geraint, Richard, Alex and Alan. Jim also in attendance, together with Archy.

Richard, Geraint and Alex want to unilaterally declare themselves Liberal Democrats and want the Parliamentary Party to do likewise. Alan Beith has demanded that I should do this immediately and if I don't, he will resign the Whip. Geraint, too, is threatening to resign unless I concede. He would then force a by-election and revert to calling himself a Liberal.

I told them there was no way I was going to concede that the Parliamentary Party had the right to decide the Party name – that was the Party's prerogative. If the Parliamentary Party unilaterally decided to over-ride Conference decision, I would resign as Leader. At this stage Alan said, 'Right, then we might as well call this meeting to a halt.'

We finished at 11.00, after which I spent a few more minutes with Matthew Taylor. Richard Livsey came back to apologize for having taken such a hard line, but said I should realize how strongly he felt about this.

I have made them look over the edge of the precipice and understand that I am not going to give in to their demands. I have also made it clear that if the name is to be changed it can only be done by the Party at large.

Back home around midnight, dog tired and very dispirited.

Tuesday, 20 June, Westminster

Into the office early to deal with a pile of post. Rather a hostile lot today – including a good number from people saying they are resigning from the Party to join the Greens.

At 2 o'clock a few minutes' thought about Prime Minister's Questions – the first after our disaster at the European polls. I wanted to press her on going for an international solution on Hong Kong. I had intended to ask a short Question, knowing I would have a very hard time, but in the end I decided just to brave it out. The Speaker brought me in right at the very end of Questions, so I was made to sit waiting to be called and getting more and more nervous. As soon as I got to my feet the House erupted with cat-calling and booing. I stood my ground with what I hoped was a faint and quizzical smile on my face – though that wasn't what it felt like inside. Dennis Skinner[1] and Bob Cryer[2] in front of me set up a chorus of 'Mister 6 per cent', while Tony Banks[3] behind me shouted out 'Bite the capsule, Paddy.' All very amusing, provided you weren't me. The Prime Minister, however, gave me rather an interesting reply, saying she would seek an international solution if events became impossible in Hong Kong.

Off at 7 o'clock to Kettners restaurant with Jane to debate Green issues with Jonathon Porritt. Alan Leaman had written a brilliant speech – we invented the phrase about the Green vote: 'Is this the first biodegradable vote?' It all went rather well and I thought Porritt was surprisingly weak on some key areas.

Then back to the House at 9 o'clock for dinner with Jane, Alan and Mark in the Strangers' dining room.

After the 10.00 vote, I met with David Steel, Alan, Archy and Ming. David tried to get me to lead the name change. He seemed somewhat annoyed that I refused to budge. I said I must let the Party decide. If I led the change, I would be letting down the old SDP and would make it more difficult for them to accept the outcome. We would, in my view, be breaking faith with the terms of the merger.

This discussion was more difficult to cope with than last night's. These are my friends who have consistently backed me. However, I ended up getting rather cross (and showing it) about my Parliamentary colleagues and the way they didn't pull their weight. Jane went to sleep on the sofa in my office.

Home by taxi at 11.30.

---

1 Member of Parliament (Labour) for Bolsover since 1970. A Labour left-winger notorious for his humour and skill in the House.
2 Bob Cryer MP (1934–94). Member of Parliament (Labour) for Keighley 1974–83, Bradford South 1987–94. Bob was tragically killed in a car accident.
3 Member of Parliament (Labour) for Newham North West 1983–97 and for West Ham since 1997.

Wednesday, 21 June, Leicester and London

At 9 o'clock to Leicester with Mark. Rail and bus strike today, so we drove.

Arrived at about 11.00 to speak for an hour with the Area Agents. They are very depressed, but stoical. I told them what the Parliamentary Party was about to do on the name, which deepened their gloom. I gave them the worst scenario and then said that I hoped that I would be able to hold the Parliamentary Party together (though I hardly feel confident about this). A lot of work to do with the Area Agents – though they seemed grateful that I had taken the trouble to come and brief them about the present situation.

Then a drive back to London, arriving about 2.00 and straight into a series of meetings with Jim and others. Things look dreadful. Jim thinks we cannot carry it and that the Parliamentary Party will break up at the forthcoming meeting. Then a final meeting with Archy Kirkwood and Ian Wrigglesworth before going in to the PPM. Archy tells me that there is no hope of holding everyone together. I asked Ian not to go over the top under any circumstances, saying that my capacity to pull it off would depend entirely on our maintaining a quiet atmosphere for the meeting, leaving those who wanted to break it up to appear unreasonable. My plan was to have a general discussion on what needed to be done in the light of the European election results, but hold the name issue over to a separate debate. Then, when the name debate started, I would encourage people to do as much blood-letting as they could on both sides, so that each could see the edge of the precipice over which they were about to throw themselves.

It was a very exhausting meeting. Richard Livsey came equipped with a press release which, by good fortune, he had not been able to put out beforehand, which said that they were going to take unilateral action and the rest of us could get stuffed.

My plan for the meeting worked well. In the first section everybody came to the conclusion that the one thing we mustn't do in the face of the European election defeat was panic or take hasty actions. The four would-be rebels (Russell, Richard, Alan and Geraint) sat together looking rather glum. There was much conferring between them, but no public statement. I noticed that Russell had actually written a speech that he intended to read out. However, the tone was set and the discussion was constructive, helpful and against immediate action.

I then moved on to the name issue, calling for a general discussion first.

Just as I hoped, everyone came out fighting. Russell made his speech, but it was rather poor. The others then came in and a strenuous discussion developed. This went on for two hours, after which, everybody having had a say (Charles and Nancy were especially good), I demanded a conclusion. It hung in the balance for about ten minutes, with Richard and Alan shaking their heads. Eventually everybody agreed that we should take the issue of the name back to the Conference. I left immensely relieved. The immediate crisis has passed.

Then off for a meal in the Strangers' dining room with Max Atkinson. He is in good form but believes the damage we will do ourselves by changing the name yet again will be extensive. I explained that the alternative was much, much worse, with the Parliamentary Party breaking up altogether.

Thursday, 22 June, London

I listened to the 7 o'clock news. To my horror, the Welsh, despite last night, have unilaterally declared themselves Liberal Democrats. In a high temper, I tried for an hour to ring Richard Livsey before going into the office. I then rang Jim and told him that either the three Welsh MPs withdrew their unilateral action or I would remove them from the team and withdraw their spokesmanships. Jim was a bit shocked. I explained, though, that I would not tolerate Members of Parliament who had made an agreement at a Parliamentary meeting then walking out and betraying it.

Jim believes that Richard Livsey allowed the press to draw this conclusion from the rather imprecise wording of his earlier statement. I told him that I couldn't give a stuff what caused the problem. Either the Welsh MPs issued a retraction or they were off the Parliamentary team. Jim immediately started to ring round and first got a retraction from Geraint. Then he spoke to Richard Livsey. Richard confirmed that he had been misunderstood and that Jim could write him and Geraint a letter for the record. I insisted that it should be made public.

Then, at a few minutes past ten, John Cleese came to see us. We spent an interesting hour discussing politics in general and what he could do for us. He agreed to help us with a Party Political Broadcast.

Life begins to look up – even if in only the very tiniest of ways.

Saturday, 24 June, Swansea and Oxford

Jane's birthday. Left at 9.30 for Swansea, for the Association of Social and Liberal Democrat Councillors (ASLDC) annual Conference. They seemed tough and determined, but a bit set back. Then off for a birthday picnic with Jane in the sand dunes at Swansea – between the Ford factory and the oil refinery! At 4 o'clock we started the drive to Oxford for an evening with Willy Goodhart. Arrived shortly after 7.00. Halfway through the evening we learned that the *Observer* would be running a front page story that Simon Hughes intends to join the Greens if we don't get our act together within four months. This cast an appalling gloom over the whole proceedings. However, we tried to be as jolly as possible.

Later it emerged that the *Observer* story, which also mentioned Matthew Taylor, was nonsense. We will do a strong letter to the *Observer*.

Sunday, 25 June, Westminster

Having driven back from Oxford, I found a huge pile of mail, the vast majority saying that to re-consider the name was bonkers and that the Parliamentary Party should be taken out and shot. Altogether a very bleak situation. Already, I suspect, people will be walking away.

A very, very black week which may well mark the end of the Party altogether. It's down to me and a few others to try and keep the thing together. The problem is that I am dog tired and very dispirited. I cannot see a way through the dilemma and I seem to have come to the end of my reserves of energy and resolve.

Sunday, 2 July, Somerset

A day spent on *Citizens' Britain*.

Hong Kong is now becoming a major issue. All the Sunday newspapers take our line on right of abode for British citizens in HK. The *Mail On Sunday* very strong and the *Sunday Telegraph* talking of Nazism and appeasement. This is excellent – though none of them, of course, even mention us. We must major on this in the weeks ahead.

The bad news of today is that the opinion polls show us down to 4 per cent. God! I thought we couldn't go lower. Surely, sooner or later, this nightmare will end.

Saturday, 8 July, Somerset

During the evening Alan Leaman rang to say that the *Observer* were running a 'Social and Liberal Democrats in Crisis' story tomorrow, added to which there was an *On The Record* quote by Geraint about not being prepared to accept any other name but Liberal Democrat and calling on Simon Hughes, Alan Beith and David Alton to do the same. I wish my colleagues would just shut up.

I now believe we can get through this terrible cascade of challenges, but only if people are prepared to give us the space to sort matters out one at a time and in a calm manner. There are times I despair. I rang Archy and Jim to warn them of what was coming and could hear the despair in their voices, too. I wonder if I will ever be able to lead a political party on the up, rather than on the down.

Tuesday, 11 July, Westminster

After the votes, a meeting in my office at 11.00pm with Charles Kennedy, David Steel, Ming Campbell, Archy Kirkwood and Jim Wallace. We pulled out the whisky bottle and talked till around 12.30am, by which time the group had shrunk to David, Jim, Charles and myself. It was an extended discussion, from which we reached the following conclusions:

1. I should take a tough line on the name. We will go for a commitment from the Parliamentary Party to accept the outcome of a ballot of the Party in the next week and to start playing a full role in the Party's affairs. In the absence of any such commitment we would simply block either a ballot or a debate. Charles undertook to persuade Bob Maclennan on this.

2. There was a general consensus, with which I strongly disagreed, that we

ought to try to block the debate on the 'named organizations' in the Party constitution.[1] I will have to reverse this on a bilateral basis later.

To bed, very tired.

Thursday, 13 July, Westminster

Just before leaving the bench after PMQs, Bob Maclennan asked if I could meet with Charles Kennedy and himself to discuss something rather urgent. He brought Charles down and they told me that Bob had been approached by John Cartwright, who said he didn't want to waste the last eight years; was there not some way that we could get closer together again?

Bob and Charles were very excited by this. I was initially cautious, but the more they explained the situation, the more interested I became. This may be a way forward. I told Bob to continue his discussions with John Cartwright. Our basic bottom line must be:

1. That Owen must resign as Parliamentary Leader (Cartwright himself seemed to suggest this).

2. That they join us on a Parliamentary basis, taking the Parliamentary Whip.

3. That we should persuade the opinion polls to abolish the name SDP in their listing of parties and substitute a single name – the Democrats – in its place.

4. That this was entirely a Parliamentary union, for activities within the House at this stage. But we could all see where it might lead (i.e. merger).

5. That there would, therefore, be no question of any electoral pacts or deals.

There are some very real advantages to this:

1. The two parties would, in the public eye, be seen to have come together.

---

1 An attempt (which I supported) to remove the word 'NATO' from our Party constitution, on the grounds that constitutions should be permanent and should not, therefore, include the names of temporary organizations. But others, especially from the old SDP, thought the inclusion of the word NATO in the constitution protected the Party from takeover by unilateral disarmers.

2. We would be seen to have won.

3. The word SDP would disappear.

4. We could then dispense with the name debate. The Parliamentary Party would refer to itself as the Democrats, with Owen and Cartwright calling themselves Social Democrats, whilst Alan Beith and Geraint Howells and Co. could call themselves Liberal Democrats. I could then simply say the name debate, ballot, etc. were off.

Bob is keen to have Owen as our Health spokesman for next year. I am against this (and anyway I don't think he would do it), but said that I would think about it. A very interesting development. But it *must* be kept totally secret until we see how much further we can go. Cartwright seems keen to pull it all off before the end of the Parliamentary session. On balance, there is probably little chance of it succeeding, as I suspect Owen will say that a single Parliamentary Whip is further than he is prepared to go [in the days of the Alliance, he always claimed that a single Whip was the same as merger]. But it is certainly something to think about.

Tuesday, 18 July, Cowley Street

As I suspected, the Finance and Administration Committee meeting was utter chaos. We will have to get rid of all the Area Agents. And even then the Party will be facing a shortfall in liquidity of £200,000 by the end of September. Otherwise we will end up half a million in debt. Meanwhile, the auditors have threatened to qualify our accounts, in effect making us bankrupt. I haven't a clue how to get out of this one. I can deal with one problem at a time, but not with all of them at the same time.

Wednesday, 19 July, London

I've had the bright idea that, on the name, it might be worthwhile having a ballot of Party representatives at the Conference, rather than Party members. This would (a) be cheaper, (b) get the issue out of the way quickly and (c) be more manageable. A useful fall-back position to reveal when I have shown my colleagues the edge of the precipice again and they have had another good look over.

Thursday, 20 July, London

Bob has seen David Owen. He promised to come and tell me about it. But we had a vote at 7.00, so I met him in the Lobby for a chat. Owen is balking (I knew he would). He wants a position which retains his credibility. But he is not making any offers, he is sitting there waiting for us to come forward with proposals. This is just what I was afraid of. We must beware the tar baby syndrome.

Monday, 24 July, Westminster

At 9.00pm into a Parliamentary Party Meeting with the Officers. The situation is dire. We are facing a £350,000 deficit that must be covered this year. The Officers are unanimous in believing we shouldn't have a ballot, which infuriated Russell, Malcolm Bruce[1] (mildly backed up by Jim) and Alan Beith. It ended with Charles Kennedy storming out and saying he felt that he had been betrayed. Events are moving to a pretty tense climax.

Later on, a discussion with Malcolm until about 11.45 over several whiskies. We talked through a number of options, including Malcolm's suggestion of simply dodging the ballot, using Democrat as a federal name and allowing the maximum laxity towards those who wish to call themselves Liberal Democrats. I am against this, as it will cause confusion and ridicule.

All rather depressing and, I suspect, as close to the bottom of this awful saga as we will get. I am now very worried whether we can survive at all. But perhaps this is just tiredness. My brain is not working properly and I find even the smallest problem almost impossible to cope with. I need a holiday more than at any time I can remember.

Tuesday, 25 July, London

At 4.30 a discussion with Roy Jenkins, who said he was strongly in favour of accommodating Owen and that we should be prepared to offer him

---

1 Member of Parliament (Liberal then Liberal Democrat) for Gordon since 1983. Malcolm was the Leader of the Scottish Party. He later became the Treasury Spokesman, and is now Chair of the Parliamentary Party. He led my campaign for the Leadership.

Deputy Leader of the Party or, if he wished, Foreign Affairs spokesman. I am opposed to the former and David Steel would not be too happy about the latter. Anyway, I don't think there is any chance he would take it.

At 6 o'clock Owen, Cartwright and Barnes turned up. Cartwright looked very shifty and Owen set and surly. I was very cheery, served them some tea and got down to the discussion.

It became quickly apparent that Cartwright had been freelancing. Owen rejected out of hand the possibility of a single Whip, putting Cartwright in a very difficult position. Owen rambled on in a most incoherent way about what he planned for the future. He talked about a kind of relationship between us in which we would all be nice to each other. I told him that this was simply not on the cards. Bob reinforced my point by getting angry with Cartwright, saying that was not at all what he had thought we were here to discuss. Cartwright seemed all over the place. Owen at one stage said, 'Well, John can take his own position, but it certainly doesn't apply to our party.'

Towards the end of the meeting, when it was clear we were getting nowhere, Owen started listing the three points he wanted:

1. no single whip,

2. no single name,

3. a purely Parliamentary relationship.

I told him that he had missed one out — we had been informed that he would be standing down as leader of the SDP. Owen flew at this and asked me where I got the information from. Bob said, 'From John.' Cartwright stammered and tried to come up with an alternative explanation (that David Alton had put him up to it). Owen immediately fastened on to this, seeing a conspiracy with the knives out behind him. I left him with that impression, but refrained from telling him that the person Cartwright had suggested might take over from him was none other than Rosie Barnes.

Rosie sat fairly silent throughout, but made it clear that she could not support Cartwright's position. I found Owen muddled and uncertain of what he wanted — but, as ever, vain and hectoring. He tried the usual tactic of insulting me and the Party. But I refused to rise, and asked him time and again, with what I hoped sounded like gentle persuasion, to tell us exactly what he wanted. We broke up after two hours, saying that we would discuss among ourselves ways of being 'kinder to each other'. I expressed my deep disappointment at having been led into a meeting in which the agenda was not as we had thought and at which an opportunity was about to be lost.

I then had a beer with Bob and Jim (Alan Leaman joined us). Bob seemed quite perky but amazed at the position Cartwright had allowed himself to be put in. Owen, who is a conspiracy theorist of the first order, must now believe that Cartwright is completely untrustworthy. On the surface, we have achieved nothing. But we will have driven deep wedges between Cartwright and Owen. We must now be kind to Cartwright and hope that at some future stage (but not too soon) he will hop off.

Wednesday, 26 July, Cowley Street

Into the office at 8.00 and an Officers' meeting at 8.30. I had a chat with Clive Lindley about the financial situation before the meeting. Apparently the auditors are saying that the Party 'can no longer continue to trade'. Meanwhile, the bank is asking for collateral to cover the overdraft. We hope this is just an opening bargaining position.

At 5 o'clock a meeting with Russell and Jim and into the Parliamentary Party Meeting. An absolute disaster. They all went off in different directions and I was simply unable to stop them. Bob made an emotional statement against a ballot. Simon made two very clear and helpful statements, but rather spoilt it by digging into the past again. Roy Jenkins then came in with a very cogently argued and powerful case that we should not have a ballot but let the name 'evolve'. He even said that he would be prepared to start calling himself a Liberal Democrat as a mark of his commitment. David Steel concurred and the meeting started to gallop off in this direction. Richard Livsey said he thought having much more flexibility and allowing the name to evolve along the lines Roy suggested was the right way. I said I was opposed; it would lead to even greater confusion. Simon Hughes and Matthew Taylor both said that they couldn't accept a decision made purely by the MPs. It was the Party's name, so the Party at large had to decide. I agreed.

At this point I had to draw stumps before the meeting deteriorated still further. We seem unable to get a consensus on anything. I thought I had stitched one together on the name. But I haven't. More time is needed on the edge of the precipice.

It is becoming clear that I will have to take a very lonely decision on this and just push it through.

I went home at around midnight, sat down and thought the thing through again. I concluded that we must take this decision (a) as fast as possible, (b) in a way which causes the minimum disruption to the Autumn Conference, and (c) in a way least likely to be open to challenge in the future.

On these grounds, Roy Jenkins' and David Steel's recommendation of an evolutionary approach falls. We must put a quick end to this damaging period of confusion and a ballot is the only way to do it. Secondly, since I can't build a consensus round this, I will have to risk going out on a limb for it.

That's my decision. The difficulty now will be applying it.

Monday, 31 July, London

The Federal Executive meeting started a few minutes after 6.00pm. There was a good attendance and most people stayed to the end (around 11.30). It was very tough. I argued for a ballot of Conference Delegates and was opposed strenuously by Charles and most of the old SDP. In the ensuing vote I won by 8 to 5. However, a good deal of my personal credibility now rests on this ballot, as I made it clear that this was my personal decision. It had better be right.

We then went into the disastrous financial position. Anthony Jacobs[1] made a superb contribution in which he said we had to be tough (i.e. cut everything to the bone, leaving us with one campaigner and one policy person). I agreed with him.

I left to do *Newsnight* on the Party's predicament. It was a very difficult interview. I said that we had to live within our financial means, but that no one should underestimate our determination to recover.

Then back into the meeting to hear the final decision. They went for the

---

1 Sir Anthony Jacobs is a long time supporter of the Party and of the old Liberal Party. He now sits on the Liberal Democrat benches in the House of Lords.

deep cuts, as I wanted. Chris Rennard[1] and others said this was 'the end of the Party as we know it'.

I went to bed happy that at least we are through this stage.

Saturday, 5 August, Somerset

A mountain of mail. Many resignations on the name fiasco. Some bitter letters attacking me. One or two from ex-SDPers objecting to the ballot.

Still going downhill, I fear.

Friday, 18 August, Somerset

We seem to be moving towards some sort of consensus on the name, at last. The deal is that we will informally 'accept', in advance, that Liberal Democrats will be the likely result of the ballot – which will take the steam out of the campaigning and make the outcome a formality. I will try and persuade Roy Jenkins to write an article in which he will refer to himself as a Liberal Democrat, then we will do some background briefing.

I think we are gently coming off the bottom. At the very least, we seem to be gaining more control over what's happening. The press, however, are still determined to write us off on every occasion. They smell blood and are doing all they can to make it flow as freely as possible – especially at the Autumn Conference.

Sunday, 3 September, London

To see Roy Jenkins at 12.30. We had a quiet session in his office over a glass of champagne. I asked him to use the phrase 'Liberal Democrat' lightly and in passing during his Conference Rally speech. He told me (rather to my surprise) that he had always been rather in favour of Liberal Democrat and was happy to do this.

---

1 The Director of Campaigns for almost my entire leadership. He was the architect of our subsequent by-election victories and has become a formidable and widely respected practitioner of political campaigning across all parties. He now sits in the House of Lords.

I left at about 8.15pm and had a pizza in Notting Hill before the meeting of the ex-SDP members of the Party at 9.30. Present were twenty or thirty leading members of the ex-SDP contingent in the Party. It was a difficult meeting, which ranged between the pragmatists and the people who believe that anybody who had ever been in the Liberal Party was a member of the 'sillies'. One or two said that this whole issue was 'a test of my Leadership', etc.

It is clear that my Leadership is now raising dissatisfaction in both wings of the Party. But this is inevitable.

Monday, 4 September, Westminster

Today is the opening ceremony of the International Parliamentary Union. Into the office by 8.00 with my morning suit. I spent the first hour or so dealing with mail, signing off letters and talking to Alan Leaman. The press are beginning to shift slightly more in our favour.

Then at 10.45, up to Central Lobby, where I met the Prime Minister, Neil Kinnock, Geoffrey Howe and John Major.[1] We processed into a full Westminster Hall and I took my seat alongside the Russian Ambassador and the Ambassador of Zimbabwe, and one up from Geoffrey Howe. We had rather an engaging conversation, but I did feel rather like one of the ten green bottles on the wall, sitting in front of around a thousand people.

In due course the Queen came in. The Prime Minister was deeply obsequious to her. She was accompanied by Chris Patten, who is the new Lord Privy Seal.[2] He looked terribly uncomfortable and out of place. He has a rather prematurely portly figure and was wearing the wrong-coloured waistcoat; the buttons seemed all askew and his hair stuck out like a haystack. To add to the general scarecrow impression, he appeared largely unaware of what he should do and got himself unerringly in the wrong position at every stage of the proceedings. My heart went out to him.

The Queen's speech was rather short, but the representative of the Secretary General of the United Nations gave a long and very rambling one. The whole thing was over in about an hour.

1 At this time Foreign Secretary.
2 At the time Chairman of the Conservative Party. Member of Parliament (Conservative) for Bath 1979–92. Patten later became the Governor and Commander-in-Chief of Hong Kong until it was handed back to China. He is now the European Commissioner for External Relations.

On the way out, I bumped into Chris. He confided how he hated ceremonial and I said I did, too. I was always a disaster at parade grounds in the Royal Marines, which is why they sent me to wars rather than risking me anywhere near formal ceremonies.

At 6.30 I went across to Cowley Street for a meeting on how to handle the forthcoming Conference, where we face a motion of no confidence in the Party Officers (and the name issue, of course). Ian Wrigglesworth, Dick Newby and Adrian Slade[1] have clearly got the wind up. Ditto Graham Elson.[2] Graham tells me that the information I was given, upon which I planned the timing for the name ballot, was now rather doubtful. I was furious about this and let my anger be known.

Tuesday, 12 September, Brighton

PARTY CONFERENCE

I woke up to receive an overnight letter from Graham Elson. All seem to believe that we will lose the motion of no confidence in the Officers, which is down for debate this afternoon. I decided in my shower that I might have to speak in this. The overwhelming consensus in the office was that I should do no such thing. I contacted Ming, who thought the same, and Jim, who thought I might have to.

I asked Charles if he would speak in the debate, but he wouldn't. I ended up being marginally persuaded that perhaps it wouldn't be a good idea for me to speak, but reserved my final judgement until I saw how the debate developed. I also rang Alan to see if he would be prepared to speak to strengthen Ming in the Defence debate (also this afternoon), but he refused.

I decided that I would not be present at the NATO debate in the morning, having made it clear what my view was on *Newsnight* last night (i.e. that the Party should take out the reference to NATO).

In the debate to remove NATO from the Constitution, Charles spoke against but well and Tom McNally, very helpfully, spoke in favour (after some persuasion from me). This meant that there were SDP people on both sides of the argument and that the issue was debated in terms of what

1 Former President of the Liberal Party.
2 General Secretary of the Party from 1989 to 1997.

was right for the constitution, rather than as a defence issue. In the end, the vote to remove NATO was carried by a hundred or so votes.

At 12.45 a meeting with the Parliamentary candidates – all very cheerful, I thought. People seem bucked up by the morning's business.

At 12.15 back in for the Party Business Report and the no confidence motion in the Officers. Clive Lindley and Ian Wrigglesworth made good speeches. They struck just the right note between contrition and resolute defence. In the end, quite a good debate, which we won overwhelmingly. The Party is behaving well in the face of very difficult circumstances.

At 4 o'clock into the Press Room, very nervous. I had to persuade them that my view of the NATO story was right. I was very firm, very direct. They seemed to take it – in fact, remarkably easily. The news coverage that evening was excellent, with NATO barely given a mention.

Friday, 15 September, Brighton

LAST DAY OF THE PARTY CONFERENCE

As always, extremely nervous about my end of Conference speech. When I got to the platform I tried two jokes, which worked reasonably well. However, I was horrified to see that we did not have the final version of the speech on the Autocue. I made a couple of fluffs, but was cheered dutifully and people were kind enough about it afterwards.

The two high points in the speech were where I said we were going to be a radical, not a centre party. The second was when I said that we would take the first opportunity to remove Mrs Thatcher. Max Atkinson and I had carefully planned this piece so that there were three clap lines before it, on the first two of which I was to hold the audience back, releasing them on the third and final clap line. It worked a charm. We also tried a little bit of audience participation with a couple of lines on Neil Kinnock, though I didn't make them work as well as I should have.

" So much for that episode — now it's heigh-ho for the open sea ! "

Friday, 6 October, London

Our opinion poll ratings have gone up to 8.5 per cent and we are ahead of the Greens again. My personal rating also seems to be rising.

Monday, 16 October, London

The results of the ballot on the name were announced today. Overwhelmingly in favour of Liberal Democrats.

That problem, at least, is behind us. Huge relief.

Thursday, 26 October, London

All-day Parliamentary Party Meeting at the National Liberal Club.

At 6.00pm Alan Leaman's bleeper went off. I paid no attention to this. He went out to make a phone call, returning almost immediately to grab my shoulder and insist that I come out. I told him I wouldn't unless it was very urgent. Then he whispered in my ear that Lawson[1] had just resigned.

I immediately called Alan Beith outside and together we concocted our initial reaction (the integrity of the Government is in ruins, its economic policy is in tatters and it is Mrs Thatcher who should consider her position, etc.).

I broke the news to the Parliamentary Party, spent five minutes outlining my strategy for the next year and then left them to it, telling them that I would call them across to the House as soon as necessary. Mark and I then walked swiftly to the House. On the way we passed the Norman Shaw buildings[2] and saw that the press and TV had congregated there. On the spur of the moment, I decided to dive in and make myself available to them there and then.

The building was in turmoil with television crews and reporters running everywhere and politicians descending on it from every corner of the House. As I walked in, Kinnock was being interviewed and they wheeled me on straight after him. Then, in quick succession, Channel 4 for the seven o'clock news (I tried a comparison between Mrs Thatcher and the last Dowager Emperor of China, which seemed to work well), then Independent Radio News and about fourteen others.

At 7 o'clock we heard that somebody would come across to the House from Downing Street and make a statement. I immediately called my colleagues back from the National Liberal Club, so they could be on the bench for the statement at 8 o'clock.

The feeling in the House was that the Prime Minister should make the statement, but would probably hand it to Geoffrey Howe to do. This was

---

1 Nigel Lawson, Chancellor of the Exchequer. Member of Parliament (Conservative) for Blaby 1974–92. He now sits in the House of Lords. Lawson resigned over Thatcher's reliance on her economic adviser, Sir Alan Walters, who disagreed with her Chancellor.

2 One of the Parliamentary buildings; once the HQ of the Metropolitan Police (Scotland Yard), now used as MPs' offices.

clearly going to be a great Parliamentary event. I did my last interview at 7.30 and returned to the office to discover that the statement would be made soon. My instinct was to take a responsible line and assure the new Chancellor of the Exchequer (John Major) that we would help him to stabilize the pound and ensure that there was not too great a financial crisis.

Then on to the bench. The place was packed and very tense. By now we knew that Geoffrey Howe would speak for the Government. As I walked down past the Labour front bench, Bryan Gould[1] said to me, 'What price a coalition now?' I responded with some crack and asked him who was going to take the statement for Labour. He confidentially told me that Neil Kinnock had decided that Frank Dobson[2] would, but that he (Bryan) considered this a serious mistake.

Shortly afterwards, Alan Beith came in and, nudging Jim to one side, said he would like to sit next to me so as to give me support. This was nice but made the bench extremely cramped (we were nearly all there). I told Alan that Frank Dobson was taking the statement and I was prepared to let him do so if he wished. He replied, 'Certainly not!' and David Steel supported this. If Labour were so stupid as to let a second-ranker take the statement, that was their problem. We certainly shouldn't. It was a generous concession.

The chamber broke into uproar with great shouts of 'Where is she?' and so on when Geoffrey Howe arrived. Frank Dobson responded to Howe's speech with a long rambling statement which he read from a piece of paper. He completely missed the target and lost the mood of the House.

After this, Sir William Clark,[3] then me. I was extremely nervous and sweating slightly. By now I sensed that something short and directly attacking the Prime Minister and the Government was needed. I said: 'I suspect that many Honourable Members feel a good deal of sympathy for the Right Honourable Member for Blaby whose job has been made impossible, whose position has been made untenable and who has taken the only honourable course open to him. Is it not the case that what is at

1 Opposition spokesman for the Environment. Member of Parliament (Labour) Southampton Test 1974–9, Dagenham 1983–94.

2 At the time the Opposition spokesman on Energy. Member of Parliament (Labour) for Holborn & St Pancras South since 1979. Frank went on to become the Secretary of State for Health before running for London Mayor.

3 Member of Parliament (Conservative) for Nottingham South 1959–66, East Surrey 1970–74, Croydon South 1974–92.

stake is not the position of the Chancellor of the Exchequer but the integrity of the Government and of a Prime Minister who has shown herself to be arrogant, dictatorial and isolated? We have been told for the last ten years that there is no alternative. There is an alternative. She must go.' The whole delivered to a rising crescendo of noise in the House – I was cheered by Labour and there was a great roar of approval from our side when I sat down. Then out of the chamber with everybody saying that we had nicely upstaged Labour.

My last interview was at 10 o'clock and I then walked with Mark to the National Liberal Club, where the Parliamentary Party and most of the staff were still meeting. As I walked in they burst into applause.

Friday, 10 November, Westminster

Meeting with Shirley Williams at 9.00 for an hour or so. She seems in very good form. She anticipates that Labour will lose the election now, and that we could move into the second stage of the break-up of the Labour Party. I said I thought there was a possibility that if Labour was to maintain a small lead over the Conservatives we were now on line for a hung Parliament, in which case we would need all the support and heavyweight people we could get. She said she would return to Britain from America the moment I asked her to. She also undertook to help Alan Beith with his committee on planning our approach to hung Parliaments, etc.[1]

Thursday, 16 November, Westminster

LAST DAY OF THE PARLIAMENTARY YEAR

The House rose today. I went through for the Ceremony of the Prorogation,[2] which requires us all to troop down from the House of Commons to the Lords. Another of those ridiculous rituals of which we have too many.

I stood almost next to the Prime Minister while we were in the Lords listening to the prorogation notices being read. I took time to study her. She really is a poor old thing. She looks lined, with her hair swept up but

1 Alan and I had agreed in September to set this up in order to prepare for the future.
2 Marks the end of the Parliamentary session.

getting very thin. She kept on staring at the ground and muttering to herself. For the first time I felt some affection for her. She looked just like any old grandmother who ought to be at home playing with her grandchildren instead of trying to conduct the ridiculous business of governing the country. She seemed alone (Geoffrey Howe was standing next to her, but carefully placed himself several feet away and the rest of the Tory Party were even further off). I caught her eye at one stage and flashed her a smile. She seemed taken aback by this, looked rather coldly and cast her eyes down to the floor again.

Monday, 27 November, London

After a day's campaigning for David Alton in Liverpool, I returned to London for the Federal Executive meeting at 6 o'clock. I stayed to discuss who should be the General Election manager. We are past the mid-point of the Parliament so I have to decide on this soon. But it's going to be difficult. My mind is hovering between Alec McGivan and Des Wilson. The former would be right if we were at 17 or 18 per cent. But at 6 per cent we really have to take risks and Des could certainly give us a campaigning edge. Not that I told them any of this, of course. I must just make a lone decision and then take the flak. Both possibilities would be divisive and each has its downside.

I think Des has the edge. We need rescuing, and for this there is no one better. And we need to be eye-catching – which he will ensure. But I must give a lot more thought to this. There will be an explosion from most of the Parliamentary Party and the Party establishment if I appoint Des, because of the book he wrote after the last election.[1] But I have no doubt that he has the flair, the unconventionality and the ability.

As always, it's a balance between taking risks and keeping the Party together. Probably the most fateful decision I will take this year – and it must be done in the next fortnight.

---

1 *Battle for Power – The inside story of the Alliance and the 1987 General Election* (1987).

Saturday, 9 December, Somerset

A quiet evening in front of the television. It is clear that Mrs Thatcher has been completely isolated in Brussels, just as I suspected she might. But goodness! They are clever. She came waddling back to Britain saying that she was still in the centre of Europe. It's completely untrue, of course. But if they say it often enough people will believe them.

Meanwhile the *Daily Telegraph* opinion poll today shows us up to 9 per cent – slowly, slowly making our way back.

1990

Monday, 8 January, Westminster

I have decided to write a regular 'position paper'[1] every year and at key moments (such as after elections) to help me sum up where we are and what we must do in the year ahead. I will use these as the basis for discussions and decision-making with the Party and my Parliamentary colleagues. I wrote the first of these this morning. I have concluded that over the last two years we have successfully established the Party, but no one yet knows what we stand for. Correcting this is what 1990 must be about. 1990 shows every sign of being just as difficult as 1989, but perhaps a little more interesting.

Wednesday, 10 January, London

In a rush, for dinner at Joe Allen's restaurant with Archy and Des, who was in ebullient form. Des kept on claiming that he didn't want the job of General Election manager, but then listed every reason under the sun why he should do it. He had even written out some organization tables and a contract between him and me! He is not someone to spend too long with. He is so damned convincing, even on madcap ideas. About fifteen minutes is all any ordinary person can take.

He said he would take time off work to do it, without cost to the Party. He is fine at this stage, but once he gets underway he will be a handful. Nevertheless, we need to take risks and Des is unquestionably the best campaigner in Britain.

Tuesday, 23 January, Brussels

Up at 5.30 to get to Heathrow by 6.30. It was blowing a gale and we had a very bumpy flight to Brussels for meetings with members of the Commission.

---

1 See Appendix A for the highlights from the position papers I wrote up to the 1997 General Election.

First, Leon Brittan[1] in his office on the top floor of the Berlaymont. He is round, avuncular and jovial. I got on well with him. He was very critical of Mrs Thatcher and clearly believes that Government policy on Economic and Monetary Union is nonsense. I hear that he is regarded as sharp-edged and tough, and is one of the few people who has the respect of Delors.[2]

At 3 o'clock David Williamson, Secretary General of the Commission and Delors' right-hand man. He is bouncing with energy and full of ideas. I was impressed. He told us that Delors' policy on Europe was what he called 'progressive structural dynamic destabilization' (I can just hear it in French). What this amounts to is deliberately introducing items on to the European agenda as 'problems'. Each problem, once solved, opens up another problem. Thus he makes progress from economic to monetary union to democratic union and eventually to political union. He never admits his ultimate destination, but merely sets the process in train (not a bad strategy for moving a political party, either).

This is more farsighted than I had previously been prepared to concede of Delors.

Afterwards, an hour's gentle fencing match, conducted with wry humour, with Sir David Hannay, the British Ambassador. He is clearly a strong believer in European unity and does not agree with Mrs Thatcher, but he made rather an elegant job of supporting her. A Foreign Office official straight out of the box.

Friday, 2 February, Westminster

At 11 o'clock it was announced from South Africa that they are about to release Nelson Mandela, unban the ANC, set free all political prisoners and suspend executions. Amazing! President de Klerk clearly sees himself as a Gorbachev and is running as many risks. I did a number of television interviews in the hour or so after the announcement, in which I suggested the British Government should be prepared to remove sanctions, but not do it just yet. Being in London on a day like this really is useful – I got a great deal of coverage.

1 Vice-President of the European Commission. Member of Parliament (Conservative) for Cleveland and Whitby 1974–83, Richmond (Yorkshire) 1983–8.
2 Jaques Delors, President of the European Commission.

Monday, 5 February, London

A very good dinner with Archy and Des, whom I have decided to make General Election manager. Archy and I applied a pincer movement, getting Des to agree to most of what we wanted as regards embedding his Election Committee into the Party structure. I even managed to persuade him that one or two of the ideas were his. He was his usual outrageous self. But I like him a good deal. I told him very straightforwardly of the likely horrified reaction to his appointment from some in the Parliamentary Party. Professional that he is, he took it all on board. I think this is going to work.

At about 11 o'clock, having gone over all the details, Des suddenly stuck out his hand and said, 'Well, do you still want me? If so, let's shake on it.' So I did. We both laughed. It now remains for me to sell him to the others. This may not be easy, as I understand there are already rumblings from the usual quarters. I left with Des promising to write us a press release, the terms of reference, a letter of confirmation and a memorandum of the meeting. I bet he has done it all before I get into the office tomorrow morning.

Today is either a Red Letter Day, from which we will all benefit, or a Black Letter Day, when I took a decision for which I will pay a very heavy price in the future.

Thursday, 8 March, London

Evening. To Hackney with Mark Payne for a meeting protesting at the Poll Tax. Throughout the day we had been hearing of huge crowds building up in front of the town hall for a demonstration. When we arrived there were already 4,000 people milling around. The town hall was boarded up and the police were under furious attack. It reminded me of Belfast.

To Mark's concern, I wandered off into the crowd to see what was going on. No doubt about who was organizing this. Militant much in evidence, but a lot of anarchists as well. And the extreme unpleasantness and brutality on their faces was rather shocking. They were using bottles, stakes from posters and anything else to throw at the police.

Mark tried to protect me from one or two flying bottles and wanted me to go inside. But I stayed where I was to observe the crowd, unrecognized.

Eventually one or two cameramen spotted me and began taking photographs. Realizing that I could be a centre for further disturbance, I pulled out, having spent about twenty minutes in the middle of the riot. The crowd was clearly organized, and intent on violence, but generally I thought the police acted with admirable restraint and courage.

On the way into the town hall I was interviewed by Thames Television, which caused another mob to gather round. They had, by now, recognized me and began shouting obscenities at me and the cameras. So we moved into the town hall, in which the Poll Tax meeting was to be held. People asked me whether we should have a closed meeting. I replied that it should be open. I didn't want to allow such intimidation to quell free speech.

It was a mistake. As soon as the doors were opened, about 200 or 300 Militants flooded into the building, screaming abuse. At one point they spotted that they could get into the main hall by going through one of the glass doors at the side. There were two heavies with Dobermann pinschers standing at these. I told them to get the dogs away as they could become an extra provocation. At this point the Militants turned on the security guards and started kicking in the glass doors. I went down to try and help.

Once back on the platform, I attempted to start the meeting. I sat patiently waiting for the Militants' shouting to stop. After about ten minutes and another two or three assaults on the platform, however, it was clear that it would not. The security guards were at risk, and, furthermore, the police outside were now extremely stretched, with a huge mob swelling up to the doors. I called the meeting to a close and we got everyone out as quickly as we could.

By now, though, we were trapped by the crowd swirling round the town hall. Fortunately, our car was parked with the police cars at the back, carefully guarded. But there was no way out. The police suggested we go into a neighbouring pub, which was being used as a sanctuary, where we had a quick beer, and waited for the crowds to move away, before driving out hurriedly.

To *Newsnight*, where I was joined by Clive Soley[1] and David Hunt.[2]

---

1 Opposition spokesman on Housing. Member of Parliament (Labour) for Hammersmith 1979–97, Ealing Acton and Shepherds Bush since 1997. Currently Chair of the Parliamentary Labour Party.
2 Minister of State for Environment. Member of Parliament (Conservative) for Wirral since 1976. Soon after, Hunt became the Secretary of State for Wales.

Soley was very stupid, saying that the rioters were all 'Thatcher's children'. This gave me the chance to round on him for not condemning the violence and call on Kinnock to withdraw the Whip from Labour MPs who supported Militant. David Hunt looked self-satisfied and supported me, so I promptly berated him for introducing the Poll Tax in the first place.

When I got home, Independent Radio News were there. They interviewed me at about 11.45, after which I couldn't sleep because of the unrelieved tension.

Wednesday, 14 March, London

Lunch with Alastair Campbell of the *Daily Mirror* at Simpsons. He thinks Kinnock can do it. He is, of course, very close to Kinnock. So I passed back some messages about the way that we should proceed if, as seems likely, there is a hung Parliament. Campbell, though, believes that Kinnock will win outright and is not prepared to contemplate anything else.

In the evening, over to the Cambridge Union. Austin Mitchell[1] there (he came without a bow-tie and had to borrow one – suitably red). We changed together and chatted about the possibilities of partnership after the next election. He believes that Kinnock is becoming a crypto-Tory and that there is every possibility of a hung Parliament. He said Kinnock wouldn't pull it off and it was time the Labour Party realized that. Altogether a useful discussion which may have laid some good groundwork for the future. At least he saw I was more flexible in private than in public. I told him there was no benefit in me raising the issue publicly until Kinnock and the Labour Party were more receptive.

Wednesday, 21 March, Westminster

To Downing Street with Jane for dinner with Vaclav Havel.[2] The Prime Minister did her usual wet handshake, after which a few words with Havel. About forty at the table. I sat next to Sandra Howard and Caroline

1 Member of Parliament (Labour) for Grimsby since 1977. Austin is on the left wing of the Labour Party.
2 President of Czech and Slovak Republic. In 1992 after the split of the countries he became President of the Czech Republic.

Waldegrave.[1] Sandra revealed that she had been Liberal in her earlier life, but was now a very wet Tory, who didn't agree much with her husband, but of course supported him fully. Caroline Waldegrave was urbane, pretty and very amusing.

Maggie gave a prepared speech on her sense of guilt over the Prague Spring and letting the Germans unite – all a bit ridiculous, I thought. Havel delivered a light speech – the kind of thing you might give having been invited to the vicarage for tea. More 'Thanks very much for having me' than anything else. Nevertheless, he exhibits a marked sense of inner strength. He is small, speaks in a quiet voice, has piercing blue eyes and almost no grey in his sandy hair. His Czechoslovak assistants were all very young, delightfully scruffy and unsure of what to do. A strange combination of naïvety and self-confidence.

As we were leaving we met the Prime Minister coming up the stairs, having said goodbye to Havel. She chatted amiably to Jane about cooking. Jane, who likes to pretend she dislikes Thatcher very much, hissed under her breath as we parted, 'She's bloody charming, isn't she?'

Wednesday, 28 March, Westminster

At 6 o'clock, into the Parliamentary Party Meeting. We discussed the impending Bootle by-election, which will be held on 3 May, along with local council elections, concluding that we have an opportunity here. David Alton, however, wants to run this on the single-issue basis of abortion. In addition, there is some question of the Doctor endorsing our candidate, which would be a mild embarrassment.

Then on to strategy. I read out my position paper.[2] It still stands up, nearly four months after I wrote it. The only real issue is that Labour are still higher than I anticipated and they have not yet peaked. On the other hand, the Greens and the SDP are lower than I predicted. A long discussion, the chief conclusions of which were that we should not talk about pacts, that we should continue to attack Labour, and that we should be patient.

1 The wives of Michael Howard (Minister of State at the Department of Employment) and William Waldegrave (Minister of State at the Foreign and Commonwealth Office).
2 See Appendix A.

Thursday, 29 March, Cambridge

KOENIGSWINTER CONFERENCE

To Cambridge with Ming for the Koenigswinter Conference. Thatcher and Kohl[1] due to give speeches in the evening.

In the afternoon Heseltine[2] made an impressive speech which was clearly intended as a challenge to the Prime Minister on almost everything. The general consensus is that he will challenge her openly later this year. He is fifty-six or -seven, so cannot afford to wait much longer. My judgement is that he probably *won't* challenge Thatcher directly, but will arrange for the men in suits to come and take her away. If he manages a changeover with Thatcher some time this year, without blood on the floor, and then calls an election next spring, the situation could be very, very tough for us. He will certainly shoot our European fox.

In the evening a formal dinner. About 150 there. I was placed almost opposite Thatcher, who sat facing the television cameras and the audience. Three places to her right sat Kohl, with his back half turned to her. He never looked at her directly, even when he spoke. Then another four places down was Heseltine. A deliciously piquant table arrangement.

I sat between David Howell[3] and Marion Grafin Dohnoff[4] – both very engaging dinner partners. I spent the early part of dinner talking to David Howell and discovered that we agreed substantially about most things. Grafin Dohnoff was absolutely wonderful. I fell in love with her immediately! She is probably about seventy-five and must have been a very beautiful woman in her day. Her now-crinkled face was set with the most superb blue eyes.

Thatcher spoke for thirty minutes, mostly about NATO, without once mentioning the EEC. Her speech was flatly delivered, completely visionless and deeply insensitive. The first part was a diatribe about how much the Germans owed to Britain for their liberty, the second about how the two

1 Dr Helmut Kohl, Chancellor of the Federal Republic of Germany.

2 Currently Secretary of State for the Environment. Member of Parliament (Conservative) for Tavistock 1966–74 and Henley since 1974. Heseltine later became Deputy Prime Minister in John Major's Government.

3 Chairman of the House of Commons Foreign Affairs Select Committee. Member of Parliament (Conservative) for Guildford 1966–97. He now sits in the House of Lords.

4 A leading member of the German Resistance during the Second World War, and the only survivor among the conspirators of the 1944 bomb plot. An amazing lady.

Germanies shouldn't reunite. Michael Heseltine's body language was fascinating throughout. He lounged in his seat with a downturned mouth and his back turned half away from her in an attitude which said more about the contempt in which he held her than any words could possibly convey.

Kohl's speech was almost a mirror image of Thatcher's. Also about thirty minutes long, full of Europe and never mentioning NATO. I noticed that whenever Kohl used the word 'Margaret', he looked in the opposite direction and injected a certain steely tone into his voice.

An altogether fascinating evening. She looked completely worn out and ill at ease.

Friday, 6 April, Yeovil

The reaction to our position on Hong Kong[1] is rather bad (there have been a number of radio and newspaper reports along the lines of 'Liberal Democrats save Maggie over Hong Kong'). This has come at a bad time and will, I suspect, affect our local government vote next month, just as it affected our Euro vote last year. Nevertheless, a principle is involved here and we cannot abandon it; besides, it gives us the identity we so badly need.

My nightmare is that ours will be the votes that save the Government from defeat. We will then suffer a terrible penalty for putting the people of Hong Kong before the people of Britain and losing the opportunity to get rid of Thatcher.

I rang Simon Hughes and asked him to check round the colleagues to make sure that everybody was on board. It seems they are. I just hope that the serious newspapers will realize what's going on and support us for a change.

Then home at 10.30 before leaving for our Easter break in France.

Wednesday, 11 April, Irancy, Burgundy

[*Jane and I soon discovered that our house in Burgundy became part of our lives as an invaluable bolt hole between Parliamentary sessions. We got into the habit of spending every holiday there. Our life there offered a*

---

1 We had announced that we would support a Government proposal, opposed by Labour, to expand the number of British passport holders in Hong Kong who could have the right of abode in Britain.

sharp contrast to the hectic pace at Westminster and we soon made many new friends in the community. In 1996, my daughter Kate was to meet and marry her husband Sebastien, who comes from a neighbouring village.]

To Auxerre Cathedral for *The Messiah.*

We arrived just before the German choir. Supposed to be a youth choir, but didn't look it. The cathedral chairs were very cramped and uncomfortable and the temperature chilly.

And the choir were awful. They were half-asleep when they sang and the conductor had been listening to too much von Karajan. The whole thing lacked any kind of pace, which is a criminal sin for Handel.

All was somewhat alleviated by an absolutely glorious young alto with wonderful Titian hair. The soprano was quite good, but the tenor, who was brought in at the last moment, was thin and seemed to have somewhat uncertain contact with the score.

The chief relieving feature to the performance were two courting pigeons who spent the whole time flapping noisily around the cathedral roof. When they weren't copulating, they were crapping on the unsuspecting audience below. I couldn't help watching who they would defile next and what the reaction would be – ranging from outrage and anger to surreptitiously wiping away the mess and pretending it hadn't happened.

Altogether not a great evening – except, of course, for the pigeons.

Thursday, 19 April, Westminster

Down to the chamber for the Hong Kong debate. David Waddington[1] made rather a good speech – well balanced and carefully judged. Hattersley's,[2] however, was a wretched affair in which the bankruptcy of Labour's position was cruelly exposed. I followed Heath,[3] who spoke well and without notes, as usual.

My speech was OK, but the end was too emotional and everybody shouted at me. You need to hold a rather cool iciness throughout a

---

1 Home Secretary. Member of Parliament (Conservative) for Nelson and Colne 1968–74, Clitheroe 1979–83 and Ribble Valley 1983–90. Waddington is now in the House of Lords.
2 Roy Hattersley. Opposition spokesman for Home Affairs. Member of Parliament (Labour) Birmingham (Sparkbrook) 1964–97. Roy now sits in the House of Lords.
3 Edward Heath, former Prime Minister. Member of Parliament (Conservative) for Old Bexley & Sidcup since 1950.

Commons speech. I suspect my style still tends far too much towards platform oratory, which is inappropriate in the House.

The Government won with a majority of 97 on the first vote and 117 on the second. A crushing defeat for Tebbit,[1] but an even greater one for Labour.

An appearance on *Newsnight*, then to Yeovil in the car, listening to *La Bohème* and singing at the top of my voice to keep myself awake. I drove too fast and, lost in the last act coming down the Wylie bypass, was pulled over by a policeman. He said the usual, 'Excuse me sir, do you know what speed you were doing?' Then, 'Hey, are you Paddy Ashdown? Oh good, I get ten extra points for you.' A pleasant enough young man, but he didn't let me off. A fixed penalty and some points on my licence. I hope it doesn't get publicity.

Wednesday, 2 May, London

Into the office early. The last press conference before the local elections tomorrow. My prediction was that we would poll about 20 per cent and confound the pollsters.[2] This reflects the mood on the ground, although I do not quite trust it. An upbeat press conference, with the press noticing we were more cheerful than previously.

A co-ordinating meeting in the morning at which we went into the question of the new logo I've commissioned.[3] I came back nervous. Opinion has turned rather against me on the need for a new Party symbol. Archy Kirkwood and Matthew Taylor wobbly; Des doubtful. Even Mark lukewarm, believing that the money (perhaps £20,000) could be spent better elsewhere.

I decided that my best way forward was to invite key campaigners to see the logo in its nearly finished form next Thursday. This will give them a part in the decision-making and a feeling of ownership. I just hope it works.

---

1 Norman Tebbit, Member of Parliament (Conservative) for Epping 1970–74, Chingford 1974–92. Formerly a member of the Conservative Cabinet and Chairman of the Conservative Party. Tebbit had previously threatened Waddington with a Tory revolt if he continued with his plan to let 50,000 in from Hong Kong. Labour, disgracefully, were going to vote with the Tory rebels against the legislation.
2 In the local elections, the respective shares of the vote were Tories 27 per cent, Labour 53, Lib Dems 14 and SDP 1. At the Bootle by-election we came third, but only 41 votes behind the Tory candidate.
3 This subsequently became the Lib Dem bird.

"YOUR FATHER MAY BE LIBERAL DEMOCRAT, RONALD, BUT HE'S NEVER FORGOTTEN HIS WORKING CLASS ORIGINS "

Friday, 1 June, Westminster

Mark came in to tell me that he had dinner last night with Ian Wright,[1] of the Owenite rump SDP. Apparently there is going to be an emergency meeting on Sunday at which a proposal will be put to wind up the SDP. The public perception will be that the call came from Owen, but in reality it has come from the Party, who are fed up with him making their lives impossible. Wright seems fairly confident they will pack it in. Having discussed the news with Mark and Ian Wrigglesworth, I have agreed to take a very conciliatory line. No triumphalism, but simply the expression of gladness that the confusion of the centre ground has resolved itself and the suggestion made to start talks immediately with those who wish to rejoin us.

1 National Organizer of the continuing SDP 1990–92. Since this meeting Ian has become a close friend and adviser who accompanied me on my Leader's tour during the 1997 election.

Sunday, 3 June, Somerset

The news broke today that the SDP has finally and formally folded.

The end of a very important week. The key message to get across to the public is not that the SDP has folded, but that the rifts in our own ranks have been healed, with most of them joining us. But it's difficult not to feel slightly triumphant, particularly since everybody once said Owen was bound to win.

I listened to the 1 o'clock news. Owen sounded statesmanlike but very bitter. He sought, even at the last moment, to dismiss us completely and encouraged his members to join either the Tories or Labour.

During the day, I spoke to Roy Jenkins and Shirley Williams, both of whom said they would issue statements supporting us.

To bed around midnight, still worried that Labour will get more benefit out of Owen's demise than we will. But at least the ground is now clear.

Thursday, 7 June, Ireland

CONFERENCE OF EUROPEAN LIBERALS

Following an all-day conference, at 9.30 we were whisked away in a bus to the Drumoland Castle Hotel. This is an imposing pile, set in huge grounds and built by a Victorian carpet magnate around a much older castle.

The dinner was very splendid, and very Irish – which means very late.

Afterwards there was a little show of delicate Irish ladies who sang delicate Irish ditties, to the accompaniment of harps. Then they all filed out and Des O'Malley[1] insisted that we all start to sing.

The first half-dozen singers were a collection of maudlin Irishmen singing sad songs about Ireland. After which John Alderdyce[2] was asked to sing. He has a wonderful voice and sang a really very moving Northern Irish song which I remember my mother singing.

After which it degenerated and we were all required to do party tricks.

I told a lengthy but reliable shaggy-dog story, as did David Steel, while

---

1 Leader of the Progressive Democrats in Ireland.
2 Leader of the Alliance Party of Northern Ireland, now speaker of the Northern Ireland Assembly and a Lord.

the Spanish Ambassador got unsteadily to his feet and in a thin, high, reedy voice sang something incredibly abstruse and Spanish while clapping his hands. As he is a portly gentleman of nearly seventy, this was amusing but not very musical.

We then dragged the Hungarians out, who sang some terribly complicated Hungarian round to general embarrassment. They were obviously stunned by the whole affair and had concluded that if democracy meant parties like this, it was clearly a Good Thing. In the end we even got the Germans singing. An ancient Swede bent over to me. 'We would never do this kind of thing in Sweden. We are all so formal there. But isn't it fun?' His rheumy old eyes shone like diamonds.

We left at 2.30am, having had a very enjoyable evening. Quite different from the usual stuffy European affairs.[1]

Tuesday, 12 June, Westminster

Saw Bob Worcester[2] at 10.15 for an hour and a half. He said that Labour has displayed their wares too early and will now be subject to more than two years of sniping. He thinks Labour probably can't do it and the Tories are likely to get in with a small majority. That's important, coming from him.

Tuesday, 19 June, Westminster

At 8.15am, a meeting with Des, Mark and Alan Leaman. Des thinks people in the Party are plotting against him. He has a terrible habit of seeing conspiracies where they don't exist. He has also strayed over the line of telling my own staff what to do in my office. This will cause trouble. My hope is that once he gets going he will become so absorbed in his task that he won't have time to plot or start at shadows.

Last night, at the General Election meeting, however, he was brilliant. His presentation lasted about an hour and a half. He put it across extremely well and convinced the whole, rather sceptical audience. I had opened the

---

1 When Jane collected me from Heathrow the following morning she told me I had the worst hangover she had ever seen me suffer from.
2 Chairman of Market & Opinion Research International (MORI) Ltd. since 1973. Managing Director of MORI Ltd. 1969–94.

proceedings by telling everyone that I wanted a campaign that was radical, fresh and risky: radical because that's what Britain needed; fresh because we wouldn't capture the public imagination unless we had new things to say; and risky because that's what we had to be at 5 per cent in the polls.

Secondly, I wanted a campaign which was targeted. It should have a simple slogan and a message which was reducible to three or four bullet points. It should also be targeted in relation to resources, because we had so few, and we should concentrate only on those seats which were winnable.

Finally, I wanted a campaign in which the lines of command were clear: I was responsible overall and would lead on the politics of the campaign; Des was responsible for organizational matters.

Tuesday, 26 June, London

At 12.30pm a two-hour meeting with Richard[1] to discuss the manifesto. We came up with the idea of writing the manifesto in four parts – the first an overall statement of intent, written largely for public consumption; the second a bald list of policies. The third part, the main body, would consist of four mini manifestos. I suggested we should write them as though we were the International Monetary Fund producing a development plan on a country: each mini manifesto should have an audit at the front saying what the Government had done right and where its deficiencies lay, followed by a series of proposed 'business plans'. Finally, there would be an appendix with costings. We had a long discussion about the theme of the document. I wanted this to be more about the redistribution of opportunities in Britain than about the redistribution of wealth: citizenship should be a strong theme and education the key. We agreed that we should be very specific about where the money came from and should target it precisely.

Later, I had a discussion with Mark about the General Election budget. The officers were proposing to increase the Party's deficit by around £70,000 for the election. I said that in no circumstances would I tolerate this: this General Election was a development election for us, which should not put the Party in hock. I wanted to use the two or three years after it to build the Party, not be forced, once again, to sack our excellent employees just to pay off election debts.

1 Richard Holme. I had previously asked him to take overall responsibility for the writing of the manifesto.

Thursday, 19 July, London

Beautiful weather; and London looking splendid.

At 12.15 off to Clarence House with a delegation from Parliament to present early 90th birthday wishes to the Queen Mum. Roy Jenkins representing us from the Lords. Also, the Prime Minister, Bernard Weatherill,[1] Neil Kinnock, Jim Molyneaux[2] and Sir Bernard Braine as Father of the House and sundry others.

We filed into the drawing room and read two petitions, the first from the Lords, the second from the Commons. She stood there, her eyes very twinkly and bright; a definitive wrinkled little old lady, somewhere between regal and the Chairman of the Women's Institute.

The drawing room was magnificent, with the sun streaming in through the window, but somehow homely as well. The most striking picture was one of the QM herself when young, painted, I suspect, shortly after she became Queen.

She read a short response to the petition and handed the text over to the Lord Chamberlain in a way which suggested she was glad to get rid of it. Then she spoke to us individually, after which she insisted that we all went into the garden for a cup of coffee and a sherry. The pompous line-up dissolved into a merry chattering group. The effect of her personality, I suppose. I noticed she made a beeline for the gin.

I had a brief conversation with Kinnock and Molyneaux and then five or ten minutes with the Queen Mother. Thatcher was at her oily worst. She looked and sounded like the Chairman of a Tory women's group meeting some visiting dignitary at a garden party. The QM's body language told me that she didn't think much of her either.

We stood around under two splendid trees, the central branches of which had been cut out to make the area rather like a green cathedral. She told me she called it her 'salle verte'. She was more homely than graceful, but I couldn't help liking her immensely – although she cannot be considered, by any stretch of the imagination, a liberal.

---

1 Speaker of the House of Commons. Member of Parliament (Conservative 1964–83, Speaker 1983–92) Croydon North East 1964–92. He now sits in the House of Lords.
2 Leader of the Ulster Unionist Party. Member of Parliament (Ulster Unionist) for Antrim South 1970–83 Lagan Valley 1983–97. He now sits in the House of Lords.

Monday, 30 July, London

Heard the shocking news this morning that Ian Gow[1] has been killed by a terrorist bomb. It appears that it was of the sort that I now look for every morning under my car. The bomb weighed 5lb! Pretty big – he would surely have seen it if he'd looked.

Wednesday, 1 August, Westminster

[*My theory of opposition politics has always been that of the great inter-war Labour leader, George Lansbury – that the temptation of opportunism should be resisted and that Opposition parties should try to behave exactly as they would in Government. This was, ultimately, the only way to win the public's confidence that they were fit to handle power. In this spirit, I agonized as to whether we should fight Eastbourne, which we had a slim chance of winning. I eventually concluded that we should not, on principle, allow the IRA to decide who was and was not an MP and to allow them the spectacle of a by-election which they had caused. I was just about to announce this decision when Chris Rennard, our director of campaigns, heard. He sent me this fax, copying it to Archy Kirkwood and Graham Elson. It was a brave thing to do, as the tone of the fax could have got him sacked. Together Archy and Chris persuaded me that I was wrong. They were right to do so.*]

Dear Paddy,

I'm appalled if I understand correctly that you were thinking of issuing a statement about the Eastbourne by-election without consulting the person responsible for organizing the party's by-election campaigns, i.e. me . . .

No decision needs to be taken about whether or not to fight the by-election for some time (certainly not before the funeral). Any statement or recommendation from you would be tantamount to a decision. How could a local party fight a by-election if it was known publicly that their party leader opposed them fighting? The reason the Labour Party are terrified by this by-election is that they know that we would probably win and that their candidate in Eastbourne is a Militant. Of

---

1 Member of Parliament (Conservative) for Eastbourne 1974–90, tragically killed by the IRA at his home in Sussex.

course, the Tories would prefer to nominate an MP instead of risking losing an embarrassing by-election.

Your job is not to do what the Labour and Tory Parties want but to stand up to them . . .

It will not be seen to be bold and courageous to recommend not fighting – it will make you a laughing stock in Walworth Road, Downing Street and eventually in the quality press that you threw away this chance.

Yours,

Chris Rennard

Wednesday, 17 October, Westminster .

The news from Eastbourne is good. Everyone thinks we are going to do extremely well. I am still doubtful.

To lunch with the PM (for the Prime Minister of Thailand). Walked through the fine autumn sunshine, down Whitehall and up Downing Street.

The standard Downing Street lunch. She is looking older and older. She made a pretty ordinary speech which was received with wild enthusiasm by the Thais. The Thai PM is an ex-general and looks as though he has only just finished murdering somebody. He made quite a civilized speech, however.

Afterwards, a chat with Alan Leaman about Eastbourne. If we do well, I want to play it deliberately low key. The news will speak for itself, without us having to hype it. And I want us to get a reputation for coolness in such matters. So, the main message to the Party is to aim for a slow and steady advance, not a dash for growth.

Thursday, 18 October, Westminster

EASTBOURNE BY-ELECTION DAY

The BBC exit poll for Eastbourne was announced on *Newsnight* – it showed us, unbelievably,[1] 1.5 per cent in the lead. The BBC were clearly

---

1 Unbelievably because this had been a rock-solid Tory seat with a majority of 16,923 at the 1987 General Election.

very worried about its accuracy – whenever anyone commented on it on the programme, they were full of caveats.

We waited on tenterhooks. Chris Rennard became more and more confident as we approached midnight. Finally, at 12.30, he rang me with the result. We'd won. Fifty-one per cent for us, and a 4,500 majority. A triumph!

But we must not overplay it. David Bellotti, the new MP, understood perfectly and gave the best acceptance speech I have ever heard.

To bed at about 3.30. I didn't actually get to sleep until 4.00 and was up at 6.00.

Friday, 19 October, Eastbourne

We arrived at Eastbourne to find a forest of cameras and David Bellotti looking a bit sheepish. I shepherded him through the usual photo sessions, etc.

Then a brief coffee to discuss the line and into the press conference. The basic line was that our vote was the Heineken vote that could now beat Mrs Thatcher in constituencies which the other parties (i.e. Labour) couldn't touch.

Into the Television South studios to do a down-the-line interview with ITN. Ken Baker[1] had said 'The parrot has twitched'. To which I replied, 'Some twitch. Maggie has been bitten hard by this one and we intend to bite again' – a little over macho, perhaps.

Tuesday, 30 October, London

Off at 11 o'clock to look over the News International plant.

Lunch with several News International journalists, the political editor of *Today*, David Montgomery (its editor), Andrew Neil (the editor of the *Sunday Times*), and, to my great surprise, Rupert Murdoch. He wandered in in a rather self-effacing way and sat alongside me. I had expected a dynamo of a man, firing off commands and sacking people over the

---

1 Kenneth Baker, Chairman of the Conservative Party. Member of Parliament (Conservative) for Acton 1968–70, St Marylebone 1970–83, Mole Valley 1983–97. He is now in the House of Lords.

pudding, etc. But he turns out to be civilized, soft spoken and rather gentle – at least on this occasion.

We discussed Europe, the general political and economic situation (Murdoch thinks the Government can pull it off and is investing on that basis), and newspapers. He believes there will be fully electronic newspapers when fibre-optic cable networks are laid across Britain. In the meantime there is tremendous pressure on all titles – in particular the *Sunday Correspondent*.[1]

David Montgomery was curiously silent throughout. I somehow got the impression of a man worried about his position. Andrew Neil much more positive. He leaned across to me and said, 'Have we got on to your position in the General Election, yet?' When I said 'No', he replied, 'Oh well, I'll take the conversation there' – and promptly did.

Tuesday, 13 November, Westminster

A blazing row with Des over who should speak for the Party on TV in the months ahead. As usual, he railed against the MPs. He also accused me of pulling the rug from under his feet, not giving him the profile that he needed, etc. His ego is seriously getting in the way of our ability to act. He went into a complete tirade, and, though I started speaking softly, I ended up losing my temper.

He wants to take the General Election management through to January but then, if I haven't given him more power, he will hand the thing over to someone else. I told him that if that's what he wants to do, he should do it. I also accused him of seeing conspiracies behind every shadow, not trusting me to argue his case, etc.

He has to understand that I was serious about putting the management of the Party into his hands for the General Election campaign, but that this cannot be done overnight. Eventually we both calmed down before bidding rather an emotional farewell.

I trust him, like him and believe in him. But he is producing problems of an unmanageable sort of which he seems wholly unaware. I'll see if Archy and others can work on him.

---

1 The *Sunday Correspondent* ceased publication less than a month later.

Down to the chamber for Geoffrey Howe's resignation speech at 4.15.[1] This was the most stunning speech I have ever heard in the House. It rocked the Government on its heels. Thatcher sat white-faced and, from time to time, bit her lip as if to stem the pain. It was the measured way in which Howe gave the speech which made it so deadly. The knife went in coolly at the beginning and never stopped turning. He made the House laugh at her expense; he made her look ridiculous; he identified the matter of substance as Europe; and he showed himself to be a powerful and witty speaker in a way we had never seen before. This was not the speech of 'Mogadon Man', but of one who came among us 'unmuzzled'.

Somebody said to me on the way out of the chamber that it had taken Elspeth Howe ten minutes to write the speech and Geoffrey Howe ten years to deliver it. Here on full display was all the venom and invective pent up after years of humiliation suffered at the hands of Mrs Thatcher.

When I went into the chamber I thought the chances of a Heseltine challenge to her leadership minimal. When I came out I knew that the opposite was the case. Heseltine will now run and he has a strong chance of damaging her. The Members' lobby in excited ferment, with Tories rushing around like scalded cats. They looked dumb, miserable and bewildered, having suddenly realized the enormity of what had happened.

I feel rather smug, since I predicted that Europe would be the issue over a year ago. Today was one of those rare days when the whole atmosphere of politics was changed by a single speech in the Commons. I fear Geoffrey stepped over the line between candour and vengeance, but the result is that she appears terminally damaged.

Sunday, 18 November, Somerset

A gloriously relaxed day – with almost nothing to do.

Judging by today's papers, and especially the evening news, Heseltine is faring better than anticipated.[2] It looks as though he will drive her to a second ballot. She seems to have completely flipped her lid and is now attacking him openly. Teresa Gorman[3] is claiming to speak on behalf of a

1 At the time, Geoffrey Howe was Deputy Prime Minister and Leader of the House of Commons. He resigned from the Government because of differences with Mrs Thatcher over Europe.
2 He did stand.
3 Member of Parliament (Conservative) for Billericay since 1987. She is on the right wing of the Conservative Party.

hundred MPs who will resign the Whip if Heseltine wins. Devastating stuff. Wouldn't it be wonderful if the Tory Party simply broke up?

Monday, 19 November, Westminster

Finished by 10.30, when I met John Baker[1] to discuss our pension arrangements. I intend to retire at sixty and so will have to start making provisions now. The penalties of living a peripatetic life and constantly changing jobs are coming home. I will be left desperately out in the cold if I lose my seat at the next election.

Arrived at the Commons at 9.15pm for voting. The House awash with rumours about the results of the Tory Leadership election tomorrow – but no one really knows.

Tuesday, 20 November, Westminster

CONSERVATIVE PARTY LEADERSHIP ELECTION DAY

After PMQs off with David Steel to Tom King's office, where we had a briefing on Privy Councillor terms on the Iraq crisis.[2]

I explained that we were very nervous about the Government invading Kuwait earlier than necessary and about lives being put at risk before all possibilities for a peaceful resolution had been exhausted.

Afterwards, David Steel and I concluded that the Allied war efforts would come to a head in mid-January, probably with the intention of trying to finish the military action by the start of Ramadan in mid-March. The Coalition would aim at a swift operation, using maximum fire power, in the hope of getting it over with as soon as possible. Air power would be used heavily, chiefly as interdiction against Iraqi targets, but ground operations would be limited to the recapture of Kuwait only.

Despite reported initial nervousness, the Russians appear relatively firm in their support of the USA. Even the Chinese seem to be on board – so the likelihood of getting an international agreement for action based on a Security Council Resolution looks good.

1 Personal pension adviser.
2 A Privy Councillor briefing is when a member of the Government or a senior civil servant verbally briefs a Privy Councillor. This briefing is strictly private, the secret contents of which may not be conveyed to anyone except, on Privy Council terms, another Privy Councillor.

But we Liberal Democrats have a very difficult decision to make. We are right to stress caution about military action, but once the Government have launched it, we will have to support them. We cannot argue in the Commons for defeat.

Then down to the office to wait for the announcement of the Tory ballot. It arrived at 6.34: Heseltine has forced Thatcher to a second vote. She will have to go.

On *Newsnight* with Ken Clarke and Tony Blair.[1] I thought Blair was awful. Clarke very clever, though. I am not sure I got much of the action, but what I did manage to say seemed effective enough. Alan Leaman took the same view.

A whisky with Alan to discuss the following day and to bed at 1.00.

Wednesday, 21 November, London

Alan Leaman rang me mid-morning to say that there is a very strong but unconfirmed rumour that the Prime Minister has resigned. She has been under severe pressure throughout the day with senior Tories in and out of Downing Street all day. I dictated a statement to be used in the event that she stepped down.

Into the office at 2.15 to map out a line for the Prime Minister's statement[2] in which I intended to be all statesmanlike – anticipating that Kinnock would attack her roundly. To my surprise, Kinnock never mentioned her present position, so what I had intended as a statesmanlike comment came out as a direct attack on her, greeted by catcalls and shouts of 'cheap'. Not at all in the mood of the House and I know that one or two of the Colleagues were troubled. I will not have done myself any good in the House, but it will have been picked up by the news bulletins. How curious that the Prime Minister should be on the ropes and we are only allowed to speak about her performance in Paris!

Jim Wallace told me that he had spoken to John Cartwright who, whilst keeping the lines open, is probably not going to join us in the near future. It would be a wonderful coup to get him just as the Tory Party is tearing itself apart. But this is an issue which can't be pressed.

1 At the time the Opposition spokesman for Employment, later to become the Shadow Home Secretary. Member of Parliament (Labour) for Sedgefield since 1983. Later Leader of the Labour Party and Prime Minister.
2 On the recent Euro Summit in Paris, from which she had just returned.

Thursday, 22 November, Glasgow

To Glasgow to campaign in the Paisley by-election. On arrival at Glasgow airport I received a message to ring the office urgently. They told me Margaret Thatcher had resigned ten minutes ago! Later, I spoke to a fellow passenger who said that the public announcement of Mrs Thatcher's resignation was made over the airport loudspeaker shortly after I left, and that everyone had burst into spontaneous clapping and cheering. I gather the same thing happened at King's Cross and Victoria.

On the way back to London the aircraft was buzzing with the Prime Minister's resignation – some people shocked, most very happy.

At PMQs, Kinnock, who had been carping most of the morning, asked a statesmanlike question, commenting on her record. Me ditto. She was in gracious mood but well in control of herself. What an iron will she has.

Then into the No Confidence debate initiated by Labour. Kinnock's speech was not good. It started well but then was rather torpedoed by Jim Wallace, who asked him to answer simply on the European single currency. He waffled uncontrollably. Lawson came in with a second question which completely floored him. The rest of his speech was lost. Her speech, however, was magnificent – completely in command of the situation, really enjoying herself and fast on her feet. The Tories must be feeling they have lost their greatest asset. They have murdered Caesar and will, I imagine, soon be looking around for a Brutus.

I rose to congratulate her on what I described as a 'bravura' performance (words which were picked up by the media). Then I launched into a strenuous attack on Labour. They rose as one to shout me down. I hadn't done enough preparation work and was severely fazed by the disruption. As bad a speech as Kinnock's. I am just glad that, but for the first ten minutes, it was not on television. Left the chamber bruised and depressed.

Wednesday, 28 November, London

To the Savoy to receive the *Spectator* 'Party Leader of the Year' award. All sorts of people there. Sat next door to one of the political columnists of the *Spectator*, Noel Malcolm, with Ian Aitken,[1] Geoffrey Howe and Nigel

1 On the political staff of the *Guardian*.

Lawson, etc. all on the table. The Prime Minister was due to come but cancelled at the last moment.

Douglas Hurd[1] made a hysterically funny speech about how receiving his award was more important to him than becoming Prime Minister. Geoffrey Howe got 'Speech of the Year', Clare Short[2] 'Campaigner of the Year' and Brian Wilson[3] – a very bright Labour front bencher – got 'MP to Watch'. I made a brief speech, but it didn't go down terrifically well. I still feel intimidated in these circumstances, but it was nice to get the award – a silver-plated thing for drinking whisky from. God knows what I will do with it.

Back to the office with Bob Maclennan and Mark Fisher.[4] Bob very positive and full of how we are in exactly the right position to build up the Party. Mark, on the other hand, very down, complaining bitterly about Kinnock. He says that they can't get rid of him and that Labour will almost certainly go down to a fourth election defeat but that, as soon as this is over, we must get the two parties together. Both Bob and I poured cold water on this, telling him that the Labour Party had a long way to go on constitutional reform before we would be interested. An insight into the thinking of a senior Labour front bencher, though.

How quickly things change in politics! Six weeks ago the press was full of how wonderful Kinnock was, how he was almost certain to be the next Prime Minister and how the Tories were in terminal chaos. Now Kinnock is regarded as having shot his bolt, the Tories have a new leader[5] who makes Kinnock look old and plodding and the Labour Party is widely perceived as on the way down. We'll have to change our tactics slightly towards Labour and help them down the slope. There is now a real opportunity for us to rebuild the old 1983/87 hope of replacing Labour as a responsible Opposition, provided we make it a long-term aspiration.

Everything has gone extremely well for us recently – except perhaps that

1 Currently Foreign Secretary. Member of Parliament (Conservative) for Mid Oxon 1974–83 and for Witney 1983–97. Hurd is now in the House of Lords.
2 Opposition spokeswoman for Social Security. Member of Parliament (Labour) for Birmingham Ladywood since 1983. Later to become a member of the Labour Government.
3 Opposition spokesman on Scottish Affairs. Member of Parliament (Labour) for Cunninghame North since 1987. Now a member of the Labour Government.
4 Opposition spokesman for the Arts. Member of Parliament (Labour) for Stoke on Trent Central since 1983.
5 John Major, who had entered the second round of the Conservative Party Leadership election after Thatcher withdrew her name.

I would like to have seen Heseltine as leader of the Conservatives as he would have smashed their party up.

Thursday, 6 December, London

To lunch with Peter Preston, editor of the *Guardian*. He thinks Labour's in a real fix and can't make it. He was very encouraging about the Party and said that we were now nicely positioned. I complained about lack of coverage in the paper and he agreed to put it right – he told me they were considering commissioning some think pieces in the run-up to the General Election. I often think that he runs the *Guardian* as a sort of paterfamilias, presiding over a co-operative. I find him very pleasant but somehow lacking bite. It's like having lunch with a blancmange.

Then back to the House and a meeting of the Kuwait Policy Group.[1] Russell, David and Ming there. I told them of my extreme nervousness about the line we were taking on the Gulf. I didn't see why we should kill young men in the third week of January just because we didn't have the patience to wait until September. The others were much more hawkish. But we decided on a more cautious line:

1. What are the results of sanctions and why has the Government changed its line on them?
2. Why does the Government want to go earlier now? They must have a good reason for launching a war in January, rather than September; what is it?

---

1 This was an *ad hoc* group I had set up to advise us in the conduct of the war, including Sir John Moberly, our former ambassador in Iraq, Admiral Sir Jim Eberle and two ex-Royal Marine colleagues, Major-General Sir Jeremy Moore MC and Major-General Julian Thompson, who had been, respectively, overall commander of land forces and commander of 3 Commando Brigade in the Falklands.

1991

Wednesday, 9 January, Westminster

[*We had spent a week skiing in France – where I had written a position paper for 1991 –* [1] *to find that, following the Iraqi invasion of Kuwait in August 1990 and a sharp deterioration in the situation in the Gulf, 'last ditch' talks were in progress between the Americans and the Iraqis.*]

Listened to the news. Baker[2] talking with Aziz[3] much longer than most people anticipated, which has raised hopes. My suspicion is that they are just a couple of windbags and there is nothing substantial going on.

At 6.30 we heard that the talks were a failure. Did a quick run round the television centres being very gloomy and beginning to lay out our position on sanctions.

Dinner with Des. Despite his drawbacks he is doing a stunning job on the General Election. We get on well, but he clearly mistrusts my handling of the Parliamentary Party. At one stage I had to bang the table and say, 'Look, Des, you have to leave the handling of my own Party to me. If I don't deliver what you want, you are entitled to take what action you think fit. But how I deliver it is my affair.' He grumbled into his soup.

We finished at 9.00 and back to the office, where I watched the 10 o'clock news. The situation in the Gulf looks very sombre. But the interesting thing is that Aziz has not commented on the talks, which must mean (a) they were substantial and (b) he is serious about them.

Thursday, 10 January, Westminster

I am really worried about losing some of our best activists because of the hawkish line we are taking on the Gulf crisis. Indeed, the potential war in the Party is taking as much of my attention as the prospective war in the Gulf.

---

1 See Appendix A.
2 James Baker. US Secretary of State.
3 Tariq Aziz. Deputy Prime Minister of Iraq.

At 6.30, into a dinner jacket and off to Downing Street for my first formal dinner with John Major.

About fifty at dinner, mostly prelates. Major is quite different from Thatcher (she was also there, very regal and generally dominating the performance). He looks just like the man next door who became Prime Minister to both his surprise and ours. Whenever I see him I think of those rows and rows of pre-war houses which line the A30 on the way into London from Guildford – he could emerge from any one of them and you would think it absolutely normal. But he is effective in his own quiet way – the sort of suburban Baldwin of our times. Gentle, pleasant, courteous. Probably the most plainly decent man we have had in Downing Street this century. And I love Norma. She has a wonderful face, full of grace and poise. I hope they make a success of it.

But I have serious doubts whether Britain will accept him as its leader in the long term – or the Conservative Party, still stunned by their matricide, in the short.

He made an engaging but rather stiff speech. Runcie[1] was splendid. Acerbic, witty and, at the end, full of meaning. I sat next door to Lady Jacobovits, the wife of the Chief Rabbi. A real Jewish mamma from New York – except she is from Paris. Bubbly and excitable.

Opposite was Ken Baker, who told me he was certain the Election would be later. He was in glowingly self-satisfied mood and said nice things about me, in contrast to Kinnock, whom he thinks is in a real mess. The usual Tory flattery.

Overall better fun than when she was here. Less like a downmarket version of Buckingham Palace.

Left at 10.45. I said to Norma Major on the way out how much Jane and I admired her for insisting on having a proper home life, rather than taking on the trappings of a Prime Ministerial court. Major appears genuinely grateful 'for the support I had given him' over the Iraq crisis.

Then home to bed, exhausted but curiously satisfied at the way events are playing out.

---

1 Robert Runcie (1921–2000), Archbishop of Canterbury. He retired later that year.

Monday, 14 January, Bexhill

At 4.30 off to do a TVS 'Questions' at Bexhill with John Smith.[1]

Terrible traffic on the way down, but the six or so hours we spent in the car getting there and back were fascinating.

Smith believes there is going to be a hung Parliament and that he can do business with us. He also has complete contempt for Kinnock (whom he considers a liability), no love for Gould and little respect for Kaufman.[2] He obviously wants to be Leader after Kinnock, but recognizes that he can't move before the election. Smith's judgement is that Major is going to do better than I anticipate, but that Labour will still overtake the Tories in the polls in the short term.

He thinks the recession is the key issue to be faced once the Gulf War has ended. It will be both deeper and longer than currently anticipated. U-shaped rather than V-shaped, with the economy beginning to bottom out around June, before rising again. He is convinced there can't be an early election and is predicting 1992.

An engaging man, with a clear and incisive brain, whose company I enjoyed. Nevertheless, he is full of his own opinions and not terribly good at listening to others. Also, an easy person to make an enemy of. He did a lot to try to extract information from me in a beguiling fashion, but I gave little away, heavily playing up the fact that we would find it difficult, but not impossible, to work with the Tories. I also let him know that we were thinking about the mechanics of a hung Parliament and shared his view that this was the most likely outcome of the next election.

Tuesday, 15 January, Westminster

GULF CRISIS DEBATE IN THE HOUSE OF COMMONS

Tension mounting over the Gulf. A deep sense of gloom settling over me. War seems now inevitable.

I went to work on my speech for the afternoon. Decided to frame this around four questions: Can peace be found? Is it necessary to use force? If

---

1 At the time, Shadow Chancellor.
2 Gerald Kaufman, Shadow Foreign Secretary, Member of Parliament (Labour) for Manchester, Gorton since 1970.

so, do we have to use it soon? And what should be its aims, constraints and objectives?

This crisis has taught me two lessons about politics. The first is that the more difficult the issue, the clearer your line should be; the second, that you cannot perform well unless you are confident about that line. It is much more difficult to be good on an ill-defined position.

Then into the debate.

Major very flat. This is his natural delivery. I suspect the Tories will say it was all calmness and strength, but I was left unimpressed. Then Kinnock. He basically made two speeches: one in favour of war and the other against.

Then Heath, who was all over the place, followed by me.[1] Shortly beforehand, someone threw a can of red paint powder from the Strangers gallery all over David Steel and myself. I managed to brush it off and they were hustled away. Quite an effective demo, though, especially with television. The speech went well enough.

After me, David Howell, who half supported my line on the French peace initiative. Major and Hurd both looked shifty. Driven by the Americans, I suspect.

Wednesday, 16 January, Westminster

GULF WAR, DAY 1

A mountain of letters on the Gulf, the overwhelming majority against our position – a disturbing number from Party activists. I worry this will have an effect on membership.

An awful sense of gloom pervades. War could be declared at any second. It all depends on the military now.

The Parliamentary Party Meeting was chiefly on the Gulf situation. Everybody agrees with the line, except Simon Hughes, who agonized in his usual Jesuitical way about the peace movement in the Party having no spokesman in Parliament and that he should do it. We listened patiently. You can always trust Simon to take out his conscience and wash it clean of all stains. He is good – on form, the best of all of us – but I sometimes wonder about the rigour.

---

1 We were on the brink of war in the Gulf. I was pessimistic about the chances of a peaceful outcome, but believed we had to continue trying for this to the last moment; I said that any war must be limited in its aims and that the following peace treaty had to be vested in the UN.

Home at 11.00 and *Newsnight*. War seems only a few days away. With this in my head, I tumbled into bed at 11.50 and turned on the radio to discover that it had started fifteen minutes ago. I leapt out of bed, called Alan, who had already got the news, and dictated an early comment.

I did a quick round of TV and radio interviews until about 2.30, saying we must support the Government and hope for a quick victory with minimal casualties.

I decided that we would have to divide into shifts while this was going on, otherwise lack of sleep would be a problem. I had woken David Steel earlier, so rang him again and suggested he go back to bed in order to take over at 8 o'clock in the morning.

Left Olly Grender[1] in charge in the Whips' Office ready to take press calls and settled Mark Payne into my office to keep pace with the news. Then I took an hour's sleep on the sofa in Jim's room. In the event, with running comments, etc., I didn't get to bed until 3.45 and was up again at 5.00.

Monday, 28 January, Westminster

GULF WAR, DAY 12

At 6.00pm, off to see the PM in Downing Street to be briefed on the war situation.

I had two issues I wanted to press him on:

1. His view on the progress of the war.

2. The aims of the war.

Charles Powell,[2] as usual, present taking notes.

Major had a bad cold and was looking very tired. I was impressed by his quiet assurance, although the meeting was slightly tetchy.

He said the war was going 'rather well' – 300 defections from the Iraqi forces. He specializes in understatement, so this is probably good news. I gained the strong impression that he will maintain the air war for some time before moving to a ground war.

---

1 Before becoming the Director of Media Communications Olly was my Policy Research Assistant. She was the Director of Media Communications for five years and is now an Account Director at LLM Communications.
2 Private Secretary to the Prime Minister for Foreign Affairs.

Nevertheless, having spoke to de la Billière[1] that day, he seemed confident. Iraqi morale is falling and the air operations are getting easier. Apparently, the Iraqi airforce has fled to Iran, although he is convinced this is for protection, rather than defection. We must be quite close to air supremacy.

We then went on to the aims of the war. He assured me that the Government was not intending any actions which were not directly related to the liberation, peace and security of Kuwait; in particular they did not want a 'Baghdad or bust' policy. I suggested that it would be helpful if he made this clear publicly but he felt he could not do so just yet.

As I left I said I would probably push him a bit on this issue in PMQs tomorrow or, alternatively, toss him a dollydrop about Arab involvement in the war. The whole meeting lasted about twenty minutes.

Despite my misgivings, the Party seems to understand our position now and resignations remain low, which is a relief.

Tuesday, 12 February, Westminster

GULF WAR, DAY 27

At 12.00 a meeting with Robert Maclennan to discuss his work on contingencies for a hung Parliament. His conclusions are:

1. We must make it clear to everybody that they will not get an answer from us on the day after polling day. We will need a week to work through our discussions with the Government.

2. The only way to force Labour into giving us PR for Westminster was for us to be convincing about contemplating a coalition with the Conservatives. I agree, but it will be God's own job to sell it to the Party.

Overnight there has been a terrible attack by Coalition forces on a bunker full of civilians in Baghdad. I decided to hang tough on this, which proved right as the day went by. At PMQs I said that, dreadful as the attack was, we should never forget that Saddam Hussein has killed more Muslims than any other human being. Well received, except by Labour.

---

1 General Sir Peter de la Billière, commander of the British Forces in the Middle East.

Tuesday, 19 February, Westminster

GULF WAR, DAY 34

Quick dash to the House, having missed PMQs, and into Major's office at about 3.40pm. He showed me Gorbachev's so-far unpublished peace proposals. They fall short on four counts.

1. Withdrawal is not going to be immediate.

2. There is no concession from the Iraqis on the legitimacy of Kuwait.

3. There is no undertaking to return prisoners – potentially deadly.

4. The Soviets have agreed to the removal of sanctions which only the UN can remove.

Major said he was going to treat the proposals with contempt. I suggested he should not slam the door on the Russians, even if he slammed it on their proposals, and that the line should be: they should be congratulated for making a step forward but further steps must be taken to fulfil the UN resolutions and create a basis for peace. But by the time I got out, Bush had already slammed the door comprehensively and Major quickly followed suit.

Wednesday, 20 February, Westminster

GULF WAR, DAY 35

David Steel is becoming terribly wobbly, expressing concern that one of our demands is that the Iraqis must recognize Kuwait. Jim agrees with him. I disagreed with rather bad temper, since I had been arguing the opposite case all day.

At the Parliamentary Party Meeting, David raised the issue again, with Ming and Jim supporting him. Alan Beith said that he trusted my judgement and that we shouldn't alter our line. Bob did an emotional outburst, all about disloyalty to the leader, which was meant to be helpful but wasn't since Ming and David are the last people to be accused of that. I grumpily restated my case and there the matter rested. The first time we have had bad blood in the Parliamentary Party over this.

Friday, 22 February, Westminster

GULF WAR, DAY 37

Ming came to my office at about 3.45pm and we watched Bush say that the Allies were setting a deadline for a ground invasion of noon tomorrow, Washington time, for Saddam Hussein to pull out of Kuwait. Bush had called Hussein's bluff. Meanwhile Saddam is laying waste to Kuwait, burning the oil wells and no doubt slaughtering the people. I think Bush is right, but we took a little time to agree amongst ourselves to follow the same line.

Unable to sleep. I have this recurring nightmare of a sergeant-major going round frightened soldiers in the dusk like a kindly uncle, checking their ammunition, morphine, field dressing and camouflage. Another one of dark figures trudging up through sand to the start-line for an attack. It's fine for us sitting in the safety of our sitting rooms, relishing the drama of war, while they are preparing to pay its terrible price. I fear ground war is now inevitable and imminent.

Saturday, 23 February, Westminster

GULF WAR, DAY 38

At about 7.20pm Major rang my office to say that the ground assault would be launched in the small hours of the morning. He had spoken to Gorbachev at length and gave me the gist of the conversation. Apparently the Iraqis were prepared to say that they would not set fire to the oil wells, but on the key issue of the recognition of Kuwait they would not give way. The Kuwaiti resistance are reporting an extensive campaign of executions and killings and many thousands are being air-lifted to Iraq. Major warned me that British troops would probably not take part for the first forty-eight hours of the campaign, but that I wasn't to say this. He was telling me so I didn't make comments based on erroneous information. A most generous and open conversation.

Ming later phoned to say Tom King had given him a start time of 1.00am.

We watched the 1 o'clock news, but there was no announcement. Mark then took my sofa, I laid out the sofabed in the other office and we went to sleep. I slept fitfully for about twenty minutes before the phone rang. The press have been told that the ground assault has been launched. I put out a statement conditional upon this being confirmed and Mark rang round saying I was available for interviews.

After about twenty minutes the phones started ringing. Then I was bundled into a car to the ITN studio, where I did a piece at 3 o'clock in the morning. We are hours ahead of any of the other parties.

Back to the office for an hour's sleep.

Wednesday, 27 February, Westminster

THE LAST DAY OF THE GULF WAR, AND MY FIFTIETH BIRTHDAY

Up at 6.00 to listen to the news. Immediately obvious that fighting would continue throughout the day.

Into the office at 9.30 or so to scribble a press release. I am worried about the attitude of some American pilots. There seems to be a blood lust developing in the last phases of the war, with terrible carnage being wreaked on a retreating enemy. I feel desperately for the young Iraqis who didn't want this war and who are trying to get home under such a murderous air attack. My press release quoted Churchill's famous words 'In war: resolution. In defeat: defiance. In victory: magnanimity. In peace: goodwill'. I said that the quality of mercy should never be absent even from the battlefield, and especially from the victors.

Almost immediately word started coming through about further concessions from the Iraqis. During the afternoon they agreed to all of the UN resolutions. As usual, with conditions attached. Why can't they just go the whole way? It would be so much easier. This giving with one hand and taking away with the other makes everyone regard each movement the Iraqis make with suspicion.

At 2.00 an office party. They had bought me a bottle of champagne and a cake.

At the end of the afternoon Iraq accepted all UN resolutions. I issued a press release saying the ingredients for a cease fire were now in place.

Then to the Parliamentary Party Meeting. A huge card signed by all my Parliamentary colleagues and another vast cake. It is really very difficult to eat a chocolate cake and run a serious meeting at the same time.

A light agenda. Ribble Valley[1] seems to be going very well. Chris Rennard thinks we can actually win it.

---

1 David Waddington, the Conservative Member of Parliament for Ribble Valley, had been elevated to the House of Lords, thus forcing a by-election.

Also received a huge bunch of flowers from the Kuwaitis.

Home at 8 o'clock for dinner cooked by Jane. To bed at around 10.30. At 12.30 I was woken by another call. Bush will announce at 2 o'clock a suspension of action, followed by a permanent ceasefire. Hooray!

Thursday, 7 March, London

RIBBLE VALLEY BY-ELECTION DAY

Mark rang at 11.15pm to say that the exit poll puts us ten points ahead. My Office team then came round to my flat at Methley Street at 11.30 and, over a few bottles of wine, we watched the result.

By midnight the exit poll had been confirmed and the rest of the TV programmes were predicated on the basis that we had won a handsome victory. And so it turned out: a stunning 48 per cent.

Straight to a radio car parked outside where I did a phone interview and conducted a 2.30 press conference on the steps of my flat with five television cameras filming.

To bed about 3.00.

Thursday, 2 May, Westminster

LOCAL ELECTION DAY

I had a very nasty sense of a bad night ahead. Little did I know what was about to happen. I went back to Cowley Street.

Tim Razzall came to me with a results table at about 11.30pm, based on 10 per cent of the votes counted, which indicated about 600 or 700 gains for us. Unbelievable news, which I simply dismissed.

Soon, though, councils were falling to us all over the place. The BBC results programmes (the dreadful David Dimbleby again) as usual reported only the Labour successes and ignored us completely. We had to prompt them hard to report ours as well. We gained control of Torbay, Cheltenham and, to my great delight, Jackie Ballard[1] won Taunton Deane. She has done a wonderful job there.

And so the night rolled on. By close of play next morning, we had

---

1 At the time Jackie was Leader of South Somerset District Council. She is now our Member of Parliament for Taunton.

won 520 seats. Despite the fact that we fought about half the seats Labour fought we had gained more than them, winning control of nineteen councils.

To bed at 4.15am very tired after twenty-four hours non-stop.

Saturday, 4 May, Glasgow

To Heathrow Terminal 4 and straight on to an RAF Tristar flight to Glasgow for a service of thanksgiving for the safe return of our troops from the Gulf.

St Mungo's Cathedral filled with service people. I gave a very large wink to the Royal Marines contingent as I walked up.

David Steel and Ming in the congregation. I was shown to my place in the front row, next to Kinnock. There followed the best part of an hour's wait. Kinnock and I chatted about almost everything, including the Cathedral, religion, music, our families, etc. We finally got round to politics. To my immense surprise he agrees with me that Britain is now voting tactically and seems quite pleased about this. 'If what happened [on Thursday] night happens at the General Election, then we [by which I presume he meant the both of us] would change the nature of this country as it's never been changed before.' I wonder whether he is conceding that we have to be part of that, even if he's not saying so publicly. I pressed him a bit further but he didn't want to go too far, so I backed off.

The Queen was late because her train had broken down. We were given this information by one of the ushers and it fled like a bush fire along the row of Ministers who were sitting behind me. David Steel turned to his next door neighbour, a Government Minister, pointed to Thatcher at the end of the row and said in a fully audible stage whisper, 'It would never have happened in her time.' Edward Heath growled, 'It only happened *because* of her time.' The row erupted with giggles while she (she must have heard it) sat there stony-faced. If the television cameras had been on us we would have looked like a bunch of mischievous school children.

In due course Major arrived. When she used to walk in to these things, the congregation would stand up. But no one moved a muscle for him. He sidled in and sat down like an usher who'd finished his work and was waiting for the service to start.

Then the Queen and Prince Philip. She looking furious – no doubt because of the train delay. She is scrupulous about time, apparently, and gets extremely angry when she keeps people waiting.

A lovely service. Just the right mix of commemoration and thanksgiving. With a glorious touch at the end when they had young children from the Muslim, Jewish and Christian faiths come up to the top of the Cathedral and give a little reading. Most moving of all was that, though they were dressed in their national and religious costumes, when they opened their mouths, they sang in pure Glaswegian.

A good sermon by Habgood.[1] Sensible but profound, using simple words. I stood between Kinnock and King, both of whom have excellent singing voices. Kinnock a deep baritone and King a tenor, but always perfectly in tune. I felt a bit out of place.

Sunday, 12 May, Wembley

To Wembley with Kate for the Simple Truth concert in aid of the Kurds of Iraq. Everyone gathered in the VIP lounge, including Mary Archer, who is much prettier than she appears on television. He was there too, poncing about and generally being obnoxious.

Kinnock and I stood in line to meet the Princess of Wales. She is very charming, but there is still something of the overgrown girl about her. Then into the auditorium for two hours of cacophonous din. Diana sat behind us. I could feel her knees pointing at the back of my neck.

Kate was in great form. Although plunged into the company of some pretty dizzy names (Marmaduke Hussey, Michael Checkland,[2] Princess Diana, etc.) she was totally unawed by any of them and chatted away as though she had known them all her life. I was very proud of her.

Diana left at 9.00 and Kinnock shortly afterwards. We stayed until about 10.15 so that Kate could hear her favourite, the Gypsy Kings (awful noise). We then left through the back of the stage, where Kate had a chat with someone called Chris de Burgh, who was obviously terribly exciting but of whom I had never heard. Apparently, he had organized the whole thing.

We drove back together and stopped in Notting Hill for a meal in a rather swish Chinese restaurant.

1 John Habgood, Archbishop of York.
2 Director General of the BBC.

Wednesday, 19 June, Westminster

I had been warned we were going to have a very difficult Parliamentary Party Meeting. It was. Bob launched into a long and virulent attack on Des, saying he was a wonderful campaigner but absolutely hopeless on television. He used words like 'maladroit, deeply unimpressive', etc. Bob has a habit of overstating his case.

I had expected some support from Archy, Jim and Matthew, but none came. Bob was followed by Russell, then David Steel, Alan Beith, and Ming Campbell – all very magisterial, all very powerful and all deeply critical of Des. I defended Des strongly, reminding them that he had been working for us for nine months and had stuck strictly to the line. He was also one of the chief factors in our recovery. The choice was either to have him as he was or to lose him completely – and this was nothing to do with his vanity. You couldn't ask someone to be responsible for a campaign internally while somebody else appeared to take responsibility for it publicly. I was particularly incensed at Bob's suggestion that I had done some kind of bargain with Des, in which he organized our election campaign in return for me feeding his ego. I was also angry at the extent of misunderstanding in the Parliamentary Party. Old scores being settled and, in some cases, old prejudices being rehearsed.

Didn't get to sleep until 2.00, turning the events of the Parliamentary Party meeting over in my mind. Then woke up again at about 4.30. It takes me back to the days when the Party was in disarray. Des is not only the best we can get, he is also the best at this sort of thing in the country. He is doing a superb job from an impossible starting position with a weak organization. I must stick to my original judgement on this.

Saturday, 29 June, London

I have fixed to do *TV AM* tomorrow on the dreadful complexities of the growing crisis in Yugoslavia. Tim Razzall had to show me maps as I didn't even know where all the countries were. We spent an hour or so over a couple of whiskies talking about Yugoslavia and what I would say the following morning.

Thursday, 11 July, Westminster

At midday a meeting with Des. Archy had managed to wind his arm up his back in order to persuade him to come to my office. Des was fuming. He unleashed a fifteen-minute long diatribe, his chief complaint being that he should be on all by-election TV programmes. He began and ended by saying he was packing in as General Election Co-ordinator. I waited until he became exhausted and then responded, trying to rebut each of the points in turn.

I reminded him that who went on by-election programmes was my decision. The problem was that what had started for him as an eight-month job was turning into nearly a two-year one. His relationship with the Parliamentarians, especially David Steel [with whom he had a particularly vituperative relationship], was for him to sort out. I wasn't going to act as a nursemaid for grown-ups. Des responded very badly, losing his temper. He accused me of cowardice and of abandoning him in the face of attacks from the MPs. We spent an hour talking, then he left in a huff, saying he was off on holiday and that while he was away he would consider his position.

I dictated a long letter and made arrangements for him to receive it before he leaves. Then I called in Alan Leaman and started making dispositions as to how we would (a) handle Des's resignation and (b) deal with the aftermath. First we must pull his name from the Conference programme, so that if he does resign (which I anticipate), it will be less obvious.

At 10.30pm I was just about to leave the office when the phone rang. It was Des: 'Do you want the good news or the bad news?' I said, 'Oh God, I can't cope with any more bad news.' 'Well, the good news is that I think you are right about by-elections. The bad news is I think you are wrong about the MPs. But I am not going to abandon you. I don't want you to have to wait to see what will happen over the next six weeks. Count me in.' To do this in this way is typical Des, who can be very generous personally.

I was immensely relieved. My relationship with Des is difficult to manage, but I still think it's worth it. He is such a genius.

I told him that I had dictated the letter, but we agreed that I wouldn't send it.

Friday, 12 July, Westminster

Up at 6.15 to meet William Wallace[1] over breakfast at the Horseguards. I asked him to start mapping out how we would move towards Labour after the next election, in the event of a Tory victory. There were two things I wanted to do:

1. Make a speech on the Saturday after the Election saying that the country's difficulties and the failure of democracy were now greater than the difference between the parties.

2. Ensure that, when I did this, we would get a positive response from Labour. Could he arrange this? The best outcome would be an agreement between us and Labour to set up a Scottish Convention-type exercise[2] under the umbrella of, say, one of the national newspapers.

Wednesday, 17 July, Westminster

A meeting with Ming. I outlined my private thoughts on what would happen if the Tories won the next election by twenty or thirty, and told him about my proposed speech.

I explained that I would need a positive response from Labour. Ming has the most trusted relationships with the Labour party, so could he speak to John Smith on the subject? Ming told me that he had better contacts with Donald Dewar[3] but that he would see what reaction he got from both Smith and Dewar over the summer recess.

I am now beginning to assemble the ingredients for our post-election strategy in two of the three circumstances from which we can benefit. God knows what we will do if Labour wins an outright victory. But I don't think that's likely.

1 A friend, academic and adviser, mainly on foreign affairs. William now speaks for us in the House of Lords on foreign affairs and defence.
2 The Scottish Convention was a cross-party exercise to bring together all those who wanted to have a Scottish Parliament. It included the Liberal Democrats, Labour, the trades unions and the Church among other groups representing a wide spectrum of Scottish opinion – but not the Conservatives. It produced a plan for a Scottish Parliament which formed the basis for the Scottish devolution legislation Labour subsequently introduced in 1998.
3 Shadow Secretary of State for Scotland. Member of Parliament (Labour) for Glasgow, Garscadden, since 1978. He is now First Minister of Scotland.

Thursday, 18 July, Westminster

Andrew Adonis[1] came to talk the Parliamentary Party through the three scenarios for a hung Parliament.[2]

The most difficult option turns out to be the first; with Labour refusing to talk to us and putting down a Queen's Speech which has most of the things we want in it (e.g. Scottish Parliament with PR, PR for local government, PR for Europe), but not PR in Westminster. The Colleagues all agree that, in these circumstances, we must be prepared to work with the Tories in order to keep Labour out until they accept Westminster PR. But the hard fact is that, whatever they say now, most of my Scottish Colleagues will find it impossible to vote against a Labour Queen's Speech which contains legislation for a Scottish Parliament but not PR for Westminster. It's all too clear just how much Labour will be able to drive wedges through our ranks should this happen.

Altogether a successful meeting, even though it didn't reach conclusions. My main aim is to get the Colleagues to think through the horrors of the situation. At least now, when I say I am not enthusiastic about a hung Parliament, they know why.

A hung Parliament would not be a dream. It would be a nightmare.

Tuesday, 22 July, London

Off with Jane to the state banquet for Mubarak.[3]

Over coffee afterwards I saw Princess Diana out of the corner of my eye flexing her arm muscles to one of the waiters. I suppressed a giggle and she flushed very red, then came over to explain that the man she had been signing to had been the physical training instructor on board HMS *Britannia* and had shown her how to use weights. We had an engaging, flirty and

---

1 At the time a Fellow of Nuffield College, Oxford and at the time a Liberal Democrat. He subsequently joined Labour and now works in the Prime Minister's Policy Unit, in No. 10 Downing Street.

2 The three positions were: Labour the largest party and the only one with whom we could combine to produce a majority in the House; the Tories in the same position; and us holding a 'true' balance and capable of giving either a majority.

3 President Hosni Said Mubarak of Egypt.

rather amusing conversation. It's the first time I have spoken to her. She is fresh and sharp; not at all the Sloane I had been led to believe.

The Duchess of York told me that she thought I was doing 'awfully well – though I suppose I shouldn't say so'. Also, that all her friends are voting for us!

As we were leaving, the Duchess of Kent came up. She was extremely indiscreet about the recent service cuts, telling me that she had 'lost' five of her regiments that day and now had no remaining connections with the British Army. She was nearly in tears about it.

Talked to Mubarak chiefly about squash.

Home around midnight.

Monday, 19 August, Somerset

Woken up by a phone call at 5.15am. Gorbachev has been deposed, supposedly on grounds of ill health. I immediately rang Alan, who got the press machine into gear. My first interview was with *Breakfast Time*, then *TV AM*, then the *Today* programme.

A very worrying situation developed through the day. It is clear that the right-wingers have taken charge and kept Gorbachev at his holiday retreat on the Black Sea. But they failed to get Yeltsin to support them. He later appeared on top of a tank appealing to the Russian people to take action on the streets. Mrs Thatcher came out of her door like a rat out of a barrel and started spouting all sorts of nonsense. She now looks quite mad.

Monday, 23 September, Westminster

A discussion with Richard Holme and Alec McGivan until about 5.30 on my plans for what should happen in the case of a fourth Labour defeat; we would then have a historic opportunity to set in motion the realignment process while Labour was entrenched in a Leadership election. My intention is that, perhaps within a week of the election, I would come out publicly and say that (1) the Labour Party has failed and (2) the system has also failed and it is now up to the progressive parties to put together a force capable of beating the Tories.

I would propose putting a group together modelled on the Scottish

Convention[1] who would draft a 'Plan for Britain' around which all the forces of progress could gather. We would then see if we could engineer 'positive echo' from Labour, welcoming this proposal (perhaps from some progressive MP like Geoff Rooker).

This is very risky stuff and could lead us into pacts etc. But there will also be great opportunities. I told Richard and Alec that I am prepared to invest my future and popularity in the Party in order to seize this moment if we can. Richard and Alec agreed to be the core of a group who would start laying down some contingency plans. We will meet again when they have given it further thought.

The trick will be for the Party to be seen as the focal point of the realignment process.

Friday, 1 November, Somerset

Barbara Amiel looking absolutely drained![2] She may claim to be a political journalist but she has no idea what life as a politician is like. Nevertheless she was a good house guest, and easy to talk to. I just hope other people didn't lower their guards. She is a very sharp lady with winning ways and a marked capacity to get under the skin of her subject. I had been strongly warned about her beforehand.

Saturday, 2 November, Somerset

Up at 7.30 for surgery beginning at 9.30, with Barbara Amiel. Actually rather a light surgery. I must have seen only about eight or ten people and was finished easily by 12.30.

I then bundled her into the car and we drove back to London. We talked easily on the way back. She said she was amazed at the pace at which we worked and at the nature of surgeries, which she had never seen before. She thought this was an admirable part of the British political system which could be sacrificed if we went over to PR. She may be right.

God knows what she will write, however.

1 i.e. including the Greens, other progressive parties, the Church, TUC, etc.
2 Barbara Amiel had come down to Yeovil to do an in-depth piece on me for the *Sunday Times* for the Election. She had stayed with us and had been with me for the day, which started very early and ended with a Liberal Democrat fund-raising event in the evening.

Thursday, 7 November, Westminster

BY-ELECTIONS AT KINCARDINE & DEESIDE, LANGBAURGH, AND
HEMSWORTH

At 9.45, a meeting with David Stephen,[1] the 'secret agent' I had sent off to make contact with Labour and the Tories. He has done very well. He has established contact with Charles Clarke[2] in Kinnock's office. At first Clarke was suspicious and asked that their relationship should be validated by a discussion between Kinnock and myself. In the end, however, David Stephen convinced him he was on the level.

Stephen was impressed at the amount of thinking that Labour has already done on hung Parliaments. He believes, like me, that Labour are much more amenable to a coalition with us, based on PR, than they are saying publicly. He confirmed what I suspected, that Labour are suspicious of me. They regard David Steel as a sort of 'half brother' – of the centre-left – but think I am probably 'centre-right'. Exactly what I want. They need to know before we go into any negotiations that I will not be a soft touch. I asked Stephen to pass back through Clarke our deadly seriousness about going in with the Tories, if the mathematics add up, unless Labour give us PR.

Stephen has also made contact with Andrew Turnbull[3] in Major's office. Turnbull made it clear that official contact on the question of hung Parliaments should be through Robin Butler,[4] but that anything Stephen tells Turnbull would go straight to Major. Useful.

After the 10 o'clock vote, into my office with the team for the by-election results. Excellent results in all of them. We won K & D convincingly, with 49 per cent of the vote, the Tories back at 32 per cent and Labour and the SNP nowhere. Second place in Hemsworth (19 per cent) and 17 per cent in Langbaurgh.

---

1 Former Liberal/SDP Alliance candidate in Luton North and adviser to James Callaghan when he was Foreign Secretary. Currently Director of the UN mission in Somalia. I had previously asked David to explore, on a highly confidential and deniable basis, the views of the other two Party Leaders on a hung Parliament.
2 At the time, the man running Neil Kinnock's Office. He is now Member of Parliament (Labour) for Norwich South, and a Minister of State at the Home Office.
3 Principal Private Secretary to the Prime Minister. Turnbull is now the Permanent Secretary at the Treasury.
4 Secretary to the Cabinet. He now sits as a Cross Bencher in the House of Lords.

Good local council by-election results as well. Wins from Labour in Brent and the Tories in Harrow, among others. A good night.

Tuesday, 12 November, Westminster

Down into the chamber at 3.15 for PMQs. Major feigned to misunderstand my question, which enabled him to dodge it. I went particularly strongly on the NATO policy on Yugoslavia.[1] I am becoming really worried about what is happening there and suspect the public are well ahead of the politicians in wanting to do something actively to protect Yugoslavia.

Friday, 15 November, London

At 2.00, picked up by an anonymous Jaguar from MI5 and driven across London to their headquarters in Gower Street. Dingy, anonymous corridors leading in various directions and a pervading atmosphere of the Civil

1 The question I asked was, 'In view of the daily increase in the oppression and brutality of Croatia and the bombardment of Dubrovnik, does he realize that many of us sometimes wonder whether we have done all within our power in that tragic situation and whether we have done enough to stop those events?'

Service. I was ushered to the top floor and whisked into Sir Patrick Walker's[1] office, where, in the company of a lady assistant secretary, he ran through the security situation for me.

It appears that the KGB are still operating at full blast in Britain. They haven't heard the news yet that politics has changed and MI5 are having to put a lot of effort into them. The Eastern Bloc organizations, however, have fallen apart and are providing everybody with a lot of information. The main threat is terrorism. Sir Patrick thinks there is an IRA active service unit operating on the mainland. We also talked about what the security services hope the Commons will do about oversight. They are in favour of doing this through a select committee of Privy Councillors.

I only spent half a hour with him. I was then ushered into the MI5 Jaguar and whisked back to the House.

Monday, 25 November, Westminster

At 2 o'clock off to the Cabinet Office where I looked at the minutes of David Steel and David Owen's 1987 meeting with Lord Armstrong[2] on the question of hung Parliaments. To my surprise, it turns out that they went there only after the election had been called, so they didn't have a very well-prepared position. Their conclusions were, however, much the same as ours.

Tuesday, 24 December, Somerset

Left Vane Cottage at 10.45am for the five-mile walk to the Rose & Crown.[3] Crisp, bright, and very Christmassy. We got there in an hour and a half. My lesson was Matthew 2:1–12. The usual wonderful service, with the carols sung very lustily.

At 11.15pm off to Chiselborough for Midnight Mass. Very high flown

1 Director General of the Security Services (MI5) 1988–92.
2 Robert Armstrong, Lord Armstrong of Ilminster. In 1987 he was the Secretary to the Cabinet. He is now a cross bench peer.
3 Part of our traditional Christmas is to attend a Christmas Eve service of nine lessons and carols held in our favourite pub, the Rose & Crown in the tiny hamlet of Dinnington. Although the bar is open, the service is properly held, officiated over by the local vicar. By tradition, as the local MP, I read one of the lessons.

with too much ringing of bells, etc. I dislike high church. Nevertheless, the little church was a joy to be in. All lit by candles, the light bouncing warmly off the whitewashed walls and reflected in the glistening humidity on the stone floors. To celebrate in the company of your fellows an event of 2,000 years, ago on such a bright, moonlit night and in such surroundings, says more about the existence of God than all the texts ever written.

Afterwards home and a whisky with Kate and Simon before going to bed about 1.30, having filled the stockings.

1992

Saturday, 11 January, London

At 7.00pm a meeting with key members of the General Election team at my flat in Methley Street. Des, Matthew Taylor, David Bellotti and myself sat twiddling our thumbs for about twenty-five minutes until Charles turned up, and then had to wait a further half-hour for Simon, who, having specifically asked for the meeting at 7.00 because he had a constituency engagement at 8.00, arrived at 7.55 and stayed until 10.00. I was cross, but it's impossible to be too tough on him. He is so charmingly vague.

We occupied much of the hour spent waiting for him telling Simon-Hughes stories. Des told one about Simon's adoption meeting as Parliamentary candidate, at which he arrived so late and went on so long that his own mother got up to leave, saying she had a train to catch; followed by three Indians in the front row, who went to pray, apologizing loudly; followed, progressively, by most of the rest of the audience. Des described the event as rather like a speech version of Haydn's *Farewell Symphony*. He had us in stitches.

Des has done a superb job in preparing us for this General Election. Having himself insisted that everyone dresses properly, he now turns up sporting a sharp tie and polkadot handkerchief to match. He clearly took to heart our ribbing of the dreadful tie he wore on TV at the Kincardine & Deeside by-election.

Sunday, 19 January, London

At 7.45 off to dinner with Roy Jenkins.

He lives on the third floor of a large, draughty Victorian mansion in Kensington Park Gardens. His flat is very elegant, as you would expect: tall ceilings, comfy sofas and a general feeling of being lived in. We had some very good claret over a dinner of veal, ham and egg pie. We talked about contingencies in the unlikely event of a hung Parliament. Roy believes that:

1. Ming, Alan and David are all candidates for the Cabinet.

2. There must be at least four Lib Dems in the Cabinet. Fewer, and we would be trampled on.

3. The ex-SDP should be included.

I asked him at one stage whether he had ever wanted to be PM. He said yes, very much. He believed he had the intellectual capacity for the job, though Crosland was cleverer and Healey more of a political operator.

Tuesday, 21 January, Westminster

I have been thinking about meeting Neil Kinnock on a bilateral and deniable basis. I need to know how his mind is working. I also need to ensure that, if we do get a hung Parliament with the serious prospect of negotiating a partnership, the messages I send are not misunderstood in the turmoil after polling day. I fear the impression he has of me and our Party (too right-wing etc.) has been distorted and magnified by the press. He needs to know that I'm serious.

I must also assess the likelihood of bringing about such a partnership. There is a danger in building it up beforehand if there is no possibility of it happening. We would look ridiculous and damage the Party's morale. The risk to both of us if these talks are revealed is about equal. For him, it would be an admission of defeat; for me, it would do severe damage to our vote in the South West.

I put my proposals to Bob, who said we ought to make a parallel approach to the Conservatives to give us cover if it came out. We agreed that Bob himself would do this through Nick Hinton,[1] at a social occasion with Chris Patten, in which Nick would be prompted to ask Patten for their understanding of the constitutional position if there was a hung Parliament. Bob and I agreed to go ahead on this basis. I will shortly be seeing David Stephen, our 'secret' courier to the other parties, to discuss the matter.

---

1 Nick Hinton (1942–1997). The Alliance's Parliamentary Party Candidate for Somerton and Frome, my neighbouring constituency. Nick went on to become President of the International Crisis Group.

Wednesday, 22 January, Westminster

In the afternoon a meeting with David Steel. I told him of my thoughts on what Cabinet posts we might take if there were a partnership Parliament. I prefaced my remarks by saying that this was only a contingency plan, as I thought the chances of it happening were slim. I could imagine three Colleagues immediately carrying out departmental responsibility: himself, Alan Beith (as Chief Secretary) and Ming Campbell. One option might be to ask for him to do Northern Ireland (where Labour might be prepared to give way on McNamara,[1] who is not widely liked). Would he be willing? He would. An alternative might be to ask for the Foreign Secretaryship. He was keener on this, not surprisingly.

The Chancellor announced today that the Budget will be on 10 March, which cleverly leaves the options open for either a 9 April or 7 May election. My hunch is still 9 April.

Thursday, 23 January, Westminster

At 4.30 a meeting to discuss how we would react to an outright Conservative victory. We agreed we can't produce as detailed a plan as we have on HP [the plan for a hung Parliament].

We settled on meeting on the Saturday after the election to review the situation. We should be prepared to come out for some co-operation between ourselves and Labour in the event of either a Tory minority government or a clear Tory victory. But the timing and nature of this will be very tricky.

We agreed the most likely outcome of the election, in descending order of probability, is:

1. Tories largest party, but without an overall majority,

2. Tory outright victory with a majority of about ten or so,

3. Labour largest party,

4. Labour outright victory.

---

1 Kevin McNamara, Opposition spokesman for Northern Ireland. Member of Parliament (Labour) for Hull since 1966.

Tuesday, 28 January, London

Home to Methley Street with Des to discuss our election strategy over a Chinese meal. Des again very sensible and sharp on the detail. Towards the end of our meeting, the phone rang. It was a tearful Tricia Howard[1] saying that the *News of the World* had been round to question her about our past relationship. My heart sank. I tried not to show my shock to Des. We completed our dinner, after which he left and I phoned Tricia back.

Apparently, the *News of the World* had suddenly turned up at her door. A nice lady, but clearly briefed by somebody – she seemed to know everything. Tricia was in a terrible state – her stepfather is about to go into hospital, her world is collapsing around her and she needs support. I tried to give her as much as I could and promised that I would put Andrew Phillips[2] in touch with her tomorrow.

I didn't tell Des. Spent most of the night awake, worrying.

Wednesday, 29 January, London

I gave Des a call early to say I would like to drop in on him on my way to work. I told him the whole story. He reacted typically well. Then to the office, where I rang Andrew and we agreed to meet at midday.

The rest of the day needed an incredible effort of discipline as I tried to keep my mind on what I was doing, while being worried stiff about what was unfolding elsewhere. Tired, as well. I don't think I have had a worse day.

At 9.45pm the phone rang. It was Tricia. She had been visited again. They appear to have more information now. She is distraught. She had rung just before the vote, so I asked Andrew to call her. He said he didn't want to do so on an open line, so he had asked her to go out to a phone box. This she did and they had an hour-long conversation. Meanwhile, I went to see Des and waited until Andrew's line was free.

---

1 Tricia had been my secretary before I had become Leader of the Party. She worked for me from 1985 and we had had a brief affair which ended when she finished working for me in 1986.
2 Friend and close adviser. Andrew is my personal solicitor.

When we got through he said that the *News of the World* are putting huge pressure on Tricia and we must support her. I suggested we might ask my brother Mark, who lives nearby, to visit her the following morning.

Then Andrew told us what he believes could be the origin of this whole wretched story. In 1990, when the issue had first raised its head, I had gone to see Andrew, asking his advice. He had written a note of our meeting and put it in his safe. About ten days ago his safe had been burgled and all the money had been taken together with some documents. His note of our 1990 meeting may well have been among them and the thief, on finding it, had gone to the *News of the World*.

I rang Tricia back. She was calmer, having spoken to Andrew. I explained how it could have happened. We started to map out how to cope with this bombshell.

I left Des about midnight and went home to a very fractured night's sleep.

Thursday, 30 January, London

In early to ring Mark [Ashdown], who responded magnificently, saying that of course he would contact Tricia immediately.

Got back to the office to find that Tricia had rung again. Before I could return her call, Andrew Phillips phoned. 'They' had been round again, this time offering large sums of money, which Tricia had turned down. They had then returned a few minutes later and taken photographs of her. Oh, God!

Talked to Des about all this. Andrew, bless him, has decided to come to London from his home in Suffolk to meet up with Tricia. (It subsequently turned out that Mark was already accompanying her to London.)

I rang Cathy[1] first thing. She is coming up tonight, so I can talk the situation through with her. I will have to tell other people in the office and, possibly, cancel all engagements on Friday, travel down to Yeovil and inform the constituency officers. This whole business is only two days old and already it feels as though it's been going on for two weeks!

At about midday I left the office, saying I was off to lunch with Des and Andrew, and took a taxi to Andrew's offices in Charterhouse Street, where

---

1 Cathy Bakewell, my constituency secretary.

I was greeted, for once, with good news. Andrew had had a call from the crime reporter on the *News of the World*, who said that a document had come into their possession on which his signature was appended. Was it accurate? At last we definitely know the source. The *News of the World* are working from a stolen document, so there is a good chance we can get an injunction.

Andrew called in William Garnett, his litigation solicitor, who says there is a 90 per cent chance that a judge will grant an injunction since (a) the document was confidential, (b) there was no proof attached to it, and (c) it was tainted, having come by way of a theft. Andrew rang Tricia's ex-husband, who is as shocked as we are. We will make no comment. The last loose end is therefore tied up.

We then talked through a contingency plan in case we couldn't stop the news breaking: I would continue with my programme, Des would handle the press, and Mark Payne would go down to Yeovil and support the constituency officers, whom I would now inform of what was happening.

We also fixed the line for me to use in response to questions – that it was a pre-election smear. Having working out the details, William Garnett set off to get our injunction.

Tricia is very low. She will need our help. I said, however, that in no circumstances should the Party be seen to provide anything by way of money etc. Nor should we be seen to act in a way which we wouldn't be happy to explain in public afterwards. Emotional support is one thing – and that will be provided by me and my brother Mark between us. But any other kind of assistance is absolutely out.

We have a story to tell and, if I have to, I shall tell it.

Mark and Tricia arrived at around 3 o'clock. Though wan and ill-looking, she was more composed than she had been the previous night. We went through the situation with her and agreed the form of words we would use if the story broke. I told her that I would support her in any way I could, but Des remarked very sternly that, until the General Election was over, she and I should not communicate at all. Any contact should be via Andrew or, as a last resort, Des. We agreed that she would stay with a female solicitor from Andrew's office tonight and then with a friend for the next couple of days.

I returned to my office at the House. There has been much buzzing among the office staff. They know something is going on. I briefed Mark Payne and Alan Leaman, but told them that nobody else was to know for the moment. We then went through the contingency plan and each of their roles in it. Control of events must lie with Andrew, Des and myself. Everyone else must act as conduits to us. It is essential to keep as tight a grip as possible.

At around 6.00 I got a call from Andrew to say that the judge had accepted the injunction in the widest possible terms, requiring the *News of the World* to provide the name of their source. The police were moving in to arrest whoever was involved. I rang Des, who was overjoyed. I think we have closed off all avenues, but I can't be certain whether the rats will find another way out.

Andrew has been magnificent as, indeed, has Des. We have had to move very fast, but we have probably done all we can.

I rang Jane and told her that we had a problem but that the injunction should cover it. She was equally relieved. What a terrible coincidence. That a thief should have broken in; that it should have been just before the election; that the Clinton/Gennifer Flowers saga is running at the same time; and that it should have all ended up in the hands of the *News of the World*.

Much relieved, I got my mind back on my job. Down to dinner with David Bellotti and Ray Michie.[1] David was endearing. He said that he had heard some extraordinarily good news. He really raised my hopes. *Old Moore's Almanac* (which had apparently predicted his win at Eastbourne) foretold that the election would be in April and the Lib Dems would do terribly well!

Friday, 31 January, Oxford

Left London at 2.00 and drove through the fog to Willy Goodhart's house outside Oxford.

Rang Andrew. He and the solicitors are still pretty nervous. Apparently Whitehall is buzzing with it; I have heard, from Don Macintyre[2] by way of Alan Leaman, that the *Sunday Times* was going to publish a major story on a party leader.

This seems an extraordinary coincidence. We decided that we really couldn't take the risk that the *News of the World* (who are in the same building) had not passed the story on to the *Sunday Times*, despite the

1 Member of Parliament (Liberal then Liberal Democrat) for Argyll & Bute since 1987.
2 Political correspondent of the *Independent*.

injunction. So we decided to issue injunctions[1] on all the national news-papers.

Saturday, 1 February, Oxford and Sussex

Up by 8.00 to do a local radio broadcast and something for Greater London Radio. Then a chat with Des and Andrew while we finalized the details of the injunctions. God knows what all this is going to cost us!

Off at 9.15 to a very foggy Abingdon RAF base for a campaign visit, followed by a rally in Oxford.

Afterwards, into the car and down to Romsey, through the fog. I slept a bit on the way. Meanwhile, Alan Leaman had been contacted by Charles Lewington from the *Express* to say that he had heard in the lobby[2] that I had placed an injunction against the *News of the World*. What was all this about?

By now the *Sunday Times* story was becoming clear. It's not about me at all, but some KGB telegrams which had been dug up in Moscow which record interviews between Kinnock, Hattersley, Callaghan and others and various Soviet diplomats. These are to be published tomorrow. Labour is shouting foul. Des said it would do us no harm to join them, in a mild sort of way.

At 9 o'clock I heard that the *News of the World* had cheekily published a piece saying, 'Outrageous, outrageous! Documents stolen from solicitors of senior politician' and hinting heavily. This is a blow we didn't expect. Andrew is not sure whether it's within the terms of the injunction; however, it was almost certainly done after careful legal consultation, so we will have to live with it.

We mapped out a position for tomorrow, including an answer I could use to the likely question from the press of 'Does the *News of the World* story refer to you?' Roughly along the lines of: 'I don't read the *News of the World*, never have, don't intend to and I make it a policy never to comment on articles in this kind of paper. There are enough smears going around and I don't wish to add to them.' It was the best we could do.

---

1 Andrew has since reminded me (confirmed by others) that the original intention of the injunction was to buy time so as to 'get our ducks in a row' before the story broke. There was little real expectation that the injunction would hold. My diary entries here probably reflect the triumph of hope over expectations – for obvious reasons.

2 The lobby system is a way for MPs to talk to journalists without being directly quoted. The term refers to the Members' lobby in the House of Commons where most lobby briefing is done.

Mark rang with further details on the *Sunday Times* piece. The piece itself may just be legitimate reporting, but the *Sunday Times* billboards have the words 'Kinnock, the Kremlin connection' emblazoned across them in red. I don't find it difficult to defend Labour on this outrageous smear. The Tories are clearly up to pre-election tricks.

Back to the Goodharts' in the evening.

Sunday, 2 February, Oxford

The *Sunday Times* is, as predicted, plastered with Kinnock this morning. Totally over the top, with a very unpleasant photomontage on the front page showing him against a red flag.

Discussions with Des and Andrew. So far, so good. Nothing in the other papers. I suspect the storm is yet to break. I got down to chairing the Policy Committee meeting, which was the reason why we were here.

The day was spent with Alan Leaman rushing backwards and forwards, speaking to Des, etc. We have agreed that I should tell Jim Wallace, Charles Kennedy and a handful of other senior Party Officers.

Arrived back in London just before 7.00, unpacked, ordered a Chinese and sat down to a quiet evening. I suspect I will not have a quiet day tomorrow. We must weather the storm for a further two or three days before we know we are safe. I have a strong sense of foreboding.

Monday, 3 February, Westminster

I didn't sleep very well and was up early to meet Des. Today's press is looking seriously leaky. The *Independent* has run the *News of the World*'s story on stolen documents juxtaposed with a picture of me in a highly suggestive way. Less and less likelihood of the injunction holding. A very gloomy meeting, but we still believe it's worth sticking with for a little longer.

Richard Holme has now joined the team. The lawyers believe we have a fifty–fifty chance of sitting it out. I have decided to tell the constituency, and will drive down tonight.

Did a press conference on a speech I am giving to the coal industry at lunchtime. As I walked in there was a huge mob of press, cameras and so on. They have scented blood. It took some doing to keep them off what they wanted to talk about.

Then up to my office for my papers and off to the Coal Society lunch. Seven photographers there. This is all looking bloody dreadful.

Back to the office and a couple more meetings with lawyers. Des is mapping out contingency plans for all eventualities and we have begun to work out statements.

At 4 o'clock into the car with Mark and off to Yeovil. I was silent for almost the whole journey, terrified of what lay ahead. The constituency officers came round at 7.30. A pretty glum meeting. Most people took it well but Nick Speakman[1] looked particularly hurt and bewildered. I have not felt worse in my life.

Watched the news and then to bed. This is where Jane's composure collapsed. We spent three hours talking the whole thing through. I will, of course, have to speak to the kids, too.

She fell asleep in due course. I had a terrible night.

Tuesday, 4 February, London

Left at 8.00am for London, arriving in time to do the Party Political Broadcast. I was hardly in a mood for it! We were to talk about what happened if there was a hung Parliament, but I couldn't face it and cancelled.

I am feeling terribly tired and worn down. The constituency are being wonderful. Cathy, however, is very upset – and understandably so. Who knows what damage this will do?

After PMQs another meeting fleshing out our contingency plans. Then off to the BBC for a dinner on election coverage. In the taxi my mind was turning over what we should do. Over dinner I suddenly decided that *we* should break the story. During the pudding course, I wrote a note to Alan and Des, asking them to come back to my flat afterwards and passed it across the table to Des. He looked at me startled, and I nodded firmly. He nodded back and passed it on to Alan.

Des, Alan, Olly Grender and I drove back from the dinner in a BBC car. We dropped off Olly, then went back to my flat, where I poured Des and Alan a whisky and told them what I wanted to do. They were rather nervous, but quickly saw the point. Having tested the law as far as it would go, I must now break the story myself before it is broken elsewhere. Better to do it on our terms than be forced. I made up my mind by midnight that

1 My constituency agent since my first election contest in 1979.

we should fix Thursday as the day, subject only to a confirming decision tomorrow from Richard and the lawyers.

But before I got to bed the phone rang. It was Nick Assinder from the *Express*. Did I have any comment on the *Scotsman* article? I said 'What article?' He explained that the *Scotsman* had run the story that I was the person who had issued the injunctions on the papers and was also the person referred to in the *News of the World* story. At this stage I knew that we had to go and we had to go tomorrow.

I disconnected the phone and went to bed.

Wednesday, 5 February, London

Anticipating that the press would come and camp outside my front door, I got up at 5.30 in order to beat them.

I left the flat at 6.25, having made sure there were no lights in the window as I got dressed. My timing was out by thirty seconds. A car had just drawn up. The *Daily Mirror*. They asked questions and took photos of me as I walked up Methley Street.

I walked through the darkness to the House, losing them in the maze of back alleys on the approach to Lambeth Bridge, but they were there waiting for me at the entrance to the House of Lords and took more photos.

I went into the office, drafted what I thought were suitable words for a press statement and made a number of phone calls. Alan arrived at 8.00, followed by Des and Richard. Then the lawyers. I rang Jane and asked her to come up. She was, naturally, in a bit of a state, but, trooper that she is, agreed to do so. The rest of the morning was spent preparing statements. We read and reread them. We decided that I would make a brief statement, then the lawyers would issue a letter containing full details.

We fixed the press conference for 11.00. A ferment of interest by this stage. We booked the Jubilee Room[1] and arranged for me to arrive through the back door. I was terribly nervous.

Kate came to see about 10.30. I told her the full story (I had told Simon the night before). She flung her arms round me and burst into tears. In the middle of this emotional scene Clare[2] knocked on the door of my office. I told her to go away, but she said it was the Prime Minister on the phone.

1 One of the Committee rooms in the House.
2 Clare Conway, my Personal Assistant.

He had heard what was about to happen, and had rung to wish me good luck and say that if it would help, he would read out a prepared statement. Three lines and very supportive. Typical of the decency of Major. I was very moved.

Then a nervous twenty minutes as we finished off the texts and I walked down the stairs through the Members' lobby to the Jubilee Room – the loneliest and longest walk in my life. Mark and Alan came with me.

The room was heaving. I put the bravest face on it I could. Then I made my statement and left. Someone – Mike Brunson from ITN, I think – shouted after me, 'Are you going to resign?', but I ignored him.

Back in the office, I suddenly remembered that Jane was coming up by train. Methley Street would, of course, be full of photographers. So, in panic, we rang through to Waterloo and asked them to put a call out for her. (She later said she had heard some kind of muttered announcement but didn't realize it was for her.) I had also asked Mark to meet her at the platform and escort her home. But he missed her, too, with the result that when she arrived at Methley Street she had to break through a barrage of press questions. She was taken off balance, but reacted magnificently.

We had also failed to anticipate that the press would start besieging the flat whilst I was in the Commons. They rang the door bell at around 8.00am. Poor Simon, unwarned and unsuspecting, was in the bath and went to answer in his bath towel. He opened the door to a battery of flashing cameras and his startled picture, dripping wet hair, towel and all appeared in the next day's *Sun*.

Mark turned up shortly after Jane arrived and found her principally concerned that our dog, Luke, whom she had brought up on the train, hadn't had a pee. Since she couldn't take him out because of the cameras, Mark offered. As soon as he emerged he was pounced upon by no fewer than five TV crews who followed him and Luke step by step. The Sky crew even shot them from low level as if from the dog's point of view and insisted on covering in close-up poor Luke's performance of his natural functions!

We decided we must give the press a photograph of the pair of us together, so at 2 o'clock I returned home and submitted myself to standing on the steps with my arm around Jane. ITN was late, so we had to redo it later.

I tried to work at home but couldn't. I was very miserable but decided I must go back into the office to finish my work. I left through a crowd of photographers and reporters.

Into the Parliamentary Party Meeting, again through a mass of journos. I thanked the Colleagues for their support but said that they should feel free to ask any questions they wished. David Steel immediately moved to 'next business' and we got down to our regular agenda.

The constituency are being wonderful. Cathy, who stayed on late, tells me there has been a flood of support. Huge numbers of faxes coming in as well. This is just the initial reaction, though.

Then home for a very emotional dinner. The kids are being superb. Having held myself up all day, I collapsed. Simon flung his arms around me. Watched *Newsnight*, which was very good, with Richard Holme and the Bishop of Bath and Wells being highly supportive.

To bed at about 11.00, but couldn't sleep. Jane very disturbed again. God, the damage you do. I now have to steel myself for tomorrow's press.

Thursday, 6 February, London

A review of the papers. They are irretrievably awful. The *Sun*'s headline is 'Paddy Pantsdown'. Dreadful – but brilliant.

I left early for the office. The press were still besieging the flat. This left Kate and Simon trapped inside and unable to get to work. Over breakfast they concocted a plan with Jane to draw the press away. Jane said that it was her that the press were after, so she would take the dog out for a walk and the press would follow her, giving the kids the opportunity to get away. It worked brilliantly. The press followed Jane in a huge crowd, photographing her at every step as she took Luke to the local park. One of them asked her why she was walking the dog. She replied 'Because he needs it and to draw you lot away from the flat, so that my children can leave in peace.'

I rang Tricia mid-morning, to make sure she was all right. She has her photocall today – she and I decided that it was best for her to do one, so that they might then leave her alone.

Then a series of meetings including a review of how things are going. We will try and shut the story down. Des held a press conference about the break-ins, in order to turn the story away from the personal. The name of the game was to try and get something positive in after Tricia's photocalls.

I was delighted to see that we were beginning to go down in the news now. Called up Jim, who told me that most, but not all, of the Colleagues were being highly supportive.

The office is under terrible pressure. As Richard said, the press could say almost anything now – true or not, it was the rumour-mongering and innuendo that would do the damage. If they went too far, we would have to sue for libel. But the short-term story would stick and in the long term the results of a libel action would be damaging, unpredictable and hugely expensive. It could destroy the whole election campaign.

Into PMQs at 3.15. There was a slight but supportive murmur as I went in. They let me ask my question in silence. I asked a question on Northern Ireland and hit the jackpot. The Prime Minister announced the start of talks.

Then into the car and home to Somerset. Jane and I had a long chat on the way down. When we arrived home, the press were of course camped outside Vane Cottage.

After a stiff gin, we unpacked everything and had dinner together, with a bottle of wine.

I don't think I've slept properly for more than fifteen minutes over the last two days and am now extremely tired.

Friday, 7 February, Somerset

Up at 7.00. The press is not bad. But the cameramen are all back. Spent the morning sorting through a huge pile of supportive mail.

Cathy came round with Wendy Doherty.[1] At 10.30 I took some coffee out to the press camped outside our front and they all had a wonderful snapping time.

Then to the Liberal Club bar in Yeovil with Jane. A change in atmosphere. Jane says I am being paranoid, but I thought people here were a little wary. Embarrassed, perhaps, not knowing quite what to say.

Off home, where I went to bed for a couple of hours to catch some desperately needed sleep before drafting a speech for the Constituency AGM (it *would* have to be tonight!). Crowded with press photographers, as we went in to the meeting. Television cameras in the hall, etc. I was greeted by a hundred or so of our members, who gave me a standing ovation and stamped their feet. It was, of course, a staged show, but it did my morale no end of good and was good for the press, too. Afterwards, some questions, then down to the White Horse for a pint. Jane has had

---

1 A constituency activist and close friend.

excellent coverage in the press (she deserves it) and is holding up extremely well.

To bed about midnight, having heard from Olly about what's in tomorrow's papers (mercifully little).

Saturday, 8 February, Yeovil

Up early. The press still camped outside. A very busy Yeovil surgery, which we got through by 11.30. Then home.

The day was punctuated by phone calls from various people about the probings of the wretched press. They seem to be chasing every female I have ever known on a generalized fishing trip. Even the (female) mayor of Yeovil and a (ditto) reporter on the local paper have been approached. Photographers and reporters crawling all over the town, and, I gather, all over the country as well.

Spent the rest of the time handwriting replies to seventy or eighty very supportive personal letters from MPs, members of the Party, etc. Then got changed and went off to Steph and John's[1] party. Jane meanwhile has spoken to Simon and Kate in London, who seem to be bearing up reasonably well, though the press keep ringing them and knocking on the door of the flat.

The party was very jolly and we left at about 11.15. Alan rang to say that press coverage was OK and none of the rumour-mongering had come out. We went to bed relatively relaxed – for the first time in ten days. I am drained and so is Jane. At last the tidal wave may be subsiding.

The opinion polls show an extraordinary surge of support. Up from 34 to 47 per cent on the question 'Would Paddy Ashdown make a good Prime Minister?' Strong condemnation of the press as well.

Sunday, 9 February, Somerset

Up late after a lie-in and off to get the papers. The press is not too bad. I think the issue is now fading. I expect it will all come up again once the General Election starts, though.

---

1 Stephanie and John Bailey, our next door neighbours. Steph is active in the local constituency party and a key volunteer in my office. She has helped with surgeries since 1988.

Discussed matters with Des, Alan, Mark and Richard before taking the dog for a walk. I agreed to do an Andrew Neil interview on Northern Ireland. But of course he got me on to the subject of Tricia and I made some comments which ran on Independent Radio News.[1] Extremely annoying, since we are trying to kill the story.

A long walk with Jane and Luke; otherwise a quiet day, reading and listening to music.

Monday, 10 February, London

Spent all day replying to letters from the public. We must have had 600 in total – almost all expressing support.

Back to the flat to change into a dinner jacket and straight off to Covent Garden to see *Don Giovanni*(!!) We stopped short of the Opera House, which was closed off, and walked into a battery of cameras. Kinnock also there. The national anthem, then the Queen came in looking rather grey and grumpy. Why will she never smile?

Dinner, then home by about 1.30am and straight to bed, feeling tired and dejected. Jane is still sleeping poorly, which is always a bad sign.

Wednesday, 19 February, Westminster

In for a press conference. Only one question on the Tricia Howard affair – from Alastair Campbell of the *Daily Mirror*. He asked me a rather rude question (I can't remember exactly what), to which I answered 'No' and moved on. He looked chagrined, but it's what he deserved.

It's clear to me that the Tories are now in such a mess that they have only one shot left in their locker and that's the Budget. I now think they will take considerable risks with it and raise public borrowing in order to drop taxation and dare us to suggest raising it again. A carefully laid trap which is supposed to ensnare Labour in particular, but could catch us too.

On the other hand, I am not sure they haven't missed the mood of the public, who are not for tax cuts but for investment in public services. But

---

1 Neil asked me to comment on the fact that the opinion polls showed that support for me had risen sharply after the revelation. I said this was more to do with the generosity of the British people than the acceptability of what I had done.

then the public always says they would prefer services to tax cuts – until they have the money in their pocket, when they react pretty strongly against politicians who want to take it away.

Thursday, 20 February, Westminster

In the afternoon David Stephen came in to report back on his meetings with Charles Clarke from Neil Kinnock's office. David said Clarke seemed genuinely interested in a meeting between Kinnock and me. Clarke had discussed the possibility with Kinnock, who had decided (in my view, correctly) that it would not be a good idea just at the moment. Clarke also pumped David about our negotiating positions.

David is convinced that Kinnock thinks he can win. But that's the psychological attitude candidates have to adopt. Labour is also convinced that we would not, in the end, dare to sustain the Tories in power. We will have to disabuse them of this. They must be made to realize that we are prepared to sustain a government with the Tories as the largest party, unless and until Labour agree to PR for Westminster.

Saturday, 22 February, Faro, Portugal

We arrived at Faro[1] with quite a wind blowing but clear blue skies. We were picked up by the caretaker, Natalio, and driven to the villa.

What a place. Rambling, with an indoor fountain at every corner. We chose the upstairs bedroom, which is clearly the grand one and has a floor space as big as the whole of Vane Cottage.

Having unpacked, we had a cup of tea and spent an hour rather emotionally doing what we said we would do ages ago – discuss the whole Tricia Howard affair from start to finish. Jane, thank God, seems to have come to terms with it in so far as anyone can, but I felt unutterably wretched. We walked round the garden together, poring over the details.

1 Ian Hutcheson, a longtime supporter and friend, had suggested that Jane and I might like to spend a few days in his villa near Faro to give us a break before the Election.

Friday, 28 February, Westminster

At 10 o'clock off to see Robin Butler and Robert Fellowes[1] in the Cabinet Office.

We talked through what would happen in a hung Parliament. I made it clear to them that we would not want to see a minority Conservative Government removed until there was an agreed Government to put in its place (unspoken – until Labour had agreed to PR). In other words, we would operate on the basis of a 'constructive vote of no confidence'.[2] Both Fellowes and Butler seemed relieved, as this would take the pressure off the Queen, although Fellowes did say that it was perfectly possible the Queen would grant a second dissolution to Major if the Tories were the largest party and he really pressed for it.

This came as a bit of a shock, as we have always worked on the basis that she wouldn't do that. But Butler told me that in those circumstances, everybody would be advising the Prime Minister not to put the Queen in a difficult position.

I warned him that we would be asking for the Civil Service to help in any hung Parliament negotiations and that, if he wanted to know our thinking, he might send someone over to see the FDP[3] in Germany, as we would be modelling our approach on what happened there.

Monday, 9 March, London

Alan Leaman rang at about 3.30 to say that GQ magazine had published a scurrilous piece about me being in SIS[4] and having been observed gambolling passionately with a female SIS officer at a training camp in the south of England. Complete fiction.

1 Sir Robert Fellowes, Private Secretary to the Queen 1990–99. He is now in the House of Lords.
2 Under a 'constructive vote of no confidence', the Government doesn't fall until there is a stable alternative Government to put in its place (e.g., the parties who would wish to replace the Government have agreed to work together to provide such an alternative).
3 The FDP is Germany's Liberal Party and, until recently, has been in continuous coalition with the ruling party since the war. As part of my preparations for a hung Parliament I had flown over to see them and spent two days discussing this subject, concluding that we should follow a very similar approach.
4 MI6.

I blew my top. For the next two hours we had a detailed discussion on how to handle it with Andrew Phillips and others. In the end we decided to brush it off. Andrew will send the magazine a letter saying that we would take action for libel against them after the election[1] and I will simply say I wouldn't dignify this kind of ridiculous gossip.

I subsequently read the article. It was written by Annika Savill, who came to stay with Jane and me at Vane Cottage and whom we both liked. But she has written the most unpleasant piece I have ever read about me. There isn't a good word in it. The piece hurt both of us very deeply. She had clearly been fed a pack of lies and published it without any kind of checking. The fact that it is untrue does not diminish either the hurt to our family or the damage to the Party. Exactly what I have been fearing – and I fear more of it once the General Election campaign starts.

Tuesday, 10 March, Somerset

Budget Day. But I stayed in Yeovil. In the afternoon we took the dog out for half an hour's walk. Spring in the air and early green shoots beginning to show. What a pity I am not going to have the chance to enjoy it.

Lamont has produced a remarkable Budget. It's caught everybody by surprise. He has established a new 20 per cent tax rate. This will be a difficult one to deal with. Much of the day spent talking through what line we should take. By the evening I had decided that we ought to reverse the Lamont tax cut and go for a responsible Budget based on long-term investment.

Managed to have a full night's sleep, which was blissful.

Wednesday, 11 March, London

Up at 6.00 to go to London.

As soon as we arrived we heard that Major was off to see the Queen at 12.00 and would announce the election date when he returned. There followed a frantic series of interviews which seemed to occupy most of the day. Major duly announced at 1.00 (as expected – 9 April) and I went

---

1 Which we did. They settled out of court.

across to Cowley Street for a photo-op with Des and a chat with the campaign people.

Des is very pleased. The campaign is off to a good start. He has done a stunning job and there is a good team in place.

At 5 o'clock into the Parliamentary Party Meeting to clear the manifesto. Des did a brief presentation on it, then we got on to Budget issues.

We had three options; to accept the Tories' 20p rate and cut back on our investment programme substantially; to accept the 20p, put 1p on the basic rate in order to fund our education package and to drop our investment plans; or to reverse the 20p and put 1p on the basic rate (which I thought was the right position).

A very long discussion which I closed as soon as I saw it wasn't going my way. Unfortunately, Alan Beith[1] was on the bench covering the Budget. I needed him with me to help argue the case. I made an impassioned plea, saying that we really had to be radical or we would lose all edge on our message. I also argued that the Tories were being irresponsible with the economy and we could paint them as such. Alan came in at about 6.45 and we had a tortuous debate until about 7.30.

At the end I said, 'Well, nothing further can be said. We will have to vote on the issue.' Bob immediately chipped in, saying that was not the way that Cabinets were run. He said that if the Leader and the spokesman both recommended the same plan of action, then everyone ought to accept it. The Colleagues agreed. I was amazed.

It is the toughest decision we have taken and could be crucial in determining our position after the election. If there is a realignment of the left between ourselves and Labour, this was the moment when it became possible.

Labour, of course, has already said they would reverse the 20p, though they won't go as far as us in adding an extra penny for education.

I am well pleased. I think we have an excellent, sharp-edged and pretty radical manifesto. But it is also a manifesto which could cost us a fair amount if the Tories are effective in their campaigning against tax increases.

---

1 Then our Treasury spokesman.

Friday, 13 March, London, Edinburgh, Cardiff, Somerset

FIRST OFFICIAL DAY OF THE ELECTION CAMPAIGN

Got up feeling great. Moved our things into the Horseguards Hotel, where Jane and I are staying for the campaign.

The first press conference seemed to go well. Afterwards, out in a coach to Heathrow with a Sky crew and ITN and BBC reporters in attendance. We had a pretty bumpy flight to Edinburgh in a little private aircraft, fighting against 140-knot headwinds which made us nearly an hour late. We were then rushed off to a hotel not far from the airport, where Malcolm Bruce and I held a press conference launching the campaign in Scotland and I succeeded in being photographed coming out of a Ladies' loo which I had gone into by mistake! Then a dash for the airport and off to Cardiff, this time with the wind behind us and a very bumpy landing at the other end. Here we launched the Welsh campaign with Richard Livsey. Then back to the airport and off to the Royal Naval Air Station at Yeovilton, from which we were whisked back to Vane Cottage. An hour or so at home where I tried to catch a little sleep before going to Yeovil for more campaigning. Then Bridgwater, where I did an impromptu speech for about twenty minutes, and Taunton, where I launched Jackie Ballard's campaign. She is in great form and everybody is determined that she is going to win. After a brief speech in the drizzling rain, dashed off to Ilminster with the campaign team for more canvassing, then to Muchelney and finally the Rose & Crown for a pint. On the way home we heard that the Prime Minister was about to give a speech attacking me directly. Wonderful. To the delight of the Rose & Crown regulars, I did a piece in the corner of the bar to all three television channels. Many jokes flying backwards and forwards. If this is to be the pace of the whole campaign, I will be pretty tired by the end of it.

Sunday, 15 March, Somerset and London

Up at 8.30 feeling refreshed. A lot of coverage for the Tory and Labour Conferences. Our coverage has concentrated on us being the high-tax party. The Barbara Amiel piece in the *Sunday Times* was published today. The photographs are wonderful, particularly the one of me and Luke on top of Ham Hill. But the piece is awful! It's very insulting and totally unfair about Jane. She was very upset, saying she would never have a journalist stay in her house again. It was Amiel's comments (totally inaccurate) about the house and the way Jane treated her as a guest that hurt most. I felt furious, miserable and guilty all at the same time. Glenys Kinnock had previously warned Jane that Amiel had done her at the last election, but that this time Glenys had refused to let her in the house because the piece had been such a hatchet job. Jane wishes she had taken Glenys's advice. I tried to cheer her up by saying, 'What can you expect of a Tory paper at election time?' – which probably wasn't very helpful.

Left at 11 o'clock for London with Special Branch in attendance and a police escort.

In the evening, after our opening rally, a short rest and into a strategy meeting. Afterwards, off with Alan, Des and Jane to Joe Allen's. All very merry. Then back to my suite, where we watched Des on television: highly competent.

Monday, 16 March, Westminster

Richard Holme warned me that Peter Riddell[1] thinks I am getting rather too presidential and self-righteous. Richard also said that the buzz about post-Tricia fishing expeditions is still going on and there are about to be further 'revelations' in some foreign newspapers. We are having to cope with a nerve-racking build-up throughout the week towards the Sundays, with much rumour-mongering – which is very, very wearing.

I met Des at 9 o'clock. We had dinner in his room and watched the press coverage. Cowley Street is taking longer to bed in as a headquarters than I had anticipated.

Tuesday, 17 March, London

An unpleasant piece by Peter Riddell along the lines Richard Holme warned of yesterday. Otherwise the press coverage for our manifesto, though not great, is good. An excellent *Guardian* editorial and quite a sympathetic *Independent* one, too.

A strategy meeting at 8.30 in which we planned the morning's press

1 Political columnist for *The Times* since 1991, assistant editor since 1993.

conferences – then into the battle bus, a magnificent canary yellow affair in which I have a little mobile bunker with smoked glass. Off to a health centre in Bermondsey, where I met Simon Hughes. I tried to have an ordinary conversation with some people in the waiting room, but this became impossible in the crush of photographers.

Des and I met at 9.00 for a meal at Joe Allen's. Early pressure is beginning to slacken slightly and his office is now up and running well. Two opinion polls tonight put Labour five points ahead of the Tories. Looks as though Labour are opening up a permanent lead, but we cannot be certain. Bad news. If Labour has a permanent lead, our vote will be fiercely squeezed.

We returned to the hotel to watch the news on television: a good piece on Kinnock and Glenys on ITN. Our profile is tomorrow. Generally speaking Labour has had it all its own way today. Organizationally, they are running away with it. The Tories, by contrast, look wobbly[1] and uncertain.

To bed at about 11.15, very tired.

Wednesday, 18 March, London

LAUNCH OF ELECTION MANIFESTO

The organization has worked well today. The press seemed pleased and I am much buoyed up by the reaction on the streets. Two polls to be published tomorrow put us at 17 and 18 per cent. One of them puts the Tories ahead of Labour and the other Labour ahead of the Tories, so our fears of last night that Labour is pulling away seem groundless. The weekend opinion polls will tell.

To Cowley Street at 7.45pm and wandered around the headquarters. Morale is high. There is a real sense of purpose within the team and the word coming in from the grass roots is that our campaign is perceived as organized, effective and targeted. A tremendous difference from 1987.

Then up to our room to watch the 10 o'clock news. We did well on press coverage today. It should have been the other two parties who dominated, but we managed to get our message across. Des went off pleased and I tumbled into bed at 11.15.

---

1 For the Tories this day subsequently became known as 'Wobbly Tuesday'.

Wednesday, 25 March, London

There is a real spat developing between Labour and the Tories over a Labour Party Election Broadcast, which uses a child who could not get an ear operation to highlight the deficiencies of the NHS. I thought it pretty effective when I saw it. However, it turns out that the mother of the child is furious. But the father, a Labour supporter, is in favour. The Tories are making the most of it.

Meanwhile, we are down to 14 per cent in one poll and up to 19 in another. Polls out today show an extraordinary 78 per cent support for our policy on education. Two polls show me as the most effective campaigner of the three leaders, though the press are saying it's all the result of the Tricia Howard stuff, which hurts.

Halfway through the campaign, now.

Thursday, 26 March, Edinburgh

The spat over Labour's Party Election Broadcast, which is becoming known as 'The War of Jennifer's Ear', is getting very messy. Des wants me to make much stronger comments on it, but I refuse, saying it would be best not to be involved in this 'ridiculous brawl'. Some of the day was spent resisting London trying to get me to take part in the row.

On our walkabout around Edinburgh West I met James Douglas Hamilton,[1] who the previous day had accompanied Ian Lang[2] to Edinburgh Zoo for the daily Tory photo-op, which, for some reason best known to them, was set up with the zoo's resident orang-utan. However, when they got there, with the press in full attendance, they discovered that the orang-utan had died – eight years ago! So they had their photograph taken with some passing penguins instead.

I was in hysterics when I heard this and used the story as a pre-speech warm-up joke in the evening. The audience loved it.

---

1 Previously Secretary of State for Scotland. Member of Parliament (Conservative) for Edinburgh West 1974–97.
2 Secretary of State for Scotland, Member of Parliament (Conservative) for Galloway 1979–97; now sits in the House of Lords.

Saturday, 28 March, London

The press has gone completely mad. The current rumour being spread around (by the Tories?) and apparently causing great media scurryings worldwide is that I have a hidden illegitimate child. It's even reached our activists out in the country.

Very good news in the polls, though. We are up to 20 per cent in two of them and rising in all bar one of the rest.

Thursday, 2 April, London, Devon, Cornwall, Sussex, Norfolk

Up at 6.00 and off to an uneventful press conference. Then started the longest day of the whole campaign. The press now see us as central to the campaign, so we are getting a lot of attention.

On to the plane to Plymouth, where we were met by local candidates before driving to Saltash. Here I stepped out of the bus with the words, 'It's good to be back in Devon' – when, of course, we were the other side of the Tamar and firmly in Cornwall.

We did a walkabout, then back on the bus to Torbay, after which by plane to London. Major has said no to PR and Kinnock has promised that he will allow other parties to join in the Plant Committee[1] on electoral reform. How very generous of him.

Into the car and down to Lewes, and then on to Eastbourne for a rally. This went brilliantly. Very crowded. The theme was democracy and the audience clapped almost every line. These rallies are becoming much more enthusiastic and revivalist.

I left feeling elated. On leaving the hall, however, I detected there was a problem from the serious looks on Mark's and Dick Newby's faces. They said everything was all right, but I had a sinking feeling that it wasn't.

Afterwards off to do a *World Tonight* interview and a couple of others. By now the adrenalin was ebbing away and I was beginning to feel quite tired. Then up to the Eastbourne golf course, into a helicopter and off for Norwich where, on arrival, I was taken straight into a television studio to answer (live) questions from members of the public. Then upstairs for a

1 Labour's internal commission set up under Professor Plant to consider electoral reform.

snack with the local Lib Dem candidates, who were all very buoyant, and a dash across town to the BBC, where I recorded a piece for local television. By now it was 11.15.

The helicopter pilot warned that the weather was coming in and we needed to get out of Norwich before too long. Mark and Dick still very serious. Something afoot.

I went off to ring Jane for my usual nightly call, to discover that Des had already rung her. He had received a call from a journalist saying that the *Sun* were going to publish a diary piece about a 'Romeo MP', referring to me. They are apparently trying to scare us into moving injunctions, etc. I was terribly shaken. Jane upset, too.

This kind of news makes my legs go wobbly, because of the damage more rumour-based publicity will do. Back in the helicopter to Elstree. Arrived at the Horseguards at about 1.45. I went up to my room with Mark and Dick to discuss the situation. Des heard us arrive and came in to talk. He showed me the *Sun*, which wasn't nearly as bad as I had been led to believe. Heavy innuendo and threats of things to come, but nothing specific. Pre-election smear stuff. Des's view – backed up by Richard and Andrew – is that they are trying to frighten us.

Des pleased with the television for the day. It appears we are now leading the agenda. I didn't get to bed until 2.30 and was up again at 5.30. Slept fitfully.

Saturday, 4 April, London, Wiltshire, Somerset

I had intended to get up at 7.30, but Luke leapt on my bed at 7.00 and scratched my face. Then a bath and the mail. Another one of those horrid anonymous letters which unsettle Jane and me so much. This one 'revealing' some completely mythical mistress I am supposed to have in Rugby!

During the morning we heard the first of the Saturday polls putting us at 22 per cent. Subsequent polls, however, not quite so good. Labour are slightly ahead of the Tories, but not enough for them to get more seats. We don't seem to be suffering, however, from the squeeze.

Off for a day's campaigning across the West Country by helicopter. At Warminster we met a few drunken squaddies from the army base and some very unpleasant Tories who kept on shouting insulting comments, particularly to Jane, about the Tricia Howard affair.

Then into the car with Jane to London. Conversations with Alan and Olly on the way. Now the rumours are about Gordon Brown, Peter Lilley etc. All complete nonsense, I'm sure.

Back in London, Des says that there is an injunction being placed by, he thinks, the Labour Party against the *News of the World*. Rumour feeds on rumour.

We had a bite to eat, then met up with Des briefly. Shortly afterwards Alan came in. He had received a call from Olly telling him that *The Times*'s front-page story was about us demanding four Cabinet seats with names attached (David Steel, Ming Campbell etc.). I rang Dick Newby. This plainly came from an indiscreet briefing he had given to Robin Oakley.[1]

Sunday, 5 April, London

A very full day. Strategy meeting first thing in the morning, then I filmed the Party Election Broadcast.

1 Then Political Editor of *The Times*; soon to become Political Editor of the BBC.

At the National Reform Club I did Jonathan Dimbleby's *On The Record*. Not good. I got awfully tangled up on hung Parliamentaria.

Afterwards straight on to *Walden*. This seemed to go better. Walden started by getting me to answer four questions. I could have answered yes to all of them, but I decided to disagree with him over something, to give me time to think. He is very clever. Being interviewed by him is like playing chess in three dimensions.

At 5 o'clock a strategy meeting. Afterwards off to Joe Allen's with Des for the final meal together of the campaign. He thinks things are going extremely well. I hope he is right.

Monday, 6 April, London

To the *Granada 500*[1] at the Grosvenor House Hotel. Sue Lawley chairing. I did a twenty-minute session with the five-hundred specially chosen people from Bolton. I responded fairly toughly and didn't have too bad a time, though there were a few hisses when I talked about my determination to put PR on the agenda. They were a tough audience, well educated, well rehearsed, who didn't accept inadequate answers.

Major came on after me and was actually booed. Last was Kinnock, who refused to give an answer on PR and was almost shouted down.

Afterwards back to the hotel, where we picked up Des, then off to Richmond. On the way we heard the polls. Our top rate is 23 per cent and the PA 10,000[2] puts us at 20.5 per cent. Des thinks we are about to deliver a triumph, but he qualified it by saying we can't be certain of anything until polling day.

The Tories, meanwhile, are mounting a strenuous attack on us on hung Parliaments, instability, etc. Baker gave an outrageous speech, building on the result of the German elections (which had resulted in some right-wing fascists getting elected) to say that PR would mean rioting in the streets. Clearly a panicky man. But it will have an effect.

1 A Granada TV programme, run at all recent General Elections, in which each Party Leader is grilled by five hundred voters.
2 Press Association Poll, which questions 10,000 electors.

Tuesday, 7 April, West Country

More campaigning in the West Country, then on to a rally in St Austell. We heard the opinion polls as we went in. They were OK, but the Tories are now putting out scare stories about a hung Parliament meaning Kinnock in Downing Street. I think it's beginning to have some effect.

Nevertheless, the rally was a huge success – about 2,000 people there. The speech went down well. We left in high spirits and returned to the plane to go back to London. At midnight I met up with Des, who is also concerned that the polls are beginning to show a check in our rise. He thinks we have to get off hung Parliament for the last day of the election. To bed about 1.00.

Wednesday, 8 April, London and Somerset

Chatted with the constituency. Nick Speakman thinks I am on my way to a 10,000 majority. I have some doubts. Now getting very nervous about a last-minute rise in the Tory vote.

In the evening, our final rally in Taunton. I don't feel happy, though. I am now pretty certain the Tories are on a lift at our expense. Playing the Kinnock card.

After the rally, out on to the balcony to speak to a torchlit gathering. I made a reference to the Monmouth Rebellion in the West Country, ending, 'Only we are going to win this time.' Jackie and David Heath[1] there as well. They are all very confident. I wish I was.

Thursday, 9 April, Somerset

POLLING DAY

Off to vote. A beautiful misty spring morning. Masses of photographers, etc. Jane and I walked to the village hall and voted for the cameras, then did a photo-op with Luke on the playing fields. . .

The exit poll at 10.00pm was disappointing. It predicted a hung Parliament, putting us at 18 per cent and showing the Tories ahead. A later BBC

---

1 Our candidate in Somerton & Frome.

poll confirmed this. The first result for us was Portsmouth South, which we narrowly lost. A bad sign. Then Torbay, which we also lost. I have an awful feeling this is not going to be a good night.

At 11.30 I couldn't wait any longer and drove off to Yeovil for my own count. When I arrived I was startled to see the Tory vote up. My worst fears realized. But it turned out all right and my majority was increased to more than 8,000. Still, it is frightening the way the Tory vote has held up. Nick was expecting a 10,000 majority and was a bit stunned not to get it.

Whilst there we heard that we have won Cheltenham. But we lost Ribble Valley and, shockingly, Ronnie Fearn in Southport has also fallen.

Then back to the Liberal Club, having done a raft of interviews. The highlight of the night was Don Foster winning Bath from Chris Patten by a narrow majority. But we will not get anything like the number of seats we thought.

As I left for London at about 2.30, it became clear that we were having a bad night. We lost Nicol Stephen at Kincardine and David Bellotti at Eastbourne, but gained North Devon, and North Cornwall. Elsewhere we missed, although we did shorten the distance between us and the Tories in a number of seats in the south and west. But by 2 o'clock, the stunning news was that Major had a majority and Labour had lost. A terrible night for Labour. I saw Kinnock on television and he looked broken.

I arrived at our campaign headquarters at the Horseguards at 4.00am to be met by a couple of hundred photographers, cameramen and press. I said that we had made some stunning gains but these were counteracted by some sad losses. I then met with Graham Elson, Alan Leaman, Dick Newby and Des in my room for an hour or so to map out the line. We agreed to put a brave face on it. Alan didn't want me to do press in the morning at all, but we have to get a reassuring message across to the Party.

So to bed at 5.00am.

Friday, 10 April, London

Up at 6.45 for a round of interviews. I did my best to put a reasonably presentable face on it. The fact is that we have more MPs, even though our vote has declined.

Then off to breakfast with Olly Grender, Mark Payne and Alan Leaman. They are all pretty low and I expended a lot of energy trying to raise people's spirits. But I am pretty exhausted myself.

Afterwards to a strategy meeting in which I covered a number of points, including the possibility of playing up to Labour. We decided we wouldn't attack them too strenuously. There is a real opportunity now for us to drive a wedge in Labour on PR. Despite the disappointment, this is the result I always said I wanted, with the Tories ahead and Labour going down to a fourth defeat and into an internal battle. We must make use of this opportunity to realign the left.

To the final press conference at 10.45. Des led off rather emotionally, claiming a triumph, of course. I followed, also rather emotionally, and then we took some questions. We gave them the best we could, but they weren't terribly impressed.

There has been a recount at Brecon, but Ray Michie has held her seat in Argyll & Bute.

Then home. On the way I heard that we had in fact lost Brecon and Radnor. Final count, twenty MPs. Rang all the old MPs and the new ones. The most poignant was Geraint Howells, who was in tears. I think he was more upset at the loss of Richard Livsey's seat than his own. God, what a terrible game this is! Why on earth do we do it?[1]

In the evening Jane and I walked across the fields with Kate and Luke to the Cat Head, then back again after a couple of beers. A glorious evening. How beautiful the Somerset countryside is. Whatever personal events, these powder blue spring days with a light mist gathering on the fields, the soft colours of the countryside and the mellow stone of Somerset cottages always restores.

Back home, dinner and to bed, early and exhausted.

Saturday, 11 April, Somerset

There is real trouble breaking out in the Labour Party. The headless chicken tendency has taken over. Some discussion that John Smith will be elected Leader unopposed. I doubt if they will let him.

I plan to throw a little hand-grenade into the Labour leadership election by suggesting a broad-ranging national debate on PR along the lines of the Scottish Convention.

I started writing notes for what needs to be done. I must get the Party

---

1 In total we lost: Ceredigon & Pembroke North; Brecon & Radnor and all our by-election gains: Eastbourne; Ribble Valley; Southport; and Kincardine & Deeside.

off its backside and working again, though I am not in much of a position to do this since I am pretty exhausted myself.

We are much better placed now than we were in 1987. Then, we had eighteen MPs, were in disarray, our membership was falling and our funds were in total chaos. Today we have two more MPs, a higher-quality Parliamentary Party, record membership, sound funds and it's the Labour Party who are in a mess.

Monday, 13 April, London

To London and into the office. Mark came in to say that I really mustn't push everyone too hard, or I would have a rebellion on my hands. I told him it was my job to get the Party moving after the election.

At 2.15 I walked with Matthew Taylor along the Embankment to the Parliamentary Party Meeting, which went on for a full two hours. There is a distressing tendency for people to climb back into their bunkers. I am determined that we stay out on open ground so that we can have a dialogue with the Labour Party, which I hope will develop into a genuine partnership and perhaps even, in the long term, an electoral pact.

But everybody said that we should stress our independence, our distinctiveness, and that we should treat the Labour Party as 'a corpse'. It's certainly not a corpse. It may be going through some pretty serious difficulties, but the idea that the Labour Party is going to lie down and stick its legs in the air is simply ludicrous.

Wednesday, 15 April, Westminster

At about 11.45, when Jane was in the office, I got an urgent call from Mark. He asked me whether I was alone. I said I was and he told me that one of the Yeovil workers had been stopped by an unnamed journalist outside the Liberal Club, saying that I was about to be delivered with a paternity order. Bizarre nonsense. Why are they still hounding me?

Monday 27 April, Westminster

At 12 o'clock a Parliamentary Party Meeting to discuss the election of the new Speaker. We agreed to support Betty Boothroyd, but to demand from her and Peter Brooke (our other acceptable candidate) a commitment to treat us properly as the third party in the House of Commons. Russell Johnston was sent away to pass our message on to our preferred contenders.

At 2.20 he returned to say that Peter Brooke had made a categoric undertaking to respect our rights as a third party, but that Betty Boothroyd had gone no further than to say she would carry on the same policy as the previous speaker, Jack Weatherall. Then into the debate about the Speaker.

A very full House. While we were in the Lords to hear the Royal Proclamation[1] instructing us to elect a new Speaker, Alan Beith managed to bag the bench, so at least we had somewhere to sit. He persuaded the Labour Whips that if they wanted us to support their candidate (Betty Boothroyd), the very least they could do was get their people off our bench. Clever, and typical of Alan.

Peter Brooke's nominees put up rather a poor set of speeches. But Biffen[2] did extremely well, proposing Betty, and when a vote was taken she carried by more than 100 votes. She was duly 'dragged'[3] to the Speaker's Chair, to spontaneous applause which was taken up by everybody, including (rather reluctantly, I thought) John Major.

My welcoming speech was the only one which was slightly contentious, reminding her to take heed of the special position of Scotland (where the Tories have almost no MPs) and the requirement to give us a fair voice in the House. Everybody started shouting at me. As usual. But at least I made my points, rather than indulging in silly sycophancy.

Then into the Parliamentary Party Meeting, the main business being my strategy paper,[4] in which I had suggested closer relations with Labour. It went badly right from the start. Alex Carlile opened up by saying that he would join Labour if this was the way we were going. It was a very

---

1 Recalling Parliament after the election.

2 John Biffen MP, Leader of the House of Commons 1982–7. Member of Parliament (Conservative) for Salop Oswestry, 1961–83, Shropshire North 1983–97; now sits in the House of Lords.

3 By tradition a newly elected Speaker has to show reluctance to take the job so has to be 'dragged' to the Chair.

4 See Appendix A.

tough meeting at which almost nobody, except Matthew Taylor and Bob Maclennan, supported me. I was left very isolated and got rather angry towards the end. However, I told them that I was determined to make them reconsider the comfortable strategy of equidistance we'd had in the past in favour of something much more fluid, and that I would return to this, etc. I may have lost the argument but am determined to win the overall battle.

Over a couple of whiskies later in the evening I discussed the Parliamentary Party Meeting with Jim Wallace and Alan Leaman. Alan, who had been present, said that what I had seen was a typical first reaction after a disappointing election: refusing to consider the new events, refusing to consider new ideas and fighting me. But he felt I would get my way in the end. Wise old bird, he is probably right.

He then drove us home, dropping Jim and me off in Methley Street. To bed at about 2.00. I slept badly turning over in my mind what needed to be done. I have yet to make up my mind about whether these are the conditions we need for a realignment. But if they are, I must be prepared to stake my leadership on it. I have to keep the Party out of the trenches, mobile and free to take part in what I think will be a very fluid period of politics. Up again at 5.30.

Wednesday, 6 May, Westminster

QUEEN'S SPEECH DAY

A particularly crowded Chamber. Ken Baker spoke first, and wittily. But Andrew Mitchell[1] gave an even better speech. No notes and very self-confident. Kinnock followed with a few very barbed witticisms at Baker. I saw Baker wincing as Kinnock had the House rolling about with laughter, largely at his expense.

Then Major, who was flat and boring. To my surprise, he started engaging in the Labour leadership battle. What a stupid thing to do. He doesn't know when to rise above it. This will be a weakness of his to watch out for. His speech contrasted strongly with how 'She' might have reacted under the circumstances. No triumphalism, just boring. I then made my speech, which was by no means flawless but a good deal better than his.

---

1 Member of Parliament (Conservative) for Gedling 1977–97.

Afterwards a meeting with Andrew Marr.[1] I took him through my realignment thinking on a totally non-attributable basis. He agreed with the thrust and said he was writing an article along exactly the same lines. He seemed relieved that somebody was thinking about opposition politics again. I think we will get a good article from him.

Thursday, 7 May, Westminster

POLLING DAY IN THE LOCAL ELECTIONS

At 3.15 Alan and I left to see Andreas Whittam Smith of the *Independent*. I showed him an advanced text of my Chard speech.[2] He seemed genuinely interested. I suggested that we needed a neutral forum in which all sides could meet to map out the new politics. Would the *Independent* play this role? It was the 'only paper capable of doing the job'. He agreed. But I don't think he will help, since he cannot find a practical way to do this without risking egg ending up on the *Independent*'s face. Nevertheless, he will print an editorial, hopefully a helpful one, on the speech.

To dinner in the evening with regular dining friends. Left at about 10.00 and walked back down the Embankment to Cowley Street, where I met Jane for the local election results. I had had two or three glasses of excellent claret and some brandy at dinner, so I was in a pretty jovial mood, expecting good results. We started well enough, but it soon became clear that we weren't going to hit the high marks of our expectations. In the end we gained only sixty seats and no councils.

But the Tories did wonderfully. The election result was not a flash in the pan at all. Labour had a catastrophic night, losing nearly 400 seats. That will increase the nervousness of their already highly active headless chickens.

1 Then a political columnist for the *Independent*; now Political Editor of the BBC.
2 This is the speech which I had planned to give if there was a fourth Labour defeat, in order to launch, as I hoped, the process of the realignment of the left through closer co-operation between ourselves and Labour. I decided that I would give this in the little town of Chard in my own constituency and had fixed the date for 9 May – exactly one month after polling day. See Appendix B, The Chard Speech.

Saturday, 9 May, Somerset

DAY OF THE CHARD SPEECH

Encouraging pre-pieces on the radio and in the newspapers for my speech. Charles did well on *Today*.

Off to surgery with Steph Bailey. There hadn't been an advert in the *Chard & Ilminster News* – so we only had three cases!

After surgeries, we had about forty or fifty people and all the television cameras in the Chard Guildhall. I had taken some trouble to make sure that the shot looked all right for the TV cameras. The audience had come from as far away as Honiton, West Dorset and Bridgwater. Very gratifying.

A quiet afternoon and evening. Jane cooked a special meal and we had a bottle of Irancy rosé. The evening news programmes were excellent: no other major news items in the day, so the Chard speech had first or second place on both. And they said that my proposals had split Labour. Couldn't be better!

Monday, 11 May, Westminster

A very strong reaction to my speech from Liz Lynne and also from Simon Hughes. Liz happened to be in the Whips' Office, so I asked her to come up to mine. She said she has had a very tough time in the constituency and accused me (a) of doing things that the Parliamentary Party had not agreed to; (b) of failing to listen to the Parliamentary Party; and (c) of putting my personal ambitions before the interests of the Party. She was furious, but fairly incomprehensible.

She said that she would lead a public revolt against me herself. I told her that of course that was her entitlement. She also said I would get a very strong reaction from the Parliamentary Party on Wednesday – she would see to it.

I tried to point out to her that I had consulted my colleagues more than any of my predecessors. That I had told people I was going to make this speech and had even circulated the text. And that I had heard not a single tweet from any of them, despite the fact they had had four days to look at it.

She stormed out of the office, slamming the door. It was the most difficult meeting I have ever had with a Parliamentary colleague.

Tuesday, 12 May, Westminster[1]

There is a good deal of anger now building up in the Parliamentary Party about Chard. They say that I am railroading everybody into positions they don't want to be in.

PMQs today very muddled and lacking in bite. Nobody seems to know how to attack the Government. It's like punching blancmange. No one believes that Major would abuse a cat, let alone his power. And what he is doing seems to be such a relief from the red-in-tooth-and-claw Thatcherism that went before that you almost can't criticize it. No doubt a line of attack will develop on the Government, but I can't see it yet.

At 9.00 I rushed off to Joe Allen's, where I found Des in bubbly form. He has found a publisher for his book;[1] meanwhile he is 'resting'. He will get back to work about August or September. He wants nothing further to do with the Party, he says.

We also talked about the Chard strategy, to which he is generally opposed. But I explained the situation to him, and he seemed to come round. We talked about a confidential discussion with John Smith. Des said he would certainly investigate the possibility. I said that I would much rather speak to Smith before he became Labour Leader than afterwards. This move could be risky for me if it ever got out and I would like an equivalence of danger on both sides. Once Smith has become Leader, there will be much less downside for him for letting the thing become public. Des will work on this.

I also discussed with Des an idea I have had of spending two or three days a week during the first half of next year going round the communities of Britain. I hated what I had to do in the election – descending on people for ten minutes, 'conferring the Westminster blessing', then dashing off. I want to refresh my sense of the real issues and of how people live in Britain now. It would re-energize me. I would try to live and work with people, without the press being there.[2]

Des gave me some very useful thoughts on how the idea could be developed.

I had a fitful night's sleep, worrying about reactions in the Party to the

---

1 A pot-boiler romance/thriller aimed at the holiday market entitled *Campaign*.
2 I subsequently wrote my second book, *Beyond Westminster*, about these visits.

Chard speech and the problems I will have with the Parliamentary Party tomorrow.

Wednesday, 13 May, Westminster

At 6.30, into the Parliamentary Party Meeting. Liz Lynne attacked what I had said at Chard and stated her intention to make her opposition clear in public. Otherwise it was much easier than I had anticipated, though Simon Hughes did ask for a proper debate on strategy before the Conference, which I agreed to.

Sunday, 17 May, Somerset

An interesting piece in the *Sunday Times* today about the so-called 'NERDS', a group of scandal hitmen who operate in America and are said to have been active here – for the Tories, of course. Their technique is to set a piece of scandal running, often totally unfounded. This disconcerts the opposition, makes them spend time rebutting it and so puts them on the back foot. Some of it sticks in the minds of the press and of the electorate. Real Goebbels stuff. Their job is to destroy people's reputations if they can, but failing that to unbalance them. I wonder if this is what happened to us over the election?

Tuesday, 19 May, Westminster

I asked Mark and Alan today whether I was getting a reputation for being grumpy. They confirmed that I was. I also seem to be rubbing my colleagues up the wrong way. It's all very well for people to say I am pushing them too hard, but that's my job. I am desperate to get through this uncertain period after the General Election as quickly as possible. Strong reactions still coming in on the Chard speech – pretty well all anti.

Tuesday, 2 June, London

I woke up at about 6.45 dreading going into work. I have temporarily lost all enthusiasm for the job. Just can't get people going again. I am very worried indeed about our lack of coverage. Opinion polls now down to 13 per cent.

This job is like pushing a stone up a hill. Leave it for a moment and it begins to roll down again – and electorally I feel it's only me holding it up at the moment. Post-election depression with a touch of the persecution complex, probably.

I have became increasingly worried about the reaction to the Chard speech. Apparently *On The Record* (which I am doing at the weekend) have been asking round my Parliamentary colleagues and have failed to find a single one who would speak enthusiastically in favour of it. Liz Lynne is being particularly difficult.

The Danes have voted against Maastricht in their referendum today. I quickly dictated a statement saying this was a testing moment for Major and rearranged my diary for tomorrow, since this news will dominate.[1]

To bed after midnight.

Wednesday, 3 June, London and Epsom

DERBY DAY

The Danish Maastricht referendum result is the major news story, so I made arrangements to stay in close contact with London while at the Derby.[2] I thought I wouldn't have to return since it seemed unlikely that Major would speak on the matter. Into a helicopter and a fifteen-minute flight to Epsom. I was surprised at how empty the stands were. A chat with

1 The Maastricht Treaty, signed at the recent intergovernmental conference in Holland, laid out the next major step towards European integration. Some countries' constitutions required this to be put to a referendum. (Ireland, France and Germany voted yes; Denmark, on this occasion, voted no – although the Danes subsequently held another referendum at which they reversed the decision.) In Britain the Maastricht Treaty had to be ratified by Parliament, a process which dominated politics for the next year, divided the Tories and, ultimately, holed the Major Government below the water-line.
2 We had been invited by Ian Hutcheson to join him and his wife at the Derby.

Peter Sissons,[1] who is clear that (a) the Labour Party is in a pretty disastrous state; (b) we have a real chance; and (c) the BBC needs a shake-up. Meanwhile, Jane talked to his wife Sylvia, whom she likes. The conversation turned to Barbara Amiel who, to Jane's great delight, was roundly despised and insulted by all.

We were just about to sit down to lunch when the phone rang. It was [my secretary] Clare. The Colleagues had met earlier and the unanimous view was that I should return. I spoke to Alan, who told me that the PM was going to make the statement on Maastricht. I outlined what I thought should be our response. The Colleagues had strongly disagreed with my view that the Maastricht legislation should, nevertheless, continue. They said this was dotty. How could a Bill based on a Treaty continue, when the Treaty has just been broken by the Danish 'no' vote?

I got back at about 2.30 and into the chamber. Major's statement took me completely by surprise. I presumed he would continue to sit on the fence, but he decided to ignore the Danes and press on with the Bill (as I had argued earlier). He has staked his reputation on driving the Maastricht process through. I immediately changed my statement to one congratulating and supporting him. He is, of course, absolutely right. Kinnock responded with a pretty wobbly comment which nobody could make head or tail of. I suspect it was designed to cover over divisions in the Labour Party.

As soon as I was called by the Speaker they all started shouting. The anti-Europeans wanted to vent their wrath on somebody and I was the obvious target. I hardly said a word before Dennis Skinner shouted, 'Make way for Captain Mainwaring.' This caused everybody to fall about in mock mirth. God, I hate this place. It is puerile, pathetic and utterly useless and I long for the day (if it ever comes) when we have the power to change it completely. I left incandescent with rage, but trying not to show it.

The Labour Party, especially the left, are now making it very difficult for me to speak whenever I get up. Clearly the Chard speech has struck a powerful chord and I am a figure of hate for them. No harm in that.

---

1 A senior BBC television news presenter whose many programmes have included *Question Time*.

Thursday, 4 June, Westminster

At 2.15 off to the meeting of the Lib Dem peers. Roy Jenkins chaired in his usual magisterial manner and I took them through my position paper. The Chard speech was generally welcomed by all of them, but especially Roy himself, Bill Rodgers,[1] Conrad Russell[2] and Emlyn.[3]

It's becoming clear that *On The Record* is going to be a tough interview. Some of my colleagues have been telling them that the Chard speech was a madcap idea, cooked up over a bottle of Burgundy on a hot sunny afternoon in France.

Tuesday, 9 June, London

Dinner with the A1 Group.[4] All the discussion on Chard and realignment. At the end I said that 500 years ago Columbus set out across the Atlantic to discover India, but discovered America instead. I felt there was a new political world waiting to be found out there and that we now had a vessel capable of making the journey and a crew who were courageous enough to try. But that we wouldn't discover America if we kept the vessel in port. There was a brief round of applause.

Monday, 22 June, Westminster

I feel as though I am wading waist-deep through treacle. I am also nervous about the Conference. I have never felt so uncertain about where to go and how to lead the Party as at present.

---

1 Liberal Democrat Peer. Member of Parliament (Labour 1962–81, then SDP) for Teesside Stockton 1962–79, Stockton North 1979–83. One of the 'Gang of Four'; formerly a member of the Labour Cabinet. Currently Leader of the Liberal Democrats in the House of Lords.
2 Earl Russell, Liberal then Liberal Democrat hereditary peer and distinguished historian.
3 Emlyn Hooson, Liberal then Liberal Democrat peer. Ex-Liberal Member of Parliament for Montgomeryshire.
4 A1 Dining Club. Established in the days of the old Liberal/SDP Alliance, A1 standing for Alliance First. The Club was crucial in bringing the parties together during the merger in 1988 and consists of senior ex-Liberals and ex-SDP members who generally support co-operation with Labour.

Speaking to a lobby journalist, I was encouraged to hear that the other parties seem in the same state. He told me that he had never known the political situation so uncertain and that all the parties were stumbling around: the Government trying to find what to do after an election they didn't expect to win; the Labour Party sunk in internal strife; and ourselves trying in coded terms to make people talk about realignment.

I will have to knock myself out of this mood before Conference.

Tuesday, 23 June, London

At 7.20pm to John Cleese's for dinner. Cleese and his wife Alyce Faye hosted it superbly. Among the guests was a man called Ian Johnstone, who had made a film about the making of a *A Fish Called Wanda* (and said that he was now in the process of writing a second film to be called *Death Fish Three*!) and his Scottish wife.

There was also Peter Luff[1] and his wife Caroline and somebody called Virginia, who turned out to be in tennis. I suppose I should have recognized her. I knew she was something important when they kept on mentioning winning the Championship. I vaguely thought that she belonged to a lawn tennis club and had done rather well there. But then they said that she was a commentator on the BBC. I finally twigged that I was sitting next to Virginia Wade! We talked at length. I found her amusing and sharp.

Friday, 3 July, Copenhagen

MEETING OF ELDR[2]

Managed to have half an hour with Roger Liddle.[3] He has been in touch with Peter Mandelson.[4] The general view is that Labour will not be in a position to respond to the Chard speech until next year, when they put their constitution right. Smith is withdrawing from his earlier suggestions

---

1 Director of the Royal Commonwealth Society.
2 European Liberals, Democrats and Radicals. The European grouping which provides a co-ordinating body for liberal parties in EU countries.
3 Then a Lib Dem.
4 Member of Parliament (Labour) for Hartlepool since 1992. Previously he was the Director of Campaigns and Communications for the Labour Party. Mandelson is now Secretary of State for Northern Ireland.

about cross-party discussions on social justice, etc. Liddle assures me that Cook[1] is still very much in favour. Mandelson takes the view that Labour's job is to make themselves into an SDP Mark II and to either work with us or destroy us, depending on which is easier. A pretty gloomy prospect.

Sunday, 5 July, Eastbourne

ANNUAL CONFERENCE OF THE ASSOCIATION OF LIBERAL DEMOCRAT
COUNCILLORS (ALDC)

Off to Eastbourne. A perfectly miserable journey down, all traffic fumes and stifling heat.

As I was on the way down, Alan called me to say that there had been a strong anti-Chard mood at the discussions yesterday, so I should be aware that I was walking into a hornets' nest. I arrived and found people reserved, but not openly hostile.

After my speech, an hour's worth of questions, which were all pretty tough. I had to argue my case with some vigour – perhaps too much. If this is a dress rehearsal for the Conference I am in for a very tough time.

Chris Rennard has been warning me of this for some time. Why is it so difficult to get people to see beyond the end of their noses? At the Autumn Conference I will have to use up a lot of the goodwill that I have created over the last three or four years, if I am not to be defeated. Nevertheless, I am quite clear that this is in the best interest of the Party and if I don't do it I will feel I have wasted my Leadership. We must have a very flexible strategy over the next few years so as to allow us to take such opportunities as present themselves.

We got back at 11.15. Almost immediately I had a call in the flat from Jane, who had terrible news. My Aunt Joyce died a few hours ago. I was terribly shocked: she was my favourite aunt. I recall so well her meeting me off the train at Lime Street Station in Liverpool, and taking me out, aged eleven or twelve, to the greatest luxury of my life – fish, chips and peas in a hotel. She didn't have much of a life. The man she fell in love with was already married and they had to wait for his disabled wife to die

---

1 Robin Cook. Member of Parliament (Labour) for Edinburgh Central 1974–83, Livingston since 1983. Cook is now Secretary of State for Foreign Affairs.

before they could wed. They had only a brief few years together before he too died.

Tuesday, 7 July, Westminster

I am worried that the oncoming economic depression will be much deeper than most people think and could seriously unfix the whole political and economic system. I don't want us to get out of the ERM – indeed, I think that would be a disaster – but it may well turn out to be less of a disaster than the alternative. I just hope my sense of foreboding is wrong.

Politics seems completely up in the air at the moment. Nobody knows which way to go. It's like when the birds stop singing and the air goes still just before the thunderstorm breaks. Or that moment of stillness at slack water before the tide starts moving in the opposite direction.

Some Channel 4 stuff on Yugoslavia (an issue which I think we have rather dodged recently).

I am really worried about the Conference, which now has three motions to do with sex on it and only one on the economy. I told Alan Sherwell[1] that I believed that when it came to sex, Liberal Democrat Conferences could do it once a week, but probably couldn't manage three times!.

Down to dinner. Afterwards Don Foster[2] had a word with me on the bench while we were waiting for the result of the vote. He said I was awful at the Councillors' conference at Eastbourne on Sunday. We went off to my office and had a whisky, which cheered me up a bit. I think Don is right. I desperately need help moving the Party. Don, typically, said he would organize some.

Wednesday, 15 July, London

In the evening, a dinner at Methley Street for Joe Rogaly[3] and Don Macintyre and their partners. Don reckons that Tony Blair is 'a real soulmate' and is up for all the stuff I have been saying, but that Smith is over-cautious, conservative and unimaginative. Nevertheless, in his view, Labour may just be able to do it though, on balance, he thinks they won't.

1 Chairman of the Lib Dems Conference Committee.
2 A close friend and adviser. Member of Parliament for Bath since 1992.
3 *Financial Times* columnist.

Tuesday, 21 July, Westminster

At 10.55 to Downing Street, going in the back door. The PM was a little delayed. I saw Richard Ryder looking sheepish outside. It occurred to me that he, as Chief Whip, may be the person who is doing the investigation that Major had said he would institute into Kelvin MacKenzie's allegations that a Cabinet Minister had tried to peddle rumours about my private life to the press during the Election.[1]

I had a good forty minutes with Major. He looked relaxed – I was rather impressed. He has a most engaging manner and a very neat mind, though not one of very wide scope. Here is an extract from my confidential minutes of the meeting:

1. The Mellor affair[2]

The Prime Minister started by assuring me that he hoped that today's reports in the Sun *newspaper were not true, but if they were he wanted me to know that he knew nothing about them and would have strongly deprecated them. I asked him what he was doing about investigating the allegations and he assured me that an investigation was underway.*

2. Maastricht

He was very frank about Maastricht. We covered the following points:
  He was personally totally committed to Maastricht and would not resile from this even if it meant leaving Downing Street. (A defeat on Maastricht would, he said, have that outcome.)

  I made it clear that we would support him on the Maastricht Bill, but PR for the European elections was essential to us. We would not co-operate with the Government over any timetable (guillotine) motion if they were dismissive of PR for the European Elections. The Prime Minister said that he had given an answer on PR (opposed) in the House at PMQs and that he could not go back on this. Whatever the case for

---

1 The *Sun* had published a story this same morning about these allegations, which had just been made by its editor Kelvin MacKenzie on a radio programme discussing the Mellor affair.

2 David Mellor, Member of Parliament (Conservative) for Putney 1979–97, had resigned as Minister for National Heritage after huge press interest in his affair with an actress.

PR (and he conceded that there might be one for Europe), he could not carry the Tory Party. I reminded him that maintaining our present electoral system would be particularly beneficial to Labour and would increase the number of Labour MEPs.

He does not want to bring the Maastricht Bill back to the House until after the Danes have had their second referendum. He is extremely reluctant to timetable the Maastricht Bill and would only do so if three conditions were satisfied: the House had debated the Bill for a substantial number of days (including weekends); it had become clear that a small group was filibustering; and only then if it was also apparent that there was a genuine mood in the House to bring this to an end.

He says there are thirty Tory MPs prepared to vote against the Bill in any circumstances and fifteen who would rather bring down the Government than see it passed. He divided these into three groups: long term anti-Europeans; those who were pro-European, but believed Maastricht was a stage too far; and those who opposed the Bill for, to use his words, 'less creditable reasons'. This latter group were those who were opposed to him personally and were prepared to use the Bill as a vehicle to bring him down.

Saturday, 25 July, Somerset

We were woken at around 8.00 by a call from Joyce Hopkirk, a journalist with whom Jane gets on well. Apparently the *Mail On Sunday* had a team in Yeovil working through last week on a story which, they said, was well-sourced – that Jane and I were about to break up 'because of the revelations of the last week'.[1] A total invention.

Jane told her this was complete rubbish. Hopkirk asked if she could pass that back to the *Sunday Express*, from whom she'd got the story. Jane said she could. Twenty minutes later we received a call from a *Sunday Express* journalist. Jane repeated that the story was 'laughably inaccurate'.

Twenty minutes later a car drew up outside. My heart sank. Back to the period of the Tricia affair. They are so obvious, these sharp-suited girls, obviously from London in their smart little well-polished cars. This one sat there making notes, so I went out into the front garden with a

---

1 The Kelvin MacKenzie interview, etc.

cup of tea, ostensibly to admire our roses in full bloom. Sure enough, she came over to me and starting asking questions. Also on behalf of the *Express*.

I told her that I had said all I intended to say. She tried to drag more out of me, but I went back in, gathered my things and set off for my regular Saturday surgery in Yeovil. On the way out I stopped for a chat with a neighbour. The girl from the *Express* was still there – waiting, presumably, to question the neighbours. At this moment Jane came out of another neighbour's house, where she'd been to feed the cat. The journalist immediately ambushed her. I shouted to Jane, 'This woman is from the *Sunday Express*, don't talk to her.' But the woman persisted, asking Jane the usual offensive questions. Jane put her arms round my waist and said, 'For God's sake, can't you see we're together?' I was furious. We must learn to say nothing to the press. Now they have their story: ' "We're still together," says Jane Ashdown, with her arms round her husband's waist, etc. etc.'

For the rest of the day I felt like a hunted animal, waiting to meet the press round the corner.

Saturday 1 to Sunday 2 August, Zagreb and Sarajevo[1]

MY FIRST VISIT TO YUGOSLAVIA

A boiling hot day. Having drunk rather too much with Russell Johnston last night, I found it difficult to get up. Down to breakfast in the ornate dining room of Zagreb's Esplanade Hotel. I can just imagine British intelligence officers meeting with their spies here in the First and Second World Wars.

There are reports of a rather troublesome day in Sarajevo yesterday, with a lot of mortar attacks and the airport closed for some time.

Out to Zagreb airport where, after an intelligence briefing, I loaded on to an RAF Hercules and met the crew. We flew at 19,000 feet for about an hour and three-quarters, first of all south-west along the Croatian coast and then east towards Sarajevo. A beautifully clear sky with the whole of the coastline laid out splendidly below us. The team on the aircraft were

---

1 Two weeks earlier, in a casual conversation about the 'current slack' period of politics, Alan Leaman had suggested, half jokingly, that I should go to Sarajevo, where the siege of the city by the Bosnian Serbs had just started. I decided to go, so beginning a long involvement with the Balkans which lasted most of the 1990s.

real professionals. It turned out that they were from the same squadron that used to drop me to submarines when I was in SBS.[1] The British flyers here are widely regarded as the most proficient.

As soon as we got over the disputed territory of Bosnia we dropped to 11,000 feet and, from being thoroughly relaxed on the flight deck, everybody became intensely serious. We flew over a ridge where some Surface to Air Missiles were known to be positioned. At one stage the alarm on the aircraft missile warning system came on and people moved very fast indeed, but it was a false alarm. (Apparently the Serbs have a habit of locking their missile radars on to UN aircraft as they come in.)

I was told that they were going to do a 'Quey-Sanh'[2] landing which, they said, only the British here do. But nothing prepared me for what happened next. We saw the Sarajevo strip from about thirty miles out. Having crossed the final ridge, we approached the airfield threshold, then, when it seemed almost directly below us at about 1,500 feet, the pilot pushed the aircraft nose down and the Hercules flew seemingly vertically at the ground. At about 400 feet he pulled out the flaps and landed promptly and smoothly on the airfield. The G-forces when he turned the aircraft round were extraordinary. We landed very short, as the end of the runway is mined, and quickly turned towards the shattered airfield buildings.

I was immediately met by Larry Hollingsworth, an ex-RAOC[3] colonel with a huge flowing white beard, who is in charge of United Nations High Commission for Refugees (UNHCR) operations out here. He looked an incongruous figure amidst the ruins. A courageous man who carries a terrific burden on his shoulders. He had a convoy going into Dobrinja, a Bosnian Muslim suburb close to the airport, which has been shelled to the point where barely a building is left standing. Would I like to come? I agreed.

There has been a lot of mortar fire over the last two or three days, including a few hits on the airfield itself. Three Ukrainians manning a UN mortar-locating radar there were seriously wounded and one killed. The Canadian general in charge (Mackenzie[4]) claims that the Bosnians are not averse to mortaring their own people in order to blame the Serbs.

---

1 The Special Boat Section, Royal Marines, in which I served in the mid-1960s.
2 Named after the famous siege in Vietnam.
3 Royal Army Ordnance Corps.
4 Major General Lewis Mackenzie, Chief of Staff of the United Nations Protection Force in Yugoslavia.

The airfield is surrounded by completely destroyed buildings. Beyond, the city of Sarajevo with its high-rise blocks is visible through the haze. Hardly a window remains in the town and almost every building has been hit. Sarajevo is surrounded by mountains, all heavily wooded and providing perfect emplacements for Serb artillery positions.

We had a quiet day, however, with nothing landing.

The Dobrinja convoy couldn't go in because the Bosnians refused to accept the Serb drivers of the UNHCR trucks, so we did a distribution run to food warehouses in the city instead. Larry was particularly nervous driving along the road from the airfield, which is very exposed. I asked him if I could go on further to take a look at a feeding point in the city, but he said that this was too dangerous. However, he arranged for me to tour the town with one of the Bosnian drivers. Mid-afternoon and there was a good deal of firing going on. We drove at a fairly leisurely pace with a television camera-crew behind us. These press people go round almost completely unprotected.

Shortly after we got back to the UN force headquarters in the PTT [post office] building, word came through that President Izetbegovic wanted to see me. We dashed off to the presidential building, where I spent forty-five minutes with him. He understands English, but would speak only Serbo Croat to me. The Presidential Palace is splendid and full of lovely furniture, though all its windows have been blown out by the shelling. As we were talking, there was an almost constant mortar and artillery barrage going on about 300 yards away: 120 mm and 81 mm mortars, at a guess. And, somewhere in the distance, a duel between a heavy and a light machine gun.

Back to the PTT building, from which we made a fast dash back to the airport. We travelled along the most infamous snipers' alley. Sporadic machine-gun fire, some passing over our heads, quite close.

I spoke to Alan Leaman in London on a satellite phone and told him of my plans to go back to Britain on Monday. I also asked Zagreb to arrange a visit to some Croatian refugee camps tomorrow. Then I rang Jane. Very odd speaking from here about domestic political arrangements. It certainly makes Britain's economic problems seem rather less exciting.

We had a scratch meal from some army rations then went down to see the French troops. One of their captains took me up to the airport control tower to see the regular evening battle which was just starting. I watched a tank at the end of the runway blasting at a Bosnian position and saw a number of snipers dodging in and out of the window openings of buildings.

I felt a little as I imagine the Duchess of Richmond's picnic party would have on the hills above the field of Waterloo.

Later at 9.00pm standing outside the hangar we saw a tremendous artillery duel take place about 400 yards away. Quite a few rounds came over our heads. You could hear the zing of the shrapnel. Out on the airfield, I suddenly realized we were being fired at by automatic rounds. We quickly retreated behind a shelter and watched the firework display for about an hour before going down to a very well-constructed bunker with iron bars and corrugated-iron revetments in which the eight of us were to spend the night.

We sat outside talking and drinking a bottle of whisky I had bought until about 11.00. The sky was so clear that you could see shooting stars above the tracer – the Milky Way mirrored by the fires burning in the city. Then to bed at about 11.30 in the dug out. I had great difficulty sleeping. At about 4.00, I got up to pour myself some water from a jerry can and wandered out in my underpants. The battle was still raging. The earlier artillery duel had been replaced by a much more vicious-sounding exchange of small-arms fire in the streets around us. From what I could tell, these were professionals, firing in short bursts, rather than the long, ammunition wasting ones beloved of war films and amateurs. I finally got to sleep, only to be woken at around 6.00am by a very heavy crump quite close to us. Big enough, I thought, to be a 155 mm. It was time to get up, anyway.

I emerged from the bunker to a beautiful cloudless day with mist lying in the valley below. How beautiful the countryside is, with the wooded hills of Mount Igman sweeping down into the Sarajevo valley. I was having a wash and shave in the cold water at the back of the hangar when a shell landed a little distance away. I was still dressed only in my underpants.

By 7.00am the battle had finished. My companions said both sides would now go home or back to their trenches to sleep. At 8.00am the British Hercules came in with the first aid load of the day. I said goodbye to Larry and co., thanking them for looking after me so well. Then on to the aircraft, with a different British crew. They did a Quey-Sanh take-off, lifting the wheels up as soon as we became airborne and flying at about four feet above the ground, gathering speed, until we reached 200 knots, then slamming on the flaps and climbing almost vertically upwards to present a minimal target to any ground fire. At about 1,500 feet we levelled out, climbed to cruising altitude and headed for Zagreb.

We arrived at around 10.30am, to be met by Colonel Mark Cook, an ex-Gurkha officer with whom I had served in Borneo in the 1960s. He is now the senior British officer supporting the UN operation in Croatia and had promised to take me on a tour of the UN areas. We were driven by Anton, a Serb working for the UN, and accompanied by Lidija, our interpreter, who was a Croat from Sarajevo and desperate for news of the city.

We dashed down the main Zagreb–Belgrade motorway at full speed towards the recent Serb/Croat battle area. It became emptier as we got closer to the first UNPA (UN Protected Area). We weren't supposed to go into the actual protected zone, but we talked our way past Jordanian troops manning a UN road block.

The drive through the war zone was uneventful. All the crops had been left unharvested for two years. This must be how Europe has looked during the wars of the past ten centuries: full of wild flowers and unkempt fields. We headed for Slavonskibrod, where a single bridge is the main crossing point on the Sava river over which refugees from Bosnia are fleeing.

The river, at this point, is about 300 yards wide. The bridge at Slavonski-brod had been rocketed and shelled several times. Across its rickety struc-ture still trickled a thin stream of refugees on foot and one or two in cars.

We stayed for about half an hour, talking to the fleeing refugees, to the accompaniment of a few desultory incoming shells.

Then off for the market town of Djakovo, where we had a look at the splendid eighteenth-century cathedral, which had also suffered attack – probably aircraft rockets. Apparently the Serbs, being Orthodox, particu-larly target Catholic churches.

Lidija pointed out the nunnery next door. Outside it stood a nun, jangling some keys, who offered to show us the superb 200-year-old cellars underneath. These turned out to be full of huge barrels of wine. I asked what the wine was for. It is a communion wine, came the reply, but they also sell it. Would we like to try? Glasses were swiftly produced and we had a little tasting – the wine is strong, but not sweet. I bought a couple of bottles and some Slivo.[1] It seemed a curious thing to do in the middle of a war zone.

Then off to a nearby refugee camp. I was quite unprepared for this. I was, I suppose, unconsciously conditioned to see refugees as they appear on television, from some Third World country. What I found was people (around 3,000 of them) who could just as easily have been my Jane or Kate. The majority were Muslims, although there were a few Croats as well.

---

1 Slivovic or plum brandy.

I walked gaily into a tent and started talking to a mother with young children, who had left her husband and fourteen-year-old son behind 'to fight for their homeland'. She described her journey out, which was harrowing in the extreme. Her dignity was immense. As she spoke of her son and husband, the tears started rolling down her face and then down mine. I made a complete fool of myself and had to stumble unceremoniously out of the tent.

Conditions here are pretty bad. The tents are leaky and it must become a sea of mud when it rains. But the refugees seem reasonably well fed. They keep themselves remarkably clean and the children are delightful. There had been some talk about the Saudis (who run the camp) removing books that they think are not appropriate for Muslims, but I could find no evidence of this.

At the end I went into a hut which housed the very elderly. I spoke to a woman who told me that she and her friends – all over seventy-five – had been herded by the Serbs, a hundred at a time, into railway trucks and shunted around the railway lines of Bosnia Hercegovina for seven sweltering days. They had to sit on each other's laps. There were no facilities; several had died. I thought such things had ended with the Nazis.

We left the camp and headed off through well-cultivated countryside which the war had not touched and back into the next UN Protected Area. More burned-out houses and uncultivated fields before arriving at Lipic, where we stopped for a beer and sat under the trees in the sunlight, much as one would in any other European city in the summer. Except in this one most of the buildings had been bombed and burned out – some, including the local hospital, shelled into a heap of concrete and twisted metal.

Mark took me to an orphanage which had, apparently, been the first building to be shelled when the battle started. It was totally wrecked, with traces of blood on the walls. Mark told me that this orphanage had affected him more than anything else in the war. The children had taken refuge in the cellar, where they had been subjected to twenty-one days of bombardment before they could be evacuated under the cover of darkness. Mark's dream was to rebuild the orphanage and care for the orphans of this war.[1]

---

1 Shortly after this, Mark Cook resigned from the Army and did just this, founding a charity of which I am a patron, Hope and Homes for Children, which now operates worldwide, helping the orphans of war.

Tuesday, 4 August, Westminster

At 11.45am to the Foreign Office to see Douglas Hurd. I told him of my concerns about Sarajevo; about the ridiculous situation with the French, Egyptians and Canadians there, none of whom could speak to each other, and the fact that there was no single military commander. I said that it was a military disaster waiting to happen. I also told him of my concern about the refugees and the need to prepare their accommodation for winter now, and of my interview with Izetbegovic.

He said that Major had instructed him to tell me everything that was on their minds. There had been a full military appraisal of the situation over the weekend, in which they had decided against the use of air power – although the decision has been a finely balanced one. They were also considering having UN safe havens in Bosnia – the question was whether to establish them in contested places such as Sarajevo or in areas where there was no conflict. They are moving – at last!

Wednesday, 5 August, France

THE FIRST DAY OF MY SUMMER HOLIDAY

Having sailed into Le Havre on a flat calm sea, we set off in good time for Giverny.[1] By the time we arrived it was too late for us to get into the Monet museum, so we looked out a decent restaurant and booked into a pleasant little family hotel.

As soon as we arrived I collapsed on the bed, hoping to snatch a quick nap, but the phone rang. It was Russell Johnston. The office had received a letter from Radovan Karadzic,[2] who was furious at my interventions in Bosnia, complaining bitterly that we hadn't seen the Serb side and inviting me to do so. Not wanting to disturb my holiday, the office had not told me of this until Russell had insisted. But the news today has been full of terrible stories of Serbian death camps – something I hadn't believed when the refugees in Croatia had told me of them last week.

I asked Russell to ring me back in half an hour, while I thought things through. When he did, I agreed that we had to go – to Jane's intense

1 Jane and I had planned to see Monet's famous garden there.
2 President of the Bosnian Serbs.

disappointment. We would be the first Western politicians to enter the war zone and we couldn't give the Serbs an excuse to duck out.

I said that we would go, providing:

1. we had a personal undertaking from Karadzic that we could go anywhere, including the 'death camps' and Gorazde,[1]

2. the Serbs would allow whoever we wanted to come with us.

Saturday, 8 August, Hungary and Yugoslavia

The flight from Paris was smooth, through clear skies over the Alps, across Austria and down into Budapest.

I met Russell at the airport. John Kennedy,[2] the ex-Tory candidate and pro-Serb contact in London, was with him. Maggie O'Kane from the *Guardian* was also there, and a host of other press people, who had been sent out to accompany me. We sat around for half an hour or so before being bundled into an air-conditioned car (thank God, it's stiflingly hot) and off for the six-hour journey across the plains of Hungary to Belgrade. Flat and featureless. You could easily imagine the Mongol hordes riding across them – or the Russian and German armies fighting their great tank battles here. Great seas of maize, little hamlets and occasionally a muddy, slow-flowing river. Very much a peasant culture.

Shortly after we crossed the border, Kennedy suddenly burst into laughter. He had been listening to Serb radio, on which it had just been announced that the descendant of Gladstone[3] (me) had entered Serbia!

On our arrival in Belgrade, we went to the Intercontinental Hotel, where we were to have had dinner with Karadzic's right-hand man, but this fell through.

There is, apparently, a Croat advance in progress and the Serbs are under considerable pressure. Also there is much anger here about 'pro-Muslim' Western press reporting. This could get tricky.

---

1 A predominantly Bosnian Muslim city, then under fierce siege by the Serbs.
2 Conservative Parliamentary Candidate in 1992 and 1997. I later discovered that he had initiated Karadzic's invitation to me. He was to become the Private Secretary to Prince Michael of Kent.
3 Serb spin doctors at work! Gladstone was of course a predecessor as leader of the Liberal Party and was famous throughout the region for his opposition to Balkan atrocities in the nineteenth century.

Sunday, 9 August, Belgrade

Up at 7.00 and down to breakfast with some of the journalists. There then ensued a good deal of hanging about, finding of flak jackets and general preparation until finally, at 10.30, we were picked up to go to see the President. I thought it would be Milosevic, the Yugoslav President, but it turned out to be Chosic, President of Serbia. Yugoslavia seems to have more presidents than postmen.

We went into the Russian-style government buildings and sat down chatting until protocol collected us and took us upstairs (you could have been in Moscow) to meet the great man. The door opened. I expected to see one man, but instead I was confronted by a row of sturdy Slavic faces. I knew one of them was President Chosic, but which one? No one made a move towards me. I selected one who looked even more sturdy than the others, walked up to him and held out my hand. Fortunately, I got the right man.

My first question to him was, 'The West believes that the Serbs are the aggressors in this conflict. How do you respond?' The interview was quite fascinating. Chosic did a number of things I didn't expect him to do. Firstly, he responded fairly rationally to my quite aggressive questioning; secondly, he took pains to separate himself from Milosevic; thirdly, he indicated quite strongly that he found the association of the actions of the Serbs in Bosnia with the Yugoslav state (his terms) pretty embarrassing. I asked him whether he would think of recognizing the borders of Bosnia Hercegovina, even if he couldn't recognize its government? He said he was seriously thinking about this. He also specifically renounced the aspirations of a greater Serbia and told me that Milosevic was not as important as everybody took him to be.

The whole interview lasted about an hour and a quarter, after which we were informed that the helicopter was delayed for a further hour. We hung about until about 2.00, finally leaving, with the attendant press, in a long convoy heading for the helicopter pad, where we sat around in the boiling sun waiting for our aircraft and making jokes. Here I met Nikolai Kolyevic, Karadzic's number two and a one-time English-literature professor at Sarajevo University. He, too, was flying out to Pale. He could hardly speak a sentence without including a quotation from Shakespeare, a trait for which he has, apparently, an international reputation.

Two hours later, our helicopter arrived. It was blazened with false UN markings and red crosses – one of the pilots told me that it was safer to fly over the battlefields with these, as it 'confused the Muslims'. We all piled on board in a mighty disorganized rush. The helicopter interior looked more like a utility van than an aircraft – nothing apart from the spare fuel tank to sit on, no seat-straps, out-of-date gauges and the ever-present, disconcerting smell of leaking fuel. Unlike Western helicopters, this one was armoured – an advantage for which, given the journey ahead, I was happy to exchange all the dials and seat-belts in the world.

The pilots then lifted the thing off the ground, hovered for a bit, put it down again and shouted, 'Too heavy – throw four out!' At first nobody moved, then after a ten-minute dispute, four press people got off. We took off. More hovering and we were finally away.

We lurched along at about 400 feet, following the Danube for a bit before swinging up into the mountains. Just like Switzerland: steep peaks, sharp cliffs and Alpine pastures. Initially, there were no signs of war, but gradually the land began to tell its own tale: wasted villages below us and, in the distance, the minarets of mosques. We were entering the battle area.

I motioned to Russell and John Kennedy to put on their flak jackets and others followed suit, although there was a good deal of bravado among the younger press people, who declined. After about forty-five minutes the pilot suddenly began tactical flying. He was superb. He used every inch of the land, at times flying at only ten feet above the ground, along the side of cliffs, clipping the tops of trees on the crests and dropping almost vertically into the valleys below. Once or twice I heard a sharp crack outside – shots fired from some distance away, I presumed. Many of the villages below us now were burned out shells.

After about half an hour of this, the aircraft suddenly steadied down. We were out of the battle zone, and back in Serb territory. We later heard that we had been delayed that morning because the aircraft originally coming to pick us up had been shot down.

In due course we came into Pale, where we were taken up to the Ski Hotel, Karadzic's base. It bore little sign of a military headquarters. Karadzic himself was talking to a Russian delegation when I was brought in and introduced to him. Coffee was served and I told him that I wanted to go to Gorazde. He said it was too late in the day, but agreed to take us to Lukovice.[1]

---

1 The main Serb Sarajevan suburb on their side of the front line.

We left almost immediately, driving up over the mountain and into the Sarajevo bowl in three black cars. Ours was driven by a Serb of devilish looks who insisted on driving five or six feet behind the President's car. Russell, who sat in the front, noticed that he had a half-empty bottle of Slivovic beside him. We passed some horrific-looking people in gun emplacements on the mountainside overlooking Sarajevo; all beards, knives and ammunition belts.

As we came down into the city we also passed the gun emplacements from which I had been fired upon the week before. A T55 tank, 40mm cannons and some heavy artillery positioned in the woods. Down, then, into the Serb outskirts of Sarajevo, ending up at their frontline headquarters at Lukovice, about 200 yards from where I had been the previous week. By now the routine evening bombardment was underway, with a sniper particularly active just behind us. The Serbs claimed that it was a Muslim firing at us, but I could tell that he was firing away from our position, because all we could hear was the crack of the rifle, not the thump of the bullets.

We were given a briefing by the Serb military commanders over a map laid out with blue and red Chinagraph markings showing the positions of both sides. The Serbs show themselves in red and the enemy in blue (Russian practice – NATO is vice versa).

Sitting round the table were a bunch of people [including Mladic[1]] who could, from their uniform and look, have been Russian senior officers. I said I wanted to see the UNPROFOR[2] observer team and was taken upstairs to meet a New Zealand naval lieutenant-commander and a captain in the Canadian Army. I talked to them for about half an hour. Impressive people. They had been here for a year.

I then asked to see a prisoner-of-war camp which I had been told was only a few hundred yards away. There was a discussion with Karadzic as to how we would get there and eventually one of the interpreters, who didn't want to go, persuaded the UNPROFOR lieutenant-commander to take us. I noticed he put on his flak jacket, so we put on ours and jumped into his Land-Rover. It had a UN sign on the side, but then so had our Serb helicopter – and the Land-Rover was not armoured.

Karadzic went ahead of us at about a hundred miles an hour, but our

1 Ratko Mladic, commander of Serbian troops in Bosnia. Now an indicted war criminal.
2 United Nations Protection Force in Former Yugoslavia. The UN military force in Bosnia, who had observers on both sides of the front line.

unarmoured Land-Rover couldn't manage more than about thirty (or so it seemed). Unfortunately, the UNPROFOR man had never been to the prison before and missed the turning, driving merrily on until we came to the Serb front line, where we were stopped by a rather beautiful woman with a gun. We asked where the prison was. She sent us back and eventually we found it.

As we drove in, under the glare of the television cameras, we were met by a group of prisoners who seemed in remarkably good shape. They were brown, fit and showed every sign of being well fed. Probably a show camp. But we saw what we wanted to see, including some quite good accommodation and a dining room where, the UNPROFOR man told me, the food 'laid out' for the prisoners was better than the Serbs got at Lukovice.

I had a chat with one or two of the prisoners. They were all Bosnian Muslims. Some complained of beatings in the early stages of the war but said they were in good condition now. Karadzic announced he wanted to let some prisoners go in order to celebrate my visit, and asked me to hand out their freedom certificates. Obviously a propaganda stunt. I said I wouldn't even watch him doing it, but quietly asked the press to stay to see that it was done while I went off to look at the kitchens. Then back in the UN Land-Rover.

We left the camp at around dusk. Our driver, who had by now finished his bottle of Slivo and was visibly drunk, this time drove right up the back of Karadzic's car. At one stage Karadzic stopped his car and told him to calm down. But it didn't seem to have much effect. We stopped at the driver's house to 'fill up with petrol'. An excuse to have several more glasses of Slivovic. Having met his family, we sat on the veranda with Karadzic as the dusk gathered and talked of the war, drinking homemade plum brandy and Lozha.[1] Apart from the distant boom of the evening battle in Sarajevo, who would know there was a war on?

Then back to Pale for dinner with Karadzic, whom I found charismatic and, to me, apparently honest, admitting that, of course Serbs had committed atrocities, like everyone else, but that these were out of his control. Russell (who had come here very anti-Serb) and I agreed that he was extremely plausible. Maggie O'Kane told me later that he was a pathological liar. If so, a very good one.

At 2.00am we said goodnight. There then followed a farcical circus in

---

1 A spirit made from grapes, similar to Marc and Grappa.

which we drove up the mountain to the old Jahorina Olympic village with a driver who didn't know which lodge we were staying at. We eventually found our beds at around 2.30, in a totally darkened ski hotel. The electricity had been cut off by the war, but our rooms had fresh linen, clean towels and specially wrapped soap.

An extraordinary day.

Monday, 10 August, Pale, Yugoslavia

Up at 6.00 and off at 7.00, having had a coffee with an eye surgeon who had escaped from Sarajevo and who had horrific tales to tell about what the Muslims had done to her and other women.

We drove back down the mountain to Pale in bright sunlight. Again, I was struck by the beauty of the place. We had to wait in Pale for an hour and a half while all the formalities were completed and the car was filled up with petrol. Eventually we left, on one of the most horrendous journeys of my life.

It was very long and very hot. We drove up the whole length of Bosnia, across the top through the narrow Posadena corridor against which the Croats forces had been pushing, and down to Banja Luka.[1] We got separated from the bus carrying the journalists and frequently passed through areas where the war had just been, with a lot of torched and shot-up houses. Most of the journey was on dusty narrow tracks, avoiding pockets of fighting and bypassing blown-up bridges. It took us over seven and a half hours.

We saw a lot of armaments on the road and several tanks, mostly T52s, one T20 and a lot of PT76s. I was especially struck by the military bearing of most of the soldiers that I saw. I had expected a rag, tag and bobtail guerrilla army, but they were well disciplined and well turned out. Any idea that the Serb military is not under proper command is nonsense.

We finally arrived in Banja Luka at a little before 3.00. To our surprise the press bus had got there before us, because we had been forced to take a diversion to avoid an ambush at one point.

Then started an extended war of nerves with the local military, all Russian-trained and up to the usual tricks. I told them I wanted to go to

---

1 The Bosnian Serb capital.

Manjaca – a prison camp which had not been visited by anyone from outside and was suspected of being another 'death camp'.

First they kept us waiting for an hour. Then they sent the Minister of Information to see me, an earnest, rather frightened little politician, who explained that the military couldn't take us to Manjaca and that was that. I told him that I had received personal undertakings from Radovan Karadzic and that if he would not give us permission I would go anyway with the press and then there would be stories of the military stopping me going to a camp that I had been promised I could go to by their own President. He dashed off to speak to the military again.

I quickly reasoned that I would have to see the military myself – stony-faced Russian-trained mid-forties generals all. So I went off to see them with a *Financial Times* interpreter. The press immediately started taking pictures and gathering round, so I suggested we went to a private room. There, one of the generals explained that there was a curfew that started at 5.00pm and anybody seen out after that would be shot. I told him that it would be very bad news indeed if: (a) we were prevented from going, or (b) we were shot. He agreed.

I then indulged in a piece of brutish name dropping, telling the general that I was to see Chosic, the President of Serbia, for dinner tomorrow evening and that he would hear about it, as indeed would Karadzic, who was arriving in town any moment. I explained that the press had heard Karadzic tell me at dinner last night that I could go anywhere I wanted. I would attempt to go, even if it put our lives at risk, and if they stopped us, or shot us, then the Western press would be full of the news that Serb soldiers didn't obey their own President. There was a thoughtful silence, then one of the generals said, 'Well, we could take you, I suppose, if we arranged it properly. But you would only have half an hour in the camp before dusk.'

I said fine, told the press and left with Russell immediately. There was no sign of a 5 o'clock curfew. They were just giving themselves more time to clean the camp up.

We drove for about forty minutes, finally coming to a barbed-wire enclosed prison camp, situated in the middle of a Yugoslav army tank firing range. Hanging on the barbed wire were signs warning of mines on all sides.

We were taken into a briefing room, where the camp commandant, a rather bluff and simple soldier, started shouting at us, mostly the usual propaganda. He said he wanted objective reporting and that it was disgraceful that the press reported only the Muslim side, not the Serb point of view (which is probably true enough). He told us he was observing the Geneva Convention and showed us a copy. (We were later told that was the first time the Geneva Convention had ever been seen in the camp.) Then we went off to see round. I particularly asked to see the people from Omarska,[1] whom I knew had been brought here three or four days previously. At first I was refused. But a little more blustering and we were taken to see them. They were pathetic. Emaciated and cowed, sitting in six rows of 200, in two huge sheds. With the crush of television cameras and the commandant and guards there, they said they were treated better here than they had been at Omarska; that they had better food and they weren't being beaten or taken out and killed. Nevertheless, they were sleeping on the ground with neither covering nor protection.

I told the commandant and his guards to go away so that I could speak to some of them privately. After some reluctance, they did so. The prisoners still gave the same story. This was bad, but at least they were alive. These were the brothers, sons and fathers of the refugees I had seen last week. Again, I couldn't keep the tears from starting in my eyes.

We went off to have a look at the medical facilities, which were primitive. I spoke to the camp doctors – all prisoners – who told me that they were worried about three people from Omarska who had been sent off to intensive care, but that the others were generally on the mend. We saw about 400 or 500 prisoners being lined up for feeding. They looked in much better condition. We also met a Canadian mercenary who had been shot in the upper femur with a 7.62 bullet. The shock wave from the bullet had smashed his pelvis and he was half-encased in a rudimentary plaster and lying there looking extremely thin. His leg smelt awful.

I knew I would soon be asked by the press for my comments, so I had to make a judgement. I discussed it with Russell and we concluded that the commandant, brusque and inappropriate though he was, had been either ordered or scared into trying to get these people better. Their conditions were improving. This was not the same as the press had described the Omarska death camp to be. I was determined to try to be objective.

So, I took the risk of blowing the whole tour by saying to the press that this was not a death camp and nor was it a concentration camp. It was a very tough military prison, where, so far as I could tell, some attempt was

1 The infamous death camp exposed a couple of days before by the press.

being made to observe the Geneva Convention. It was now vital to get the Red Cross in as fast as possible and start prisoner exchange before the winter arrived.[1]

I could see the looks of surprise on the faces of one or two of the press people, who had clearly expected me to say that it was a death camp and to play to their prejudices.

Later that night, back in Banja Luka, we were approached by Penny Marshall of ITN about going to look at another camp, Trnopolje. This, she said, was an open camp, in which people can come and go. It's being used as a gathering point for refugees. Just the kind of place the UN should use as a safe haven.

Went up to my room at about midnight with Russell for a glass of whisky, after which the lights went out in the city and I fell into a deep sleep.

Tuesday, 11 August, Yugoslavia

Up at 7.00 with the sun shining through the window and the electricity still off. I lay in bed for a few minutes trying to remember where I was. Then up wanting a shower. No water in the hotel! In fact, the whole town has been cut off. I should have thought ahead.

Called Russell to warn him. But for the first time he had got up before me, had a shower before the water ran out, and was all bright and spruce. He pulled my leg about this unmercifully for the rest of the trip.

After breakfast off with a military escort, driving at a ridiculous speed, waving people into the side and even pushing some of them off the road. We went first to Prijedor, the regional capital, where we met the local paramilitary commander, a huge bull of a man with a very powerful frame but, I thought, kindly eyes. With him was someone called Simo Drljaca, who described himself as the mayor. If there was a villain, I suspect this

---

1 Later, in November 1995, I gave evidence to the War Crimes Tribunal on conditions in Manjaca. The war crimes investigator who took my testimony had also interviewed many of those I saw on this day as witnesses. Several had said that, though Manjaca was better than the infamous camps at Prijedor, Omarska and Keraterm, treatment had been harsh 'until one day a British MP arrived with TV cameras', after which the Red Cross arrived, conditions improved and there were no further deaths in the camp. I still regard this as the most useful day's work I have done in politics.

was him. Narrow, cold eyes and very arrogant. He was said to be the man behind the horrors of Omarska.[1]

We then drove out to Trnopolje. Just like driving through the narrow winding lanes of Kent, except that the road was filled with trudging, hopeless, pitiable little groups of women, old men and children carrying all they could under the roasting sun. I was, nevertheless, completely unprepared for what I saw when we arrived.

A scene of indescribable squalor. Perhaps 3,000 people there, mostly Muslims, but some Roma[2] and a few Croats. Absolutely no facilities. They had taken over an old school and had camped out on the playground. The Red Cross were visiting when we arrived, getting them to fill in identification forms in return for packets of cigarettes. Penny and the ITN team were there already.[3] I was taken into the medical area and met the doctors, who were completely overwhelmed. Outside in the boiling sun the wounded were lying on filthy flyblown mattresses.

Near by, on the school playing field, was camped a miserable heap of humanity: old men and women, mothers with children, the sick and the disabled, but no young men. They had come, in most cases, with literally nothing. Some were lying under makeshift awnings, suitable for shade but hopeless when it rained. I stopped to talk to them, but found it once again difficult to keep the tears back. In the sleeping areas were old men, women, children and some young babies. I spoke to one man who had been a well-known economist in his local community, but was now made equal with the others in misery. I could hardly speak for emotion.

In one area were four rough earth lavatories, with a few tattered make-shift curtains stuck around in a pathetic attempt to provide some privacy. But most didn't bother and crapped outside. The ground within yards of the tents was covered with human faeces. No one had any dignity left.

Some cooking was going on, largely a dreadful stew of noodles made from Red Cross food parcels. Why is the UN not setting up protected havens for these wretched people? They have nowhere to go, having been turned back from Croatia and terrorized by the Serbs.[4]

1 It later turned out that he was indeed the villain of Omarska. He was later shot dead by the SAS when, after the Dayton Peace Accords, they raided his house to arrest him for trial in The Hague.
2 Yugoslavian gypsies.
3 Penny Marshall later won the BAFTA news award for her filming this day.
4 I subsequently learned that hundreds, some claim thousands, of these wretched people were taken away during the following days by the Serbs and tipped to their deaths over the cliffs of the Vlasic mountain, some thirty miles to the south.

We stayed for a couple of despairing hours before heading back for Banja Luka and Belgrade.[1]

Saturday, 5 September, Somerset

To Wincanton where I spent an hour and a half with refugees from Bosnia. Four families. About eighteen adults, together with kids who have been brought over by the good people of Wincanton in a bus. They had arranged an amazing reception for them. The refugees were avid for information, so I sat down with a map and showed them where I had been. They came from Gorazde, Sarajevo and Prijedor. One man asked me to see if I could find his three-year-old son Adnan, whom he and his wife had left behind when they fled Gorazde. The man had had a nervous breakdown from the guilt of abandoning the child when he fled. I told him I would try when I next went out, but that he should not expect too much. Most were professional people, doctors and lawyers.

Sunday, 13 September, Harrogate

FIRST DAY OF THE LIBERAL DEMOCRAT PARTY CONFERENCE

Breakfast with Jane, then off to a meeting of the speech team. My Leader's speech is now fairly well set up, but we need a few more jokes.

In the afternoon I attended an informal discussion of Party members on the Chard speech, etc. It was pretty scrappy and rather low quality. But the overwhelming mood was anti-Labour. As always, those who claimed purity and said they would not sacrifice their birthright got the best applause. Why is it that the rebels always have the best tunes? The Party appears firmly opposed to what I am trying to do on equidistance, so it is going to require a clear line and a lot of hard work to pull them round.

Today's press is dominated by worries about the ERM. The Italians have devalued and the pound will now come under pressure.

To the Parliamentary Party meeting. They, too, are in a dreadful mood. Fractious and difficult to control.

---

1 Bumping across the appalling roads on the journey back to Belgrade, I wrote an angry letter to John Major calling for urgent UN assistance for the Trnopolje refugees and specifically for the creation of safe havens. The letter was subsequently published in the *Guardian*.

Monday, 14 September, Harrogate

In the afternoon I went on to the platform for the start of the New Agenda[1] debate. Jackie Ballard spoke in the debate. She made a technically brilliant speech, but a dishonest one, in which she deliberately set up an Aunt Sally by distorting what was proposed, in order the more easily to knock it down. Jackie is a fine politician with all the gifts, but there comes a point when you have to shift from being admired for your populism to being respected for your integrity. But she certainly moved the audience.

In the end, we won agreement for the New Agenda, but only by a handful of votes out of 500. I was deeply shocked by this. Not because people were speaking against me, but because I had so comprehensively failed to gauge the mood of the Party.

At the Parliamentary Party Meeting, more rows. Alex livid about a motion on gypsies and another on hunting. There is a view that the Conference has gone back to its bad old ways, that the 'old Liberal Party' is reasserting itself.

It was Nancy Seear who gave a more measured opinion. She pointed out that the Conference had been wonderful for the last four years. This was the delegates' first year 'off the leash' and they were bound to flex their muscles. We shouldn't judge the nature of the Conference or the Party 'by their first day out of prison for four years'. She was, of course, right.

Tuesday, 15 September, Harrogate

On to the platform for Charles Kennedy's speech. The buzz throughout the morning was that interest rates will go up. This was supposed to happen at 10.00, but didn't. Charles gave a beautifully delivered, calm, and intelligent speech supporting the Chard position.

At the Parliamentary Party meeting, a discussion of tomorrow's resolution on strategy (the Chard speech). It became quickly apparent that this was going to be a disaster. Alan Sherwell took us through the resolution

---

1 The New Agenda was a manifesto type document which we produced and debated at this Conference as the start of the process of reformulating our policies.

chosen by the Conference Committee.[1] I saw Richard Holme at the other end of the table shaking his head and saying that in the form it was drafted, we would lose it. I agreed. We told Philip Goldenberg[2] that it was unacceptable in its present form; but he replied that he did not have the constitutional powers to change it.

This was a major crisis. The resolution in the present form would provide for a very bad debate and one which I would almost certainly lose. Liz Lynne was, of course, delighted, sensing, rightly, that she would win.

The consensus opinion in the Parliamentary Party was that this was Eastbourne[3] all over again. We would first have to make the best of it we could. But I left feeling intensely angry and determined to use the next few hours to try and pull the irons out of the fire.

I went out into the bar and sought out someone from the Association of Liberal Democrat Councillors (ALDC). [One of my rules for running the Lib Dems is that, whenever the Leader and the ALDC act together, we can always get our way.] I quickly found Bill Le Bretton,[4] who has been very helpful throughout this, and sent him off to get Andrew Stunell[5] out of bed. Tony Greaves,[6] Andrew Stunell, Alan Leaman and myself then went up to our room, to be joined in due course by Simon Hughes and Liz Barker.[7] Meanwhile, the Party in the bars downstairs is in a complete turmoil of conspiracy and protest.

We had a long discussion over a beer in my office which went on until 3 o'clock. Eventually, I decided that we had to put a gun to the Conference

1 The Conference Committee is elected by Conference delegates and decides on the motions for debate.

2 A legal adviser to the Liberal Party and Liberal Democrats and our candidate in Woking in the 1992 and 1997 General Elections. He was later the originator of the idea of forming a Joint Cabinet Committee with the Labour Party after the 1997 General Election.

3 The Eastbourne Conference in 1986. At this Conference the Leader David Steel was defeated on defence policy, doing the Party terrible damage and, effectively, beginning the end of his term as Party Leader.

4 Chair of the Association of Liberal Democrat Councillors and a party activist. After helping Martin Bell in the Tatton constituency at the last election, Bill is now an adviser to the Lib Dem Group on Liverpool Council.

5 Head of the Association of Liberal Democrat Councillors. Member of Parliament for Hazel Grove since 1997.

6 Liberal Democrat activist and adviser to the Association of Liberal Democrat Councillors. Now sits in the House of Lords.

7 Chair of the Federal Conference Committee. Liz is now a member of the House of Lords.

Committee's head and insist that the ALDC's motion (which was better and we could win) should be put to the Conference instead. We were able to put together an agreement, ultimately brokered between Tony Greaves and me.

We then got Archy out of his bed and obtained his agreement to take it to the Conference Committee in the morning. Graham Elson also came in and we distributed the work that needed to be done to square off Liz Lynne, Philip Goldenberg and Alan Sherwell.

I wanted to make sure that people knew there was no option but to do what was necessary.

We also divided up who would speak to whom in the morning in order to get a majority on the Conference Committee.

I went to bed at a little after 3.00 feeling worried about the morning, but happier than I had been at midnight.

Wednesday, 16 September, Harrogate

At breakfast, Liz Lynne came in and asked why the resolution had been changed overnight. I tried to explain. She immediately accused me of a conspiracy (true) to undermine her position (also true).

I went off to the office, where we had a council of war. Archy thought he could get the necessary words for debate through the Conference Committee and that we should be all right. Now we can relax.

But too soon.

I was told, as I sat on the platform at about 1 o'clock, that interest rates had gone up by 3 per cent. From here on the day was conducted largely in front of television cameras as we mapped out our position on each successive and frequent rise in interest rates, while trying to prevent disaster on the Chard debate.

At 4 o'clock down to the strategy debate. It all worked a charm. The final vote was 600 for and only 300 against. It was a very high-quality debate. Liz Lynne made a good speech, upon which I congratulated her afterwards. If we'd lost, down would have gone my whole Chard strategy and probably me with it. Now only the pound to deal with.

The currency markets are in total disarray – the peseta is under pressure, as is the escudo and, still, the lira.

A piece on the economy at 7 o'clock for Channel 4, then the VIPs' reception. As I was coming out I was stopped and told that the pound had dropped out of the ERM and had effectively been devalued. Pandemonium from here onwards.

I snatched a brief dinner, then went off to practise tomorrow's Leader's speech. We would have to rewrite the whole thing because of the devaluation.

Back to the hotel room, where I hit a terrible block. Alan called up Ed Davey[1] and between them they saved my life – effectively guiding me through a complete rewrite. We finished at 3.00am and I fell into bed.

Thursday, 17 September, Harrogate

Alan Beith made a brilliant speech in the economics debate. So the Conference was in splendid mood when I was brought on at 2.18 precisely.

I was nervous to start with and on one occasion I nearly knocked the water all over Susan Thomas,[2] who was sitting alongside me. But otherwise the speech worked all right. Still not using my voice properly, though. They laughed in all the right places. Fifty minutes.

Monday, 19 October, Westminster

Off to see Smith at 9.00pm in the Leader of the Opposition's office.[3]

He drank two large whiskies and was in the process of consuming a third when I left. The meeting was best summed up in his parting words: 'Let's develop the habit of friendship, even if this is not the time for formal co-operation.'

He does not agree with pacts or alliances and neither does he believe they are deliverable. I made it clear that we could not have any formal working relationship unless he adopted PR. He said Labour would in due course adopt PR for the Euro elections, but that they were now in retreat on PR at Westminster, because of the way it had been handled by Kinnock at the last election. He was disparaging of Kinnock and made it clear that

---

1 Economics adviser to the Liberal Democrats, now the Lib Dem Member of Parliament for Kingston & Surbiton.
2 Baroness Thomas of Walliswood, Lib Dem peer and Surrey County Councillor.
3 John Smith had been elected leader of the Labour Party on 18 July 1992.

he intends to run the party on a more collegiate basis. He would not even consider Chardism.

I told him that informal agreements between our parties at the grass-roots level should increase. He had no objections to this.

He is not prepared to vote for Maastricht unless it includes the Social Chapter. He thinks that the defeat of Maastricht would mean the end of Major, but not necessarily a General Election. I told him we were already committed to Maastricht and would not change. But in order to tempt him, I said that the only circumstances in which we might possibly vote against Maastricht would be if it were followed by a General Election, the winners of which would ratify Maastricht as a first or early act.

We agreed that the closer our spokesmen worked together the better and that Alan Leaman and his Chief of Staff ought to set up a framework for co-operation on Prime Minister's Questions.

He is very bitter about the SNP. 'If there is one area in which we can work together, it is in squeezing out that lot.'

He believes he is running a marathon, not a sprint, and is determined not to do anything to upset the equilibrium of his Party. He obviously does not share my analysis of the scale of his task, or of the limited time available, or of the potential of the moment. But we got on well and I will have an easier relationship with him than I had with Kinnock.

Tuesday, 27 October, Westminster

I have now worked out the line I want to follow in the Commons on the Maastricht Bill.[1] 'If it is about Britain's future in Europe we will vote in favour of it. But if the Government make it about their survival, we will have to vote against.'

We are now in a very fast-manoeuvring game, with the Government desperate for our support and Labour ready to really damage us if we provide it.

Labour is going to vote against Maastricht in the forthcoming 'paving' Bill and have already said so – even before seeing its wording. This will undoubtedly give them some short-term dividends – it's also probably the only way that they can hide their internal splits on Europe. But if we play this right we will severely damage their European credentials and show that

1 To ratify the recently signed Maastricht Treaty.

the Lib Dems are prepared to hold to their principles. Though damaging in the short term, this should help us establish our distinctiveness and credentials in the long term.

Wednesday, 28 October, Westminster

In the Parliamentary Party Meeting, the main discussion was on Europe. Alex said we should try to negotiate more from the Prime Minister. The overwhelming view, however, was that we should hold to our present line, with only Alex dissenting. But Liz Lynne not there. Nor Charles.

The new MPs very impressive, especially Don Foster. I was proud of them. They know how difficult this is going to be, and how dangerous.

Monday, 2 November, London

Lay awake much of the night worrying about the effects on the Party of the position we have taken on Maastricht. We are coming under heavy attack from Labour and are receiving about 150 phone calls a day in Cowley Street, half from members resigning. Also about 300 letters into the Office and many messages on the constituency phone line. People even ringing me directly. There is strong kickback from Westminster, too. Charles Kennedy is getting wobbly. He has been under pressure from his local councillors. The Labour Party, however dishonest, are being highly effective. It's going to be tough to hold the line.

Good support for us, however, in the *Financial Times* leader and the *Indy*.

I do find these times unbearable. I risk seriously damaging something which I have put so much effort in the last three or four years creating. And I am also beginning to have doubts about whether we will benefit from it as much as I had hoped. Labour's action may well bring down the Prime Minister and, therefore, seriously weaken the Government. They may then be able to recover their pro-European reputation later. We will consequently be seen as rather naïve and outside the main action. But there is no other option for us. Whatever the damage, it would be greater if we ditched our commitment to Europe.

At a grim-faced meeting in the Whips' Office Simon Hughes suggested that we should put down a motion of No Confidence in the Government, so as to lessen our difficulties. I said this was not the time to wobble. We must look absolutely confident about what we are going to do. To vote with the Government at the same time as putting down a No Confidence motion against them would be weak and lack confidence.

Tuesday, 3 November, London

A call from Shirley Williams in the States last night at around 11 o'clock. She was convinced we were right, and if there was anything she could do to help she would. Tom McNally also called with support.

But the effects on the Party are worrying. Cowley Street is being hit by a tidal wave. They have had nearly a thousand letters on the subject and are still getting about a hundred calls a day. We are playing for extremely high stakes.

At 2.15 we held a special Parliamentary Party meeting. I opened by asking if there was anybody who had changed their views from last Wednesday. Charles burst forth, reminding us in his first sentence that he hadn't been there last Wednesday. He said he was desperately worried. He had defended our position loyally, but believed it was totally wrong. He could not continue to support it. He finished with: 'If we follow this line that will be the end.' There was a stunned silence.

Roy Jenkins waded in in support of my position, followed by David Steel and others. At the end I said, 'Right, there is an overwhelming view that we should vote with the Government, unless anybody dissents?' No one spoke. 'In which case I expect to see nineteen votes with the Government.' Again no dissenters.

Into the Chamber at around 3.00 for PMQs. I am glad I had my prayer card in.[1] The Labour Party were hovering all round us. Smith asked a question but (once again) couldn't go on Europe because the Labour position is so fragile. This left the way open for me, so I pushed the single message I had been asking everyone else to stress: that failure to ratify Maastricht would damage the economy and destroy jobs. I had warned Major of this beforehand, so that he could prepare an answer attacking Labour.

He responded perfectly. I don't particularly like doing this but we are in

1 MPs can reserve their place in the chamber by placing a 'prayer-card' with their name on it in their chosen spot before the start of the day's business and then attending prayers.

a knockdown, drag-out, win-or-lose fight with Labour and we have to use what meagre resources we can muster.

Left at 7.15, changed and off to the state banquet with Jane.

Prince Andrew was there, and Prince Edward. Much talk about Prince Charles. I spoke to Sir Robert Fellowes, who told me that if Major asked for a dissolution and an election if Maastricht went wrong, the Queen would seek to persuade him not to do it. He also told me that the newspapers were now sensing the end of Charles and Diana's marriage and are circling for the kill.

Wednesday, 4 November, Westminster

THE DAY OF THE VOTE ON THE MAASTRICHT PAVING BILL

Bill Clinton was elected today by a large margin. Change in the air.

Tremendous tension building up for tonight's debate. Down to the chamber at 3.30. Standing room only.

Major was the best I have seen him. Smith was poor. Once again, having such a weak case to argue really showed. As anticipated, he turned his whole speech away from Europe and into a generalized attack on the Government.

Then Heath, who delivered a devastating attack on Smith, all about failure of principle, etc. Then me. I had an appalling time. They shouted, booed, catcalled and generally made life impossible for me. I thought the speech went badly, but the Colleagues said it was all right and lots of people – mostly Tories – said it was excellent. [The following day some of the sketch writers wrote that it was my best ever Parliamentary performance. Not, I suspect, because of the speech but because I fought my way through the heckling.]

Then a Parliamentary Party meeting, in the middle of which Archy came in, ashen-faced, to say that the Government's calculation was that we [the Government and Lib Dems combined] would win by nine; in other words, Lib Dem votes would hold the balance. We tried to put pressure on Nick Harvey[1] to change his position or at least abstain. But Nick stuck to his guns. He has done well in this. I disagree with him, and his position is an

---

1 Close friend and adviser. Our Member of Parliament for North Devon since 1992. Chair of the Campaigns and Communications Committee. Harvey had not attended the previous day's Parliamentary Party meeting.

embarrassment to us, but it's the position he argued for at the election and he has stuck to it honourably and with a good deal of courage.

We discussed the line to take in each of the three possible scenarios for tonight and reached an appropriate set of conclusions. The three options were:

1. The Government would win by our votes (our message would then be 'Europe and jobs have been saved').

2. The Government's motion would fall and so would Labour's (the mother of all chaos: 'Labour has brought this about and threatened the country's future in Europe and thousands of future jobs').

3. The Government's amendment would fall and Labour's would carry (variation on 2, but more strongly).

Down to dinner with the Colleagues and then into the vote at 10.00. Real tension. The Tories welcomed us into the lobbies, which was very uncomfortable.

Back into the chamber to vote in the first of two divisions. Word ran round that the Government had survived by six. And so it turned out.

As soon as the vote was announced, Labour MPs gathered round, pointing their fingers at us and shouting insults. It was pretty unpleasant. But I felt really proud that we had held to our principles.

Then the second vote. At this stage, the word came back from the Whips that the Government had lost narrowly. The Prime Minister looked very glum, but they came in with a majority of two. Even more anger and cat-calling from Labour. There was open hostility and almost fisticuffs, I think chiefly because Labour don't believe in the position they have taken and are seeking to put the blame on others. Smith was furious.

Off to do a round of interviews, where I bumped into Jack Cunningham,[1] who was vitriolic and bitter. Patricia Hollis[2] came up to him, threw her arms around him and then pointed an accusing finger at me and said, 'You are a traitor. And you can forget any prospect of PR from now on and for ever.' This was real anger, too. Not the mock stuff we so often get in the Chamber.

Thursday, 5 November, Westminster

At 3.30, off to see the PM. He saw me alone in his room.

He said he wanted to see me to thank me and the Party for 'standing by our principles'. He did not see me before the vote last night because he wanted to be able to say hand-on-heart that there had been no discussions between us and no deals.

I pressed him about the programme for the next stage of the Maastricht Bill. He said that the information he was about to give was known only to the Cabinet. The Tory rebellion at the time this process started numbered 100 and it had taken two months to whittle them down to three.

He was very critical of the press – especially Murdoch and Conrad Black,[3] who wanted to destroy the Treaty by any means possible, including personal attacks on him. Among others he mentioned in this 'cabal' (his words) were Simon Jenkins,[4] Charles Moore[5] and Sir Peregrine Worsthorne.[6] He said he had to 'untie the various knots around which the rebels were congregated, a little at a time'. He confirmed that he would use the guillotine for later stages of the Bill, but only after it became absolutely necessary.

1 Shadow Foreign Secretary. Member of Parliament (Labour) for Whitehaven 1970–83 and Copeland since 1983.
2 Lady Hollis, a Labour member of the House of Lords and Labour Party Whip.
3 Owner of the *Daily Telegraph*.
4 Columnist for *The Times*.
5 Editor of the *Sunday Telegraph*, 1992–5, editor of the *Daily Telegraph* since 1995.
6 Former editor of the *Sunday Telegraph*.

He is well in control of himself. But I sensed a real underlying fear, particularly about the press and about the level of poison now running through his party. He used the words 'civil war' on a number of occasions. He is obsessed by Maastricht. When he dies, it will be found engraved upon his heart.

Wednesday, 9 December, London

At mid-morning my secretary, Clare, contacted me to say that Alex Allan from No. 10 Downing Street had been trying to reach me. He had to come and warn me that the Prime Minister was going to make a major constitutional announcement at 3.30.

He came over and showed me the Prime Minister's statement which announced that the Prince and Princess of Wales were about to separate.

The statement was very simple, claiming there was no constitutional issue. I am not so sure.

Major is describing the purely legal position. But it seems inconceivable that Diana could be Queen now, or that there would not be a problem about the alternative Court that Diana is likely to set up. She will have no private life and any man who ever visits her (or any woman who visits Prince Charles) is bound to be under public scrutiny. This is just a gradual way of stepping into divorce.

The constitutional implications of that would be very considerable. Perhaps even the disestablishment of the Church (hurray).

Thursday, 10 December, London

Sarajevo has been completely surrounded by the Serbs, who have cut off the road to the airport and are preparing to strangle the city. At PMQs, I asked the PM whether he would let Sarajevo fall. Having given him a warning of my question the day before, I hoped I would get a fairly stiff-backed response, but he gave me the flabbiest answer I have ever heard. Little more than a green light to the Serbs. If they tried to take Sarajevo we wouldn't stop them. I was outraged.

Saturday, 12 December, UK and Yugoslavia

THE START OF MY THIRD TRIP TO THE FORMER YUGOSLAVIA

Up at 2.30am and off at 3.00 with Debs[1] and Nick[2] to Lyneham airbase and on to our Hercules for the flight out. All three of us were seated on the flight deck, with about twenty troops in the main body together with a full load of stores. We had a smooth flight through to Zagreb, which I used to catch up on some reading. On arrival we rushed around the airport trying to get a flight on to Sarajevo. A Russian turboprop was supposed to be going in, the first aircraft into Sarajevo for several days, but the pilot decided it was too dangerous at the moment. So back to catch the Hercules just before it took off for Split (in Croatia). Better to be closer to Sarajevo and travel overland than kick our heels in Zagreb.

Sunday, 13 December, Split

Up at 5.15 and off at 6.00 with Bob Regan[3] and Nick South in a Land-Rover.

We left Split in darkness, but dawn came up over the mountains as we crossed the first ridges, which rise like huge steps from Split to the Dinaric Alps. A short stop at Tomislavgrad to visit the logistics unit which services the front-line British troops.

Then over the Dinaric Alps on an indescribable little dirt track which the Royal Engineers have turned into a one-lane earth road with passing places. Icy and covered in snow. Croat tractors, a few lorries and wandering cattle were the only other users. God knows what it was like before the Royal Engineers took over. The Royal Engineer commander told me he had bought the road for Her Majesty from the local landowner for 10 dinars (10p). He paid too much.

We stopped several times. Firstly, to put on snow chains, then to call at the Royal Engineer post at the top of the mountains. Then down the other side. Very slippery. We passed lorries coming the other way up a track

---

1 Deborah Chapman. Debs worked in my office and I had asked her to accompany me to look, especially, at the refugee situation in Croatia while I went into Sarajevo.
2 Nick South. At that time a policy adviser and speech writer in my office. Later to become my Head of Office.
3 Political adviser to the British mission.

which was no more than one vehicle wide with a vertiginous drop to our left. Eventually, the inevitable happened. We came round a corner to find one of the huge British trucks had slipped off the side of the road, but had been prevented from crashing into the ravine below by trees. There followed an hour's discussion and much movement of trucks backwards and forwards. Bloody cold and the skies beginning to cloud over. Snow coming, I think. Waiting for the road to be cleared, I met a *Jane's Weekly* man. He told me the British troops here were by far the best in the theatre. He's right. I am especially impressed with the young officers and NCOs. Far more professional than the Services I belonged to.

We cleared the blockage by about 4.00 and dropped off the mountain to a very beautiful lake dotted with wooded islands and small villages. Tito's summer palace used to be here.

Then down to the village of Prozor, which brought us back to reality. This is a Croat village from which all the Muslims have been ethnically cleansed. The black-shirted quasi-Nazi Hoss in evidence everywhere. If ever things become nasty for the British troops further up the line, Prozor is where the withdrawal will get difficult. All the lines of communication run through this village.

Then on a further two hours to the British camp of Vitez. Here fifteen television cameras were poked up my nose and I met the famous Colonel Bob Stewart.[1] I did an impromptu press conference in front of a Warrior tank and then went off with Stewart for a briefing. He is a bluff 'hail fellow, well met' officer, who leads from the front and is much respected by all.

Afterwards, to the sergeants' mess and then dinner with Bob and his officers.

Monday, 14 December, Vitez

Up at 6.00. Breakfast, a couple of interviews by telephone and then off on patrol with Bob Stewart in his Warrior, together with his Sergeant Major, Nick and Bob Regan. Colonel Bob said before we left that he would get into trouble because he was taking me up to the front line, where he had not taken anyone before, including visiting generals.

1 Lieutenant-Colonel Bob Stewart, Commander of the 1st Battalion of the Cheshire Regiment.

We passed through Travnik, where there had been a good deal of shelling. The whole valley is dominated by the Vlasic mountain, which is currently covered in deep snow. This is where the Serb guns which shell the valley are positioned. We could see them when the light was right.

Then further up the valley to the front line at Turbe. Evidence of regular fighting here – shell holes and bullet marks everywhere. But still quiet. We were met by the Muslim commander, who looked sunken-eyed from a night of fighting.

As we went in to see him, a few rounds opened up over our heads. A long chat over the inevitable glasses of Slivo and strong Turkish coffee. At one stage he pulled out his pistol, laid it on the table and said, 'This is my arms. The problem is my opposite number has a howitzer.' Probably true. But not much evidence that the Serbs, even though better armed, are prepared to close with their enemy. What I saw was not a regular unit, just a collection of home guard. All looking exhausted and unshaven.

On the way back down the mountain, I was leaning out of one of the Warrior's hatches talking to Colonel Bob when I suddenly heard a loud bang and felt a hot blast in the back of my neck. I ducked down behind the armour of the Warrior faster than I thought possible. A single mortar round had landed ten yards from us. Bob shouted 'Shit!' over the radio and I could smell the acrid whiff of cordite. I expected the next stick of rounds to follow immediately, but they never came. The Serbs on the mountain above obviously had a pre-registered spot on the road and were telling us they knew we were there.

The Colonel said it was the closest round they'd had. Martin Bell and the BBC people following on behind got the whole lot on film. This became the running story of the day – and headlines in Britain. Isn't it funny? It's not what happens, but what happens on film that matters.

On the way back, I was asked for a comment on being mortared. I heard my mouth utter the unbelievably embarrassing phrase, 'Oh, one mortar round is very much like another!' What I intended to indicate was that, for the troops out here, and even more so for the locals, this was an everyday occurrence. But it must have sounded awful. I winced all day about it.

To Sarajevo. We travelled the first leg by Land-Rover, then transferred to an armoured personnel carrier. We passed through Oatez, where the Serbs had launched a recent major attack. Barely a building left standing. But the Bosnians, who are much better close-quarters fighters, had held on and inflicted heavy casualties. Serb morale had plummeted during the assault and their commanders had admitted to the UN that they didn't

1. Thursday, 28 July 1988, Cowley Street
'We then returned to the steps at Cowley Street, where I gave my acceptance speech'

2. Thursday, 29 September 1988, Blackpool First Conference
'I was surprised at how well the speech was received'

3. Monday, 29 August 1988, Irancy
'Having spent a glorious and much-needed two weeks in Irancy...'

4. Sunday, 18 June 1989, Somerset
'Sat out in the courtyard at home, did some work and read the papers in the morning'

5. **Thursday, 4 May 1989, Somerset**
'A photo-op outside Vane Cottage, then off to vote at the village hall'

6. Monday, 14 September 1992, Harrogate
'In the afternoon I went on to the platform for the start of the New Agenda debate'

7. Thursday, 9 April 1992, Somerset
'A beautiful misty spring morning ... Jane and I walked to the village hall and voted for the cameras, then did a photo-op with Luke on the playing fields'

8. Thursday, 2 April 1992, Sutton
'The press now see us as central to the campaign, so we are getting a lot of attention'

9. Monday, 10 August 1992, Manjaca, Yugoslavia
'We finally came to a barbed-wire enclosed prison camp … Hanging on the barbed wire were signs warning of mines on all sides'

10. Monday, 10 August 1992, Manjaca, Yugoslavia
'I asked to see the people from Omarska … They were pathetic. Emaciated and cowed, sitting in rows of 200 in two huge sheds'

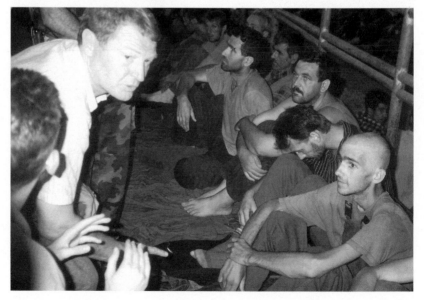

11. Saturday, 12 December 1992, to Yugoslavia
'A smooth flight through to Zagreb, which I used to catch up on some reading'

12. Sunday, 9 August 1992, Pale, Yugoslavia
'To Pale for dinner with Karadzic, whom I found charismatic' (he is showing me a rocket grenade)

13. Sunday, 13 December 1992, Dinaric Alps, Yugoslavia
'We came round a corner to find one of the huge British trucks had slipped off the side of the road'

14. Sunday, 13 December 1992, Vitez, Yugoslavia
'I did an impromptu press conference in front of a Warrior tank'

realize it would be so tough. One Serb brigadier who went up to the front-line to stiffen his troops' morale, promptly got killed for his pains. UNHCR told me the place was littered with bodies afterwards.

Then through to the airport, where I met Larry Hollingsworth. Great to see him again. We bundled into the back of his Land-Rover and drove down into the city. Sarajevo has taken a terrible pounding and is in much worse condition than last time. The people on the streets are grey and seem to be wandering in a dream. A general background cackle of machine-gun fire in various parts of the suburbs and the occasional crump of artillery, light, medium and sometimes heavy, was a constant accompaniment. Nothing intense, just continuous.

Into the PTT, where I met the Egyptian general. Dazed, ineffectual, hadn't a clue what was going on. I wouldn't put him in charge of a jumble sale.

To bed, shattered, around midnight. I made Nick sleep under the window as the building was subject to occasional shelling. He asked me why and I explained that if a shell did hit the room, the blast would go over our heads and the shrapnel would land in the far end of the room, just where he wanted to put his bed.

Tuesday, 15 December, Sarajevo

Up at 6.30, a blessed shower and what passed for breakfast in the French soldiers' canteen. As I was eating I looked out of the window and saw a bunch of haggard, unshaven people hanging around just outside the barbed wire, like ghosts from a Stanley Kubrick film. They were scavenging in the rubbish thrown out by the UN troops. A French soldier was trying to keep them at bay. These were the ordinary people of Sarajevo, now brought to begging from the UN. A truly terrible sight. Wrecked buildings all round and these gaunt figures in long coats trying to scavenge what food they could. I felt ashamed that UN personnel were living in such relative comfort inside.

Off with Martin Bell in the BBC armoured Land-Rover. He is an extraordinarily brave man. He was wounded in the stomach by shrapnel not long ago. He tells me the city gives him a pain in the stomach but he can't keep away. I know the feeling. It haunts me, too, when I am back in the UK.

We drove into the centre of the town. I had some parcels and mail to deliver from the Wincanton refugees and it took a little time to find the address. The family were still in bed at 10 o'clock in the morning. There is nothing else to do in Sarajevo. The old man was very sick. I gave them their Christmas presents – medicine. They were living in terrible conditions in a single room in a foetid atmosphere. Several floors up, so also subject to bombardment. But hanging on to life grimly.

Then to the cemetery. Newly dug empty graves everywhere. They have dug about 150 to 200 of these before the ground freezes. Nothing in Sarajevo is as horrible as these black mouths waiting for the snipers and the mortars to fill them and the names to be written on the markers.

Afterwards to the hospital. We went into the intensive-care unit, where a surgeon showed me an operating theatre which had been shelled yesterday. Two huge holes in the wall.

Then to visit some patients. One man with his throat blown away breathing through a tube and clearly close to death. Another who had been hit in the leg yesterday and had it amputated. The surgeon showed me the stump. Blood everywhere, old and new. On the sheets, on the patients and on the trolleys. The doctor told me in a matter-of-fact way that the patients started to come in between 10.00am and 1.00pm. 'That's when the shelling starts, when the gunners on the hills wake up.' They have no blood, no plasma, no antibiotics and only local anaesthetics. And this six months after the siege had started.

Then down into the town again. Shell and mortar holes everywhere. To the old French (now State) Hospital, where they took me to their intensive-care unit. No more than a room with haggard nurses doing what they could. What struck me most was the blankets. The kind of blankets my mother gave me when I was sent away to school – coloured or tartan or brightly patterned. Again no blood, no plasma, no antibiotics and anaesthetics in very short supply. People dying here of the most terrible wounds. I walked over to one bed to find a six-year-old child there. His face and his hair shone. He lay there for all the world like any six-year-old dreaming of Christmas. The difference was that he was not asleep, but drugged, having had his stomach ripped open by a piece of shrapnel earlier in the morning. The nurse told me with a shrug that he would shortly die. I couldn't stand it any longer and had to stumble out, making a fool of myself once again in front of people for whom this is a daily and inescapable fact of life. I don't know which was the stronger emotion, the anger or the shame. If we can't protect these people, at least we can provide them with the means to keep themselves alive. But we have failed in both.

Then to see Ganic[1] in the Presidency. They have replaced the windows since I was last here. An intelligent man – a teacher – but, like everyone else, desperate for intervention. I doubt if he will get it. I spent about half an hour with him, chatted to the press afterwards and then off round the town again and down to the warehouses. Met a very impressive Royal Corps of Transport captain called Peter Jones, who has been sent here to organize warehouse distribution for the city. He told me that he was desperately worried about their plight. There was not enough food to feed the city's 380,000 on a regular basis. He thought people would start dying very soon, especially when the weather got colder and the January fogs close the airport. The Serbs now had their units across the supply route so they could cut the city off at any time. And reserve stocks are so low that if the Serbs cut the supply lines, the city would feel it next day. How can we not even have accumulated reserves, six months after this started? It's a scandal.

I wanted to go across to the Serb side of the city to see Karadzic again, but Larry received a message that this had become much more dangerous, as both sides were shooting people crossing the line. We decided to go ahead, nevertheless. At 3 o'clock we left, crossing over to the Serb side at the suburb of Butmir, where the road runs for 400 metres between the two front lines and is subject to sniping from both sides. Again that horrible itchiness in the back of my neck.

A shot or two over our tops, but nothing serious, and we arrived safely into the Serb positions at Lukovice. Here I was met by a very smart Serb lady with fat thighs called Svetlana. She bundled me and Nick into the back of a car and, after saying thanks and goodbye to Larry, we were driven over the top to Pale. It was clear that the Serbs had heard what I had said about intervention and I wasn't terrifically popular.

However, we arrived at our hotel without incident. Then off to see Kolyevic, with whom I spent an hour and a half. Not so much Shakespeare this time, but I became convinced that he genuinely wants peace, probably because the Serbs want to legitimize their gains.

I fulfilled the purpose of my visit, which was to tell him bluntly that if the Serbs went further into either Travnik or Sarajevo, intervention was unavoidable.

---

1 Ejup Ganic, President of Bosnia.

Wednesday, 16 December, Pale to Sarajevo

Up at 5.30 to be ready to go back over the mountain to where Larry had arranged to pick us up and take us back to Sarajevo. The generator had gone off in the night, so we shaved with cold water and got dressed in the dark.

At 7.45 no car had turned up. 8.15 still no car. So we placed a few phone calls and were told that Svetlana of the fat thighs had arranged everything for 9.00; which, of course, was too late to catch the shuttle out of Sarajevo for our journey back. Eventually, I persuaded a Serb accompanying a French television team to drive us over the hill in his Fiat Uno. One of the French cameramen was wearing a green beret – being macho, I think. I told him he should take it off if he didn't want to get killed. Green is the Muslim colour and the worst Muslim atrocities were said by the Serbs to have been committed by the Bosnian green berets. Not a good thing to wear on the Serb side.

We bundled into the back of his Fiat and went over the hill, the French team following us. A hair-raising journey. The car tyres were totally treadless. The roads were very icy and we slid around all over the place. We met a French UNPROFOR patrol and tried to flag them down so that I could hitch a lift with them. But they refused to stop.

Eventually we got down to the Serb barracks at Lukovice to discover that Larry hadn't come across. There had been, according to the Serbs, a Bosnian 'massacre' of 120 Serbs in a town about forty miles away last night and the whole front line was in ferment. The Bosnians were now furious, too, having taken a terrible pounding during the night. There was also some talk that they were preparing their own assault. They said they would shoot anybody who crossed the airfield.

Eventually, however, Larry did get across, contrary to the advice of the UN. Typical Larry. He turned up smiling as ever in his Land-Rover, loaded us in the back and, now with the French APC column following us, we crossed the front line by a back route. Fortunately the fog was down, so the snipers couldn't see us and we had an uneventful crossing.

We arrived at the airport. The shuttle hadn't left. So we jumped into the back of a Danish APC to find ourselves sharing it with members of the Royal Canadian Mounted Police and some bewildered-looking Nepalese. What an extraordinary war this is! The flotsam and jetsam of the world's armies thrown together in strange vehicles in the middle of a conflict which no one understands.

Thursday, 24 December, Somerset

Christmas Eve, foggy. The weather has been beautiful. As I was clearing up my work before Christmas last night, the phone rang – the Prime Minister from Downing Street. He briefed me on his Christmas tour to visit the troops in Bosnia and said that he was opposed to the imposition of a no-fly zone. The Serbs, he was certain, would treat this as a one-sided act and take it out on us. I replied that I couldn't see how preventing both sides using excessive force against civilians through air power was taking sides. On the contrary, it was standing up for international law. He said the options we faced were double or quits, and that nobody else in NATO would double with us. Britain would be left alone. He complained bitterly about the uncertainty of the Americans, who were between Presidents. The French also getting nervous. I thanked him for ringing and we wished each other a Happy Christmas.

Later in the day, a call from Larry Hollingsworth. He had flown back to the UK for three or four days. Apparently Sarajevo had been rather quiet for the last week. He thinks it may even be the beginnings of a cease fire. I doubt it. He says the Bosnians are the ones to fear now.

1993

Tuesday, 19 January, Monktonhall, Yorkshire[1]

Up at 6.15, a quick breakfast and off to the mine by seven. Bitterly cold and threatening snow. We arrived at Monktonhall pit just as dawn was breaking – an angry red sky under heavy clouds.

I was fitted out with a pair of boots, belt, a hat and some overalls. Then off to collect my brass tag and down for a briefing on the use of the survival kit and lamp.

To the entrance of the shaft with Angus McDonald,[2] Jackie Aitcheson[3] and my fellow shift workers. We entered the cage, a rusting, dripping affair. The doors closed and the cage dropped like a stone down the black hole of the shaft, three thousand feet in a minute and a half. When we got to the bottom, we entered a gallery about sixteen feet high and as broad as a London Underground tunnel. The air was warm and filled with dust, which gave a soft focus to the light thrown by lamps set in the walls. A pit train rattled past us out of the gloom.

We picked up our gear and started to walk down the large service passage. After about fifteen minutes we turned into a smaller tunnel down a sharp incline which was wide enough for a conveyor belt and a narrow path alongside. We descended in single file through the gloom towards the coal face.

Then, at the bottom, into a wide intersection between two tunnels, where we turned into a yet smaller passage and passed through an airlock into the working area of the face. All the time a steady blast of air blew in our faces, providing vital ventilation for the coal face. We made towards the face, heads bowed beneath the low ceiling. By now it was hot and humid, though the strong breeze kept it bearable. Then across the conveyor

1 This visit to Britain's deepest pit, Monktonhall Colliery, to work a shift with the miners was part of my 'Tour of Britain' trips, which took up much of the early part of 1993 and formed the basis of *Beyond Westminster*. Other visits included two days on a fishing trawler off the Cornish coast, a period in a drug-riddled Moss Side estate in Manchester, working in a silk mill in Suffolk, some time in Toxteth in Liverpool and visits to the Orkneys, Bristol, the East End of London and Solihull.
2 The foreman of my shift.
3 The Chairman of Monktonhall Mining Co-operative, with whom I stayed.

belt and into the tunnel, which had been cut relatively recently. As we came nearer to the face the ceiling dropped down to two or three feet, propped up every foot or so by hydraulic rams. We crawled about a hundred and fifty yards across rough stones up to the face itself. The air was filled with dust and somewhere ahead a great machine roared. Like a scene from Dante's Inferno. By now we were in darkness, except for the lights on our helmets.

I was taken up to the cutting machine, which bellowed and bucketed like a great subterranean dragon as it cut into the coal face, kicking out showers of sparks from the gouged-out rock.

For the next three hours I worked with the miners, shovelling coal in this tiny slot of space nearly four thousand feet into the earth.

The face was, at most, three feet high, but in places much lower, forcing me to crawl or crouch.

Angus took me to the 'stall', an area hewn out of the end of the face in order to allow the cutting machine to turn. He showed me the raw coal above us, and pointed out the ancient bole of a fossilized tree, perfectly etched in coal. Angus hit this with his pick and a huge chunk crashed to the floor. All the while there were ominous crackings and bangs and thuds, as the roof settled above us.

And all the time the banter of the miners, pulling my leg, mainly about politicians doing a decent day's work for a change.

We had our 'slice'[1] at midday. I shared mine with Paul the photographer, and with Angus, who hadn't brought anything for himself. Everybody shares everything.

In the afternoon I was put to work with 'Big Andy' – a giant of a man, who seemed to fill the whole of the tiny cavern in which we worked. We sweated and cursed and laughed as we cleared a pile of rock from the mouth of the main tunnel. He told me as we worked that he was waiting for the birth of his first child, which was a little late. He made some very rude, but obviously affectionate comments about his wife, whom he first described as being like a film star. Then he laughingly corrected himself: 'Actually she's built like a brick shit-house – but that's what I like about her.'

Beneath the macho talk he was really worried about her and the baby. 'Can't wait to see the wee lad. When he's older, I shall give him a share of the pit[2] – then he will be a mine owner and won't have to come down here

1 Sandwich.
2 Monktonhall is a co-operative, owned by the miners, who each have a share in the pit.

like his dad.' Andy's capacity for work was phenomenal – he shifted at least twice as much as me.

When we finished clearing the pile of rocks, he took me back up the tunnel on all fours to show me the cutting machine. It was a huge beast with fearsome tines spinning on a pair of discs at the front. After a face is cut the machine is moved forwards and hydraulic rams are used to prop up the passage it has forged. I kept on hearing the roof creaking over our heads and the area we'd just cut immediately collapsing behind us. Andy said that the roof collapsing was a good sign, but I found it very disconcerting. All the time we sweated and swore in the dust and darkness, our helmet lights the only illumination in this inky narrow space squeezed somewhere between the centre of the earth and daylight.

At one stage there was quite a large roof fall and a rock skidded to a halt just beside me. I ineffectually put my hand out to stop it, and cut myself slightly. If it had fallen on my leg it would certainly have broken it. I kept thinking that for three hundred and fifty million years this stuff had lain in the dark, only now to be ripped out into the sunlight, from which it had first drawn the power of its creation.

Later, the word came down that they were about to do some blasting. We were moved away from the blast area and told to lean against the sides of the tunnel with our backs to the explosion. The machines stopped, and about five minutes later there was a dull, heavy thump that reverberated right into the pit of my stomach. No bang, just a deep momentary shivering of the rocks around us.

Then, for several minutes, the strong smell of cordite, which was soon blown away by the current of air which took it up towards the mine mouth somewhere far above us.

By now it was two or three in the afternoon and we were all liberally covered in grime. The most distinguishing characteristics of my shift colleagues had become their teeth and the whites of their eyes.

An extraordinary sense of teamwork and unquenchable humour. No demarcation, no rank, no distinctions. Just people confident in each other's skills. Despite my earlier fears, I too relaxed, relying on my shift mates to keep me safe in this creaking, roaring world. And in the end, I almost enjoyed it. We dug about six hundred tons of coal of reasonable quality. I felt proud. We left the face at about 3.20. The path out felt much steeper than on the way down. Then into the cage and up into light.

I was exhausted, but felt a real sense of achievement. The other men kept on teasing me, saying they'd give me 7 out of 10 for a politician, but I still had some way to go before I could take up a job as a miner.

Afterwards, a cup of coffee, a cigarette and a chat before contacting the office in London to catch up on the news. No problems over Maastricht and the Colleagues quiet. I am to see the Prime Minister on Thursday.

Friday, 5 February, Westminster

A beautiful, crisp, cold day, with a bright blue sky. I really enjoyed the walk across Westminster Bridge to Century House, the headquarters of M16. The old building has changed hardly at all.

I was whisked up to the eleventh floor to see Colin McColl (now Sir Colin)[1] in his curiously dingy office. He told me the décor hadn't changed since Maurice Oldfield was there. I was introduced to the Director of Requirements, the Director of the Secretariat, the Controller for the Middle East and another man who looks after [Soviet] Bloc intelligence. They are doing extraordinary work, particularly against drug rings. They also gave me a lot of very useful information about the political situation in the Soviet Union and elsewhere. They have good sources in a number of key areas, but their work, particularly their operations against drug rings, is rather more dangerous than before.

I had a very full briefing then lunch with them all, which we finished at 2.30. Then back to Westminster in Colin's car.

Friday, 19 February, Sudbury

A WEEKEND AT ANDREW PHILLIPS' HOUSE

Dinner at 7.30.

Anthony King and Ivor Crewe[2] and their wives were there. We had a terrific meal cooked by Andrew's wife Penelope – one of the best I have ever had.

The conversation turned largely on politics and opinion polls. Both King and Crewe are clear that Labour cannot do it and think that they are on the way down, though much slower than perhaps some in my Party would

---

1 Head of MI6 from 1988 until 1994.
2 Two academics who write books about elections and British politics in general.

like to believe. King, in particular, is an avid 'Chardist' and believes that's the only way forward.

In the course of the evening we had two bets. One, which I initiated for a bottle of Irancy Burgundy, that there would be an election before June 1995. King and Crewe took this with alacrity. The second (King's proposal, I think) was on the outcome of the next General Election. Both King and Crewe were remarkably close to each other, though they denied ever having discussed this before. They both bet there would be a Tory majority and that we would get either twenty-five seats (King) or thirty seats (Crewe). Andrew said we would get thirty-two seats and I said we would get forty. I predicted a hung Parliament, as did Andrew.

The bets were all duly formally written down amid much laughter and filed away in Andrew's wonderful, untidy filing system.

King made his apologies at around midnight, complaining of bad sinusitis. The phone rang at 12.15. It was King, who had heard on the radio that there was to be by-election in Newbury, the incumbent MP Judith Chaplin having died during an operation.

Newbury must be one of our top hundred or so seats in the country. We control the council there and we have a good candidate in David Rendel.

Thursday, 11 March, London

Off to lunch with Anthony Lester[1] at the National Liberal Club. He told me that Robin Butler, whom he knows well, is in despair with the Government. Robin, who is usually a deeply discreet man, could not control himself the other day and told Anthony what an appalling shower he thought they were. Can't make their minds up about anything, jockeying for position, stabbing each other in the back, speaking separately to the press, etc.

Anthony said that it was not insignificant that there had been an attack on Butler in the *Guardian* the previous day. 'It comes to something when the Cabinet are so split they not only attack each other but their own, very excellent, Cabinet Secretary.'

---

1 A human rights lawyer, who now sits on the Liberal Democrat benches in the House of Lords.

On the Chard front, he agreed to get alongside some of the Labour MPs he knows, particularly Tony Blair.

I told him that I was now determined to try and initiate the realignment but that I could get no interest from Smith. So he said he would try and fix dinner with Blair.

Monday, 15 March, Downing Street

Breakfast with the Prime Minister at 8.00am. The discussion was all about Maastricht and how to get the Bill through.

I told him that, whilst our two Whips worked together adequately on short-term tactics for the Bill, we were getting dangerously out of touch with each other's long-term thinking and we needed to open a supplementary line of communication. We agreed to see each other on an extremely private basis whenever either felt the need. He wanted to propose a meeting every week, but I thought that excessive. This arrangement was to be known only to the Prime Minister and myself, and to the two Chief Whips.

He then went into a long and highly defensive explanation of why he thought it was necessary to get the Bill through on time: the economic situation in Europe was fast deteriorating; all the European leaders were in serious trouble at home – even Gonzalez, who had looked certain for re-election (Spanish unemployment was now running at 20 per cent). 'If we don't get the Maastricht Bill completed by July, the Treaty could become unstitched in the rest of Europe by the autumn,' he said.

There are about fifty rebels in the Tory Party who are totally implacable. Even with our support, he would have to shift twenty of these. And the rebellion is growing.

He was obviously very hurt by comments I had made over the weekend about 'kow-towing' to his right wing. I explained that I was certainly not prepared to slacken off my attacks on the Government. The fact that we were co-operating on Maastricht didn't mean we should give up our job of opposition.

Finally, he asked me not to keep him hanging around for information on how we would vote until the last minute. I responded that this depended on our having a rather better knowledge of the Government's overall strategic positions. I also made it clear that we would vote for the Social Chapter whatever, but I didn't see how this would destroy the Bill. It may destroy the Government – but that was up to him. And if our insistence on the Social Chapter caused the Government to withdraw support for the Bill, that was their decision, not ours.

I left at 8.45.

Wednesday, 31 March, Westminster

At 6.00pm into the PPM. This went well until we came to discuss Maastricht. I could see that Alex Carlile had something up his sleeve.

The proposal he unveiled was that we ought to give the Government a waiver on the Social Chapter in return for an extra seat on the Council of the Regions[1] (on which he is under pressure in Wales) and a chance to reconsider the Social Chapter in two years' time. David Steel supported him.

I couldn't be sure of defeating them, so I postponed a full debate until the Wednesday after Easter, saying that the Colleagues needed time to think about it. But I made it very clear I thought the proposal would be a disaster. We would be seen to be taking crumbs from the Government's table, voting for British workers to lose their rights and getting in return an extra seat on a body no one even knew existed. If we abandoned our principles for such grubby deals, we would also destroy all our credibility in the next election.

After the ten o'clock vote, I asked Don Foster back for a whisky in my office, where he agreed to mobilize the Parliamentary vote against this proposal.

Thursday, 1 April, Westminster

Meeting with Anthony Lester at 10.30am. He has discussed the possibility of realignment with Blair and Graham Allen.[2] Allen says he personally is strongly in favour, but is working against the tide in the Labour Party. Blair says the same thing, but has suggested we might have dinner on some neutral territory so that we could get to know each other as 'he doesn't really know me'. Anthony will fix this.

1 A pan-European body set up under the Maastricht Treaty as a forum for Europe's regions.
2 An Opposition spokesman on Home Affairs. Member of Parliament (Labour) for Nottingham North since 1987.

Monday, 12 April, Irancy, Burgundy

EASTER HOLIDAYS

The apple tree outside our bedroom window is just coming into flower. Green leaves and blossom against the Burgundy tiles.

I have done a lot of thinking this holiday. It has only recently dawned on me that this is my last chance. If we end up with the same result after the next election, I will have to stand down. And even if we don't, I need to think about it on grounds of age.

I am getting very tired, I am pushing people too hard, I am snapping their heads off and am generally beginning to look a bit brutal. All the dreadful signs of an old man in a hurry! It's been very tough getting the Party moving again after the election. But by and large we have succeeded. We are also now well placed in the county elections in May and at Newbury [the date for which had now been fixed for 6 May], upon which everything depends. But I cannot have been much fun to work for. And nor am I coming across very well to the public – too manic. All in all I am not doing either myself or the Party any favours. It is time to relax a bit.

Wednesday, 14 April, Westminster

The Parliamentary Party Meeting at 6.00pm. Rather a small turn-out, though more people drifted in later. We rattled through the agenda fairly quickly until we got to the Maastricht issue, when Alex re-stated his proposition of two weeks ago. He ended up by saying he thought the Party had taken a wimpish position and this had done us no good. But he didn't make a very convincing case. I went round the room asking who agreed with him. It was eight to two against. Alex made a generous and elegant withdrawal.

Tuesday, 27 April, Westminster

At 4.00pm, to see the PM, who was in a chirpy mood, in his office. He wanted to explain the Government's position on Bosnia.[1]

---

1 Talks between the Bosnians and Croats had broken down and fighting had intensified.

In an extended and rather impressive monologue he ran through all available options:

1. *Lift the embargo* The USA favours this option because it is the only one which does not involve the use of American forces. The PM regards this as dishonest. In fact, he is 'passionately opposed to it'. In his view, this is the single option most likely to widen the war. I agree.

2. *Air strikes on Serb supply lines* The military have said this is possible, but there would be the following disadvantages:
    a. Humanitarian aid in exposed areas would have to cease.
    b. It is unlikely that it would be completely effective.
    c. The Yugoslavian air force might get involved, which would widen the war.
    d. It would almost certainly result in civilian casualties.
    I formed the view that he could be persuaded to this as a last option.

3. *Safe havens* He believes that these would require substantial extra reinforcements of troops on the ground and no other Western or NATO country was prepared to support this.[1]

He would, therefore, prefer to keep the policy as it is.[2] But of all the options listed he would consider (2) and (3) provided that, in the latter case, troops from other nations were forthcoming.

He is presently considering issuing an ultimatum to the Serbs in the case of further attacks on, for instance, Tuzla. But he has only discussed this with the Foreign Secretary. He is not certain of support in the Cabinet for this and is even more doubtful of support in the wider Conservative Party. I told him that, in the worst case, if he did decide to follow the ultimatum route, he could probably count on our support.

For any of the above courses of action, he felt it necessary to first strengthen the 'fire break' to prevent the conflict spreading into Kosovo and Macedonia. It might be possible to increase UN presence in Macedonia, but we had no capacity to do this in Kosovo. He is very worried that military intervention by the West would lead to the Muslims rising in Kosovo, while the Serbs concentrated on UN attacks. But his chief concern

---

1 The Serbian nationalist-held town of Srbrenica had been designated a 'safe haven' by the United Nations.
2 i.e., no further deepening of our involvement, no lifting of the arms embargo, no further use of air power and no safe havens.

lies in the widening gulf between the USA and European members of NATO. The Clinton administration is more hostile to Europe than Bush's was. The PM fears that failure to provide Clinton with support for whatever action he favours could accelerate the withdrawal of US troops from Europe and mark the beginning of the end for NATO.

I left at 4.30pm.

Later I saw Liz Lynne, at her request. She told me that she is taking soundings in her constituency about the Maastricht vote. If they opposed Maastricht, she would too. I told her not to be so ridiculous, and persuaded her not to act on whatever soundings she got unless there was more than a 25 per cent response, which of course she won't get. I also said that if she voted against the Party in the Maastricht third reading debate I would have to reconsider her spokesmanship. She told me she was pretty bored with adhering to Parliamentary Party discipline, anyway, and was thinking of joining David Alton,[1] with whom she had discussed the matter.

Left at 7.40 for Buckingham Palace, for the usual state dinner palaver. This time for the President of Portugal, Mario Suarez. He made rather a political speech, as I thought did the Queen. I sat next to someone whose name card told me that she was one of the Queen's Ladies-in-Waiting. An appallingly right-wing old Tory dragon. I attempted to steer clear of contentious subjects, but at one stage her prejudiced opinions were just too much for me and I responded sharply to some point she made, whereupon she glowered and turned to her other neighbour.

On my other side was a rather shapely lady who was the wife of the Brazilian Ambassador. She was put between John Smith and me and said that she had been told by a friend that she was sitting between the two most interesting men in London! Smith and I had quite a flirty little banter with her, saying that at the end of the dinner we would decide which one of our two parties she'd join.

After dinner, Jane and I spoke to Sir Robert Fellowes. Also his wife Jane, who is the Princess of Wales's sister. The Princess herself is looking thin, hook-nosed and predatory. Somehow being separated from the Royal Family has had an effect on her. She is already beginning to look like an outsider.

---

1 i.e., as a 'semi-detached' member of the Parliamentary Party who took no spokesmanship role.

Thursday, 29 April, Westminster

In early for the co-ordinating group meeting. Alan presented a paper on what we should do after Newbury. I said that I was determined to use the Newbury result to reopen the whole question of realignment. Almost everybody advised caution on this. But this is too important a moment to miss.

Tuesday, 4 May, Westminster

At 5.30 Russell, Archy and I went to see Douglas Hurd and talk about the Maastricht Bill (still trundling through its House of Commons procedures), on which the Government is facing defeat.

I opened by saying we would vote against the Government on the Social Chapter, as we had previously warned, unless he could show us that such a move would threaten the survival of the Bill. Hurd tried to do this in a rather blustery way, but I don't think he even convinced himself.

Hurd then went on to tell us about Bosnia. Russell also reported on his latest visit – he had seen things from the Serb side. I said that:

1. We would support the Government in opposing the lifting of the arms embargo.

2. We were unconvinced about generalized bombing unless backed by ground troops to stop the conflict.

3. We were, however, in favour of the limited use of air power in defence of safe havens.

4. It was important to try and establish further safe havens in some of the hot spots.

5. We should immediately re-open Tuzla airport for the supply of troops and transport of humanitarian aid.

Friday, 7 May, London

To Cowley Street for the local election and Newbury by election results. By 3.30am, all the local election results were in, but not Newbury. I decided

to go home and get a little sleep, asking the office to ring me when they knew the majority. At 4.20am Graham Elson rang to say that David Rendel had got in by 22,000. I said yes, that was his vote, but what was the majority? Graham said, 'That was his majority.' I told him not to be so silly, I wanted to know the majority not the total vote. 'Paddy, that is the majority.' I was gobsmacked.

Thursday, 13 May, London

I have decided on four aims for our policy towards Labour: two national and two local; two overt and two covert.

The open national aim is to be congenial and co-operative towards them where this improves our standing as an opposition party in Westminster and drives forward the politics of co-operation.

The covert national aim is to promote debate within the Labour Party between the modernizers and the traditionalists, in order to split them.

The open local aim is to co-operate with Labour where necessary in council chambers in order to give us power and strengthen our status as a party of local government.

The covert local aim is to do everything we can to win council seats from them where they are vulnerable, especially in the inner cities, in order to erode their base and widen ours.

I have also devised a 'rule of thumb' for when it might be possible to promote co-operation with Labour, which I am referring to as 'the Labour unpopularity threshold':

'As long as the Labour Party is regarded by voters in Lib Dem target seats as more unpopular than the Tories, then any formal relationship would damage our election performance. But, if it was the other way round (and with a collapsing Government and a bland John Smith, it might just), then formal co-operation with Labour would boost our electoral performance.'

Wednesday, 9 June, Westminster

At 1 o'clock, lunch with Andrew Phillips. Just before I left I heard that Norman Lamont[1] has decided to make his resignation statement this afternoon. Why?[2]

I thought about this in the taxi on the way to lunch. He must have chosen this time because it was the most damaging for Major. His statement was therefore intended to be a bombshell. I rang Alan Leaman to tell him we must plan for the possibility that Lamont would try to do to Major what Howe had done to Thatcher.

We agreed that Alan Beith would sit alongside me for Lamont's speech, and if it was as I suspected then we'd coin a line on the spot. Alan would go and sell it to the media and I would incorporate it into my speech in the main debate.

Lamont got up at 3.30pm. He opened his speech quite quietly. A hint of steel there, but no real damage until right at the end when, under the guise of giving advice to Major, he excoriated him. Exactly like Howe's speech, but not nearly as good. The key sentence was, 'We seem to be in Government, but not in power.' We hastily agreed the line that this was the beginning of the end for Major.

Then Smith got up. To my surprise, he responded hardly at all to

1 Norman Lamont had been replaced as Chancellor a month before, in May 1993, following a number of embarrassing events for the Government, most notably Britain's suspension from the Exchange Rate Mechanism.
2 This was curious because the debate of the day was one initiated by Labour, on a motion critical of the Government's Economic and Social Policy.

Lamont's speech, seeming not to recognize its significance. But he gave a brilliant performance. Funny, very jokey and extremely disconcerting for the Government. But no policy in it and no indication of Labour's views.

Then Major. He was very flat, and didn't receive the support of his back benchers. I preceded my speech with the words, 'I believe that what we have heard and seen this afternoon is the beginning of the end of the Right Honourable Gentleman's premiership . . . If he had bothered to turn round during his speech he would have seen his fate indelibly written on the faces of Conservative Members.' No cat calls from the Tories. They listened to me in silence.

Thursday, 1 July, Westminster

At 2 o'clock I saw Richard Holme to discuss the possibility of him running the next General Election campaign. We talked through the structure we would need and how we would sell it to the Party. He clearly wants to do it and I think he is the right person. But it will cause ructions in some quarters. We must make sure we get the internal politics of this right.

Friday, 9 July, Westminster

An opinion poll out today. It puts us in second place at 27 per cent, with the Tories down to 24 per cent!

Wednesday, 14 July, London

Dinner at Anthony and Katya Lesters' with Cherie and Tony Blair.[1] When Jane and I arrived they were already there.

Blair and I spoke at some length over the meal, while Anthony kept the others talking at the other end of the table. We struck up a good rapport. He wants modernization, but thinks it must be taken step by step. He is scared to death of being squashed by the unions and the left wing. His most interesting comment was, 'The history of the Labour Party is littered with nice people who get beaten. I don't intend to be one of them.'

---

1 By now Shadow Home Secretary.

He appears to want what we want (i.e., realignment), though Anthony wondered later whether he is showing enough courage in doing what is necessary to get it.

He left at just before ten to get back for a vote, having agreed that we should meet again after the Party Conferences were over. I spent another hour with Anthony.

Wednesday 21, July, Westminster

I am fearful that the Government will spot the weakness of our position on Maastricht and make us choose between the survival of the Bill and the inclusion of the Social Chapter. I shall be delighted if they win the vote tomorrow and even more delighted if they don't push the vote for another week, when we will be past the Christchurch by-election.[1] I know only too well that being forced to choose between ratification and the Social Chapter will split the Party from top to bottom. Privately I have decided that I will put my own leadership at stake rather than see us act in a way which destroys Maastricht and with it our European credentials. But I realize that this will cause terrible problems and may even lose us the Christchurch by-election. It has been keeping me awake at night. Never mind Major's leadership, it could be the end of mine if things go wrong now.

Into the Parliamentary Party meeting. Fairly plain sailing, but I went into the Maastricht position in detail, describing graphically the mantrap that lay ahead of us. Now if we get caught in the wrong position, at least we all know what's coming.

Thursday, 22 July, Westminster

PARLIAMENTARY VOTE ON THE GOVERNMENT'S 'OPT-OUT' ON THE INCLUSION OF THE SOCIAL CHAPTER IN THE MAASTRICHT TREATY

At PMQs, Smith wisely stayed away from the Social Chapter and I asked the Prime Minister whether or not we would take any action to save Sarajevo.[2] Disgracefully, he said no. Then into the Maastricht debate at 4.15.

1 A by-election had been called at Christchurch for 29 July following the death of its MP, Robert Adley.
2 Serbian forces had launched further attacks upon the mountains surrounding the besieged city. This followed their attack on Gorazde, a UN safe haven.

Major made rather a good speech, very self-confident and much of it attacking me. He pulled me up from the bench three times to intervene. I was pretty angry. There was quite a personal clash between us.

Smith was rather pedestrian. Next Tim Renton,[1] who went on and on. By now it was approaching 6 o'clock and I was going to fall into the ten-minute rule.[2] I rose at 5.55 and finished at 6.04.

Later on, the summings-up. David Hunt delivered a positively dreadful speech. Joe Ashton,[3] sitting next to me, discouraged Labour members from intervening and instead organized a background hum of chatter to put him off. Rather successful, too. Hunt is usually so good.

We then went in for the vote. Huge tension on the first vote. Word came in that the Ulstermen had done a deal with the Government and, sure enough, they all filed in to vote with them. Labour Whips told us they thought we could still win by two. Early indications were that the Government had won. Nods and thumbs-up on the Government's side.

But in the end the most dramatic result of all: 317 to 317. Betty rose and did her constitutional duty by casting her vote for the Government. We were in high spirits, as this was almost the worst result of all for them. So out for the second vote, which we were now confident of winning. A majority of sixteen. Major rose immediately afterwards. His smile had vanished and he looked really troubled. He announced that they would link a vote of confidence with one on the Social Chapter the following day.

I went home at around 12.15am, poured myself a whisky and fell into bed. An extraordinary night.

Friday, 23 July, Westminster

To the chamber for the confidence debate at 3.30. Major wasn't bad in the first half of his speech, but fell away a lot in the second. At least he was feisty and laid his own position on the line.

Then Smith, who was absolutely brilliant. Funny; superb with interventions; a real Parliamentary performance of quality. He had an open goal and he shot several balls into it. Then Tom King in an almost empty

---

1 Member of Parliament (Conservative) for Mid Sussex 1974–97. He now sits in the House of Lords.

2 The rule in the House at the time was that speeches after 6.00pm had to be of less than ten minutes in length.

3 Member of Parliament (Labour) for Bassetlaw since 1968.

chamber, then me. My speech lasted five or six minutes. The Colleagues said it was OK, but I thought it was below par.

Into the chamber again at 9.15 for the summings-up. George Robertson[1] made a rather pedestrian speech. Hurd a very elegant and effective one, which included a sustained attack on me that had his back benches roaring. Difficult not to smile myself, even though I was the butt of the attack.

We have seriously riled the Tories, who are now desperately worried. But they have paid us off in pretty miserable coinage for the support we gave them on Maastricht earlier in the year, when they were in such trouble with their own right wing. And there is real animosity between me and Major now, which has been picked up by the press.

Then to the vote: 299 to 339, a majority for the Government of forty.

Thursday, 29 July, Somerset

THE CHRISTCHURCH BY-ELECTION

On the way home I dropped in to Wincanton to see the Bosnians [ahead of my forthcoming trip to Bosnia] and pick up some mail to deliver to their friends and relatives in Sarajevo. A huge parcel which is going to take up half my case. Very affecting. All of them desperately seeking news of their relatives. I have six or seven letters to deliver and several to leave in the desperate hope that they will get to other parts of eastern Bosnia.

Word started coming in on the Christchurch count at around 10.30. A high poll, nearly 80 per cent. Chris Rennard said he was confident we would get a five-figure majority. At about 12.45 he was tempted to say 12–15,000. At about 2.00am the result came through. A 16,000 majority for Diana Maddock.[2]

Friday, 30 July, Somerset and London

Up at 7.30. Bathed, finished packing my gear for Bosnia and left at 8.45 for London. On the previous evening, two Sarajevan refugees living in Taunton

1 Opposition spokesman for Foreign Affairs. Member of Parliament (Labour) for Hamilton from 1979–99. From 1997 he was the Secretary of State for Defence until he went to the House of Lords in 1999, which coincided with his appointment as Secretary General of NATO.
2 Member of Parliament (Liberal Democrat) for Christchurch 1993–7. Now sits in the House of Lords and was, until recently, our Party President.

came across to deliver a couple of packages with medical stuff in them for friends in a suburb of Sarajevo. They were so dignified and gave their precious parcel of medicine for the coming winter to me with such reverence and hope that Jane and I were very moved. We both wondered how we would cope if Simon and Kate were separated from us like this. We agreed we wouldn't.

Saturday 31 July, Hungary and Yugoslavia

Nick and I had a smooth flight through to Budapest, arriving at about 4.15pm. The usual tortuous journey across the Danube flood plain. Finally into Belgrade at 11.00, to be met by John Kennedy. The chance of seeing Milosevic as originally planned had now evaporated. Kennedy took us down to the Turkish quarter, where we had something to eat. The usual Serbian food, six different kinds of meat and half a lettuce leaf.

Kennedy in good form, having just come back from Geneva.[1] Full of the old bullshit, however. He told me that the Serbs had excellent anti-aircraft missiles on Mount Igman [above Sarajevo] and would shoot down any planes that attacked them. He also claimed they had tactical nuclear weapons in the area. He clearly thinks they have won and has seventy-three different reasons why we should not support the Muslims. A remarkable man. Extraordinary self-confidence but lacking in plain common sense. Somehow, he is good company, even if – or perhaps because – he is so provocative.

Back to the hotel at about 2.00am, where he checked we had a car for the morning. Kennedy couldn't get through to the villa where the car was based, so he phoned Karadzic in Geneva. This at 2.30 in the morning! He put Karadzic through to me. I had quite an extended conversation with him, but there was not much we could really talk about. As usual he said the Muslims were holding up the peace process, the Serbs and the Croats having already agreed everything. He tried to persuade me to stay on at Pale for when he arrived back on Monday. But I explained that this was simply not possible.

We all went to bed, having fixed to meet for breakfast at 6.00am.

---

1 Where peace talks between both sides, under the chairmanship of David Owen, were in progress.

Sunday, 1 August, Yugoslavia

Up at 5.15, a shower and some coffee, then downstairs for 5.55. As I feared, no car. Went to have a chat with Kennedy, who was still in bed. He claimed they hadn't given him an alarm call.

Each time we rang the Serbs asking for progress on the car, they had a different excuse: it was coming; it had to be filled with petrol; it would be there in ten minutes; it was going to be Karadzic's car; they couldn't find it; it was away at Pale. The usual Belgrade urgency. I held my temper until about midday, then exploded all over Kennedy. Eventually, we decided to go up to the villa. I went there in an exceptionally brutish mood, to be met by Serbs smiling and saying they were terribly sorry, etc. But the tactic worked. We were on our way in fifteen minutes, driven by a man who told us his name was Vladimir Ilyich. I said, 'You mean Lenin.' He said yes, he had been born in Lenin Street, Sarajevo.

We crossed the Drina by the bridge at Svornik, where we were stopped by Serbs with huge beards and even bigger machine-guns. To my astonishment one of them looked at my passport, saw the name, pointed a finger at me and said in Serbo Croat (or so John told me), 'You were the one who beat Major at Christchurch the other day!' Another listener to the BBC World Service.

Then followed one of the most hair-raising drives I have ever taken. Up over the mountains, through Han Pijesak, the site of the old hunting lodge of the Yugoslav kings, now the army headquarters of the Bosnian Serbs.

We drove higher and higher up into the mountains. But neither height, nor road conditions nor oncoming traffic made any difference to Vladimir's breakneck pace. I decided I preferred the helicopter of our last trip. It may have been three times as frightening, but at least it was ten times shorter. Nevertheless, indescribably lovely countryside on a very beautiful day. I slept a bit, while Kennedy and Nick hung on to the sides of the car.

As we sped through the recent war zones, we saw that the crops hadn't been harvested and most of the houses had been destroyed. Once again, it's very difficult to adjust to the contrast between such a beautiful place and such a terrible war. John told us that Serb women wear black when a close member of their family has been killed. About 80 per cent of the women walking on the roads or hanging around the villages wore black.

We arrived in Pale at around 7.00pm and were immediately taken to meet Rajo Kasagic, Prime Minister of the Bosnian Serbs. He told us that getting to Mount Igman, as we had planned tonight, was an impossibility. There were a lot of Muslim guerillas about and he couldn't guarantee our safety. We should go tomorrow. So we briefed the press and went off to look at the local hospital.

It was bad, but nothing like as bad as the one at Sarajevo, with which the Serbs constantly compare it. They have antibiotics, plasma and plenty of anaesthetic. I was shown one or two mine injuries. The young surgeon there, who looked haggard, showed me some of his microsurgery work. It was remarkable, given that he had done it with the naked eye.

Then off to dinner with the Republica Srbska Prime Minister at the Presidency and the general in command.[1] A great bull of a man who was largely monosyllabic. At one point I asked him directly when he estimated he could take Sarajevo. Whenever he wanted, he replied. 'Then why don't you?' 'I was Russian trained. They teach that, if you are given the chance to kill an enemy or shoot his balls off, always shoot his balls off. That way his own people have to use resources they could be using against you, to care for him. Why should I take Sarajevo when you lot are spending so much effort keeping it alive? As long as you are doing that, you are not chasing after me. We can take any of the safe havens when we want. And we will. Sarajevo will fall to us like a ripe plum when the war is over. It's not worth the hassle for now.'

I said I wondered if it wasn't more to do with their costly failure to take Oatez[2] earlier in the year. But he grunted and said that was irrelevant.

Also there was the Minister for Information, who was even more hardline than the Prime Minister. Nick and I concluded that they desperately want to sue for peace, because they think they have won and want to legitimize their gains. I kept on saying to the Prime Minister that he couldn't have peace for his grandson (whom he told me had been born two weeks ago) unless he gave a proper deal to the Bosnians. The Minister of Information kept on referring to the Bosnians as the Turks. Once or twice he let slip that he thought the best thing was to wipe them out.

But the Prime Minister was more subtle and intelligent – although not a patch on Karadzic. He is desperately concerned about intervention and talked of little else. Would it come? Would Pale be hit? For all their bravado the Serbs are worried about NATO's aircraft. Word is coming through from the talks at Geneva, with the Americans saying that intervention will be necessary. A particularly stupid piece of timing by the United States.

1 A manuscript note in my diary records that this was Ratko Mladic.
2 A Sarajevo suburb. (See 14 December 1992.)

To bed a bit befuddled by wine in the old Jahorina ski resort at about 2 o'clock, having planned to meet the others on the Sarajevo road at 7.00. Light and warm water here this time. I needed no rocking.

Monday, 2 August, Yugoslavia

Downstairs at 6.30 for a bite to eat and a cup of sweet tea without milk, which is all the restaurant had. Another cloudless day. The Jahorina looks beautiful, desolate and lonely. Abandoned ski lifts on all sides. We had arranged to leave at 6.45, but Vladimir was still in bed. In the end we weren't at the checkpoint until about half-past seven.

Halfway down the hill from the checkpoint we stopped at one of the Serb gun positions to view Sarajevo below us. Much more knocked about than a few months ago. Then down the hill to Lukovice, past Butmir and the snipers' positions which command the road here. The old familiar prickling at the back of my neck.

But we got through safely, and at high speed. Then up the narrow valley to Trnovo. Every house burned out. The Serbs explained that the Bosnians had destroyed everything when they had been forced to withdraw. But I knew that Trnovo was a predominantly Muslim community. When we got there, there were a few Serb women in black wandering around. They showed me the freshly dug grave of the local priest and the burned-out orthodox church. According to the locals, the priest had been taken away and tortured for three months. Both of his legs had been broken. Then he'd been shot. They also dug up a woman who had been strangled and a man who, they said, had been beaten to death by the Muslims. But where is the truth in a war like this? Evil deeds are committed on both sides.

We drove further up the valley, to the headquarters of a Serb unit. We had 'breakfast' (Spam) with them. I joked to John Kennedy that Spam was the one thing standard to all armies. But on the principle that you ought to eat when you can, we did. I got talking to a rather impressive young Serb second-lieutenant who could speak a bit of English. The soldiers are well turned-out and have all the signs of a professional army. I suspect the Bosnians are not so well equipped. About half an hour there, then further up the valley, and to the right to get behind Igman. We ran through a series of burned-out villages. I was told they were Serb villages, but I noticed a lot of Muslim graveyards and minarets.

The track, now getting rougher and rougher, soon turned to dirt. Very beautiful high alpine pastures where a number of people, both Serb and Muslim, had had holiday cottages before the war. We stopped at one with an outhouse. Apparently sixteen Serb prisoners had been kept here by the Muslims in a space no more than ten feet by six. The guards tortured them routinely, then shot them and refilled this Balkan Black Hole with more. I couldn't help thinking what happiness there had been here when it was used as a summer house. And, if the stories were true, what memories of terror must now be embedded in its walls.

From this makeshift prison we went up a small mountain track into the woods. Here I was shown three recently excavated graves, those of a priest and two others. I was told how the priest had died. Apparently, he had been taken up there with another Serb. The priest was in too bad a condition to dig his own grave, so the other man had been ordered to dig two. After this the man was ordered back down the hill. On his way down he heard two shots. Subsequently he had taken people back to the grave. They had disinterred the priest about three days ago. We stood for a moment on the site where the priest had been killed, by the grave in which he had lain for several months. In among the pines in the silence, with the birds singing.

Then out on to the road again to a Serb gun position. Three 120 mm howitzers, a few old branches thrown over them in a pathetic attempt at camouflage. Stacked behind the guns were rows and rows of ammunition boxes. The Serbs claimed the guns were simply in reserve. But I doubt it. They were properly prepared for firing. Compression marks behind each gun site told me they had been fired recently and I saw traces of carbon inside the muzzle of one of the guns from fairly recent use – say, in the last two or three days. It was pointed towards Bjelasnica, the highest mountain in the Igman feature, which the Serbs had taken only two days before. These gunners have clearly never experienced counter-battery fire or air attack. Their ammunition was lying immediately behind the gun position and the guns themselves sat like pimples out in the open with no protection. NATO will have a turkey shoot if we ever attack these.

We then dropped down to an observation post, at which the colonel in charge showed me a map of all the gun positions. One of these was near by, so I asked to see it. While there I heard the clatter of a helicopter. One, with clear Serb markings, flew past just below us. So much for the NATO no-fly zone. The Serbs with us panicked, saying that helicopter flights were OK if they had been agreed through Banja Luka. We will check on this later.

Then, having passed two further gun positions, we dropped down into the glorious open bowl of a valley, round the rim of which were five burned-out villages. We stopped in one idyllic spot, where a village had once nestled in a group of trees, surrounded by alpine pastures on which, judging by the churned-up ground, tanks had recently stood. I went to look at some of the burned-out houses. We were told they were Serb, but the graveyard and mosque told a different story. Then we said goodbye to the soldiers who had come with us, and also to a Reuters Viz News man who had come along to interview me, but had decided to stay behind.

The commander told us that this was the only day there had been no mortar rounds coming into the valley. Too soon! Very shortly after we left, a mortar round landed where we had been standing, terribly wounding the Viz News man, taking away one of his kidneys and half his liver.

Then back down the valley to Lukovice and through the Butmir crossing again. The buildings here are now reduced to complete wrecks. But Sarajevo at the moment is remarkably quiet; its inhabitants out on the street, wandering around as though it were an ordinary sunny afternoon. An occasional sniper's round going off and an explosion or two. People simply ignoring them. And they look healthier than last time I was here. The effects of the summer, I suspect. They must be dreading the winter. Barely an intact building or window pane anywhere. And all the trees cut down for firewood.

We booked into the Holiday Inn. My first time there. It has the air of one of those hotels that Hemingway wrote about which was used by journalists and soldiers in the Spanish Civil War. No electricity, uncertain water and limited supplies. But a great atmosphere of camaraderie. No doubt there will be a Hemingwayesque novel written about this in due course. Booked into my room on the fourth floor. There are, of course, no lifts, so we had to carry everything up the stairs, which are referred to here as the 'Sarajevo lifts'. Then off to deliver two of the Wincanton packages, after which to the Presidency to see Ganic.

The last time I met him I thought he was intelligent and sharp. This time he railed at me. He refuses to accept any kind of partition and is living in an impossible world. A good man brought down by the pressures of the siege. We had a rather difficult discussion. Finally remembering I was on his side, he ended by saying, 'We have had a very frank discussion, I just wanted you to know how I feel. But we recognize you as a friend.' Not a good man to be guiding a troubled people at such a difficult time. I wonder if he is in touch with the reality of their ordinary lives here. I suspect they want peace on almost any terms.

Then back with Tony Land [now the resident UNHCR man here] to the Holiday Inn to pick up the litre of whisky I had brought with me, and out to his place in the old Olympic village about 150 metres from the front line.

A typical block of Sarajevo flats. The residents were playing football and sitting on the doorsteps in the sunshine when we arrived. I sat down, opened the bottle of whisky and soon a group of about forty or fifty joined us. We were still there two hours later. As I thought, they want out of Sarajevo. I was particularly struck by the fact that none of the young people want to stay. Even if peace comes, which they desire at any price, they will still leave. They have given up on the city.

One woman got extremely angry, telling me it was all Britain's and France's fault. 'If you will not help us, why do you stop others doing so?' It took me a good half-hour to explain to her that I disagreed with my Government. 'You wouldn't judge every Serb by Slobodan Milosevic – you mustn't judge every Briton by John Major.' Eventually we became quite friendly.

Nick sat surrounded by youngsters, including some young girls who thought he was wonderful. At the end we asked everyone what they would all like most. Most of them said peace, one said a bottle of whisky and the angry woman said a U2 record. Surely she would prefer peace or a bottle of whisky to a U2 record? I asked. But she insisted on the U2 record.

The Sarajevans do not seem to be starved. Indeed, we saw one or two fat people. But morale is terribly low after eighteen months of siege. There are also early signs of sectarian killings and gangsterism in the city. The black market is run by Ukrainian soldiers, the last battalion of which reportedly walked away with 26 million deutchmarks taken from the desperate inhabitants of the city.

A World Health Organization official told me that he was amazed there wasn't typhus and cholera in the city, given the lack of water. He described the Sarajevans as heroes of survival with extraordinary standards of personal and public hygiene. A Sarajevan woman will risk sniper fire to carry water four or five kilometres and up ten floors to wash her baby, he said.

We sat there in the gathering dark, with the faces becoming more and more indistinct, the circle closing in on us listening and questioning more intently as the evening bombardment continued over our heads and tracer lit up the sky.

Wednesday, 15 September, Westminster

PREPARING FOR THE PARTY CONFERENCE

To the gym. I was just going for a sauna but then decided that I would do some exercise and finally did the whole round – 624 metres on the rowing machine. John Smith came in later and pedalled on the exercise bicycle for a bit. At one moment we were on adjacent running machines – John walking with the machine set on a slight hill incline while I was running flat out next to him. He said he was practising for his Munros[1] – what was I practising for? The Olympics?

In the changing room afterwards we both agreed that the Government was in a mess. John believes he may not get OMOV[2] through his own conference, but I don't believe that. They will pull it off at the last moment; they always do.

Thursday, 28 October, Westminster

This morning I drove to the House in the new car I had been lent by Rover for my duties as Lib Dem leader. Past Millbank I pulled out to turn right into the House of Lords. I looked down Whitehall and thought I could only see one motor cycle about 250 yards away with its light burning full. To my horror there was a second motor cycle which I hadn't seen.

As I pulled across the road, he hit me hard, smashing open the wing of the car and sliding 150 yards down the road. I was absolutely horrified. I parked the car and rushed over to him. He turned out to be an Irishman called Cornelius Martin O'Driscoll, or Connie for short. I asked him if he was all right and he said he thought he was. Something wrong with his leg, though. I acknowledged it was my fault, apologized profusely and then waited with him for the ambulance. He asked me to ring the Tate Gallery to tell them he wouldn't be in for work. This I did from my car, but his boss thought it was a wind-up. Apparently, Connie is something of a practical joker and often calls in pretending to be all sorts of people to explain why he's late for work.

1 The 277 Scottish mountains which are over 3,000 feet in height. Smith was on a programme to climb all of them after a heart attack.
2 One Member One Vote. Smith was trying to extend democracy in Labour and weaken the grip of the Union block vote.

By now a passing policeman had arrived. Thoroughly shaken, I walked back to my car having seen O'Driscoll in the ambulance. The press had already heard of the incident and it was becoming a story. Kate saw it on the 9 o'clock news. I rang Jane. The police subsequently took my details and cautioned me, saying that they may have to charge me with driving without due care and attention. I said the fault was clearly mine and gave them a statement.

Spent the morning fending off the press, particularly the tabs, who soon got hold of the idea that this was a 'free car'. I passed the rest of the day in misery at my own stupidity. Everybody very nice, however, with MPs stopping to ask me if I was all right. It's been all over the news. You can't fart without them wanting to know the details. I feel an absolute fool.

Later I rang Connie at home to see how he was. He's been inundated with pressmen and photographers, but he won't speak to them. I told him how to contact me if he needed my help and I promised to do everything I could to push through the insurance as fast as possible, since his work depends on his bike.

Thursday, 4 November, Westminster

At 1.30pm a meeting with John Hume,[1] who is to see the Prime Minister this afternoon. I have never seen a man look so terrible. His eyes are watery, his face lined and his skin has a deathly pallor. He spent most of the time justifying his position. I gently explained that I thought there was no prospect of Hume–Adams,[2] unless he was prepared to give up exclusive ownership of it and allow it to be folded into the Government's own proposals. This could be his Kitty O'Shea.[3] He's clearly under a lot of pressure, including the threat of assassination from the Ulster Volunteer Force, who have declared him public target number 1. He can also feel the

1 Leader of the Social Democratic and Labour Party since 1979. Member of Parliament (SDLP) for Foyle since 1983. John is now a Member of the Northern Ireland Assembly (SDLP) for Foyle.
2 Hume–Adams was an initiative jointly put together by John Hume and Gerry Adams. It ran into the sand, but from it eventually sprang the whole Anglo-Irish peace process.
3 Kitty O'Shea's love affair with the nationalist Leader Charles Stewart Parnell led to a scandal which ultimately ended Parnell's career, divided public opinion and delayed Home Rule.

ground moving under his feet politically and is desperate to be baled out, but refuses to accept the lifelines that are thrown to him. I think he wants to go down in history as the man who forced the Irish and British Prime Ministers to act. I told him to put maximum pressure on the two Prime Ministers to take over the initiative and stake their own political careers on it. I am very worried about him; he looks appalling. I like him, but he is often the architect of his own difficulties.

Tuesday, 9 November, London

State banquet at Buckingham Palace for the King of Malaysia. We swept into the Palace with me sitting in the back of Lisa's[1] two-door Ford Fiesta. When we rolled up, one of the flunkies opened Jane's door on the passenger side while another tried to find the back door to let me out.

In the usual reception line-up, the Duke of Edinburgh boomed to the King, 'This is a jolly good fellow. He was in the Royal Marines.' I had a quick chat with the King who had been briefed that I could speak Malay.

After dinner I was standing talking to the Chief Executive of Westland and his wife when the Duke of Edinburgh came up. He asked me why I had learned Malay. I told him that I had been in the Commando Brigade in Singapore as a bachelor and had discovered that in Malay there was one word which meant 'Let's take off our clothes and tell dirty stories,' so how could I resist? He roared with laughter and followed up with some pretty salty jokes, including a very fruity one about wanting a pee in China. Much giggling.

Then a word with John and Elizabeth Smith. Almost the first thing Smith said to me was that he didn't think it was time for them to put down a motion of no confidence in the Government. They were doing themselves enough damage and didn't need our assistance. He would 'keep his cavalry over the hill' until they were needed.

Wednesday, 24 November, London

To the Diplomatic Reception at Buckingham Palace. I had a word with Owen, who told me that he thought there was a chance for peace in Bosnia

1 Lisa Dorse (now O'Brien), my PA at the time.

before the winter ended. But it would only be temporary. All three sides would use the time to rebuild their forces for a spring offensive. He's looking grey, lined and rather ill. He also thinks we cannot keep the troops there much beyond the spring.

I also talked to Rifkind,[1] who told me that he's not going out until January. Picking up on the Owen line, I said surely our troops could not actually do anything and wouldn't it be difficult to keep them in Bosnia until next year? He got very confidential and said that this was the case. As I suspected, the Government is thinking of withdrawing.

Wednesday, 1 December, London

After the Parliamentary Party Meeting I gathered up my things from the office and dashed home to Methley Street for the Blair dinner. [We had arranged this at the Anthony Lester dinner, over which we agreed to meet after the conference season. I had subsequently written to him at his home and he responded almost immediately suggesting dates around the Budget.]

Blair was very forthcoming. A number of specific points arose from it:

1. He believes there is a desperate need to reformulate the politics of the left and that he and I could prepare the ground for this. In his view, there is no case for a formal process. We ought to assemble a set of *ideas* based on the central one of 'community' and the new contract between the citizen and the state, around which both parties can gather. He is very nervous about setting up any kind of organization that will stimulate the process, because he believes that its existence is bound to come out. He is also nervous of his position inside the Labour Party and kept on saying that he would have to review whether or not there was 'room in the Party for this at the moment'. He wants to start with both of us making parallel sets of speeches which the press and public would come to realize amounted to very similar messages. We could then let things take their natural course.

2. He said that there were difficulties about continuing Labour's internal reform process. The reformers in Labour were not as weak as they appeared

---

1 Malcolm Rifkind, Secretary of State for Defence. Member of Parliament (Conservative) for Edinburgh Pentlands 1974–97.

to be, and for the moment it was quite useful to let the opposition within Labour be lulled into a sense of security by letting it be understood that 'the reform process has ended and the reformers have lost heart'. However, come the New Year, he, Gordon Brown and others will make a series of speeches to push the reform process forward.

3. John Smith is at present hostile to co-operation and more internal reform. Indeed, Blair let me know that he was very hostile, 'but his mind could be changed'.

4. It is clear that Blair and Brown have a very close relationship and that this is the real axis which is driving Labour's reform process. He mentioned other Shadow Cabinet names who are also sympathetic to the process. Amongst these were Michael Meacher, Harriet Harman,[1] Robin Cook, Jack Cunningham and Jack Straw.[2]

5. He thought that the best thing to do was to establish close personal relationships between some of our people on both sides and let things develop from there. Names which are well regarded by them are Charles Kennedy, Ming Campbell, Jim Wallace, Don Foster, Simon Hughes and, possibly, Nick Harvey.

6. Blair himself is rather depressed. I said that I was disconcerted by the lack of any sign of a breakthrough against the Tories – though I was sure it would come. He too thinks that the Tories are on a bounce and that Labour has lost a valuable opportunity. Cherie, rather revealingly, said that he was very low and at one stage we began to discuss what it was like being an eternal opposition politician and the attractions of 'real' life outside. He and Cherie both said it was pretty miserable when there is no prospect of government, which there isn't at the moment.

7. We agreed that the prospect of co-operation would only re-emerge when the Labour Party had come to an understanding that it would not win the next election on its own and this would be unlikely to happen before the autumn or winter of next year. He thought it was a bad thing that the Tories had done so badly last year, as it enabled some, including those at the top in the Labour Party (Jack Straw?) to crawl back into their burrows

---

1 Shadow Chief Secretary to the Treasury. Member of Parliament (Labour) for Peckham since 1982. Harman was a Cabinet member in the first years of the Labour Government.
2 Shadow Home Secretary. Member of Parliament (Labour) for Blackburn since 1979. Straw is now Home Secretary.

and believe that everything would come their way without them having to try too hard or do too much new thinking.

8. The centre of the agenda as far as he is concerned is the formulation of a new contract between the citizen and the state. He is very interested in *Reinventing Government*[1] and in the whole concept of community. He has been much influenced by Clinton on this.

I found Blair engaging, very intelligent and constructive. There is very little difference between his thinking and mine. We have come to the same analysis from different directions. He seems utterly committed to ensuring that the Labour Party does modernize its approach and rethink its ideas, and sees nothing inconsistent between an approach which is based on these lines and socialism in its modern guise. I told him that I, too, was committed to the reshaping of the centre but that I was not interested in Lib/Lab electoral pacts. I was interested in creating a pluralist system of politics, not in preserving the present structure in a new configuration. Blair agreed to go away and talk to Brown and Peter Mandelson. He is suggesting a further dinner at his house in January. Mandelson may come to this and I may think it right to invite someone from our side – probably Charles Kennedy. A useful, friendly and constructive dinner.

Saturday, 11 December, Sarajevo[2]

We landed smoothly at Sarajevo airport. Much better protected than last time. Earth mounds all around to protect people from flying bullets. They say that almost every aircraft that enters has been fired at and a Norwegian aircraft recently came in with a bullet through its wing, almost certainly fired across the runway.

At 1.30pm, a meeting with Izetbegovic. He, of course, pressed heavily for the lifting of the arms embargo. I found the Bosnians much more cocky than last time. They gave up on the international community around May and decided to go it alone, no matter how long it took. They have just won some little victories in Grbavica.[3] When I asked how much territory they

1 *Reinventing Government: How the Entrepreneurial Spirit is Transforming the Public Sector* by David Osborne (1992).
2 By now I had developed what became almost a routine of visiting Bosnia twice a year – once in mid-summer and once around Christmas.
3 A hotly contested suburb of Sarajevo.

had actually gained, they said two buildings. I pointed out that at this rate it would take them a hundred years to recover Sarajevo, but they replied that, nevertheless, time was on their side. People on the streets looking pretty gaunt; wandering about with a permanent impression of tiredness. But the war leaders seem much more confident of their position.

David[1] dropped our kit off at a flat that Bosnian Liberals had fixed for us in the town, the occupants having fled a year ago. By now it was dark. No lights anywhere, and very cold; minus 15°C at night and a heavy covering of snow. The inevitable accompaniment of sniping and machine-gun fire, and from time to time some quite stiff bombardment. Perhaps more active than the last time I was here. We grabbed a quick whisky, washed in cold water, then went down to join the Bosnian Liberals at the Holiday Inn. They had booked a table for members of the Liberal Party and we had a good meal accompanied by some wine they'd found in the cellars, left over from before the war. We offered to pay, but they insisted.

Then back to the hotel, where we spent an hour and a half talking to Nias, one of the young Sarajevan Liberals, and his Serb friend Dragan. We sat talking by candlelight to these two perfectly ordinary Sarajevans, who, despite the siege and the murders, are utterly determined to hang on to their multi-ethnic way of life. In the area where we were staying they get four hours of electricity every four days and gas and water every three days. They fill up baths, basins and every receptacle while the water is on. They don't have any batteries, so no torches.

We wandered around in pitch blackness, occasionally lighting our way with a candle. But even these are scarce. The price of a small box of candles is 5 DM (the common currency in the city), coffee goes for about 100 DM, and wood for about 400 DM a cubic metre. Meat is almost unobtainable. They're living off something like 600 grams of food every fifteen days which is around 60 per cent of what is needed to keep alive. People look very thin, but there are no visible signs of malnutrition.

To bed at about 1.30am absolutely exhausted.

Sunday, 12 December, Sarajevo

To the State Hospital. Things are better than when I last was here. The very impressive Dr Nakas, whom I met last time, is still in charge. He gave

1 David Vigar. At the time my Head of Press.

me a list of medical supplies they need, though at least they now have a reasonable supply of the basics. Their main problem is lack of power. They often have to operate on very serious cases by torchlight. Ten people had been killed the day before, when the Serbs mortared a school in the city. Twenty-seven injured. They're keeping going, however.

I was taken around the wards. As usual, I found it impossible to cope with the sight of young children with amputated legs, and horrible wounds from sniper fire and shrapnel. I spoke to one seven-year-old who had been injured in her thigh by a piece of shrapnel when the Serbs had mortared her school. She had been standing next to the teacher when the mortar fell and cut her teacher in half. We walked back along the street. I carried my flak jacket. I couldn't wear it, as nobody else had one. We called in at the market to see a pathetic number of goods being traded. Scraps of tiny lettuces grown presumably in window boxes around the city, and some potatoes brought in from the small area of land still in Muslim hands outside it. The stalls are empty. But people cheerfully and stoically gathered there, under the lightly falling snow, deliberately ignoring the fact that the market is a favourite target for Serb mortars.

Then to the black market, which was full of gear from UNPROFOR. Someone asked me if I would sell them my flak jacket. The black market is held in an old hall with a concrete roof which has been hit by a mortar. There are many more people here than in the official market outside – buying and selling everything. The product of a city under siege. A lot of stuff from UNHCR, but most of what I could see was from soldiers' ration packs, possibly given away, more likely sold. Sarajevans all believe that the UN soldiers are making huge sums of money at the city's expense.

At 5.30, a two hour phone-in at a local radio station, answering calls from people round the city. Much shelling, so a lot of noises off.

I was closely, and often aggressively, questioned. David Owen is seen as the arch-demon and the British Government comes next. What really frightens me is that these people believe that all this is the result of the eighteenth-century Anglo-French pro-Serb policy in the Balkans. They simply won't believe that the West's sin was carelessness, not conspiracy. But in their position, I suspect, neither would I.

1994

Thursday, 20 January, Westminster

A meeting with Ming on the Bosnian situation. This has been getting worse. Last night the European Parliament voted to get rid of David Owen as the chief peace negotiator. I think he is being scapegoated. The fact that he has failed is not his fault – he has done the best that was possible with the chaotic organization and muddled policies he had to work with. The fault lies with the Western leaders (especially Major) for vacillation, failure to co-ordinate what the military were doing on the ground with what the negotiators were trying to achieve in Geneva, and weakness towards all three Balkan players.

Wednesday, 2 February, London

A 2.00pm meeting with Don Foster. He told me that I was getting a reputation for being rather separate from the Colleagues and too serious and tense. He is probably right. Also, that the national press are saying I am overly pompous. Probably right, too. Pushing too hard again.

At 5.30pm Lisa came and said that she had received a phone call from Tricia Howard asking me to ring her as soon as possible.

Tricia told me that she had been visited that afternoon by somebody from the *Sunday Express* offering a large sum of money to tell her side of the story 'from February 1991 onwards'. The woman who approached her said that she had spent the previous night in Shepton Mallet 'trying to dig up who Paddy Ashdown is seeing now'. I told Tricia that any statement from her would be painful for me, but that I would think about it and call back. Ten minutes later I rang back and said that she must, of course, do what she believed was best for her. I hoped I might assist her in some material way, but I didn't see how I could do that. But I would ponder on it overnight and come back to her with a more substantive answer in the morning.

At home, I told Jane all about it. She is worried, of course. A troubled and turbulent night.

Thursday, 3 February, Westminster

In the morning, a meeting with Andrew Phillips and co. to talk through the latest Tricia situation. Andrew said that Tricia must have full editorial rights for any article she sanctioned, and would need our support. I will just have to sit this one out again, as will poor Jane. I can't stop Tricia earning what money she can out of it. Andrew kindly offered the services of the female solicitor who had given Tricia such support last time.

I called Tricia. We had a long discussion, during which I told her that she must go ahead as she wished. She had behaved impeccably previously and she should not now turn down offers if they were in her interest. She assured me that she would be terribly responsible and delicate. No doubt – but it's not what she says that matters but what the press writes.

I told her of Andrew's offer of the solicitor. She had been offered a considerable sum for her story, but she would ask for more if she was to 'tell the story' before February 1991. She has decided to get as much as she can out of this situation, which fills me with gloom – but she is entirely within her rights.

In the evening, I went with Jane to the Queen's Theatre to see *She Stoops to Conquer*, at the invitation of the actor Donald Sinden. In the taxi on the way to the theatre I told Jane about events on the Tricia front. She was crestfallen, having hoped that we had seen the end of all this. However, we soon cheered up by the time the play started. It was beautifully done.

After the performance, we were taken to Donald Sinden's dressing room. He chatted away, then took us to the Garrick Club. He is a wonderful old man with a splendid deep voice. Smokes like a chimney. We were the last to leave, at 1.00am.

A brief discussion on the Tricia thing before we fell asleep. It is affecting Jane more than I had hoped – and me. Throughout the evening while I was enjoying myself, I would suddenly feel that old sinking sensation in the pit of my stomach.

Friday, 4 February, Sheffield

YORKSHIRE REGION'S PARTY CONFERENCE

Throughout the day I worried about the Tricia article in the *Sunday Express*. A great effort of will to keep going without letting it show. Shades of the General Election all over again.

Halfway through the day the word from London was that the article may be put off until next weekend, but it became apparent in the afternoon that they were pressing ahead for this Sunday.

Although absolutely exhausted I still couldn't sleep from worry. Jane coping extremely well, but I can sense the tension in her.

Saturday, 5 February, Sheffield and London

To the conference centre at Sheffield Hallam University for press interviews. A weaselly, wizened-faced man with a camera was trying to grab shots of me. I immediately put him down for a newspaper photographer and guessed that he was from the *Sunday Express*. So I sent Nick to find out. He confirmed my fears.

I gave my speech to the conference at 10.30. My throat played up terribly, no doubt owing to tension. It wasn't a bad speech, but I didn't make the best of it.

During the day news came through of a terrible bombing in Sarajevo.

After my speech, into a car driven by the local Party Chairman to Beverley for Clare's[1] wedding. Unfortunately the *Sunday Express* photographer found out where we were going and followed.

We arrived at Beverley Minster in good time. The church looked very pretty and the service was good. But I kept on looking round to see if the photographer was about. Afterwards we watched the wedding party leave and Alan and I left through the back door in order to avoid the photographer, who was waiting at the front. My bleeper went off as we wandered down to the pub for a beer. Sarajevo – sixty killed in a mortar attack.

Then to the Memorial Hall, where we had a long wedding breakfast. Clare looked wonderful – her eyes shining and her cheeks flushed.

1 Clare Conway, my ex-PA.

At about 4.30 I was bleeped again by David Vigar.[1] He had had the Tricia article read out to him and it was much better than we could have expected.

We got away as quickly as we could, around 6.00pm. The photographer was waiting outside, but we lost him as we left for London.

Arrived at Methley Street at 9.15pm expecting photographers, but there were none.

David rang me again to say he had got hold of a copy of the *Sunday Express*. He came round with it immediately. The article was very painful, but much better than it could have been. Tricia promised to be delicate and she had been.

After David left, Jane read the article. I couldn't bear to watch while she did this, so went off to ring Kate in France. Kate has received *Beyond Westminster* and thinks it's terrific – which gives me some joy. I go a lot by her judgement. If she finds it fun, then other people will like it, too.

Jane also had a word with Kate, whom I had warned about the *Sunday Express* article. She took it with her usual equanimity.

Then to bed at about 11.15. Still couldn't sleep. Kept myself awake until about 3.00. I noticed that Jane was awake most of the night, too.

Sunday, 6 February, London and East Hendred

Breakfast With Frost in the morning. No photographers outside. Met David Owen in the make-up studios. He was nicer than I have ever known him before.

Frost was very delicate about the *Sunday Express* article, though it was commented on, both in the review of the papers and in my interview. Jane, David and Olly thought the programme went well, but I felt tired and lacking in spark.

Then back to the flat before leaving with Jane for lunch with Roy Jenkins in East Hendred. When we arrived, we found Sir Crispin Tickell[2] and his wife Penelope, a lady called Thea and, of course, Sir Robert Fellowes. Champagne first and then an excellent claret. There was much talk about the Queen and past Prime Ministers, of Wilson and how to deal with him. Roy said that, in his experience as Chancellor, when you went to see Wilson

1 My new press officer.
2 Warden of Green College, Oxford. He was previously a senior member of the British Diplomatic Corps, serving as our Ambassador to the UN.

you had to be prepared to come out drunk two hours later in order to get five things agreed!

Afterwards, we sat in front of the fire and Robert Fellowes, Roy and I talked about hung Parliaments. Fellowes was clearly pumping us so that he would know how to advise the Queen if such a thing happened.

We didn't get away until 5.00pm. By now a beautiful day had turned to rain and wind.

Monday, 7 February, Westminster

PUBLICATION OF *BEYOND WESTMINSTER*

Much of the day spent signing books and giving them out with appropriate letters to journalists, Party members and those who'd helped me on the tour. Very satisfying. I must have got rid of eighty or ninety books.

At about 5.00 the news began to break that Stephen Milligan,[1] the bright young Tory MP for Eastleigh, had been found dead in his flat. The place immediately became alive with wild rumours. Karina Trimmingham[2] came in and said that he'd been found strangled, in a pair of women's stockings.

The Tory Whips put the word around that he had been murdered. But the gutter press are on to the story like vultures and are rushing around spreading scandalous rumours which no doubt they will print.

Tuesday, 8 February, Westminster

At the Leader's Co-ordinating Committee meeting today, we talked through our chances in the Eastleigh by-election. This is now a real prospect for us. If we can pull off a double on 5 May,[3] winning seats from Labour in the metropolitan elections and Eastleigh from the Tories, it will give us a tremendous boost for the June European elections. We mustn't muff it.[4]

1 Member of Parliament (Conservative, for Eastleigh, 1992–4).
2 Previously of the Lib Dem press office, now a member of the Sky TV team in Westminster.
3 The first Thursday in May is always local-election day. It was considered likely also to be the day on which the Eastleigh by-election would be held, although this did not, in fact, take place until 9 June.
4 In the event, we did very well, increasing our number of seats to 1,098 – over 200 more than the Tories (who lost 429 seats and control of over half of their Councils). We were now the second-largest party in local government behind Labour, who also improved their position.

There's a problem now over financial resources, as well as human ones. But Eastleigh must be our first priority.

Political Party finances are always tightest in the mid period of a Parliament when political interest is at its lowest. We are having to be careful again.

Wednesday, 9 February, Westminster

Labour is going to run the next few months as though it were a General Election. I have heard via press contacts that they will target Eastleigh specifically in the hope of stopping us winning. They know how important it is to us.

Thursday, 10 February, Westminster

David Steel and I met at 9.15 and walked down Whitehall in the crisp sunshine to see Douglas Hurd for a briefing on Bosnia. We were ushered into his office, where he gave us a pretty vague and airy talk.

I questioned him about contingency plans for feeding Sarajevo if the West opened hostilities against the Serbs. He had no idea.

I asked him whether they would put mortar-locating radar on the airfield. Again, he had no idea.

We then talked about Srebrenica and the condition of the troops there. That hadn't been thought about.

I said that there was a real danger that the Muslims would use the suppression of Serb heavy weapons and the NATO-policed peace to launch an offensive to regain territory the Serbs had taken from them. They had considered this. The Americans had offered to act as the Bosnian advocates in the peace talks, provided they undertook not to move from their current positions. This at least is a reasonable view.

I concluded during our meeting that Hurd is deeply opposed to the action NATO is taking but that Britain cannot resist a NATO decision without risking severe damage to the Alliance. I concluded that Hurd and Rifkind are opposed but that the Prime Minister has driven them to it. There was deep unhappiness and uncertainty in Hurd's voice and his whole demeanour.

Wednesday, 16 February, Westminster

A chat with Chris Rennard about developments on Eastleigh. Labour will open their campaign by getting Jack Straw to hold a press conference even before the inquest on Milligan's death has finished. Unprecedented.[1] But their intention will be to draw attention to themselves as the challengers by deliberately stirring up a row.

I am feeling very scratchy and bad-tempered. I have two years left to achieve the summation of a whole life's work. If I cannot pull this off in the next couple of years, then the things I know can be achieved won't be. But I already drive people very hard, and there's a limit. I must try to be more relaxed.

The Bosnian situation is slowly clarifying. Britain has been asked for troops. I bet Rose[2] asked some time ago but it's only just come to light. Typical non-response from Douglas Hurd. Fancy turning down the request of a British general. The Serbs will be rubbing their hands.

Friday, 18 February, London

Overnight, the Russians have pulled the irons out of the Bosnian fire by persuading the Serbs to withdraw their guns from around Sarajevo in exchange for the use of four hundred Russian peacekeeping troops. This is a real coup, which plays the Russians into the centre of the game.

Sunday, 6 March, Somerset

Jane and I have been knocked backwards by the fact that Fiona Miller,[3] who came to interview her two months ago for *She* magazine on a cast-iron promise not to raise the events of two years ago, has had her article taken over by her editor, who, Fiona tells us, has slipped in a piece about Tricia Howard and juxtaposed it with Jane saying that she felt people were staring

---

1 It is convention not to start campaigning in a by-election caused by a death until after the funeral.
2 General Sir Michael Rose, Commander of the British troops in Bosnia.
3 A journalist and Alastair Campbell's partner.

at her behind her back. The editor has built a whole press release around Jane's reaction. I am absolutely furious and so is Jane. You can never trust the press.

We rang Andrew Phillips, who said there is probably nothing we can do about it. I spoke to Fiona Miller who, to her credit, has publicly dissociated herself from the article. Jane says that she will never speak to the national press again.

I'm in the blackest depression I can remember for a long time. I really feel like packing it in.

Monday, 7 March, London

At 2.00 I picked up Jane and we drove up to London. As soon as we left, Jane Bonham-Carter[1] rang to say that there'd been stuff in the *Mirror* and in the *Mail*. They'd used the *She* magazine interview in a highly destructive way, misquoting Jane and re-running the whole miserable thing of two years ago. I was very angry and rang David Vigar. He says that only the regional editions of the *Mirror* and the *Mail* had carried the story. Alastair Campbell, bless him, had pulled it from the later editions.

Wednesday, 9 March, Westminster

Polls out today. Labour are doing very well. They were up 9 per cent in the by-elections in January and February, whereas we were only up 3 per cent. Apparently the MORI poll at the weekend will show Labour up 3 per cent and us down – it will also indicate that the public believe Labour can win the election and, for the first time, want them to.

Thursday, 24 March, Westminster

At 5.00pm off to see the Prime Minister. I had gone to talk to him about peerages, which only took a few minutes. But as I got up to leave, he motioned me to stay.

There followed the most extraordinary meeting I have ever had with a

---

1 Director of Press and Broadcasting for the Liberal Democrats.

senior politician from another party. Alex Allan[1] was the only other person there and I could see him out of the corner of my eye shifting from one embarrassed buttock to the other.

On several occasions over the next half-hour I made to finish the conversation but Major insisted I stayed and talked.

He started by telling me he thought Britain was becoming ungovernable. He complained bitterly about the press who, he said, had other scandals they could have unleashed in January, but insisted on covering only those connected with the Government. I was amazed at how blunt he was.

I told him of my fears about the Isle of Dogs.[2] This opened the floodgates. He told me:

1. He was prepared to tolerate a Parliament for Wales, but this was not possible since it would mean the Scots would also have a Parliament, which they would use then to break away from the rest of the UK.

2. He wanted to see the devolution of power away from Westminster as it was the only way to govern the country. ('Parliament simply isn't working and I can't make it work. I hate Prime Minister's Question Time; it is an utterly pointless and futile exercise. We are forced to attack each other. I used to look at Italy and think we in Britain could never become so ungovernable – but now I am not so sure'). I said that if he believed devolution was right, why didn't he do it? He claimed he didn't have the majority for it and the Tory Party was opposed.

3. He complained bitterly about his right wing, who were hamstringing him.

4. On the Scott Report,[3] he claimed he couldn't understand why the nation believed that members of his Government would send innocent men to jail. 'How can they believe this of people like Michael [Heseltine] and me?'

5. There were thirty to forty anti-Europe MPs, backed by a substantial portion of Tory Fleet Street, who would do anything, even bring down the Government, to get rid of him.

1 Principal Private Secretary to the Prime Minister. Allan became the High Commissioner to Australia from 1997 to 1999.
2 There was an impending Council by-election there and there were real fears that the British National Party (BNP) might win it.
3 This enquiry under Lord Justice Scott had looked into the 'Arms to Iraq' scandal. This had come to light as a result of the collapse of a prosecution of two businessmen who had turned out to be working for MI6, but whom the Government appeared ready to allow to go to jail.

He struck me as a man who is near the end of his tether – and who needed someone to talk to. He displayed none of the animosity he shows me in public. He seems in the most profound depths of inner despair.

Friday, 15 April, London-Edinburgh

Off on the 10.55 to Edinburgh for pre-local election campaigning.

Mo Mowlam,[1] who was on the same train, came briefly to sit with me. We spent about thirty minutes talking. She wanted to know whether the recent Andy Grice[2] article was accurate. I said it was an accurate reflection, not of how things were, but how they could be. She's clearly very keen on co-operation. We agreed to meet up after the mid-year elections were over; 'meanwhile, let's keep lines open'. She said that John Smith was essentially a pragmatist and would do whatever was necessary. He didn't have an intellectual commitment to co-operation, but that would come later. At one stage she rather engagingly asked me whether there were any people in the Shadow Cabinet who shared her view and mine. I said, 'Mo, you should be better informed about that than me.'

The Serbs are now attacking Gorazde. Two British soldiers have been wounded – one fatally. It's blowing up again.

Thursday, 21 April, Westminster

I've decided privately that our next move should be to abandon equidistance,[3] accept publicly that we can't support a Tory Government after the next election and then set some very tough conditions for our relationship with Labour. What I now have to do is persuade the Party to adopt this position, to which they are very hostile. I have shared my thoughts with Alan Leaman and a few others.

---

1 Opposition spokesperson for National Heritage. Member of Parliament (Labour) for Redcar since 1987. Mowlam is now a member of the Labour Cabinet.
2 Article in the *Independent* discussing the possibility of the Lib Dems and Labour forming a 'common front', but not a formal pact, before the election.
3 The Party's official policy on relations with the Tories and Labour was known as 'equidistance', i.e. we would maintain an equal distance between ourselves and both of them, and would not favour either party.

Monday, 25 April, London

At 7 o'clock, with Jane to a bash at the American Ambassador's residence in Regent's Park. An extraordinary affair over which he presided with great grace. Three or four hundred people there – all the establishment, including most of the Cabinet and a lot of senior journalists and commentators. I had a long chat with Cathy Ashton.[1] She told me that Blair was thoroughly fed-up. Everybody thought Smith was an awful Leader, and that Labour had real problems which just weren't visible at the moment. Apparently, relations were so bad at one stage that Blair and Brown could not speak to Smith.

We stayed there until about 8.45, when I had booked a taxi. As we were leaving we met Denis and Edna Healey waiting for a taxi outside. We invited them to share ours. Healey was ebullient. They really don't build politicians like that any more. 'Question: What should you look for if you see a pin flying through the air? Answer: John Major with a grenade in his mouth.' Vintage Healey.

Thursday, 28 April, Westminster

David Vigar came in rather white-faced to say that the Yeovil office had faxed through a document which had been left in a phone box in the town. Apparently, one of our supporters had found it and rung the office. Another copy has been sent to the District Council. It shows a picture of a thirteen-year-old boy who, it claimed, was my child and I had failed to provide for the mother! I told David to treat it lightly as nonsense. No doubt, however, it will be all round Yeovil. The Nerds at work again?[2] Politics can be such a dirty business.

---

1 Freelance policy adviser connected with the Labour Party. She now sits on the Labour benches in the House of Lords.
2 See entry for 17 May 1992.

Cartoon published in *The Times* on the day of John Smith's death.

Wednesday, 11 May, Somerset

Arrived home at a few minutes to ten and sat down with a whisky to watch the television news. Smith on, going to address some meeting in London. He emerged holding hands with his wife, Elizabeth, and looking absolutely terrific. I turned to Jane and said that for the first time he looked like a potential Prime Minister.

To bed at around midnight.

Thursday, 12 May, Somerset-London

On our way to London in the morning Jane and I stopped off at a garage for petrol. When I got back in the car I made a call to London. Becky[1] said, 'Have you heard the news? John Smith is dead.'

We were polaxed and drove on numbly and silently.

We were due to visit a school in Richmond and I said we should carry on. But at the school I just went round in a daze.

Then David rang to say that Westminster was going mad and I ought to get back. Apparently the Speaker is going to suspend the House this afternoon.

In the chamber at 2.30pm. Betty announced that we would replace the day's business with an adjournment debate for tributes to John. Everyone looking very sombre and there were one or two red eyes on the Labour benches.

Back into the chamber at 3.30. Blair went first. He was very good. Then Margaret Beckett, who was exceptional. Then me. I only spoke for three or four minutes. Before going down, I had read Jo Grimond's tribute to Hugh Gaitskell on his death in 1963. I could have re-read the first three paragraphs of Jo's speech word for word. At 4.15 the House adjourned.

Dinner with senior journalists and political observers in the evening. We discussed Smith's successor, in the usual ghoulish Westminster way. The overwhelming view is that it will be Blair.

It's extraordinary how an event like this suddenly changes everything: the Prime Minister's position is strengthened; Heseltine's is weakened; and the Labour Party has a real problem to solve. We will know, from whom they elect to replace John, if they are serious about implementing the changes necessary to make them electable.

I fear that media attention after the June elections will be on who will be the Leader of the Labour Party rather than on us. I will have to re-think our position again, right from the beginning.

Caught a taxi home to watch *Newsnight*. John Prescott and Gordon Brown on. I'm damned if I'd have gone on television on a day like this. Prescott clearly positioning himself. Everybody else has steered off the subject, except Healey, who has of course blundered in with size-ten boots and become the subject of some criticism. I penned a private note to Blair, saying that I hoped he would stand. 'You are mad if you don't, and the Labour Party is mad if they don't elect you.'

To bed about midnight.

1 Becky Vye, my PA.

Sunday, 15 May, London

A beautiful sunny day, which clouded over in the late afternoon. We had a wonderful walk in the park, with the dog running at full tilt after his ball. Stopped off for a beer at the Prince of Wales, near Methley Street. On the way back we spotted Dick Newby at Roger Liddle's house near by. Dick came out to talk to us and, subsequently, so did Roger and his wife, Caroline. Roger believes Blair will split the Labour Party. And Dick feels he will make it much more difficult for us.

I think Dick's right. But I still can't decide how Blair will turn out. He's an absolute shoe-in for the leadership. The press is going flat out for him and the opinion polls put him well ahead of the others. He has one disadvantage for us, and two advantages. The disadvantage is that he'll steal our clothes and appeal to our voters. The first advantage is that he will lower the 'unpopularity threshold' by making Labour less frightening to potential Lib Dem voters who flood to the Tories for fear of Labour in the last few days before every election. The second is that he's very interested in co-operation. But all remains to be seen.

Friday, 20 May, Edinburgh

JOHN SMITH'S FUNERAL

I stayed the night with Ming and his wife Elspeth in their Edinburgh house, where David Steel joined us before setting off for the funeral. A cold May wind under a grey sky.

The area outside the church was crowded with television crews and there were about 200 people who couldn't get in.

Ming, Elspeth, David and I sat together four rows back, with the Prime Minister, Edward Heath, Malcolm Rifkind and Ian Lang. Then a small gap and Ian Paisley.[1] Behind, members of the Labour Party and friends and to the right the press and more Labour MPs.

It was a dignified and moving service. Donald Dewar spoke exceptionally

---

1 Revd Ian Paisley, Leader of the Democratic Unionist Party. Member of Parliament (Democratic Unionist) for North Antrim since June 1970. Member of the European Parliament (Democratic Unionist) for Northern Ireland since 1979. Member of the Northern Ireland Assembly since 1998.

well, as did one of Smith's other close friends. A soloist sang 'The Lord is my Shepherd' in Gaelic. A beautiful, haunting tune which evoked with ineffable sadness the desolate, windswept landscape of the Western Isles.

Then a reception in the old Parliament building. Had a chat with the beautiful Smith daughters, who seem amazingly composed. Elizabeth, too, was full of dignity. I only stayed half an hour, then went to catch the 2.40 shuttle to London.

On the way up to Scotland yesterday, I had a long chat with Robin Cook, whom I found leaning at the bar at Heathrow waiting for the plane. He told me that he had lost John Smith last week, followed by his father-in-law this week and preceded by his father earlier in the year. He was 'fed up with politics' and felt like packing it all in. I asked him about the leadership campaign. He said, 'They have written some very nice things about me in the press. But apparently I am too ugly to be the next Labour Leader!'

Saturday, 4 June, Portsmouth

D-DAY FIFTIETH ANNIVERSARY DINNER

Showered and changed into my dinner jacket, then off to Portsmouth Guildhall.

We were all led to an anteroom. When I arrived, Montgomery's son was there, Admiral Ramsey's son, and Thatcher. I had a brief conversation with her. Later Jim Callaghan and the whole caboodle arrived, including the Prime Minister, who looked grey, and Norma, who looked lost. Also Bill and Hillary Clinton.

Clinton was rather unprepossessing – doubtless tired. Grey hair and a blotchy, over-fleshed face. Difficult to imagine he is the most powerful man in the world. Hillary looked much more the part, though perhaps she had somewhat overdone it. Her hair over-lacquered, her dress over-shiny and her facial expression over-satisfied.

I had a chat with Clinton. He didn't impress in conversation any more than in appearance. But he did know that we had done well recently and congratulated me on our successes. Clearly well briefed.

Then into dinner. We sat at one of the top tables just beside the Queen, to whose right sat Mitterrand[1] looking pale, cadaverous and foxy. His eyes

---

1 François Mitterrand, President of the French Republic.

had narrowed to slits and his mind seemed a million miles away. Behind him his interpreter whispered in his ear, like a plotter at the court of Cesare Borgia. He affected to pay no attention, his face remaining impassive, but his eyes roved ceaselessly around the room, as though he was disdainful of the company but totally at ease with himself.

On the Queen's left was Clinton, looking even more blotchy under the television lights. They had a brief, animated conversation, but I was struck by how much time he spent looking rather lost. Hillary, two down, was next to Major. She obviously became bored by him and started to talk to the man on her right, whom I didn't recognize.

I sat on a table with some D-Day veterans. To my right, a Major Rathbone. He had been a signaller at Pegasus bridge. On my left, an American called Jack Campbell who, with his skipper sitting opposite him, had taken one of the US Coastguard cutters from Poole over to Juno Beach. A nice man who got slightly tipsy and kept on asking me why I couldn't be President instead of Clinton.

Opposite him at the table was an X-craft captain who had taken his midget submarine in two days before D-Day and had spent more than sixty hours submerged because of the postponement of the operation. On D-Day he'd stuck up his beacons for the first wave to use as transit points into the beach, and then surfaced after they had passed, for a grandstand view of the whole thing.

The Queen made an excellent speech. The whole event was rather moving, although let down slightly by the tatty atmosphere of the Guildhall dining room.

Thursday, 9 June, Somerset

EUROPEAN ELECTIONS; BY-ELECTIONS AT NEWHAM NORTH-EAST AND EASTLEIGH

To vote at 8.00 at Norton village hall, accompanied by Luke and lots of cameras.

Having toured committee rooms throughout the constituency during the day, Jane and I finally got back home at 10.00pm, absolutely shattered. We had a glass of beer and waited for the results to start coming through. Labour doing very well. We lost our deposit at Newham North-East.[1]

1 A by-election called due to the death of the incumbent Labour MP, Ronald Leighton. Our candidate, Alex Kellaway, defected to Labour on the eve of the election.

The Eastleigh result came through at about 2.15am. A 9,000 majority for David Chidgey.[1] But Labour came second, beating the Tories by 2,000. This takes the gilt off the gingerbread. There was much BBC comment about Labour's strength holding up in the south – from the very same commentators who had said at the start of the campaign that Labour must win this seat in order to prove that they could win in the south.

The press are in a frenzy of excitement over Blair. Although, of course, what they puff up they will subsequently pull down.

To bed at about 3.00am.

Sunday, 12 June, Somerset

ANNOUNCEMENT OF THE EUROPEAN ELECTIONS RESULTS

The papers are having a full-scale love affair with Blair. I did *Breakfast With Frost* down the line from the cottage. It seemed to go quite well. Watched Blair's interview. He started off terribly defensively – body language all wrong. Good on general stuff, but bad on specifics.

Spoke to Richard Holme, who came up with the nice thought that Blair was the Prince Charming who was supposed to kiss Britain awake again.

The first European result to come in was Sheffield, which showed Labour doing rather badly. Winning, of course, but a substantial rise in our vote. Our spirits lifted, but they needn't have done. From then on we had a series of near misses, usually by less than 5–6,000.

Labour's vote up right across the country, sweeping out the Tories and holding up too high for us to win the seats we had targeted in the south. The joy of the night was winning Somerset for Graham Watson. Our first ever European seat.

Then we heard that Robin Teverson had won Cornwall. Some further consolation.

On the wretched David Dimbleby results programme, which was, as usual, heavily weighted against us. Charles Kennedy got very touchy with Peter Kellner and Peter Snow. Snow brought back the bloody swingometer, which even denies our existence!

The Tories got away by the skin of their teeth in the south as a result of a rise in the Labour vote. We made that point, but it didn't make much impression and probably sounded rather defensive.

---

1 Our candidate at Eastleigh. He has held the seat ever since.

In the end we left, quietly satisfied by the two seats in the South West but disappointed by our narrow failures. We've had some great election nights – but this wasn't one of them.

Wednesday, 15 June, Westminster

A long discussion at the Parliamentary Party Meeting today on the Euro elections. My brain was too tired for me to chair it properly, so I became a bit crotchety. The Colleagues were nervous and I didn't deal with them very gently.

There is strong resistance to an immediate reshuffle. The natural reaction of exhausted people after an election. I will have to accommodate this, though I must try and press the reshuffle through before the start of the recess. But at least they have accepted my analysis that we still have a lot of work to do to get ourselves back into the action.

In the evening, a diplomatic dinner at the Foreign Office. As Jane and I were walking across from the House to the Foreign Office, I saw somebody I thought I recognized standing opposite me at the zebra crossing. It looked just like John Major. It *was* Major! Accompanied by two heavies, but otherwise strolling up Parliament Street in a very unconcerned and inconspicuous way. Just the kind of thing Prime Ministers should do more of. As we crossed the road I said to him, 'Better not stay in the middle of the road too long. That's how you get run over.'

Hurd's speech at the dinner was spine-chilling. He painted a very gloomy picture of what was happening in North Korea[1] and a gloomier one still of Bosnia.

Afterwards I went to speak to Lynda Chalker,[2] who confirmed that Hurd is indeed very depressed. He finished his speech referring to 'the cloudless blue summer days before 1914'. He is normally a great underestimator of threat and drama, so this from him is powerful stuff. He actually said that if there wasn't peace in Bosnia the war would probably spread to the rest of the region. At last he sees the danger of which we have been trying to warn him for the last two years.

1 A deadlock had been reached at talks between the USA and North Korea at a conference to discuss denuclearization.
2 Lady Chalker, Minister of State at the Foreign and Commonwealth Office. Conservative peer since 1992.

Friday, 1 July, Westminster

Peter Riddell has written a glowing piece in *The Times* about Tony Blair's speech yesterday on economics, which largely borrows phrases and ideas I was using five or six years ago. Very galling that when Blair repeats them now he is hailed as a brilliant new thinker in British politics!

Thursday, 14 July, Westminster

Malcolm Bruce and I walked across in the sunlight to John Smith's memorial service in Westminster Abbey. A beautiful day. Quite a moderate crowd outside as we went in, which had swollen to about a thousand when we came out. The Abbey itself was completely full.

At the back, rows and rows of solid Labour faces from local parties up and down the country. It suddenly occurred to me that many of them were there not just to mourn John Smith, but also the passing of the old Labour Party, of which John was almost the last bastion. Plain, trusting faces, most of them. But unsmiling at me. Sitting opposite me during the service were Elizabeth Smith and the three girls. Elizabeth dignified and grim. The girls, however, are stunning. Somehow out of place in this sombre and ordinary group – like fashion models who had suddenly emerged from a catwalk into a Presbyterian convention.

It is extraordinary how his death has affected us all. Ming told me that he felt really low because two of his best friends had gone: David Steel was leaving politics and John Smith ('I am still grieving for John,' he said) was dead.

Friday, 15 July, London

A lunchtime beer with Jane. We sat out on the square and were just about to return home when I saw a familiar figure walking across Cleaver Square – Peter Mandelson.[1]

I shouted to him and he came over and chatted for a few minutes. Very pleasant, considering what he used to write about me in the *Sunday People*.

1 At the time, Labour Party Whip. Member of Parliament (Labour) for Hartlepool since 1992.

Richard Holme later told me that Blair rings him about twenty times a day and will hardly move an inch without seeking Mandelson's advice. But this is hidden carefully from the Labour Party, since many – especially Straw – dislike Mandelson.

Mandelson told me he was getting fed up and wanted a spokesmanship. He stood chatting there with a bottle of wine under his arm and then wandered off to Roger Liddle's house to 'go and have my tea'. I was struck by the jarring and rather affected use of the working-class term.

Thursday, 21 July, Westminster

Blair elected leader of the Labour Party today. I wrote congratulating him on his election, saying that this was an excellent thing for Labour and for our plans. I suggested that we meet when the dust had settled – after his holiday, but before the House returned.

Friday, 22 July, Westminster

Blair's 'coronation' went well yesterday, though I thought his speech depended too much on easy rhetoric. On the way to work I bought a *Guardian* and an *Independent*. Full of paeans of praise for him. He has a lot to live up to.

A real problem is developing on our forthcoming Sarajevo trip. The Foreign Office are being very helpful. But the Serbs are shooting explosive rounds at aircraft flying in and hit one yesterday. I am beginning to wonder if we will get in.

Thursday, 28 July, London–Frankfurt–Zagreb

Up at 5.30am and off at 6.00, leaving Jane asleep.

Arrived at Heathrow at 11 o'clock. Fifty minutes in Frankfurt, then to Zagreb. But Sallyann's[1] bags have been left behind in Frankfurt. She was very calm about it. We were picked up at the airport by an Embassy car and taken to the Intercontinental Hotel.

---

1 Sallyann Marron, my PA who accompanied me on this trip.

Dinner with the Ambassador, Gavin Hewett. A typical Foreign Office man. Lean, chinless with a drawling voice. Also at dinner were the Croatian Deputy Foreign Minister, Sergio De Mello,[1] and the American Ambassador. The morale of my fellow dinner guests was very low indeed. They think the Contact Group[2] have made a complete mess of it and the Serbs will inevitably resume fighting both with the Bosnian Muslims and eventually with the Croats. All our worst fears confirmed.

Friday, 29 July, Zagreb and Sarajevo

The Embassy have managed to get me on the UNPROFOR flight to Sarajevo. Beautiful weather. Thunderstorms last night, but rain-washed today.

Sallyann and I were equipped with flak jackets, then we piled on to the RAF Hercules. Much talk of being shot at from a colonel in Rose's bodyguard, who told us blood-curdling stories about aircraft being hit coming into Sarajevo. Distinctly unhelpful – especially for Sallyann on her first military flight. As I felt the aircraft turn over Split and begin to descend towards Sarajevo I got Sallyann to put on her flak jacket. Everybody else followed suit. The landing in Sarajevo was a bit bumpy but otherwise uneventful.

A beautiful cloudless day in Sarajevo. Only occasional sniper fire and one or two rocket-propelled grenades (RPGs). By Sarajevan standards, peaceful. Robert Barnett, the British Ambassador, picked us up and took us into the city. I have never seen Sarajevo so calm. Droves of people wandering around the streets; like Taunton with shattered buildings. A strong sense of foreboding, though. Everybody stockpiling food and market prices going up. The Serbs are refusing to let anything through.

We went off to UNHCR headquarters. A new man there who is totally useless. He has allowed the warehouses to run out of flour and the bakery now has only two or three days' supply left.

Lunch at an old inn down in the Muslim quarter. A beautiful place. Cobbled courtyards and heavy oak beams, built in the early 1700s.

1 UNHCR Special Envoy and a much-respected figure.
2 The Contact Group of the former Yugoslavia is made up of representatives from six nations (United States, Russia, France, Germany, Britain and Italy). They meet to discuss the problems encountered by the nations of the former Yugoslavia.

We had a huge Bosnian lunch, with vast amounts of meat, as usual. Poor Sallyann, who is vegetarian, referred to it afterwards as 'Flintstone stew'. With us was a man called Fred Price, an impressive Royal Naval lieutenant commander from Rose's staff. He thinks there is nothing we can do now to stop the Serbs. Any actions that the Contact Group recommend are militarily impractical. They cannot enforce the exclusion zones, or widen them, without producing a near-disaster for UNPROFOR.

There is much talk of withdrawal. But Price believes (as do others) that this is also impractical. UN troops wouldn't get two miles down the road before they had all the citizens of Sarajevo out in the streets blocking their exits and, if necessary, shooting at them. The UN has become a hostage in its own operation. Most people on the ground believe that the best option now is to 'muddle through'. Not much faith in what the Contact Group will come up with. It is evident that there is little or no political liaison with the military here. What a disastrous situation.

Then back to the Embassy, where I met the press. Martin Bell turned up, saying he had just come over Igman and wanted to go back the same way on Monday. But it all depended on whether they closed the checkpoints. If so, Sarajevo would be plunged into chaos again. Martin took quite a risk coming over Igman. The hairs stood up on the back of his neck when he rounded the final hairpin in the sights of the Z88 anti-aircraft guns which had killed a British soldier here two days ago. But he is going back out in two days – would I like to come with him? I said yes.

The press then departed. I sat out on the hotel balcony contemplating the relatively peaceful city laid out below me in the sunlight. How long would this last before something worse happened?

Only occasional sniper fire today, mostly over from Grbavica. One or two fiercer exchanges, as usual, as dusk fell. Two people shot on the trams running along 'Murder Mile' today. Both badly wounded. Ordinary passengers out shopping. A quiet day in Sarajevo.

Saturday, 30 July, Sarajevo

Perfect blue skies. Sarajevo at its best – cool and dry. Breakfast, then to the Embassy, where I sat around trying to make my modem work so as to pick up my e-mail.

Robert Barnett came back. He had been to see UNPROFOR. Rose is out of town. Robert is desperately trying to persuade me not to go over Igman with Martin Bell. He offered to take me down to Kisseljak,[1] where I could wait for Martin. Robert told me London would make his life impossible if something happened to me. I said it would probably spoil my afternoon, too. But the Embassy have been good to me and I mustn't make life even more difficult for them. So I agreed to go with him.

At about 11.00am word started coming through of bad news from Geneva. The Serbs have made a declaration which is being taken as a 'No'. Robert is very gloomy. He thinks they will shut off all the checkpoints and start shelling the city again very soon.

Sunday, 31 July, Sarajevo

A meeting with Haris Silajdzic, the Bosnian Prime Minister, in the Majestic restaurant, close to the Presidency. When we arrived, the place was surrounded by sinister people with submachine guns.

The meeting got off to a sticky start, but he soon warmed up.

He is an extraordinarily driven man. A young, agile face with great strength in it. We took to each other, chiefly because he spoke bluntly to me and I spoke bluntly back. At one stage he got himself into a 'looped tape' about how awful the British Government was. I said, 'Look, Prime Minister, there is no point in your saying rude things about the British Government, because they won't be ruder than anything I have said already.'

Robert got restive at 10 o'clock, saying we had to move because he was worried about keeping the Prime Minister up, etc. But Silajdzic interrupted, saying he was enjoying himself and wanted to continue.

So we did for another half hour. Silajdzic was fascinating on Izetbegovic and admitted the possibility of a link between the Bosnian Serbs and Serbia proper. He said that the Bosnians' attachment to the arms embargo was symbolic rather than substantive, but 'Please do not press me too far on this. There is a diplomat present [Robert], who will pass my words on to his government.' I found him likeable and impressive. A potential leader of a new Bosnia.

---

1 A Bosnian town outside the Serb siege.

Monday, 1 August, Sarajevo

Off to see General Rose. I was quite shocked by him. I expected somebody cool, calm and intellectual, but I found him very defensive. The gap between him and the Contact Group is, as others have said, very wide and very dangerous.

He said quite openly that the Contact Group could suggest what they liked in Geneva, but if he couldn't carry it out on the ground he wouldn't even try. 'They can pull me out of here anytime and put somebody else in.' He kept saying that he was regarded as pro-Serb, which he wasn't, and as going soft on peacekeeping, which he also wasn't. He said at one stage that he had had the initiative and lost it because of the political shenanigans. He now intends to take it back.

I concluded that, though he is a man much loved by his troops, he is not, in these circumstances, the right person to be in charge of a situation as difficult, dangerous and delicate as Sarajevo.

I wrestled with my conscience afterwards but finally decided that I must see Douglas Hurd about him.[1] Having such a man in charge at Sarajevo, in such a mood, is not a good idea.

Wednesday, 3 August, London

Bill Rodgers has written a rather stupid piece in *The Times* which criticizes me and says Blair is wonderful. I wrote him a very angry letter. In the end I didn't send it, but it made me feel better.

Tom McNally, however, wrote a splendid response in the *Guardian*. What Bill and Shirley have done is give Blair yet another boost, as well as ensuring that the issue will be discussed in detail at the Autumn Conference and that the Party will be split, or appear split. The papers are already running 'Row within the Lib Dems'. What Bill and Co. don't seem to realize is that we all want the same end, but that I must be given room for manoeuvre.

My unsent letter ended up, 'There's not much point in splitting the Party – surely you have split enough of them already?'

At 11 o'clock I did a press briefing on the Bosnia trip, at the end of which a journalist asked me, 'What do you think of the "Gang of Four" now supporting Tony Blair?' I reacted in what I thought was a (carefully

1 Which I did on my return.

rehearsed) jokey manner, but the press, of course, reported the following day that I was getting rattled. Probably right, too.

Monday, 8 August, Somerset

Richard Holme arrived at Vane Cottage at 3.00. We set off over the hills shortly afterwards. We talked chiefly about our General Election plans. I started off by saying that I had been very depressed. I seem to have completely lost direction. I have been building the Party to fill a certain gap in politics, which I know is there and which would give us real electoral appeal. But then along comes Blair with all the power of Labour behind him, and fills exactly the space I have been aiming at for the last seven years!

I was seriously wondering whether I wanted to continue in this job; whether I had the energy and the ideas; and whether I was the right person to take the party forward. He said that of all the leaders he had known, I was the one who he really felt could get us somewhere. Kind flattery, of course. But it cheered me up for a couple of days.

He tried to persuade me to make the break from equidistance now. But all my instincts are against this, since I think it's still too early. It will look like a panic move, responding to Blair, without knowing what he will do. I would much prefer to prepare the ground with the Party in September and move in the spring.

I also received a letter from Tom McNally today:

Dear Paddy,

I hope the trip to Bosnia went well. It really does seem to be crunch point now. Whether the West has the balls to do the crunching we will have to see.

As Jane will have told you, I was asked to pass on a message to you by a mutual friend [Blair]. In essence the message was:

> *Thank you for your personal note, which was much appreciated. I hope you have noted that I have not attacked you or the Liberal Democrats in recent months. I have emphasized that opposition to the Tories comes from a broad spectrum of opinion on the centre-left of British politics. Both the lack of attack and the loose definition (i.e. not single party) of the opposition were made with you very much in mind. I hope we have the opportunity for a quiet word once we are back from our respective holidays.*

Make sure you have a good rest . . .

Love to Jane . . .

Wednesday, 24 August, Irancy

ON HOLIDAY

In the evening, a quiet dinner with Jane. At about 8.00pm Cherie Blair rang (I think from the South of France) asking us to dinner when we got back. She said that Tony thought it would be useful for us to meet privately before the Conferences. We will go back by an earlier ferry on Sunday so that we can do this on 4 September.

Jane rang Cherie back a couple of hours later. Blair had strained his back and was in bed. Sunday is difficult for them, but they are keen, so she is going to discuss it with him and call back later. The whole negotiation was conducted between Cherie and Jane.

Can we lead our parties into what needs to be done? Is it possible at all?

Thursday, 25 August, Irancy

Cherie rang during the morning. We fixed to go round to their house the evening we got back. Tony, she said, believes we must meet as early as possible. I had anticipated that he would leave it until after the Conferences, but it sounds as if he has something specific to propose. I am enthusiastic. The key will be to make sure I have sufficient room for manoeuvre and also the time to carry the Party with me.

Sunday, 28 August, Irancy

There is a village picnic today. It started raining in the morning, quite heavily at first. But it slackened off a bit by lunchtime and became a glorious afternoon.

We all went to the field next door to the cemetery, which everyone refers to as 'Hyde Park' (pronounced ' 'Ide Parke'). Quite a turnout. René and Jacqueline Charriat[1] came to sit at our table, where we had a little contingent of English, including frequent visitors to Irancy, Jill Chapman and her husband.

---

1 French friends who are *vignerons*.

Jill got delightfully merry, as did most of the rest of us, and insisted on standing up at the table and singing 'God Save the Queen' in a very loud but tuneless voice, to our mortification. The French retaliated with several increasingly imaginative renderings of 'La Marseillaise', accompanied by a lot of hand waving and some pretend playing of musical instruments, which suddenly coalesced at one table into a mock military band marching up and down.

We finished the picnic at about 4.00 and rolled back down the hill to the village to the accompaniment of the tattered remnants of various national anthems. Entering the village meant passing René Charriat's *cave*, which we obviously couldn't do without dropping in for another *coup-de-rouge*,[1] followed by some of the family *bru-de-noix*[2] and the local eau-de-vie. We stood out on René's front patio and people passing by on their Sunday afternoon walks came in to join us until there were twenty or so people there, drinking and laughing.

Soon Jill came by to collect her bicycle, which, she claimed, she had left there earlier in the day. She accepted the obligatory invitation to a glass of wine from René. After half an hour or so, she announced unsteadily that she must go as her husband was waiting for her. She then made four attempts to get on her bicycle – all unsuccessful. Eventually she gave up the unequal struggle with equilibrium and, using the bicycle as a prop, retreated down the main street in an extremely unsteady manner.

We left at about 5.00. Jane and I had a snooze before meeting up again with the others at the village bar. We stayed until around midnight.

A typical Irancy day – over-indulgence and joy in equal measures.

Sunday, 4 September, London

We arrived at the Blairs' house in Islington at 8 o'clock.

Tony was dressed in jeans and appeared very relaxed, as was Cherie. We had some sparkling wine to start with, then a bottle of white and a very good claret. We also met the boys, Euan and Nicky. Kathryn was upstairs, but we didn't see her. The house is very elegant; he has collected some fine paintings ('Derry Irvine is my art consultant').

1 Glass of red wine.
2 *Bru-de-noix* is a highly potent but delicious Burgundian liqueur made from walnuts immersed in eau-de-vie.

We got down to serious discussions early. He confirmed that he wanted to create the impression that we could work together in government. He was determined to change the Labour Party, its policy and its image, in order to make it electable again, although this was the most difficult bit. He hadn't discussed our relationship with Jonathan Powell[1] or anybody else, other than Anji[2] in his office. We agreed that Anji and Jo[3] should get together. He also said that he would discuss the whole project with Jonathan.

Blair's main reason for seeking co-operation was that he didn't want to waste talent. We should get the sensible people in his Party together with the sensible people in ours. 'You have to understand that I am not playing a tactical manoeuvre on you. You can trust me on this.' I said I believed him and this was what I wanted, too. 'Your task is to make the Labour Party electable and also accept that we have the right to exist. My task is to persuade the Lib Dems to accept co-operative politics.'

He said that many in his Party wanted to destroy the Liberal Democrats, but that he thought this silly. We should change the culture of politics so we could work together. He thinks Major is done for, but is determined to plan for the worst case, i.e., that both the Tory Party and Major will recover – even though he thinks it unlikely.

He said that he was 'not persuaded' of the advantages of PR. I made it very clear that, for us, this would be a 'road block to progress'. We would accept a referendum on PR, but we were not prepared to find ourselves in a position in which, in such a referendum, the Labour Leader was campaigning against change. He said, 'I have been as generous on this as I can be, at the moment. But let's see where we go in the future.' I did no more than mark this as the chief area of difficulty between us.

He is determined to stick to Europe and will make a pro-European speech at his Conference: 'It is one of those issues on which you have to mark your line, then stick to it through thick and thin.'

He is also going to make internal changes to the Labour Party, including streamlining the policymaking procedures. He suggested that the next step might be for us to get some of our spokesmen together – he thought Charles Kennedy and Ming Campbell, in particular, were good.

He wanted to do this directly after the Conference, but I thought this

---

1 Tony Blair's Chief of Staff.
2 Anji Hunter, Tony Blair's special assistant.
3 Jo Phillips, the new Head of Press in my office.

was too early. The project for both of us at our respective Conferences should be to move our parties forward, not push them so far that they revolted. He had a big job to do, and so had I. I said, 'You have a more difficult task, but I have more to lose.'

We agreed:

1. There was nothing we could do to stop our parties fighting each other where they had traditionally done so, but that there was everything to gain from the people at the centre working together as co-operatively as possible on issues that they agreed on.

2. That we (the Lib Dems) had to concentrate on our identity. Otherwise we wouldn't exist. But that would be difficult for him, he said, if I played the line that we were the 'third party insurance' for change with safety, as this would work against making the Labour Party electable (which was in our interest, too, since if their 'unpopularity threshold' was lowered, there would be much more tactical voting against the Tories).

3. That our offices would work closely together, especially on PMQs.

4. That I would send him a copy of the pamphlet I was writing,[1] and also a copy of my Conference speech shortly before I gave it, so that he could react appropriately. He, in return, would send me copies of a leaflet he was doing on strategy and his speech.

We got on well together (as did Cherie and Jane), although there is still a certain wary distance between us. He thinks he can carry the Shadow Cabinet with him. He is also well aware that his present popularity levels won't hold up.

At the end of the dinner (which finished at about 10.30), I said that the SDP had unlocked one wave of hope, his election as Leader of the Labour Party had unlocked a second and that, if we could pull this off at the beginning of 1996 (a year before the election), we would unleash a third and decisive wave which would sweep the Tories away.

I said that our aim must be to keep the Tories out for the ten years or so it would take to modernize Britain.

Blair has a slightly disconcerting habit of sometimes not looking at you while he is speaking, as if his mind works better without eye contact. But

1 'Making Change Our Ally', a pamphlet about the challenges facing Britain in the run-up to the end of the century.

it's not offensive, nor does it appear that he is avoiding you. The impression given is one of thoughtfulness.

At one stage I asked him about the minimum wage. He said that they would hold to the policy but wouldn't put a figure on it.

At the end, he said: 'We ought to keep in touch on issues like Bosnia as well.'

I noticed, as we came to leave at around 11 o'clock, that they both hung back from the door, saying goodbye to us in the hallway and leaving us to go out alone.

They must have agreed it beforehand, so as to avoid any possibility of our being photographed together.

It was a good evening. Jane and I agreed in the taxi on the way back that it could even prove a historic one.

Monday, 5 September, Westminster

After our regular morning meeting I kept back Tom McNally, Alan Leaman, Nick South and Richard Holme whom, together with Jo Phillips, I decided to call the 'Jo Group'.[1] I told them about the previous night and asked them to be prepared to advise me on the developing relationship.

Sunday, 11 September, East Hendred

To Roy Jenkins', arriving at 12.40. We went into his study, as usual, and had a glass of champagne sitting in front of his fire. He has been ill, but looks much better now.

I told him about Blair and asked his advice. We agreed that following their nice words about Blair it would now be very inappropriate for the Gang of Three to start rushing around declaring their loyalty to me at the Conference. He also promised to put pressure on Blair, whom he will see again soon, on the question of PR. I told him that this was the one area on which Blair had to be moved. It was our only guarantee that pluralism would last beyond the election of a Labour Government.

---

1 Later I was to add people to this committee until it numbered about ten. The 'Jo Group' became the key steering group who advised me and planned and controlled all our relations with Labour on the 'project'.

Monday, 12 September, London

At 7 o'clock, with Jo to Rupert Murdoch's cocktail party. What a gathering! And what a flat! All brightly coloured walls, chromium-plated knobs and rather garish modern pictures. There was a lady harpist in the foyer as we came in. She played well, but looked ridiculous.

Then upstairs. The whole of the Murdoch empire there. And some interesting others as well: Tony and Cherie Blair, Michael Howard and Ken Clarke. Also Anthony Lester, Richard Branson,[1] Arnie Weinstock,[2] Woodrow Wyatt,[3] Mo Mowlam. Tony and I nodded briefly to each other. I had quite an extended conversation over several glasses of champagne with Mo Mowlam. Later I heard that John Major had been invited, but had demanded to see the guest list. To which Murdoch said, 'Stuff him, this is my party, not his' – so he didn't come.

Thursday, 15 September, Westminster

The papers this morning are full of equidistance. There will be an attempt at Conference to prevent me from abandoning this position. Yet almost everyone in their heart of hearts must know that we can't have an alliance with the Tories. But we have to maintain the pretence, at least until we see Labour's hand.

Friday, 16 September, London and Belfast

MEMORIAL SERVICE FOR THE MULL OF KINTYRE CHINOOK HELICOPTER DISASTER

A bumpy flight over to Belfast. On the way out Blair and I started chatting cautiously, while keeping a wary eye on an air vice-marshal sitting in the corner. In the course of the conversation, mostly on mundane matters, I

1 Entrepreneur; founder and chairman of the Virgin group of companies.
2 Lord Weinstock, Managing Director of the General Electric Company.
3 Woodrow Wyatt (1918–97). Member of Parliament (Labour) for Birmingham Aston 1945–55, Leicester Bosworth 1959–70. Later elevated to the House of Lords. Political commentator and columnist for the *News of the World* and *The Times*.

established that his driver's wife was ill. I said I had driven myself so I could give him a lift home and then there would be time to talk later.

Archbishop Eames[1] spoke at the service. His voice is full of wonderful cadences. Afterwards to the BBC, where we both did local and network stuff followed by ITN. Our Special Branch driver became rather fractious, as it was getting late and he had had a call from the plane telling us to hurry up. A quick dash to the airport and back to the jet. There we found the Chief of the General Staff and Nico Soames,[2] already ensconced, and drinking wine. It was obviously Nico who had sent for us.

We landed back at Northolt and walked towards my car. There followed a slightly embarrassing couple of moments while Tony got into my car and Soames got into the ministerial limo.

I opened by saying, 'Let's not beat about the bush. We have both embarked on a process here and we need to be clear about where it might end up. Neither of us, of course, knows exactly where the journey might finish, but we need to know what the possible final destinations are. What's your view?'

He thought for about twenty seconds, then said, 'Look, this is for you and you alone. There are a number of destinations we could arrive at. One is that there should be a sort of generalized agreement that the public knows exists, but is left unarticulated. The second is that we allow our local constituencies to stand down in favour of the other party, if they wish, but we don't push it. The third is that we should have some formalized agreement between us before the next election. I would like to get to the third, if that's possible.'

I nodded: 'That is exactly my view. And I think we can get there if we are clever and careful. The point is not to frighten the horses – or at least, if we have to frighten them, to do it in a planned way. We should let things develop gradually within our parties and then see where that gets us. But we should remember that uncertainty was the killer at the last election so the more up-front we can make our relationship the better.' We agreed that our next meeting should be à deux, but that after that we would invite others.

I dropped him at the corner of his street and drove back to the flat.

---

1 Most Revd Dr Robert Eames, Archbishop of Armagh and Primate of All Ireland.
2 Nicholas Soames, Minister of State at the Ministry of Defence. Member of Parliament (Conservative) for Crawley 1983–97 and for Mid-Sussex since 1997.

Monday, 19 September, Brighton

LIB DEM PARTY CONFERENCE

I am tired and grumpy with everybody. I am very worried about the drugs debate this afternoon, when there is a half-baked resolution down which our enemies will be able to misrepresent as legalizing cannabis. We also have a debate on the minimum wage, which I am likely to lose, and one on the monarchy, which is open to misinterpretation.

CHALLENGE TO THE MONARCHY

I interrupted a speech meeting in the morning to go into the end of the drugs debate.

It was immediately apparent that the vote was going to be very narrow. But when they raised the cards to vote, I could see that we were probably beaten. Somebody called for a recount. As soon as I had cast my vote I decided it would be best to leave the platform, for an appointment for which I was already late, so that the cameras weren't on me when the vote was announced.

[This subsequently became the biggest event of the whole conference. The press accused me the following day of 'stalking off the platform in disgust'. This proved a major error of judgement for which I paid throughout the rest of the week.]

In the event my meeting was delayed, so I sat in front of the television in total gloom watching the recount. Richard came in and, just before the vote was announced, bet me ten pounds we had won. But we lost by about seventy. He grimaced and handed over his £10 note.

My heart sank. I know exactly what this will do to us. But everybody else seems delighted. A great cheer went up in the conference hall. To add insult to injury, John Sergeant[1] then came on the 9 o'clock news saying that we had voted for the legalization of cannabis. This was plain wrong. We had voted for a Royal Commission to look into the issue of drugs. But it would be impossible to put things right, now.

Couldn't sleep a wink all night. Everything has combined. Bad presentation, a piece of total unprofessionalism from the BBC, and silliness on the part of the Party. I have spent the last seven years trying to change the image of the Party to one that can be trusted with power. That will have been very severely damaged by today. And having Blair in the ascendant makes it even worse. Do they not see the danger?

Saturday, 24 September, Chequers

DINNER FOR BORIS YELTSIN DURING AN OFFICIAL STATE VISIT

The house is magnificent, with some wonderful paintings. There were about forty people there, including Yeltsin, his ambassador, Owen, Sir Nicholas Bonsor,[2] Douglas Hurd, Arnie Weinstock, Bryan Forbes[3] and his

1 Chief Political Correspondent of the BBC.
2 Chair of the House of Commons Defence Select Committee. Member of Parliament (Conservative) for Nantwich 1979–83, Upminster 1983–97.
3 Novelist and award-winning film director.

wife and Kozyrev.[1] I was surprised, again, at the size of Yeltsin. He looked healthy despite all the vodka he is supposed to be swilling.

Major gave rather a banal speech and Yeltsin an even more banal one. At the end of the evening, Owen sought me out and we talked for five or ten minutes on Bosnia. He is very gloomy. He can't see how we can get through the winter without a major catastrophe – the Russians are backing us in everything and fully understand the situation. But the Americans are being utterly dreadful. Rose and the French general are toughies who are holding out against political pressure to do more against the Serbs. The problem is that the UN forces have effectively become the Serbs' hostages. Our capacity to take strong action against the Serbs is very limited, given the implication for our own troops on the ground. Meanwhile, the Bosnians keep taking advantage of the fact that they have world opinion on their side to continue aggressive operations against the Serbs. Owen's view is that it was a Bosnian attack that put paid to the Pope coming to Sarajevo – for which, of course, the Serbs got the blame.

Owen looks brown and fit. But his wife Debbie said he wants to move on. I should think so. He must be desperate to get out of this mire. It looks as though Bosnia is going to descend from bad to worse in sharp order.

Sunday, 25 September, Somerset

On the way down to Somerset today I began thinking again about Blair and my relationship with him. I came up with a proposal that would be worth testing out on him.

Blair's interest in us is, at least in part, because we can counteract the effects of his left wing in government. If he can count on us, he can ignore them. This will be especially useful in a government with a small minority (say, twenty or thirty). Secondly, if he wins the next election by a narrowish majority, he is likely only to have a one-term government. He cannot do what he wants to do in a single term and so must be attracted by the idea that a relationship with us could give him a solid government lasting at least two parliaments. In other words, there are benefits to Blair in having a relationship with us which both precedes and follows the General Election, even if he has a majority.

I will ask him at our next meeting whether he would work with us,

1 Andrei Kozyrev, Russian Foreign Minister.

even if Labour won a majority in the next election. It would be hugely advantageous to both of us to force Major to fight on two fronts. The best way to do this would be if he and I were to say in the near future that we had set our two parties to work on a 'heads of agreement', covering four or five areas on which we could jointly stand at the next election and co-operate in the next Government. This would electrify the political scene. Our relationship would then be 'issue driven', not personality driven. And I could put to the Party a manifesto part of which contains commitments to work with Labour on, for instance, constitutional issues with which they would find it difficult to disagree.

It's a hazardous throw, which will require considerable courage from both of us and, especially, a great deal of statesmanship from him. But it would be an extraordinary coup.

Sunday, 2 October, Somerset

Not much in the papers. But there is a Blair interview by Andrew Rawnsley[1] in the *Observer* in which he says that yes, there is a place for the Liberal Democrats (well, thank you!); that Labour doesn't have the monopoly of ideas; that there is a broad movement of the left; and that the task for us all is to find a definition of what we stand for and a central set of ideas to gather round. Very much what we agreed. It gathers pace.

Tuesday, 11 October, London

I met Jo Phillips at 9.30 at the House of Commons. The previous evening Anthony Lester had rung me at home to say that he had been given some extraordinary information by Mohamed Al Fayed. Apparently Al Fayed claims to have Tiny Rowland on tape alleging that he gave £1,000,000 which ended up in the hands of Michael Howard, then Minister for Corporate Affairs, in return for which Howard put the Inspectors on to the Al Fayed takeover of Harrods. This, after both Leon Brittan and Paul Channon had refused to put the Inspectors in, saying there was nothing to investigate. What an extraordinary claim – the Home Secretary receiving

1 Chief political columnist and Associate Editor of the *Observer*.

a £1,000,000 bribe! I don't believe a word of it and neither does Anthony.[1]

Anthony Lester says Al Fayed feels he has been cheated by the Government and wants to get his own back on them. He has just lost a case in the European Court of Human Rights and so believes that he can't pursue his claim further through legal channels.

Al Fayed also says that Neil Hamilton[2] has been 'paid vast sums of money' to put down questions for him (Al Fayed). Also Tim Smith.[3] He has evidence too that Jonathan Aitken[4] had his hotel bill in Paris paid by Saudi Arabian arms buyers when he was Minister for Procurement.

At Anthony's request, I agreed to go and see Al Fayed. I asked Ming to come with me, but he couldn't, so Alex Carlile came instead.

At 10.00pm Alex, Jo and I all went round to Al Fayed's. We were shown into his penthouse off Park Lane, and then Al Fayed himself walked in. He told us that he has already given the whole story to Peter Preston of the *Guardian*. He then produced the transcript of the Tiny Rowland interview and said we could look at the video if we wished (we declined). Al Fayed claims that Rowland agreed to have this conversation taped in return for Al Fayed dropping his libel action. I wouldn't trust Al Fayed an inch. But his bitterness towards the Tories gives him a motive. He says all Tories are 'buyable'. He then produced documentary evidence to show that Neil Hamilton had been given money to ask questions. Then the stuff on Howard, which he claims proves he took bribes. But in my view this allegation seems totally unfounded.

If, of course, he does manage to pin the acceptance of bribes on the Home Secretary the Government will fall.

Al Fayed is a curious man. Curiously naïve, in a way – but also rather engaging. His language is totally chaotic and full of expletives and his words tumble over each other.

I said before we left that we really couldn't open this can of worms. Only a newspaper could do it. But if the *Guardian* started it we would support them in Parliament. I will speak to Preston in the morning.

---

1 This view was subsequently confirmed in the report of the Commons Standards and Privileges Committee, chaired by Sir Gordon Downey, of 2 July 1997.

2 Member of Parliament (Conservative) for Tatton 1983-97.

3 Member of Parliament (Conservative) for Ashfield 1977–79, Beaconsfield 1982–97. Smith did not re-stand at the 1997 General Election.

4 Chief Secretary to the Treasury, formerly a Minister of State at the Ministry of Defence. Member of Parliament (Conservative) for Thanet East 1974–83, Thanet South 1983–97.

As we walked out, Al Fayed tried to thrust some carrier bags into our hands, full of, he said, Harrods goodies. Each with the face of a teddy bear staring through the handles. 'Not the real stuff you buy over the counter, all promotional goods.' We politely declined, with me winking at Alex. We giggled in the lift going down about the fact that we could have been photographed leaving Al Fayed's flat clutching bag loads of teddy bears.

An electrifying evening.

Wednesday, 12 October, London

The taxi picked me up at 6.50am to drive me to Blair's house. We covered the journey more quickly than I had thought and so had to wait outside for five minutes. He answered the door looking rather bleary-eyed in a green tracksuit. He said, 'I'm not used to early morning meetings like this – I hope it's not part of the psychological warfare!'

I congratulated him on his Conference and said that he'd had a splendid couple of months. He said he hadn't seen today's *Guardian* poll, which put them seventeen points ahead of the Tories.

We went downstairs and made a cup of coffee. Nicky, his son, was sitting in a chair looking as bleary-eyed as his father and watching television. Blair made a wry comment about him not normally being allowed to watch television at this hour, but at least it would give us some peace.

We then went upstairs to his back study, Where we had an exceptionally constructive discussion:

PA: What do you think is going to happen next?

TB: What do you mean? [Thinking that I was referring to Labour and us.]

PA: On the broader scene – the Tories.

We agreed that over the next year or so we should assume that the Tories would improve their position which would diminish both his lead and our vote. I then returned to the question left unresolved at our last meeting.

PA: We really must try and get clear between us what we see the end position as being. Let me see if I can be more specific than I was last time. If we had a hung Parliament would you see us working together in government?

TB: Yes.

PA: Good, now let me go a stage further. If you got a majority do you still see us working together in government?

TB (after a three-second pause): Yes.

PA: In which case I think we have the opportunity to do something really historic in politics. Lib Dems will abandon equidistance in the expectation that you will make it clear that you see us as partners in a hung Parliament. That leaves us with three options. The clearer we are the bigger the dividends. The three options for us are:

1. *Independence* i.e., sitting on the Opposition benches and taking things on a case-by-case basis. [We both agreed that this was not the best way forward.]

2. *The love that dares not speak its name* We create the expectation that we will work together on the broad outlines of an assumed programme, but without being clear about it.

3. *Full open partnership* In this we would say quite openly that we would work together in the next government, whether you have a majority or not. And we would do so on an agreed programme which we would get both parties to agree before the election.

TB: That's a very big step and one I will have to think about. But broadly, I am in favour of doing something along those lines if possible. We will need, in particular, to look at opinion polls.

I agreed and said that we were already doing some opinion polling on these issues. He suggested that we could piggy-back a few of our questions on some polling they were doing at the same time.

He went on to say that the task was to assemble a new set of core ideas for the left, 'or progressive politics, since you seem to prefer that word'. The Tories have lost this and are seen as intellectually bereft – we must fill that vacuum. The project must be driven by ideas and programmes, not just by an alliance to beat the Tories. I agreed.

We then discussed specific projects on which we could work. He is keen that we should manage the response to the Borrie Commission[1] as effectively as we can. I said we would do the same for Dahrendorf[2] when it came.

We then discussed other areas in which we could work together. He

1 A Labour Commission set up by John Smith to look at Social Justice.
2 A Lib Dem Commission set up by me to look at the creation of an enterprise-based economy within a socially just society.

proposed health, but I said that we may not necessarily agree on health policy. It would be damaging to seek an agreement on something and then fail.

The two areas we could work on, though, were long-term unemployment and Europe. In both these, agreement between the parties could be useful to both of us.

We decided that our next meeting should be held with three from either side, plus ourselves.

He told me that he would want Peter Mandelson, Gordon Brown ('I will have to discuss all this with Gordon') and probably John Prescott. He had been inclined to leave Prescott out at the beginning of our meeting, but by the end, when he saw the breadth of our discussions, he decided that would be wrong. He thinks that Prescott has 'changed remarkably'. 'He is really one of the people I depend on most, now.'

I said that, from our side, I would probably want Ming Campbell, Archy Kirkwood and Richard Holme. We needed to fix a date as soon as possible. We should also make policy contact between us through David Milliband[1] and Nick South.

We covered a lot of ground and some of the earlier reserve is now vanishing.

As I left the house I noticed that a number of the occupants of cars taking children to school recognized who I was. I hope it doesn't get out. We can't afford to meet there again.

In the evening, a Jo Group meeting, at which Richard commented, 'Goodness! you two have moved ahead faster than I would have thought wise at this stage.' They all recommended caution, Tom saying that we ought to 'let the situation settle down and clarify a bit'. We need to keep up the tension between us and Labour. For every step we take Labour must give something in return. I asked them at the end how they felt about it. 'Scared to death but exhilarated,' was Alan Leaman's response. We agreed that the three representing us at the meeting with Labour would be Ming Campbell, Archy Kirkwood and Richard Holme, but that I would take Bob Maclennan, Jim Wallace and Alex Carlile into my confidence.

I faxed Blair the following:

1 David Milliband was the Secretary to the Borrie Commission before going on to run Tony Blair's Office. He is now a Special Adviser to the Prime Minister.

Conclusions of the Meeting of 12 October 1994

1. Anji and Jo will set up a meeting for eight people sometime in the next month. An evening meeting would be best from our side. I would wish to have me, Ming Campbell, Archy Kirkwood and Richard Holme. Most have yet to be approached, but will be shortly.

2. Borrie You will arrange a briefing on this. On our side it will be dealt with by Alex Carlile who is not yet in the know, but soon will be. I will arrange reciprocal action on Dahrendorf.

3. Polls You discussed mentioning this to Philip Gould.[1] Richard Holme is handling these from our side. He is in the know and can be contacted by Philip Gould as and when you think appropriate.

4. Policy Nick South will handle this in my office and has been initiated. I suggest that David Milliband and he make contact as soon as appropriate.

5. We will need to have a clear agenda for the next meeting. I will make some proposals through Jonathan for Anji.

Tuesday, 18 October, Westminster

At 11 o'clock Anthony Lester came in with Alex Carlile. We discussed the Al Fayed affair. Anthony brought with him the article drafted by Peter Preston to be published in tomorrow's *Guardian*, culled from his conversation with Al Fayed last night. [Preston and I had talked the previous day about co-ordinating our efforts. He had seemed quite surprised that we knew all about it. I told him that I had sight of all documents he had seen.]

What Peter has written is absolutely devastating. We all agreed that we should send a very strong recommendation to the *Guardian* that they reveal the safest stuff first, i.e. the material on Hamilton and Smith.

Anthony Lester seemed concerned about this, although up until now he has been very relaxed about the whole thing. I was also very worried that, although we had clear evidence that the money had gone to Greer,[2] Greer was the only person who could say whether the money had gone on to

---

1 An adviser to Labour on polling. He also advised the Clinton campaign.
2 Ian Greer, Chairman of lobby company Ian Greer Associates 1982–96.

Hamilton. I was nervous that everyone was double-crossing everyone else. But all three lawyers – Alex, Ming and Anthony – pooh-poohed this, saying there was enough circumstantial evidence for it to stand up in court. I wonder.

We agreed that Alex should handle this for us in the Commons and that we should meet again later.

At 11.30am Archy came in and I briefed him first on the Al Fayed stuff and then on the Jo project.

His hair stood on end at the latter. He read the papers through, whistling through his teeth on several occasions, then said to me, 'You'll never get away with this, you know – everyone is opposed to it and you can't go against them.' I told him that I wanted to take it slowly, get the Party to cross the fences one at a time – the first one being an agreement that we couldn't support the Tories in a minority government. Having done that – which might take three months of me tramping round the country persuading the grass roots – we could then look at what our relationship with Labour would be. A far cry from what I had originally intended, but the only practical way forward. In his usual way, Archy warned me that I was moving into very dangerous territory.

During the course of the morning I looked at the Order Paper[1] and considered how to progress the Al Fayed material at PMQs. I had been tempted to come in myself with a question on whether the Prime Minister was confident that his Government was free of sleaze. At the mid-morning meeting, however, Alex suggested 'Can the Rt Hon. Gentleman assure the House that his Government is a sleaze-free zone?' A superb question. But not one that I can ask, since I have been making public statements saying that I hoped Blair's advent at PMQs will make the atmosphere of the House less 'yah-boo' and more reasonable. Eventually we decided that Paul Tyler,[2] who already has a question on the Order Paper today, should take it. There is much talk of sleaze today, so it should work well. I raised Paul on his mobile phone and asked him to make sure he was in for his PMQ and explained that we had a question framed for him which he should say word for word and shouldn't ask why.

At PMQs Paul sat alongside me. Previous questioners rambled on with different kinds of questions, including some about sleaze. But the question Alex had given Paul was perfectly targeted. The Prime Minister went into

1 This lists the day's business in the House.
2 Member of Parliament (Lib Dem) for Bodmin since 1992. He is currently our Chief Whip.

a long pre-prepared statement (why pre-prepared?) saying that 'wrong-doing will have to be rooted out wherever it is'. A great success. The press came up to Paul afterwards saying that the answer we had got out of Major would be much quoted back at the Government as things develop. I had anticipated that Paul would be asked by the press whether he knew of anything coming down the track, and briefed him on how to reply to this. Paul has been brilliant. He has done exactly as we asked him to do, and he hasn't asked why. A real trooper.

Wednesday, 19 October, Westminster

The big day for the Al Fayed stuff.

At 11 o'clock we had a meeting on how to play Al Fayed tonight in the House. The *Guardian* will publish its first edition at about 11.00pm. I got Peter Preston's agreement that we should raise a point of order in the House simultaneously with the *Guardian* being published. We have now laid out our plans and will meet again this afternoon to discuss what will happen next.

At 5.45pm Preston rang to say he agreed that it was best to run just with the Hamilton stuff at the start. I am very glad. But I am still doubtful whether even that is safe.

No sign that Labour has heard any of this yet, though there is talk in the press gallery about something big coming tonight. *Newsnight* are interested. They have asked Preston to appear on the programme but he has refused.

Archy has been sent off to tell Neil Hamilton that we are going to raise a point of order on his conduct later,[1] but without mentioning specifics. But Alex got to him first. Hamilton categorically denies that he has been paid for questions. Archy then got hold of a faxed copy of the *Guardian* article. It was immediately obvious that there was a potentially dangerous section still in it. The *Guardian* have completely missed the fact that, although Greer sent Al Fayed seventeen questions he said Hamilton was going to put down, there is no evidence that they had actually been put down. Furthermore, just as I thought, the *Guardian* cannot connect Greer

---

1 It is House of Commons protocol that a Member should be warned if another Member is going to raise his/her name in the Chamber.

to Hamilton in a way that proves that money changed hands. I immediately started having a serious attack of cold feet about all this.

After dinner I decided that it would be wrong for Alex to raise the point of order himself, but that we are safe going ahead with an Early Day Motion[1] asking for a full independent review into general standards, etc. This falls significantly short of what we had originally intended. But the *Guardian* have really blown the gaff by taking the story further than we think is supportable at this stage. It appears they might not even have checked that the questions went down on the Order Paper. And since we have no copies of them, we can't find out either. All we can find in Hansard are three questions from Hamilton which are not at all helpful to Lonhro. The *Guardian* could be in deep trouble.

We showed the *Guardian* article to colleagues and warned them not to quote from it in any way whatsoever, as they could lay themselves open to action. At 10.45pm we suddenly got word that Stuart Bell[2] was going to raise a point of order. On reflection I think the *Guardian* tipped off the Labour Party. But later Archy told me that the matter was briefly alluded to in the Chamber at 10.30, so it's just possible Labour were quick enough to get something together. We immediately despatched Alex to the bench, and I followed.

A very fevered atmosphere in the House. Bell was trying to get in with the Deputy Speaker, but the latter refused to interrupt the votes on the Criminal Justice Bill. I leaned across to Alex and said we should stick to our judgement. If Bell wanted to use the *Guardian* allegations, let him do so. Alex could then follow up with our more sensible suggestion. In due course, at about 11 o'clock, Stuart Bell rose and made an absolute hash of the point of order (though of course, he had got himself a prime slot on television because he mentioned the names and allegations in detail). But it appeared to all of us that he was reading from the *Guardian* transcript. At one stage he said that Hamilton had 'received pounds two thousand', indicating to everybody that he was reading from a printed text. Alex sat next to me, muttering.

To my shock and anger the Deputy Speaker then called Dennis Skinner

---

1 An Early Day Motion (or EDM) is a means by which a Member or Members can get a resolution printed on the Order Paper. These are not debated, but Members who agree can add their signatures, indicating the support that the resolution enjoys in the House.

2 An Opposition spokesman for Trade and Industry. Member of Parliament (Labour) for Middlesbrough since 1983.

second and Alex third. Alex did his usual competent job, but the moment had slipped from us.

It was all over the midnight news, but Labour has shared the running with us, which is annoying since we have been preparing for so long. Sometimes impetuosity pays.

Thursday, 20 October, Westminster

PMQs. The House in a very nervous and excited state. Major made a statement announcing that Al Fayed had been in touch with him, but not saying about what. Not very convincing.

Blair then asked a very direct question to an almost silent House. He carried it off brilliantly.[1] Major completely failed to answer it. A direct hit for Blair, and his back benchers were absolutely delighted.

Then some wretched Tory. I decided immediately that I would back Blair up and said how disappointed I was with the Prime Minister's answer to the 'three questions from the Rt Hon. Gentleman, the Leader of the Labour Party'.

Afterwards, a meeting in my office with David Milliband on the Borrie Commission. I told Alex and Willy Goodhart that I wanted us to respond in positive terms. 'A very important contribution to a very important debate.' We smuggled Milliband out of the back door.

Saturday, 22 October, London

A blessedly free day. Particularly useful since the sleaze situation is gathering pace nicely. Hamilton under a lot of pressure. I have spoken again to Tony Bevins of the *Observer* who tells me that an injunction had been put out on the *FT*. Bevins's initial opinion was that this was because the *FT* had something the *Observer* didn't have.

Bevins tells me that he is thinking of putting it on the front page of the *Observer* tomorrow and will I stand by in case they too get an injunction placed against them? If this happens they will print a blank page and we

1 He demanded that 'the cash for questions enquiry be broadened, made deeper, held in public and made fully independent so that the confidence of the British people in their government can begin to be restored'.

could go round saying, 'Why is the Government gagging the *Observer*?' He also tells me that there is a clear majority of MPs now in favour of the independent inquiry we have been calling for.

Tuesday, 25 October, Westminster

During the morning I had been contacted by Downing Street. The Prime Minister was going to make a statement about establishing a committee under Lord Justice Nolan to look into standards in public office. Almost identical to what Alex Carlile had suggested more than a week ago!

I had arranged to speak to Blair at 3.15. Before I could do so, though, Robin Butler rang to tell me the remit for the Committee. Typical Major – he is being driven to this. If only it had been done a week ago he could have helped himself enormously and taken the sting out of the sleaze allegations.

Spoke to Blair at 3.20. We agreed that we would welcome the report but put down an early marker for Major that he still had the specific allegations about his individual ministers to answer. I said, 'I don't think I am going to come in this afternoon – I'll keep myself for the statement at 3.30.' He paused then said, 'I agree. I will do that as well.' He was as good as his word and never asked a question during PMQs, leaving it to the back benchers. Smith would never have done that.

Blair delivered a rather good statement, with me largely echoing him, saying that whilst the Nolan Committee was right, individual allegations against ministers must be investigated in the open, by the Privileges Committee. Major spotted what Blair and I were doing and accused me of being a copycat.

Saturday, 29 October, Scotland

Two hours with the Scottish Lib Dems.[1] They are strongly opposed to a closer relationship with Labour. But they see it from a very narrow Scottish

---

1 I had decided that I was going to use the next four months, until the Spring Conference of 1995, tramping round the country seeing each region and many constituency parties in order to prepare the ground for the abandonment of equidistance. I set myself the task of taking this big step, not by forcing a division – that might have to come later – but by consensus. My first 'consultative session' was in Scotland.

point of view. I emphasized that we didn't have to take this decision now and we ought to avoid any kind of discussion of it at Scarborough,[1] since this would be suicidal. I am not sure we will get away with it. I need more time. But I managed at least to get them to see a point of view other than their own, even if they didn't agree with it.

Wednesday, 2 November, London

A call from Andrew Phillips this evening. He told me that at the A1 meeting last night, Dick Newby, Roger Liddle and Tony Halmos[2] had said why didn't I get a grip and drive the relationship with Labour forward? This is outrageous from Roger, given that he knows what's going on. Andrew was concerned that Roger and perhaps some of the others were in danger of defecting to Labour. I rang Roger and found him in good form. I fixed for him and others from that wing to come and see me as part of the consultation process.

Thursday, 17 November, Westminster

Saw Roger Liddle at 8.30. He is very low. Talking about joining Labour, saying that everybody else (from the old SDP) is low as well. Mandelson has told him many of the details of my meetings with Blair anyway, so I confirmed this and gave him my analysis.

Tuesday, 29 November, Westminster

At 12.30, a meeting with Jo, Nick, Richard Holme, Alan Leaman, Tom McNally, Bob Maclennan, Archy Kirkwood and Ming Campbell, to discuss what steps we could take to manage the equidistance debate next year. I won myself an extra six months at the last Conference. But I still have to turn the Party and make sure it doesn't smash itself apart. In the process of our meeting, Bob made it clear that he did not believe we should go into the next election in any kind of formal relationship with Labour. He thinks

1 Our Spring Conference was to be at Scarborough.
2 A former adviser to the Party, now Director of Public Relations for the Corporation of London.

independence is the best option. I didn't argue with him on this. I merely said that we should leave final destinations until later and keep our options open for as long as possible.

I am beginning to meet real opposition. It's not at all likely that we will have a relationship with Labour, but I am determined to keep the option open.

Tuesday, 6 December, Westminster

VOTING ON THE VAT ON FUEL BILL

Tremendous drama building up about tonight. All the news broadcasters are questioning rebel Tories. The word in the tea rooms is that the Government have got it by one or two. But they always say that, and then rebel Tory MPs lose their courage at the last moment.

I arrived in the House just as the division bells were going. The division lobbies were crowded to bursting, with a palpable sense of excitement.

After voting we sat hunched on our benches, watching nervously for the Whips to return.

The Government benches looked cheerful. I saw Richard Ryder[1] come back and the smiles never left their faces. The word went round that they had won. But I noticed that Ken Clarke had a prepared statement and that Major and he were continuing to work on it after Richard Ryder returned. I leaned across to Archy and Alan and said that I thought that they had lost, otherwise Ken wouldn't be continuing to amend his statement. I said 'Look at Major's face!' It was ashen, although he had a thin smile painted on it.

But the rest of the House became convinced that the Tories had won.

There was a delay. It turned out that Toby Jessel[2] had voted Yes with the Government, then wandered into the No lobby to go to the loo and now he refused to come out and had locked the door. Everyone piled in to try to get him out, much to the hilarity of the House. Eventually the Labour Whips, having done a count, realized what the outcome would be and let the thing go. He could have been there all night. What an idiot.

Ian Bruce from Dorset voted twice, too. What a state they are in!

Just before the Whips came back, it became evident that we had won

---

1 Government Chief Whip. Member of Parliament (Conservative) for Mid-Norfolk 1983-97.
2 Member of Parliament (Conservative) for Twickenham 1970-97.

and the word went round like wildfire. Then they marched back, the Labour Whip following on behind so that they could take position to the right of the mace [indicating that we had won]. There was a great cheer and much waving of order papers.

A majority of seven for us. A terrible defeat for the Government.

1995

Wednesday, 11 January, London

At 12.15, lunch with David Montgomery[1] in Canary Wharf. He spent half the time telling us about the damage Murdoch was doing. But he is very enthusiastic for constitutional reform. I told him about my long-term plans and said that we might need the *Mirror*'s help to persuade people to vote tactically at the Election. He wants the *Mirror* to take a broad centre-left view rather than just support Labour, although it is clear that he gets on well with the Labour front bench and has considerable respect for Blair.

Tuesday, 17 January, Bosnia

HALFWAY THROUGH MY SEVENTH VISIT TO THE BALKANS

A beautiful day. Bright, crisp, still and very cold.

Up at 7.00 and off at 8.00 to Maglaj, northern Bosnia with Jo Phillips. I have always wanted to go there. They suffered most terribly in the siege of a year ago.

Arrived with the forward unit of the Household Cavalry, who took us up to the Observation Point, which commands a grandstand view of the fight between the Serbs and the Muslims in the valley below. They pointed out both sides' battle positions to me, including a tank on the horizon which lobs the occasional shell into Maglaj.

Every year since 1992 I have been bringing out parcels from one of the Wincanton refugees for his brother, Stefan Drago, trapped in Maglaj. But I had never been able to deliver these because the town had been under siege. I asked if someone could find out whether Drago was still alive. He was, and was brought to see me. I gave him his parcel. I was delighted when he told me that the previous ones, which I had left with the Bosnian authorities in Sarajevo, had eventually got to him. I offered to take a letter back to his brother in Wincanton, which we picked up from his flat before heading off to Sarajevo.

1 Chief Executive of the *Daily Mirror*.

Sarajevo looks much better since the current ceasefire. Snow covering everything, which gives the hard, jagged edges of the demolished buildings a slightly softer look. The light is yellowish, like a Turner painting, because of the city's pollution, trapped in the valley through weather inversion.

I paid my usual courtesy call on Izetbegovic, whom I found more optimistic than before. He told me what I had already concluded – that the federation with Croatia is a sham and will never last. Nevertheless, he believes that the Serbs will be forced to open the routes across the airport and in the end will have to accept the peace terms.

I noticed on two occasions during our meeting that somebody tried to signal to him that it was time to move on, but he waved them away. My relations with him are deepening. But he is a frail old man, and I wonder how long he can last.

Wednesday, 18 January, Bosnia

At 8.30am an interview with General Rose. He sprayed the usual optimism over me like a garden hose. He can't hide his dislike of the Bosnians. He said that they were a crooked shower who couldn't be trusted. Nevertheless, he seems optimistic – unreasonably so – about the future.

He claims that routes across the airport would not be opened because they would destroy the economics of the tunnel the Bosnians have dug underneath it.[1] 'What needs to be said in front of a television camera sometime is, why are young Bosnian boys being sent to the trenches to fight while the children of their leaders are at university abroad?'

It's a good thing he's going. His blokes love him but I continue to have severe reservations about his judgement.

Then to Ilidza on the Serb side. Kate Adie[2] came along with a TV camera. The Serbs gave us hassle at the checkpoint. Whether it was ex-Communist bureaucracy or a deliberate attempt to get at me, I don't know. Probably the former.

---

1 The Sarajevo tunnel was dug in secret by hand by the Bosnians in the first year of the war, when they realized that the West was not going to help them break the Serb siege. A kilometre long, it passes under the main runway of the airfield. The tunnel, which connected the city to Bosnian-held territory beyond Serb lines, was used for three years to get people in and out of the city and weapons, ammunition and other vital supplies in. The tunnel was funded by private sources and a charge was made for all non-military personnel and material using it. See 16 July 1995 for a full description.
2 Chief News Correspondent for the BBC since 1989.

Off to look at some flats being done up for the Serbs by the ODA [Overseas Development Agency]. One of the terrible things about this war is that the innocent suffer for the sins of the guilty. The wretched people here have been driven out of their houses by the Muslims.

Then to a Serb refugee camp, where they were huddled together in the snow, eating at a communal kitchen. But there is a greater sense of community spirit among the Serbs. They turn out to help the UN rebuild their houses and band together to help refugees more effectively than the Bosnians.

Then a meeting with the Mayor. The obligatory two large glasses of Slivo. I felt the blood rush to my cheeks. The Mayor himself seemed a nice enough man, but he had a political apparatchik at his elbow who started to lecture me on how Sarajevo had been a Serb city. I told him to cut out that shit (a phrase which the interpreter found difficult to translate); I didn't need a lecture on history.

I remarked at the end of our meeting that it was strange to be in the office of a mayor of a republic and see a picture of a king on the wall (King Peter). I asked the Mayor whether he really wanted a monarchy back, and he said he did. To which Kate Adie, at the back of the room, muttered very audibly, 'Well, you can have ours.' I joked that we could export them under the auspices of ODA, if they wished. Much mirth all round.

Dinner with Silajdzic. He arrived wearing an overcoat, which he didn't take off all evening, and stayed until about 11.00 – practically unheard of. A very effective, subtle and likeable man. Good company, too. According to him, the arms embargo should be lifted in order to 'radicalize the situation'.

'Everything's stuck,' he said. 'I know we are taking risks in lifting the arms embargo, but it would provide a new dynamic. Although I don't expect to get the arms in, of course. They will be blocked by the Croats.'

'So it's only symbolic?' I suggested. 'Designed to put pressure on the Serbs?'

'What else can we do?'

We talked a lot about NATO. He knows Clinton well and says he is a young man with an old heart. He doesn't trust the Americans as a whole. He thinks they are gauche, but he will use them for the moment. He hates Owen and thinks Rose has been a complete failure. At the end of the evening I taxed him on the corruption Rose spoke of and repeated Rose's opinion that the Bosnian authorities wouldn't open the routes across the airport because it would break their stranglehold on the supply of food to the city through the tunnel, from which their friends made profits. He said that if Rose gave him the information he would act.

'Time is on our side. The Serbs know it. If we can continue this war, we can win it.'

I replied, 'Yes, but at what cost to your young men and your country – what will be left?'

He dissembled only once that I know of. I asked him whether or not he could still count on the will of his population to fight. He gave me the answer every leader has to give. But I know that the ordinary people are tiring of war.

Sunday, 29 January, Yeovil, London and Peterborough

The 6.15 train from Yeovil to do David Frost. I had hoped to read the Sunday papers, but snoozed instead.

Into the studio, where I watched Rory Bremner do a very funny imitation of me before they wheeled me on. I went hard on Europe, hoping that my comments would carry through the day in the news bulletins, which they did. Heath on before me, strenuously attacking the Government. God, they are in a mess. Open civil war.

We finished at 9.15 and Mandelson, who had been on to review the papers, came up to me (I had been fairly critical of Labour) and patted me on the back and gave a sort of resigned sigh. Afterwards up to breakfast, chatting with Mandelson and Frost on the way. Mandelson is good company. He is sharp and clever, but not to be trusted.

Then in the car to Peterborough for a General Election planning meeting, where I led the strategy discussion on the 1995 position paper.[1] I made it clear that I did not want any high-profile razzmatazz rallies. I wanted to talk to people, not at them.

Richard Holme will fight a different kind of election from Des. Much more a teamwork affair. Just what we need at this stage of our development.

To bed around midnight.

---

1 My regular review of 'where we are' – see Appendix A.

Tuesday, 21 February, UN Headquarters, New York[1]

A meeting with Kofi Annan[2] and the Under Secretary-General[3] of Peace Keeping. I took to Annan, whom I knew as a fellow diplomat when I was in the Foreign Office in Geneva. He is gentle and sophisticated; but he was accompanied by a couple of UN bureaucrats who persisted in getting the wrong end of the stick. I was very blunt about the UN's inadequacies on military matters and the consequences of this for our soldiers. He said, 'You are just about to see the Secretary-General. Make the point to him.'

So to see Boutros Boutros-Ghali.[4] A funny little man. Bright, amused eyes, lots of lines around his face and a disarmingly naïve attitude. Ming and I sat on the sofa, all attentive and respectful, while, to my astonishment, David Hannay, the British Ambassador, lounged in a rather louche fashion in one of the chairs.

I repeated what I had said to Kofi Annan: we must take the war in Yugoslavia seriously if we aren't to lose troops and the UN has been appalling at organizing this. Marrack Goulding intervened: 'You ask why we aren't any good at fighting a war. It's because we aren't supposed to be fighting a war.' To which I responded rather sharply 'That distinction isn't likely to be very important to the young UN soldier who is unfortunate enough to take a bullet in the back. The real question is whether his life is at risk. And if you continue to conduct military operations as you have been doing so far, you will shorten the lives of lots more young soldiers, the UN will end up being discredited and peace-keeping operations will stop.'

We discussed the American cut in funding for the UN down to 25 per cent of their fixed contribution. I asked Boutros Boutros-Ghali how serious this was. 'Not serious, really, other people will chip in.' At which Hannay exploded from his semi-supine position, saying, 'That's nonsense, Secretary-General, and you'd better stop saying it. If the Americans pay less, then don't think we will just pay more. We won't. If you come out with

---

1 Ming Campbell and I had agreed to do a joint visit to the UN in New York and the US administration in Washington earlier in the year.

2 UN Special Envoy to the Former Yugoslavia. Annan is now the Secretary-General of the UN.

3 Marrack Goulding, Under Secretary-General of the UN, formerly the Under Secretary-General for Peace Keeping Operations.

4 Secretary-General of the UN.

this kind of nonsense, it will encourage the Americans to continue as they are. This is a crisis and it would be better to recognize it.'

Boutros-Ghali waved his hand as though dismissing Hannay. 'My job on the thirty-sixth floor is to take a constantly optimistic view. These bad messages don't get through to me.' Hannay spoke to him as if he were a schoolboy. I suppose that's what happens if you are a member of the Security Council – you view the Secretary-General as little more than the figurehead of an organization which you fund, and can therefore boss about.

Hannay complained bitterly afterwards. 'The Secretary-General can be on good form, but he wasn't today.'

Wednesday, 22 February, Washington

To the White House to see Vice-President Al Gore.

In the lobby of the President's office there was a constant flow of young men and women and a general air of chaos. Not at all what I had expected to find in the most powerful office in the world. It felt more like the ante-chamber to a Persian pasha.

Gore, however, was totally different. A rather serious man. He was half an hour late for our meeting, having been to watch his child play basketball. He regretted that this would mean that he could only give us twenty minutes, but in the event we had about an hour. We spoke of Bosnia, but his responses to my questions were pretty straight and reserved. He knows Silajdzic and likes him.

We then got on talking about the Internet and the new technologies. (Ming later described this conversation as the two of us 'ascending to heaven on a cloud of cyber speak'.) Then a further conversation about the nature of government, of democracies and what needed to be done to make them more effective. We agreed about a good deal.

I am not sure how much the Ambassador got out of it. He had wanted to use the meeting to lobby against Gerry Adams's forthcoming visit to Washington for St Patrick's Day. But I found it fascinating.

Thursday, 2 March, Westminster and Somerset

A meeting in my office of the Jo Group this morning. Tom McNally started to go backwards and ask whether we should abandon equidistance at all. I got rather tetchy. At one stage I said in exasperation, 'Well, if we are not going forward with this, what the hell have I been doing flogging my guts out for the last three months, tramping round the country trying to persuade the Party?'

After which a very tough meeting with the MPs' researchers, also very hostile to the abandonment of equidistance, reflecting, they said, the views of their MPs.

Archy keeps telling me that I haven't got the Party on my side nearly as much as I would like. And here, now, was the proof.

In the late afternoon I drove back to Norton through thick snow and in a near catatonic mood of depression. Had a whisky with Jane, a late supper and to bed about midnight. Is this the time to pack it in?

Tuesday, 7 March, Westminster

At 4.00pm the key meeting of the team leaders[1] to discuss strategy. It went quite well.

On the strategy question, Alan Beith said we should not declare our hand with the Tories and were comfortable where we were. But Malcolm said that he didn't mind it being known that we would oppose the Tories, provided it was also made clear that we wanted to win ourselves. Exactly contrary to his previous position. He meant his intervention to have one effect but it had entirely the opposite one, enabling me to say, 'That's exactly what I am after, too!'

A dangerous moment. But we have now been through this twice, so there is probably no going back. To my delight, we also agreed the format – i.e., we would write a document containing the abandonment of equidistance, to be published in June.

---

1 I had divided the Parliamentary Party into teams covering each of the key spokesmanship areas (Education, Health, Foreign Affairs, etc), each with a team leader. The team leaders' weekly meeting was, therefore, in effect our 'Shadow Cabinet'.

Monday, 13 March, Westminster

After the 10.00 vote last night Charles Kennedy told me that Peter Mandelson was furious about my Conference speech at the weekend.[1] Apparently he had said, 'I need to know whether you lot are serious about this project or not.'

At about 4.45pm, just as I was leaving my office, Anji from Blair's office rang. Blair, on his way back from an NEC[2] meeting, had told her to fax through to me drafts of the new sections of the revised Labour constitution which they had just agreed. I asked her to send them to Methley Street. They turn out to be extraordinarily convoluted stuff. The thoughts of Blair, but the punctuation of Prescott! But tougher than I had expected. A testimony to Blair's courage.

Anji later rang to say that Blair could be reached on his car phone. I rang him, saying I would instruct my colleagues not to comment to the press on this, but if they were forced, they should say 'Good words. But will Labour follow them with the actions?'

Blair seems cheerful – and he has every right to be. He will get great crits tomorrow. He said he was absolutely knackered. I am not surprised. He has had a hell of a punishing schedule. He was now, in his words, 'going to spend a couple of days at home'. Oh, to have that luxury!

Friday, 31 March, London

On the way back from *Any Questions*, Michael Meacher told me about Labour Party attitudes to Blair. They are all very suspicious. 'He has our heads but he hasn't got our hearts. He can ride roughshod over us. But only for so long. I don't know what the next Labour Government is going to be like under his leadership. The place seems to be run by Mandelson and sharp suits.'

He kept on asking me if I'd met Blair. Of course I wasn't going to tell him. He's very suspicious – though he claims to be in favour of the project.

1 In my end of Conference speech at our Scarborough Spring Conference in the previous week, I had attacked Blair for timidity.
2 National Executive Committee – Labour's ruling body. Blair had taken his proposed changes on Clause IV to them that day.

Thursday, 20 April, Westminster

I had arranged to see Major about honours after PMQs. Again he wanted to engage me in conversation even before our business was finished.

We had a long conversation in which he complained about the Labour Party broadcast last night.[1] At first he had thought Blair didn't know about the broadcast. 'I don't know everything that goes on in Central Office, you know.' But he concluded that Blair did know, because he had run it at his press conference. Major was deeply offended at being called a liar. I said that I thought it was a mistake by Labour.

He then went out of his way to explain to me that he didn't expect to put up taxes. In fact he intended to bring them down, if he could. 'If Labour had any courage they would take your position, which is very courageous and terribly honest.' He was being ironic, of course.

He then briefed me on the Nolan Committee report – due out in mid-May.

Finally he briefed me on Gerry Adams, saying that, having returned from a very successful fund-raising tour of America, Adams had overreached his position on arms decommissioning. As so often happens with Irish leaders, he had found that the IRA at home wouldn't go as far as he had promised abroad (to Clinton). So Adams couldn't go on with the decommissioning process unless it was part of a deal which also included demilitarization (i.e., withdrawal of troops from Northern Ireland) by the British Government. Major said, 'We have, of course, been having extensive meetings with him.' Major told me he cannot demilitarize, but that he is prepared to outline the basic principles and programme for the progressive withdrawal of *all* parties (which would, of course, include our forces), and if the IRA wanted to read this as demilitarization they could do so.

He appears to have found some inner strength. I think he now knows he is going to be defeated at the next election, has come to terms with it and is concentrating on securing his place in the history books – hence the Ireland thing.

---

1 Which repeatedly referred to Major as a liar because he had raised taxes when he promised in the 1992 election not to.

Wednesday, 3 May, London

At 7.30pm Archy and I arrived at Derry Irvine's[1] house in Hampstead, to be met at the door by Irvine himself.

Blair was already there with Robin Cook. Blair looking very crumpled with his jacket off and his tie undone. He had just come from the Hilton, where, he confessed, he had missed a couple of lines in his speech, fluffed the soundbite that Alastair Campbell[2] had drafted for him and then plunged on for several sentences making no sense whatsoever. I told him that I knew what it felt like!

Throughout the evening Irvine took trouble to remind us in many little ways of the master/pupil relationship between him and Blair. He seems to act as a kind of godfather to Blair. At one stage Irvine said that the relationship between him and Blair had been reversed. 'I do what he tells me, including making my house available at the drop of a hat – all at the command of Tony!' Blair revealed that it was only when I had expressed my concern about going round to the Blairs' house that he had hurriedly rearranged our meeting at Irvine's.

However, despite his reputation for egotism, Irvine took little substantive part in the ensuing conversation, apart from suggesting that if devolution proved difficult in Wales, we ought to do Scotland and London first.

He and his wife Alison arranged the whole thing very well. Shortly after we arrived, we were taken round the house, and the rather sumptuous garden in which there were some splendid trees and shrubs and a mosaic showing Dante's Inferno, which included Mrs Thatcher among the figures in hell. Derry's little joke.

We then had a look at Irvine's paintings. There were some original Stanley Spencers, including some from the *Christ Preaching at Cookham Regatta* series, which were wonderful, and some very nice Sickerts. Also three nudes in the dining room that looked to me like Lucian Freuds, but aren't (though they are, I was assured, by someone just as important, of whom I had never heard). I found that eating my dinner confronted by moist images of female pudenda did little for the appetite.

The meal itself was excellent. Chablis throughout and a carafe of claret

---

1 Lord Irvine of Lairg. Shadow Lord Chancellor, Lord Chancellor since 1997.
2 Previously of the *Daily Mirror* but Press Secretary to Tony Blair since 1994.

which Irvine kept on saying was very good, but which somehow I never
got to taste.

We were all in shirtsleeves except Robin Cook, who didn't take his
jacket off all evening.

I had intended to start the ball rolling, but Blair got in first saying, 'How
do you see things?'

I was pretty cagey, then batted his question back. 'Just describe to me,
so that we know how things have changed, what you think the best and
the worst outcome of this will be.'

He was noticeably less forthcoming than he had been when we were alone.

TB: Well, the worst outcome would be that we ended up fighting each other. The
best would be that we created a climate for co-operation, which sent messages to
the British electorate without us actually putting anything specific on paper.

PA: But surely there is a better position. If everything went well, we could work
together in a hung Parliament?

I particularly wanted him to repeat in front of Cook what he had said
to me previously. He confirmed that, even if they had a small majority,
there would be advantages to us working together. But he was not as
unequivocal on this as he had been to me before, or as he had been to Roy
Jenkins.

I went on to explain that we intended to abandon equidistance by July
and seek to get this confirmed by our Autumn Conference in Glasgow.
Archy Kirkwood, being cautious, said that none of this would be absolutely
certain until after Glasgow. I told Blair that when we did this, what we
needed from him was an echo which would give momentum to the process.
In particular, we wanted a commitment that, in the case of a hung Parliament, we could work together.

Blair agreed and said that we could discuss the details later.

We then discussed local government co-operation. We agreed that, whilst
it would be inappropriate for parties to lay down hard and fast rules about
local government co-operation, we should not do anything which would
impede it.

TB: There is some ridiculous clause 7 or something in our Constitution which
prevents co-operation – but we should be able to get around that.

Robin Cook: I know exactly what that clause says because I wrote it. There
shouldn't be co-operation which damages the distinctiveness and identity of the
Party.

PA: I have to give my Party a sense of mission and a role to play. The danger is that if we abandon equidistance we will be seen to be in your camp. So, as soon as we have done this we will have to compensate by taking strong measures to assert our independence. That may mean attacking you. It's absolutely vital for us that we are not seen to be the *demandeur* in this process and that we maintain our distinctiveness. So we must maintain a healthy tension between our parties.

Robin Cook wanted to know if 'independence' meant we would do a deal with the Tories?

I replied that it could not mean that.

RC: What exactly does it mean, then?

PA: Well, in the next government we must have a role, whichever side we sit on. That role must be one that can be filled only by us. We shall be the force that keeps you to your promises, where we agree, and prevents you from doing damage to the country, where we don't.

Tony went on to outline what he was going to do during the summer, including tightening up his policies on health, education and the economy.

I commented that one major block to progress on the whole project was taxation.

Tony launched into a monologue about how they couldn't take too clear a position. 'The public thinks Labour means tax, whatever we say at the next election – and we can't encourage that.'

I responded that that might be his position, but it wasn't ours. One of our points of distinctiveness was to take up positions on tax that they couldn't take.

Robin interjected that we could do things they couldn't do 'because, whatever you say, you are not going to be in power, whereas whatever we say, we are'. Typical of the sharpness of Robin, whom I found constructive and realistic throughout the meeting.

The other real block to progress was PR. Robin said that Labour's position was that there would be PR for Europe, PR for regional government, PR for the Scottish and Welsh assemblies – surely that was enough?

I responded, no, it wasn't. We could not enter into a relationship with them unless there was a reasonable prospect of PR for Westminster as well. To do so would be to invite our own destruction – and I wasn't going to do that. I added, 'Surely you have also committed yourself to PR for local government?'

Robin replied that they hadn't formally come to this position yet, but that it was the next thing the Plant Commission[1] was going to address.

As for PR for Westminster, I was happy to launch the constitutional project with them, but not if it was bound to fail. And it would fail if we couldn't agree on PR for Westminster.

Tony reiterated that his position on PR was that he is 'unpersuaded'.

Irvine said that surely it would be enough to have a referendum? I pointed out that Labour were already committed to a referendum, so that would require no move from them. I repeated that a position in which the Prime Minister was either hostile or agnostic in a PR referendum would be unacceptable to us.

RC: I am the person who is most enthusiastic about PR. But I am prepared to accept this position, why aren't you?

PA: Of course I am not prepared to accept a position which would mean, in the end, the destruction of my Party.

I wanted to close down the discussion because it was becoming a negotiation rather than an identification of problem areas, so I said, 'Look, this isn't the place to negotiate this. I feel certain that intelligent minds can come up with solutions. But what I want to mark out for you guys is just how difficult this is for us and how much of a block it could be.'

TB: Yes. But it's equally difficult for us, and I don't see how we can resolve it. There is no point in us going into this without a clear knowledge of each other's positions. I understand yours. You have to understand mine. I can't go further than 'I'm unpersuaded.'

At that point we decided that we should have one MP from each party get together and see if they could come to an agreement about what the end position on PR would be, before we started casting wider.

We then turned to the constitutional project, which Robin said he and Tony were fully on board for. I replied that the first step was for them to decide who should manage the talks between us. There ensued an interesting discussion between Tony and Robin. I said Bob Maclennan would do it from our side, but we needed to know who they would nominate. Archy and I made it clear that Jack Straw would be impossible for us to deal with, whereas Robin would be helpful.

TB: What do you think, Robin?

1 An internal Labour Party commission looking at electoral reform.

RC: You know perfectly well what I think. I am the person in charge of policy. I am the appropriate person to do it.

Tony said he would think about it.

I then proposed that the remit for the group should be 'to investigate the legislative procedure that would prevent the Tories blocking the passage of constitutional reform in the next Parliament', and that we should assemble teams from both sides to begin work immediately on the modalities; the aim should be to arrive at an agreed position on PR by June. There should be no public announcement about the start of the wider constitutional project until that agreement had been reached. Depending on the outcome we could then, perhaps in June or July, begin the second stage, i.e., public work to produce a report in 1996. We agreed to have four politicians from our side and I mentioned the names – Bob Maclennan, Alex Carlile, Jim Wallace, and Anthony Lester.

TB: If at the same time that you abandon equidistance, we start joint constitutional work, the press will know what to make of it.

I agreed, but said that the important thing was to have a rational explanation for what we were doing. On our side, we could explain that to engage in such a discussion with Labour was no more than the kind of co-operation we had already with the Tories on Maastricht, though accepting that, as a cover story, this fig-leaf was pretty thin.

The substantive business done, we talked about the local elections.

They think the Tories won't lose more than 1,200 seats. Tony's belief, like mine, is that Major won't go afterwards, but if he does Heseltine will be the replacement and that he will make more effective opposition than Major.

Archy and I left at 10.20pm.

Blair has changed quite a lot. He has grown in self-confidence. There is even, perhaps, a tinge of arrogance showing. Much talk about 'that's the way you lead parties'. I was also especially struck that he is suddenly using rather cruder language than I remember from him before, with quite a few 'bollocks' thrown in. All part of a leader becoming a Leader.

Saturday, 6 May, London

VE DAY FIFTIETH-ANNIVERSARY DINNER[1]

At 5.20 a taxi to the Guildhall.

There was a reception first. A couple of glasses of champagne and a long chat with Walter Cronkite, the splendid World War Two correspondent in London. At one stage I found Cherie Blair wandering around looking for Tony, so I grabbed her and introduced her to Kronkite, while I went off to pester Robin Ross[2] to come and meet an injured Royal Marine I had found in a wheelchair.

At dinner I was seated next to Franjo Tudjman.[3] Somebody in the Foreign Office with a sense of humour! Particularly since he wasn't even on our side in the war.

During dinner I was careful to keep Tudjman's glass full of white wine, and he got drunker and drunker. Over the pudding I asked him to draw, on the back of my menu, a map of ex-Yugoslavia as it would be in ten years' time. I drew the coast, marked in Zagreb, Belgrade and Sarajevo, and left the rest to him. Without hesitation, he drew a broad 'S'-shaped line, starting in Slovenia and running along the Sava River, including Tuzla, back to just east of Sarajevo and down to the sea. Everything to the right of that line, he said, would be Serbia and everything to the left would be Croatia.

I pointed out that this would mean that they would have to exchange Tuzla[4] for Banja Luka.[5] He said, yes, the Muslims would have to give up Tuzla to the Serbs and the Serbs would have to give up Banja Luka to the Muslims. (Some hope.)

He then told me that, when the UN mandate ended, the Croats would launch an attack on the Knin Krajina,[6] probably in August or September, and that this would take eight days and cost no more than 1,000 lives. I bet him a bottle of Croatian white wine that he couldn't do it in eight days and that his causalities would be more than 1,000. He took the bet without hesitation.

---

1 I sent a copy of this diary entry confidentially to the Foreign Secretary, Douglas Hurd, the following day.
2 Commandant General of the Royal Marines and an old friend of mine.
3 President of Croatia.
4 Currently held by the Bosnians.
5 Currently held by the Serbs and the capital of Karadzic's breakaway Bosnian Serb Republic.
6 A Serb enclave of Croatia.

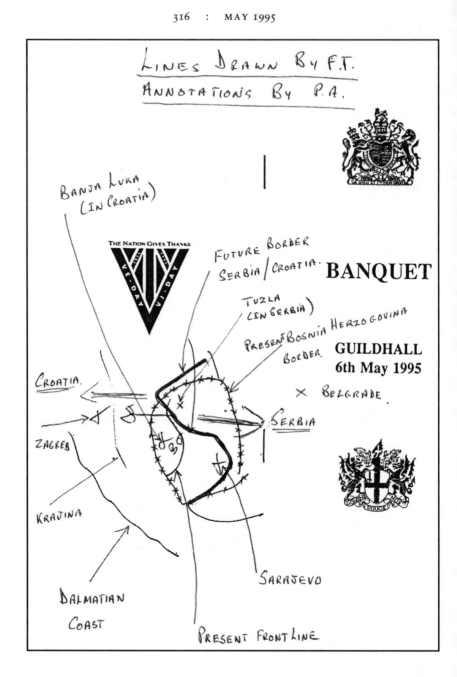

LINES DRAWN BY F.T.
ANNOTATIONS BY P.A.

BANJA LUKA (IN CROATIA)

THE NATION GIVES THANKS
VE·DAY VJ·DAY

FUTURE BORDER SERBIA/CROATIA.

TUZLA (IN SERBIA)

PRESENT BOSNIA HERZOGOVINA BORDER.

BANQUET

GUILDHALL
6th May 1995

CROATIA.

× BELGRADE.

SERBIA

ZAGREB

KRAJINA

DALMATIAN COAST

SARAJEVO

PRESENT FRONT LINE

What a terrible thought. On the day we celebrate the end of the last war in Europe, the president of a European country calmly betting a bottle of his own country's white wine that he would kill only 1,000 of his own people in a piece of military adventurism.

I detested the man very early on and decided to press him as far as I could.

As he got more and more drunk, I asked him with whom he would prefer to do business, Milosevic or Izetbegovic? He said, 'Izetbegovic is a wog and an Algerian and a fundamentalist. Historically I find it easy to do business with Milosevic. He is more intelligent, sticks to his word and anyway he is "one of us". The Muslims are only Serbs and Croats who were too weak to stand up to the Turks.'

It's perfectly clear what his game plan is. He will come to some kind of agreement with the Serbs that, as soon as their armies have taken as much as they can from each other, they will both turn on the Muslims and wipe them out. In the meantime, he is going to take on the Serbs in the Krajina at Knin, either towards the end of the period of the UN mandate or as soon as it is over. A truly horrible man.

Sunday, 7 May, London

VE DAY THANKSGIVING SERVICE

Slightly hungover today. The papers are full of my comments on *A Week in Politics* saying that we have to tackle equidistance this year. It's the lead in the *Sunday Times*: 'Ashdown and Blair prepare anti-Tory pact'. This will cause trouble among the Colleagues. But it is what I anticipated. The press can only think in black and white; if we are not on one side, then we must be on the other. It will take us some time to get the real message through.

To St Paul's, which always takes me by surprise. The sheer grandeur of the place. With all the television arc lights, the ceiling above us glittered as though set with precious stones. The choir sang a beautiful anthem by John Tavener. Ghostly trebles from the back pushing against the basses singing about beating swords into ploughshares. It made my spine tingle.

Afterwards the crowds outside clapped me and Blair as we emerged together. We then piled into a bus and drove back to Buckingham Palace. When we got there I used their phone to ring Archy to find out the Colleagues' reaction to the anti-Tory pact story. Predictably a lot of kick-back. Paul Tyler says we are in for a real bloodbath at the Wednesday Parliamentary Party Meeting.

Tuesday, 9 May, Somerset and London

The Party is in turmoil. They assumed the *Sunday Times* stuff is a result of a briefing and that I am about to lead them into deals with Labour. Bob Maclennan has had phone calls saying I am not fit to lead the Party and my e-mail is full of messages from outraged councillors. We will just have to stiffen our sinews to see this through until people understand what it is I am trying to do.

Andrew Marr, though, has written a perceptive article in the *Independent* today. It's as though he has been living inside my head for the last month.

When I got up to London Archy called me, very worried: the Parliamentary Party also believe that the *Sunday Times* story was the result of a special briefing put out by me. I am in for a very tough time tomorrow. I told Archy that, having spoken to all the MPs, I was confident tomorrow would be OK. He said I was wrong.

Wednesday, 10 May, Westminster

I rehearsed with Archy what I am going to say at the PPM. How I would put myself in listening mode and outline the origin of my thinking, and the outcome of the national consultation exercise.[1]

He remains very nervous. He particularly wants me to speak to Diana Maddock and David Rendel. So I cancelled my programme to see them.

The local government people, meanwhile, are being terrific. Real politicians who are used to dealing with power. I faxed the draft document I am going to use to end equidistance through to Andrew Stunell and Bill Le Bretton. They think it's fine but caution against delay on releasing it, to avoid leaks.

Then Diana and David. I had a terrible meeting with them. They both think we should continue the myth that we could support the Conservatives. If this is a prelude of what is to come, I am in trouble.

The Parliamentary Party Meeting was the worst I have ever experienced. Those who promised to back the proposal didn't, despite the fact that they

---

1 I had been exhaustingly tramping the country from end to end since January, meeting local parties, explaining my vision post the Chard Speech and telling them of the need to abandon equidistance.

had all received a brilliant and supportive minute drafted by Chris Rennard. Alan Beith said that if we abandoned equidistance we would be misunderstood. Malcolm Bruce agreed. Don Foster was helpful, but stressed no pacts, no mergers. Bob Maclennan hardly said anything. Liz Lynne said it was appalling and she wouldn't stand for it. Charles Kennedy came in late and was very equivocal. Alex Carlile was utterly clear but totally unhelpful, saying that he wanted a pact with Labour now.

I gently said that if we got on to what the position might be with Labour in a year's time, we were dead – let's concentrate on one thing at a time and talk about the abandonment of equidistance. At which point Simon Hughes entered the debate in a thoroughly confusing way and lost everybody after half a minute.

The whole thing then spun steadily out of control. I had to send a message out to Jane halfway through saying we'd have to cancel our attendance at tonight's Guildhall dinner for the 200th anniversary of the Red Cross, for which she had come in all dressed up. The message came back that they had laid a place for me next to Mrs Dole[1], the Queen was going to be there, we couldn't cancel, etc. But I insisted, and wrote a letter of apology afterwards.

Alan Beith tried to sum up by saying that we must oppose the Tories but that we shouldn't actually say this or close our options until after the next election.

I jumped in with my own summing-up: 'I just want to say two final things to you: If you duck this decision you will lose much more than you will by taking it. You will lose members and you will certainly lose voters. And you will be made to look very foolish.

'My second thing is more difficult. So I had better put it bluntly. If you want a leader who will argue the myth of equidistance at the next election, it can't be me. You'll have to get someone else to do it.'

Everybody said, No, no, that's not what we are asking. What we were actually saying is we just don't want it now.

I told them I couldn't agree to that. And I would have to make my views clear if necessary.

At 7.45pm the meeting broke up in disarray. I went out, weak-kneed with despair.

Up to the office for a much-needed drink with Jane. In drifted Don and Paul. They said it wasn't as bad as I thought it was. But I refused to be

1 Wife of the US Senator Bob Dole. He was Republican nominee for President in 1996.

consoled and complained bitterly at the extent to which individuals in every party would much rather be comfortable in their bunkers than take decisions, particularly difficult ones.

I then took Jane off to dinner. We talked the whole thing through and concluded that I had to follow my instincts – even if it threatened my position. And the more clearly I did this, the greater my chance of success.

As we were talking, I noticed that Peter Mandelson was at a table not far from us. I said to Jane that I might take him to one side and tell him that I had had a very difficult Parliamentary Party Meeting and please tell Blair that the most useful thing from him would be silence. I knew that Mandelson would then go straight to the press and tell them that I'd had a bad Parliamentary Party meeting. And they would then go straight to Liz Lynne, who would spout it all, which would give me the chance to get it out in public and mobilize support from the Party and the friendly press. Jane said I shouldn't. It would be wrong. And probably too Machiavellian to work anyway. I agreed and was rather ashamed to have even thought of it. So I should be, she said. Indicative of my frame of mind, though.

Then at 10 o'clock, a further meeting with Bob. He agrees that we won't get this through unless I am prepared to risk my own position on it. Archy and Alan Leaman also there. All of them trying to persuade me to sit tight, play it long. Archy said that if I did say anything it would make his life more difficult. I replied rather snappily that it was my job to lead the Party, not to make his life easier. This was unkind. I couldn't have survived the previous years without him. Of all people, Archy has been utterly dedicated and totally loyal. As Chief Whip, he, of course, had to stay silent during the Parliamentary Party Meeting.

What they don't understand, I continued, is that if the decision goes against me, I am dead anyway, so I have no option. At the end I said to Archy and Alan that I had listened to their advice, but that I must trust my judgement on this.

Richard came in later. He thinks that if the Parliamentary Party was so divided, I would probably get my way anyway. Not a bad conclusion – probably the most helpful of the night.

I staggered home at midnight, dejected.

Thursday, 25 May, Westminster

At midday news started to break that Nick Jones of the BBC had got a copy of the equidistance letter.[1] We had to decide what to do. My instinct was to unveil the draft document immediately. That of others was to hold it, and build up the suspense so that we could get two bites of the cherry. In the end I agreed that this was probably correct, provided that the resulting press speculation went along the right lines. So everybody was sent scurrying off to the press gallery to tell them that it was just speculation, while doing what they could to ensure that if it was reported, the press got the right story.

In the afternoon I rang Blair, having previously sent him a copy. He was clearly disappointed by what he thought was its lack of clarity. 'Will the press understand that this is the break of equidistance?' he asked. I said, 'You can be sure of it.' He asked what sort of response we would like. I said, nothing too enthusiastic – a quiet welcome would do.

Across to the Federal Executive, where I expected a replay of the Parliamentary Party Meeting of a week ago. But they were full of praise. Even Gerald Vernon Jackson[2] was in favour. I said, 'Gerald, I am as grateful for your support as I am terrified by it!'

Slowly, slowly, I think we are winning.

Sunday, 28 May, Irancy

The Bosnian situation is getting worse. British soldiers taken hostage today. We had invited friends round to dinner and were sitting round the fire at about 10.30 when the phone rang. It was Downing Street, would I speak to the PM? They put me through, much to our friends' amusement. Not knowing who it was, Jane came in from the kitchen and said something very salty in a loud voice about people who ring at this time of night. Everybody burst into suppressed giggles and I tried to be serious.

Major said he was so worried about the Bosnian situation that he was going to send reinforcements out – an extra 6,000. I responded, 'I see. You are trying to achieve two things at the same time; send a message to the

1 See Appendix C for an abridged version.
2 Liberal Democrat activist and agent.

Serbs but also get us in a position where we have sufficient troops on the ground for withdrawal.'

'Exactly.'

I promised our qualified support, though I expressed doubts about the definition and command. He said he would take this into account. He also told me that Parliament would return on Wednesday.

My heart sank. We will have to go back home tomorrow night.

Wednesday, 31 May, London

COMMONS DEBATE ON SENDING MORE TROOPS TO BOSNIA

I spoke to Malcolm Rifkind late last night. He told me that they were considering the possibility of withdrawing from the safe havens. I asked him what they would do to protect them afterwards. He said he would provide them with assistance to protect themselves. I responded that, since the Serbs had declared that all those left in the enclaves would now be treated as enemies, that could only mean one thing. He pooh-poohed this.

So I challenged him publicly in the chamber during the summing-up speeches at the end of the Bosnia debate and he admitted that UN protection for the safe havens was 'under review'. This can only act as a green light to the Serbs to attack the safe havens, so I dashed off a letter to Major asking 'what undertakings [he] would seek as to the safety of the Muslim populations in the besieged enclaves. Or would it be acceptable [to him] to leave them to their own devices?'[1]

Sunday, 4 June, Westminster

In the evening I spoke to Chris Rennard, who was driving back from Littleborough & Saddleworth.[2] He said Labour are working really hard – no leaflets yet, but a lot of telephone canvassing. They will wait, then bring the big guns in later.

1 This, which I have since come to believe may have been a reflection of a secret agreement made by Western governments ultimately not to defend the safe havens, was the beginning of the chain of policy decisions which ended with the massacre in Srbrenica of 8,000 Bosnian Muslims in July 1995.
2 A by-election had been called in Littleborough & Saddleworth because of the death of the sitting Conservative MP, Geoffrey Dickens.

I have asked Jo Phillips to contact Blair's office. I want to see whether he will back off from a full-scale campaign in Littleborough & Saddleworth for the good of the project. I doubt it, but it's worth a try.

Friday, 9 June, London

Finally got through to Blair on the telephone at 8.00am.

I said, 'We need to discuss when the work on the constitution should start, who will do it from your side and who the contact person at a lower level in your office is going to be.'

He said, rather elliptically, 'Yes, we do need to discuss that. I was talking about it with Robin the other day. I will get Anji to fix something early next week.'

I was taken aback by this. I had expected him to reply, yes, we have decided on who. It's X and Y and let's get together to discuss the remit, etc., etc.

This could be chaos, bad organization or overwork, or all three. Or it could be (in my view, more likely) that they have gone cold on the project until after their Autumn Conference.

PA: I also want to talk about Littleborough & Saddleworth to see if there is anything we can do to prevent our people from using language which damages the long-term prospects.

TB: Yes, I am concerned about that, too. One of the reasons why I put Peter Mandelson there was to ensure that the language was properly controlled. [I have less faith in Mandelson's abilities in this area. He was terrible at Eastleigh.] But your candidate is all right on the broad project position, isn't he?

PA: Yes. But you need to understand that while no doubt it would be nice for you to win Littleborough, it is vital for us. If you are serious about the long-term project, our capacity to win seats where we are challenging the Tories would be fatally undermined if we weren't able to win Littleborough and Saddleworth.

He knew perfectly well what I was hinting at, but didn't reply.

I went on, 'This is a test case of whether you are prepared to make the sacrifices to get the project to work.'
Still no response.

He has been got at, I suspect. I will wait until our meeting next week to go harder.

Sunday, 11 June, Somerset

A little snooze and then a walk with the dog. Blair got all his policies through his policy forum in Reading today.

I am becoming really worried. I can't see a role for us. If the Tories collapse completely I suppose we could become Her Majesty's Opposition. But then what? Our policies are too close to Labour's for us to be a genuine Opposition and the Tories would simply recover again. Meanwhile, Labour has stolen our ground comprehensively. If I do manage to construct something distinctive, it's going to be very much a smoke-and-mirrors job.

In the past I have been able to see what the Party should do next. But with the advent of Blair it's becoming much more difficult. So much depends on Littleborough & Saddleworth.

Thursday, 15 June, Westminster

To Blair's office at 10.45am. He had his jacket off and was sitting in a rather crumpled fashion in the chair. But he was looking jovial and we had a good forty-five minutes' discussion, despite the fact that both of us said we only had half an hour. I started by saying that I thought he had been disappointed by our equidistance document.

He said yes, he thought we had been too delicate about it. 'From my experience, you have to take your Party members and shove their faces in it before they really understand. What you did was phrased far too carefully.'

I replied that the press knew that it meant the abandonment of equidistance. And that was what mattered.

I then took him on to the territory which I knew was affecting him. 'I think you are upset because I have criticized Labour. Is that true?'

TB: Yes, I am. I don't see why you should play the Tories' game. Saying that we are unelectable, can't be trusted in government etc., only plays into their hands and diminishes your capacity to pull votes where you need to.

I replied that it was absolutely vital that we maintained a strong tension between the parties. I had to ensure that my Party wasn't swallowed up by his. And this meant identifying not only the policy differences but also the role that we had to play.

TB: Yeah, but I think your role is to be more distinctive than us.

PA: That's not sufficient. You don't have to answer the question, 'Why vote Labour?' because it's obvious. People vote Labour because they could be the next Government. But I have to answer the question 'Why vote Lib Dem?' The answer to that comes in two parts. One is about policy (distinctiveness) and the second is about our role in the context of the new Government. The answer to that second question is that our role will be to make a change to Labour safe. That way we pull votes in areas where the Tories are still frightened of your Party.

TB: So your position is to be strong and independent?

PA: Exactly! And that means that we have to correct the impression that we are in your pocket. Which means that the next four or five months will be a period when we mark out our differences from you and our suspicions about what you would be like in government.

TB: The Shadow Cabinet thinks something is going on behind the scenes but don't seem to object to it. The Labour policy forum in Reading was very relaxed about working with the Lib Dems. There are grumbles in some corners of the Party. But only a few.

I said I believed we were now ready to move to the second stage, creating the climate for co-operation. This meant widening the base from bilateral discussions between him and me. He agreed that it was time to 'build some super-structure around this'. He talked about getting Labour people to attend our conference and sending out invitations for us to attend theirs. I said this was a matter we should treat with some caution. However, I agreed that Archy Kirkwood would discuss this with Jonathan Powell to see what could be done.

We also agreed that the work should start on the constitutional project. Robin Cook will do this for them and Bob Maclennan can contact him as soon as possible. But this process ought not to be made public until after the Conferences.

He also thought it was time he made a statement which echoed the equidistance statement. He would do this before the summer recess.

We discussed Littleborough & Saddleworth at some length.

TB: If this was a Newbury then I would be hauling my people off – but it isn't. We stand a chance of winning and we have to go for it.

PA: You are damaging our ability to deliver seats in the South and West, where you can't beat the Tories. Littleborough & Saddleworth is vital for us. We will do whatever is necessary to win.

We also talked about the South West:

TB: I had some figures produced the other day. You lot *really are* in a very commanding position in the South West indeed, aren't you? And we are nowhere. I wonder if we can do anything about that?

PA: I don't think there is anything we can do about it, beyond informally encouraging tactical voting by creating the expectation that we will work together in the next Parliament.

I sensed he would go further, if we came up with a reasonable proposition for his people to stand down in the West Country in order for us to gain these seats.

Afterwards, back to the office.

Monday, 26 June, Westminster

Into the office late, about 9 o'clock, cleared the mail then walked down to the Westminster Hall for the fiftieth anniversary celebrations of the UN. I was part of the platform party. Blair arrived very late, flustered and sweating coming down the steps that the Queen would enter by. Shortly after he sat down Major came in from the back of the hall like the rest of us. Blair turned to me with panic in his voice and said, 'Oh my God, were we supposed to come in that way?' 'Yes, the other steps are for the Queen,' I said and winked at him. He blushed to his roots and said, 'That's terrible. I was told to come down that way.' Then through clenched teeth and in a low voice (we were surrounded by Tories), 'This lot are in a real mess. You and I should have a chat. I have asked my office to ring yours to fix a time today so we can co-ordinate the line.' I said, 'I am speculating on an early election.' To which he replied, 'We think there may be. There is some very sharp thinking to do and we have started doing it already.'

Wednesday, 28 June, London

I have decided to make another visit to Sarajevo, where the situation has deteriorated sharply. The Serb ring has tightened and life is extremely hard there. A lot of shelling today. We sent a message by secure fax through the Foreign Office network to Rasim Kadic[1] in Sarajevo, saying that I would like to come, but the UN wouldn't get me in. Could the Bosnians get me into the city?

Spoke to Martin Bell, who has just come out. He tells me all routes are closed, except some old logging tracks over Igman.

He believes, as I do, that the Rapid Reaction Force[2] is actually all about withdrawal.

Meanwhile, word from Littleborough & Saddleworth is good. Chris Rennard tells me that the polls show us slightly ahead, but it's very tight.

All the news is of Major in trouble.[3] I spoke to one Tory MP in the lobby today who told me he would either vote against Major or abstain because he wanted Heseltine. In the middle of our conversation his local newspaperman came up to him and he said, brazen as you like, that he was going to vote for Major and he should put it down in the local newspaper that he is a firm Major supporter – bloody liar!

Wednesday, 5 July, Stockholm

ELDR MEETING

A lovely bright day. Stockholm is rather beautiful, though all built in the style of the Midland Bank.

At the hotel I bumped into Hasib Salkic,[4] who had been waiting for me. He had come out of Sarajevo over Igman four or five days ago. Rasim Kadic had told him of my intention to try and get into the city. He agreed to take me through the lines, crossing the old logging tracks over Igman and then through the tunnel into the city – I would be the first non-Bosnian to go through it. We fixed a rendezvous at Jablanica at 2.00am on Sunday 16 July.

1 President of the Liberal Party in Bosnia.
2 Major's reinforcements.
3 The Tory leadership election, which Major himself initiated, was in full swing.
4 Secretary-General of the Bosnian Liberal Party in Sarajevo.

Wednesday, 12 July, Cowley Street

To Cowley Street for the 8.30am Co-ordinating Group meeting. Party structure looking better and finances are stabilizing – we will probably have a £30,000 deficit at the end of the year, but £15,000 of this may be taken away because of a tax break. Membership stabilizing, too. And some evidence of increasing branch activity.

A very cheerful meeting, until at 9.15 Alan Leaman said, 'This is all very well. But what about the front page of the *Independent*?'[1] He then passed it down the table for me to read. Archy said, 'Oh, it doesn't look too bad to me.' I said, 'Yes, it *is*' – and threw the paper at him to read.

Hurt, I said, 'I don't give a damn about me, but I really object when our party slugs its decent guts out in Littleborough & Saddleworth, while MPs in Westminster help journos write the Labour Party's campaign literature for them. The Party will be furious, and quite rightly, too!'

After the meeting, back to the office in a towering rage. I could see everybody steering a path around me.

Thursday, 13 July, London

At an early morning BBC programme I met Martin Bell again. I told him of my plan to go into Sarajevo over the weekend. He said, 'Good luck, mate – absolutely right you should go in, even if they do try and stop you.'

Over the morning the Foreign Office started kicking up about my going over Igman – too dangerous, could damage a fragile situation, etc., etc. By PMQs I still hadn't heard whether they would try to stop me, so I scribbled a note to Rifkind saying I needed a final view by 4.30, and passed it across the floor of the House to him.

Later his office phoned to say that the Foreign Secretary had said I should go. He followed this up with a letter later saying he couldn't arrange for UNPROFOR to take me in and it wouldn't be possible to get UN

---

1 An article by their chief political correspondent, Colin Brown, headlined 'Liberal Democrat MPs Put Ashdown under Pressure' and reporting 'rumblings . . . of discontent . . . about Ashdown's leadership'; criticism of me 'spending too much time in Bosnia' and trying to 'steer the party towards . . . Labour'.

clearance. But it would be useful if I went and he would like to talk to me when I came back.

I am more nervous about going in this time than ever before.

So I found myself writing Jane one of those notes you write in these circumstances and told Sallyann where to find it if anything did happen.

Saturday, 15 July, Bosnia

Arrived at Jablanica in the early afternoon. Yesterday four Belgian trucks were destroyed by tank fire on the road over Igman that I am to travel tomorrow. But it appears they went in daytime, the fools.

I stayed the night with a Bosnian family Hasib had fixed up for me in the town. We sat around chatting in very broken English and drinking a bottle of whisky I had brought. At around 11.00 we received a message that Hasib would arrive after midnight. So I went for an hour or so's sleep, asking the family to wake me when he came.

Sunday, 16 July, Bosnia

At 2 o'clock I woke up. No Hasib.

I thought to myself, 'we can't be going in tonight' and went back to sleep.

Woke again at 3.20am. Hasib had just arrived. His plane from Germany to Zagreb had been late.

He said we should go in tonight. I looked at my watch. Surely there wasn't enough time to get over before daylight? He replied, 'Never mind, I think we can do it, so let's go. I will give you fifteen minutes.'

I said I only needed five. I piled my stuff into the back of his Renault 5. The car was so full that there was room for just one in the back. I insisted that the girl travelling with Hasib, a twenty-two-year-old Sarajevan called Amerla, should sit in the front while I clambered into the back seat with my gear piled up around me.

As soon as I saw Amerla I realized that even if I'd wanted to put on my flak jacket I couldn't, since she didn't have one.

By 3.30 we were off at breakneck speed up the valley through Konic and then on to a route marked 'Sarajevo Igman – 30 km'.

As we left Jablanica, Hasib looked up and said, 'A perfect night for going in. The fog is down over the mountains.'

As we drove up the mountain, however, we broke into a cloudless, moonlit night. But no one mentioned it.

The ascent started off on a tarmac road, but this soon deteriorated into an indescribably nasty little track which had started life as an Ottoman logging route.

The sky was, by now, getting disturbingly light. To make matters worse we repeatedly had to pull in to let through traffic which had left Sarajevo earlier under cover of darkness. An occasional lorry, a few armoured Land-Rovers – and one or two Bosnians coming out. Everybody going at a breakneck speed. I suppose if you have been shot at and shelled for so long, you don't care about dangerous driving.

Then we got a puncture. We changed the wheel in record time and hurtled off again.

But we were still an hour away from Sarajevo and it was becoming evident that we would arrive in broad daylight. My heart started to sink. Knowing Hasib, he would go in anyway.

I decided the only thing was to pray and submit myself to what would come next.

Another thirty minutes and we passed a UN base in the dawn mist before turning up an even more vicious track. Finally over the top and down the other side, through a Bosnian frontline base. Hasib turned to me and said, 'This is the last road block – I am not sure if we can go in. I will look when we get there. Perhaps we will walk down the mountain into the city.'

Good, I thought. At least there was an alternative. I replied that walking sounded a good idea. Hasib said he didn't think so – we'd have to cross a minefield!

So, finally, we got to the point that I dreaded most. By now I could see the city lying below us veiled in a thin fog which seemed to start too many feet below us to be much help.

I longed to get down into its shelter, but it seemed to move down ahead of us. We then turned on to the final kilometre of road which descends into the outskirts of the city. The Bosnian on the last road block said, 'It looks pretty tricky. Are you sure you want to go?' But then he mentioned to Hasib that there was a UN convoy on its way up. Hasib reasoned that the UN convoy would have clearance and decided to give it a try.

There was dead silence in the car as we hurtled down the final kilometre.

The mountain falling away vertiginously to our right, the dreaded school-yard with the Serb heavy Z88 machine guns dead ahead and the city emerging into sunlight from the early morning fog. There was safety, but would we get there?

I recall consoling myself with the thought that if it was going to be nasty, at least it would be quick.

Hasib hurtled the little car down the track, dodging the huge UN lorries which were hurtling up. They weren't stopping for anything – especially an insignificant Renault 5.

We passed the burned-out remains of previous UN convoys that had been shot up, the one from two nights ago still smoking. Then some private cars totally destroyed by the dreadful Z88s.

Mercifully, fog briefly shrouded the Ildje schoolyard where the Serb guns were positioned. But I knew they would be on fixed lines. One press of the button would be sufficient.

At one stage a UN lorry flying past us up the hill hit the back of the car with a bang, breaking the window beside me. I was covered in broken glass. Hasib turned round, thinking that we'd been hit. I said simply 'It's OK.' But the car was quite severely damaged. We could easily have been barged off the road, down the mountain and into the minefield.

Eventually, we made it to the bottom of the hill. We were safe.

Hasib and I both had unlit cigarettes in our mouths all the way down the hill but no light. I had given up smoking six weeks before but Bosnia made me start again. So we borrowed a match from one of the UN soldiers at the first Sarajevo checkpoint. Hasib swore about the damage to his car. 'Better to be hit by a UN truck than by a Serb shell,' I said. We laughed and agreed that could be the motto for Sarajevo in this war.

We then drove to the start of the concealed route to the tunnel.

Hasib stopped at the side of what looked like an ordinary bit of road and pulled back a bush to reveal a shallow communications trench leading away from the road at a sharp angle. We humped our stuff on to our backs, left the Renault with one of Hasib's friends and started off down the trench.

We walked for about 400 metres out into no-man's land between the two front lines to a single isolated house. On the way we passed people who had come through the tunnel from the opposite direction. Mostly soldiers, young girls and old women carrying vegetables.

We entered the tunnel itself under the house we had been heading for. Here was an underground waiting room lit by low-wattage bulbs powered by a generator which we could hear quietly thumping away somewhere close by. We waited in the semi-darkness and were then shown into a second underground chamber. As my eyes grew accustomed to the light I saw that the place was full of people waiting to go in. Some soldiers swapping jokes and occasionally blowing smoke into the dark; a disabled man making his way back into the city following a leg amputation; three schoolgirls going back to their families; and some old men and women sitting hunched in a corner.

The atmosphere was foetid and foul smelling – not least, I suspect, from us, as we were sweating profusely from our walk along the trench.

Eventually, we were called forward into another room, where our passports were checked. Hasib spoke to the commander of the tunnel, a friend of his (Hasib knows everybody in Sarajevo). The commander asked to see my passport and said to Hasib, 'But he's British!' Hasib said I had proved myself a friend of Sarajevo and could be trusted.

He waved us through.

Shortly after the entrance, the tunnel was joined by another one from the right. We stopped here and loaded our stuff on to a trolley, which Hasib and I took turns to push ahead of us on a pair of railway lines made of upended angle irons.

The tunnel started about seven feet high but quickly dropped in height as we went further in. Hasib told me to make sure I didn't bang my head, which I nevertheless did about four times during the kilometre walk to the other end.

By now we were bent double, the tunnel having reduced to around 4ft 6in high and about 3 feet wide. The whole length of the tunnel is well engineered, with wooden joists holding up the ceiling. To start with, we were just below the surface and there were little air holes above us through which I could see daylight. Every hundred yards or so there were passing places, lit by softly glowing bulbs. We were told to keep silent because of fear of detection by Serb listening posts.

As we went deeper the temperature rose and the air got staler. By now the ceiling of the tunnel was dripping with water. At the deepest point (going under the airfield runway) the water was up to our ankles.

In due course we made it to the tunnel mouth and came out, blinking in the daylight, into a small square in the suburb of Dobrinja to be met by a group of Bosnian soldiers. Their commander said, 'Why didn't you tell us you were coming earlier?' Hasib replied, 'Look, this bloke has come in like a Bosnian. He is a senior politician in England. If he'd told you, you would have made it even more difficult. Anyway, we didn't want the bloody Serbs to know, did we? He is not very popular with them.'

We waited patiently outside with a group of fellow tunnel travellers while Amerla went off to the Liberal Party office. Dobrinja, as before, totally wrecked. Several fresh mortar strikes on the ground. Hasib said the Serbs regularly mortar this square, to catch people using the tunnel. Still can't wear the flak jacket, though, since nobody else is.

We picked up a car and dropped Amerla off at her home. Sarajevo has gone rapidly downhill since I was last here. The trams were running at Christmas. No sign of them now. But at least it's quiet. I heard one large shell landing in the distance; perhaps a 155. An occasional crack of sniper shots.

Hasib dropped me back at his flat where I fell asleep for three hours, getting up at 7.00pm. By now the city, which had been quiet all day, was reverting to its usual noisy self for the evening.

Monday, 17 July, Sarajevo

A midday meeting with General Sir Rupert Smith.[1] He has briefed me before. I liked him then and I like him even more now.

He wanted to press home that he had suffered one defeat as a result of politicians failing to back up the action he had taken and couldn't afford to suffer another. If we were to ask him to take any action, we had to realize its consequences, and make sure we were prepared to see the issue through. 'All the ambiguities and illusions of the Bosnian operation are now being cruelly exposed.'

He was very honest, very forthright and impressed me considerably. He said that we ought to recognize that opening Igman meant breaking the siege of Sarajevo, the consequence of which could be going to war with Mladic. If that's what we wanted him to do, fine. But he needed backing for the operation. There was no point in taking the first step, then shouting ouch at the second and stopping at the third.

It was an excellent briefing. A million times better than Rose. He is said to be much respected by the Bosnians, too.

By eight o'clock the sirens were wailing. We were in for a bumpy night. A lot of machine-gun fire and mortars hitting the buildings quite close

1 Commander of the UN Forces in Bosnia. Smith had replaced Rose earlier in 1995.

to us. The UNPROFOR headquarters appears to have been especially targeted.

Dinner with Haris Silajdzic in a restaurant with the shells banging away around us. I found him weary, with sunken cheeks and in a despairing mood. He thinks everybody is against him. The West want him to divide Bosnia and the right wing of his party are telling him he is not fundamentalist enough. Haris loves to feel persecuted.

I told him about my conversation with Tudjman. He asked me to send him the map on the menu. Finished at 11.00 and Silajdzic dropped me back, at Hasib's flat.

I packed my kit by candle- and torchlight and set my alarm for 2.00am. A very noisy night with heavy fire-fights around the Presidency, just opposite the flat. I moved my bed directly under the window so that I wouldn't be hit by flying glass and slept rather soundly.

Tuesday, 18 July, Sarajevo

Up at 2.15am. Dressed in the dark, shaved by candlelight and walked down to a nearby street corner where I had arranged to meet the UNPROFOR people. They turned up exactly at 3.00, as agreed, and drove me to their headquarters. Then into a Land-Rover with a French officer, Colonel Coiffet, and a couple of British officers. We rumbled on to the airfield in the dark with our lights off.

I looked up nervously at Igman. The usual shroud of mist not there, but the night itself was quite thick and foggy. I could see the loom of the hill but not much more. We drove up the hill as fast as possible to our rendezvous point with the helicopter which was to take us to visit British troops in Kisseljak.[1]

Thursday, 27 July, Somerset

LITTLEBOROUGH & SADDLEWORTH BY-ELECTION DAY

Just before leaving Yeovil I had put a message through to Nick South that I wanted to speak to Blair. He rang me from his constituency office.

---

1 This period became known retrospectively as 'The Battle of Igman'. Shortly afterwards, NATO at last used air power and troops to break the three-year seige of Sarajevo. A ceasefire followed in October, and the Dayton Peace Accords shortly thereafter.

I told him that there were going to be hard words about the Littleborough & Saddleworth campaign. 'We really can't go round pretending that we are creating a new kind of politics based on respect for other people's parties, then spend three weeks character assassinating the other's candidates.' He said maybe he had misunderstood the campaign, but he thought it was fine. 'Anyway it doesn't matter, you are going to win.'

We agreed that we should see the next two or three days through and that it would not alter anything in the long term.

At 10 o'clock we were all getting terribly nervous about the predicted closeness of the result. On *Newsnight*, a good attack by Alton on Mandelson for the dirtiness of their campaign. I expected the result at a few minutes past 12.00. At 11.45 I got a bleep saying that the team in the count thought we were safe, but not by much, perhaps 2,000 votes. In the event the result was much delayed and there was a great deal of biting of nails. The final majority for Chris Davies[1] was 1,993.

Huge relief.

Friday, 28 July, Littleborough and Saddleworth

To Littleborough and Saddleworth to celebrate Chris's victory. A good deal of riding around in open-topped buses. At the post-election press conference I was asked about the Labour campaign and replied, 'I think New Labour should let the dust settle and then go away and decide whether this is really the kind of politics they want to be known for in Britain.' Later in the day Nick told me he had spoken to Blair's office. Apparently they had received calls from lots of people, including the *Guardian*, asking whether this was the end of co-operation. They wanted permission to say that Blair and I had spoken. Certainly not. What on earth has got into them? They must be under pressure.

I authorized a statement to go out saying that of course the dialogue of ideas would continue, but that everything has been far from lovey-dovey. Still, we have rattled them, I think.

The papers are very good, saying we have stopped the Blair surge and that we are now the most powerful third party force Britain has had for sixty years.

---

1 Member of Parliament (Liberal Democrat) for Littleborough & Saddleworth 1995–7. Now a Member of the European Parliament.

Somebody said that Labour had come a good second; couldn't I congratulate them?

I said, 'I remember the days when we used to celebrate good second places. I am more than happy to let Labour have the opportunity on this occasion.'

Tuesday, 1 August, London

The only time Blair can see me is 6.30 at his house. Sod it! I will be very late back from London and will have to drive to Yeovil through the rush hour.

Anji didn't realize that I didn't have a driver or a government car and said, 'Good God that's scandalous, we should do something to alter that!' They do live in cloud-cuckoo-land.

I was with Blair by 6.30. He suggested we sit out in the garden. It was very pleasant, but we were overlooked by houses on either side. I hope nobody had a camera.

We had a rather rambling discussion, much of it on PR. He told me that intellectually he had serious reservations about PR and didn't believe that the public would want it. 'If the tabloid newspapers really take against it, we could lose and find the public opposed.' I reminded him that he was bound to lose if he wasn't prepared to stake out his position clearly and argue for it. 'It would be out of character for you – and, more importantly, for your image as a decisive leader – to do a "Kinnock" and sit on the fence on this.'

I explained that I wanted my Party to be committed to co-operation. But there was no point in doing this if the result was political suicide. If he hit a period of unpopularity – which was bound to happen sooner or later – he would suffer; but we could be wiped out. PR was the mechanism which would ensure that we could survive and therefore be able to support a Labour Government in a stable and dependable way. Secondly, if he was really committed to pluralism, then PR was the non-return valve for a pluralist Britain.

He is still very hesitant. It is going to be the big block.

Eventually I said, 'Let's get off this subject. We have discussed it to death. You know my position and I know yours. The important thing is what happens next. Our forthcoming Party Conferences should now be consolidating ones, at which we should pocket what we have done over the last year. You with your modernization; me with our position on equidistance. When they are over and those positions have been accepted by our parties, then we can begin to move to the next phase.'

We then got on to Littleborough & Saddleworth.

PA: I don't mind playing hard ball with you. We have to compete and we have to compete strenuously. And it's right and proper that we should do so. It's not that that we are objecting to. What we are objecting to is the importation of American-style politics, which is deliberately designed to play the man, not the ball. You didn't discuss your policies. You simply spent four weeks character-assassinating Chris Davies. He is one of my Party's favourite sons and to be dealt with by Labour like this is not the way that we build respect between our parties. If you intend to import these kinds of negative campaigning tactics into British politics I don't think our project can stand it and I don't want any part of it.

Towards the end of our meeting he again returned to the dominance of the Lib Dems in the South West.

TB: You guys really are in such a dominant position down there, surely there is some way we can rationalize this?

PA: If you are thinking about pacts, forget it. It is not sensible for you and me to spend the next two years wandering up and down the country winding our candidates' arms up their backs to persuade them to stand down, when we should be attacking the Government. The best we can do is create the expectation of co-operation so as to encourage tactical voting.

Cherie came in halfway through, having been to the gym. Blair said that he had to get me to come to his house, because he had been looking after the kids all day! He is looking forward to his summer holidays, he is very tired and desperately in need of a break.

I left at 7.30, walking out to the car and feeling very exposed. I saw one resident turn his head to watch me.

Friday, 4 August, London

Tudjman's predictions to me at the VE Day celebration dinner at the Guildhall are coming true. The Croats are attacking Knin, just as he said they would.[1] And they are making a success of it. They are gobbling up the Serbs very quickly. The Serbs in Croatia look defeated.

1 I decided overnight to leak to *The Times* the map which Tudjman drew for me on the back of the VE Day menu at the Guildhall on 6 May. It became known as 'The Map on the Menu'. My intention was to alert the international community to the Croats' long-term aims in the Knin operations, which included the division of Bosnia between themselves and the Serbs.

Monday, 7 August, London

Most newspapers have the map on their front pages today. The Croats have started kicking back, saying that it wasn't Tudjman's handwriting, etc.

Sunday, 20 August, London

VJ DAY FIFTIETH-ANNIVERSARY PARADE

In the afternoon, to Horseguards for a VJ Day parade. As I was chatting to the new Chief of the Naval Staff, Admiral Mike Boyce [now Chief of the Defence Staff], who as a submariner had landed me in my bygone SBS days, the PM came up for a chat. Blair joined us. The three of us stood there talking for about five minutes with the press frantically photographing us. Major was in a rather odd mood. Bosnia is going really badly – he thinks the Croatians will open up in eastern Slovenia. He told us that he had worked two and a half hours every day while on holiday.

Blair said he had done absolutely nothing, not even read the newspapers.

Then Major suddenly said, 'Do you know that goldfish can get sunstroke?'

Startled, we confessed we didn't.

He then launched into an extraordinary tale about how some of the ornamental carp in the pond he had constructed in his garden in Huntingdon had spent too much time basking on the surface in the sun and got badly sunburned. He had had to take them out and put suncream on them.

But the next day a heron came and ate them all. 'Most distressing,' he said.

It somehow seemed so typical of Major, poor man. The only Prime Minister in history to have tried to save some goldfish – and even then to have failed.

The USA and Germany, who were especially close to the Croats, together with other members of the international community, responded to the Croat offensive by putting pressure on Tudjman to halt the offensive before it was complete. I have since come to believe that what Tudjman drew for me on VE day were not just his aims, but the agreement he had reached with Milosevic about how they would divide up Bosnia, at their secret Karadjordjevo 'hunting lodge' meeting of March 1991.

In March 1998, I went to the International War Crimes Tribunal in The Hague to give evidence, which included both the map and my account of the Guildhall dinner, in the successful prosecution of the Croat General Blaskic for war crimes during the Knin offensive.

I joked, 'Well, over the hols, you had trouble with your goldfish. But Tony has had similar trouble with his Party.'[1]

Blair said, 'Nothing a few piranhas wouldn't put right.'

To which I replied, 'You have plenty of those.'

We all laughed.

1 Whilst Blair was on holiday, Prescott was involved in suspending Walsall's local Labour Party. This led to a Labour MP attacking Blair as having an inner sanctum that controlled the Party. Further condemnation of this action followed.

Thursday, 7 September, Irancy

END OF OUR HOLIDAY

I am not sleeping again, worried about the conference. I lay awake for three hours last night.

We packed slowly, shut the windows and closed everything up. I wandered round our house. It is already ghostly. Standing in the little lane outside I could almost hear the laughter around our dinner table as the stars shone above us on one of those black, black Burgundy nights. And, in my mind's eye, see our friends' faces lit by candlelight and our table laden with empty dishes and spent wine bottles.

Now the house looked unbelievably lonely. I remarked to Jane as we left that one of the advantages of having a second home is that you are always in your own house during the holidays. But one of the disadvantages is that when you leave it's not just a hotel room you leave behind, but a piece of your heart.

Wednesday, 13 September, Westminster

At a press conference today someone asked me when I'd seen Blair and I said, 'I can't remember.' 'But you had an hour and a half with him on VJ Day.' 'No, the only time I saw Blair on VJ Day was with him and the Prime Minister. And we weren't discussing politics, we were discussing the Prime Minister's goldfish.'

This became the story of the press conference. I said that the Prime Minister had, I understood, rescued his goldfish by putting suntan cream on them, but in vain, since they were then eaten by a heron.

They all dashed off to Downing Street for comment. Downing Street responded, 'We are not prepared to confirm the detail. But we can confirm that the Prime Minister has a long-standing interest in goldfish.'

Then they asked Blair's office, whose comment was, 'These are not our goldfish to comment on.'

Sunday, 17 September, Glasgow

EVE OF LIB DEM ANNUAL PARTY CONFERENCE

A photo-op over breakfast with Jane and then an interview with Frost. It seemed to go quite well. The Party is in a positive mood.

More work on my end-of-conference speech. Very slow. On the fourteenth draft now.

At 7.00pm a story began to break that Blair had done an interview for *The Times* tomorrow all about co-operation.

I was furious. This is not the moment for stories about co-operation.

I told Nick that I really had to speak to Blair and find out what the hell was going on. Eventually I got through.

PA: What's the meaning of this? I don't understand what you're trying to do.

TB (in that puzzled voice of his): Oh dear, has it played that big? I didn't mean it to.

I said that was strange, since he gave the interview to *The Times* on Thursday, presumably in the knowledge that it would be used on the first day of our Conference, and Alastair Campbell had gone out of his way to brief *The Times* on the significance both of the substance and of the timing.

TB: Well, the right thing for you to do is to welcome it.

PA: You must be crazy! This has thrown a hand-grenade into our conference. And I am now going to have to try and settle them down. Remember we agreed that these would be consolidating Conferences? I'll be as welcoming as I can. But I will have to distance myself from this.

I then started to plot the counterattack, to regain control of the Conference.

I eventually decided that the line we would take was: 'We meet here strong, united and confident. If Tony Blair is responding to the agenda that we launched three years ago – well and good. But you can't co-operate if you don't have any policies. We do, and he doesn't. So the next move is up to him.'

We then fixed for me to do the *Today* programme tomorrow morning. I must give the Party a lead on this early, or the Conference will descend into chaos.

Tuesday, 19 September, Glasgow

Up blessedly late at around 7.00. The press and radio reports from yesterday are excellent. Even a couple of cartoons showing Blair paying court to me. Though I'm still worried about the tone.

My speech at 2.20. It didn't go nearly as well as it should have done. It sagged in the middle, although it picked up in the second half. Afterwards a dreadful anticlimax. I was covered in sweat from head to toe.

I suddenly felt horribly drained. I didn't think I had done a very good job. But Bob Maclennan said he thought it was terrific; the delegates were buzzing with it. Then the messages started dribbling in. I watched the television on which there was a phone-in programme where people rang in saying they would be joining us because of what I had said. Extraordinary. I thought the speech had been a failure in delivery. I can never judge these things.

The Conference has gone well. Good press coverage. And we have turned the pressure back on Blair.

"IT TAKES TWO TO TANGO, TWO TO TANGO..."

Saturday, 7 October, London

Just before we arrived back in London from Hong Kong[1] I turned on the World Service to hear that Alan Howarth[2] has defected to Labour. A tremendous coup for them and a blow for the Tories at the start of their Conference. Labour are getting their act together. I wanted them to show some fallibility this week.

I am filled with deep foreboding. I had assumed that we had survived last year with Labour at its high-water mark. It now looks as if they can go still higher. I am really worried about how they will eat into our base.

We landed at Heathrow at 6.30pm and I immediately contacted Alan Leaman. He is sounding very tired and fed up. He has had a tough week. But there is good news. Archy has seen Peter Thurnham.[3] Thurnham says he will join us, but probably not until after the General Election is called. I said we should try and bring him in earlier. It would be wonderful if we could announce a defector on the day of Major's speech at the Tory Conference.

Archy thought the chances very slim, but I asked him to try. He later reported back that Thurnham didn't want to go to the Tory Conference, but that he had to, since he had a fringe meeting to address. He would find out what was happening. He believes that a number of Tory MPs are feeling the same way as him and Howarth, but most of them won't join another Party, they will just leave politics. Archy said there was not much chance of getting him earlier. Pity – we could do with a lift at the moment.

Monday, 8 October, Westminster

A glorious bright, sunny autumn day.
At 11.30 Alan Leaman and Nick South came round to discuss a minute Alan had written me. They both expressed strong reservations about taking co-operation with Labour any further. I told them of my concerns about the

1 I had been invited by the Chinese Government to take a small delegation to visit China.
2 Member of Parliament (Conservative 1983–95, Labour since 1995) for Stratford-upon-Avon 1983–97, Newport East since 1997.
3 Member of Parliament (Conservative 1983–96, Liberal Democrat 1996–7) for Bolton North-East 1983–97. He had previously sent messages that he was exasperated by the Tories.

Party's general position. The local government election results of the last two to three weeks have been disastrous for us. And I was very concerned that what Labour was now generating was one of those twenty-five-year political tidal waves which would carry into the next election and well beyond. There were now two possibilities. The first was that the tidal wave for change would continue to run. If so, we must be seen to be part of it – indeed, preferably at its leading edge. If, on the other hand, the mood for change subsided, then the Tories would recover, mostly at our expense. So our job was to tell people what we stood for and to keep our options open.

Monday, 16 October, London

A meeting with David Steel over a cup of tea. He thinks we must keep the co-operation process going but that a joint position with Labour before the next election would not be wise.

I told him that Blair had committed himself to working with us, even if he had a majority. So there are huge advantages in us going for deep co-operation and entering the next election with a broad joint programme on which we can agree, say, five or ten points – a programme for Britain.

This will have the effect of:

1. Protecting our position in places where Labour is beginning to eat into our support especially in the South and West.

2. Setting in train a process of re-alignment, leading to a breakaway of the left and all sorts of distant possibilities.

3. Encouraging the same thing to happen to the Tories.

But this can only be done if we get commitments on PR; otherwise, close co-operation would mean suicide for us. For Blair PR is the guarantor of a second and third Parliament. A change to the voting system is also what the Tories fear most. I still don't understand why Blair doesn't see this. We will have to persuade him.

I think there are now three possibilities:

1. That we have a loose *ad hoc* co-operation that could lead to anything – most likely sitting on the opposition benches. This in the absence of PR.

2. That we put together a broad programme for Britain and say these are the areas that we will work on together. PR is an essential precondition

for this. But the end position could be either in government or on the opposition benches.

3. The full works – unveiling a complete programme for government before an election, on the assumption of a coalition after it.

I favour the second of these three options. The third would probably leave too many embarrassing questions for us to answer, especially about areas where we don't agree. David is in favour of the first only.

Then across St James's Park in the darkness to No. 11 Carlton Gardens, Gladstone's old house, for the launch of Roy's book on the Grand Old Man.[1] Roy started by playing us the only extant recording of Gladstone's voice, recorded in 1888 by Edison. Not what I expected. I had imagined a deep bass, but it was a rather thin, high-timbred tenor with a strong trace of a Lancastrian accent, particularly in the vowels. Extraordinarily eerie.

Thursday, 19 October, Westminster

We lost two more activists who defected to Labour today.

At 11.30 a meeting of the Jo Group. A full turn-out. I started off by saying that I realized there were people who wanted to go no further on the project, but that I still wanted to push on. In my view, there was a real opportunity to do something extraordinary in British politics, perhaps even to reshape it completely. If we were successful we could look forward to the Tory Party breaking up and perhaps the left of the Labour Party splitting off, too. We could certainly keep the Tories out for ten years. But if we let the momentum of co-operation die, the moment would pass. Bob Maclennan supported this. Alan Leaman and Richard Holme in favour of staying in our present more comfortable position. I rather snapped at Alan and said, 'The job of leaders is to ensure that people don't get comfortable, especially if they're a third party.' Somebody else used the expression that we were all neatly camped. I said that as far as I was concerned it was a base camp and I was determined to explore the slopes above us.

I then outlined the three possible end positions: we could go for marriage, or we could go for an affair, or we could go for casual sex. I wrote off marriage (full coalition) on the grounds that this would open up more questions than we could answer (in particular, it would highlight the

1 *Gladstone* (1995).

differences between the two parties and make sure that the whole General Election debate centred on who fulfilled what post in any subsequent Cabinet). On the other hand, casual sex (co-operating on an opportunistic basis) would not generate the wave of hope I looked for. In my view, the next election was about hope against fear and we had to persuade people that hope was the safest option. So we must do the maximum to generate the hope that the two parties would work together in the context of the next Government. This led me to the belief that the affair (co-operation; encouraging tactical voting and options open after the election) was the best end point.

We should therefore map out, by next autumn, four or five key points on which we and Labour could agree. We could then announce that we would work together on these in the next Parliament, without being specific about whether this was to be done in Government or from the opposition benches.

Tuesday, 24 October, London

To dinner with Roy at the National Liberal Club.

He is very close to Blair and sees him quite often. He said, 'I think Tony treats me as a sort of father-figure in politics. He comes to me a lot for advice, particularly about how to construct a Government.'

I said I didn't want to talk to Blair about who would be in any joint Government. But I had views about who was good and who was bad.

Roy replied, 'I think that is very wise. But you can use me as a bridge.' His names for inclusion in any future joint Cabinet (he is pressing Blair for four Lib Dems) were the same as mine: Ming, Alan and Charles. I said that Alex Carlile, though difficult at times, could certainly hold down a Ministry. Roy agreed.

He told me that Blair had said in August, 'I would prefer to have a Government in which Liberal Democrats were present, than a Government entirely made up of Labour Party – and that applies whether I get a majority or not.'

I told Roy of the importance that we attached to PR, and of the absolute necessity of pushing it forward. Whether or not we got PR would determine how far we could go on co-operation in other areas. I told him there were reasons why Blair should be in favour of this as well. Roy undertook to put pressure on Blair. He thinks Blair's opposition to Westminster PR is rather 'unthought-through' and 'ill-considered', and that he is 'moveable'.

Wednesday, 25 October, Westminster

A meeting with Bob Maclennan. He and Robin Cook have agreed to put together a group of five Labour, five Lib Dems and six 'lay' outsiders, jointly chaired by the pair of them. The outsiders are important, as they can overturn the combined Labour cohorts on PR. A significant advance that Bob has won for us. Cook had also said to Bob, 'I'd be delighted if you'd push as much as you can on PR. But if Blair is pushed too hard he will still say no at this stage.'

I told Bob about my conversation with Roy and asked him not to go any further until I had really pushed Blair on PR.

At 10.00 Andrew Phillips came to discuss Peter Thurnham. We agreed that from now on we would use the code name 'Wolseley' (after the vintage car he has a passion for) for him. I said that he was a classic defector. They came in three guises: the first was the ideologue who would defect whatever; the second was the person in mid-term crisis wanting to relive their youth; and the third (Wolseley's case) was someone who had been slighted by their own side and this had caused him to re-think his position.

What we needed to do was to move in friends to restore him to the feeling of worth that he had lost from own side. We agreed that Jane and I would invite him and his wife to dinner. I'm not sure if this will work, but it's worth a try.

Sunday, 5 November, London, Northolt, Tel Aviv and Jerusalem

Up at eight, cleared my desk, and then started to do my exercises at around ten. At 10.30 the phone rang. Downing Street. The Prime Minister was flying out to Rabin's funeral,[1] did I want a seat?

Damn! I was really looking forward to a weekend at home. But it didn't take me long to decide to go. Blair is going, too.

I arrived at Northolt a little after 4.00 to find Malcolm Rifkind and his officials already there. In due course Blair arrived, together with the Chief Rabbi Jonathan Sacks and the Israeli Ambassador, who had come to see

---

1 Yitzhak Rabin, (1922–95), Prime Minister of Israel. Rabin had been assassinated by a Jewish extremist.

us off. Blair looked tired and pale and his suit exceptionally crumpled. Then Major swept in from Chequers looking spry, neat and full of cheery bonhomie.

We all sat in the same part of the small jet. Major and Rifkind sat opposite each other at a small table and, to the side, Blair, Major's Personal Private Secretary, myself and Jonathan Sacks.

Everyone worked for the first couple of hours or so. Rifkind read his red boxes[1] and Major spent some time working on a speech about monetary union.

Just before we arrived in Rome to refuel Major stood up, clapped his hands and said, 'I think it's time for a drink.' They had whiskies and gins and I had a glass of Chablis.

Blair seemed curiously uneasy. I suddenly realized that the clash between the Leaders of the two major parties was, inevitably, more intensely personal than mine could ever be with either. Blair was on Major's territory and he didn't like it. Major was equally nervous about this interloper who was after his job. Both showed it by reacting out of character – Major by being brash and rather showing off and Blair through reticence.

Sacks was pleasant but declined the food on board, eating instead the buns that his mother had prepared for him (rather sweet). We had a long discussion about Jewish mothers.

On the two-hour flight from Rome to Tel Aviv the conversation roamed widely. Major and I talked about the current Divorce Bill and Domestic Violence Bill, both of which the Government had been forced to withdraw (Major insists they will bring them back), about PMQs (Major hates them), about the Privacy Bill (he was in favour, I was against and Blair was equivocal), and about the Queen Mother (she loves *Dads' Army* videos). Finally we got on to Europe. Major said, 'Your and my views are not far apart, but we have reached different conclusions.' He thinks monetary union is impossible by 1999 because the French and Italians won't be able to meet the criteria. But it will happen by 2002. He also thinks that if monetary union happens too early and fails, it will wreck the whole of Europe. He shares my view about the importance of holding Europe together.

At one stage I said to him, 'But if you will the ends, you must will the means. If you want to enlarge Europe, you must reform its institutions.' And he said, 'I agree. But you can say that, I can't.' I said, 'But that won't

---

1 Government ministers receive their mail and papers in Government red boxes.

stop you attacking me, particularly on the reform of the veto.' He smiled wanly. 'But you have to realize that politics is the art of the possible. I don't disagree with you about the veto. It has to be reformed. But I can't say that, not with my Party.'

What a disaster! On something so important. Yet he will go attacking us at the next election for doing exactly what he believes in!

We arrived at Tel Aviv at around midnight and were driven at high speed up the road to Jerusalem, where there was a great mêlée of VIPs and police cars, television cameras and press.

I got to bed about 3.00am, Israeli time. I tried to sleep in late but, as usual, failed.

Monday, 6 November, Jerusalem

YITZHAK RABIN'S FUNERAL

A beautiful morning. Bright, crisp and with an almost unblemished blue sky. Breakfast, then a walk around the back of the King David Hotel and across the valley to the East Wall of the city and the Jaffa Gate. It looked strong and clean in the morning sunlight. Almost, I imagine, as it was when Suliman the Magnificent built it in the sixteenth century.

I wandered through a public park and noticed what looked like excavations in the side of the hill. These turned out to be tombs of the sort that Christ had been buried in. This is not far from Gethsemane. One of them actually had a stone rolled across the front.

At 11.00 we all went outside, got into our cars and drove off to President Weizman's[1] official residence. The Prime Minister, Rifkind, Blair and I walked in with Sacks. Weizman greeted us and we then joined the mêlée of the great and the good. In due course Prince Charles turned up, King Hussein, Chirac, Mubarak, Kohl, etc., etc., all with their retinues and security guards. It was wonderful turmoil.

We were then driven through the streets of Jerusalem to Mount Herzel. I was with Sacks. We both commented on the number of people on the streets. About a fifth of the population has visited Rabin's lying-in-state. Lines of people all along the route to the cemetery. I was struck at how sombre they looked – and how youthful. This is a very young country.

1 Ezer Weizman. President of Israel since 1993. Weizman was a former pilot in the Royal Air Force, before becoming Commander of the Israeli Air Force.

Then into a tent at the edge of the cemetery. As we left the Presidency, Major said, 'I've already done two bilaterals in the loo!' To my delight, I later saw him going off again to a bank of Portaloos the Israelis had installed, this time with Bruton, the Irish Prime Minister. International diplomacy is obviously best served by a weak bladder. When the two Prime Ministers arrived at their destination there was a long queue and they had to wait in line, trying to talk without being overheard by their fellow waiting potentates. Eventually Major's turn came and he went in, leaving Bruton outside shifting from one foot to another, whether from embarrassment or a full bladder it was impossible to tell.

We were then all herded up to the ceremony.

By now Clinton had turned up and I saw Blair fall behind in order to talk to him. He later told me that Clinton was confident of being re-elected and that he had brought 238 security guards.

When we arrived at the cemetery I was surprised to be welcomed by a small man with a permanent grin creasing across his face. I suddenly recognized him as Menachem Begin.[1]

The Israelis are astonishingly informal and scruffy. And totally chaotic. A scrummage quickly developed of Prime Ministers, Princes and Presidents and Shahs all greeting each other as long lost friends while a distraught official on the loudspeaker repeatedly asked everybody to *please* sit down.

Eventually order was restored and Rabin's coffin brought in. A siren sounded and I looked at the watch. To my astonishment, it was exactly 2.00 – the planned start time for the funeral. I saw what Sacks meant when he had said earlier that the Israelis were hopeless at organization but wonderful at improvisation.

Then the speeches.

Hussein's[2] was remarkable. I looked across the sea of heads in front of me and wondered at the fact that here, in the midst of Israeli Jerusalem, was this brown Arab face wearing a shemagh among all the skull caps and rituals of Jewry.

He repeatedly referred to us all as 'children of Abraham' and spoke of 'our one God' – and I felt the lump rise in my throat.

At the end, he looked towards Rabin's coffin and said, 'Here I am in Jerusalem to mourn the murder of my friend. The last time I was in this

---

1 Former Prime Minister of Israel.
2 King Hussein ibn Talal of Jordan (1935–99), one of the main architects of peace after the Arab–Israeli war.

city was when I stood alongside my grandfather when he was shot by an assassin. I hope I end the same way.'

Weizman's speech was very cold and hard. He said, starkly, that he regretted Rabin's passing but that he had warned him he was going too far, too fast.

Shimon Perez[1] was moving and powerful. Clinton's speech was perfectly crafted and clearly tailored for a Jewish audience.

But the most extraordinary speech was that of Rabin's granddaughter. Personal and powerful, a young girl grieving for her beloved grandfather. The tears rolled down my face and I noticed that Sacks was also weeping gently.

The return journey to Tel Aviv airport took about forty minutes. Major was off to New Zealand while Rifkind stayed behind to continue a Middle Eastern tour. So, in the aircraft for the return flight were only the Prince of Wales, his private secretary, Sacks, Blair and myself.

The Prince of Wales called Sacks over for a couple of hours. Otherwise he worked most of the time.

At one stage, however, we had an interesting discussion about religion. Blair revealed to Sacks that he is reading the Bible nightly and has got as far as Ezekiel. This led to a discussion about the disestablishment of the Church. Sacks said one or two things to which the Prince of Wales immediately said, 'Are you making an argument for disestablishment?'

Sacks retreated. But I said, 'Yes of course he is. And he's right.' Charles looked at me, smiled broadly and said, 'I really can't think why we can't have Catholics on the throne.' I gulped. It seemed such an obvious reference to Camilla Parker-Bowles.

Blair and I spent most of the rest of the flight talking in a corner seat, so as not to be overheard.

This was our longest and most constructive meeting so far. (The total flight time from Tel Aviv was seven and a half hours).

We started off by discussing the Conference.

I said, 'Just tell me what you meant by what you did at Conference.'

He turned in his seat to look me straight in the face and said, 'Look, you and I are going to work together for a long time so you need to trust me on this. I promise you, we did not mean it to be taken the way it was. I thought I had only repeated what had been said since the L & S by-election.'

I told him that that was not the way we heard it. Both Martin Kettle of

1 Prime Minister of Israel.

the *Guardian* and Peter Riddell of *The Times* had been specifically briefed by Alastair Campbell that this was the biggest story out of the interview and that it was to be played up.

Then he went into a puzzled sequence about how he couldn't understand our reaction at Conference. Why were we saying such nasty things about them, and him? I told him that was the problem. 'Every interview we do concentrates on only one thing - our relationship with you. I needed a Conference which was about us. So your intervention forced me to push you to one side in order to recapture my own Conference.'

He responded, 'I just can't understand why you are playing it this way. I expected you to welcome what I said. I have thought about how I would play it if I was in your position . . .'

I retorted rather sharply that he should concentrate on running his own Party and leave me to run mine. He smiled and we left it at that.

Then I explained that I couldn't afford to divide my Party, but that there was also no advantage to him in weakening it. 'That will only save more Tory skins. In order to maintain our distinctiveness and identity, it is absolutely vital that there is a sharp differentiation between you and me. The moment we lose this, the case for voting for us ceases to exist, with the result that the Tories will win seats we both need them to lose.'

I then asked him again to define his end position. He said, 'This is between you and me, but the position I would like is that we do a deal on seats in the South West so that we stand down in favour of you.' I said I thought this was totally impossible. And that we would waste a lot of time dividing our parties if we tried to do it. It would also look like a grubby plan to gain power and votes for ourselves, instead of one based round principles and what was best for the country. I had experienced this during the Alliance. It was very painful and, in the end, counterproductive.

I repeated my view that the better way would be to lay out a small number of points of real interest to the public on which we agreed, and then make it clear that we would co-operate on these in the next Government. This would get over the difficulty of having two programmes which were identical, and of having to answer who would serve in which position in what kind of government. And it would encourage people to vote tactically in the seats where we could beat the Tories. He responded, 'That is a very interesting idea. I will give it some thought.'

We then got into a discussion on voting, etc. He seems to think that our combining with Labour will ensure every Labour vote will switch to us in the seats where we could win. And the Tories who vote for us would still stay with us. I disagreed. There are many seats in the South and West where Labour, even New Labour, is still regarded as such anathema that people would rather return to the Tories than vote for us if they thought we were supporting Labour. I agreed that this anti-Labour vote was probably now diminishing, and pointed to today's poll, which showed the Conservatives were now more feared than Labour.

These were the conditions I was waiting for. 'There is absolutely no point in my taking actions which allow your votes to rise in our seats at our expense, so saving Tory skins in seats where we should be beating them.'

We then got on to a discussion on Scotland. He said, 'I am really worried that the West Lothian question[1] could damage us.' I told him that I didn't think it was a real question. There were plenty of places (e.g. Spain) with asymmetrical devolution, where people who had a regional parliament in one area could still vote in the national Parliament. But Kilbrandon[2] was a real problem. There was no way he could get devolution legislation through the Lords without reducing the number of MPs after devolution. And since Scotland was overwhelmingly Labour this would in future reduce Labour's ability to get a majority. But again, PR and a relationship with us would solve the problem.

He then asked me, rather pointedly, 'What system [for elections] do you want?'

I told him that there were only two systems that were acceptable. The system that George Robertson and Jim Wallace had agreed upon in the Scottish convention (Alternative Vote Plus). We were not at all keen on this. It might be OK for Scotland, but for the UK, Single Transferable Vote (STV) was best. He agreed with me that if we had Proportional Representation, the Tories would break up 'and some on the far left of my Party would probably leave us, too'.

We had a brief discussion on the Maclennan/Cook operation. I made it clear to him that without PR I was reluctant to even start this. I was not prepared to be put in the position where PR was the leftovers, having assembled the whole of the rest of the constitutional agenda. He said, rather

---

1 The question posed most famously in recent years by Tam Dalyell, Labour MP for West Lothian, roughly: 'How is it right that Scottish MPs, who have a Parliament of their own, vote on English matters at Westminster, when English MPs don't have equivalent rights to vote on Scottish matters?'
2 The Kilbrandon Commission looked at whether the over-representation of Scottish MPs at Westminster, which came as a result of the Act of Union of 1707, should continue if Scotland had its own parliament, and concluded that it should not.

quickly, 'does that mean we can't make any progress at all?' I said to him, 'Well, we could doubtless make some, but on purely technical things.'

I asked, 'What do you want to achieve out of this?' He said, 'Well, we should be able to put together, pretty quickly, a programme of what we want to do, on an agreed basis.' At one point he asked me, 'Have you spoken to Major about PR?' I was quite taken aback. 'Of course not.' His reply was, 'Oh, I don't know, I just wondered.' He seems worried that I may be playing a double game and bargaining with the Tories, too.

We then got on to taxes. He is obsessed with the idea that the Tories can recover by cutting taxes. I agreed that taxes were important, but much more important was to put forward a convincing alternative programme to the Tories. 'The great mistake of generals is to fight the last war, rather than the present one.' I knew that he had read Hillary Clinton's book, *The Agenda*, so I reminded him of how she had said that the lack of a clear project for the Clinton administration, or anything that was convincing to the electorate, had really dogged them in the first years. Blair said, 'That's what the next year is about.'

We turned to talking about the Tories. I said that I thought they were probably beaten, but we had to plan on the basis that they could recover. He said that his tactic was to keep the Tories moving. He believes that the 'sellable' line to the press, and internally in the Tory Party, is that Major can't lead and can be pushed all over the place. So he is really trying to push them back to the centre ground so that the right wing start to complain and Major has to tack back to find consensus again.

We then touched on Europe. Apparently, Chirac had said to him that Blair's position and Major's are indistinguishable. Blair is in favour of a single currency in principle. But Labour are not going to commit themselves until the battle can be won on the basis of what is good for the country.

Our conversation drifted back to the relationship between the two parties. Again I emphasized the importance of PR to us. Again he said that he would think about it. I told him that he shouldn't go on thinking about it for too long. We had a lot of work to do if we were to complete the course before the election.

Blair also has a very high opinion of Donald Dewar and of their new Whip, Nick Brown, whom he considers 'brilliant'.

Relations within the Shadow Cabinet are, apparently, better. John Prescott is still very supportive. The stuff over the summer was nonsense, but has had the effect of getting Prescott to experience what it was like to be under fire as part of the leadership team.

Then we got on to PMQs. I said that it would be very helpful if we knew what subject he was going to raise, since I have to prepare two or three subjects, in case he takes the ones I want first. He said he was perfectly happy for Nick South to ring his office on a regular basis to find out what he was doing, if this would help. From time to time it might be possible for the two of us to co-ordinate as well.

Earlier I said to him, 'I understand that you had dinner with Roy last week and had said to him that you would want to work with us, even if you had a majority. You have, of course, said this to me before. Is it still your firm view?' He confirmed that it was.

We didn't finish our conversation until we landed at Northholt. It was, I think, the easiest conversation we have had. Light, good-natured, funny, and with each listening closely to what the other was saying. My worry is that I haven't managed to tie him down. I know where I want to get to, but I don't think he has thought this thing through in much detail yet.

We were back in London by 10.00. I went home, looked through the papers and tumbled into bed.

Sunday, 12 November, Methley Street

REMEMBRANCE SUNDAY

The Blairs arrived at 7.45, driven in his official car. The dinner was friendly and fun. Cherie didn't drink because she is working tomorrow, but he had a couple of glasses of white and some red. Jane cooked pheasant.

The first half an hour was spent on pleasantries.

I told him that I had had a brief chat with Trimble[1] at the Cenotaph earlier in the day, when Trimble had made it clear that he couldn't support the Government. Blair said, 'But can we trust him?' I said I thought we could, though it was the nature of Irish politicians to face both ways at once, as it was necessary for their survival.

Blair said that he was under great pressure from the Irish and the Americans, but that he had told them, 'You are asking me to do things that you won't do, which is to come out and attack my Government. Well, I won't do it either. Firstly, because I don't know what's going on behind

1 David Trimble MP, Leader of the Ulster Unionists. Member of Parliament (Ulster Unionist) for Upper Bann since 1990. Trimble is now the First Minister of Northern Ireland.

the scenes and I would be getting involved in a process whose mechanics and movements I can't predict. Secondly, because I can't think that there is anything in this for New Labour.'

I said that I thought the Government had managed to put the IRA at the centre of the stage, which was foolish. We should support them over their position on decommissioning, but tell them that getting themselves into rows with the Irish Government would benefit nobody. What was important was to find a way to take the IRA and Sinn Fein out of the centre of the project and work towards bilateral talks with all parties.

We got down to real business over dinner. He started by saying, 'Look, I'm just not sure how far this thing can go – what do you think?'

I said that perhaps it would be helpful if I outlined our position to him again, so that he wasn't in any doubt about it. I stressed the importance of maintaining a strong distinction between us. But he said, 'I don't understand what your line will be. What will you say to the electorate?'

PA: We will be the force which holds you to your promises where they were good for Britain and prevents you from doing damage where they were not.

TB: Well, that's OK. It's certainly better than joining the Tories in a generalized attack on us. Saying that you will keep us up to the mark is one thing. Attacking us because you believe there are people in our Party who would prevent New Labour from governing, is another.

PA: Don't be ridiculous. If we do not have a partnership and go into the next election fighting two separate cases, then we will have to make use of all the opportunities that we can get. It is absolutely vital that people know why they should vote for us. One of the reasons they should vote for us is because they can believe us on issues like constitutional change. Another is because you have rebels, and everybody knows that. So the stronger we are, the less trouble your rebels will be able to create in a future Labour Government. So don't expect us not to criticize you. Except, of course, in those areas where there is formal agreement.

If, however, we put a partnership in place, we would each be reinforcing the messages and campaigns of the other. We would, in fact, be fighting a totally different kind of election.

So, there are effectively two sorts of elections ahead of us. The first is one in which we might be more friendly to you than before, but would still be criticizing you in order to ensure we had a role.

The second is where we have had a partnership on an agreed basis. But you know that this cannot be done without PR. I will do a lot to get this project off the ground. I will take a lot of risks. But I'm not prepared to take actions which risk obliteration for my Party and I hope you don't expect me to.

He said that he didn't, but that he couldn't see why we placed such importance on PR.

PA: Frankly, I'm surprised that you lot can't see why PR is in your interests, too. It is the means by which you get a stable relationship in government and a second term of government. As far as I'm concerned, if we put together a deal, it is for two parliaments, not one. That's what this is all about.

TB: You need to know my concerns about PR. I think the arguments from an electoral point of view are pretty evenly balanced. But I have two other major objections. The first is that the adoption of PR will encourage my people to duck the tough decisions we must make in order to gain power.

Secondly, and more importantly, the Tory press seem reasonably well disposed towards me. If that means they won't support the Tories in the next election that's an immense plus for me. They believe that, since I am hostile to PR, I can provide an interregnum between the current Conservative Government and a future right-wing one, possibly under Portillo. But if I support PR they will think they are out not only this time, but for good. And then they will throw their lot behind the Tories again.

He is absolutely obsessed with the thought that the Tories could recover.

He continued, 'You can't expect the Labour Party to support PR openly.' I repeated my point about taking our chances in a referendum, but not if he was openly against.

TB: Well, I could see myself perhaps coming to a position which would make it possible to adopt that course, but only after the election.

PA: And that means that anything we do will have to wait until after the election and you will lose the advantage of it beforehand.

Later on he again returned to PR, this time in more positive terms.

TB: The huge advantage of PR is that it releases the bounds of the whole system, allowing a reshaping of politics along more rational lines.

PA: Exactly! In any normal system of politics, you and I would be in the same party, whereas Dennis Skinner would be in a different one. And the same applies to some Tories.

At this stage Cherie said, 'But surely the point about PR is that it would be possible to be in different parties.'

TB: No, you miss the point. With PR, our left may break away, but the anti-Europeans would also break away from the Conservatives, too. This would leave everyone else to regroup themselves, perhaps into the same party.

PA: I hope you realize just what a huge prize that would be. And the only thing that stands in the way is your inability to accept PR. Overcome that and almost anything is possible.

We then got on to tax again. He is certain the Tories will reduce taxes by 2p in the Budget for this year, then put a further 3p reduction next year 'on account' if they win the election. He doesn't think there will be an election in the spring, but he has put his people on alert nevertheless. The most likely date is in the autumn, before the next budget. He is determined to avoid a position where Labour say they will raise taxes at the next election. I explained that, in all probability, we would vote against a tax cut in this Budget, 'but then we can do things you can't do. I will not reverse the penny for education. But I have no intention of allowing the Lib Dems to propose tax increases in the next election, just for the hell of it.'

Returning once more to PR, I said we didn't expect public statements of support from him at this juncture. An understanding between the pair of us would do. But before a deal could be done he must make his own personal position on PR (i.e., that he was in favour) clear, even if only privately to me. If Bob Maclennan and Robin Cook put together a commission of the sort we had talked about and it came up with a constitutional package recommending PR, then that was the time to shift position. He responded, 'In other words, you would be satisfied with me saying that I had become convinced at that stage that a change was necessary.'

'Exactly!'

At one stage he went into a fascinating discussion about his family background. It turns out his father was adopted and his grandparents had been in vaudeville. We discussed the curious fact that both the current PM and he had had recent forebears in showbusiness. Apparently, after the details about his grandfather were published, Cyril Smith rang to say that he had actually known Blair's grandfather. Cyril had been one of his grandfather's supporters in the last years of music-hall. Blair also said, 'Of course, all my ancestors were Irish, and pretty rabble-rousing at that.'

Towards the end of the evening, we again got on to the question of a national seats deal. I told him that in my view this was simply out of the question: 'It can't be done; it will waste time; and it would look exceedingly grubby.

'It is vital to portray whatever we do as being in the interest of the nation, not of ourselves. But that does not preclude local seat deals if local parties want them.'

TB: Surely we should encourage this.

PA: We certainly shouldn't oppose it – the Lib Dem constitution allows for this to happen. The best way, however, is not to deal cards in smoke-filled rooms in Westminster, but to put together a programme which is good for Britain. Then let whatever happens, happen naturally at the constituency level. In most cases, this would mean no more than tactical voting. In some, however, constituency parties may agree not to field candidates in order to leave the other a free run. But in my view not many.

We also talked about co-operation at council level – Blair was astonished to learn that Labour allies with the Tories in some places.

He said that he would get Gordon Brown to come and speak to me about the forthcoming Budget. Apparently he has some wheeze up his sleeve to get round this year's projected 2p tax cut. Gordon is deeply suspicious of Malcolm Bruce, however, whom he thinks may be 'unsound on economic matters' (the second time he has mentioned this). I told him that I thought Malcolm Bruce was doing an excellent job and that he shouldn't be judged by a single Conference speech.[1]

Finally, we discussed what should happen next.

We agreed there should be a meeting between representatives of the two parties. I emphasized, however, that substantive discussions between Bob Maclennan and Robin Cook could not take place until we had settled the PR thing. They could talk on an *ad hoc* basis about individual items. But that was all.

At the end of the evening, as they were leaving, I said, 'You just need to know how committed I am to this. I really think we can change politics. I believe that, despite your strength and all you have done, we Lib Dems have a very important role to play. And I will do whatever is necessary to ensure we play that role. But we have to be given room to survive and grow. How far we can go on this is now up to you.'

---

1 Malcolm's first speech as our new economic spokesman at our recent Party Conference had been rather badly received.

My worry about him remains that he is not prepared to take risks, even for great prizes, at least at the moment.

I don't think we have had a more enjoyable meeting in the three years this has been going on. Our relationship now is very friendly and relaxed. The presence of Cherie added greatly to this. She and Jane seem to get on well together.

But his bottom line remains: he is not prepared to concede PR, at least for the moment. The door is probably still ajar, but only just. We can proceed further only if he understands where our bottom line lies and is prepared to amend his own position. I don't think he is going to do this, but it is worth one last push at the January meeting. We will have to script that meeting very carefully. In short, a less antagonistic relationship between the two parties is possible, but there will be little slackening of our 'no let-up on Labour' policy; we may be able to co-operate, but only on an opportunistic basis. They will have to move more for that to happen.

Tuesday, 14 November, Westminster

At 7 o'clock off to see Roy Jenkins in his room. On PR he said, 'He [Blair] is being very, very cautious. It is extremely disappointing. Of course I will do what I can do to put pressure on him. It is a ridiculous position. He must realize how much is at stake here.' Good. Roy has a lot of leverage with him. And if Roy is taking our position and thinking that we are being generous (which we are) then he is more likely to put pressure on Blair.

Monday 20 November, London

At 4 o'clock a meeting with members of the Former Yugoslavia War Crimes Commission, who had flown out from The Hague to see me. Russell Johnston and I spent the best part of two hours with them. They took us through my diary note for my visit to the Manjaca prison camp on 10 August 1992.

Sunday, 26 November, Somerset

Bright and blustery with patches of cloud.

At 10.30 in the evening I went into Yeovil, where I had arranged to meet Mark Ellis at the Viceroy Restaurant.[1] Everything seemed very quiet, so we decided to stroll around the town.

As soon as we left the restaurant, one of our fellow diners came out and introduced himself as a plain-clothed policeman, keeping an eye on the situation. Mark and I wandered around the town and chatted with a couple of uniformed policemen. Then into Middle Street, where we saw three lads striding up the road throwing things at the windows and doors. As I came level with them they recognized first Mark and then me. Not wanting to provoke an incident, we went down to the bottom of town and sat watching them from a couple of hundred yards away, ready to call the uniformed police if they started breaking windows.

One of them started to urinate in the street and shouted obscenities at me, Paddy Pantsdown, etc. – the usual stuff. They were then joined by an older man. Previously they had kept their distance, taunting us. But when the older man arrived, they all came up to us. He was obviously very drunk.

He was large, unkept, with a huge beard and a fearsome face. Probably in his early fifties. I decided the best thing to do was to draw the older man away from the younger ones, so I started to walk. He immediately joined me. Mark stayed behind with the other three. The older man and I walked up Middle Street, turned left into Wyndham Street and then down Earl Street. He wanted me to stop and talk, but I refused to do so. I wasn't about to stop in any of those dark alleyways with him. He kept on saying

1 In late September, I had read in my local paper, the *Western Gazette*, that a Turkish kebab restaurant close to my constituency office had been fire bombed. When I started to look into this, I uncovered an extensive series of incidents against ethnic restaurant owners in the town – especially Indians. What stunned me was that this had been going on for some time and had taken place no more than a hundred yards from my office. Not only did I not know what was going on, but when I asked the Asian restaurant owners why they hadn't come to see me, they replied that they thought MPs were for the locals, not for them.

It turned out that the perpetrators were a gang of local criminals who had, for a long time, held many of the weakest in our community to ransom through intimidation and violence. I was determined to stamp this out, so we set up a local anti-racist partnership under the chairmanship of a local vicar and friend mine, Mark Ellis. Mark and I agreed that we had better see things for ourselves and arranged to meet this Sunday to visit the worst areas.

things like, 'I bet you've got a microphone and you're leading me into a police trap.' But he wasn't especially aggressive.

By the time we got back to the kebab house to rejoin Mark, the wife of one of the gang members had turned up. She started shouting at me: 'They are the racists, not us' – pointing at the Indian restaurant across the road. Suddenly the older man lashed out with a knee to my groin. I moved backwards before he could get me. Then he pulled out a large flick knife and started waving it around. I persuaded him to put it away. Then, while I was talking to the woman, he suddenly reached over from behind me and put the sharp edge of the blade to my throat. As soon as I felt it touch, I knocked it out of the way and started to walk away with Mark (who had joined us). At this stage the plain-clothed policemen came out and arrested him.

The next three hours were spent in the police station. We were asked whether we wanted to press charges against my assailant who was, I was informed, a local man, well-known to the police, called Chris Mason. I felt we had to. If we weren't prepared to stand up to these people, how could we ask others to?

I didn't get home until about four, by which time the press were going absolutely mad.

Monday, 27 November, Somerset

The *Sun*, ahead of events as ever, had already heard the news by about three in the morning. Extraordinary how quick they are. And how scare-mongering. In the early hours they had rung Pat Martin[1] saying that I was in hospital with my throat cut, having the Last Rites read over me while Jane held my hand. Poor old Pat dashed off to the hospital to find a perplexed emergency ward wondering what on earth she was talking about.

I had about an hour's sleep before the telephone started ringing at six. From then on, a constant stream of telephone calls through to 10.30, when Jane and I held an impromptu press conference outside Vane Cottage. Photographers and television crews everywhere. I tried to play it down, because I did not want Yeovil to get a reputation as a centre of racism. But the press concluded that playing it down was just another way of hyping it up. Once they are in a feeding frenzy you just can't win.

1 The Mayor of Yeovil.

Later, I heard that Mason was publicly claiming that the row had been about one of his prostitutes, of whom I was a client. My heart sank. Apparently he was trying to sell his story to the *Sun*. I told Nick and Mark Ellis privately, then tried to ring Andrew Phillips, without success, so spoke to one of his solicitors, Willie Garnett, instead. They will slap an injunction on the press if they start anything silly.

Up to London. Much hilarity in the office and among the Colleagues.

At 6.15 a meeting with Hugo Young.[1] I took him into my confidence about our relations with Labour and asked him if he could help shift Blair on PR. He seemed almost angrily sad that Labour are being so timid. His view is that Labour is playing into the hands of the Tories, especially the Tory press. He said that he would do an article next week in which he would propose that a group from both parties should get together to discuss constitutional change but that this couldn't be done until PR had first been acceded to. Very helpful.

Wednesday, 29 November, Methley Street

The Wolseleys arrived for dinner pretty well on time, he in a large 'Emil and the Detectives' mac and hat bought specially for the occasion. He sidled in like a middle-aged vicar entering a brothel. But we liked them both very much. He is a very decent man and she is lovely.

Wolseley told me that the Tory Party, especially in Cumbria, is in a terrible state. Factionalism is rife. He said, 'I would like to stand for you in Westmorland, but it must be with Stan Collins'[2] agreement. I am not having him treated the way I was.'

I pressed him to take the step to join us now, but he is held back by three things. First he does not want to let down Bolton – they have been good to him and he has worked hard with them. Secondly, he is really worried about the reaction of the Tory Party. They will be absolutely vicious, and he wants to avoid what Alan Howarth had to go through. Thirdly, he doesn't want to give the Tories any prior notice in Westmorland. He says they are very complacent there and doing very little.

At the end of the evening he called a taxi, but wouldn't give my address and asked it instead to park up at a nearby road junction. My last sight of

1 Chairman of the Scott Trust, which owns the *Guardian*, and a columnist for the paper.
2 Liberal Democrat prospective candidate in Westmorland & Lonsdale.

him was of a figure skulking away into the darkness, mac collar turned up and hat firmly pulled down over his eyes with his wife struggling along behind.

I think it will be a real culture shock if he comes into the Party. Nevertheless, he is much closer to a Liberal in his attitude and the way he works than almost any other Tory MP I've met. He is clearly very fed up indeed with the Tory Party but wants to go on being an MP. His wife said, 'I really want him to continue as an MP. It's what he is best at.'

Monday, 4 December, Westminster

At six Dick Newby rang to tell me John Dickie[1] had decided to join Labour and would defect shortly. For some reason I feel more betrayed by this than I did by Roger.[2] Apparently Andrew Adonis is going as well. Of course, Labour will make the most of it. And I am worried to death that an atmosphere of mistrust will be generated in the Party towards old members of the SDP.

Tuesday, 5 December, Westminster

John Harris[3] came to see me in the morning. He told me of a rumour circulating in the Lords that Emma Nicholson[4] wants to leave the Tories.

I decided that we should see if there was anything in this. So, just before the 10.00 pm vote I found Nick Harvey and asked him to approach Emma. Nick said that she was in the tea room, so I sent him off with a script to use: he should be straightforward, disarming and open, and say, 'Last year there were rumours circulating about me [Nick] joining the Tories. It was, of course, absolute nonsense. There is now a rumour circulating that you want to join us. Is it true?'

---

1 Former SDP member who had joined the Lib Dems.
2 Roger Liddle had defected to Labour some weeks previously.
3 Lord John Harris of Greenwich, Liberal Democrat Chief Whip in the House of Lords. Entered the Lords as a Labour peer in 1974, where he became a Minister of State at the Home Office.
4 Member of Parliament (Conservative 1987–95, Liberal Democrat 1995–7) for Devon West & Torridge 1987–97. Former Vice-Chairman of the Conservative Party, now a Liberal Democrat member of the House of Lords and a Member of the European Parliament for the South East.

He came back, white in the face. 'She said: "I might if you asked me."'

I immediately feared she was playing a double game. Our previous candidate for her seat, Matthew Owen, has just resigned and we are in the process of selecting a new one. I feared she might be trying to tempt us into asking her to stand for us, so that, when our new candidate was elected, she could destroy him by revealing that we had asked her first.

So I took Archy out of the chamber and said that in no circumstances should Nick tell her we were interested. I would set up a 'cut out' who could approach her in a deniable fashion, so that if it was a trap we could refute authorship and preserve the position of our candidate. If, however, she followed up herself with Nick, the very most he should do was suggest that if she wanted to join our Party, she would be welcome – but on no account mention anything about standing for us.

We then returned to Archy's office with Nick to sort out our next move. Later Emma did indeed seek Nick out to ask him for Matthew Owen's address so that she could write to him saying how sorry she was that he had resigned.[1] Good. This gives Nick the excuse to contact her tomorrow.

Returned home with my mind in a turmoil. If she really wants to join us, it would be a terrific coup just when we need it most. But I am worried that it's a Tory trick. She is, after all a vice-chairman of the Party. On the other hand, I cannot see why, if someone approaches you out of the blue, you would respond as she did unless you were serious.

Wednesday, 6 December, Westminster

As I walked to the House with Richard Holme I told him the Emma Nicholson story and of my need to find a 'cut out'. He said that he had a friend who knew Nicholson's husband Michael[2] very well and who may be able to do it. I asked him to follow this up. Shortly after I got back to the office Richard rang. His friend was very enthusiastic and said that Emma was 'exceedingly dissatisfied'. So I left it to him to arrange.

---

1 Emma has subsequently told me that she did this deliberately to maintain contact, as she didn't understand why, having shown interest, we then dropped her.
2 Sir Michael Caine, Chairman of Booker plc.

Friday, 8 December, Westminster

We are down two in the polls today and the story of the John Dickie and Andrew Adonis defections has broken. I am suddenly beset by a terrible pessimism. 12.5 per cent! At this level we are going to be squeezed out. And with good people going to Labour as well, I will have to grit my teeth, otherwise everyone will start panicking.

Monday, 11 December, Westminster

I saw Alex Carlile between the votes this evening and talked to him about the Mason case, which will go to court in the New Year. Mason's associates are spreading lies to the press about me in an attempt to embarrass me into withdrawing my charge. Alex said that there was nothing I could do about this. Mason was allowed his day in court and could say anything he wanted. So it is going to be tough.

Mason is apparently making two allegations: that I had touched him on the bum and that I had been a client of their brothel in Yeovil. He is trying to sell this to the newspapers for all it is worth and, after he has said it all in court, they can publish it.

Meanwhile, the more I see of the Party the more I think we are in a desperately fragile state. People squabbling, etc.

Tuesday, 12 December, Westminster

Into the office early and a call to Roy at his Kensington flat. He told me that he was seeing Blair for dinner, together with some senior Whitehall mandarins on 16 January. All part of Blair's preparations for government.

I told him that I thought things were coming to a head on the PR front. He said he had had lunch with Mandelson, who said that Blair was moving from a neutral position to welcoming PR. Roy said he would really press this matter home with Blair and let me know how he got on.

A long discussion with Richard about Emma. He told me that he had spoken to his friend Jonathan Taylor, who has already made contact with Emma, whom we agreed to code-name 'Austin' (as distinct from 'Wolseley').

Austin had told Jonathan she was deeply unhappy and had proposed a breakfast with Richard. Excellent. Last night I also learned that Paul Tyler is in touch with Bob Hicks[1] who is going to have dinner with Ming Campbell. This gets exciting!

To lunch with Adrian Lithgow from the *Mail On Sunday*, who said, 'Incidentally, I gather you are dropping the charges against the knifeman who attacked you.' Mason's poison has clearly got through to their newsroom. Very menacing. I told Lithgow I certainly was not pulling charges.

Thursday, 14 December, Dublin

DURING A VISIT FOR TALKS WITH THE IRISH GOVERNMENT

I was driven though the gloom and rain to Glasnevin cemetery to visit O'Connell's tomb.[2] On the way, the Irish Government driver said to me over his left shoulder, in the manner of drivers the world over, 'I gather you are the great-great-grandson of Daniel O'Connell.'

I said I believed I was.

'Do you know what they used to say about him?' he asked.

'No.' I said (not wanting to admit that I knew they called him 'The Liberator'). 'What did they use to say about him?'

He said, 'They used to say about him, that you couldn't throw a stone over an orphanage wall, but you would hit one of his children!'

It was a glorious put down, done completely without malice.

Monday, 18 December, Somerset and London

I finally got a call from Richard during the morning. To my delight, he told me that the meeting with Austin had gone very well. He likes her and thinks she is now four-fifths on board.

She doesn't want to fight her seat at the next election. She is happy to

---

1 Member of Parliament (Conservative) for Bodmin 1970–74, 1974–83, Cornwall South-East 1983–97. (Paul Tyler was the Member of Bodmin between the two 1974 elections.)

2 The Irish Government had got to hear that I am a direct descendant of Daniel O'Connell, the man who won Catholic emancipation for Ireland and who, as the father of Irish Nationalism, was known as 'The Liberator'.

leave that to our man.[1] But she does want to have a crack at a European seat. Richard has stressed that she will have to go into open competition for this, and she accepts that. She has promised to have a chat with her husband and then report back to Richard in two days.

I clambered into the car and drove up to London, my mind buzzing on how we were going to handle all this. It is potentially a very big event. We have lost Hicks, who is standing down at the next election, but there is still Wolseley, and if we can pull Austin, that would be a great prize. If this comes off it will take up a lot of my Christmas. But I still fear it won't, even though Richard sounds pretty confident. I will be on tenterhooks until she makes her final decision.

At seven o'clock I had a long chat with Richard and Archy about how we would handle Austin. If she responds positively, I will see her over the Christmas period. But we will also have to do something to ensure we get the right response from the Lib Dems in her Torridge & West Devon constituency. It will be all too easy for people to criticize her, not knowing what the situation is. My view is that she should come to us clean, but Richard and Archy are dubious. This will require a lot more thinking.

Thursday, 21 December, Somerset

Early this morning Jane gave me a message from Richard saying that he had met Austin and everything was set up. She is nine-tenths on board and has agreed to meet me over the Christmas holidays.

A long discussion with Richard later. He thinks everything has gone very well. She also revealed that she had been chased by Labour for three months, but 'didn't feel like a socialist'.

During the evening I spoke to Graham Elson about using his cottage near Exeter as a 'safe house' in which to meet Austin. I didn't tell him what I wanted it for – just that it was very important. Goodness knows what he thought. But he was happy to assist and promised me the keys.

I hope to see her on Saturday and then perhaps again later in the week.

---

1 John Burnett. Elected as MP for Emma's old seat in 1997.

Friday, 22 December, Somerset

Up at seven and a chat with Richard about Austin. I told him where I wanted to meet her and he faxed her a letter to see if this could be set up.

At 6.15 Richard rang to say that he had fixed with Austin to call me in twenty minutes. Austin duly rang, exactly on time. We fixed to meet tomorrow at two o'clock – after she had finished her Christmas visits programme for the day.

At about 7.15 Graham and his wife Jane arrived on their way up to London. He gave me a key and a very detailed set of instructions to find his house, which I faxed through to her, together with full instructions and my contact numbers.

Saturday, 23 December, Devon

Arrived at Graham Elson's house comfortably by 12.45. Then off to the local pub for a pint of Guinness and back to the house to turn on the heating and lights, make a pot of coffee and wait. She was a few minutes late.

I took her to the sitting room and we went through the usual pleasantries.

My first question was whether her husband knew we were meeting, to which she replied 'Of course. He dropped me here!'

She went on to say that she is fed up with the Tories. The Whips have given her a very hard time. They told her that she had stuck a knife into the heart of the Tory Party when she voted for public disclosure of MPs' outside financial interests. And they were furious with her last year for her comments on disabled people and on single mothers. They said that she had been personally disloyal to John Major.

We talked a lot about her work with the Marsh Arabs.[1] I didn't realize that she had created such a large organization. Her Chief Executive was with me in the Royal Marines.

I let her talk and talk, knowing that it was important for her to have her motives understood. She ranged across all areas, but particularly foreign affairs. I found her pleasant and impressive.

---

1 The Ma'dan people who live in the southern wetland area of Iraq and who have suffered terrible persecution by the Iraqi Government.

I was particularly struck by the extraordinary courage she must have shown to have done what she has done, given her disability.[1] She is also deeply concerned about how her defection will be received by her constituency and especially her agent, for whom she has a very high respect.

I then said, 'Why do you want to join the Lib Dems? What do you disagree with about our policies?'

She said she disagreed with STV.[2] She agrees that the electoral system needs to be reformed but prefers the French AV system. She also doesn't want to get rid of the assisted places scheme.[3] Otherwise, she has no difficulties.

Eventually I said to her, 'Well, what do you want to do, then?'

At this stage she appeared to draw back a little. 'Well, I couldn't fight the seat for the Tories next time, though I think I could still win. But it would be very tough and I would be in a Party that I have come to like less and less. I like the old people in the Tory Party but they are all leaving. I want to continue in politics and I like the Lib Dems. I don't really want to fight Torridge and West Devon again, but I would love to be in Europe.'

She then let loose about all Tories hating foreigners, in particular Douglas Hogg,[4] who referred to her Marsh Arab and Iranian friends as 'your friends with bath towels round their heads'.

I gently brought her back and asked her what she wanted to do. She said, 'Stay in politics, preferably at Strasbourg.' So I said, 'OK, then. Here is a proposition. If you want to join us, I suggest you do so on the following terms:

1. That you cross the floor at a time we should discuss in a moment.

2. You should not fight the next election.

3. That you should put your name forward for a European seat, but you need to know that isn't in my gift. You will have to compete in the normal fashion.'

She swiftly responded, 'I would be very worried if it were any other way.'

---

1 She has been 80% deaf from birth.
2 For discussion of different kinds of PR, see footnotes on p. 381.
3 A scheme introduced by the Conservatives to help some children who would otherwise attend state schools go to private schools.
4 Minister for Agriculture, Fisheries and Food. Member of Parliament (Conservative) for Grantham 1979–97, Sleaford & North Hykeham since 1997. Formerly a Minister of State at the Foreign and Commonwealth Office.

We then got talking about timing. She said that she would like to do it about the time we select our new candidate. I thought this unwise. I suggested the New Year.

To my delight, she said, 'Well, I have been thinking that – I have been thinking, why not just do it on the first of January and have done with it.' I said that the advantage of this was that it would give her a week or so's break before having to return to the House of Commons and the nastiness of the Tories.

We should now begin to draw up a plan aimed at handling her change-over in the most dignified manner possible.

She agreed, but said, 'I would like another meeting with you. Just one more and then we can get down to talking about the details.'

My heart sank, but I tried not to show it.

We then talked about the next moves. I said that I would want to tell people down in Devon. She baulked strongly at this, saying she thought it would get out if that happened. She had to tell her agent first.

I responded that I would need to have Alan Leaman and Archy Kirkwood present when we next talked. Again she was very nervous about this.

But I said, 'Look, you have to realize it is going to be very nasty. The Tories will throw everything at you. It will be a very big story. It must be handled professionally, and that means preparation.' She reluctantly agreed.

At this stage I suggested that I should come up to London to see her on Wednesday night and, on the assumption that we went ahead, I would call Archy down from Scotland and put Alan on standby (without telling either of them why) for a meeting Thursday at 11.30am.

As she was writing down details of where she would be, I went out to collect her husband Michael, who was by now sitting outside in the car.

She then returned to the agent question, saying she was really worried about letting him down. But Michael was wonderfully tough and said, 'Look, this is going to be difficult and painful. You are going to have a lot shit over this. There is no way you can do this without hurting some people. The trick is to do it in the most honest and reasonable way possible.'

We parted at about four.

We are not yet there, but we are as near as dammit. This last inching of the fish on to the shore is going to be tricky.

Wednesday, 27 December, London

Left for London about midday, arriving at about four. Then round to see Austin. She lives in a very elegant house in Maunsell Street. I do like her husband. He is thoroughly supportive. We had a chat for about an hour and a half, during which she confirmed that she would like to go ahead over the next few days. So we began to discuss when we should do it.

She had been contacted by the *Today* programme on something to do with the single currency. This has made her very frightened that we have been found out. 'They have a way of knowing. They somehow sense it in people's body language.'

She is also now very aware of how nasty the Tories are going to be.

I found her more and more impressive. She is very courageous. Much influenced by her father, who suffered much for voting against Chamberlain and for Churchill after Munich. 'I will never forget what they did to Father.'

We went through the plan in detail and agreed that we would all meet at her place at 11.30am tomorrow.

I was delighted. If we can now just manage the press aspects of this right it will be devastating for the Government.

Went home and left a message on Richard's answerphone. Also rang Alan Leaman, Chris Rennard, Nick South and Archy. Archy could not believe it, but readily agreed to come down from Scotland on the night sleeper – bless him. We arranged to meet tomorrow at Methley Street at ten o'clock.

Thursday, 28 December, London

Up early to go through the Austin plan one last time. Archy arrived at about 9.30. The house is full of my family, who have come over for Christmas.

We sat down to talk through what would happen, first of all taking the decision on when to do it. We decided on tomorrow night – we couldn't afford to wait until Sunday, New Year's Eve, because of the danger of leaks. This decision was confirmed when we heard that Major was doing a *Today* interview on Saturday morning. So we drew up a plan which involved releasing news of the defection to the BBC's 9 o'clock news on Friday followed up by the 10 o'clock ITN news, and then going flat out on Saturday and Sunday to capitalize on the advantage, before putting Austin into purdah for the following week.

We bundled into my car and drove to Maunsell Street. I didn't want us all entering the street at the same time, as it is full of Tory MPs' homes. So I dropped Alan at the end of Horseferry Road, making him walk the whole distance of it, so that he came late from one direction. I then dropped Richard more or less outside; but to my horror he started walking in the wrong direction so I had to lower the window and shout at him to turn round and go back the other way. I then dropped Archy at the other end of the street and, having parked the car, gave myself about five minutes before setting off.

We all arrived from different directions at different times – perfect (apart from Richard).

We went through the plan with her. She wants to get her word in first. She is keen to honour an agreement she made to John Pienaar[1] some weeks ago that, if ever she decided to leave the Tories, he would have the first exclusive interview, provided he got the other journalists off her back later.

We were dubious about this. Richard tried to persuade her otherwise. I stayed silent, but then came in, 'Look, if this is what Emma wants to do, and believes is right, then this is what we must do.' The meeting was all over in an hour or so.

Richard went off to lunch and Archy and Alan and I went back to the flat where Nick joined us and started to draw up a detailed plan. By 4.30 it was completed.

We faxed it through to those who had left (Archy had gone back to Scotland, Chris to Liverpool and Alan to Dorset). Nick and I then went to the House, where we did a little work on the final details.

I have been dreading that the news would break all afternoon, but it hasn't. Journalists are saying to me that there are no stories at the moment. I keep looking at the TV news thinking how different it will be tomorrow.

Friday, 29 December, London

Out at 7.40 for the *Today* programme. When I arrived, I was horrified to hear that they are going to record Major this afternoon for tomorrow (i.e. the Austin story would break between the recording and its broadcast).

1 BBC journalist.

I agonized over what I should do. I couldn't help reflecting just how much things would have changed by tomorrow. On the way out, after doing my slot, I bumped into Roger Mosey.[1] I asked him whether they were really pre-recording Major and he said they were.

I decide to take a risk. 'Look, I can't tell you why, and I cannot give any details, so do not ask me and do not go beating the bushes. But I will share a very private confidence with you. If you interview the Prime Minister today it will look exceedingly silly by tomorrow, because something is going to happen that will change everything. So, here's a tip for you. If you do him today, make sure you get a commitment from him to return if anything big breaks.'

Mosey tried to drag more out of me, but he didn't succeed. I then met up with Nick and we walked through the bitter cold but bright sunlit morning to Richard's flat.

When we arrived, Austin and her husband were already there. We made a number of changes to the programme. We produced a single document which would run the whole operation from this afternoon, including telephone numbers and all other details. Our plan included faxing to Nick Harvey and Paul Tyler in the West Country the letters Austin had written to her constituency chairman and officers. Nick and Paul were instructed that they would get these by six and were then to cut all distinguishing marks off the faxes and put them into sealed and addressed envelopes. These were to be given to activists from their local parties, who should not be told of the contents but must be instructed to deliver the letters, by hand, to the addresses shown, at exactly eight o'clock (neither earlier nor later).

Austin then showed us the article she and Michael had drafted. I left Richard working on this. He was to knock it into an article for the *Western Morning News*.

We then discussed how we would send it to the *Western Morning News*. Austin said she would go directly to the editor. Meanwhile, in a corner of the room, a friend of hers was drafting an article for the *Daily Telegraph*, which we would offer them before their last deadline of 8.20. Then Nick and I returned to the office, where we finalized amendments to the programme. Alan Leaman, at the same time, rang his press team and, without telling them what was afoot, asked them to come into the office.

By now there was great speculation in the Party. Was I going to announce

1 Editor of the *Today* programme.

my resignation, or what? We were now running on the programme which had started at 11.00am.

At about 2 o'clock, Richard rang me to say that they couldn't get hold of the editor of the *Western Morning News*. There ensued a long discussion, during which Richard and Austin suggested giving the story to *The Times*. But I said it had to go to the *Western Morning News*, because of the effect in the South West. I then contacted a *Western Morning News* reporter I knew personally and said, 'Look, I can promise you an article which will be in my name and will be a real bombshell. It will be not only on your front page, but on the front pages of every other newspaper in Britain as well. But I cannot tell you the subject and I cannot get it to you until 7.45pm. Trust me.' He agreed.

Next, we couldn't get hold of John Pienaar, so we agreed that the best alternative would be Robin Oakley. I rang him at three. I couldn't get him, so we bleeped him. When he rang back I said, 'Robin, I have a big story for you. I am not going to tell you what it is. Richard will do that. He will ring you at 4.15. Will you be at home?' He said that he would be. When Richard rang him, he took the story immediately.

At 6.00 the team started to arrive to prepare the press packs, to be released by fax and e-mail on the Party's internal system to all our candidates and activists. We had finished this by 6.15, then downstairs for a light supper. The news still hasn't broken. And the Tories are still in the dark.

At 7.10 exactly we started to follow the plan by the minute. We piled into the car and I dropped the team off at the House to gather in various other people from the press office. None of them knew what was happening and were amazed when they heard.

Then back to Emma's house at 7.40 through the now foggy streets of London, passing by a BBC outside broadcast van already on the green outside the House. And still the Tories do not know!

I picked up Emma and Michael and dropped them off with Richard at Millbank to do the Robin Oakley piece.

We then started to contact our key candidates in the South West to prime them for the local press.

By now the whole team was hunting. At 8.15 we heard that the drop of Emma's letters to her constituency officers had been completed. It was 8.30 I think before anybody in the Tory Party knew.

At 8.10, on Austin's behalf, I faxed her handwritten letter[1] through to

---

1 See Appendix D for a transcript.

the Prime Minister at Downing Street. [He was later to claim that he never received it].

Emma and Michael came back at about 8.20. I put them in my office and said, 'This office is now yours for the rest of the night. I will make you some coffee and here is a decanter of whisky and a bottle of wine.'

She then settled down to ringing her ex-supporters, constituency chairman, etc. She was very, very nervous, but stood up to it well. She told me that about 50 per cent said they supported what she was doing.

By now the press were going absolutely mad. We watched the 9 o'clock news together. She was excellent. We then sent her home before the paparazzi turned up on her doorstep. She got there just in time.

The whole operation went absolutely perfectly. It took the Tories and the press completely by surprise and dominated every news bulletin through the night and into the following morning. [Peter Riddell was later to say that it was the best coup he had ever seen.]

I got home at about eleven. Jane said that it looked great on television. We listened to the midnight news and then to bed. We've done it!

Saturday, 30 December, London

The papers are full of Emma's defection. All the later editions lead on it. I heard her on the *Today* programme. She was really excellent. By now the Tories have got their act together and are throwing the shit at her.

At 9.30 a photo op with Emma in the freezing rain and afterwards to Millbank for more interviews.

Perhaps this is, at last, the turning point.

1996

Monday, 15 January, Westminster

I told Archy today that we need to pull off Wolseley, if we possibly can. The Government is reeling like a punch-drunk boxer. We must continue jabbing at its chin, keep it off balance. Emma's defection has dealt it a real blow and we need another. If we could force the Government down in these circumstances (their morale is very low and an atmosphere of civil war pervades the Conservative benches) then, in the next election, the Tories will be fighting each other rather than us. The General Election would already be a goner and the real fight would be for the Leadership of the Party afterwards.

Wolseley is apparently convinced a coup is being mounted on Major and that a leadership election is going to come sooner rather than later. But I don't think he really knows. I suspect what goes on in the upper echelon of that extraordinary organization which is now devouring its own intestines is as great a mystery to Tory back benchers as it is to those who sit opposite them.

Tuesday, 16 January, London

With Jane to Simon's graduation at the Barbican.[1] We caught a brief glimpse of him in his gown in the scrum of graduates. The presentations went on for two hours. I had a real thrill to see him pick up his degree. He looked very handsome and relaxed.

Then back to the House.

Roy is giving dinner tonight for Tony Blair and Jonathan Powell, to meet some permanent secretaries in Whitehall. All part of preparing for government. I said to Roy, 'I think Blair is moving on PR. It is really important that we push him as far as we can. I have sent you a copy of the speech I am making on Monday.[2] Please feel free to tell him this is a

1 Where Simon had received a BSc in Music Technology from the New Guildhall University.
2 This speech, which became known as the 'Bridge speech', was about the next Government launching a great decade of reform to modernize Britain and 'build a bridge' between this century and the next. In it I said that the Liberal Democrats and Labour should commit themselves to working in a long-term partnership in order to form the cornerstone of this decade of reform.

proposition for a full two terms' partnership in which we could be stable and reliable partners – if only he would shift his position on PR. I am hoping you can push him forward. He has a very high regard for you.'

Wednesday, 17 January, Westminster

At 12.30 I went down to see Roy. The meeting had gone well. Blair impressive – more impressive than some of the permanent secretaries. They had spoken together briefly beforehand and afterwards. Roy had explained to Blair what I was trying to say in my speech. He then put pressure on Blair on PR and concluded that he was 'becoming convinced intellectually', but that if he adopted PR it would split Labour. Roy told Blair that I needed a commitment from him (if necessary a purely private one) that he would support PR before the election.

Apparently the main part of this conversation was held on the doorstep after the meeting with the permanent secretaries. He thinks that Blair is at last moving. I will find out how far the next time I meet him.

Friday, 19 January, Somerset

A meeting with Detective Constable Jim Midgely, who is handling the Mason business. We had a long discussion about Mason's allegations. Apparently the *Sun* has offered £50,000 for the transcript of Mason's police interview. This is not going to be comfortable. Midgely thinks that the County Court, to which it is bound to go, will be difficult. And the press are very interested.

Friday, 26 January, London

I saw Chris Rennard for breakfast at Methley Street. I wanted to push Wolseley as hard as possible. Chris understands how important this is and will speak to Archy, who is seeing Mrs Wolseley this weekend. The key is to get our people in Westmorland & Lonsdale to move. We must put the Government on the back foot again. There is evidence of a recovery in the Tory vote and they are becoming far too bouncy for my liking.

Then off to catch the bus. It's minus two or three this morning. I was freezing to death at the bus stop when an old banger drew up. It was Jack Straw. He offered me a lift and we chatted as he drove. He started off with the Harriet Harman situation[1] – they believe it hasn't done them much damage with voters, although they expect to see some decline in their opinion poll ratings. But there is real anger among teachers and Party members.

They appreciate that they cannot duck tricky issues by shifting the agenda. 'That was a lesson we learned in the last election. If it is one of "our" issues we will just have to fight it through.'

He also said, 'I am aware of the discussions that are going on between you and Tony and between Robin and Bob. I also know that the block is electoral reform. Frankly, it is going to be very difficult for us to argue against the Alternative Vote[2], since we use it in the Labour Party and for Shadow Cabinet elections. If I could persuade people like Margaret Beckett to go for the Alternative Vote would that satisfy you?'

I said it wouldn't. Our view was STV.[3] But the important thing was to concentrate on the principle of electoral reform. We could argue precise systems later, if Labour accepted before the election that the current system had to be reformed. He said that nevertheless, and for the record, he would be prepared to recommend AV. No more. It was vital for him, and others in the Labour Party, that we should retain a position where one member represents one constituency. 'That's the problem with AMS.'[4]

I said it was not good enough simply to propose a referendum, they

1 Harriet Harman had decided to send one of her sons to a grammar school ten miles from her home. It caused great controversy, not least in the Labour Party.

2 *Alternative Vote.* Single member constituencies. Voters list candidates in order of preference 1, 2, 3 etc. If no candidate has 50 per cent of the vote, the candidate with the least support is eliminated and votes are transferred to second preference. This process continues, until one candidate has 50 per cent of the vote. This is not a proportional system; it tends to exaggerate swings and can produce results even more distorted than first past the post (our present electoral system in the UK).

3 *Single Transferable Vote.* Multi-member constituencies. Parties generally stand several candidates and the voters number them in order of preference. Candidates with least support are eliminated and a quota system determines which of them are elected. This process ensures proportionality so that the number of MPs elected reflects the number of votes cast for that party.

4 *Alternative Member System/Additional Member System.* Some MPs are elected in single-member constituencies whilst others are elected as additional members. The number of additional members awarded to each Party is based on the number each Party needs to make its overall number of MPs reflect the votes cast for each Party. It is usual for voters to cast two votes – one for the constituency member and one for the Party.

would also have to take a position and they would look ridiculous if they didn't. We had a brief discussion about referendums. He is against the New Zealand-style 'Preferendum'.[1] He thinks we would have to get the legislation through the House of Commons and then present perhaps two clear options to the electorate in a referendum 'in the first two or three years'. I said it would have to be much earlier than that.

He then said, 'We realize that we must take a position on this and will almost certainly end up recommending AV in a referendum. We cannot keep saying nothing.'

I repeated that timing was vital. If they came out in favour of a referendum before the election, all sorts of things were possible; but if they did it after the election they would (a) look silly at the election and (b) not be able to deliver the maximum blow to the Tories.

He replied, 'Frankly, it will be very difficult before the election. But it is certainly something we will look at. I will have another chat with Tony.'

He was very friendly. I was surprised that he supports electoral reform, even if he favours the wrong position. He said that he had practically blackmailed the Party into accepting a referendum at Conference, and that his personal position had shifted and he thought the Party's was shifting, too.

He said that they had to attack us over Tower Hamlets[2] because we were 'carving great chunks out of them in local government. But that's part of politics, isn't it?' I replied, 'Yes, and you can expect us to attack you, too, unless a fully co-operative approach is followed. We have been more restrained than we would otherwise have been on the Harman affair because we wanted you lot to understand what it is like if you only had the Tories to deal with. But you can't expect such kindness in the future, unless we do a deal. We can't produce such big guns as the Conservatives, but we can snap at your heels pretty effectively.'

In the late afternoon, Blair rang me, apologizing for not fixing a meeting. 'We've had a hell of a week.'

Commenting on my 'Bridge speech' last week, he said, 'I don't think our people are going to kick up a fuss. I have been surprised by how matter-of-

---

1 In New Zealand they had recently had a referendum on PR (overwhelmingly in favour), in which citizens were allowed to state a preference, not just for PR as a principle, but also for a particular system of PR.

2 The Lib Dems in Tower Hamlets published leaflets which were subsequently found, by an internal inquiry that I set up under Anthony Lester, to have pandered to racism.

fact they are about it.' I said that I had been surprised by the lack of reaction from our lot, too.

He went on, 'Perhaps both our parties think we are so wilful that we will do what we are going to do anyway.' That may be true of his lot, but it certainly isn't true of mine.

We fixed to meet on Monday at eight for an extended discussion. I said that I would want to talk about PR again as this was our main concern now. He replied, 'Yes, I have one or two thoughts to put to you on that.' It was a brief and cheerful conversation.

Monday 29 January, London

To Blair's house just before 8 o'clock. As we drove into the road his red Rover was departing, having delivered him back from his evening speech. I rang the bell. The door clicked open and in I walked. Tony looked tired and dishevelled as he came up the stairs from the kitchen.

He left me in the sitting room while he went to get changed into a pair of jeans.

At first I didn't notice Euan in the corner, working away at the computer. He is a very nice lad, who seems completely unspoilt by being the subject of so many front-page articles.

We then went down into the kitchen and had five or ten minutes over a glass of wine discussing the present political situation. Cherie is out tonight, so Tony is left babysitting and is not going to the 10 o'clock vote. We sat down to some food which had been brought in from a restaurant – fettucine cheese with lentils, dried tomatoes and bressaola for starters and then a very good duck with red and green peppers for the main course, followed up by some kind of Italian gâteau. We had a fine bottle of white Burgundy. He said it had been recommended to him by Derry Irvine 'who acts as my wine merchant'.

He also told me that last week had been the worst of his life. He had been terribly upset with Harriet, not for her decision, but for the stupidity of its timing. 'It was bad enough when I chose the Oratory[1] for Euan – surely she should have known the chaos this would cause.'

The incident had done little serious damage with the voters, but it had badly dented the Party's morale and resuscitated the whole 'New Labour/

---

1 Highly regarded grant-maintained Catholic comprehensive school in Fulham.

old Labour' issue. He had had to sacrifice a lot to defend her. I reminded him of Lord Melbourne's dictum that 'It is more important to stick with your friends when they are wrong than when they are right.' He said, 'Well, if that's the case I shall have saved up great store in heaven. We had a terrible internal row about this. John Prescott was very angry with her for being so stupid. The real danger is that it has given the Tories breathing space. We've just got to realize that these people are bastards and are now capable of doing almost anything. We must hit them down again. If they are up on both feet and fighting, they are very dangerous.'

This was a theme to which he returned time and again during the meeting. He said, 'I have studied the Tories for a long time. I have fought them in court cases at the Bar. I know what makes them tick. And I know how deadly and unpleasant they can be. Their really nasty quality is that they will do anything to save their own skins. And say anything, too. We have people who are just as powerful, just as efficient, just as professional, but we don't have people who are just as nasty.'

Later, on PR, he said, 'I know people decry me whenever I say this, but my main reason for not wanting PR is because I understand the power of Murdoch and Black. At present they are prepared to let me have a go at government while the Tories sort themselves out. But they will change to a terrible opposition if they believe I will keep them out for ever. It's the one thing that could unite the Tories. Did you see the *Daily Mail* on Lib/Labbery last week? The possibility of us getting together has really sent them into panic in Smith Square.'

PA: Tony, I am just amazed at you. These people are not going to do you any favours. I very much doubt that you can alter the tone of what they will say in the election, anyway. You don't have to spell out to them that you will keep them out of power. They judge you by themselves. If they have power, they try to change the rules of the game. And they expect you to do the same. In the heat of an election they will attack you as though you were keeping them out of power for ever. And they will use that as an argument. Major will specifically say, 'Please re-elect me one more time so I can kill socialism for ever. And if you don't, socialism will kill us for ever.'

TB: I don't mind about Major. I don't rate him highly and we don't get on particularly well, but he's decent. It's the people who are behind him who are terrible. Terribly powerful and terribly ruthless, as well.

We then discussed what we would have to do to knock the Government down again. He said, 'What we need is another defector – you haven't got one have you?' I said that there were faint rustlings in the undergrowth, but nothing definite. Did he have anybody? 'One who is just possible. But extremely unlikely and not to be counted upon.' I suspect we were both bluffing!

Yet again during the meeting he returned to the subject of the South West. 'Surely there is some way we can indicate to our people in the South West that they shouldn't oppose your lot.' I told him that the only way to do this was to give them a good reason to vote tactically.

Later, we got on to discussing the economy. His economic advisers say that it is currently in a sticky period, but that growth and consumption will take off from the middle of the year. If the Tories leave it too late, however, the Governor of the Bank of England will press them to raise interest rates early next year, because the economy will be expanding too fast and inflation will have become a real danger. There is an 8 per cent growth in the money supply at present.

TB: If this had been the 1980s people would say we were in a real crisis. The difference now is that the new relationship between the Governor and the Chancellor is such that the Tories can't get away with over-inflating the economy before the election. But I can see some good economic reasons for them going earlier in the autumn, when the consumption/growth boom has taken hold and before inflation hits. But my own view remains that they will wait until spring next year.

We also talked about our relative teams. He said that his relationship with John Prescott was good and that he had said to Prescott, 'Look, John, you must stop looking grumpy when you are sitting on the bench. People think you are being grumpy with me rather than grumpy with the situation.'

He thinks that Donald Dewar is superb, 'a real discovery'. Jack Straw isn't a problem, as he reckons 'in the end he will do what I ask him to do', but Margaret Beckett is 'more difficult'. 'Robin appears fully in favour of what we are doing, but that's because he is totally committed to PR. I'm not sure how far he really believes in the project, however.' Gordon Brown is a surprising opponent to the whole project. He believes that we will diminish their appeal. 'Contrary to what you read in the papers, Gordon and I get on very well together. He is extremely sharp and if he says that I should reconsider something, I do. He thinks you lot are too undisciplined to cope with the situation we will find ourselves in when we get into government. But then he is thinking rather smaller than I am . . .'

We then got on to talking about our people – he has a high regard for Ming Campbell and Alex Carlile.

We discussed who on his side was in the 'circle of knowledge'. He told me Robin Cook, Gordon Brown, Peter Mandelson, Donald Dewar and John Prescott. I told him who was in the Jo Group and said that we must broaden our communications channels if we were to expand the relationship.

I said that on positioning we were now quite satisfied with where we were. We believed that Labour had now done their worst to us. They had eroded our position as much as they could, but we had held our territory, and even improved it. The likelihood was that their overall popularity would decline and we could hold our own quite adequately without them.

So if we had to go into the next election on the basis of my Bridge speech, making general noises about co-operation, then we could. We would then fight what was, in all respects, a perfectly conventional election. We would attack them and the Tories more or less equally. Of course, the tone might be different. But I couldn't even guarantee that.

The other option was the larger project. We could use the next election to launch a reshaping of British politics. We could set in train something which would lead to him and me jointly proposing around the autumn, say, two to four key projects. One would have to be constitutional. But the others could relate to people's real needs (e.g., education and health). We could then say the two parties would stand on their independent manifestos, but would work together on the agreed issues in the next parliament. Not necessarily in a coalition. Across the floor of the House, if necessary.

In my view, such a project, unveiled at the right time, would convert a Conservative defeat into a Conservative rout. It would also create the best conditions for a Conservative split afterwards. And, most important of all, we'd be creating a partnership that could genuinely deliver ten years of solid reform in government.

But the precondition for this was Blair's own personal support for PR. Without this, I couldn't carry my Party. Any kind of relationship along the lines that I suggested would be certain death for us without PR, and I didn't intend to ask my party to commit suicide. Finally, PR was the key ingredient to achieve the kind of pluralist government he said he wanted.

TB: That's all very interesting. I am of a bold frame of mind. I like big projects rather than small ones. This proposition is one that we have thought through at length and it appeals to me. But I am still undecided on whether PR will prove to be good for the governance of Britain.

At this point I stopped him.

PA: Look, I think PR is good for the country but I cannot persuade you intellectually. You have to persuade yourself. You shouldn't be in any doubt, however, about its political advantages to you and to the project.

TB: What kind of PR do you guys want?

PA: Well, you are going to find it difficult to argue against AV, since you use it internally in the Labour Party. But you need to know that it is unacceptable for us. These are matters that would have to be decided, of course, in a referendum. At the moment the principle is more important than the detailed system. We will take our chances in a referendum, and to a certain extent we will take our chances with an appropriate system as well, provided it isn't just AV. But whatever the system, we cannot win a yes vote in a PR referendum with the Prime Minister arguing against change.

TB: Yes, I understand that. But you must know how divisive that will be in my Party, and what a big leap it is for me to make.

PA: Well, that is your choice. You can achieve something small which removes the Tories from power for one term. Or you can do something big which will lay the foundations for a decade of reform and reshaping of British politics. Surely you cannot go into a referendum without telling people what your opinion is?

TB: Yes, I know. I must take a position.

PA: And it will be impossible for you to call a referendum and then recommend 'no'.

TB: Yes, that is probably true as well.

PA: In which case, the choice is between you saying 'yes' before an election and 'yes' afterwards. You must decide where the advantage lies.

I told him we would need a statement from him before we made any public announcement on major co-operation (e.g., on the constitution), but that it wasn't necessary right now. It would be sufficient for him to indicate to me privately that he agreed with our end position and that he would recommend PR. Then we could start building towards it.

PA: There isn't much time. I wanted to press you on your decision tonight. If we are to go for minor co-operation, then of course we can keep things as they are and we needn't make any further changes. But if we decide to go for major co-operation, then there is a hell of a lot of work to be done. And if we are to assemble our proposals in time for an autumn election, then we must start work in the next few weeks. Which is why we need an answer from you in the next two to three weeks.

He agreed, and promised to clarify his position by our next meeting.

At one stage he said, 'I can see a huge advantage in having you chiming in with us. It would really have helped last week if you lot had come out and accused the Government of hypocrisy themselves.' I said that we were aware of the importance of the Harman affair, which was why we didn't join the Tory attack. Quite deliberately I had said to my people, 'I'm not sure if she's right, but I am sure it is right to defend her against the Tory attacks.' He said he had spotted this.

Towards the end of dinner Euan came down and sat with us. He said that he liked John Prescott best of all the Shadow Cabinet people and then Gordon Brown because he talked to him about football!

When I left for the vote at 9.40, Blair said, 'I will let you know how we stand on all this soon.'

Tuesday, 30 January, London

A wonderfully relaxed day. I saw Andrew Phillips over breakfast today to discuss with him both Wolseley and the wretched Chris Mason witness appearance I have to do next week. He thinks that there is not going to be as much fuss as I fear and that Mason's allegations will be dismissed out of hand, although the press will have some fun with it. I wish I was so sure.

Meanwhile, I am really worried that Blair, who can be very broad brush, will not have hoisted on board some of the details from last night. It is important that Labour understand exactly what we are proposing. So I have decided to send them a minute explaining our position. But in case this leaks, I will write it as though from a well-informed Labour researcher,[1] and Archy will give it to Donald Dewar. That way they will have a piece of paper they can legitimately circulate which lays out our position clearly.

I fear Blair thinks that this is all going to be terribly lovey-dovey. I do not want any accusations of bad faith later.

During the morning, things started to move on the Wolseley front. He is intending to go very soon. I will have to see him.

---

1 See Appendix E.

Wednesday, 31 January, Westminster

Alan and I went to Andrew's office at nine. Wolseley was already there. I sat down and said to him, 'Now, tell me what you want to do.'

He said he had decided to go early so that he can explain how badly he has been treated by the Tories. His constituency has been wiped out by the Boundary Commission and the Tories have refused to select him at Westmorland & Lonsdale. I said that it would be a disaster for him to be seen to be moving because of that; he should move on grounds of high principle. The Tories would anyway be quick enough to paint him as acting from pique.

He has a plan to cover this point and it is a good one. He will carry out an opinion poll in his constituency about attitudes to the Government. When he has the results, he will say that his unhappiness is his constituents' unhappiness as well. Since he is, above all, a person committed to representing them, he would go away and think about this. He will then have a meeting with Major during the week to see if Major could persuade him that the Tories would change. Then, on the following Sunday he would announce he was going independent.

We could then manage the transition across to us in slow time.

I asked if he realized just what that week would be like. The Tories would be dreadful. And he would be pursued everywhere. Nor could we give him the support we had given Emma. He would be out on the high seas in a dinghy, on his own, with huge gales blowing – and we feared for his safety.

I then left him with Alan and asked Alan to draft Wolseley's first statement, his resignation letter to the Prime Minister and other articles. These all need to be in the can before we start.

Friday, 2 February, Somerset

At a little before 4.00am the telephone rang. Jane went to take it. I could hear from the sound of her voice that something was wrong and leapt out of bed. Jane said, 'They have got our car!'[1] It was Steph from next door saying that our car was on fire. She had rung the fire brigade.

---

[1] When I had driven back from London the previous night, I had parked my car in the garage belonging to our next-door neighbours, the Baileys, for safekeeping. Following the knife attack by Mason, my car windows had been broken several times while it was parked outside my house overnight.

I immediately rang the police, dressed and dashed out, locking the door behind me and telling Jane under no circumstances to come out into the road. Almost immediately I met Steve[1] running out of his house. We rushed round to the garage at the end of Steph's drive to find the car well and truly ablaze.

I immediately panicked about John's car, which was parked alongside mine, so belted back to Steph, who gave me the keys. As I ran back I shouted to Steve, 'I am really worried my petrol tank is going to blow'. Steve said, 'Then for goodness' sake stay clear.' I said, 'But we can't let John's car burn, too,' so Steve and I dashed into the garage. With my heart pounding, I jumped into John's driving seat. I could feel the heat from my car burning only a few feet away. Already the garage roof was dropping flaming shards around us.

I managed to get John's car out and went back for Steph's, which was also there. But the car wouldn't start, so we had to push it out of the garage.

By this time the fire brigade had arrived, followed by the police. My car had by now burned out completely, together with the roof of the garage.

The police took statements while Jane made tea for the firemen – all thirteen of them. Then Steve came out with some more tea and flapjacks. It became quite a midnight party.

We didn't go back to bed. I rang Nick at about six, having spent a long time thinking about whether I wanted this to get out to the press. Then I rang Mark Ellis, told him what had happened and said to look out for his house. What I didn't know was that Kate, Mark's daughter, who is a reporter on the local paper, was in his kitchen at the time. So the story was out. We issued a brief factual statement on what happened to the Press Association.

As I was having my bath at 7.00, we were amused to hear on the *Today* programme that car crime has gone down in the Avon and Somerset area!

The world started to go mad from about 7.30am. A succession of people came to the door and we spent the rest of the morning dealing with the press. We decided to say nothing other than that a criminal investigation was underway and I would be happy for it to take its normal course. The nine o'clock and midday news bulletins were full of it. They did the 1 o'clock news from outside the garage with the burned out car in the background.

---

1 Steve Radley, our other neighbour.

I am now scared to death of the house being fire-bombed with Jane inside. I rang the burglar alarm people to order a new security light and some smoke alarms, and then permanently closed off our letterbox as the police said there was a danger of petrol being poured through it.

Saturday, 3 February, Somerset

The town has been full of press people and Mason's associates have been filling their ears with scandalous lies, on which they promise to expand in court on Thursday.

So I was chased throughout the day by, in particular, the *Sunday Times* and *News of the World*. I spoke to Andrew Phillips, who says that the main thing is not to give them anything to hang a story on – even an angry denial, he says, will give them something to print and insinuate.

In the late afternoon, the police came by. They have decided to have somebody in an unmarked car outside our house all night.

We settled down to a quiet evening, but it was soon interrupted. Apparently there is a scandal story about me in the *Sunday Times* tomorrow. Many telephone calls back and forth. The *News of the World* – Eben Black – rang to ask whether I had any comments on the story that I had been going to a local brothel and massage parlour.

I was absolutely furious. I said it was outrageous and I couldn't dignify it with a comment.

Then I rang Nick and Andrew Phillips. At this stage the pressure was getting through to me and I exploded. 'These shits! How can they believe these lies? It is one thing to be fire-bombed. It is quite another to have the press then publish the smears given to them by people with criminal records, who are almost certainly involved in fire-bombing my car and who they know are trying to intimidate me.'

Andrew was very cool. He had discussed this with the *Sunday Times* and believed that, in the end, they would not dare to publish and that I should keep calm. It wasn't out on the streets yet, anyway, and he doubted if it ever would be. Next came a call from Roland Watts of the *Sunday Mirror*. He said that the *Sunday Times* weren't publishing their first edition, the rumour being that we had injuncted them. Was that correct? Then a whole flood of calls.

Nick rang at about eleven to confirm that the *Sunday Times* had pulled their first edition, the front page of which ran with the headline, 'Paddy Rubdown' and retold the whole pack of lies. I said that if they did publish I would throw the book at them. But Nick said that their own lawyers had stopped them. They had, he said, actually pulled the newspapers back from King's Cross. Must have cost them a mint.

Andrew was right. They didn't publish. But I would rather have my car fire-bombed every night than go through the absolutely terrifying business of having a remote battle of wills from my sitting room with the newsroom of a vast organization like the *Sunday Times* – knowing that if I got it wrong I would give them the grounds on which to publish, whether the allegations were true or not.

Sunday, 4 February, Somerset

Bright, clear, crisp and frosty.

The *Sunday Times* has rewritten the story so that it comes out in my favour, indicating that I will stand up to the smear campaign.

The *News of the World* is worse. Three pages. The headlines read 'Ashdown in brothel vendetta'. Inside, a re-run of the Tricia stuff. Nasty, but not libellous. Nothing I can do.

There are now more newspaper reporters outside the door. Late last night there was a knock on the door. I opened it and they said, 'I am sorry to disturb you so late at night.' I replied, 'Yes, too late' and closed the door. It was the *Sun*, I think – with a photographer. They got fed up and went down to the Lord Nelson for a drink.[1] While they were gone, I nipped out to take a cup of tea to the poor policeman who was protecting our house.

This morning they are back. Somebody from the *Sun* again and three photographers. Jane took them a cup of coffee. I suppose they have a job to do, even if it is a revolting one.

At 11.15 we left with Luke for the five-mile walk to the Rose & Crown. The photographers snapped away, walking backwards in front of us. But they didn't come more than a couple of hundred yards before getting fed up.

We had a lovely walk, discussing the arrangements for Kate's wedding.[2] A low winter mist hung over the levels between Over Stratton and Chiselborough, though this was soon burned off by the sun. The birds beginning to sing, probably under the misapprehension that it is spring. Out of the sunlight it is still sharp and cold, with a hard frost on the ground.

To bed about midnight. Two undercover policemen have moved into a nearby house to keep an eye on us. I looked out of our window for them, but they were completely invisible. Bizarre to think of them watching the house all night. There was a police car tucked round the corner as well, but apparently this broke down and they had to get the low-loader round in the middle of the night to pick it up.

A quiet night, thank God.

1 The pub in our village.
2 Our daughter Kate had recently become engaged to her French boyfriend, Sebastien, who lives in the next village to Irancy. They were to marry in August.

Monday, 5 February, Somerset and London

Up early to ask the London office to fax through the pops, to see how they covered the smear stories of yesterday. All fine. Some even quite good. But I wish it wasn't on the front pages at all.

I then asked the Yeovil office to fax through the *Western Daily Press*. To my horror, they had simply regurgitated on pages one, two and three all the lies told to them by Mason's associates. I had heard of these, but had not seen them in detail. Now they are printed on the front page of my local newspaper.

The story quotes informants saying that a prostitute called Zoë gave me 'sexual services' three years ago. Zoë ('not her real name') has gone into hiding. I was furious and rang Andrew.

It is a clear libel and, he says, probably contempt of court as well. Suddenly I felt the deep black pit in the bottom of my stomach again. I was going to meet the press at eleven and this is what they would talk about. Goodness knows what other rubbish they will get from Mason's cronies as well.

I cannot understand how the *Western Daily Press* has been so stupid. I shall never forgive them. They know this gang and what they have been doing in the Yeovil community for ages. They publish high-minded editorials on law and order – then print a load of lies like this.

Andrew and I agreed that we would have to sue them. We had a very strong case. But of course no one could be certain of the outcome. Libel trials are always an expensive lottery, so there was always a risk. I said that I had no option. I left him to work out the details and drove into Yeovil.

My problem now is that, if they ask me whether the allegations are true I will, of course, have to deny them, thereby making the denial the story and blowing to smithereens all our careful work of the weekend. They will get their front-page stories. I decided on the way to Yeovil that we should announce we would sue the *Western Daily Press* for libel immediately and demand an apology. I am utterly furious. I am also frightened that one slip now and it will all be gone.

Spoke to Andrew again. We agreed the statement: 'The press generally have been excellent and responsible, with one exception. The story published in the *Western Daily Press* today is absolutely disgraceful. My lawyers will be in touch with them and we will be issuing proceedings today.'

When I arrived at the office I was shaking with anger and nervousness. I briefed the office staff and then started to prepare for the press conference.

The press were already arriving in their droves like hyenas gathering for the kill. At this stage we got a call from Tina Rowe.[1] Could she have a few words with me beforehand? I took the phone and she handed it to the senior reporter who, I think, was the author of the story. He said, 'Paddy, I would like a few words with you before the press conference.' I said, 'There is no point. As far as I am concerned you are beneath contempt.' And put the phone down.

I noted later that he didn't come along to the press conference but sent poor Tina to do his dirty work for him. She looked ashen-faced and shaken as well. I think she knows just what a mistake they have made. I was informed that they did not believe the stories but thought they would publish them anyway. Unbelievable.

Then into the press conference. I tried to be as light-hearted as possible, pulling the journalists' legs about the London press being so interested in our local issues.

Then someone said, 'You know what we have come here to ask. What is your reaction to the way this has been reported in the papers?'

I said, 'The papers have by and large been responsible and fair. With one exception. The *Western Daily Press* report today is absolutely scandalous. My solicitors will be in touch with them and a writ for libel will be issued today.' Someone tried to ask me a second question but that was all I had to say. Someone else then said, 'But can we ask you . . . ?'

'No – this is now a matter for the legal process and for a criminal investigation. I have nothing further to say and you all know why.' I then walked out and drove home.

I was still shaking and terrified when I arrived. Jane drove me up to London. It was all on the lunchtime news, of course.

When we got to the London office, I rang Andrew, who had just had a conversation with the *Western Daily Press*'s lawyers. They have more or less conceded that they were totally wrong. Hooray! But by now all the news and reports were full of me taking a libel action against a Bristol paper which has made allegations about my private life. All that dragged out again.

At 4.30 I nipped down to discuss Blair with Roy. He had read through

1 The Yeovil-based *Western Daily Press* reporter whom I have known since I first came to this part of Somerset in 1976.

my diary record of our last meeting. He is strongly in support and recognizes that this is a very important moment. He also offered his commiserations on 'the other events'.

We have had an extraordinary flood of e-mail and mail, including a £100 cheque from a pensioner towards my car. Amazing. There have been one or two very nasty letters, too. Although I have public sympathy, this will not, I fear, do us any good in the long run.

At 7.15 Jane, who had been speaking to Kate and Simon on the phone, came in and we went down to the National Farmers Union dinner. All the other Somerset MPs there.

We were just having a drink when Nick turned up, took me to one side and said, 'The *Western Daily Press* has agreed everything.' They are going to publish a front-page apology, do a grovelling editorial and release it tonight to the press.

A huge load lifted from my shoulders. It was bad enough having my car fire-bombed on Friday, then fighting all the London newsrooms on Sunday. But to follow that up with a direct battle for my political life against my regional paper, who ought to know better, has added insult to injury. But they have caved in.

Left early for a meeting on Wolseley in my office. Jane came up later.

Chris Rennard made the point, accepted by all, that Wolseley really had to make it clear that he could not support the Government in a no-confidence vote and would move to the cross benches (in so far as they exist in the House of Commons) before coming to us. Unless he looked principled, there was no chance of getting the constituency to consider him as a candidate. So we decided that it was in his interest, and ours, to go through with the plan he had formulated before coming to us.

By this time the press calls from the *Western Daily Press*'s climbdown started to come in. We agreed a very brief statement: 'The apology speaks for itself. It needs no further comment from me.'

Tuesday, 6 February, London

At five past midnight the telephone rang and I answered it. It was a cultured voice with a lot of background noise saying, 'Is that Paddy Ashdown?' When I said, 'Yes' it said, 'You have made a lot of people angry and we are going to come and get you.' I had been warned that they might get on to us in London, so I immediately dialled 1471. That gave me the telephone number, which I called back. The same cultured voice answered. I asked, 'Who is that?' It said, 'Piers' and told me this was the home of Mr X. I asked him for the address. 'Why do you want to know?' 'Because you have just made a telephone call and I wanted to know where you are ringing from.' He put the phone down straight away. I then rang Yeovil police and gave them the details.

Again I think of petrol being thrown through the letterbox, so I didn't sleep much. For some reason I can't help thinking the caller was a Young Tory at a rather drunken dinner party. I don't know why.

Wednesday, 7 February, London

Off to buy Jane a wedding anniversary present. We agreed that we wouldn't buy each other presents this year. But she has been so wonderful over this whole thing – an absolute rock. I had never realized she was quite so strong.

At about 2.45pm to Downing Street to see the PM. We talked chiefly about Ireland.

At the end he sent out his private secretary and said, 'I am terribly sorry to hear about all this trouble. I will make sure my people do not take advantage of it.' I told him, 'There is nothing to take advantage of.' He has obviously been briefed that there is some truth at the bottom of it. He was being very magnanimous, but I didn't respond well, I fear. Oversensitive, I suppose. I said rather roughly that my wife was very strong and anyway I wouldn't tolerate these kinds of lies. He said, 'I have suffered from false rumours, too. It's very disconcerting. I had the press round at my sister's all last weekend.'

I got away at 4.30 and walked across Hungerford Bridge, past the Festival Hall. It is grey and cold, but there isn't any snow yet. Caught the 5.05 from Waterloo to Yeovil.

I am very nervous about tomorrow's court case.

Jane picked me up from Yeovil station. Thick with snow and very icy under foot.

We did the usual bit of battening down the hatches in the house against fire-bombs before going to bed.

Thursday, 8 February, Yeovil

THE DAY OF THE MASON TRIAL

The day we have been dreading.

Off early to see Ted Allen[1] in his office. Mark turned up as well.

Ted had some new information which he wanted to brief me on. First, apparently, Mason was going to be given a handgun in court. Second, all sorts of rumours were now being spread by these people about me, the police and other Yeovil personalities. Mason's associates had been delighted by the gullibility of the *Western Daily Press* and were still busy throwing mud in all directions, in the hope that some of it would stick. Last, and perhaps most worrying, two men believed to be connected with these people had been spotted testing an incendiary device in a field near Bristol last week. The police would have to keep the protection on us over the weekend and into next week, and review it later.

We then went through our various pieces of evidence and re-read our statements. I told Ted that Andrew has discovered who 'Zoë' is – her solicitor had rung yesterday. Apparently, she had been a prostitute in Yeovil and had worked for Mason's associates until she had been threatened and left. She completely refuted the *Western Daily Press* lies, had never met me or had anything to do with me and was prepared to give evidence to that effect. She is a brave lady. She will be putting her life at risk.

Andrew is delighted. So are the police. I also said that, following a discussion with Andrew, they should go ahead and prosecute the people who made the threatening telephone call to me during the week.

Finally, I gave them copies of the hate mail I have received,[2] including the following:

London W14
Ashdown,
It is with deep regret that I hear of your car being burnt to a cinder.
The regret has two aspects. One that you were not inside it at the time of the incineration. Two that the incendiarists did not have the necessary gall or brain power to set light to your thatched roof, which, with luck, would have toasted you

1 Chief Superintendent Ted Allen, the senior police officer at Yeovil police station.
2 Over this week we received more than 2,000 letters and e-mails of support. But there were exceptions.

and your ugly kunt of a wife and rid Britain of two monstrous parasites that batten
on this poor doomed country.
I think that you are sincerely (and quite rightly) hated and I hope that future attacks
on your person or property are more successful.
XXX.
(Middlesex Rgt. (the diehards))

KEEP EUROPE WHITE
Combat 18

Fucking red scum, expect a visit from our Public Relations Dept soon. We've had
your car, now we'll have your house with you inside it, you fucking traitorous
cunt. You're going to die.
One day the world will know that Adolf Hitler was right!
Death to the Reds

RIGHTS FOR WHITES!
National Socialist Alliance

Then to court. Mark and I were both very nervous. I was called in at about 10.45 and gave evidence for about thirty-five minutes. Then I was cross-examined. It was pretty simple, though the defence counsel concentrated heavily on what I had talked about as I walked round Wyndham Street with Mason. He put it to me that Mason had been accusing me of duplicity and hypocrisy, and of double standards between my public and private lives. He asked me if I had touched Mason on the bum, and a titter went round court, especially in the press gallery, which was full to capacity. Mark was subsequently asked the same question. By 1 o'clock it was all over. The police seemed pleased. Mason was found guilty and received a custodial sentence.

I badly needed some fresh air, so I dropped Jane home and went with Luke over the fields and up the hill at the back of the village. It was very beautiful. The snow is thawing a bit now and a few drops of rain fell, but the sky soon cleared and I was able to stand on Gawler's Hill and look out towards the Quantocks. The sun shining blue on the snow and the dog bouncing in and out of the deep snowdrifts. I felt indescribably happy.

Relaxed after the day's events and thrilled by the hint of spring in the air and the snow-covered Somerset countryside laid out before me, suddenly I knelt down and said a prayer at the place where they put the cross on Gawler's at Easter – a strange thing to do, since I am not very religious that way. Then I walked home.

Had a chat with Andrew. The *News of the World* and *Western Daily Press* are now chasing 'Zoë' and have photographed her. She faxed us the letter the *News of the World* had sent her:

News of the World
1 Virginia Street
London
E1 9XR

Dear Ms —,
As I am sure you are aware, there is great press interest surrounding Mr Paddy Ashdown's private life and the so called 'smear campaign' currently being waged against him.

Bearing in mind you are due to be named in court as 'Zoë' and linked 'sexually' with Mr Ashdown, it suggests you could have a great story to sell and we at the News of the World would, of course, like to buy it!

Obviously there is much to be discussed.

Please call me asap.

Yours sincerely
Ayling Fox.

It is said they offered her £30,000. Presumably Mason's associates gave her address believing that she would succumb to the temptation of money. They obviously underestimated her.

At 6.30 Jane and I went off for a walk to the Cat Head, had a pint, then came back by way of the Lord Nelson. A beautiful starlit night.

Saturday, 10 February, Somerset

Purchased some rope for Simon to escape from his bedroom in the London flat, if that is attacked. Also a postbox, so that we can seal up our letterbox in the flat, too.

At about 12.30 Les and Joan[1] came round unannounced. I opened a bottle of Aligoté and, while Jane showed them some family photographs

---

1 Our friends Les and Joan Farris.

in our dining room, I installed a light in a small cupboard – something I had been promising Jane I would do for some time.

Jane said to me that I ought to turn the electricity off. Which I did. And we continued chatting, with a candle on the table, while I finished installing the light.

After about five minutes the front doorbell rang. It was the police. I opened the door to find a startled-looking young woman PC. I said, 'Oh, how nice to see you. Do come in for a cup of coffee. I presume you are here to change the surveillance videos?' Ashen-faced, she said, 'Are you all right?'

The police alarm had gone off because I had turned off the electricity. By now the road outside was filling with police cars and there was a helicopter hovering overhead. One of the cars had been on traffic duty and had just pulled someone up for doing 100 mph on the A303. In the middle of taking his details, the alarm had gone off and the offender had been unceremoniously bundled out of the police car and left in a bewildered but uncharged state by the side of the road while the police sped off to answer the call.

I think there were six or seven police cars eventually. They had already sealed off the whole village.

I was covered in confusion. But they took it in good part. Les and Joan were in complete hysterics by the time it was over.

Wednesday, 14 February, Westminster

A whisky with Archy at around 7.30. He had seen Donald Dewar and given him the minute I had written as from a Labour researcher. Dewar had been shocked, especially about the 'big thing'. He had obviously not been fully briefed by Blair. He says that Blair is still 'intellectually unconvinced on PR'. Archy left with the very firm conclusion that the 'big thing' was not on the cards. But he and Dewar are going to fix a meeting in the near future.

I told Archy that we had to be tough with them. If they didn't want the big deal then they could expect a few warm words here and there in what would otherwise be a conventional election. But that was all.

Thursday, 15 February, Somerset

At 10 o'clock I saw two detective constables from Yeovil police station, who brought me up to date on the latest security assessments on me and our house. They also asked me whether I wanted to go further with my action on the threatening telephone calls. I said probably not, but that I would like them to find out a bit more before I took a final decision.[1]

The rest of the day was spent preparing for the Scott Report.[2]

Ming, as our spokesman, was given the opportunity to read it. Afterwards he came to me, saying, 'I really can't see how Waldegrave[3] and Lyell[4] can survive. The report is devastating.'

At 3 o'clock we saw Ian Lang's statement. The Government are going to try and tough it out. No resignations. And they are going to claim that nobody acted improperly. I can't see how they will get away with that. But it all depends on the media management, as always.

Lyell's statement was very long and very boring – deliberately so, in order to keep the temperature of the House down.

Cook got up and was adversarial and sharp, but somehow missed the target. Ming's question was short and very pointed. Quoting paragraph numbers and specific sentences from the report. It was, I thought, a better intervention than Cook's. Lyell wobbled, but then recovered his composure and began a long fight back over the next two hours. It was exceedingly well done.

In the early evening into a helicopter with some people from the training department from the Special Intelligence Service (SIS).[5] We flew down in the last light of dusk of a very calm and pleasant February evening and arrived at their training establishment in darkness. They took Jane and me to our room. A bath and a telephone chat with Ming, and then off to dinner.

I was impressed with the trainees. They are all very young – Jane joked

1 I eventually instructed that the charges should be dropped.
2 The Scott Report was an inquiry into the supplying of arms to Iraq. The report concluded that Ministers had misled Parliament.
3 William Waldegrave, Chief Secretary to the Treasury; during the period the inquiry was looking into, he was a Minister of State at the Foreign Office. Member of Parliament (Conservative) for Bristol West 1979–97. He is now in the House of Lords.
4 Nicholas Lyell, Attorney-General; during the period in question he was the Solicitor-General. Member of Parliament (Conservative) for Hemel Hempstead 1979–83, Mid Bedfordshire 1983–97, North-East Bedfordshire since 1997.
5 I had been invited by SIS to make a speech at the 'passing out' dinner of a course of trainees.

that you know you are getting old when the country's spies start looking so young!

I sat next to a girl from Liverpool. The others were from all classes and backgrounds, including one Indian. It was extraordinary to be sitting at the graduation ceremony for this year's crop of spies. Then there were a series of speeches, some from the training people and some from the students. Much laughter about individual successes and failures in learning the strange arts of their trade. A different world altogether.

I suddenly realized to what extent this was a very close-knit community whose members drew succour and support from each other. But a deeply intelligent one. The girl next to me was a pacifist and a vegetarian. She clearly found some elements of the course difficult, but had come to terms with them because, she said, people listened to her views and accommodated them.

On my other side was a young Northern Irishman. Apparently the best student on the course. Intelligent, thoughtful, and almost certainly, I would have thought, voted Liberal Democrat or New Labour. I suspect that most of those round the table would not have voted Tory. I joked with them about their skills being of use in Parliament – for instance, when we recruited Emma Nicholson, etc.

To bed about 1.30am, a bit befuddled.

Friday, 16 February, SIS Training Establishment and London

Up at seven to read the papers. At 7.50 I did the *Today* programme down the line with John Humphrys. I wasn't good; hung over from last night. It is also difficult suddenly to come back into a very big event which you have been cut out of over the past twelve hours. I didn't get the tone right.

Out at 8.30 and into the helicopter. We were in Battersea by nine. I phoned Ming, who had rung late last night to ask whether we should have a joint press conference with Robin Cook. I said I thought it was a very good idea. He has fixed it with Cook.

The papers this morning are about evenly balanced. Most of the ones you would expect are against the Government (*The Times* called for Waldegrave's resignation); otherwise they have probably got away with it. An excellent exercise for the Tories in damage limitation within the House of Commons and news management outside it.

Saturday, 17 February, Somerset

I had hoped to spend the day working on my Conference speech. I was startled to hear on the review of the morning papers that the Wolseley story had broken. It wasn't supposed to break until tonight. I rang Alan, who found out that the embargo had been broken. Anyway, the papers are fairly full of it, although only as speculation.

I spoke to Blair at 1.30, telling him that this was our fish and he shouldn't interfere. They could make as much as they liked of it, especially in the context of Scott, but I didn't want his people knocking on Wolseley's door. It had taken six months to hook him and at this stage we could only pull him halfway.

By midday, the Wolseley story was running strong. When I spoke to Blair he had heard it confirmed on the 1 o'clock news. Nothing we can do. The galling thing is nobody knows our hand has been behind it all the time. What's more, Scott is getting all the comments and we are not even in the story.

Sunday, 18 February, Somerset

Quite a lot in the papers about Wolseley, including the fact that he had dinner with me. I have been fending off press for most of the day. Andrew Phillips rang me in the evening and said that Wolseley is bearing up well. He sees Major tomorrow, and will probably publish his resignation letter shortly afterwards. He now wants to get it over with. Andrew still thinks he will come to us, although I am doubtful.

Wednesday, 21 February, Westminster

At four o'clock a meeting of the Jo Group. A full turn-out, except for Richard Holme. We decided that Bob should continue the generalized talks with Robin Cook but that they shouldn't reach a conclusion until Labour had given us what we needed on PR. We mustn't give the impression that the talks had broken up. But although we desperately wanted the 'big thing', the 'small thing' was good enough. Yesterday Hugo Young came to see me. I told him, perhaps unwisely, exactly what the plot was, including the 'big thing' and the 'small thing', which we could put in place by the autumn. He appeared startled, not having realized we were thinking so dramatically.

Monday, 26 February, Westminster

Cold today, but the bitter wind has gone.

The whole of the Commons is now hanging on tenterhooks for the Scott debate this evening.

Into the chamber at 3.15. Lang was dreadful, but probably deliberately so. He took one or two interventions and handled them competently but not well.

Then Cook. One of the most startling speeches I have ever heard in the House – a brilliant performance. Mellor tried to interrupt, but Cook destroyed him. He mastered every intervention, was sharp, very quick-footed and acerbic. He really had the Government squirming. And drew blood with every sarcastic comment. He even had ministers he was attacking laughing. Quite the best piece of debating I have ever seen, and a Parliamentary occasion to match Geoffrey Howe's resignation speech.

Ming was called fourth. He made a very good speech, but it was inevitably overshadowed by Cook's.

At 9.30 into the chamber to listen to the summings-up. Beckett was pedestrian and Freeman[1] was awful. The whole place still resonated to Cook's attack. It is extraordinary how a really effective attack can pervade the whole debate that follows. Then the vote. The Unionists have been playing hard to get – it is said they had a meeting with Major. At all events they were hiding from the press. But they came in dramatically right at the very end.

I had a hunch from the start that they were going to vote against the Government. But everybody else said they had bottled out and would abstain. It became immediately apparent that the Unionists were indeed going to vote with us. Traipsing through the lobbies I bumped into Trimble, who told me they had had a furious row with Major.

1 Roger Freeman, Chancellor of the Duchy of Lancaster. Member of Parliament (Conservative) for Kettering 1983–97.

We then filed back in and waited for the result. Most of us thought we were going to win by a narrow margin. But then someone said that Rupert Allason, Tory MP for Torbay, had voted with the Government despite promising that he would vote against. Faces started to look long on our side and brighter on the Government's.

Eventually, the Whips came out. The Government had won – by one vote. In my view almost the best result. It has saved us from a no-confidence vote tomorrow, which the Government would have won. But they have been badly exposed and have looked grubby and wheedling all day.

Then out through a thronged and excited House.

Tuesday, 27 February, Westminster

Trimble came in to see me with Maginnis[1] at 3.30. We had a long and useful discussion, the most interesting part of which was that, if the Government had lost yesterday, he would have abstained in the no-confidence vote.

He thinks the Government cannot last beyond October. I told him that depended on him, to which he said, 'Oh they can't expect anything from us now. We hate this crew and the sooner they go the better.' The old line. I wonder if he means it?

Wednesday, 28 February, London

MEMORIAL SERVICE FOR THOSE WHO SERVED IN THE GULF WAR

A wonderful semi-spring day, chilly but sunny. St Paul's cathedral magnificent in the sunlight. I was placed in the front row, which was pretty well empty except for Thatcher and Denis and Michael Morris.[2] So I wandered back to the third row and chatted with the French Ambassador. We had a long conversation about Kate and the fact that she was about to marry a French citizen. He told me that Chirac is coming over in May. He also said that the French Government is absolutely determined to go ahead with the

1 Ken Maginnis, Member of Parliament (Ulster Unionist) for Fermanagh & South Tyrone since 1983.
2 Deputy Speaker of the House of Commons. Member of Parliament (Conservative) for Northampton South 1974–97.

single currency and the British are being totally unrealistic if they think it won't happen. He agreed that the timetable may not be kept to – it could go later, but not much. However difficult, Chirac would not break from it.

Then back to the front row where I had a chat with Michael Portillo,[1] sitting two down from me. We spoke first about the single currency and then I asked whether he believed it would really happen. He thinks it will. I reminded him that he had gone further than Major on this, but he ducked the issue by saying, no, he was just ahead of the PM. But there would be real problems if there was a two-speed Europe. I said the bigger problem was that the whole European project would unravel if EMU didn't go ahead. He didn't accept this.

Then Blair came in and we had a brief chat. A good sermon from the Archbishop of Canterbury. Delicate and careful, but also moving. But he looks very grey. I hope he is not ill.

At the end there was a collection. This took Blair by surprise. He blanched and whispered to me out of the side of his mouth, 'God, I didn't expect a collection! I don't have a penny on me. Do you have any money?' I smiled at him and said, 'Yes, how much would you like?' 'A fiver.' I dug into my wallet. 'I only have a tenner.' So I gave him that. So the collection cost me twenty quid!

Robert Fellowes, the Queen's Private Secretary, who was on my right, spotted me hand the note to Blair and smiled broadly. At the end of the service he leaned across and said, 'I hope you get that back.' 'I am sure I will, one way or another!' I replied.

Then Fellowes turned to Blair, and said, 'It is the job of the Queen's Private Secretary to see everything, but say nothing.' Tony blushed and said, a little too quickly, 'Of course he will get it back!'

We wandered out together and I told Blair of my conversation of yesterday with Trimble – how he would abstain on a vote of no confidence. I said, 'We really ought to find a way to test Trimble's resolve in this.' He whistled through his teeth and said, 'If Trimble really is going to abstain that opens all sorts of possibilities. But I never get to speak to him. I don't want him to think he can start bargaining with me.' I said I would try and follow this up.

---

1 Secretary of State for Defence. Member of Parliament (Conservative) for Enfield Southgate 1984–97 and for Kensington & Chelsea since 1999.

Thursday, 29 February, London – Somerset

In the late afternoon Jane and I headed for home. An absolutely glorious day with cloudless blue skies, the first real touch of spring, though no sign of it yet in the hedgerows. The whole of Salisbury Plain and beyond lying expectant in the sunshine.

On Monday I received a call from Detective Inspector Foster who told me rather worriedly that they had received information from Bristol – one of their informers – that we were going to have our 'properties' fire-bombed over the Easter period. This has set us both worrying again. The police are taking it very seriously and will come back with a plan for our protection.

God, where will this end? It is putting real pressure on Jane. And it makes us feel uncomfortable in our own home. The information is that somebody will come up on a motorbike and throw a fire-bomb through the window. It doesn't add much to our peace of mind.

We left at 6.30 to walk across the fields. A beautiful crisp cold evening, cloudless blue skies and a wonderful russet sunset. A couple of pints at the Lord Nelson and then home for dinner.

Friday, 1 March, Somerset

Into the police station. We had half an hour with Ted Allen. The police are convinced there is about to be another attempt on us, possibly on Easter Sunday. They want to try and provoke these people into action. Ted Allen said, 'Don't worry – I can't give you a perfect undertaking that they won't get your house. But if they do it will be terribly embarrassing for me as well as you.' I said that it wasn't his embarrassment I was worrying about!

I also told him that if this was a serious threat, I must inform my next-door neighbours. He agreed.

Monday, 18 March, London

I met Richard Holme, Bob Maclennan and Archy Kirkwood at 6.00pm at the Lords Cloakroom and we jumped into Richard's car to go out to Derry Irvine's house. We ran through how we should play the meeting with the

Labour team. We arrived at the house at 6.30 and the door was opened by Derry himself, who said, 'There is something symbolic in the fact that the Liberals arrive exactly on time, but my lot are late.'

We stood around chatting, chiefly about his pictures. There had been much joking on the way about paying homage to Derry's art collection – and that's exactly what happened. I went off to ring the office while Richard and Archy did their duty.

After a few minutes we moved into the sitting room and sat down. A lot of books lying around, including Roy Jenkins' *Gladstone* and Peter Hennessy's latest book on the constitution of Britain.[1] Derry said he loved Roy's book but that he couldn't get used to Peter Hennessy's style. I asked him about Andrew Marr's *Ruling Britannia*, which I had just read. He replied, 'Oh, I keep that by my bedside.'

After about fifteen minutes the doorbell rang. It was the Labour team arriving. Derry looked at his watch and said, 'What sort of time do you call this?'

Tony responded with a mock-sheepish smile, 'I think it is rather good, given my usual performance.'

Then into the dining room.

On the way in, Robin Cook spotted that, among the books on the side table, were the Mandelson/Liddle book on the project,[2] side by side with Albert Camus. He said, 'My God, those two are strange bedfellows. How can you be reading Mandelson and Camus at the same time?'

A brief discussion on dinner placings was resolved by Robin saying, 'Let's mix it up. We don't want to look like trade union negotiations.' I ended up sitting opposite those nudes again.

Tony was suffering from a bad back – pulled muscles, apparently from a weekend game of tennis. He was in obvious discomfort, so after about three-quarters of an hour, Jonathan Powell, who sat on my right and slightly apart (like a good civil servant), brought a cushion, which seemed to ease his pain.

We had previously agreed that Jonathan should make notes and send each of us a copy. Richard later told us that Jonathan, with whom he had dinner after a US Embassy 'do', is very enthusiastic for the project.

Our side had agreed beforehand to try and get them to say what their

1 *The Hidden Wiring: Unearthing the British Constitution* (1995).
2 *The Blair Revolution: Can New Labour Deliver?* (1996).

position was. But Tony immediately turned to me and said, 'OK, let's go. Why don't you say your piece first?'

In the hope of throwing the ball back into his court, I kept my opening words very short, saying that there were two options open to us, the 'big thing' and the 'small thing', and that we were keen to come to an agreement on which they preferred.

Richard then entered into a fairly lengthy exposition. He outlined, in some detail, the differences between the two positions: 'the small thing', where they could still expect to be sniped at by us; and the 'the big thing', where we would be entering into a partnership of a different sort. He then tried to give an objective view of the advantages and disadvantages for both sides. I briefly summed up by saying that there were, therefore, two kinds of General Election we could fight: a conventional election, but with a slightly warmer glow to it, or an election in which we would be clear partners on two or three major issues, while leaving other policy areas as ones on which we should not be ashamed to have differences. In my view the second option (the 'big thing') was the right way to go, despite its risks. This could turn a Tory defeat into a Tory rout – and open the way for a historic shift in politics. I was strongly in favour.

Tony responded, 'Well, that is very clear. But I don't quite understand why you guys are following the line you are. I don't, for instance, understand why you think it is necessary to attack us.' Then his tone of voice suddenly changed. 'I really didn't like what happened over the weekend' (referring to my Conference speech,[1] heavily reported in today's papers).

This was a crucial point of the meeting which I had anticipated. He needed to know that I wasn't going to back off or apologize.

I responded, 'Look. Let's get this absolutely clear. We are perfectly happy with where we are now. We don't have to go further, although I would like to. And we are quite content to go into the next election in exactly this position. We believe you have done as much damage as you are going to do to us. We are beginning to identify policies which are clearly different from yours. So, if that is our option, we are quite happy to pursue it.

'But that will mean more public criticism. In fact my speech was badly reported and I was as unhappy about that as you were. But you must not be under any delusions. If we must attack you in order to differentiate ourselves from you, then we will. It would be death for us to be swallowed

---

1 This had contained a short passage of criticism of Labour's timidity.

up by you. And I am not going to let that happen, which means keeping a very clear tension between you and us. That will, of course, diminish if we choose the second option that Richard has outlined – but only then.'

He replied that he still didn't understand our strategy. I responded that while I was very grateful to him for spending so much time trying to understand our position, our strategy was for us to pursue.

There was laughter and the moment of tension quickly passed. One of his real strengths is responding to reality and not bearing a grudge.

There then followed a long discussion on PR. Tony kept on saying, 'Look, if you want us to deliver STV, then that is not possible.'

I suggested that we considered this in the context of the work to be done on the constitution and asked Bob to explain this. Bob then went through a detailed explanation of what we thought could be done, ending on the question of PR.

I then asked, 'Were the reports in the weekend's press that you had agreed to accept AV correct?' He said, 'Yes, broadly they were. I'm not saying that we necessarily put them across in those terms, but that is our position. However, you must understand that if you are asking us to go further, we simply cannot.'

I responded, 'That is very interesting. You accept that the voting system should be reformed, which is a start. What we now have to discover is whether there is any room for agreement between our view on how it should be reformed and yours. If you genuinely believe that there is nothing to be done to bridge the gap between you and us, and that AV is your final position, then there is no point in continuing this any further. If, on the other hand, there is a possibility that Bob and Robin can come to an agreement that bridges this, then the whole process takes on a completely different shape. What you are hearing from us is that we are prepared to be flexible. What we need to know is, are you?'

A technical discussion about PR and STV ensued, in the process of which Tony said, 'Look, I believe the important thing in politics is to recognize reality. And the reality is that Labour is now 80 per cent modernized and you guys are 80 per cent Social Democrats. So I can't see what the problem is.' We all chorused (including Bob), 'No, we are Liberals.'

Richard then said that there could be no question of us validating their constitutional programme, thereby leaving us to pursue PR alone. I continued, 'You have to understand the danger to us. For us to validate your programme and leave PR as an enthusiasm for people like Robin and myself would present the real danger of PR being left on the periphery rather than at the centre of reform. Frankly, I don't understand your opposition. If you believe in pluralism, then PR is a means to achieve that. AV is not proportional. So we must go further than that. Do you understand why we regard this as so important?' Tony laughed and said, 'Yes, I think so,' in a voice lightly tinged with sarcasm. Robin and Donald also laughed.

I came back. 'Yes, but I still don't think you *really* understand. So let me ask Bob to explain.' Bob then expounded on why we believed PR was in the public interest, rather than simply our Party's. Tony said he understood this, though it was clear he wasn't convinced.

Then we got on to a discussion about where the end position might be. I reminded Tony that we had proposed three points of co-operation, of which one was constitutional reform. Donald said that he thought that it would be very difficult to have as few points as three. Richard said that three was more than enough. But it was agreed that the other two or three points should concentrate on things that matter to 'real' people, such as the economy.

Bob then returned to the main items of the constitution. He felt 'a certain bitterness that Labour had never done what they said they would do because they were never in for long enough'. Labour should understand that we were determined to create the stability that would ensure change over a longer period.

At this stage Robin came in, picking up on a previous idea of Richard's, and suggested there may be a way around, following the New Zealand 'Preferendum' route. What would happen if we had a two-stage referendum, the first on the principle of voting reform and the second to choose the actual system? Richard immediately reinforced this and I said that it would be well worth thinking about, though I couldn't commit without very careful consideration. But if they were serious we would certainly consider it.

I said the key thing was Tony's own personal position. We would take our chances in a referendum and were prepared to accept that the Labour Party would not be united – some would fight for PR, some against – but we couldn't enter into a referendum if the case against PR was being argued by the Labour Leader and Prime Minister. At this point, Donald came in and said, 'But you are upping the ante. If we follow Robin's scenario, then it is perfectly possible for Tony to support change in the first round and, say, AV in the second – and it wouldn't be just Tony anyway, it would be the whole Cabinet.'

This was agreed round the table. I conceded that it was a way forward, and one worth thinking about.

At this point, Tony suddenly said, 'I strongly favour the second option – the "big thing". And I think that this way round the electoral reform roadblock is worth pursuing.'

A real breakthrough.

It clearly went further than Donald had anticipated, because he immediately began to backtrack, saying, 'Well, it is worth considering. But I want to say how difficult it will be for us. I don't want anyone to think that we have reached a decision here.'

Robin chipped in, 'Look, if we are to go ahead with this two-stage referendum, it is absolutely vital that it is seen to come from our side. But we will have to get it through the Party Conference. It mustn't be seen to be the product of these negotiations.'

I said it was similarly vital that we didn't appear to be the *demandeurs* on this, either. We were quite satisfied that this should be seen to come from their side and we would respond appropriately.

In discussing the evening afterwards, Richard, Bob and Archy were of the opinion that we had taken them much further than they had intended to go. Indeed, Archy told us that Donald had said as much at the end of the meeting.

At the time, however, I responded, 'Well, I prefer the "big thing" and want to explore that, too,' adding that it was important that we should do this as quickly as possible because of the work involved. First of all, we needed to check that it would work to our advantage electorally, which would mean a lot of work on opinion polls, etc. Secondly, we would need to decide the actual areas in which we would work, which could be pretty tricky, because of the animosity between Gordon Brown and Malcolm Bruce over tax and spending. And thirdly, we needed to change the attitudes of our parties in order to sell the idea when the time came.

Donald said that if we were to go for the 'big thing' it was vital to do this as late as possible so that we gave the Tories minimal time to unpick it, and ourselves maximum impact for the election itself. This was agreed.

We then got on to a discussion about whether a coalition Government after the election would be necessary. There was some disagreement about this. But in the end we all agreed that it would be possible to support the three or four points we wished to pursue without necessarily being in coalition.

I made it clear, reinforced by Donald, that we should never get to talking about who got what Cabinet seats, or what form the partnership should take after the election. It was important that we kept the whole argument on what was good for the nation, rather than what was good for our parties or any individuals. And we must retain a degree of differentiation between us. Even if we went for the 'big thing', we would need to say that we had different policies in areas outside the three or four agreed ones.

I then proposed that we give the green light for Bob and Robin to get together and work out the details. Which immediately produced an intervention from Donald: 'In the end, this is a matter for Tony and Paddy to work out face to face. It cannot be arranged between Robin and Robert.' I responded that they could do the hard work and then Tony and I would get together to fix the final deal, but Tony said, 'I will have to give this a lot of thought. Then you and I must meet to decide whether it should continue on the basis of what Robin and Robert have managed to work up.'

After a discussion we agreed that this should happen no later than the third week in April. Donald came back to reinforce this point. He sounded nervous that the weight of the decision should be carried forward by Robin and kept saying, 'It will be very difficult to get through our Party – there's a lot to think about ... There are considerations that have to be very carefully thought through,' and so on.

Richard raised the issue of negative campaigning. He said that it would be very useful, in the context of the General Election campaign, for Tony and me to agree jointly a common front against negative campaigning. We agreed.

Donald then said that it would be a disaster, even if we were to turn away from the 'big thing', for us to turn our backs on what had already been achieved. But I made it clear that there had to be a very definite firebreak between the 'big thing' and the 'little thing'. It was entirely in Labour's interest to seek the advantages of the full partnership, while not giving more than was required by the smaller one. We in the Lib Dems recognized this danger and, in the absence of PR, we had to keep a sharp differentiation between the two options.

Donald said at one stage, 'I presume that the aim of this is to maximize on tactical voting.' Tony picked up on this. 'Yeah. Surely to you the importance is the tactical vote.' I said that it was, but that we had to make sure it would be delivered. So even if we could agree the terms of the 'big thing', it should not go ahead unless it increased our votes or their impact.

At one stage, Blair said, 'The real problem is that the Tories will play uncertainty at us. And it is for this reason that I want to neutralize the

15. Tuesday, 15 December 1992, Sarajevo
'To the cemetery. Newly dug empty graves everywhere'

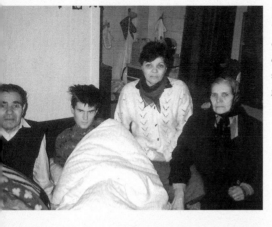

16. Tuesday, 15 December 1992, Sarajevo
'The family were still in bed at 10 o'clock … The old man was very sick … They were living in terrible conditions in a single room in a foetid atmosphere … subject to bombardment. But hanging on to life grimly'

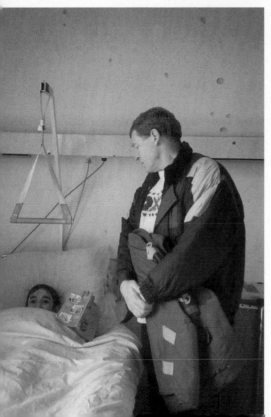

17. Sunday, 12 December 1993, Sarajevo
'To the State hospital … I found it impossible to cope with the sight of young children with … horrible wounds from sniper fire and shrapnel. I spoke to one seven-year-old who had a piece of shrapnel in her thigh'

18. Tuesday, 19 January 1993, Monktonhall

'Andy's capacity for work was phenomenal – he shifted at least twice as much as me'

19. Thursday, 11 July 1996, London
From left: Menzies Campbell, Nelson Mandela, PA
'At 5.30 with Ming to Buckingham Palace to talk properly to Mandela'

20. Tuesday, 21 February 1995, New York
From left: Menzies Campbell, PA, Boutros Boutros-Ghali
'To see Boutros Boutros-Ghali. A funny little man. Bright, amused eyes, lots of lines around his face and a disarmingly naïve attitude'

21. Sunday, 20 August 1995, London VJ Day Parade
'Then Major suddenly said, "Do you know that goldfish can get sunstroke?"'

22. Friday, 28 July 1995, Littleborough & Saddleworth
From left: Carol, Chris and Kate Davies, PA and Chris Rennard
'To Littleborough & Saddleworth to celebrate Chris's victory. A good deal of riding around in open-topped buses.'

23. Saturday, 31 August 1996, Burgundy
'Then in the French tradition, as bride and father, Kate and I led the whole wedding party ... down the main street and out through the old gateway of Cravant ... I have never felt prouder in my life'

24. Saturday, 19 April 1997
'We then had a look at my grandson, Mathias. He is absolutely wonderful'

25. Thursday, 7 September 1995, Irancy
From left: Rene Charriat, Kate Ashdown (hidden), Jacqueline Charriat, Jocelyne Lorin, Daniel Reis, Leslie Jefferies, Jacques Le Blond, Greg Jefferies (hidden), Josette Reis, PA Cilou Le Blond
'...in my mind's eye, [I could] see our friends' faces lit by candlelight and our table laden with empty dishes and spent wine bottles'

26. Saturday, 30 December 1995, London
'At 9.30 a photo-op with Emma [Nicholson] in the freezing rain and afterwards to Millbank for more interviews'

27. Friday, 19 October 1990, Eastbourne
'We arrived at Eastbourne to find a forest of cameras and David Bellotti … The usual photos sessions, etc.'

28. Sunday, 17 September 1995, Glasgow
From left: Diana Maddock, Alan Beith, PA, Don Foster
'More work on my end-of-conference speech. Very slow. On the fourteenth draft'

29. Friday, 12 July 1996, Oxford
From left: Graham Watson, David Chidgey, Alan Beith, Liz Lynne, PA, David Steel,
Robin Teverson
'All-day Parliamentary Party Meeting'

30. Wednesday, 30 April 1997
'Into the helicopter again for the last full day of campaigning. Polls still looking good'

31. Thursday, 1 May 1997, Somerset
A beautiful day. Sparkling sunshine and clear blue skies ... Jane and I came out at smack on 9.00 and went off to vote, holding hands, the dog in attendance'

32. Friday, 2 May 1997, London
The Parliamentary Party
'We must get PR eventually. And ... then the young and very talented MPs who have just been elected will, in time, be Government ministers and handle power in a way that the rest of us have never been able to do'

Tory press.' I responded, 'Yes, that is correct. But we must recognize that one of the ways of neutralizing the uncertainty factor is to be certain about the one or two things we would do in partnership, either in a coalition Government or across the floor of the House.'

We then got on to the mechanics of the relationship. I asked Archy to introduce this, saying that it was necessary to sort out (a) our main channel of communication, (b) the cover story for the whole operation, and (c) the contingency plan if it leaked. We agreed that the main line of communication should be between the two Whips' Offices. Donald again went for caution, saying, 'We should keep communication to a minimum. It only needs to expand if we decide to go for the "big thing". If, as I anticipate, we will stay with rather more limited ambitions, then our communications need only be on an "as necessary" basis.'

We turned to the contingency plan should the story break publicly and agreed that it should be sorted out by the two Whips' Offices.

We then discussed who was 'in the circle'. I said that the only people inside our circle were the members of the Jo Group. Tony said, 'Basically, the only people who are fully inside the circle are those people around this table, though Gordon Brown knows quite a lot about it, and so does John Prescott, who generally accepts it.'

Tony has moved a very long way since we last met. And we all recognize that a potential watershed has been crossed. We have opened up the way for constructive further work.

We finished about 8 o'clock, and Derry sent Jonathan out to the kitchen to bring in the food and wine.

At one stage, Robin said, 'I am delighted that my side is now genuinely engaged in a real discussion on electoral reform. We all start with AV – I spent two weeks there – but then I had to move on. It didn't make sense.' Tony quipped, 'But you're so quick, Robin!'

Derry served some very nice white Burgundy and a splendid claret. Tony said, 'Do try some of that, Paddy. It is excellent.' And it was.

As was the food: delicious sausage, crostinis, etc. There was an almost tangible sense of relief on all sides that the evening hadn't ended in disaster.

As soon as we got up from the meeting, we became just a group of friends, drinking wine and enjoying each other's company. After the wine and the nibbles, Derry's wife Alison joined us. She was, of course, previously married to Donald. As Richard remarked on the way out: 'Very Iris Murdoch.'

Just before we broke up I asked, 'What about Jonathan's minutes?' Tony said, 'Oh, I didn't know he was taking minutes.' I said, 'Jonathan, you did take minutes didn't you?' He replied, 'Of course. I'm a civil servant. I will send you a copy.' He made a quip about not giving them to my solicitor to put in his safe! Much laughter. But only half in jest.

Afterwards, I took Archy, Bob and Richard to Tiles restaurant in Buckingham Palace Road, where we talked through the meeting. We agreed that it was, potentially, a very important moment. They had come much further than we had anticipated. Richard said, 'We have agreed to fly, and Bob and Robin have been asked to design the aeroplane.'

On the way back to the House, Richard said, 'When I went into that meeting, I thought there was about a seventy–thirty chance against this happening. Now I think it is about fifty–fifty. When I said we have a real opportunity to line up all of the British people against the Tories, I saw Tony's eyes light up.'

After Richard dropped us off at the House, Archy and I walked across New Palace Yard. I said, 'I was excited by tonight. I think we have made a real breakthrough.' Archy replied 'You're excited, I'm frightened. We have made a breakthrough, but it opens up as many dangers as it does possibilities.'

Monday, 25 March, Westminster

At 3.30 down to the House for the BSE statement.[1] The first from Dorrell[2] on health, the second from Hogg on agriculture. I only stayed for the first. Harriet Harman was well below par. The Dorrell statement was fine but Hogg's was completely inadequate. So I called in Paul Tyler and, having consulted with the National Farmers' Union, we decided to call on the Government to cull animals in what we would call a 'clean break policy'. This is, I think, welcome to farmers on the ground, but not to the hierarchy of the NFU. I checked it with Anthony Gibson,[3] who is opposed, and Nigel Clist,[4] who said that the farmers in the Yeovil area could be in favour.

1 This was the day the BSE ('mad cow disease') story broke.
2 Stephen Dorrell, Secretary of State for Health. Member of Parliament (Conservative) for Loughborough 1979–97, Charnwood since 1997.
3 South-West area representative of the NFU.
4 Yeovil NFU representative.

My judgement is that the Government will have to come to it in the end, anyway. The European vets have recommended banning British beef from the continent. There is a real catastrophe in train, and the Government must act decisively. The NFU opposing us is dangerous, but in crises like these, I always think it's worth taking a risk and being decisive. The big thing is to have something clear to say.

Tuesday, 26 March, London

The airwaves are full of BSE. As I thought last night, the Government's actions have gone down very badly. Too little, too late, and not enough to restore the market.

At 4 o'clock off to see the Prime Minister at his request to discuss honours. Alex Allan also present.

But at the end I said, 'If you have a moment, I would like to talk to you about BSE. You are in a real mess.'

Major replied, 'Yes, we are. I have never been so worried about anything since I first came into the House. I think we could be presiding over the collapse of a £20 billion industry, with incalculable consequences for jobs. But I couldn't go further than I did. It wouldn't have been supported by scientific evidence. And if I start a cull, where will it stop? We could even end up culling the offspring of infected beasts. Then, in a few years, BSE could be identified as not having come through cattle at all, and we would be open to terrible criticism for panic reaction and wasting public money. In our view, the cost of a culling policy, including its impact on other areas, could be £500 million a year, with an upper limit of goodness knows what.' He pointed out the implications across many industrial sectors. Beef products even go into perfume, etc.

He looked grey and ill, shrunken and exhausted, and really, really worried.

PA: Prime Minister, you look absolutely terrible.

JM: I'm scared stiff. I simply don't know what to do next.

PA: Why not pocket the Naish proposals?[1]

---

1 These were proposals made by Sir David Naish, President of the National Farmers' Union for a cull of infected cows.

JM: Because I'm in the middle of negotiating European action, and if I accept the Naish proposals Europe will simply say that is not enough. I cannot do Naish until Europe has agreed it's sufficient.

PA: Look, the important thing is to save the industry. You can count on our co-operation if you come forward with something sensible. Let me put two propositions to you:

1. If you go for the Naish proposals we will support you. We will not call for more if you do this quickly, but if you delay, you will lose control.
2. If you want to create a cross-party consensus on Naish, we will join you and I think we could persuade Labour to take such a position.

JM: That is very good of you. I will bear it in mind, and may well call on you. I am particularly keen to ensure that we get some kind of support from Labour. Could you have a word with them about this?

I said I would do my best. I have never seen him look so worried or so distracted.

Monday, 1 April, Somerset

Into the police station at 8.45 for a chat with Ted Allen. They are going to put somebody in the house. We also went through the arrangements for the period we will be away in France.

Later I spoke to my next-door neighbour John Bailey on the telephone. The police have seen him today. He is very level-headed about all this. Also to Steve Radley on the other side, who is very calm as well, but said rather ominously, 'You and I have run many of these operations[1] – I just hope they have thought of everything. I suppose they have.'

Tuesday, 2 April, London

Jane came up from Yeovil today. She was in tears leaving Vane Cottage, thinking of them setting fire to it. The police team have now moved in with fire extinguishers.

---

1 Steve used to be in the Royal Navy.

Sunday, 7 April, Irancy

EASTER SUNDAY

Kate arrived today. Wonderful to see her.

At 6.30 off for a party in Jocelyne Lorin's[1] *cave*. We spent two and a half hours down there. Much laughing. Sitting in somebody's *cave* picking wine off the rack to drink where you sit makes for an excellent party. Back about midnight under a pitch-black sky. The nightingales are singing from the four corners of the village tonight.

This is the night they are supposed to set fire to our house. Jane got a bit emotional – not surprising. We both slept rather fitfully, waiting for the telephone to ring. But it didn't.

Tuesday, 9 April, Irancy

I am reading Roy Jenkins' *Gladstone*. I never realized what turmoil there was in the 1840s and 1850s. Full of parties dissolving and people defecting from one side to another. Gladstone himself was a Tory before defecting to the Liberals. It took four decades for the old political structures to dissolve and the new shape of politics to emerge with the Tory and Liberal national parties. I have become convinced that the same thing is happening now.

I have for some time thought that the current shape of party politics in Britain cannot contain all the different forces that are contained within it. So one of the historic roles of the Liberal Democrats, and of my leadership of the Party, is to use this opportunity and my relationship with Blair to start the process of creating a complete new shape for our politics. There is, after all, no reason why the Labour Party, any more than the Tory Party, should remain the same for ever. The Tories are in fact two parties and Labour ditto. And it is liberalism which is becoming more and more relevant. But if, as it appears, I have more in common with Blair than he has with his left wing, surely the logical thing is for us to create a new, powerful alternative force which would be unified around a broadly liberal agenda.

And the sooner we do that, the sooner we will stimulate the break-up of the Tories into pro-European, one-nation Tories like Kenneth Clarke and the anti-European xenophobes who have taken control of the party under Major.

1 A local friend.

It will be very risky, of course. And will need time. And may ultimately be impossible. But the prize is so huge it must be worth the attempt. The talks I am having with Blair could be the start of this process.

The big thing in a period of such change is to keep our minds open. I would take more from my Party into such a new formation than Blair would take from his, but we would then force a change in the Conservative Party, which would shake itself apart after the next election.

These thoughts keep turning in my mind. And the more I dwell on them the more they make sense.

Thursday, 25 April, The Midlands

After BBC *Question Time*[1] Becky picked up Robin Cook and me and drove us to Birmingham. Gaynor, Robin's assistant, sat in the front and we sat in the back.

When we got to our hotel, I suggested that he should come and have a whisky in my room, where we continued our conversation until after midnight.

He was in a chirpy mood. Very decisive. Thoughtful, as well.

He kept pressing me to give my views by asking open-ended questions. But when I did the same to him, he responded fully and frankly. He started off, 'Well, what do you want to do?'

I replied that I wanted to know what ultimate destination he thought we could get to and how we would get there.

He responded by saying that, as far as he was concerned, the end position was that we should support them in Government if they had a majority, but 'if we end up with a hung Parliament, I know nobody in the Party would have any difficulty in working with you in a coalition. What we are talking about is your support for legislation that we put through the House of Commons with which you agree and being free to vote against when you don't.'

He then asked me what I thought the best end position was. I replied that there were two, of which one was the one he described, but that this was very much a second-best position. It had the disadvantage of not putting us under the disciplines of government, and I wanted my Party to learn how to handle power nationally as it had done in local government.

---

1 Robin Cook was also on the panel and I had previously fixed to give him a lift so that we could have a private chat.

Secondly, and most importantly, we were bound to be less reliable as partners when the Government started to come under pressure than if we were within the Government.

He said, 'Yes, I know, that's what Tony thinks as well. But there is no possibility that he can get it through the Party. The Party won't accept winning a majority in an election and then having a coalition with you. Tony has vastly over-extended what he can do with the Party already. I never cease to be amazed at just how far he has been able to go. But after a General Election in which we won a clear majority he could not have a coalition with you without breaking the Party up.'

I responded that if this was the case it was vital they should make up their minds to say no and do it quickly. Otherwise, expectations would be generated which, if not fulfilled, would lead to accusations of bad faith.

His reply was that he knew what Tony had been saying about a partnership Government, both publicly and privately. But he couldn't get it through the Party. If no one else would stop it, Donald Dewar would.

Robin asked me directly, 'Do you meet often?'

I was a bit startled, since I had presumed that he knew every time we had met. I said, 'Oh, from time to time, usually in the margins of state events.' I then went on to discuss what the co-operation project might contain. The constitution, something on the economy and perhaps something on education. He said there were no differences between us on either of these. Especially on education [where Labour had more or less adopted our policy].

We then got on to talking about the details of the agreement with Bob Maclennan. I asked him to say what kind of document he thought they could produce. Would it be detailed or broad brush? I hoped it would be broad brush. He agreed that the document should be thematic.

On PR, he said that he thought Tony could be persuaded to recommend change, but that his mind was moving towards AV, no further. So the best option was a single referendum carrying two questions, the first of which would be 'Change or not?' (in which Tony would recommend change), and the second would offer the options. I made it clear that, while this was acceptable (just), it was not the best solution. Far better if the two parties could recommend a single system.

He said, 'Look, there is a system which I think we could recommend. A compromise, with AV in the constituencies and AMS lists to top up. But we have only just persuaded Tony to move towards AV. I really think the chances of getting him to move further than that are very limited – but I will have a go.'

We talked about the timing of any announcement of the 'big thing'. He agreed that it could initiate a tremendous 'third wave of hope', which would carry us into the election and obliterate the Tories. He is in favour of making the announcement, therefore, towards the end of the year.

He then talked about how a Labour Government might progress. He believes it will hit a difficult patch eighteen months or two years in, so it was important to time the referendum on electoral reform with that in mind. I said that our aim was to get a commitment from them for a referendum on electoral reform. Once this had been agreed, they would see the advantage of going with it early, since Tony would not wish to lose the referendum. He agreed.

He said there would be no difficulty in getting agreement from them to hold a referendum, say, in the first eighteen months. I replied that, in our view, the crucial point was to have the new electoral system in place at the next election. Otherwise, we would be signing a suicide note.

From other matters we discussed, a number of clear points emerged:

1. Jack Straw is not yet fully on board. He and others from the Shadow Cabinet know that something is going on, but they don't know what. 'We will have to explain it to Jack soon and I can't tell what the reaction will be.'

2. Mandelson's influence is very strong. It is Peter in particular who is pushing AV. Incidentally, Robin is in favour of a proportional system, because he believes it to be to Labour's advantage since it will 'unlock all those southern Labour votes which currently go to the Lib Dems'.

3. Gordon Brown is being very difficult. He still hasn't accepted the outcome of the Leadership election and is nursing a bruised ego. Tony defers to him a lot, however. But Robin thinks he is much closer to Tony now than Gordon is. There is clearly some hostility between Robin and Gordon.

4. Robin said, 'A number of us on the moderate left of the party are becoming increasingly concerned that we are abandoning the underclass and our historic mission to work for the poor, in favour of the middle class.' I said it would be deadly if we abandoned the dispossessed for the middle classes, for then the excluded would turn to the extreme right. He agreed. 'That is exactly the problem. And it's the way we are going unless we are careful. There are a lot of us now determined to make sure that we start mentioning the poor again.'

5. At one stage I said, 'The interesting thing about Tony is that he is not really *of* the Labour Party.' He said, 'Yes all those around him and all his predecessors as Labour Leaders have had tap roots that go deep, deep into Labour. But Tony doesn't. That's what makes him so dangerous and so frightening. But it is also what makes him so interesting, so useful and so imaginative. No doubt that's what you find exciting about him. I really don't know why he didn't join you.'

6. He has detected a strong erosion of their activist base. 'People are coming to us of the sort who came to you with the SDP. I had a constituency meeting not long ago – a social function to which many of our new members were invited. They were all very nice people – professionals, etc. – but when we started mentioning delivering leaflets and knocking on doors, their eyes glazed and they all said they had Rotary meetings to go to. I am not at all sure there is enough substance here on which to build a sustainable political movement, especially if things start to get tough, as inevitably they will.'

7. Labour are very conscious that there will be too many referendums in the early part of their administration – he mentioned two (one being PR, presumably) in the first eighteen months.

This has been an unexpectedly revealing conversation. He is a direct talker who responds to questions tidily and openly.

Monday, 29 April, Westminster

At 7.30pm, Richard came in. We must put the Party into top gear for the General Election as soon as the local elections are over. I am very nervous about their outcome, and told Richard this. History will say we got through them by the skin of our teeth.

If the Blair effect had started earlier they would have done us real damage. Or if the election had come a year later, we would have been over the top for the local elections. By this time next year our local election base will be at its peak and beginning to decrease again. A very bad background against which to go into the election. Much depends on Thursday. It is still just possible for the PM to follow next year's local elections with the General Election three weeks afterwards. Let's hope he chooses to have them on the same day.

Thursday, 2 May, London

LOCAL ELECTION DAY

So much depends on today. In the morning, to see Roy. I found him in ebullient mood. Blair had had dinner with him the day after I had seen Robin Cook. He was fascinated by Cook's views. He said, 'Blair said to me three or four times that he intends, even if he gets a majority, to have a coalition Government with two or three Lib Dems in it.' At the very end of their dinner, when they were standing on the steps of his flat, Blair had also said that he was moving towards PR.

I said this was good news, but wondered whether Blair could deliver and relayed Cook's doubts on this score. Roy said, 'I am worried about that, too. But I think he means it.' We decided that when I see Blair next week we will try to clinch the deal. And that if he wants a coalition Government it is going to be much easier to announce that before the election than after it, with Labour in a triumphant mood. We also agreed that there was a deal to be done on PR, on which Roy would continue to press Blair. Roy thinks a two-question referendum is a good idea. Our last five minutes were spent in enthusiastic discussion of Gladstone and the similarity between the present fluidity of British politics and the thirteen years after the repeal of the Corn Laws.

Good news. But can we get the final deal on PR, and is Blair able to deliver what he says he wants to deliver? If only we do well this evening . . .

To Cowley Street at around ten. The early results through were Newbury and Eastleigh; both good. We were in for a good night. But the bloody BBC, as usual, ignored us. By the end of the night we had increased our share of the vote, even in those areas outside our targets. And won over a hundred and fifty seats.

I left at 3.00am, very happy. We have resisted the Labour squeeze and are now beginning to push against it. We have done well everywhere. We couldn't have a better launch pad for the General Election.

Wednesday, 8 May, Westminster

At 1.15, to Blair's office. He was sitting, as always, in his shirtsleeves on his sofa.

He asked me if I had had lunch. I said no, so he arranged for some smoked salmon sandwiches to be brought in and some coffee. He complained bitterly that he had now grown too thin for his trousers, and had lost his belt. I thought he looked tired and much more careworn than on previous occasions.

Our meeting, though, was frank, open and very friendly.

We talked to start with about the position of the Government. He said, 'God, I wish I didn't have to wait another year for the election. I would do anything to get rid of them now. But it seems unlikely it will happen until the spring of next year.' I agreed. An election now and the Tories would be fighting each other up and down the country, rather than fighting us. Blair said he was working to see if he could 'do something' before the summer recess, perhaps in mid-July. 'The trick will be to find something which will pull the centre of the Tory Party in with us. Perhaps the Post Office.'

I suggested a referendum on Europe and we agreed to look at this possibility.

We talked about defectors. They have nobody else in the pipeline. 'One or two people are making unhappy noises, but nothing specific. If we are to defeat the Government it will have to be on an issue, rather than because of numbers.'

He is still uncertain about the way Trimble would go in a vote of no confidence. I said I thought Trimble was a constitutionalist: if the Government lost its majority he wouldn't support them in the House of Commons, not least because it would give him a bad start with the next Government. Why didn't Labour try a bit of 'hard ball' with them and let them know this? Blair replied, 'Yes. But I will put it to them the other way round. I will say that there are forces within our Party who are unhappy with our relationship with the Unionists. They will become increasingly unhappy if the Unionists are seen to support the Government beyond the time that they had lost their majority in the House.' It is clear that he has been speaking to Trimble but is still uncertain of what the Irish will actually do.

We also spoke about the local election results. He was pleased with these.

TB: But we performed somewhat under form – some signs of complacency. What fascinated me, though, as an indication of how far my Party has travelled, is that when we discussed this at Shadow Cabinet, they were all very pleased at the way people are increasingly voting tactically. In the past, they would have seen your success as a threat. Now they welcome it.

PA: Well, we now must decide whether we will go ahead with this thing or not.

TB: I am strongly in favour, and I think it can be done. I want to get it started. But I have not yet squared Gordon on electoral reform. He is still in favour of 'first past the post'. I can personally deliver to you what I think you want, which is my commitment to change, but I must get Gordon on board. I will try in the next two weeks. But we can't really get started until I've convinced him.

PA: So, let me review the situation. As I understand it, we had come to an agreement that there should be a referendum, as the Labour Party have already promised. And you would vote in favour of change to the present system. This raises the second question, in which we put forward two, or perhaps three, options. I have stated a preference that both parties should recommend the same system. I know you are attached to AV. That is unacceptable to us, because it is not proportional. But if we could both jointly recommend an AV system with a 'top-up' from a list system, then I could bring my Party to that, if you can bring yours.

He clearly didn't know what I was talking about and asked me to explain AMS. I said that he ought to have a word with Robin, since Robin had 'indicated that he would be in favour of such a system'. But, briefly, the 'top-up' would make AV fairer.

TB: It would all depend on the size of the 'top-up'. If it was as little as fifty additional MPs there shouldn't be a problem. But if it was as many as 150, that would bring the system into disrepute with the public.

He then confirmed that the position as I had described it was correct. We could have a two-question referendum, and a two-option second question if we couldn't agree on a single system. But he still has to move Gordon on this.

PA: In which case, let's move on to the work that needs to be done, on the assumption that you can bring Gordon on board. I want to put some propositions to you. However, before going into detail, let me make one thing absolutely clear. There is no point in us doing the 'big thing' at the end of the process unless (a) it is a surprise (and this means that we must be careful how we assemble it in public) and (b) it enables us to beat more Tories. We are doing polling work on this at the present, although this is difficult. Being a third party is always like working with a revolving door. With any given action you gain some voters and lose others. It's the net difference between the two that matters. My strong instinct is that the revolving door at present would benefit us, and the recent pattern of tactical voting at the local elections seems to confirm this. But if, at the end of the day, we end up losing seats to the Tories, then it's in neither of our interests that we should go ahead.

TB: Yes, we should keep our options open to the very end. We should only do it if it increases the number of seats we can both win.

We then discussed possible areas of co-operative work. On constitutional reform, Bob and Robin had already decided on their group, which should consist of four Labour, four Lib Dems and four lay people.

PA: As for other areas, what about welfare reform? Is it true, as I heard Chris Smith[1] say the other day, that you favour a Royal Commission after the election?

TB: Royal Commissions are always regarded by the public as something of a cop-out. But yes, we have come to the view that we cannot be specific about welfare reform. It is the most difficult problem Britain now faces. We must review the way our welfare system works. No options excluded. The problem is that if you try and do that in opposition, the Tories, whose capacity for negative campaigning should never be underestimated, will make life impossible by scaremongering about the costs. And it will be no picnic in government, either. So, yes, I am in favour of being very broad brush about this.

I pointed out that Beveridge had acknowledged that his reforms were only successful because they were done 'in the context of a national consensus'. Could we not do the same? Why not bring Borrie and Dahren-dorf together on a very tight remit? Working together on this would be a sign that the two parties were prepared to work seriously on an issue of wide common interest.

PA: But, even if we couldn't do this, we should still propose co-operation on welfare reform. And I'll bet you and I could agree five basic principles in very short order. I don't think there is any difference between us.

TB: I think that's right. We should be prepared to work on this area together, the only question is how and where. Your suggestion about Borrie and Dahrendorf is certainly interesting, since it would give a lot of intellectual weight to our proposals. I will give it some thought.

I suggested education as the third area, and explained that I had asked Don Foster to draw up a paper outlining the differences in policies between our two parties. Don had responded, 'I can do it for you now – there are none. Unless you want me to invent some?' So, there is real scope for a

---

1 Shadow Social Security Secretary. Member of Parliament (Labour) for Islington South and Finsbury since 1983. Now Secretary of State for Culture, Media and Sport.

joint programme to raise standards and improve investment, which would be both easy to assemble and attractive in a manifesto.

What about our '1p' for education – could he support that? He said he didn't think he could. 'If I put a penny on for education I will be under huge pressure to put it on other areas like health as well. You can get away with it, we can't.'

I replied that this was fine. 'We can only gain from this, as it will increase our differentiation from you on education.'

PA: The fourth area I think we can work together on is the economy. People want reassurance in that quarter. I'm sure if I came together with Gordon he and I could agree four or five basic principles; for instance, competition, the 'golden rule',[1] enterprise, an independent bank, the level of Public Sector Borrowing Requirement (PSBR) and the Maastricht criteria on which we would agree and work together.

TB: I think it is a rather good idea for you and Gordon to meet. This is where the major block is at the moment. And part of it is because he is not convinced about the seriousness of you guys.

I continued that I was proposing a programme of work, some of which could be assembled quickly (e.g. education) and unveiled at the last moment; some of which would look like ordinary co-operation on technical issues (e.g. constitutional legislation); and some of which would look like common sense (e.g. Borrie and Dahrendorf). But these could all be brought together quickly at the last moment in a very powerful and attractive programme. Two of the issues were defensive (welfare and constitutional change), where we needed to stand together to resist Tory attack; the other two (education and the economy) would appeal directly to voters. We agreed to consider them in more detail and I said that, over the holidays, I would start to draft what an agreement in these areas could look like.

PA: Look, there is one other thing I must raise with you. It is the firm view of some of your senior colleagues that you cannot carry the party on a coalition Government if you get a majority. I know that you have talked about this with Roy Jenkins. And I think this is what you want to do. But are you *able* to do it? It is absolutely vital that you do not allow false hopes to be generated. Otherwise, when they are dashed, the whole relationship will start off after the election in bad faith. So I must know exactly where we stand. Let me first make clear where I stand. I am

1 The 'golden rule' stipulates that, over the economic cycle, Governments should not borrow more than they invest.

perfectly happy to continue our relationship across the floor of the House of Commons, but I would much prefer to do it in partnership in Government, for the three reasons I have outlined before. If we work across the floor of the House of Commons (and I may not even be Leader in those circumstances), we would be able to support you easily at the start, but would be put under increasing strain as you become unpopular, as you must over time. Supporting you across the floor in the first year is easy. Doing so in the fourth year of a parliament is a different thing.

TB: Right. Let me give it to you absolutely straight. I repeat what I have said to Roy. The preferred option is very clear. It is to have you in the Government, even if there is a majority. There are two reasons for that, the first is because we can rely on you more in those circumstances, and the second, if I were to be blunt, is because you have some good talent that ought to be in government.

PA: That brings us to the last point I want to discuss with you. If we are to go ahead with the 'big thing' we must now think about its mechanics. My proposition is that we should, very discreetly, bring together Peter Mandelson and Richard Holme to begin discussing the outline of the programme, timings, the nature of the announcement, phrases, etc.

We agreed to do so and he promised to come back to me within two weeks, having spoken to Gordon Brown.

I now think it's odds-on that we will go ahead.

Thursday, 16 May, London

Dinner with Jacques Chirac. We ate out in a marquee in the grounds of the French Embassy. About a hundred people altogether.

Superb Sèvres plates. But the wine below par. Château d'Yquem (surprisingly) to start with, which was delicious, but the claret was served too cold.

To my right was the French colonel of the Marines who is Chirac's aide-de-camp and to my left the Countess of Airlie.[1] Ken Clarke was also on the table, together with Arnie Weinstock. We had a good giggle. It didn't finish until 11.30. A very sumptuous meal; very formal and very French.

Peter Mandelson was there, too. I had a few words with him before

---

1 Lady of the Bedchamber to the Queen.

going in. He always speaks to you as though you are a journalist, which I find most annoying. Thatcher there, looking very ill and old. And Major, with Norma, who looked sad but graceful, as always.

Still raining outside. We couldn't get a taxi to come to the residence so Hugh Dykes[1] took us off to the Lancaster Gate Hotel where we picked one up. Home at about twelve.

Tuesday, 21 May, Westminster

Throughout the morning stories have been coming in that the whole BSE thing has descended into chaos. Meanwhile, the Government has failed to get the ban lifted in Europe. A mighty stink brewing up and the Eurosceptics are angry.

At about 12.30, we heard that the Prime Minister was going to make a statement after PMQs. Westminster is buzzing with rumours that, since it's Major, he must be getting rid of Hogg.

At about 2.15 I got a call from Blair's office – Jonathan Powell. Somehow they had seen the statement, or at least part of it. Major was going to declare war on Europe by threatening complete non-cooperation. This took us both by surprise. Jonathan told me that Blair wanted to know what my line was going to be. I said I hadn't seen the statement, so he was ahead of me, but if he would fax it through, I would give it some thought and ring back.

I immediately bleeped Ming, Paul and Charles, but only Paul replied. I now had to do some very fast thinking. This is a high throw of Major's. It is designed to wrong-foot us. If we held to our position, we would criticize him for this kind of nonsense. But if he gets it right he will reap enormous political dividends, both within his party and with the wider (increasingly anti-European) public. It could undermine all our work of the past six weeks to get farming confidence behind us.

At 2.40pm, having seen the statement, I rang Jonathan back and said that my instinct was to go hard at Major. It was high risk, but we had to up the ante with him. Jonathan said Tony felt the same way. His line would be that Major was 'offering empty threats'. Still struggling to find the right phrases, I went down into the chamber. I saw Charles Kennedy on the bench and showed him the statement, but he couldn't give me a

---

1 Member of Parliament (Conservative) for Harrow East 1970–97.

clear recommendation. I then showed it to Ming and David Steel, both of whom are for holding firm to our beliefs and, whatever the risk, going for Major.

At about 3.10 Alan Beith came in and sat alongside me. He was for caution. Attack Major, but don't go overboard. I thought this was wrong and decided to go with my instincts. Someone – I think it was Ming – offered the phrase, 'They have handed over foreign policy to the sceptics.'

Major gave his statement declaring war on Europe to great roars of approval from the Tory benches. Then Blair. To my astonishment he rambled disastrously for about five minutes against a rising tumult from the Tory benches. He didn't stick to the line we had agreed. Not a good performance.

Now I was in a real quandary. If I stuck to my line I would be completely alone. I decided to go for it.

In the event the first part of the question went well – I took Ming's line about handing over foreign policy to the right wing (which ran on the news through the night). But the second part, about the problems of a specific abattoir in Cornwall, was bad and went on too long. The Tory benches bayed at me. They needed some Euro target to shout at and, as usual, I was it.

Typical Major. Do nothing for seven weeks, then grab desperately at any solution which makes him look strong. He will get good crits in the short term, but it will rebound in the long term.[1]

At least I hope that's right. We have risked a lot this afternoon.

A whisky and then to bed at around midnight. I couldn't sleep terribly well and was awake again by four thinking about the BSE problem. I listened to the news at six. Major has a lot of support from the tabloids – 'At last Major shows he has balls; we are off to war with Europe, etc.' Horrible, jingoistic stuff. But it must be music to his ears. Great support from the Euro-sceptics as well.

Significantly, we got a very good comment in *The Times*, which contrasted my intervention with Blair's. And full support from the *FT* and the *Independent* for our decision. I have been thinking what we must do today. We must reinforce the position we have taken. Major has raised the stakes and we will have to match him.

---

1 I have since come to believe that, in fact, John Major felt let down by the European Commission, having received private assurances from them that they would not be implementing a total ban on British beef. He felt he had no option but to respond in this way to what he believed was a betrayal of Britain's interests and, in particular, of our beef industry.

Wednesday, 22 May, Westminster

Sources in Whitehall say the Government is in chaos. Clarke and Gummer[1] met in a panic yesterday afternoon to discuss what the hell they should do. But today Clarke is defending the Government, though in less than enthusiastic terms. There is clearly not a solid front there. I am gambling heavily on the fact that Major is up to his usual short-term tricks. It would be best if we could get a common front with Labour.

So at around nine I rang Blair at home. I spoke to Cherie. He was shaving, but she put me through to him. I told him that my instincts remain that we should take a firm line. He said he didn't want to do that. He wanted to see how it plays out and was in favour of caution. I told him I couldn't see the benefit in that; if we were cautious we would still suffer if Major was wrong, only we would look wrong as well. We might as well be hung for a sheep as a lamb. I was going for it.

He said, 'Well, I suppose you can. But I am going to sit tight today.' I told him I would send him a copy of the letter I was writing to Major.

I got another call from Jonathan later in the morning. Tony was in a National Executive Meeting, but had asked Jonathan to pass on the message that, having thought about it again, he agreed with me. We should take a very firm position on this and act tough. I wasn't absolutely certain whether he meant that I should do this while he stayed silent, or if he thought it was best for both of us to do it. In the event, Labour said nothing during the day.

By 9.15 I had drafted the letter to the Prime Minister. I find these decisions absolutely agonizing. But once I have taken them and we are embarked on whatever course we have chosen, I feel elated. Nevertheless, a tricky moment. It had better work out. My letter was as follows:

Dear Prime Minister,

After nine weeks of confusion, indecision and delay by your Government you decided yesterday to bet the whole British Beef industry in an attempt to appease the Euro-sceptics in your own Party.

I want you to know that, if this gamble fails, then your authority as Prime Minister will have gone and the only honourable course left for you will be to resign and call a General Election.

1 John Selwyn Gummer, Secretary of State for the Environment. Member of Parliament (Conservative) for Lewiston 1970–74, Eye 1979–83, Suffolk Coastal since 1983.

We all know that there is now a near certainty that the gelatine, tallow and semen ban is going to be lifted – unless, of course, the action you took yesterday has the contrary effect of making it more difficult for Britain's friends in Europe to support the Commission's recommendation to lift the ban. Let us hope that this will not happen.

But lifting the derivatives ban, though welcome, will only have marginal impact on the beef industry as a whole, which is now in such peril as a result of this crisis, compounded by the chaos which now reigns over the implementation of your own BSE eradication scheme.

The test for your gamble, therefore, does not lie in lifting the derivatives ban (which was going to happen anyway) but in whether the outcome is an agreement on lifting the overall European beef ban by the end of June – the very latest moment when such an agreement needs to be in place if we are to save the jobs and enterprises which the actions of your Government have put at risk.

We have seen you many times before in Europe posture and then back down. We have heard you many times before use strong words to describe weak action, resulting in nothing at best, or further damage at worst.

If this turns out to be yet another of your gambles for short-term political advantage at the cost of long-term damage to Britain's interests, then you and your Government will have no further purpose to serve.

Yours,
Paddy

Thursday, 23 May, Westminster

This morning I received the following letter from the Prime Minister:

Dear Paddy,

Thank you for your letter of 22 May concerning the European Union ban on British beef. I regret that you found it necessary to write in such terms. I had hoped that, with such vital British interests at stake, you would have found it appropriate to join me in standing up for those interests. Instead, as the Liberals have demonstrated time after time, you would rather sacrifice our vital interests in the cause of European integration.

I intend to stand up for the interests of our beef industry. I am disappointed that you find yourself unable to do so.

Yours sincerely
John

PS[hand written] Offensive letters serve no useful purpose – why do you do it? *What you have written is a travesty of the truth.* John.

Monday, 3 June, Westminster

Today I hand wrote the following note to the Prime Minister:

Personal and private
  Dear John,
  I saw the personal note on the bottom of your letter.
  I am sorry you found my letter offensive – it was written in anger for what I regard as a deeply silly policy which will damage all of us.
  But I will do a deal with you. I will stop writing you 'offensive' letters if you stop giving me offensive answers to my PMQs!

  Yours,
  Paddy

Three days later, I received the following note, again handwritten:

Dear Paddy,
  Many thanks for your note.
  It's a deal!

  Yours,
  John

Tuesday, 4 June, Westminster

Labour are really worrying me now. They seem all over the place. The stuff from Jack Straw yesterday on curfews is just bizarre.[1] And supported by Blair today. Their inability to take a clear position on Europe is in stark contrast to Blair's private statements to me that they can be relied on for Europe.

I conclude that they have lost all their anchors of belief and are drifting.

---

1 Jack Straw suggested that local councils and the police should have the power to impose child curfews.

They seem to be picking on any passing idea from whatever source and using it to get a bit of short-term press, without thinking of the long-term implications.

They look less and less like a Government-in-waiting. And if they do come to power and continue in this way, they are likely to be one blown hither and thither by every passing wind. That's what happens when you don't have a coherent set of beliefs on which to base your actions. But the press haven't picked up on this yet, except with BSE.

Off in the late morning to see Arafat.[1] He is a little man, wizened and ugly. His eyes dart backwards and forwards like a lizard's. But there is no doubt about his power. He told us privately that he is extremely gloomy about the election of the Netanyahu Government in Israel and fears for peace.

Wednesday, 6 June, Westminster

At 11.00am to see Blair. When I walked in, Jonathan was there, and Alastair Campbell.

Tony was sitting on the sofa in the corner, in his shirtsleeves. We opened with a discussion about beef. He was very defensive. 'Look, I'm not at all certain that these bloody Europeans, who in the end are terribly weak, are not going to give in to this lot [the Government]. The people I have been speaking to tell me that it is possible for them to cobble together a package which might give the Tories a way out. We hear that the non-cooperation policy is really beginning to have an effect. The Europeans want this cleared away as quickly as possible. Rifkind has a point when he says non-cooperation is concentrating minds. My fear is that the Europeans are so weak, so brought up on the habit of compromise, that they will provide the Government with something that they can call a respectable outcome, along the lines of: "Lift the beef, tallow and semen ban; then separate out the grass-raised herds; then put to one side cattle over a certain age. Then allow calves in, which can be proved not to have come from BSE infected-herds." This would let the Government claim victory.'

I said I didn't see this as a strong possibility. The Europeans could provide a framework, but it would require a cull level unacceptable to the

1 Yasser Arafat, Palestinian Leader. In Britain to address the Oxford Union and meet with the Prime Minister.

Tories. I didn't see how they could get out of it with a package that would satisfy both their pro and anti-Europeans.

He said, 'Look, if I had taken your position I would have been very exposed. My difficulty is that I must preserve my position so that we don't suffer damage if they do manage to succeed in this. I have to endure the kind of attacks we have seen in the *Financial Times*, and even the *Mirror*, for the larger aim that we are both working for. I can see why you have taken your position. Indeed, it is probably the right one. But we risk too much by taking it, as I think you understand.'

I said that was his business. In my view there would have been a greater dividend in showing leadership and staking out a clear position. But in the end, he had to make his own tactical decisions. At all events we were quite satisfied with our position. It was right for us and, if they weren't prepared to join us at this stage, that would only increase the extra dimension that we could bring to a partnership on the European front.

We then had a brief discussion about the date of the election. He doesn't think it is going to be October.

Then I said, 'It is time we got this thing sewn up. Where are we?'

It quickly became apparent that although he has had discussions with Gordon, they have been inconclusive. Gordon was broadly in favour of the project, but remained wobbly on PR.

TB: I am now very confident that I can get to where I want to be. And that is recommending, in my own time, electoral reform. One of my strong objections to this has always been that it would enable the Labour Party to duck out of the hard decisions it has to take. I now think that moment has passed. The internal reforms we have made are irreversible and have their own momentum. But Gordon still believes that it's too early for PR. I must speak to him further on this. I don't want to move without Gordon. My relations with him remain very, very close, quite contrary to all the stuff you read in the papers. It is neither he nor I who is doing all this briefing. It is the people around us.

PA: Leaving aside Gordon's concerns about PR, which you say you cannot sort out yet, is he in favour of the project in general?

TB: Yes. There are problems, but he understands what I am trying to do, believes it is right and is committed to it. I really think you should have a chat with Gordon, so that he can see inside your mind. It would be greatly reassuring to him. Perhaps we should arrange it after this weekend, when I have had my final meeting with him.

I agreed, saying that I would also like to discuss with him some broad agreements we might arrive at on the economic front.

PA: How about the rest of the Shadow Cabinet? Are there any changes there?

TB: Robin is, as you know, fully on board. The others are, or will be. I recently had a long chat with John Prescott. I was surprised how easily he took it, though you always have to be careful with John.

Letting my frustration show, I said, 'Look, I accept that you haven't finally squared Gordon away, and I understand why it is important that you do so. This is going to be difficult enough and we need to unstitch our problems one by one. But we must not delay too long. There is a tremendous amount to be done. If there is to be an autumn election we will need our programme to be rough-hewn by the start of the summer recess. So delay is deadly to us.'

He said that he would speak to Gordon over the weekend and come back to me early next week. But, 'You just need to understand that I am very preoccupied at the moment with the "Roads to the Manifesto".[1] It is taking up a huge amount of my time. I don't want you to think that my inability to square Gordon in any way reflects a lack of enthusiasm for the project.'

We then had a discussion on his position on PR and on timing.

TB: When Bob and Robin have finished their work, what do you want them to consider on PR?

I replied that they should arrive at the position he and I had agreed: a two-question referendum early in the next parliament (unless we could jointly agree a single system).

TB: So what do you want from me and when?'

I replied that I wanted him to come out in favour of change on the first question, and either express an opinion in favour of his choice on the second or support an agreed solution.

TB: It's not in my nature not to have an opinion. I would state my support for AV on the second question . . .

PA: Unless we can arrive at a jointly proposed system.

---

1 Labour's pre-manifesto policy document.

TB: Do you want me to make my position clear when the Cook/Maclennan report is published?

I replied that that was desirable, but not essential. All we needed was for him to make his position clear before the election; the rest could be a matter of trust between us.

PA: I don't know whether we will actually arrive at the coherent end position which we previously described as the 'big thing'. It seems that the approach we should take is that each step is, in and of itself, useful, but that each contributes to the direction in which we want to go. We can then decide at the end of the process whether to unveil the integrated programme or simply leave the various positions as a collection of points of agreement. This gives us maximum flexibility right up to the last moment.

If we started things it wasn't necessarily the case that we were committing to complete them, especially if we found that it didn't help us beat the Tories.

TB: Incidentally, have you done polling on this?

I said that we had, but that I didn't have the results yet.

TB: We've been doing some, too. When the results are out, and I have had a look at them, I will let you see them. Our task is to unite the country against the Tories, in favour of constitutional reform and a new Government.

I finally turned to the question of the work to be done on the wider programme (education, welfare, the economy) by 'the mechanics' [Richard and Peter]. There were serious issues that had to be addressed, such as timings, forms and procedures. These would have to start soon.

He again promised to come back to me after his discussions with Gordon and the meeting ended.

Monday, 17 June, Westminster

Roy has asked for a meeting this week out of the blue. I wonder what he proposes? I suspect he may be carrying a message from Blair. I am getting nervous. No word from Blair on his meetings with Brown. So I don't know whether we are on or off at this stage. I am beginning to wonder. Richard Holme, meanwhile, has written me a letter saying that he is opposed to the 'big thing'. I am still in favour. But Labour's performance recently, in particular their wobbliness on important issues, doesn't encourage me.

Blair is in Germany at present, and taking an increasingly Euro-sceptic line on the beef ban – 'four square behind it' are the words used on the BBC news. This, of course, exposes our position. He has now said that he will back Major up to Florence, provided the policy works. Clever politics in the short term, but worrying for the long.

Wednesday, 19 June, London

At 12.30 off to lunch with Andrew Marr at Christopher's in Convent Garden. I told him that I was worried about progress with Blair at the moment. He said that he thought the problem was Prescott. He also gave me some interesting titbits. Trimble is apparently genuinely worried that Ireland is about to ignite again. Which is why he will cleave to the Government for the moment. Marr also told me that Major, with whom he has close contact, is in the deepest depression. Apparently last week, when Thatcher announced that she was supporting Bill Cash,[1] Major himself drafted the press release he wanted, calling her 'a man', for reasons no one could work out. It required the combined lobbying efforts of Downing Street to stop him putting it out. I said to Marr that what ran Major was 'I will show the buggers', i.e., if he was humiliated enough he would simply turn and fight as he did last year. Marr thinks Major is in that kind of mood at the moment. We also had a discussion about election dates. Marr believes that October is likely on the grounds that the three main items on the agenda – the economy, Europe and Ireland – could get worse. Trimble apparently believes the same.

Thursday, 20 June, London

Lunch with Roy – very enjoyable. Talked mostly about Blair. I wanted some messages passed back to Blair about our attitude to serving in his Government. Roy is convinced that Blair does wish us to serve, even if he has a majority. But his view (rightly) is that this must be made clear to his Party beforehand. I said that if that happened, we would have to appear rather cool, so that it didn't look as though we were desperate to get our backsides into a Government Daimler.

1 Cash launched an anti-federalism fund to which she said she would contribute.

At one point, Roy said of Blair, 'I am not sure that he will make a great Prime Minister. But I think of all the people I know in British politics I enjoy meeting and talking to him most.' Apparently Roy had once said to Blair, 'Things have been going well for you. You must be very cheerful.' To which Blair replied that he was in fact losing a good deal of sleep over it. 'One morning I wake up thinking I've lost the election, I've blown it. The next that I've won and am Prime Minister, but am no good at it.' Roy commented, 'I can think of no other Prime Minister or possible Prime Minister who would be so self-deprecating – I find it rather attractive.'

He said he had formed an image of Blair, which he had described to him, that he was like a man with a very large, utterly priceless crystal bowl, condemned to walk miles and miles down slippery passageways, with events like the Harman affair bowling around blind corners to knock him over. His role in history was to get to the other end without dropping the bowl. Blair had apparently laughed at this and said it was very accurate.

We went through the Shadow Cabinet members. Roy is strongly opposed to Straw, whom he thinks is dangerous. He has a low opinion of some of the Shadow Cabinet members below the top three. Apart from Brown and Cook, he thinks they are rather weak. He had advised Blair to build a very close attachment with one person in his Cabinet upon whom he could rely on all occasions. This probably accounts for Blair's reliance on Brown.

Tuesday, 25 June, Westminster

On Saturday, coming down on the train, I had read a piece in the *Guardian* about a campaign being waged by Brian Mawhinney[1] against Cherie Blair to put her into the 'Hillary Clinton' mould. I decided I would do a PMQ about this.

I forewarned Blair. He is very nervous of it. I drafted the question, and had it read out to him. I needed to make sure he gave his agreement, since it would be wrong of me to ask the question if it made Cherie's life more difficult.

Into the chamber. In the event, Major had no idea my question was

---

1 Chairman of the Conservative Party. Member of Parliament (Conservative) for Peterborough 1979–97, Cambridgeshire North West since 1997.

coming and went round and round in circles.[1] 'There is no such campaign, nor will there be. The Right Hon. Gentleman will know that I speak from some experience.' A pretty pathetic response.

Later in the afternoon, a meeting with Andrew Marr. He has picked up strong rumours that Labour are up to some kind of skulduggery on Scotland. Marr thought probably proposing a referendum on taxation powers for the Scottish Parliament, contrary to our agreement in the Scottish Convention, as a response to attacks from the Tories. Did I have any information?

I promised to beat the bushes and called Jim, Archy and Ray Michie to ask them if they had heard anything. Archy and Ray came back having drawn a blank, but Jim was more cautious. George Robertson had started off totally denying it then wavered. Jim is suspicious. I am worried. To move to a referendum in Scotland would be a real *coup de théâtre* for Blair. And the right policy, too – as I have been trying to persuade my Scottish colleagues for some time, without success. But it will cause outrage, since it goes against the Scottish convention agreements.

Friday, 26 June, Westminster

At 10.15am a meeting with Blair in his office. I thought we were at last going to talk about his conversations with Gordon Brown. But he said that he had not yet finalized them. 'I am so sorry. I am so busy at the moment that I really can't think about anything else. I know you are impatient to get on with this. I am, too. But there is only so much I can do. I have had a brief chat with Gordon and I think all our ducks are in a row. But I really want us to discuss today something which I want to announce tomorrow.'

He went on to tell me in confidence that tomorrow he would be announcing a Scottish referendum before devolution. It would be a two-question referendum [the second question being on tax-raising powers for the Scottish Parliament] held within two months of the General Election.

1 My question was: 'It is not my job to defend another Party. However, the Prime Minister had rightly committed himself and the rest of us to defending standards in politics. Will he now tell us whether he personally approves of the unpleasant campaign being run by his Party Chairman to attack the Labour Party through the Labour Leader's wife? Does he really want an election campaign run around personality attacks which extend even to our families?'

TB: I have been looking at the Callaghan Government. The devolution issue swallowed up three years of his Government and then didn't get through. I simply can't have the next Government mired in the devolution issue for so long. We know the Tories will resist devolution legislation, root and branch, just as they did before.

And then there is the whole question of English nationalism. There are English nationalists in my own Party, especially among the northern Labour MPs, and I fear them perhaps most of all. I must now get myself a proper mandate in order to drive this through the House of Commons on a whipped basis. A 'yes' vote in a referendum will strengthen my hand.

I am going to announce the same for Wales, with PR.

PA: This will be regarded as an act of betrayal by Jim Wallace[1] and my Scots, and justifiably so. Jim has been exceedingly courageous. He has put his political career on the line and faced down his own Party for the deal he struck on the Scottish Convention with George Robertson.

And the fact that we haven't been told about this beforehand will be regarded by my colleagues as adding insult to injury. It has always been my view that a referendum ought to be one of the things we should consider in Scotland. And to be fair, Jim has made it clear that he would 'never say never' to a referendum, either. But the deal we struck between our two parties in the Convention was that a referendum wasn't necessary. They feel this because of the way Labour betrayed them on the referendum in 1979, initiated by the Callaghan Government. People like Ming, on whom I will rely heavily to get our plans through the Party, are wholly opposed to this. I may even get some resignations.

If the policy is right, it is worth pursuing. But by doing it in this way, without consultation, and particularly with the second question on taxation, is very, very damaging for me. Incidentally, I am furious that I heard about this from a press person two days ago. I feel 'bounced', and so will my colleagues. At the very least, George Robertson, who has worked very closely with Jim Wallace, and with whom he has built up trust, should have told Jim what was in his mind.

Lecture over. I will now see what I can do to ensure that my colleagues respond to this without being destructive. But we are not able to welcome it. My real concern now is not with the proposition, but with the way you have acted. You risk blowing the whole Scottish Convention agreement apart, since many will, justifiably, say that this is a gross breach of faith.

He is going up to Scotland on Friday, to 'face down his Party'. He is, apparently, 'worried about it'.

1 Now Leader of the Scottish Liberal Democrats.

We then had a brief discussion about the Tories. They are rising in the polls, and we are both worried. I don't understand why they haven't suffered more over BSE. He said, 'You have done terrifically well on BSE. You really have. You took a very brave position. I rather wish we had taken it now.'

He thanked me briefly for my comment yesterday about Cherie at PMQs. I said to him that, though I liked Cherie, this was not simply about her, it was about the principle. We have got Major to say things (e.g. that wives should not be part of the election campaign) that will be useful to both of us.

Before leaving I stressed once again the importance of getting down to work. 'We really can't let more time slip away. I am particularly keen to get Bob and Robin started, and also Peter and Richard.'

TB: Then why not let them start now?

PA: No, this must be kept under tight control. There is no point in starting work until we have cleared all the hurdles, especially on PR, and we haven't. I have told my people to hold off until we have jointly pressed the button. But we really must get moving.

On the way out, Alastair said, 'Ah, the gallant Paddy!' as we stood at his door, with Anji joking about my coming to Cherie's rescue.

Later in the day, having spoken to Jim, Ming and co. and persuaded them, after a very tough discussion, to hold their fire on the Scottish referendum, I rang Blair again. 'Look, I know you are busy, but I just want to say this whole affair is regarded by my colleagues as a gross breach of faith. And they are right. Words like betrayal are being used. And those who feel strongest are those whom I rely on to support what we have been doing. The way you have handled this has seriously damaged relations between Jim and George. We must learn to deal with each other on a better basis.'

Saturday, 27 June, Somerset

I sent the following typed note to Blair today:

Dear Tony,

I am sure that your mind will be concentrated on what you must do next week [in Scotland]. But I want to reinforce what I said yesterday. It is very important that we get started on the work that has to be done once we have both agreed that the project is 'on'. In my view, the Cook/Maclennan project, in particular, should be started the week after next at the latest.

Time is running out if we are to get something we can use if the balloon goes up in the autumn. Announcing that the work has commenced would, in any case, make a very good postscript to what you do next week (for example, you've laid out your position, we know ours – so work can commence).

Please can we meet early in the following week so that we can press the button, hopefully, for this work to start?

Good luck tomorrow and next week.

Yours,
Paddy

Tuesday, 9 July, London

NELSON MANDELA'S FIRST STATE VISIT TO BRITAIN

Mandela's visit today has raised extraordinary public interest. Crowds lining the streets, especially around the Mall, and the traffic completely snarled up.

At the state dinner for him at Buckingham Palace this evening Mandela wore a black shirt without a tie. He looked splendid and somehow quite formal enough, even among the tails and medals. Wonderful grace in his face. I kept watching him while the Queen was speaking and the pipers were marching round after the dinner. Tall but frail. Yet he still does not look nearly as old as his years. How very curious to see this grizzled head and black face full of humility and grace against the crimson backdrop of the British throne. His speech was rather pedestrian, I thought, but probably suitable for the occasion. His handshake, however, was firm, his eyes tranquil and humane. I was also struck by how slowly he speaks and how many pauses he leaves between sentences. It has the effect of forcing you to listen to what he says.

Thursday, 11 July, London

Jane and I walked down into the Westminster Hall for Mandela's address to the joint Houses. It was packed. Fifteen hundred people, or so. The Westminster Hall is magnificent on these occasions: red carpet, arc lights, the Royal Heralds and three ornate chairs set out on a raised platform in front of the assembled audience. In due course the Speaker and the Lord Chancellor arrived. Betty Boothroyd looked magnificent in her robe of black and gold.

Then Mandela. He emerged into the arc lights after the fanfare, and I immediately thought of the prisoner in *Fidelio* emerging blinking into the sunlight. He looked immensely calm. He had difficulty with the steps because of the damage done to his ankles by the chains in prison, so he held on to Betty's hand. The pair then descended the steps of the West-minster Hall amid the pomp. It was both human and immensely moving. I could feel the tears start in my eyes. Jane, who had been put two rows behind me, told me afterwards that she felt the same. She had sat next to Douglas Hogg, who ostentatiously (and despite Jane's protests) ignored the whole event and busied himself with the work in his ministerial boxes.

Mandela spoke for surprisingly long. There was real tension at the beginning of his speech, in which he didn't flinch from saying that we had a bad colonial record in South Africa. But real warmth at the end, when he went through the people who had maintained faith with the blacks in South Africa. Unfortunately his rather clipped voice doesn't carry very well and got rather lost in the echoes of the hall.

Betty Boothroyd gave a superb speech, interrupted, unusually, by claps on several occasions. She said that Mandela represented the triumph of the human spirit over evil.

Then off to the Dorchester for lunch. Probably four or five hundred people there. I sat next to some South African businessmen, one of whom told me he had been approached by Labour and the other that he had recently joined Labour. Their net is certainly flung wide.

The Queen and Mandela came in. All I could see was two grizzled heads as they moved among the crowd, one short with wavy hair and the other taller with crinkly hair. But they seemed to move perfectly together. From their body language, they really seemed to like each other.

I noticed that during lunch they were leaning towards each other like an elderly couple who had known each other all their lives. I found it very affecting: the Queen with all her background of pomp and this frail ex-prisoner who was now recognized as one of the really great men of our time.

Mandela delivered a courteous speech, while the Queen gave the shortest speech I have ever heard. 'Thank you for coming. We have enjoyed having you. Ladies and Gentlemen, please raise your glasses.' The first time I have been to a dinner where the speech was shorter than the grace!

At 5.30 with Ming to Buckingham Palace to talk properly to Mandela. How immensely powerful he is close-to – despite his age. What looks like a weak body from a distance turns out to be very strong at close quarters. He suddenly has a very commanding authority in his voice. And his hands and arms are amazingly youthful and strong. I put my hand round his shoulders when we stood up for photographs. He has an immensely muscular back. He may be eighty-one, but he is anything but frail.

Friday, 12 July, St Catherine's College, Oxford

ALL-DAY PARLIAMENTARY PARTY MEETING

Dinner in the evening in the Senior Common Room. Afterwards, we met in an adjoining room for an hour and a quarter.

I mapped out the position as I saw it. With Labour and the Tories split there were now, under the surface, not two parties in Britain, but five; New Labour; Old Labour; anti-European Tories; one-nation Tories; and us. Everyone moving house. All moving to the liberal agenda. We were the only fixed point, it was up to us to use our position to move things forward. But we shouldn't do it in any way which might sacrifice our independence or distinctiveness.

During the day Shirley Williams had sent me a note saying that we must be careful of Blair. She is becoming less and less convinced that he will do what needs to be done for Britain. She will act as a powerful counterbalance to Bill Rodgers's comments recently that Blair is wonderful.

I brought Shirley into the discussion later. Ming made an impassioned plea that the purpose of his life was to get rid of the Tories and to get rid of them for good. And he didn't care who he combined with to do so. At the other extreme, Chris Davies said that in no circumstances should we do any kind of deal after the election, and that we should make that clear beforehand. However, the consensus was for keeping our options open –

much to my delight. Nigel Jones[1] introduced real tension by asking directly, as I anticipated somebody would, whether I had seen Blair. I said that I had but that we had reached no agreement (true) and that we had never discussed Cabinet places (also true).

Richard said afterwards that he didn't think I should have done this. Jones will go away and blab. But I take a different view. I must not lie to them. Archy shares this view.

At the very end, wanting to move forward, I said, 'Look, what really worries me about this man Blair is that he is not a natural member of the Labour Party. We should never underestimate his capacity to manoeuvre. Or his courage. My real concern is that he could make us an offer before the election that we can't refuse, which includes PR.'

The meeting was useful. People were able to lay out their opinions and the thing that I feared – an attempt to close off options – didn't happen. The purpose of these meetings is to 'see into each other's minds'. In the words of Emma Nicholson, we are here to defeat the Tories, and we're not therefore dealing with enemies of 'equal weight'. In defeating the Tories, however, we must never allow limits to be set on our capacity for growth. We must be part of the forces for change and not allow ourselves to be separated from this, while maintaining our independence and distinctiveness. PR was our key aim, so we must keep our options open. And lastly, we must continue to maintain a tension between ourselves and Labour.

Tuesday, 16 July, London

To the Goring Hotel to meet Roy Jenkins and Robert Fellowes for lunch. Fellowes is a compassionate and very rational man. I asked him whether the Palace had difficulties over our policy to remove the royal prerogative. He said they didn't want the Queen to lose that power as he thought she could use it constructively. He also asked me how serious I was about it. I said we were serious, and would remain so. But if there were objections we would, of course, listen to them. He also questioned me closely about our relations with Labour. I let him understand that they were getting closer and closer, and that I had a good personal relationship with Blair.

At one stage he referred to the Labour front-bench team as 'very able'. I

1 Member of Parliament (Liberal Democrat) for Cheltenham since 1992.

told him that I didn't think they were. The senior members were very good and would make excellent Secretaries of State. But further down they were weak. Until we got down to the 1992 entry, some of whom had great potential.

I took him through our position on a hung election. I said, 'I recall that before the 1992 election, I told you we would want to go for a constructive vote of no confidence if there was a minority administration. In other words, that we wouldn't vote one Government out until there was a positive vote in favour of a replacement – and that PR for Westminster would be the essential requirement for us to participate in this. This should have the effect of taking the pressure off the Queen – although I concede that it is not our primary purpose.

'This approach is still our general view. But this time we cannot support a minority Conservative Government.'

Roy and Sir Robert were very funny about past kings. He said that George V's decision to call Baldwin was one of the occasions in modern times when the monarch had seriously influenced events. The Queen's decision to accept Macmillan's advice and call Eden rather than Butler was another. In the end, though, she had no choice. The majority and the soundings that were conducted in the Conservative Party made Eden the only choice.

Fellowes also said that he was very keen for the Prince of Wales to start taking on more duties. The problem with him is that he doesn't have enough to do and languishes.

I left them together at 2.30 to return to PMQs.

Wednesday, 17 July, Westminster

At 9.15 a meeting of the Jo Group. Tom McNally and Tim Razzall abroad and Ming delayed; otherwise a full turn-out. We went over the weekend's events. I said that I was meeting Blair this afternoon and needed their advice. The overwhelming view was to delay things. Blair's betrayal on Scottish devolution and his *New Statesman* interview [in which he was reported as saying that he would campaign against PR in any referendum] have done a lot of damage. Nick South said that the Cook/Maclennan project should be put on hold, and that we should reconsider any further work on this front. Bob reported that he and Cook had met and had decided not to start work until after the Conference. I said that I was unhappy about this, but could see the sense in it.

I then launched into a rather passionate statement in which I said I understood how people felt. I also understood how things had changed as a result of the Scottish Convention decision. But I needed everyone to understand that. I had decided that one of my roles as Leader was to make change happen and to use the force that we had created to try to reshape politics. If I wasn't able to do this I would feel that I had failed. I was quite prepared to take the decision rationally and not emotionally. But I wanted people to understand that, just as I would not seek at this stage to close options on others, they must not try to close options on me. I would fight bitterly any attempt to hog-tie me at Conference.

We agreed to delay the announcement of the Cook/Maclennan work until October, but Richard Holme and Peter Mandelson could start discussing modalities straight away.

Afterwards I spoke to Richard, telling him that as my closest partner in the General Election team, he needed to know how attached I was to this. He said, 'I understand where you are coming from. I used to be fully of your opinion. I am less so now. But you must not get carried away with the film script that you have written in your head – two strong people standing up and shaping history. It must be practical.'

Then down to see Blair.

When I entered his office he was, as usual, sitting in his shirtsleeves surrounded by paper. I started with 'Tell me how you now see things.' Referring immediately to the *New Statesman* story, he said he appreciated how upset we were and recognized the reasons for this. He had spoken to Robin yesterday, who had relayed our concerns. He wanted to assure me that the *New Statesman* report had not come out the way he had intended. They had asked him, in the course of a long interview from which they extracted only a little, if he would make clear in any referendum where he stood on electoral reform. He said he would.

Would he campaign for that view? 'Obviously.'

They had taken this to mean that he would campaign against PR. In fact, all he had said was that he would campaign for his views, and that he retained doubts about PR.

He said that he was nervous about it, too, and apologized. I told him how much anger it had created on our side; it seemed to go back on what had already been agreed.

I repeated that the damage caused to me and to the project by the Scottish referendum stuff was very severe. Those who are most supportive of the project were among those who felt most betrayed. Furthermore, the experience of Lib Dems at large was that the history of our relationship with Labour was that they consistently used us when they needed to and ditched us when they didn't. His actions had confirmed these prejudices. Finally, we were very angry indeed at the lack of consultation – between him and me or between George Robertson and Jim Wallace. If we were going to make a success of our project then this kind of thing shouldn't happen again.

TB: Look, I understand the problems we caused you. Frankly, I don't think there was another way. But we will try to handle things better in the future.

PA: You have had a very bruising two weeks. Has this changed your view about the limits of what we can do together? Donald has told Archy that the events of the past fortnight have made it almost certain that you cannot do what you and I had previously discussed. If you tried, you would launch a civil war in your own Party. In other words, I have to ask you again, do you really think it is within your powers to deliver what we have been planning?

He replied that he was confident he could. He recognized that people had difficulties; and would continue to have difficulties. But in his view, there was now a much broader understanding about the need for effective co-operation between our parties. And provided he gave his Party firm leadership, he could carry it.

He then asked me whether I could still deliver in my Party. I said that depended on him, on timing and on substance. If he continued as he had over the last three weeks, my task would become increasingly difficult.

Had he now discussed with Gordon the deal that I had proposed? He confirmed that he had. 'Gordon is not happy, but he accepts that it is my view and that it is the way we will go forward.'

PA: Does that mean that you accept that there should be a referendum; that it should be early in the first year of the next parliament (in my view, at the same time as the referendum you are to hold on Scotland); that you will propose a change to the voting system; that there will be a second question, taken coincidentally on the same day, which gives you the opportunity to offer your position (I presume that's AV) and us to offer ours? Is that what we have now agreed?

TB: Yes – and that means that we can go ahead. I asked Gordon to come and speak to you. I don't know if he has done so yet [I said that he hadn't]. Then he will do. I am now committed to your proposition. I recognize that I will have to commit to recommending change before the next election and publicly. Frankly, I want to get this out in the open as soon as possible. I want people to get used to it.

PA: In that case, we can proceed and I am happy to do so.

To my considerable surprise, he immediately responded by saying, 'Right, then, I think what we ought to do is make our announcement about co-operating in given areas of policy at the end of this month.' I said I thought this was folly. We had missed five or six weeks when we should have been doing the preparatory work. We simply couldn't do it at the end of the month; we didn't have the pieces in place. It would look unfinished and would not bear examination. Also, there is no point in us announcing something which then becomes the subject of strenuous contrary debate at our Conferences. That would take the gloss off the whole thing. Apart from anything else, doing it at the end of August would also give the Tories maximum time to unpick it before a May election. 'We should only go for the "big thing" if there is clear electoral advantage to both of us, and it should be announced as close to the next election as possible in order to maximize its impact.'

We then had a brief discussion about the election date. I said that a month ago I would have thought October, but the fact that the Tories did not rebel over BSE led me to believe they would continue to support Major, which meant he would go for May next year. At this point, the phone rang. Anji said that it was Gordon. There followed a ten-minute discussion on the forthcoming economics debate. From what I could tell, Gordon was going into very considerable detail about how he should approach this. Tony kept saying, 'Well, I've given you my view, that's what I would like you to do.'

Then we returned to our conversation. I put my proposal, as follows:

1. Bob and Robin should get together to prepare for an October announcement [of the Cook/Maclennan Commission] after the Conferences. There should be no hint about their work before then. We could open the new Parliamentary session with it.

2. Meanwhile, the two 'mechanics', Richard and Peter, should start planning modalities, timings, etc. Included in this should be an exchange of each other's polling information: our polling showed that co-operation between the two parties boosted both our votes, but hints of pacts, deals, or even working in Government, appeared unpopular. However, I believed that we were now dealing with a dynamic rather than a static position. People didn't like deals etc. because they weren't convinced we could

co-operate, but the more that they saw us co-operating successfully, the more likely these perceptions would change. (He agreed.)

3. Meanwhile, over the summer recess, I would work on a document which contained 'heads of agreement' for the 'big thing'.

4. We should keep any further moves for later, probably some time in the New Year.

He noted these points down on a piece of paper, then said, 'You need to understand where I am coming from. In the long term, what we are talking about is rearranging the centre-left of British politics. It would indeed be remarkable if, a hundred years after the two parties split, they could come back together again.'

PA: That may be a long-term destination. I don't exclude it. It may happen, say, ten years from now, probably under somebody else's leadership. There are those in my Party who wish to exclude that as a destination. But I am not prepared to do so. We must arrive at it naturally, however. It can't be imposed from the top. Meanwhile, we can't even be certain that we will get to the 'big thing' by, let's say, January or February. That should be decided exclusively on the basis of whether it would help us beat the Tories. This is, therefore, a practical decision taken purely for electoral reasons. So, every step that we take (e.g., the work done by Cook/Maclennan) should be taken for its own sake. It doesn't have to connect to other things. If, in the end, we can connect the various steps together to make something bigger, fine. And if in the very long-term other options open up to us, that's fine, too. What's crucial now is to make this thing work effectively, both within our parties and with the public, but for us each to maintain our separate identities. I cannot, and will not, lead my Party into a position in which its independence is put in jeopardy. Nor will I lead it into a position which may benefit it in the long term, but is damaging in the short term.

We then had a discussion about whether our relationship beyond the next election should be in the Government or out of it. He said that he would much prefer if we were in the Government and went on to talk about Cabinet seats. I stopped him there.

PA: This must be about what we do, not who does it. I want to be able to say that I have never discussed individual positions with you. On our side, we must keep open the possibility that we will stay on the opposition benches. We can't fight the General Election on any other basis. What happens after the election can be discussed after the election. So this is not a discussion I wish to have.

You should know, however, that I would prefer for us to be involved in Government. My Party has taken power in local government right across the country, and we have managed it well. Now I want us to be subject to the same disciplines in Westminster. It would require a change of culture at national level, but I want that to happen. But if the prospect of us being in Government loses us votes and saves Tory skins at the election, then I would be perfectly happy to limit our co-operation to working across the floor of the House.

We discussed PR. He currently favours AV. He would like to go further, but thinks that his party would not accept it. But he is seriously considering alternative proportional systems (Andrew Marr at work?).

By now we were coming to the end of our meeting and I said, 'There is one more assurance I need from you. No hand-grenades into my Party Conference. I want this Conference to be about the Party, so please lay off.'

He smiled and said. 'OK, no hand-grenades, unless, of course, it is me saying that I agree with PR!'

'Ah, that would be different.'

Finally, I summed up by saying, 'You have agreed that you will announce at an appropriate time that you are in favour of a change to the voting system. You will have a two-question referendum early in the first year of the next parliament, possibly on the same day as a referendum on Scotland. On that basis we can press the button with Bob and Robin. But this mustn't be announced until after the summer recess. If we go further, it must be solely on the basis that it will do us electoral good and the Tories harm. Any other decision that we take should be the subject of discussion between Richard and Peter which should start immediately – although there is little likelihood of anything on those lines happening until the New Year. We will not interfere with each other's Conferences. We may meet during the recess, perhaps after the Conferences but before Parliament returns. Over the summer, I will draft some heads of agreement for the sort of statement we might make in the New Year.'

Later in the day, I received the following memo strictly private and confidential, from Richard Holme:

A most revealing conversation with Robin [Cook] on Saturday [at Ascot]. He described his party as being stretched tight like a rubber band. The only issue is when it will break.

He personally is very fed up, because he believes they no longer offer anything to *'their people, the working class, the poor unfortunates, the Ds and Es'. They have cut off their roots, silenced their consciences and ignored their core constituency. (He sees us as relatively 'courageous' by comparison.)*

He believes that could end up breaking the Party into two pieces.

The timing of this event may be two years into the next parliament, involving a reshuffle and co-opting us and the Tory left into filling the gap left by the departing comrades.

He believes that a hung Parliament, or a Labour majority of up to 20–30, provides a rational case for a coalition with us. But he would oppose it at any higher majority, and believes Donald would too, largely for the reasons given above.

He is personally friendly to us, still very committed to PR and devoted to competitive/co-operative pluralism rather than 'realignment'.

He is sympathetic to a combination of, say, AV single-constituency members and 1/3 AMS, to create overall proportionality.

He sees no reason why he and Bob should not agree some sort of limited constitutional package.

He asked to keep a line open to me.

Saturday, 31 August, Irancy

KATE'S WEDDING DAY

It dawned beautiful and blue, but the sky soon covered over with a light milky layer of cloud. In the afternoon, however, the cloud broke and the sun came through in patches.

Jane and I went to the church at 10.30 with a kettle of wild flowers. We both nearly wept, the church appeared so beautiful with the sunlight streaming in. The flowers looked splendid, placed just to the left of the altar and in front of where the priest will stand.

At 3.15 Simon left the house to join the English convoy for the journey over the hill to the civil ceremony in Cravant.[1] Everyone looked magnificent. Archy didn't wear his kilt, but Max Atkinson did, and looked wonderful. Dick Budd[2] in the complete English outfit, top hat and all. They lined up, perhaps sixteen cars in all with Greg Jefferies playing Rommel at the front

---

1 The village, about three kilometres away, where Kate's husband-to-be, Sebastien Theurel, lived and of which his mother, Marie, was deputy mayor.

2 A friend from Somerset.

(except he was flying a huge Union Jack), then they all drove round the village, hooting their horns in the French fashion, before going over the hill to Cravant.

Kate emerged from the house, looking magnificent. I have never seen her so beautiful. We had to wait outside while our neighbours took photographs, then off to Cravant.

We arrived at the Mairie at 4.30 exactly and deposited Kate at the steps, to a great roar of applause from everybody.

Sebastien's mother, Marie, took the ceremony superbly, even speaking some English. Then out on to the steps where gales of rice were thrown, followed by a small pause for photos. Then in the French tradition, as bride and father Kate and I led the whole wedding party through the village, with the groom and his mother at the back. The sun came out just as we set off.

Down the main street and out through the old gateway of Cravant with Kate on my arm and all our friends, English and French, streaming out behind us – I have never felt prouder in my life.

Then into the church. Much joy and laughing. Lesley Jefferies read the passage about love from I Corinthians 13 in a wonderful clear voice. And it was conceded by both nations afterwards that the English completely outsang the French ('Dear Lord and Father of Mankind').

Then off to the *Vin d'honneur* for two hours, where much was drunk and the wedding cake cut and eaten. The French, who don't do wedding cake, declared this the single known English culinary masterpiece and came back repeatedly for more.

We all left for Irancy and the wedding *repas*, just as dusk was gathering. We picked up the English convoy, whose numbers were now much swollen with French, and all had great fun hooting and blaring our way back over the hill.

We later learned that Joey Atkinson desperately needed a pee halfway over, so Max turned off into the vines to let her out. The French behind her thought that this was a new English way to Irancy and followed them in perfect convoy formation.

There followed an incredibly long evening of eating and drinking, interspersed with a good deal of singing. The pudding was not served till three in the morning!

I tumbled into bed at around 6.00am.

Friday, 5 September, London

Anji Hunter rang Jane at home to say that her boss very much wanted a meeting with me. I rang him and we compared diaries, to discover that we couldn't meet until the week after next. Then he said, 'Why not come and see me tonight? I'm having supper at around seven, then I will get down to work after the kids have gone to bed.' We agreed that I would go round at 7.30.

When I arrived Tony and Cherie were looking over their holiday snaps from Tuscany. He was in jeans and an open-necked shirt. When I walked in, Cherie, who was in a slinky black number, rose to kiss me. Having got into the Burgundy habit of four kisses on the cheek, I duly dispensed four and we had a good laugh over the fact that, in London, this seemed a bit excessive.

We had a relaxed dinner of lasagne from around the corner, some salad and a nice white Burgundy. In the middle of our meal, Kathryn, Nicky and Euan came in, red-cheeked from running around the local playing fields. Nicky said, 'We took on the local lads at football and beat them 12–3.' They are terrific kids.

The Blairs said they had had a fabulous holiday and that he wasn't interrupted at all. He didn't even read a paper, and never listened to the news.

He had, however, done a lot of reading, including the speeches of Keir Hardie and some early speeches of Lloyd George. 'The real shame is that our two parties weren't able to stay together in the early part of the century. It was such nonsense that Keynes and Bevan and Beveridge were all in different parties. Lloyd George was incomparably the most radical figure of the second and third decade of the twentieth century, but he wasn't in a party that could deliver. We have to bring these two streams back together again.'

On the way to see him, I had reflected on the language I had used during the day (in a number of statements) on the issue of negative campaigning. I said, as an opener, 'We are all allowed to make mistakes sometimes. As you know, I think you made a profound mistake over Scotland. But I think I made a mistake today in using language which is inconsistent with the agreements we have privately reached and illogical now that we have abandoned equidistance. I have criticized you and the Tories in equal terms as both being engaged in a campaign of lies. I should have said that the Tories launched this, that they had dragged the campaign into the gutter, but that you had, regrettably, responded to it, etc.'

This led to an extensive debate on language.

PA: You have to give me room to maintain the distinctiveness of my Party. We have abandoned equidistance and we must follow the logic of that. So we shouldn't be treating you as enemies equal to the Tories. On the other hand, there is a primary question in the public's mind. Put bluntly, this is 'Can Labour be trusted?' Or, in a more palatable form, 'How deep does the Blair revolution go?' I desperately need a role to play in the next election. I have to convince the electorate that we 'add value' to the process of change. I must give them a reason to vote for us. Otherwise they will vote for you in the seats that we could win and Tory skins which ought to be scalped will be saved.

I have said to our lot that we should criticize you only where the purpose is to differentiate us – and never in the same language we would use for the Tories.

TB: I agree. But there is no logic in your criticizing us in ways which help the Tories make people fear Labour more. I saw a comment you made the other day which on first sight was insulting, but on second I thought was very clever. You said, 'Blair has been making wonderful speeches. I know, because I have been making them for the last five years.' This seems to me to articulate exactly the position you should be taking. That you are the trailblazers; that you have been standing on this ground for a long time; that you can be trusted; that you are ahead of the game and the rest of us will follow. Why can't you be satisfied with that?

PA: How many votes are there in being the trailblazers?

TB: I concede. Probably not many.

By this time we were upstairs in his sitting room, with him spread on the sofa and me sitting in one of the armchairs.

PA: Look, we have little enough to play on. We will not enhance imaginary public fears about Labour, nor will we manufacture scares about you. But there is a genuine concern in the public's mind about you; the jury is still out on New Labour. We have to play to that, and you must accept it. It is not an insult to you, it is a statement of fact. There is a simple reason for voting for you – power. You don't have to be particularly distinctive. You can be vague. You don't even have to mention us. But it is not the same for us. We must provide people with a reason to vote for us, and the only sensible one is that we add to the process of change; that we make it more secure. Which also means playing off natural concerns the public has about you. We will do it in a way which does not assist the Tories in demonizing you. But our relationship can never be overtly comfortable, at least until we have reached some public accommodation.

I gave him the first draft of my paper on partnership.[1]

TB: If we can do that, we will really do something extraordinary.

PA: I think the name of the game for the next two or three months is to ensure that we increasingly attack the Tories together, that we use language which hints at our partnership but does not explicitly describe it. And that we do nothing to close off the final options which may be open to us in January or February, along the lines of this paper.

He is still paranoid that the Tories can take it away from him.

TB: You have to understand the power of the Tories and the power of the Tory press.

PA: I think your greatest error is to overestimate the power of the Tory press and underestimate the appeal you have for the country. But I don't mind if you leave that to us – if you leave us the space to be the party of conscience and reform then we will happily take it.

TB: This is an issue of judgement. That's your judgement, and it may be right. But I have made mine and I, too, have to stick to it.

We also decided that:

1. The Robin/Bob operation should get underway as soon as possible after the House returned.

2. We would continue to discuss the possibility of a January/February announcement on the 'big thing', along the lines of my paper.

3. I would meet Gordon as soon as possible. Blair thought dinner at Methley Street with Jane would be a good idea.

4. We would not interfere in each other's Conferences.

5. We would maintain a tone of friendliness, peppered from time to time with pained but constructive criticism.

At the end I said that we would want him to announce fairly soon when a referendum on the electoral system was going to be. He responded, 'I'm not sure how far you will get with that one. I nearly lost the whole referendum on PR at last year's conference. I have no wish to raise sleeping dogs again.'

We agreed to meet again after the Conference season.

We finished at about 9.00pm. It was one of our longer and more discursive, almost philosophical, conversations.

1 See Appendix E.

Friday, 6 September, London–Cheltenham

Drove down to Cheltenham [to make a Party Political Broadcast] with Richard Holme in his magnificent new Jaguar. Richard has an appalling eye infection. I joked that it makes him look like Blair's demon eyes poster.[1]

We chatted about a number of key items related to the General Election. I took him through the minutes of last night's meeting with Blair and gave him a copy of the draft partnership agreement.

We have to make a number of very important decisions fairly soon. I must start assembling all the up-sides and down-sides of the consequences of the 'big thing', so that I am able to make a decision when the time comes. And I must also start subtly recruiting others to help me sell this to the Party when the moment comes.

When we arrived in Cheltenham we went to the Playhouse Theatre for dinner.

Over the first course, my bleeper suddenly went off with a message from Jane saying, 'Guess who's going to be a grandfather?'

Kate is pregnant! My first grandchild! Jane says Kate is nervous and fearful about the future. But I tried to calm her down. Kate has the same physique as my mother, and she had babies like shelling peas.

Tuesday, 17 September, Westminster

Today I received the following note from Roy Jenkins:

Dear Paddy,

I just read the account of your latest 'conversation' and think it excellently conducted on your part. And there is nothing incompatible in what he says with what he said to me at East Hendred the previous Sunday. I have no doubt at all about his philosophical commitment to a radical centre strategy. It is the nuts and bolts which pose the problems, e.g. PR. But I think he will ultimately subordinate them to the wider strategy. The plan for a January or February declaration of first purpose is very good, and very desirable.

Good luck for next week.

RJ

---

1 The Tories had recently launched an anti-Labour poster campaign which depicted Blair with 'demon eyes'.

Wednesday, 18 September, London

I have become increasingly concerned about some of today's press, particularly the *Guardian*, apparently sourced from Labour, which portrays Blair as leading the process of reuniting the left and the Liberals. I am very nervous about the impact on our Conference next week.

I rang Blair this evening from my flat.

PA: I am worried about the tone of some of today's press coverage, which seems to be coming from your side. It is unhelpful and it will cause me to hold you at further arm's length than I hoped for my Conference next week. We both agreed that we would not throw hand-grenades into each other's Conferences. I appreciate that you may not have inspired what is coming out – but it's looking like that. If you can stop it, please do so. There are three reasons for this. The first is because it is unhelpful to me in getting my Party over these hurdles. The second is that, if ours is a project to reunite the historic schism between Labour and the Liberals, then it is for both of us as equals, not for me to follow you. I cannot allow a position to develop where you are seen as the author, and I the follower. Thirdly, in purely electoral terms, if I am seen to be in your pocket, we won't gain votes from the Tories. So please can we turn this off.

TB: You mustn't imagine that everything you read in the press is at my inspiration. The *Guardian* are undoubtedly trying to play into your Conference. I promise you absolutely that I did not initiate this. Indeed, I don't want the *Guardian* publishing editorials saying that I ought to belong to a different Party and that I don't like my Party, either. I am furious with them. I have demanded a right of response in tomorrow's paper.

As we ended the conversation he wished me luck for next week. My parting shot was to say, 'I can't guarantee the speeches of every junior Liberal Democrat delegate from Hartlepool. No doubt many of my Party from the North who are fighting you in local elections will enjoy attacking you. But I have put the word out that this Conference should be about us – about what we believe in, what we stand for and why people should vote for us. I can see no benefit in wasting our breath attacking Labour in an unreasonable way. You know my rule: where we can criticize you in a way which differentiates us from you, fine; but if it helps the Tories demonize you, that is stupid.'

Saturday, 21 September, Brighton

FIRST DAY OF THE LIB DEM PARTY CONFERENCE

I am terribly tired for some reason. I have serious doubts about whether I am up to this job. I suppose it is the tensions of the coming week. I hope I will be OK once the adrenalin gets going. On the way back to the hotel I said to Jane that I rather hoped this was my last Conference as Leader. Had a couple of beers in the bar. Then fell into bed rather nervous about the week ahead.

Sunday, 22 September Brighton

Alex Carlile is going to say in a speech tonight that he favours a merger between Labour and the Lib Dems. This has set all the press hares running. I am livid, having said to the Parliamentary Party only this morning that, while letting an unwise phrase slip during an interview under pressure was forgivable, any Colleague who didn't use the Conference platform to put across our messages rather than talk about Labour could expect a kick with malicious intent at tender parts of their anatomy. And now Alex, who can never resist mischief, immediately puts his size fifteen feet in it. The issue soon gained momentum with the press and I was forced bluntly to disagree with him – giving them a 'splits in the Lib Dems' story.

At around 6.00pm I met Alex in the foyer. The TV cameras were there waiting for a confrontation. So, just out of earshot, I went up to him with a beaming smile for the cameras and hissed, 'Alex, you are a complete shit!' To which he replied, also smiling, 'Yes, I know. It's the way I am made.'

We then turned, the television cameras upon us, and walked out, me giving him a hefty slice of my mind all the while embracing him in a jovial fashion, so that the body language expressed the opposite. He responded in kind. They showed the shots on television that night over a report that we had healed our differences.

I love Alex dearly and in the end I have to laugh at him. He played the deception game to the television cameras perfectly. He promised me, as we walked out in a comradely fashion, that he would try not to do it again.

Thursday, 26 September, Brighton

Into the auditorium at 11.15 for the Conference finale. Alan Beith spoke first – a good speech – mapping our Lib Dem territory in a clear attempt to block off moves towards Labour. Then Jackie Ballard – excellent. David Rendel's speech was bad – narrow and unreal. Nicol Stephen[1] spoke slightly inappropriately, but was good enough. Then Shirley.

I knew she wasn't going to fly across the Atlantic without getting herself a headline or two. First of all she told the Party that a Labour victory was necessary, but not sufficient. Silence from the hall. Then she said, 'We are about policies and ideas; we must not sacrifice these for a few seats in the Cabinet!' A huge round of applause, much stamping of feet, and headlines in subsequent press reports. Then I did my little unscripted piece, saying no options open, no options closed. And we left to a standing ovation. A good end to an excellent Conference.

Friday, 27 September, Westminster

Worried about her speech yesterday, I rang Shirley at about four in the afternoon. I had a long chat with her, broadly indicating what has been happening. Despite her speech yesterday, she said she would support me to the hilt.

Shirley doesn't have a very high opinion of Blair. She had previously, but it has diminished. She thinks he is a fixer and she doesn't know what he stands for. I assured her that it wasn't a burning ambition of mine to be a Cabinet minister, and she should know that.

It was my burning ambition, however, to deliver the Party to a stronger position and, if the opportunity arose, into government. I want to increase, perhaps to double, the number of MPs we have. I would much prefer to have over forty MPs in the next parliament and not be in the Cabinet than, let's say, thirty and be in.

She replied, 'Your position is much stronger if being in government is not a burning ambition for you. Most people want to be in government

---

1 Member of Parliament (Liberal Democrat) for Kincardine & Deeside 1991–92. Nicol is now a Member of the Scottish Parliament, and is Deputy Minister for Enterprise and Lifelong Learning.

terribly, but then realize how powerless they are when they get there.'

I said that she could be confident about three things:

1. I would not close any options before the next election.

2. I would not abandon our policy positions for government.

3. Whatever I did had to be carried by the Party at large.

Actually, Jane and I have, over the last few weeks, privately decided that in all circumstances except our being in government (when I would have to continue for a bit), I will stand down after the next election. But not immediately. My ambition is to deliver the Party to a position where it is strong, stable and growing, then hand it over to somebody else. I will then consider where my future in Yeovil lies. I could enjoy being a back-bench MP for another few years. Or, more likely, I will go and do something completely different.

I now feel very secure. Since I genuinely do not mind giving up this job, I will be in a stronger bargaining position when the time comes.

Tuesday, 1 October, London

Blair's Conference speech today. Same words, same notions, same sentiments, same policies as I have been trying to get on to the agenda now for eight years. And he comes along and takes it off me in one!

HOW MANY ANGELS CAN DANCE ON THE HEAD OF A PIN?

Tuesday, 6 October, Yeovil

Archy has been ringing me about Wolseley, who wants to see me. [He was by now sitting as an Independent Conservative.] I had been rather putting it off, but suddenly realized that if I can persuade him to join us during the Tory Party Conference it would be a real coup. So I agreed to see him.

Archy arranged a meeting for Tuesday. Apparently Wolseley watched our Conference and was very impressed by it. He is certainly not with us on Europe, but he is a dedicated community politician. And it would be a real blow to the Tories.

Tuesday, 8 October, London

By the time I arrived at Methley Street, I was ten minutes late and found Wolseley and Nick South installed there already.

For the first half hour of our meeting I let him explain what he wanted. His original idea was to cross the floor some time in the next two or three weeks, which he would do by initiating an adjournment debate and then just appearing on our side. He had decided that he would choose children as the reason. He would not commit himself to us, but would be a sort of independent MP, sitting on our side of the House.

I said to him, rather directly, 'Look, you have got to be more decisive than this. One of the reasons why we are having difficulty persuading Westmorland & Lonsdale to consider you as their candidate is because you haven't made a commitment to the Party.

'If you were to come to us directly I might be in a position at the end of the year to return to Westmorland and say that you have done well, that your Parliamentary colleagues like you and want you and will they please make a commitment for the future? Even so, I cannot guarantee that they will say yes. The decision is theirs. Anyway, you have said you do not want them ridden over roughshod in the way that you have been.'

He nodded.

'Secondly, you must have a good reason for coming over. It is far too wishy-washy to say that you do not like the way the Government has handled children. The reason you relinquished the Whip in the first place was because of Scott and Nolan. You have a perfect reason to say that the recent sleaze allegations have made it impossible for you to even sit among them. You must decide how you will do it. But my view is that you should do it early and that you should come to us in one go.'

There followed a long discussion in which he put forward reasons for not doing this. After about an hour I said, 'OK we have agreed that you will do it on the issue of sleaze, but you will probably want to do it later rather than earlier, and you still do not want to come to us in one go but to go through the independent line.

'If that is what you want, then of course we will facilitate it. But I think it is messy; we can't give you the support you will need and it will serve your interests less well. I now intend to call in Nick and Jane [Bonham-Carter] so that they can help you put a plan together.'

I left him with Jane and Nick, jumped into the car and drove back to Yeovil. Before leaving I said to Nick privately, 'Do what you can to get him to move early. This weekend if at all possible. Ideally I would like him to do it on Friday, so as to damage Major's speech. But if he doesn't want to because he is worried about the pain it will cause his old Party, we must respect that. In which case, this Sunday is fine. It will still help damage the Tories' Conference nicely.'

Nick said he'd try. He rang me in the car shortly before I arrived home to say that Wolseley had finally agreed that he would go this weekend. Saturday, for Sunday. Excellent.

Wednesday, 9 October, Yeovil

I have a really heavy cold, but at least I had a decent night's sleep. I got up rather late, being woken by a call from Richard at about 8 o'clock, during which I told him of the developments on Wolseley.

Almost as soon as I put the phone down, it rang again. Wolseley. 'I have been thinking things over. I think you are right. I shall do it on sleaze and do it this weekend. I shall join you in one go.'

I told him he had taken a very courageous decision and that I would immediately set the wheels in motion.

Saturday, 12 October, London

Much of the day spent putting the finishing touches to the Wolseley plan and statements before meeting the team we had assembled for the operation at 4 o'clock. We started ringing around at 5.30. Having completed all our preparatory work we got everybody working the phones. Jane Bonham-Carter, Alan and I then went to see Wolseley at his house in Great Peter Street, just a few yards from Millbank. He is very nervous. Worried about the Tory kickback. We talked him through his lines for the final time and said that we would not be able to return because he would be besieged by photographers. As we were talking, my bleeper went.

The *Mail On Sunday*. Please call. I immediately realized that they had got hold of the story about an hour and three-quarters before we wanted them to. Damn!

I rang Jane at home, who confirmed she had given my bleeper number to the *Mail On Sunday*. I asked her to tell anybody who rang that I wasn't at home. Jane Bonham-Carter rang the *Mail* man. He asked her directly whether Thurnham had defected. Jane said, 'I cannot confirm that.' But eventually she had to give way and admit it. We hung on to our seats, but nothing else happened for about an hour and a quarter, when the *Sunday Telegraph* rang.

I was furious. I do not know how the news got out.

But all is not totally lost. My immediate concern was that we would be trapped inside Thurnham's flat with photographers outside so I hustled everybody out, wished him well and went home for a bite and a bath.

Then to the office. By now things were going mad. The story had mostly broken. But we stuck to the plan and refused interviews with him. The team worked like clockwork, informing our activists on the ground from a bank of phones in my office.

Then home. I listened to the midnight news. We are leading.

Sunday, 13 October, London

The press is good and Thurnham coped with the pressures of the day extremely well. He has appeared as a decent, agonized man (which he is). Heseltine has been doing his best to rubbish him, but none of it sticks. Heseltine did, however, have one wonderful line which he used time and again. Asked by Frost what he thought of Thurnham's defection, he looked mock startled and said, 'Good heavens! I thought he had gone already.' A great line, superbly delivered, but its impact diminished with use.

There comes a moment for any defector when, all tension gone, his morale collapses. So I faxed Thurnham through a letter to congratulate him on how well he had done. Party staff will look after him tonight and Archy will take over tomorrow.

The recess ends here. It seems as though it started only yesterday. I look forward to the next three months with great trepidation. I am going to have to take the Party even further and I have a suspicion I will be totally alone on it. Not one of my key advisers now thinks I am taking the right step.

We have built up something really powerful and the Thurnham defection has put us into an excellent position. But politics is about what you can do, not what you have done. There is no point in having helped to create a party that can deliver things if we are not prepared to take risks to deliver them.

Monday, 14 October, Westminster

THE HOUSE RETURNS

At 12.30 off to see Andrew Marr. I have been worried about Nick [South], who has become increasingly hostile to the project, so on the way I tried to explain to him what it was I was trying to do.

I said, 'Look, you must give me room to manoeuvre and develop my relationship with Blair. This has been going on for two and a half years now. He has never yet let me down on something he has said he would do. I know this whole thing makes you nervous. I know you are trying to stop me. But this is not the way to do it. Politics is also about personal relationships and I have developed one with Blair. He might let me down in the future. But I see no signs of it yet. And anyway, there is so much at stake that I have to take the risk. If in due course you want to oppose what I am trying to do, that is fine. But please don't try to cut me off before I get to the pass. It is becoming boring.'

Nick, being Nick, understood and accepted this.

Marr was excellent. He wants the *Independent* to play a big role in it. I also told him that I may need a newspaper to help me move my Party as well – darting a look at Nick.

On the way back from the lunch with Marr I said to Nick, 'If I decide to go ahead with this, starting with Cook/Maclennan, it has become increasingly obvious that I will have to do it alone. In which case I suspect I may not be able to keep you working for me. Is that right?'

He said, 'Well, I have given it a good deal of thought. I will not give you an answer now. But suffice to say that if you do decide to go ahead and I think it is wrong then it would be difficult for me to continue to work with you.'

This went through me like a dagger. I have grown to trust Nick utterly. He has been a superb colleague and the thought of the next election without him is terrible.

When we got back at 2.45 Richard Holme was in my office and we talked for nearly an hour. It emerges that he had a dinner with Ming Campbell and David Steel while attending the Democratic Convention in Chicago. They have agreed to oppose what I am trying to do on a detailed pre-election agreement, though not on Cook/Maclennan. Later on I learned from Archy Kirkwood that they had all separately rung him to voice their opposition. Richard and I had a minor row about it.

It appears that I am totally alone. I asked Richard whether he could continue to lead the General Election campaign if I went ahead on this. He said, 'If you go against the advice of the Colleagues, the answer is no.'

I will have to work much harder to shift people.

At 5.30 a meeting with Andrew Duff,[1] who is very much in favour. He is under pressure as chairman of the English Party, but fully in support of the operation.

At 6.15 Don Foster. He is also in favour, but thinks we shouldn't make an issue out of PR. He is wrong about that.

At 6.45 Jim Wallace. He seems broadly in favour as well. Good. But how long can I hold them?

At 7.15 a meeting with Archy. Archy told me of the Chicago conversations. He is very concerned about where it will all lead.

Tuesday, 15 October, Westminster

After PMQs, Alan Beith came to see me. He is opposed to doing anything, though he also said there wasn't a halfway house. We couldn't sit on the other side of the House and support the Government without missing the credit when they did good things and taking the blame when they made mistakes.

---

1 Vice-President (England) of the Liberal Democrats and Director of the Federal Trust. Andrew is now a Member of the European Parliament (Liberal Democrat) for the Eastern Region.

Afterwards, Paul Tyler. He is very open-minded and broadly in favour. But, again, people initially seem to see the logic of the position, then get cold feet about it.

After the Parliamentary Party Meeting, Richard again in my office. I explained why I thought I was right to press on. 'Look, we now have a deal on PR. It is the best we will ever have. But it comes as part of a package. If you ditch the rest, you lose PR. There is no earthly reason why Blair should accept PR if he doesn't get the rest. He is not really interested in PR anyway and will simply kick it into touch later in the parliament and we will have lost our best opportunity for fifty years. Are you really prepared to lose that prize?'

We had a very useful discussion, which we shall return to later. But I am determined to press ahead with Cook/Maclennan and will just have to take a little more time to persuade people that going further may be the right thing to do.

Back to the House for a vote at ten.

Then Ming upstairs. I showed him the minutes of the last Jo Group meeting and I told him I knew about the Chicago dinner. We had a long talk which ended with me rather emotionally saying that we had worked together for a long time and I couldn't carry this without his help.

Ming and Richard have been my courageous and totally dependable props in all this up to now. To lose them would be disastrous.

Afterwards I spoke to David Steel and I let him know roughly what was going on. He listened carefully, then said, 'You can rely on my support. But I am worried about this. It is a very risky move and I am not sure you can carry the Party on it.' I said that I certainly could not carry the Party unless he helped me.

Back to Methley Street at midnight. I am desperately worried about my position. I am very exposed and with very few supporters for the project. But I am still determined to go ahead.

Sunday, 20 October, London

Rainy and miserable. At a little after two o'clock today my bleeper went. It was Jane; please ring her. I did so. Apparently, a close friend of ours, who is in a position to know, overheard a conversation in Yeovil at the weekend. They intend to burn our property again. The same people. She has been in touch with the police, who are taking it seriously. They will keep a close eye on the house and reinstall all the alarm buttons when we get back. Oh dear.

Rang our neighbours to warn them. I lay awake most of the night waiting for the phone call at three in the morning. But it never came.

Monday, 28 October, Westminster

Over the weekend I had called Tony asking for a meeting, just as he was leaving for Mass. We had a very brief discussion, saying that we could keep everything until this meeting.

In to see him at a little after 5.30. He was looking very strained and tired – he kept on yawning throughout our meeting.

We discussed the timings of the Cook/Maclennan announcements. Then the larger project. 'Over the last two or three weeks we have been looking closely at the electoral implications of all this,' I said. 'We have done some focus-group work. Frankly, it is not very encouraging. It seems to indicate that while we would gain some votes from you if the co-operation was overt, some of our potential voters would return to the Tories if the relationship with you was too explicit. I am not sure our focus groups got the questions right – and this runs counter to my own intuition. But it is sufficiently worrying for me to want to look at it again.'

He immediately started writing furiously on a piece of paper and said, 'I agree with you. I don't understand why this should turn people off. It is entirely counterintuitive to me, too. Surely people don't fear us that much in your seats?'

I said that this was probably a West Country phenomenon. The Liberals there were long established. And people perhaps didn't like it if we were seen to be too closely associated with anyone else.

But this is where 'the revolving door' came in again. We needed to gain two Labour votes to compensate for one vote lost to the Tories. 'For instance, take Taunton, which is the seat I have my eye on. If, say, we were to gain 6,000 Labour votes but lose 3,000 votes to the Tories, the Tory majority would still be the same. I need to look at this information in some detail, which will require a bit more work and a bit more polling.' It wasn't qualitative (focus-group) work we needed, but quantitative work. We needed to have a proper poll done.

He said, 'Fine, we will do it for you.'

I said that this would be inappropriate, and anyway I didn't think their polling operations would operate in our target areas. It couldn't be piggy-backed on to his existing polls because they would be in different constituencies. I said we should make an approach to Rowntree[1] for some more money.

He dismissed this, saying that he thought it too dangerous. He would initiate some polling of his own and we could compare notes. Richard and Peter could swap information and report back soon.

At this point, Anji put her head round the door, saying he had to leave at 6.00pm and was already late – and that Alastair wanted to speak to him about the Cook/Maclennan stuff. Alastair was duly ushered in with the secretary of the Cook/Maclennan group and ran through the options. Blair suggested we should make an announcement in ten days.

I said that I didn't think we could keep it quiet for that long. Since the Shadow Cabinet and my Parliamentary Party would soon know, it was bound to leak. Alastair agreed and said that Donald Dewar had proposed that the whole thing should be kept secret permanently. Alastair and I both thought this was ridiculous – it was bound to come to light – but if we wanted to play it down, the right way was to make a minimal press announcement.

By this time, Tony was putting on his jacket and going for the door. 'Look, Ali, you deal with this, can you? I have to go.'

Alastair and I talked for a few minutes after he left. We agreed to issue a press release tomorrow afternoon.

Tuesday, 29 October, Westminster

ANNOUNCEMENT OF THE COOK/MACLENNAN COMMITTEE[2]

I sent the following unsigned minute to Blair today:

We are now moving to a new phase in the project.

I am concerned that we should have a clear idea of the options that are open to

---

1 The Joseph Rowntree Reform Trust. A company which makes grants for the reform of the democratic system.
2 The membership of the Committee was as follows:
Labour: Robin Cook MP, Donald Dewar MP, Jack Straw MP, Ann Taylor MP, George Robertson MP, Ron Davies MP, Baroness Symons, Lord Plant; *Liberal Democrat*: Robert Maclennan MP, Jim Wallace MP, Nick Harvey MP, Lord McNally, John Macdonald QC, Professor Dawn Oliver, Michael Steed, Lord Lester QC. The Committee also from time to time drew on the expertise of outside advisers.

us. And a planned route to get to where we want to. With the other things that are now crowding in, there is a danger that we will run out of time to make the necessary decisions in a rational and careful manner. Since the success of this will largely depend on how it is presented it is crucial that we prepare the ground as thoroughly as possible.

I had these thoughts after our meeting yesterday:

1. We have always agreed that, ultimately, this stands or falls on the electoral effect. If it helped us, we should continue. If not, we should find another way of achieving the same outcome. The early indications about the consequences that we have received from our focus groups appear, on the face of it, worrying. I am doubtful about this as it runs counter to what my intuition tells me is likely to be the effect. But I will need to do some more research – this time of a quantitative nature. I am setting this up in our areas, with the aim of completing it by early December. Polls will, of course, not take our decisions for us. In the end we will have to make a judgement. But I don't yet have enough information on the effect to confidently make that judgement. You indicated that you would probably do some more work on this, too. It is vital that we have a date for this to be completed, so that we can share information. Could we agree, say, the second week of December for a get-together with Richard and Peter to share the outcome?

2. The Cook/Maclennan work has started. I don't think that we should admit publicly to any deadline for this – not least because it can't be seen to fail. So if they are unable to reach agreement, we will want their work to run on without conclusion into the General Election. But if we are to do anything along the lines of the 'big thing', then the window for this is likely to be mid-January to mid-February. This means that we should privately be asking Bob and Robin to reach conclusions by the middle of January at the latest, to allow for decision making and proper preparation after that. Since we have already agreed the outcome of the most contentious area (PR), this should not be difficult.

3. We will need to have a larger meeting between both sides to explore options, share perceptions and discuss how to present whatever we decide before taking the final decision. In my view this would best be done after Cook/Maclennan have finished their work (i.e., mid-January). I don't see this as a final decision-making meeting. That will be for you and me to do later.

4. Meanwhile, we should continue to reshape the climate by continuing with the smaller-scale, self-contained co-operative projects of the sort we have been doing over the last two months. It would be useful if we could initiate one of these soon.

Sunday, 3 November, Somerset

A piece in the *Sunday Times* today saying that we have gone down 3 per cent in the local government by-elections (on Thursday). We lost some key seats in Wales. Very worrying. Strong signs of a Tory recovery.

Thursday, 7 November, Westminster

At 10.30 a two-hour meeting of the Jo Group.

They spent the first hour once again trying to persuade me to abandon the whole project. Ming Campbell in a quiet way; Archy not intervening; only Tom supporting me as best he could. Meanwhile, Alan Leaman stayed fairly quiet but Nick South and Richard Holme went at me hard. I got rather bad-tempered.

Eventually I said, 'I know you are trying to get me to abandon this now. It is a vain effort. I am not prepared to do so. The purpose of this meeting is to set in place some key decision-making points and to gather more information. It may be that I have to abandon this project in due course. But you are not helping me or yourselves by pushing me into trying to do so now. I won't.

'Later, if the polls show conclusively that it will lose us votes, perhaps. But not without that information.

'I still remain intuitively of the view that this will do us a lot of good. Clearly you do not. So let's see who is right from the polls. Meanwhile, we must draw up plans and gather information in order to make rational decisions in the months ahead.'

Saturday, 9 November, Methley Street

AFTER THE REMEMBRANCE DAY FESTIVAL, ALBERT HALL

The Blairs arrived at our flat about twenty minutes after me. Apparently they had to wait for their car and had been besieged by autograph hunters.

Jane let them in through the front door. He came in carrying a change of clothes and a hanger and immediately dived into our bedroom saying, 'I can't wait to get out of this bloody suit.'

I poured them both a glass of wine and took his in to him. To my horror he was getting changed with the light on and the curtains open. I pulled them closed, saying, 'Now, that would make a really good photograph!'

He returned in a pair of jeans and an open-necked shirt.

They seemed in good form, though he later confessed to not sleeping very well. The strain is beginning to show. They sat side by side and swiftly wolfed down a couple of bowls of peanuts. She said she was terribly hungry.

In due course we went down to dinner – a rather good fish pie that Jane had made, together with some baked Somerset apples. We also drank a couple of bottles of Irancy wine.

Tony was tired and constantly yawning. Cherie, however, was bubbly and dominated the conversation for the first part of dinner, taking it off on to subjects well away from what he and I wanted to talk about.

She kept going on about how awful the Tories were, at one stage saying, 'Of course, it would be terrible if I said all these things in public. Tony is so restrained in public. But I don't feel that way at all.'

We had one very funny moment when she said that there was a *Sunday Express* poll tomorrow on the sexiest MPs. She looked me straight in the eye and said, 'Tony's third, you know, behind you. I wouldn't mind that, but the one who has come top is Peter [Mandelson]!' We all roared with laughter.

Cherie was fascinated by news of our grandchild, due in April. They both thought it would be wonderful, electorally. But I said I didn't think it was good at all. 'There you are charging all over the country, being fêted as the young, thrusting Blair, while I'll be going round on a metaphorical Zimmer frame being referred to as Grandfather Ashdown.'

He asked me whether I was becoming increasingly isolated on the project. (Someone on our side talking?) I said that my position wasn't easy and nor would it get any easier. I am counting on the fact that if the Cook/Maclennan talks succeed and we come to a conclusion on PR, that will change the climate.

She said, 'I think that what you two have already done has changed the climate. It is very encouraging.'

After dinner, he and I went upstairs, leaving Jane and Cherie talking at the table. It is clear that he is keener and keener to pursue the project. He talked about wanting to do it in January. I had to put him off, pointing out that this was not possible, particularly in the light of our conference in March. I also expressed worry about the polls. He said he would get Philip Gould to do some work on this, particularly in some of the northern seats.

He went on to say that the task now was to encourage tactical voting. He wanted to tell his people that it was OK to vote Lib Dem, but has had a strong kickback on this, particularly from activists in the South West. 'No doubt your people are saying the same things to you in the North.' He concluded, 'If you are going to win the big prize, then we'll just have to press ahead – but it isn't going to be easy.'

I asked him whether he was aware that in some of our target seats, e.g., Eastleigh, Christchurch, there was a great deal of telephone polling going on by the Labour Party. He said he would look into this. There was no point in wasting their efforts in seats that we needed to win. On the other hand, there was a limit to how much he could tell his people to hold off.

We also spoke about the Budget. He thinks the Government will bring in tax cuts, probably quite large ones. I asked him what Labour would do. 'Well, provided they are not too blatant, we will just have to support them. We must play this thing tactically. If the tax cuts look tawdry and really irresponsible then we might look again, but basically as they tack we will have to tack to cover them. We simply cannot go into the election proposing tax rises.'

I replied that we took a different position, but then perhaps we could afford to – we would definitely vote against Budget tax cuts.

This led to a discussion about the General Election. He is desperate to get the Government out early, but can't see how it will happen. He thinks the Unionists will be bought off over BSE and I agreed. So the BSE debate next week is unlikely to present a serious opportunity for defeating the Government.

He said, 'The economy is the main thing. We must undermine the Tories' capacity to take advantage of any economic recovery. We will chip and chip away at this. We would like to play the debt issue, which you are doing very well, but we can't. I have spoken to Gordon about this. I am keen, but he says that the moment we concentrate on debt people will ask us how we are going to pay for it, and then we don't have an answer. I am really worried that if we can't get them out soon the economy may deliver for them.'

We had a brief discussion about what the outcome of the next election might be. I said 45 per cent for Labour, 35–37 per cent for the Tories and 15 per cent for us. He said, 'God, if we get that I would be a very happy man. I think it will be much, much narrower.' I asked him to give me a prediction, but he said no, he would prefer not to. This is the only time he has kept his personal views from me. The politician's superstition! He also deeply distrusts the positive messages he is getting from his pollsters – 'The same people told us we would win last time!'

I asked him about their attitude to monetary union. He said, 'This is very complex and very difficult. I don't think we can join in the first wave. If we were to join in 1999 it would require a huge effort which would distract from other things. It just doesn't seem practical. But I am committed to joining if it works and is good for the country, though I still retain a very strong doubt that it will happen at all. The possible seeds of its own destruction are already evident: I have no doubt about the commitment of other European leaders to it, but I am not at all sure they can withstand the pressures from their populations brought about by the austerity which will be necessary to meet the Maastricht conditions. However, I am quite happy to make a declaration in favour of joining monetary union if it's in Britain's interest, as soon as the election is over. We can then join at the earliest feasible moment after 1999.'

Then we discussed PMQs, and he said, 'I can't understand why the press haven't spotted that we work very much in tandem. It seems to work very well.'

We agreed to have a larger meeting in January when we should discuss (a) the polls, (b) the 'big thing', (c) areas of co-operation, (d) when the 'big thing' could be done, and (e) how it would be presented. Then, having got all these practical matters sorted out, we could decide whether to go ahead with the 'big thing' or not. He thought that his side would consist of Peter, Gordon, Robin and himself. (I have subsequently given this further thought and suggested we increase the group to six on each side.)

They left just before midnight. His car was waiting for them outside.

After they left I made notes of the meeting and we got to bed at about quarter past twelve.

Sunday, 10 November, Whitehall

REMEMBRANCE SUNDAY

At the Cenotaph, I walked out with Trimble, as usual. I asked him how he was going to vote on BSE. He looked me straight in the eye and said, 'Haven't made up our minds yet. It depends whether they will give us anything – they haven't given us enough yet.'

Wednesday, 13 November, Westminster

Down to see Roy at 11.00.

I wanted his advice. I told him I was having severe difficulty over the polling information, which was pointing the wrong way for the 'big thing'. Also that I was having problems with one or two of the Colleagues, whose support I needed. He said he would take them to one side and see if he could persuade them.

We had an interesting discussion about Blair's character. He, like me, thinks that the most important thing to realize about Blair is that he is a man on a journey who hasn't yet arrived at his destination. But he is impressed with him and really enjoys his company.

I received the following note from Nick Harvey:

Paddy,

Alan Meale MP (who is John Prescott's PPS) asked me if we would consider giving Blair unofficially a list of those seats we are fighting seriously (he assumed about 70).[1]

He suggested that they would find subtle ways of getting their people to 'back off' in them. I stressed that this should all be off the record, and any action would have to be oral not written.

It was interesting that they should make such a move. He stressed how essential they see it that we make significant gains. Obviously, there would be a handful of clashes (Falmouth, Rochdale, Birmingham Yardley). What do you think?

Nick Harvey MP

Thursday, 14 November, London

To see Bob Maclennan at his house following his operation. His wife Helen welcomed me and I sat in their very pleasant front room talking to Bob for an hour and a half. The operation had taken five hours and they had warned me he would look very gaunt. In fact he looked rather well.

I took him on to what I wanted done and by when on the Cook/ Maclennan front. I said that we should paint in broad strokes. 'You are

---

1 Chris Rennard subsequently passed them a list.

painting a Gauguin, not a Canaletto.' The more detail we provided the more open we would be to attack from the Tories. So it would be much better if we could get the Labour Party to agree to a 'broadly proportional' electoral system rather than going into AMS plus or AV minus, etc. He said that was exactly the way his mind was going as well.

I asked him to finish if at all possible by the end of December or, at the latest, mid-January. Any later and I would get very nervous.

I also told him that I was now becoming isolated on further moves toward's the 'big thing', but that I was determined to press ahead. I didn't know where he stood. He said we ought to press ahead with it, but exercise caution.

Friday, 15 November, Westminster

I am really downcast. An opinion poll in the *Daily Telegraph* has us in single figures. The Party is in a desperate position and I do not know what the hell to do about it. We are being totally squeezed out.

Monday, 18 November, Westminster

Our latest private polling shows that we would indeed get a boost if we did the 'big thing', as I have always suspected. So I am now clear in my mind. If Blair delivers on PR, I shall do it. If the Party doesn't want it they can say so and somebody else can lead them into the election. I couldn't fight an election, anyway, in which we were following a strategy I didn't agree with.

I am not so desperate to hang on to the Leadership of the Party anyway. I have done all I wanted to do with it, except take it into power and win PR. I have now clarified my thoughts and feel much relieved.

Tuesday, 19 November, Westminster

At 4.30 a word with Bob Worcester. He thinks we have sunk to our lowest position and will not get any worse. In fact he thinks we will do well in the election. I told him that my best guess was Labour 43 per cent, Tory 37 and ourselves 17–18. He thinks it will be 41, 37 and 20, respectively. I bet him a pint of beer we wouldn't get to 20 per cent.

Wednesday, 20 November, Westminster

Co-ordinating Group at eight o'clock. We had quite a long discussion about Lib–Labbery.

I ended up saying, rather emotionally, 'Look, before I pass over this job I want to leave two things. The first is to do at national level what we have done at local level – get our hands on power. This does not necessarily mean being in a coalition, but it does mean being prepared to make the compromises necessary to put what we believe into practice.

'Secondly, I know what comes next. It is this. In due course the next Labour Government will fall. And when it does we will suffer more than they will. The growth that we have sustained over the last eight years and, hopefully, the next few, will crumble overnight. Labour will suffer when they fall. But we will suffer more – we always do. There is a kind of iron law in British politics: when the Tories go down, we go up. But when Labour goes down, we go down harder and further.

'So my second ambition is to try and inoculate the Lib Dems against that swingback. Which means PR. And I will take almost any risk to see that we get it. So I am determined to follow this through. We are now closer than ever before to PR. And we mustn't let it slip.'

Nevertheless, I accept that I am becoming increasingly isolated.

Monday, 25 November, Westminster

I dropped off my coat and walked up to the Speaker's apartments for the dinner with the Queen.[1]

There were about thirty there.

The Queen turned up at ten past eight. She came round each of us for a chat. No tiara, no fuss, no ballgown. She looked rather like a smiling grandmother pottering around her Sunday lunch guests.

---

1 By tradition, the Queen dines once with each of the Speakers who serve during her reign – and this was her dinner with Betty.

Then we filed into the Speaker's magnificent dining-room. Amazing silver on the table.

I sat with Sir John Wheeler[1] on my left and Sir Michael Morris on my right. Wheeler has been a disaster as a minister in Northern Ireland, but underneath there is a likeable decency. He told me that he thought Trimble was really dangerous, that Hume had a death wish and that there would be another major IRA spectacular before Christmas.

I also got into a conversation with the Duke of Edinburgh, two down from me, about the death railway in Thailand and conditions in the Japanese war.

After about three-quarters of an hour, somebody suddenly appeared bearing a fax. This was delivered to Tony Newton, who was sitting alongside the Speaker.

Newton looked at it and blanched. Then handed it, across the Speaker and across the Queen, to Major, who blanched too.

Then the Queen peered over the fax, read it and said, in a cheery voice, 'Oh, the press! They are so unhelpful.'

It later transpired that the fax said that the entire bundle of Budget documents had been given to the *Daily Mirror*!

I was amazed to watch Major's body language with the Queen. They appear rather good friends. I suppose they would have to be, since they meet every week. But they were very relaxed, with Major gently teasing her.

He is very good in these circumstances. On his right sat Margaret Beckett. At the end they brought in some delicious ice-cream, on top of which were little biscuit maces. Many jokes flying around about this, but I heard Major lean across to Beckett and say, 'Would you like a nibble of my mace.' The *double entendre* was perfectly plain. He is a terrible flirt!

We got into an argument about the media. Major complained bitterly that you couldn't get a fair deal out of the press, who were driving politics. Margaret Beckett joined in and then, one down from me, Ann Taylor[2] chipped in too. Soon the whole of my end of the table were engaged in the discussion.

I said I thought they were talking nonsense. Eventually, when they had

---

1 Minister of State for Northern Ireland. Member of Parliament (Conservative) for Paddington 1979–83, Westminster 1983–97.
2 Shadow Leader of the House. Member of Parliament (Labour) for Dewsbury since 1987. Taylor is now the Government's Chief Whip.

all gone on being miserable about the press, I added, 'Oh for God's sake, stop whingeing. By and large we get the press we deserve. They don't run Prime Minister's Questions, we do. And if we can't change it then nobody can. It is up to us. Otherwise, what on earth are we here for?'

Major went into a long explanation about how in 1992 he and Kinnock had tried to change PMQs, but they couldn't because of back-benchers' criticism. I said that didn't sound much like leadership to me.

Tuesday, 3 December, Westminster

To see Blair in his office. He asked for this meeting in order to discuss, as I understood, constitutional reform and the Cook/Maclennan talks.

As usual he was sitting on his sofa in his shirtsleeves, looking a bit crumpled.

Initially we discussed PMQs for the day.

Then he said, 'I want to talk to you about two things, both to do with the Cook/Maclennan talks.

'I have been speaking to Robin today and there are a couple of points I just want to clarify. First of all, we are in danger of getting too detailed. The important thing to realize is that this is a political event, not just a constitutional policy one. We will advance the constitutional agenda if we are seen to stand broadly in the same position. It is the impression on the public that matters.'

I said that I fully agreed with this. I told him, however, that there was another difficulty which caused us concern. Apparently, his side were saying that nothing could be done to change their Party's policy. There was no way we could achieve agreement unless we could also achieve compromise. We were not there just to validate Labour policy. 'In the end it will be up to you and me to make sure that our people do the necessary and accept the compromises that are essential to success. But it is vital that your people understand they will have to go further than the positions they have taken up in the past if we are to get an agreement out of this.' He said he thought this was possible, although there was a real difficulty over PR.

We then went into a detailed discussion on PR. I prefixed this by reiterating the position on which we had previously agreed. 'Firstly, we have agreed between us the conclusions we will arrive at. So now it is up to us to make sure that they happen. Our key agreements, you will recall, are these:

1. That whatever is done will be instituted before the election after next.

2. That you personally will commit to changing the voting system.

3. That we could follow this up with a two-question referendum in which each Party puts forward its preferred option for electoral reform.

4. But that, preferably, we should arrive at an agreed position on electoral reform to recommend to the electorate.'

He said that he believed that the fourth option – arriving at an agreed position – was very, very important. We have to be looking, he pointed out, not at the agreement we can reach now, but at one that is saleable to the British electorate in a referendum later. This is where the difficulties lie.

Did I expect the Labour Party to adopt the policy that Robin and Bob came up with? I said I didn't, but I did expect him to support it personally. He replied that he couldn't necessarily support it the moment it came out – 'that would look bizarre' – but he would find his own means, his own timing and his own language to support it at some later date. I replied that I could see no reason why he shouldn't arrive at his position at the end of the Cook/Maclennan talks, presuming they were successful. But the timing was up to him, provided it was done sufficiently in advance of the next election for us to pick up any further possibilities for co-operation that sprang out of the newly created climate. I reminded him that time was very short.

TB: I cannot, of course, commit the Labour Party to this. In this sense, what my people say is correct. We are not changing Labour Party policy. But I can take a position myself and of course that would carry through into the new Government. But it's not going to be easy.

He then went into some of the details about PR. He said there was no possibility they would accept STV, although they could easily accept AV. I conceded that this was the case.

TB: Robin came and spoke to me the other day. Now I'm not promising anything, but I found his propositions, about AMS, which retains the single-member system, and adapting this, very persuasive. I might just be able to get to this myself. But I don't want you to underestimate the huge row it would create in my Party. I am agonizing about it at the moment. Though I certainly can't see us going any further than that.'

It was clear to me that he was, in fact, outlining what their end position could be. Or maybe even what he had already agreed with Robin.

PA: Look, you know our enthusiasm. It is for STV. And sooner or later I am sure that you will conclude that that is the best system. But maybe we can't get to where we'd like in one leap. And anyway, I have severe doubts about whether the British public will allow us to change the voting system so as to remove the one thing they think is valuable – the single-member connection with the single constituency. So a compromise along the lines you have outlined is difficult, but can be achieved, I think. My suggestion is that we let the two of them get on with it and see what they come up with.

He responded by saying that he would have God's own job with his Party on this.

TB: There are senior people who are really entrenched opponents. Including on the Committee. I am not sure I can get them off these positions.

I said that we had two different kinds of problems. My Party's problem was with the concept of co-operation at all – which was natural for a small party dealing with a large one. His problem was with policy. We both had to demonstrate our own kind of leadership to overcome this.

We then went on to talk about the next Government.

TB: Look, let's assume for moment that we have a majority or a hung Parliament and we wish to work with you. My real fear is that, two years down the line, when things get tough, you can't hold your Party to the disciplines of Government. That's what Gordon and others are telling me and I can see the force of that.

PA: But that is exactly where PR comes in, don't you understand? If we Lib Dems are always looking over our shoulder because we know we will suffer in the forthcoming election, probably more than you, then the temptation to break away will be substantial. If, on the other hand, you have committed to PR and are in the process of making it happen, that will act as a lever of control over my Party. We cannot achieve PR unless we stay in partnership with you, because it won't have been fully delivered.

And secondly, once we have PR, we will be protected against the electoral backlash which comes from working with you. So we can concentrate fully on working with you. My greatest ambition is to get my Party to face up to the exigencies of power. And to learn the internal disciplines that come with that. If, at the end of the day, we enter into a partnership with you and we don't have the discipline and internal cohesion to carry that off and we break our relationship with you, say, mid-term, then my Party will have effectively self-destructed. I am taking a terrific risk here. Under those circumstances, for instance, all those people who joined us from the SDP and are important to our strength and respect would leave. And the voters would leave with them as well. We would become once more a rump party of no significance. And it would be Labour who would benefit. You would be able to grow in areas of Britain where you can't expand at present because we are there. So you are taking a risk with us, but I am taking a risk, too, if I can't deliver. You may suffer if we withdraw from partnership, but we would suffer more.

I asked him how I should approach my meeting with Gordon Brown tomorrow.

TB: The point I made to you a moment ago about Lib Dems being untrustworthy in power is very much Gordon's point. He thinks you guys are nice and he has a respect for you, Ming and others individually. But he thinks you simply don't have the cohesion to be in power, will never be in power, and therefore will never act as though you can safely handle power. In other words, you are not to be trusted. Gordon is exceedingly clever. But once he gets an *idée fixe* he will wheedle and wheedle away until he arrives at a satisfactory answer.

We agreed to meet before Christmas, depending on how the talks progressed. As I left I said, 'Look, these talks are not going to succeed unless we provide the leadership to make them succeed. Both of us must be sure we don't let the small things get in the way of the big thing, and we must tell our people what we want them to agree on.'

Wednesday, 4 December, Methley Street

Gordon [Brown] and I had arranged to meet at 10.15am and he arrived pretty well on time. I made some coffee and we sat alone in my sitting room, the sun streaming through the window. He asked immediately, 'How long have we got?' We agreed on an hour, since he had a Shadow Cabinet meeting at 11.30. We exchanged pleasantries about houses, then got down to business pretty swiftly.

It was one of the most interesting meetings I think I have had with anybody on their side. The difference between Gordon and Tony is that, while Tony is all about positioning, Gordon is a man whose head is literally bulging with ideas. We very quickly found we were speaking the same language and talking about the same concepts.

Very refreshingly he said, 'I reviewed the situation after 1992 and discovered that you lot were right. In all the economic policies you've been trying to pursue, especially competition, and enterprise and equality of opportunity, you have been leading the agenda. I thought the book you wrote about your tour around Britain was spot on. More of us should do stuff like that. I have decided that what we have to do is basically adopt the classic Liberal agenda, in favour of competition, in favour of enterprise and centred around equality of opportunity.'

Throughout our meeting he kept using phrases we have been using for the last five or six years, but which have been entirely absent from Labour Party dialogue until now. Our discussion was chiefly given to an enthusiastic exploration of common ideas, not positioning – although we had to bring it on to that rather reluctantly at the end, as time was running out.

I started off by explaining my view that politics was at a moment of change. That there were five political parties, not three: two Conservative parties, two Labour parties and (plainly) us. That we were now faced with a real opportunity to reshape British politics in a historic way. Ultimately, this may end up with a more broadly European shape to politics – a Christian Democrat Party, a Social Democrat Party and the Liberal Party. I wouldn't exclude any ultimate destination. I was not interested in a short-term merger between the two parties. I was, however, interested in whether we could work together sensibly and within our separate identities, to create a more pluralist structure to our politics. And to assemble a sufficiently powerful intellectual project to be the driving force for a decade of reform for the modernization of Britain.

He said, 'That's very interesting. I see things slightly differently. But I recognize what you are saying and think it a perfectly logical conclusion to what we should be doing. Let me tell you what I believe. I believe that we on the left have completely failed to assemble a cogent intellectual project that is similar in strength, coherence and relevance to that assembled by Thatcher in the late 1970s. The ingredients are there and I can see many of them: we live at the end of corporatism and collectivism; this is the age of the individual. Our economies, therefore, must be highly internally competitive. We need to encourage enterprise, small businesses, self-employment. Our taxation system and our welfare system must be reformed. My view is that you cannot reform one without reforming the other. I have looked at tax credits. I see there are flaws. But ultimately I think that is the best way forward. You cannot divorce tax from benefits. You must take them both together and formulate a system which creates opportunity for all.

'When we propose our 10p tax, everybody thinks that is just an opportunistic response to the Tory Party. What you fail to understand, and what we have failed adequately to explain, is that actually this is the centrepiece of the whole new approach, not only to taxation but to benefits as well. We must reform the benefits system if we are in government after the election. But we will lay the groundwork now. If you go to America, you will find that there are millions and millions of people who receive, in one way or another, a top-up for low wages. But in this country topping-up wages is regarded as unacceptable and only for the few. We must change that.

'My worry is that in this country, when people are driven out of work, they find it impossible to get back in. And if they do get back in, they can only do so at a very low wage. We must make it easier for the unemployed to re-enter the job market. And that means topping-up low wages as part of our taxation and economic structure. That is what I am working towards.

'But the project must be far bigger than that. I have been trying to think of a single, central theme which expresses all our ideas and ties them all together. It would be wrong to call this an -ism – that sounds too ideological. I have decided that the central idea is "equality of opportunity" – something you were talking about in your book *Citizens' Britain*. Like you, I have come to believe that we cannot engineer outcomes. What we must have is a Government that is prepared to intervene to provide equality of opportunity for all. Some of that is done through education. Some of it through a proper tax and benefits system. Some of it in the political sphere, through constitutional reforms and giving people rights, responsibilities and power. Competition itself is about equality of opportunity in the economic sense, and enterprise is about encouraging it. I think that is the coherent idea that ties it all together.'

I responded that this was the kind of thing we have been saying for a long time, and, in particular, that I had tried to persuade my Party to pick up even before the last election. I suggested that we could not reform the welfare system ('a new Beveridge for a new age') unless this was done on a cross-party basis. He agreed.

He said that he believed that this was, in effect, the biggest task facing the next Government because it depended on a whole new attitude to tax, a whole new attitude to welfare, and any chance we had of lowering public spending as a percentage of Gross Domestic Product down to levels sustainable in the global economy. I said that if we got it right it should be possible to lower public expenditure to below 40 per cent of GDP within the next decade, and he said that this was his view, too.

We then went on to discuss the present economic situation. He said, 'You are absolutely right to have been going on about the mounting public debt. But you can do this. We can't. You are also right about the problem that faces the next Government, whoever runs it, after the election. You used the term a "smoke and mirrors" job to describe the Budget. That is exactly what it was. The Tories are telling lies on several fronts. First, they say that inflation will be lower than it will be, and growth higher than it can possibly be if inflation is within the target range. Secondly, the VAT receipts will not be as high as they pretend. Thirdly, they are ducking the issue on debt and borrowing. I would not be surprised if, at the next election, we too were forced off our agenda on to a new agenda which accepts that, whoever comes into power, there are going to be tax rises. My whole strategy for the past three or four years has been to shift the tax argument from high tax/low tax on to fair tax. If we can do that, we will win the argument. But before that we must persuade the public they can trust Labour. That we will not return to our old ways of tax and spend. If we come to power I will have to spend a long time persuading people that Labour will not tax, before we can show them that Labour will spend.'

We then went on to our various policies.

He said, 'Frankly, we are exactly the same on most of the main issues. Fundamentally, you and I don't disagree on Europe. Our parties don't disagree on the whole of the social agenda, including education (with the single exception of the penny on income tax). We agree now broadly on our economic approach. There is a difference on the environment, but not as much as you like to make out. I am generally in favour of some environmental taxation, I just don't think it is sensible for us to say so before the election.

'The real problem we could be confronting in the context of the election is on individual details of our economic policy. I am worried that you will join in attacking our economic policy in a way which helps the Tories replay their tax bombshell of the last election.'

We agreed that it would be foolish to embroil ourselves in too strenuous a battle in the early days of the election.

He responded, 'It is quite clear that the Tories will kick off the election on economic policy. The likelihood is that they will do this day after day. If you take a position too critical of us, that could throw the whole election campaign off balance in a way which will damage what we both want to achieve.'

I said I would have a look at this.

By this time our hour had nearly passed, so I took him on to constitutional change and PR. He is fully on board for the whole constitutional agenda and has doubts only about PR: 'Look, I am not opposed to PR. You need to understand that. But I think it has some difficulties, potentially very big ones. I am really frightened about factionalism in politics and really frightened about running a Cabinet in which individuals would have to run back to their own sections or groups to get validation for what they are doing. I am not just referring to you here. I am referring to my own Party as well. There are those in the Labour Party who push for PR because they believe it will enable them to push Labour back on to a conventional left-wing agenda.' (I gained the strong impression he was talking about Robin here.)

I agreed with him about the dangers of factionalism: 'It is a growing element in British politics, but you don't need PR to make it grow. Look at the factionalism in the Tories, which has wrecked Major. In my view, PR is a means of channelling factionalism in a positive way, while the present system ensures that factionalism does maximum damage to a party's internal cohesion, and therefore its capacity to govern – again, look at the Tories!'

We agreed that we would meet again soon for a more extensive discussion, perhaps in the New Year.

It was a really fascinating meeting. He has an extraordinarily fertile mind and, quite contrary to my expectations, a warm personality. Not at all the reserved person I had expected.

Thursday, 12 December, Westminster

Saw Tom McNally about post-General Election arrangements. I said I wanted him and the Hung Parliament Group to take over from Richard and the General Election team at midday on Polling Day +1, in order to arrange dealing with Labour and coalitions etc., if that was relevant. I would then ask Richard and the GE press team to stay on to help Tom for another seventy-two hours in order to facilitate the transition.

I asked Tom if he could take the last week of the General Election off, if it looked like we were in coalition territory with Labour. I hoped he would concentrate on what happened after the polls closed. Those who had fought the election would be in the wrong mood and too tired to cope with things, so he would have to do the thinking for us until we got some rest.

I also told him that, when we decided what our plan was, it was important to tell Labour. They needed to know, confidentially, what we would do, so that they didn't misunderstand our actions in the exhaustion of the post-polling day period. However good our intentions, it was perfectly possible for people emotionally drained from the election campaign and still in campaigning mood to make false moves. So the more we knew what the other expected the better.

He asked me to fix for him to see Sir Robert Fellowes. He wants some guidance on what the Queen would do were there a hung Parliament. I agreed to do this.

Richard came in to see me and report back on his meeting with Mandelson. His chief concern was that Mandelson doesn't know what Blair wants him to do. Blair hasn't briefed his people nearly as closely as I have. Mandelson asked Richard, 'What does Paddy think he has agreed with Blair?' When Richard asked the same question, it was clear that Blair had hardly briefed Mandelson at all.

Tuesday, 17 December, Westminster

At 11 o'clock over to the Queen Elizabeth Conference Centre in Vauxhall Bridge Road to meet about 150 Lib Dem councillors. They are very hostile to closer co-operation with Labour and partnerships in government.

I said, 'But many of you are now in power because you had the courage to go into partnership with other parties, chiefly Labour. If you were clever enough to do that, why not us?'

I also said that, while I valued our local government asset and recognized it as our most important electoral possession, I could not run the Party nationally on the basis that I could never take any action which risked losing a council seat anywhere in Britain. I wanted the Party to get used to handling power nationally, just as it had locally. And I was prepared to take risks to do that. It was all rather blunt – and, although they opposed me, they took it constructively.

The chairman of the group, Keith Whitmore,[1] said at the end, 'It has been a very refreshing discussion, Paddy. Not many of us agree with you. But at least you haven't come along to give us guff.'

Wednesday, 18 December, Westminster

At 11.15, down to see Roy.

I said that it was really crucial we put as much pressure as possible on Blair over the next few weeks. He said, 'We have moved him a long way, you know. This will be a really important point in the history of the development of the two parties, if it all comes off. I will try and see him again before the House returns [from Christmas recess] probably in the second week of January, and I will try as hard as I can to move him to a position that we could accept on PR.' He then told me that he had seen David Steel, who was 'basically on board' and would be seeing Ming Campbell.

I told him of the work that Tom was doing on the HP Group and asked him to give Tom his advice.

Tuesday, 31 December, Somerset

The last day of the year. Beautiful, but terribly cold with clear blue skies. Heavy snows across the south of England, but apart from an occasional tiny flake nothing has touched us yet.

I have spent much time thinking about the New Year. I will settle down tomorrow and write a new version of the Partnership Agreement. The coming year fills me with trepidation. The whole of my life will probably come to its peak in the months ahead.

And I fear that it will all go wrong. We may not do well, and the whole thing could collapse around my ears. One way or another, however, the next year is the one that matters; it will decide whether my political career ends here or continues.

I am nervous about the Party's position; I am nervous about my own capabilities; I am nervous about the mud that the Tories can throw. I desperately want to do well by the Party, but I enter the New Year deeply concerned about my capacity to deliver.

1 Leader of the Liberal Democrat Group on Manchester City Council.

It is also a big year for Kate, whose baby will be born this year. And for Simon, who will probably decide what he will do for the rest of his life.

A New Year to look forward to with mixed feelings. But the old year has ended well enough.

1997

Wednesday, 1 January, Somerset

During the morning I completed the new version of the Partnership Agreement[1] and spoke to Archy. Donald Dewar is off in the Cotswolds living like a hermit in a cottage. He has taken a suitcase full of books with him. Apparently, this is his dream way to spend the New Year. What a strange man.

Hard frost again and a clear, brilliant night. The ground is now deep, deep frozen. We dug the garden last week so this has come at just the right time.

Friday, 3 January, Somerset

I had asked Archy Kirkwood to give me his considered, private views on where we stood over the Christmas and New Year period. This is the memo he faxed to me in reply today:

From: Archy Kirkwood
To: Paddy Ashdown
The first objection you will meet is that you are moving the Party's hard fought political positioning from 'no let up on Labour' to 'we will work together whatever the outcome of the election'.

A significant and controversial change for which you have no authority. Any previous planned moves made by you have always been constitutionally authorized – eventually! If you were to achieve your proposed objective with this project you would have to bounce the Party. Bouncing the Party has never been your style.

You would start the process almost entirely on your own (maybe Tom McNally, Andrew Duff and a few others could be mustered) but there is no stomach among the Colleagues for such a change at this stage.

The centre of gravity of opinion still revolves around the proposition that 'nothing should be ruled out, but we are prepared to contemplate joint activity in agreed areas after the election'.

1 See Appendix H.

Indeed, after the next election – and subject to the precise make-up of the new Parliamentary Party – you are likely to have a considerable amount of room for manoeuvre, particularly if the Party is left feeling good about the result and you personally have had a good campaign.

You will also be subject to the charge that you have no power in Standing Orders to commit the next Parliamentary Party in advance. That was certainly the message I got when I met the target-seat Parliamentary candidates in Brighton last autumn.

Referring now to your 'Partnership document' your view that these four selected areas are 'above' party politics does not wash. They are the very stuff of political campaigns.

A cursory glance at Labour's recently published Candidates' Handbook *makes it clear that Labour have already invested an unprecedented amount of time and energy to establish the shape of their forthcoming campaign. Compare this with your much more radical approach in 'Partnership'. For them to change tack now would be almost unthinkable. They have the same difficulties as we do in getting any changed policy positions ratified in time for the election.*

I am sending you all of this to try to illustrate that, although your idea sounds visionary and full of common sense, the reality is that if it were to happen there would need to be a great deal of work done to make sure that our policies were actually the same in a way that would stand the scrutiny of Tony Bevins in a bad mood and that they were clear, practical and deliverable.

As you already know, I think it is mad to put any figures on the level to which public spending would be reduced as a percentage of GDP during the life of a parliament. I could be made to be in favour of 'bearing down on the increase', but I am not in favour of being responsible for the level of drastic cuts necessary to achieve reductions of even 2 per cent in the next five years in the face of the in-built pressure for higher levels over that time. It is not practical politics.

I therefore think that you would have difficulties with the spokespersons in their own individual areas. Not just Conrad [Russell] on Welfare, but also Malcolm [Bruce] on the economy and Bob [Maclennan] on the constitution. They have been struggling to achieve a coherent and distinctive set of policies, which your ideas would effectively supplant.

The final thing you have to confront is the level of suspicion about your personal understanding with your opposite number. There are already frequent references made to the disposition of jobs. (Incidentally, if it ever comes to this we need a method of getting Parliamentary Party approval for the package.) But you would be harassed to the point of exasperation during the campaign about ministerial cars, aided and abetted by the Rochdale tendency [i.e., Liz Lynne and co.].

In addition to all this, the most obvious practical difficulty is lack of time. If we had eighteen months, it would be worth a run. At this stage it's all great fun, but it is actually a massive diversion from the more mundane but essential tasks that have to be sorted out to enable our existing election plans to get successfully off the ground.

My honest opinion is that you have a less than 10 per cent chance of achieving your objective in good order before polling day. You only have that prospect of success if further and more detailed work is done on the existing areas of genuine policy overlap and a bankable commitment is secured to reforming the voting system before the election after next.

Archy

To which I faxed this response:

Dear Archy,

Thanks for your fax; I think that my paper could be amended.

But your fax seems to indicate that the best place would be in the dustbin!

However, your fax confuses me for more reasons than that.

You will remember that the last two Jo Group meetings concluded that the polling information indicated there was advantage in sensibly pursuing the co-operative agenda, but that this should now be limited AT MOST to co-operation on 'above politics' matters in a way which was inclusive to others, rather than exclusive to us. We defined 'above politics' as sorting out sleaze (especially party funding), welfare reform and whatever Bob and Robin agree on the constitution.

I have merely tried to find words to express these conclusions.

Of course we will 'work with Labour whatever the outcome of the election'. We have always done that where we agree. We worked with the Tories on Europe, despite the outcome of the last election. What else can co-operative politics mean? So this is nothing new. The real point is that the agreement does not predicate any specific shape to the post-election House, since we said we would work on these things 'wherever we sit in the House', i.e., our room for manoeuvre to sit on the opposition benches is specifically and explicitly preserved.

You say that I am 'likely to have considerable room for manoeuvre' after the elections. I have severe doubts about this in the light of candidates' comments and your own experiences with them. One of the reasons why I feel I have to do this is precisely to stake out my ground before the election, so as to strengthen my hand after it. I am really worried that our party will have a large tranche of people elected who have never been beyond their own constituency boundaries and will, naturally, want to resist the opportunities which we may then have. I want them to be elected with this as a part of the reasons why they are elected, rather than something they can claim was unconnected to their success.

You say that these are Labour's policies (from their handbook). But they are also our policies. And that is the whole point!

They are policies where we both obviously agree.

You say that, 'having invested so much time and energy' in their campaigns they will not want to change these. But why not, since it doesn't involve policy changes for them (with the exception of independence for the Bank of England)[1] or for us? Just an admission of what is obvious anyway – that there are some areas where we agree. And anyway, if they are not prepared to consider this, why is Tony talking to me about it?

On the issue of the welfare percentage, this is a hoary old problem which I can amend or abandon. But you persistently continue to misunderstand what I mean. You continue to claim that getting below 40 per cent means a slash-and-burn approach to welfare. It means nothing of the sort. It means getting more people back to work. Australia (not a perfect example, I concede) has, in many ways and areas, more protection for the vulnerable than we have, yet they have already achieved a level of expenditure below 40 per cent.

You mention jobs and being harassed. This is coming whatever we do. Doing this will certainly make it no worse. I am anyway able to say that I never have and never will discuss jobs with Tony or anyone else before the election.

Next, you say I will have trouble with Malcolm (true) and Bob (false). The whole point about all this is and always has been that, unless we get what we want on constitutional reform (including PR), then none of this is on anyway. It doesn't even start. No satisfactory arrangement for PR – no arrangement for anything.

Every instinct and fibre of my body tells me that this, or something like it, will hugely increase not just our seats, but also our bargaining power. Of course I have never 'bounced the Party'. But there are times when leaders have to lead.

We are still discussing this. I have not yet concluded. But time is shortening.

Thanks for your detailed response.

Let's talk. But please – no sight for others of this just yet.

I'm contactable by e-mail.

Happy New Year to you all,

P

---

1 This was Lib Dem policy for successive elections, opposed by Labour – but, to everyone's surprise, they announced Bank of England independence in the days after the 1997 election.

Saturday, 4 January, London

Overcast, gloomy, grey, and with a very light dusting of snow. The flakes are invisible in the air but gather in little rills that are blown by the wind into the cracks in the pavements and into the gutters.

A message from Peter Kellner.[1] There is a poll out in *The Times* tomorrow: Labour on 50 per cent, Tory 30, Lib Dem 14. I think that means we are up a point. But the really good news is that there is a very substantial proportion of Labour voters who positively favour a Lib–Lab partnership in a Labour Government. Thirty per cent. Astonishing. And 80 per cent of Lib Dems. This confirms our recent polling and will strengthen my hand enormously.

At about 10.30 Nick rang to say that tomorrow's papers, led by the *Observer*, would be full of reports saying that we had reached agreements with Labour on constitutional change. This sounds to me like a Labour leak – probably from Robin Cook. And probably to put pressure on Blair on PR.

The papers will say that we have reached agreement in four areas – the Bill of Rights, freedom of information, reform of the House of Lords and reform of procedures in the House of Commons – leaving Scottish devolution and electoral reform yet to be decided. This is a dangerous moment. We must make it clear to Labour that our agreement comes as a package and cannot be subject to 'pick and mix'.

Sunday, 5 January, London

Up at eight and out to get the papers. All full of the agreement between ourselves and Labour, which they describe as secret. Watched Major on *Breakfast With Frost*. He was good. He looked calm and confident. He also looked rational. He went straight for us in the early part of the programme, describing the discussions with Labour as secret, etc. The Tories are obviously frightened to death by what we are doing. Nevertheless, an impressive interview, considering the pressure he is under.

Bob rang me this morning to tell me that Robin Cook had said that a 'well-respected' Conservative MP (name unknown) was going to back PR

1 Political correspondent for the *Evening Standard*.

and wants to make a contribution to the talks on constitutional reform. Tony was trying to reach me all of yesterday and today – I suspect this is what it is about.

In the middle of lunch with friends I got a call on my bleeper – 'Ring Tony'. He told me that the Tory MP was Hugh Dykes.[1] He will make it clear that he probably won't leave the Conservative Party; nevertheless, he is going to exchange letters with Jack Straw, which will be published tomorrow. Very good news.

We agreed to meet tomorrow. I need to know where Tony is on PR.

I also got a call from Mandelson. He didn't mention the Dykes affair, but did tell me the line he recommended Labour MPs to use on this morning's reports of Lib–Lab agreements.

Alastair Campbell called at about 11.00am to tell me that the news of Dykes would break at seven this evening and then again to say that it would break at 6.30.

To bed. Difficult to sleep.

Monday, 6 January, London

On the way out of the *Today* studio this morning, I met Donald Dewar. He had just come back from his cottage in the Cotswolds. I said, 'What a bizarre way to spend Christmas.' He smiled wanly and said, 'Yes, I suppose it is. But I enjoyed it. It gave me a real break and time to think.'

I said, 'Isn't it good news about Hugh Dykes?' To my astonishment he hadn't heard. His eyes widened. 'Yes, that is terrific news!'

To see Tony at 12.15pm.

When I walked in Alastair and Anji were there. Alastair was looking suitably dishevelled after what had apparently been a very convivial Christmas.

They left and we immediately got down to talking.

He showed me some photographs sent to him by a supporter in Scotland. They were of his grandmother on a cart, with the words 'Peace and Socialism' emblazoned across it – obviously addressing a public meeting. He told me that she and his father had been Communists in the 1920s and

---

1 Hugh went on to fight, and lose, his seat of Harrow East for the Tories at the May election, and joined the Lib Dems in September 1997.

that his father had been a member of the Young Communists League.

He opened our discussions with: 'I've been giving a lot of thought to the PR thing. I have to tell you that the events of the weekend have not been terribly helpful. They have put a lot of pressure on me.'

PA: Well, you know we are convinced that it came from your side. Indeed, we have almost had confirmation of that.

TB: Our guys think it's you. But I decided long ago that chasing leaks is a completely fruitless exercise [I agreed enthusiastically]. However, the echo in the press today is of 'Blair doing a flip-flop in order to accommodate the Lib Dems.' This is not easy for me and damages my reputation, not least with my own Party. I have concluded that changing the electoral system while preserving the single member constituency but having an element of proportionality – what you call the AMS system – may be the way forward. But I really do not want to be seen to be doing flip-flops in order to do deals with you.

I said that he needed to understand that this was an absolutely irreducible minimum for us. I could not tolerate a situation where all we did was validate the portions of their constitutional agenda which we agreed with, while leaving PR aside as a fringe concern of the Lib Dems and 'a few madcap constitutional enthusiasts'. As I had said before, it either comes as a package or it can't be done.

PA: I am also getting very concerned about the time constraints here. The election is closing in on us. We have to ensure that the Cook/Maclennan talks are concluded by the end of January or early February. We can, if they fail, let them run on into the election. But we should not delude ourselves. If they don't produce a specific outcome, then they will be perceived by the outside world to have failed, however much we spin it. That will damage both of us . . .

TB: And I definitely don't want that to happen.

PA: . . . So, we can neither let this run into the election without a conclusion nor let it continue beyond February. So I must ask you to make up your mind pretty quickly.

TB: Well, I can't see a way around this. It is not going to be easy and I will have to spend a bit more time thinking about it.

PA: OK. Then let's talk about the step beyond that. Our polls are now quite clear. If we are to go a stage further – and I am not yet fully convinced that this is wise – then the very most we could do would be on the basis of issues we could claim were 'above politics'. The Hugh Dykes thing over the weekend has been of great assistance to us. I have always taken the view that the best way to get this out of the 'deal' territory is for us as two leaders (not the parties) to reach an agreement which we could describe as the cornerstone of a broader consensus which could incorporate members of other parties (e.g. Hugh Dykes), as well as those beyond politics, in order to build a wider consensus for those issues which everybody knows need changing.

I told him that I was in the process of redrafting the partnership agreement I had shown him last year, in which I proposed that we could commit to working together on:

1. The constitutional package that Bob and Robin would arrive at.

2. Cleaning up politics and political sleaze (e.g. political funding, quangos, etc.).

3. Welfare reform.

4. Some broad cornerstones for economic stability.

He said he thought this was a good idea. I agreed that I would try and draft something provided always we agreed on Cook/Maclennan.

He then turned to my meeting with Gordon. 'From what I hear, Gordon had a very good meeting with you. He enjoyed it. [I said I had, too.] But we are left with one major problem: the issue of tax. I have come to accept, as does Gordon, that you and we have different views on tax. You will want to put forward your own tax proposals and this should not be inimical to our wider co-operation. You will want to say that the only way to fund education properly is to put a penny on income tax. That's fine. But the really devastating thing would be if we started the election campaign with you parroting the Tory campaign about a Labour "tax bombshell". And Gordon is quite right in saying that whatever the advantages might be of co-operation in other areas, if the result of this was that you strengthened the Tories' economic attacks then that would be unacceptable.'

I said that I had had a long discussion with Gordon on this. I had understood the point rather differently. But if their real concern now was that we would join with the Tories in persuading the public that there was a Labour tax bombshell lurking round the corner, then I could put his mind at rest. We would attack both parties equally. We would play the role of the boy who said that the emperor had no clothes. We would say that neither of them could fulfil their promises without raising taxation. We would say that it didn't matter who got in, taxes would go up. We

THE MAN WHO SAID TAX MIGHT HAVE TO RISE   after H.M.BATEMAN

would argue that Labour were wrong in pretending they could improve public services without increasing taxation, but that the Tories had an appalling record on economic management.

I returned, at the end, to PR.

PA: You will just have to make up your mind about this. I can think of ways in which we can make life easier for you when you change position. I can think of finesses we can put into place to help, and I believe that Hugh Dykes throwing his weight behind this will help that process. But in the end it's up to you.

TB: I come back to my core concern about this: (a) I do not like doing flip-flops in order to put together deals. It is not my style and it is not what I want to be known for. (b) I am really nervous that this is the one thing that could unite the Tories. If they feel that we are going to change the rules so that they will be out for ever, then that could bring them back together again.

PA: If that is what they believe, they probably believe it already.

I left at about 3.10pm.

Monday, 13 January, Westminster

Into the office. Trouble brewing up on the Blair front. Richard came to see me at 5 o'clock to tell me that Mandelson says there has been a considerable wobble on PR. The events of last week have not helped. I am seeing him tomorrow.

In the evening I had a chat with Archy about Liz Lynne, who has come out with the announcement that she will reject any possibility of a coalition with Labour, even if the Party as a whole votes in favour of it. I said that I would have to act. I must set down some guidelines on collective responsibility. Both Archy and Ming, to whom I also spoke, thought this unwise. But I explained that if I do not make it clear now that those who won't play as part of the team cannot be part of the team, there would be real trouble during and after the election. We must set some rules for collective responsibility, otherwise the whole thing will become totally unmanageable if we go into a coalition with Labour.

Tuesday, 14 January, Westminster

At 12.15 Bob Maclennan came to see me with Chris Rennard. Some progress in the talks with Labour, but some setbacks as well. The Labour team have proposed an electoral commission to sit after the election. This would report after a year on appropriate ways of reforming the voting system. There would then be a referendum on that. But they weren't making any undertakings about whether this could be done in time for the next election. Robin Cook said it would depend on 'the weights of the votes in favour'. Jack Straw had said that he saw the referendum as a means of reaffirming the present voting system. And, of course, Blair wouldn't have to make his position clear. So this is inadequate.

To makes matters worse, they now seem to be reneging on getting PR through for the European elections. Bob thinks this is a bargaining position, but I have my doubts. They say they cannot get it done in time, which is, of course, nonsense. Callaghan did it in one go in 1978 – or could have done.[1] Either they do not understand the technicalities (which would not surprise me) or they are playing fast and loose.

1 At the time of the Lib–Lab Pact in the Callaghan Government, David Steel had negotiated a commitment from Callaghan to introduce a Bill for PR in European Elections, but it never got through the House of Commons.

I sense that Blair is now rescinding on our agreement. I am worried and angry about this. I must ensure that when I go to see Blair this afternoon I make clear my disappointment.

I arrived in his office at 3.00, to be hustled into the Shadow Cabinet room. The *Financial Times* were apparently with him. After about five minutes, Anji came in saying, 'This is like a bedroom farce, shuffling you from room to room.'

When I went in I found him in his usual place in his shirtsleeves.

It was a long meeting. And something of a crisis one.

I had heard that he was upset by the language we had used to criticize Labour, so I opened the conversation by saying, 'I gather you are upset by the tone of what Alex Carlile and Simon Hughes said last week.'

TB: I don't want to make too much of this, but it does identify the problem that Gordon was talking about. Our people are complaining bitterly. They ask what is the point of coming to an agreement with you lot when it is all one-way traffic? We are conceding to you, but you continue to attack us. And, what's more, using the same language as the Tories. It doesn't help the whole project, and it certainly doesn't help me. I am coming under a lot of pressure now. We really must sort this out.

PA: I said to you at the start that, although we could agree about some things, we had to maintain our distinctiveness from you. And that we will continue to disagree – sometimes strenuously – about issues on which we don't have the same policy. You must give me room on this. To do any less would simply smother our identity in yours. That would mean the Tories keeping more seats which we would otherwise win from them. Apart from anything else, we haven't even got a deal yet, and it doesn't look to me, from the reports I have received about the constitutional meeting today, that we are going to get one. Naturally, if there is a deal on the constitution, that will alter the terms of our relationship. But until that happens, the kind of thing we saw last week has to continue. Where we disagree with you we will have to say so, sometimes bluntly. We expect you to do the same with us.

He said that he didn't want to be oversensitive about this. However, he couldn't quite see what strategy we were pursuing. He thought it was confusing to the public to see us agreeing with Labour on some things and disagreeing on others. I responded that it wasn't so much confusing as necessary. Of course I was trying to work a delicate balance. Maintaining a tension with them on some issues while agreeing on others was an essential part of that. To do otherwise, as our polls had clearly shown, would merely encourage more Conservatives who might vote for us to return to the fold.

TB: But why should people vote for you if your policies are, on the face of it, more dangerous than ours?

PA: I don't think they are. But let's, for a moment, accept your premise. They are voting for us because the memory of 1979[1] still lingers. They are voting for us because they consider us to be a sensible, moderate party. And they are voting for us because they have a local Lib Dem council which governs effectively, efficiently, responsibly and well. You may not like that. You may not even consider it logical. But the polls show that it is a fact of life and we must play to it.

We finally agreed that this whole business of what language we use should be the main subject of our discussion when we next meet.

We then turned to the constitutional talks.

He said, 'Why do you think the talks aren't progressing well?'

I responded that there were three areas in which I thought they were going badly. First, it appeared from today's meeting that Labour didn't understand the absolute imperative to us of getting change to the electoral system in place before the election after next. Second, we were very disappointed indeed to hear that there was some doubt about introducing PR for the European elections – this would be a deal breaker, not least because we had understood this to be Labour Party policy.

Third, the key basic requirement which he and I had agreed upon was that he personally should state a preference for change. But this now appeared, both from his latest interview on *Frost* and from today's constitutional discussion, to be non-deliverable. Was this so?

He said that it was very difficult to see how he could now make that commitment. The leak last weekend hadn't helped. 'My guys are saying to me that I am being pushed around by you. If I make the statement you want me to make, then I fear it will look to the Tories as though I am wobbling and prepared to do a deal with you on issues that are important to you, but not to the country. That will be dangerous for me, dangerous for the whole project and, I think, dangerous for you.'

I reminded him that I would not have let the Cook/Maclennan talks start had it not been for the fact that he and I had made a private agreement that, before the election, he would make a statement in favour of change.

1 The Winter of Discontent.

If he was now changing his mind on that, then the best thing we could do was to withdraw as elegantly as possible.

He responded, 'I don't understand why you guys can't accept that a referendum is a good enough commitment. I have told you privately I am in favour of a change to the voting system provided we retain the single-member system. Can't you just accept that this is the position I will arrive at?'

I replied that of course I couldn't accept that. It was, after all, the same position that John Smith had taken. In which case, how had our relationship moved forward? At the end of the day, any vague agreement to introduce the possibility of PR without a commitment from him to support change was merely a return to the Lib–Lab pact with the Callaghan Government in which the Liberals lost out. I could not recommend that to my Party. If he couldn't deliver on our previous agreement then we should stop now. We would then campaign as the only party clearly committed to electoral reform and he would have to explain, like Neil Kinnock, why he was calling a referendum, while not saying how he would vote in it.

PA: After all, as Cherie said, we have still come a long way. Indeed, we have come further than we ever thought. I have no intention of going back. The concept of co-operation is now well planted in the public's mind and an amicable relationship has been well established. That's a lot to have achieved. But without you fulfilling your undertaking to me that you would personally make a statement in favour of change, and do so before the election, further progress before the election is impossible.

Of course, if you were prepared to make that commitment after the election, we could continue then to build on the ground we have already established. But that would be a disappointing end to a process which has started so well.

TB: I have become convinced of the need for electoral reform in Britain. But it is not as important to me as it is to you. I don't see it as fundamental. In due course, no doubt, we will bring in reform. But I am only prepared to put this up the agenda of priorities because it will open the way to a relationship with you. But I don't want it to end here. We should see where Bob and Robin get to. We thought that the proposition that we made to you, about holding an electoral commission, was a useful one. I can say that I am open-minded about the outcome of that and, when it produces its recommendations, I can announce that I am in favour of them. That gives me the cover that I need to change my mind. But that will happen after the election, not before. For the time being I must preserve my own position and I must not be seen to be being pushed around by you. I cannot therefore go further than 'I am not convinced of the need for electoral change.'

He pointed out to me that this was a different position from that of Margaret Beckett, for instance, who was definitely opposed.

Finally, towards the end of the meeting, he said, 'I have looked back at history. The great mistake was that Labour and the Liberals fought because they misunderstood each other in the early part of this century. They couldn't in the end bring themselves to make the agreements that were necessary to prevent the divisions of the left which have given the Tories so many chances they shouldn't have had. It would be a tragedy if we made the same mistake. I will give this matter some more thought. But you need to know how difficult it is. Nevertheless, I recognize the prizes that are on offer. At the end of the day, who knows, the two parties may combine again and we can mend the divisions on the left which have done so much damage in the early part of this century.'

I said that it would be an extraordinary achievement. I had made it clear to my people that, at the end of a long process of working together, who knows what the outcome may be? I was not closing off any options. We could do all sorts of things immediately the other side of the election. But what we had to do now – and time was running short – was to decide on what basis we went into an election only weeks away.

When I got home at 11.15 I rang Roy and told him about the meeting. I explained that this was a crucial moment. Blair was going back on the agreements we had privately made and I couldn't go further forward on this basis. I said that I found it extraordinary that Blair could put a halt to a potentially historic opportunity, simply because of a press leak. He promised to give Blair a call.

I went to bed feeling a bit better. I know that Roy's influence on Blair will be strong. The good news of the day, however, is that Bob has at least got the commission to agree that any new voting system will be a proportional one, so it won't be just AV. A step forward. But, taken with everything else that has happened, particularly the retrograde step on PR for Europe, I fear we are still making no real progress. We *must* change Blair's mind!

Friday, 17 January, London

Very nervous today. The *Daily Telegraph* has published a poll under a new system which gives us only 10.5 per cent. My heart sinks. I thought we were going up again. But our private polls in the constituencies, Chris Rennard tells me, look good.

Yesterday Roy Jenkins gave me a call – could we meet at lunchtime? He has fixed to see Blair on Sunday. I ran through the points I wanted him to make. The first was Blair's personal position. For Roy's own information only, I was prepared to compromise on this, but not yet and only if they reversed their retreat on Europe and injected some urgency into the proceedings. They think this can be delivered at any time. But for us it must be in place before the next election.

Then home by tube and a quiet evening in front of the television.

Monday, 20 January, Westminster

At 12.15 down to see Roy. He was not in as positive a mood as I have seen him before.

He said, 'My brain didn't seem to be working last night. Tony and I had a good dinner. But I am bound to agree with you that the project is not looking good. He feels he cannot now deliver what he promised you. Indeed, on the way out, he said, "Look, I am going to find it difficult to do what I want to do even to incorporate the Lib Dems in the next Government. My view is that if my majority is very large or very small then I may have more room for manoeuvre. But if it is in the mid range then I won't have as much [Roy didn't understand the logic behind this]. I don't suppose it would be acceptable just to have Paddy in the Cabinet?"' Roy, bless him, said, 'No, certainly not. That would destroy Paddy and I know he wouldn't accept it.' Roy continued, 'I could have got down to thinking about words last night but I didn't. However, I began to think about them this morning and have produced a wording on which I could act as honest broker between the pair of you. I have not put these to him yet. I wanted your view first.'

He then produced a typesheet. I made a minor amendment to it, then spent about thirty seconds in silence. 'Look, Roy, I need time to think about this.'

This was a cover for the fact that I do not think the words Roy has produced are acceptable. I promised to contact him before tomorrow to let him know whether to incorporate them in a letter he is going to send to Blair. This letter will say that he is pretty disappointed and believes that things are now going backwards. I took his form of words and went back to the office to consider them. I reworked them twice, once in a medium position and once in a tougher one. In my view, the tougher one is the very minimum that would now be acceptable.

Tuesday, 21 January, Westminster

Last night's Jo Group meeting agreed that Roy should not intervene at this stage. Instead, I should go and see Blair and tell him that we were close to breaking point and that I felt let down. I would not do this in anger, but in sorrow. The words I should use were that he had 'failed to deliver'.

At 12.00pm, off to see Tony.

PA: I suppose we have all anticipated that this project would hit rough water. And I think it has. I have come to mark up for you just how important I think this moment is. I am not sure I explained my concerns and disappointment as clearly as I should have done when we met before. But I want to flag up to you that this is, if not a crisis, then very close to one.

You will remember the meeting we had at Derry's house. You will remember that Jonathan Powell took minutes at that meeting. I have been looking at these. They are quite clear about our conditions for opening the Cook/Maclennan talks. We asked you to announce, before the election, that you were in favour of change (but not necessarily of PR). You said you would think about this. I have looked through my diary of the meeting that we had on 17 July. It is quite clear that we reached agreement that you would say publicly that you supported change, without necessarily supporting PR, before the election. It was on that basis alone that we went ahead.

Of course, I understand that things change in politics. But I am very disappointed indeed that you now feel you cannot deliver on this. I have been led into the position I feared most – that we would validate your agenda but leave ours unresolved, thereby exposing ourselves to the danger of holding out for what would be perceived as a private selfish enthusiasm of the Lib Dems [PR]. This is exactly the danger I now run because of your change of mind.

Secondly, I am bound to tell you that I find it very disturbing indeed that the very first time you and I reach an important private verbal agreement, you can't deliver. Frankly, I am not sure how much further we can go on this. You know how committed I am to it. This is a big event. But I cannot lead my Party into a position where the risks outweigh the advantages – and that is where I now find myself.

TB: In short, you see this as a breach of trust.

PA: That's too strong a word. We have made progress and I don't want to go backwards. But I want you to understand the depths of my concern and disappointment. We on our side are now having to think of exit strategies, and I do not want us to do that.

TB: I understand how you feel. I didn't expect things to turn out like this. But I have real problems with colleagues who say that to accede to what I agreed with you would be damaging to us and helpful to the Tories. I don't want PR to be part of the electoral agenda. [I confirmed the same view.] I don't want it to be discussed during the election at all. In my view, if I accede to what we have agreed, then this would become the centre of the General Election campaign. Which would be bad for us and good for the Tories.

PA: I think you are making a profound mistake. You are replaying the position taken by Neil Kinnock. You privately agree to change. You even privately agree to a proportional system. You want a referendum. But at very worst, you say you are going to vote against it (which is illogical to me), and at the very best, you say you are uncertain about it – which is exactly what Neil Kinnock did.

TB: Dear God, I don't want to get into that position. But I don't think I am. I can quite happily say that, while I am presently unpersuaded, this matter will be decided by a commission, when I will be able to consider it again.

PA: Well, that is exactly where you can't be as far as we are concerned. On the present presumption, you would vote 'no' in any referendum. That is intolerable to us. And it is precisely the opposite of what you promised.

TB: But I would respond to questioning along the lines of, 'If I was asked in a referendum how I would vote today, I would vote no' and leave it open as to whether I might change in the future.

I started to get a little angry.

PA: But that is exactly the opposite of what you promised you would do. To be open-minded is bad enough. But to publicly say that you are going to vote against change in a referendum is just unacceptable. You cannot be surprised that we are beginning to prepare exit strategies from this. And that we feel pretty aggrieved in the process.

TB: I don't understand why you guys aren't prepared to accept that we have come a long way in committing to a referendum. After all, it could have been kicked into touch. But thanks to me, it has been brought forward so that it will be held in the next parliament. Why is that not enough for you? Particularly since I have now given you a private undertaking that I would be prepared to accept a proportional system recommended by the commission. But I need the commission's cover to change my mind.

I wanted to shut the discussion down here, before it got worse.

PA: It is clear we are hitting a major blockage here. We may have to think about how we break this off in good order. The main thing is not to have a public rupture, and to try and make sure that we can claim the outcome as a success, even though we know it isn't. But let's at least leave it to the Cook/Maclennan team to see if they can close the gap further. In the end I suppose it will mean you and I coming together to cut a deal – if there is one to be cut.

We parted, saying that we would fix the larger meeting soon.

Wednesday, 22 January, Westminster

Into the office for an hour's work. Then saw Bob at 9.15. We talked over how to handle the PR roadblock and looked over the words we had been working on. Bob suggested that Blair couldn't be asked to move the whole distance from the position he was now in, to where we wanted. The best thing would be to get him to use the Roy Jenkins form of words first and then, when the constitution talks had finished, ours. This would enable him to lever himself forward in small steps. A good suggestion.

Tuesday, 28 January, Westminster

Bob tells me they had a dreadful meeting on the Cook/Maclennan committee. Labour have started unstitching all their agreements. A concerted attempt to try and break up the talks. Bob responded pretty strenuously.

Cook, apparently, was livid with his colleagues, and went with Bob to his office afterwards and, in his presence, rang Blair saying, 'The talks are in crisis and I am furious. I want a meeting with you within thirty-six hours.' It was clear that the other participants, whether with Cook's knowledge or not, are trying to wreck the thing. A bad day.

Wednesday, 29 January, London

Breakfast with the Jo Group. This was actually quite fun. A full cooked breakfast and a full turn-out. We talked through the words we wanted Blair to use on PR. And also the end position we ourselves wanted to reach.

Then I gave them the partnership document that I had composed on 1 January. Strenuous discussion about this. Every person around the table advised me against it. They all said it was a step too far. And all of them listed in loving detail why taking that step would be so very dangerous.

I let them all have their say, then said, in a controlled but increasingly angry voice, 'Look, of course you all see the downside to this. But why do we always look at the worst aspect of things and why do we agree things which you want me to achieve and then, when I have done them, blow them out of the water?

'We all agreed to go ahead on the basis outlined in this partnership paper. We agreed it had to be substantially changed from the first one. So I go away and write this, then you tell me it is wrong and produce a hundred reasons why it cannot be done.

'It remains my belief that Blair and I saying this kind of thing will give an immense shot in the arm to a very tired and jaded electorate looking forward with some trepidation to a miserable and negative General Election campaign. The effect could be really dramatic. And I cannot see that we are saying or doing anything different here. I am proposing no more than we have already agreed. In most incidences things Tories can agree with, too. You miss completely in your calculations the positive aspects of this. I am grateful to you for all your views. But you need to understand that if I am to do this it will be a personal decision made between the two leaders.'

At 2.30, to see David Montgomery of the *Daily Mirror*. We discussed the 'pincer movement' that we and Labour could pull on the Tories with the help of tactical voting. I left him with a list of seats where the Tories could be ousted by the Lib Dems if the *Mirror* encouraged Labour voters to vote for us.[1]

Monday, 3 February, Westminster

I am feeling absolutely lousy this morning. Terribly stuffed-up and a vicious sore throat. I cannot remember feeling like this for ages – perhaps not since the 1992 election.

At 3 o'clock we had a manifesto costings meeting in the flat, with David Laws[2] and William Wallace, at which we went through some of the key issues. There is a hole of about £700m in our costings. We had some very tough decisions to take about core issues: parental rights; 16- to 18-year-olds' benefits; the restoration of rights to asylum seekers; and child benefit. Conrad Russell will be the key in this. I asked William to try to get him on side on some of the key issues. I can see a way through, but it is not going to be easy. So we will keep the approval process for the final version of the manifesto by the Parliamentary Party and the Federal Policy Committee until the last minute so as to diminish their ability to unstitch it.

At 8 o'clock David Steel came round for dinner. He quickly revealed why he had asked to see me. He had apparently been approached by 'very senior and influential people in the Parliamentary Party', who said they had anticipated that I would have a bust-up with them all at last July's all-day Parliamentary Party meeting in Oxford, and that I might have walked out.[3] They are now worried that I might put forward a similar proposition for a relationship with Blair which would be rejected and that I would resign as Leader. Would he then be prepared to step in as a caretaker? He had sent them away with a flea in their ear. But I need to be aware of the danger.

---

1 This list was later reproduced almost word for word in the *Mirror* with the recommendation to its readers that they voted tactically to remove the local Tory. It was also reprinted in other friendly national newspapers to whom I subsequently gave it.
2 Economic Senior Researcher for the Party. David went on to become the Director of Policy. He is now the Prospective Parliamentary Candidate for my seat of Yeovil.
3 See diary entry for 12 July 1996.

Friday, 5 February, Westminster

At 11.15, I had asked for a few minutes with Tony alone before the larger meeting of 3+3 (TB and myself, Robin Cook and Peter Mandelson from Labour, Ming Campbell and Bob Maclennan from our side). In the fifteen minutes before the others arrived he explained the problem from their point of view.

He showed me a letter from Ann Taylor, which listed the referendums they would have to have 'if we acceded to the Liberals' demands'. This included referendums for PR for Scotland, PR for Europe, PR for Wales and PR for Westminster, and ended up with the phrase: 'If we do all this, we will appear plain daft.'

TB: That's not necessarily my view. But what I am concerned about is that if we come to an agreement at this stage which introduces a mass of constitutional reform legislation, then that will immediately send signals that I have done a deal with you. That won't help me and it won't help you. But more importantly, it will enable the Tories to portray the whole thing as a ludicrous stitch-up.

My own private view is that we can do the Europe thing [PR for the Euro elections], but we shouldn't flag it beforehand. We should stick to our present position, leave it to be assumed by the public that that's what will happen in 1999. I want to leave that opaque. And, similarly, I think we can get the referendum on PR for Westminster through in time for the election after next. But I don't want to say so beforehand, because it will open us up to the attack of being more interested in constitutional reform than real things that matter in Britain. I am trying to ensure that PR isn't discussed during the campaign.

PA: This is the second thing we have agreed on which you now appear to be backtracking. I have already explained to you that PR for Europe by the next Euro elections is an absolute essential requirement of ours – a deal breaker. If we are to get ourselves into any lasting relationship with you, PR is essential. No need to rehearse the arguments. But why are we going into reverse again?

He said that we weren't going into reverse. It would be put into effect. But there was no point in flagging this up before the election.

PA: I simply don't understand what you are trying to achieve here. PR for European elections is Labour Party policy. The public assumption must be that you want it for 1999. If you leave the question open someone will ask you, 'Well, are you going to do this by 1999?' If you then sound equivocal, it will be reported as a retreat over PR on Europe as well. We cannot, we simply cannot, be tied into negotiations which produce an outcome which, far from enabling Labour to progress on PR, actually covers your retreat.

At this point the rest of the group came in. Mandelson very pointedly took his coat off and sat on the sofa alongside Tony. One of Robin's office staff was there to take notes.

Tony opened up, repeating much of what he had just said to me.

At one stage he said, 'Look, I live in a different world from you lot. I have to deal on a day-to-day basis with this ravenous beast [the Tory press]. They are out there waiting for me on this. It would be simply incredible if we filled up the agenda of the next parliament with constitutional things.

'Then there is the question of language. Our lot are getting very nervous. They are saying, "Why are you going so far to accommodate the Lib Dems when all they do is attack us?"

'These are the two things we just have to get sorted out.

'Finally, there is my own position. I have to do what I am comfortable with on this. I can't be driven by you lot into making constitutional change *the* issue at the next election. I want to emphasize other things. If the Tories can drag us on to PR they can get away from their record. I know why you guys want something different. You want the whole PR issue up in lights because then it will show that you have achieved something. But my aim is the exact opposite.'

I immediately came in. 'Two brief points. The first is that we absolutely do *not* want the PR issue up in lights. If it is never talked about again I shall be perfectly happy. I would like to fight this election on bread-and-butter issues, too. But we do need substantial progress on PR. We can't enter talks at the end of which your commitment to PR is actually weakened. My Party is already suspicious of you on this. And I will tell you why. It is because, whenever we have got into these discussions with you lot before, you have stuffed us. There may be – there is – trust here. But there is none in my Party at large that if you say you will do something, it will be done. That's why a clear commitment is absolutely essential. It would be particularly intolerable to us if the outcome of the Cook/Maclennan negotiation was a retreat from your current position on PR for Europe. I would then be torn apart by both my party and the press. And rightly so. To use our relationship to move forward is one thing. To use the talks to provide you with cover for a retreat is quite another.

'Secondly, there is the question of the language we use in attacking you.

I want to make it clear again that we use this language precisely because there isn't a deal. And it will have to be like this if we continue on the present basis, without agreement. But the moment there is a deal, we fully accept we will have to change our language. I have said to my people that, under those circumstances, we would want to follow two principles. The first is that we would not use language that echoes the Tories in attacking you. The second is that our general principle would be to "play the ball, not the man" – we attack your policies, not your people. I would expect all our main players to adhere to these disciplines, but only if we put a deal together.

'You don't have to explain to the press and the public why you exist,' I continued. 'We do. And to be precise, we have to explain why we are not the Labour Party. That means pointing up some of the differences between us. But surely that's what all this is about? We agreed long ago that co-operative politics ought to be about agreeing where we agree, and respecting our differences where we don't.'

Bob then spoke at length about the constitutional stuff. He prefaced his remarks by saying that he really wanted the talks to succeed. It was the biggest opportunity he had ever had during his life in politics. Of course there would be those in our Party who would object to it; it was simply unthinkable, however, that we should fail. That would be a terrible blow to the whole cause of reform, and a gift to the Tories. However, Tony and his team needed to realize that there were some things on which we really could not compromise. Labour's policy for PR on Europe was one. How could they possibly withdraw on that now?

Tony responded about the dangers of legislative overload and finished with some comments on PR for Europe. 'Look, if I were suddenly to announce that Labour policy for PR on Europe was going to be in place by 1999, that would be a big story.'

I interjected that I didn't see how it could possibly be a big story since they had already said that. Interestingly, Peter came in for the first time to say that he didn't think it would be a big story either, 'But of course, I defer to you on this matter.'

Tony came back, 'No, I defer to you on these things.' It was meant ironically, but it was closer to the truth than a joke.

Peter said that, though he didn't think the press was the problem, legislative overload was, and he went through the various pieces of legislation we would have to get through. He continued, 'I am really worried that we could get totally bogged down in this. That we do nothing else in the next parliament but constitutional reform. That the Tories are able to fight a sort of guerrilla war against us on every front. I just don't see how it is going to work.'

At this stage it became apparent that there is a clear split between the position Tony is taking (that it can be done, but that we shouldn't say so beforehand) and what Peter is saying (that it is very difficult to do).

Bob swiftly interjected after Peter had finished, saying, 'There is a clear precedent for a legislative programme which changes the face of Britain. It has been done before. By Herbert Morrison. He had the political will to get it through.' It was a deadly jab (Morrison was Peter's grandfather) and drew an immediately riposte from Peter, 'But he was a great man.' We all laughed.

Robin came in, saying that if Labour threw PR for Europe beyond 1999, then that *would* be a story. It would be portrayed as yet another Labour retreat from an established commitment. He said, 'I think we can arrive at an agreement here. In the case of a referendum for PR for Westminster, we can express due urgency. For instance, we could say that the commission should get started in the first year. And that the referendum should happen as soon as possible after that. Whether or not it went forward from the referendum result to legislation would in large measure depend on the result of the referendum anyway. A large majority would make it urgent; a small one less so.'

I said, 'I think these two [pointing to Bob and Robin] can sort this out. But we must make sure that those on your team who are clearly hostile will be told what the outcome will be. If the Labour team on this were as co-operative as we all are in this room, reaching agreement wouldn't be difficult. But they are not and we know that.'

Robin responded, 'Yes, there is going to have to be a meeting in which those who want to hold this up will be told what the score is.' (A clear, but unspoken reference to Jack Straw.)

Tony responded by saying, 'No doubt those who look as if they are trying to hold it up are merely expressing caution.' Bob then reminded him that one of the (preposterous) reasons that had been put forward by their side for not holding an earlier referendum was that it would be a spending commitment and Gordon wouldn't agree. Much laughter. We agreed at this point to leave Bob and Robin to see if they could find a form of words on two areas: Europe and PR for Westminster. Tony interjected, 'I will want to have a look at that very closely.'

I said to him, 'There is the final point about you and the form of words that you use. Let my explain what I think we have to do. Your present position is one of assumed hostility. At the very least, we must find a way for you to move to a position of positive open-mindedness. I have a few words that may help towards this.'

To which he replied, 'So have I, let's meet.'

I had a chat with Robin afterwards in the corridor of the Shadow Cabinet room. I said, 'I think we can find a way around the referendum timing. I simply don't understand Tony's position on PR for Europe. He has to move off this.'

Robin replied, 'I quite agree. His position is untenable. He can't fudge on this one. We have a commitment already and the presumption is that it will be enacted by 1999. There is, as Bob pointed out in the meeting, a Labour Bill already in existence[1] which can be taken down off the shelf. His idea that he can maintain neutrality simply won't stand up to scrutiny.'

We agreed to keep in touch.

Monday, 10 February, Westminster

At 11.40, to see Tony.

We got quickly down to business.

TB: I have seen the leak in today's *Times*.[2] I greatly fear that this probably did come from one of the Shadow Cabinet. I have just dealt with it at the press conference. I disposed of it swiftly. It wasn't difficult.

PA: We really must stop this negotiation by leaks. Of course it can happen from both sides, and no doubt it has happened from ours, too. But it is very unhelpful.

I know you are meeting with your people this afternoon, so I thought it was worthwhile to lay out our position very firmly. I have brought with me some suggested words which we worked on over the weekend. They concern both Europe and the issue of the commission and timing. If you can agree with this, we can go along with it. I understand that these words are broadly those already negotiated between Bob and Robin, though I have added a few of my own.

---

1 The Callaghan PR for Europe Bill.
2 Jill Sherman of *The Times* had written a piece, backed by an editorial, which stated that Blair was 'expected to drop his party's pledge to stage a referendum on proportional representation during the first term of a Labour Government, in a U-turn which could sour relations with the Liberal Democrats'.

I then gave him a copy of the words:

The European Parliament *(Cook/Maclennan proposed words)*
It is the purpose of both our Parties to improve the democratic account-
ability of the European Union institutions.

The next elections to the European Parliament will take place in 1999.
Member countries are due to consider, in the Inter-Governmental Confer-
ence (IGC), the implementation of the obligation to introduce a common
system of election to the European Parliament.

The last Labour Government, with Liberal support, introduced a Bill in
1977 to give effect to a proportional system (the Regional List System) and
since then the Plant Commission has confirmed that system for European
Elections.

It remains the policy of both Labour and the Liberal Democrats that
member countries should seek agreement on a common system of election
and that, prior to that agreement being reached, elections in Britain to the
European Parliament should be by the system set out in the 1977 Bill.

TB: This is going a long way. It is very strong. I am now hitting very strong resistance on the issue of Europe in particular. We still have some difficulty with individuals on our side. I just can't go this far.

PA: In which case you must realize that this is a break issue for us.

TB: I am keen, as you know – and as I have repeated to you on several occasions – to ensure that PR is not talked about during the election. So I don't want to raise this spectre just at the moment.

PA: I understand your view. But if we can reach an agreement on this, then it won't be discussed. It will be tied up with a bow and put in a cupboard until afterwards. So the best way to achieve what you want is not to leave things vague, but to be sufficiently clear for everyone to know where you stand.

We then went on to the wordings on the commission and the referendum:

Electoral Reform *(Cook/Maclennan proposed words)*
It is the policy of both Labour and the Liberal Democrats to give the British
people an early opportunity, through a referendum, to decide whether they
wish to reform our electoral system and to implement that choice, as
appropriate.

The Joint Committee proposes that, in order to offer a clear choice of
voting systems in such a referendum between the status quo and a suitable

proportional alternative, a commission should be appointed immediately after the General Election, following consultation between the two party leaders, and other parties as appropriate. The commission will be charged with the formulation of that alternative to first past the post, as soon as possible.

The commission would be broad based and have the following remit: 'To recommend a proportional voting system for subsequent elections to the House of Commons which, taking account of all relevant factors, is most suitable to be put to the British people in a referendum, as an alternative to the first past the post system.'

He had no objections to these. Finally, we turned to the words he would use to describe his own position.

PA: You no doubt want to find your own words. But I have drafted a few which we think would meet our concerns, for you to think about. The important thing here is for us to have from you an expression of opinion which shifts away from the perception of hostility to change, to, at least, open-mindedness about it.

I handed the words to him.

Suggested words to be used by Tony Blair on PR when Cook/Maclennan announce

I well know the flaws in our present system and recognize the case for change. Yet, as I have said previously, I remain unpersuaded of the case for any particular alternative system.

However, I have agreed with Paddy Ashdown that a broad-based commission will be established, following the formation of a Labour Government, to see if a proportional system can be found which gives the advantage of fairness and fuller choice for the voters, without the disadvantages of severing the links between a Member of Parliament and their constituency, or creating instability.

If such a system can be identified, I would be prepared to support it. I certainly would not have committed Labour to a referendum on this issue of electoral reform if my mind were firmly closed to its merits.

TB: I can't say the first sentence of the last paragraph.

PA: Why not? After all, if the commission does come up with a sensible proposition, we both know you are going to accede to it. This is only common sense – no more.

He went off again about the Tory press.

TB: Look, I know what goes on inside the Tory press. My antennae are very good on them. I have a better judgement on this than almost anybody else, including you. I believe that they don't mind having me in for a term if that means that they can put their Party back together again under a right-wing leader and then have a chance to come back next time. But if we change the rules on elections they will know they can never get back again. And then the whole mass of the Tory media will be deployed against me. I don't want that.

Our meeting ended with an agreement to leave this unresolved and return to it later.

I left feeling betrayed. He knows perfectly well what we agreed before this whole process started and he has not delivered.

Bob contacted me at 11.30 in the evening. He thinks that the talks are going well, suddenly. A much better mood. Donald Dewar is being particularly helpful. And a deal seems to be emerging. Our private meetings appear to be having an effect. They have now agreed that they will exchange a firm date on PR for the European Parliament for an agreement from us to cease hostilities over the two-question referendum in Scotland. I am nervous at being seen to make concessions on Scotland in order to deliver something for England, but providing Labour does not ask for too much we should be able to arrive at a sensible agreement with Jim (Wallace). Bob thought so too.

I went to bed at about midnight but lay awake most of the night. I was half cheered up by the possibility that we were now out of the thicket. But half worried about the fact that, in order to tempt Blair to accept the deal, I had more or less agreed to make a joint statement. What impact would this have? When would we do it?

After our meeting, I sent the following unsigned, hastily prepared minute to confirm the points discussed:

One of the reasons why I was keen for you and me to agree to the components of the 'end position' of the Robin/Bob talks before they started was to avoid just this kind of last-minute hassle. But needs must.

First, my aim in all this is, as yours, to ensure that we don't discuss PR, etc., in the election. My view is that the best way to do this is to come to an agreement which closes the door on this now. If we cannot agree, then our differences will be part of the election campaign, not least because, on our side, we will no doubt be pointing them up as a point of differentiation, not agreement.

Secondly, I hope, as you do, that this is the cornerstone of a wider ranging co-operation between us. If we can agree on the constitutional package, then I would want to consider going further before the election, along the lines we have already discussed.

Failure to agree would, therefore, be a tragedy. It would mean that it would be much more difficult to start the process of a wider rapprochement after the General Election. And that the Tories would celebrate and that PR would be a matter to be debated between us in the open at the election, instead of locked away 'out of sight' in the agreement.

I do not want this to happen.

But we still have three key points which are bottom line ones for us:

1. Your attitude   *Of course your words are for you to find. But I have made it clear over the past two years that they are, nevertheless, an integral part of the deal. As I have often said, we could not commit to a process which included a referendum where you were arguing for no change . . . We have compromised a lot in the substance, etc. But we could not put our hand to a deal where the public perception of your position is hostility (even though I know this is not your private position). I can, under the circumstances, live with a perception of open-mindedness, but not one of perceived hostility – which is where we are at present.*

2. Europe   *The difficulty over Europe has come as a complete surprise. We had no inkling before that this was a problem. We can no doubt leave this open in suitable words. But you are bound to be asked about it. Since the public perception of Labour policy is that PR will be in place for 1999, anything less than reaffirmation of this will be taken as a retreat. This is a break point for us.*

3. The electoral reform commission   *It seems from your reaction that we have found an acceptable form of words for this. The key thing for us is to start the commission work straight away after the election with the referendum as soon as possible afterwards. I hope this is now OK?*

If we fail to agree on all this, we can no doubt find agreement on the other elements of the constitutional agenda and then preserve our differences over PR. But this will mean that the other steps which ought to flow from agreement, can't; that our 'language' will be bound to reflect this; that we will be making PR an election issue and a point of difference between us;

and that the larger scheme we had hoped to achieve will be much less likely now, and much more difficult in the future.

Tuesday, 11 February, Westminster

A very busy day, mostly discussing the manifesto.

We spent until 1.30 going through the manifesto document. We only got through half of it. We will need another day.

Blair had been trying to reach me, so I rang his office to say I was available. We fixed to speak in the afternoon. I hope this results in the breakthrough. Bob is optimistic.

At 4 o'clock Bob came to see me about today's talks. Very good atmosphere. They were making progress, he thought. He was due to see Robin Cook later on today.

At 5.40 a telephone call as pre-arranged with Tony.

TB: I'm sorry I haven't managed to get back to you before now. Life has been very busy. I am meeting some very heavy-duty opposition. I think we broadly agreed about the commission and the referendum. I gather you guys want this to report within a year? That seems a pretty short order to me.

PA: I think it's a *long* time! Surely a commission like this ought to be able report well within a year? We would hope for something before that.

TB: Look, my lot are in a pretty rebellious mood at the moment and I am finding it difficult to hold them to this. They also tell me that, apparently, you are demanding that we should exclude AV from the systems that the commission would investigate.

PA: Yes, they agreed that in the committee some time ago. They agreed that the commission would investigate proportional systems only.

TB: And that excludes AV?

PA: Yes, you said so yourself on the *Frost* programme. AV with a top-up system, fine; but AV by itself is not proportional.

TB: But the point is this, we don't think it should exclude AV.

PA: This is becoming intolerable. We are now going backwards. That's what was agreed and it now appears that you are reopening the whole thing.

TB: You mean it was agreed at the meeting that was held this morning? Because I certainly didn't hear from my lot that they had agreed it yesterday.

PA: No, this was agreed some weeks ago and our capacity to compromise on other things has been as a direct result of our accepting this as an important concession on your part that needed a response from us. If you are now retracing your steps, we might as well pack the thing in now. I get the impression your right hand doesn't know what your left hand is doing. This habit of reopening issues that have been closed makes the whole negotiation process quite impossible. I will check this out again with Bob. But I am quite clear, and so are the rest on our team, that this is something that was agreed with your lot some time ago. And that it was explicitly accepted that AV by itself was excluded from the Commission's remit.

TB: Well, look, I will just have to speak to our people again about this.

Secondly, though, I want to talk about Europe. Of course we remain committed. But if we are asked to expand on this, we cannot commit ourselves definitely to doing it for the 1999 Euros. The best I can say is that we will try and do it.

PA: But the public perception is that you are committed to PR and the presumption is that this is for the 1999 Euro elections. If you now say that you will only try and do that, then we will be giving you cover for what will be written up, quite rightly, as a retreat.

TB: But we are not going to be asked that question. If you don't prompt it, no press person is going to ask it. Why don't we just leave it like that?

PA: You are wrong about this. Someone is certain to ask whether PR for Europe applies to 1999. And unless you give a clear answer the whole thing will come apart. The very least you should say on this is that it has always been your intention and remains so.

TB: No. I can't go that far. I am happy that it is presumed to be 1999. And I am certain that no one is going to question us about this.

PA: Well, I am certain they are and I can't take the risk.

Wednesday, 12 February, Westminster

Andrew Marr came to see me at 8 o'clock. Blair and the *Independent* have had several run-ins.

Marr said, 'I just don't know that he is a reformer. I just don't know that when he gets in there he is not going to get together in cosy little huddles with people like Paul Dacre[1] and sort things out from inside Downing Street.

'I used to be certain who he was. But I am not certain now. We have had one or two run-ins with them and we are probably going to have to say that we are not clear that he is a reformer and that it is the *Independent*'s job to push him. I think you should be playing the same role.'

I told him about the European retreat. He said of course we couldn't tolerate this. He would understand and so would others if we broke over this issue. It was a small issue – perhaps even a rather technical one. But it was a talisman. If they retreated on this they couldn't be trusted on anything else.

Sunday, 16 February, London

Following our failure to agree on Thursday, I arranged to go to Tony's house for a drink at 6.00pm. I arrived promptly and we talked for about an hour.

I started by saying, 'We need to decide now how far we can go. But first of all, I need to know why you can't deliver what you promised last October.'

TB: I'm sorry about that. I recognize how exposed it leaves you. But my perception hasn't changed. I must do what I believe is deliverable. I have become increasingly certain that a change on PR would both weaken my position and help the Tories. They are just waiting for me to do it. That's why Major has opened up on the constitutional agenda and, in particular, why he has been careful recently to mention PR in that context. I think we are already at risk of going too far. But I recognize what a difficult position I have put you in.

We had several minutes' discussion on this.

1 Editor of the *Daily Mail*.

He then talked about the words he would use on electoral change.

TB: I said to you that I was in favour of AV and making an announcement to that effect. Or, if we couldn't do that, I would just say I was in favour of electoral change. I can't do that now. I can, however, find a form of words which I think will satisfy you. I have been thinking of saying in an interview in the next few weeks, something like, 'You know my position on PR. I remain unpersuaded. However, I would not have agreed to this commission with Paddy Ashdown if my mind was entirely closed. Let's see what the commission comes up with and I am happy to reconsider then.'

I said that these were the right kind of words. They closely reflected what I had given him last time, but that they didn't go far enough – he needed, at the very least, to say that he recognized the flaws in our present system.

TB: To be fair, I have already done that. But I am prepared to go further and recognize that there are unfairnesses in the present system. I don't think we will have difficulty about that.

I moved the conversation on.

PA: Well, that means that the single outstanding item which we need to resolve is PR for Europe by 1999.

TB: I don't think it will be a problem. It can be delivered. But I just don't want us to say so. It is going far too far, what with everything else we have on – Wales, Scotland, a referendum for Europe, Freedom of Information, a Bill of Rights, etc. And, of course, a referendum on PR. I just don't want to add Europe to the list.

PA: But nobody cares about Europe. This isn't the one that matters. I really can't see the Tories getting upset about this. The Tories' newspapers are certainly not going to object to PR for Europe. It's Westminster, not Strasbourg, that is the big deal for them – particularly since everybody has assumed that your position is PR for Europe in 1999, anyway. But if you leave the door the slightest bit open then that will be portrayed as a retreat. If that happens, you will do yourself more harm than good. Robin and Peter both reminded you of that during our last meeting.

TB: There really is a hell of a lot to do in the next parliament. I am not sure that we can get it through. How would we find the time? This is a big piece of legislation, not a small one.

PA: No, it is a small piece of legislation.

TB: Look, I know the legislation exists. But it will be tough to get through the House. And then we will have to redraw all the boundaries, etc.

PA: No, you don't have to redraw the boundaries. You have been badly advised on this. It is a regional list system. We can keep the boundaries as they are. So it really is a small thing.

TB: But we would have to reselect our candidates.

PA: Oh, so that's the problem. You are worried about problems with your candidates.

TB (defensively): Of course I'm not worried about my candidates, I can easily deal with them. But what about the system?

PA: We have already agreed the system. It is a regional list system. Your party's policy and mine are exactly the same.

He agreed to go away and think about it again. We then had a long discussion about language.

TB: We have to find a language that we can criticize each other in. I do not want you, either in the course of the election campaign or before, to so provoke our lot that they start attacking you. The key thing, however, is that you and I get our language right. I think we have done that and can continue to do so.

I told him, in general terms, about our chosen electoral theme – 'Liberal Democrats will make the difference' – but I also said that we would be telling the voters, 'Your teachers have been sacked, your hospitals are in crisis. The Tories have done this. But Labour won't put it right. We will. That's how we will make the difference.'

TB: I recognize that's what you have to do. I much prefer that to some of the other stuff that is going on. You keep on attacking us and our people keep on wanting to respond. I have told them not to. I don't think it helps, particularly since I can tell you privately that our polls are showing us dangerously high in some of your seats. It doesn't do us any good to drag you down. But it doesn't do you any good to demonize us, either. Our polls are also showing that, whereas you used to be viewed as a moderate party, you are now seen as moving to the left. That's why I am saying to our people that they really mustn't make the case that you are the high-tax party. That won't help you win seats. There is no point in us coming a good third in your target seats, if that means local Tories getting back in. I am, again, particularly struck by our polls in the South West – not only by how high we are in them, but about what a commanding position you have in seats we can't get at. There is just no point in acting in a way which gives the Tories ten extra seats that you could win. What can we do about this?

PA: There is no way you and I can get involved in this. That would be a disaster. You know that I have privately reached an agreement with the *Mirror*?

TB: Yes, I heard. That's a good thing. The *Mirror* will be very important in this. I have encouraged them to help you. What else can you and I do? I must give this some more thought.

PA: I already have. As I said, we can't get directly involved. But we could perhaps license some mavericks to say things we can't say. We could then mildly deny them – but the effect would have been created. I was thinking of perhaps letting Shirley Williams and Bill Rodgers call for tactical voting. I could say, 'Oh, it's just old Shirley. She's always up to this.' Who could you have do the same thing? Callaghan, for instance?

TB: No chance of that. I don't think he's in favour anyway.

PA: What about Hattersley?

He gave this some thought and said, 'Yes, that is a possibility. I might have a word with him. He thinks you lot are necessary to keep us radical. So it may be worth a try.'

I then suggested Kinnock and he responded first by saying, 'No, he couldn't do that. Not as an ex-Party Leader.' Then he gave it a few moments thought and said, 'But I am not absolutely certain. Perhaps Neil could do this. I will have a word with him. I think it is a very good idea and I will pursue it.'

I told him about how we would handle a hung Parliament and that we had already had discussions with Robin Butler and Robin Fellowes.

I said we had drawn up plans which will be finalized shortly. 'When we have done this – and to avoid misunderstandings in the crucial few hours after the election – I will give you a bowdlerized version of our plans for a hung Parliament which you can put in your safe for after election day.'

TB: I have been giving this a lot of thought as well. I now know what needs to be done. The question is how I do it. It is going to be tough. I must work out what the process will be.

PA: The important thing is that you know how we believe things should develop so that you don't misunderstand what we say and do in the immediate aftermath of the General Election. But what happens then will be up to you. I will respond in the light of the circumstances we find ourselves in.

I left shortly after 7.00pm.

Tuesday, 25 February, Westminster

I have had long telephone discussions with Bob today about preparing for the day's meeting of the Cook/Maclennan Committee. He came into my office late last night and, over a glass of whisky, showed me the form of words on which he had agreement from Robin Cook. We agreed that the words themselves were all right but much depended on what Labour said in answer to questions at the press conference. In particular, the words they are proposing on the European Parliament still leave open the possibility for Labour to delay beyond 1999. I said we had to get agreement from Robin Cook that, in any response to questions, he would use words which would confirm the 1999 position. The important thing is to get Cook to do this ahead of Blair.

Bob reported back later that the Cook/Maclennan session had gone well. Cook had got through the words, slightly amended. A negotiating triumph for Bob.

But we're not there yet. On questions about PR for Europe the door is still too wide open. I have to tie Blair down. And that can only be done between us personally. I will go and see him for a final crunch meeting.

I don't want them running away with the idea that it has all been done, however. So I phoned Tony's office to say that it was good that they had agreed, but he and I still had to confirm and as far as I was concerned, everything was 'in square brackets' (i.e., we could agree nothing if we couldn't agree everything). It all depended on his possible answers to questions on PR for Europe.

I am not in a strong bargaining position, however. The main items have been agreed and it will be difficult for me now to exercise any leverage on him about the words that he uses on the crucial issue of PR for Europe.

I am still worried about next Wednesday's launch of the Cook/Maclennan agreement. So is Nick. We agreed with Labour that we will not sound triumphalist. I don't even mind Labour claiming a success out of it. I think the press will see through that, anyway. And the fact is that we have almost everything we want.

Wednesday, 26 February, Westminster

At 4.30 Rosie Boycott, the new editor of the *Independent On Sunday*. I asked her what her paper was going to do during the election. Back Blair, was her answer. She thinks Blair is right and she trusts him. But she is up for 'the project', too.

I told her that Blair and I had, of course, been meeting for a long time. That our relations were close. She asked me whether there was anything in the agreement about targeting seats. I said that the figures spoke for themselves. There didn't have to be an agreement. Could I leave her with a list of seats so that she could see the way that in some areas voting Labour would simply be letting the Tories in?

I gave her the same document we had given to the *Mirror*. I said that the most useful thing they could do if they wanted a Blair Government was to advise people to vote Labour where Labour could win, but to back us in places where we could beat the Tories. She said she would do this. A useful meeting.

Now only the *Independent*, *Guardian* and *FT* to go.

At about five past seven the phone rang: Jonathan Powell from Blair's office. 'Look, I have bad news. The *Observer* has just rung. They read out to us sections of the constitutional agreement. It is clear from internal checks that they have the latest document. There are only two documents in existence. One is Bob Maclennan's and the other is Tony's.' The clear implication was that we had leaked it. I assured him that we hadn't and immediately bleeped Bob and Jane Bonham-Carter. We had a swift discussion on what we should do. Bob confirmed that during the latest committee talks, people had been scribbling extensive notes while the document was in their hands. I rang Jonathan back. He had revised his earlier view and said that the *Observer* didn't in fact have the document – they had just read extracts from it. But these were extracts from the latest one. I said to him, 'Yes, well, that is almost certainly somebody noting it down during the committee meeting.' I assured him again that it wasn't one of us. Then I bleeped Richard. We quickly decided that if the *Observer* was running this on Sunday (the worrying thing from the Labour point of view was the *Observer*'s spin that Blair had caved in to us on PR), we really must pre-empt them.

I suggested that we should launch early, perhaps tomorrow or Friday. I put this to Jonathan, who, having contacted Blair, came back saying, not surprisingly, that Blair was against this. Blair is very angry. And justifiably so. He still thinks it is us trying to bounce him.

I then rang Jonathan and said, 'Look, it is not in our interest to have this story run in the way the *Observer* wants to run it. Please tell Tony that we are partners with him in this. We will do what we can to persuade the

Observer not to publish the story as a victory for us and a defeat for you. I want him to know that tonight. How we do it, we can discuss when we meet tomorrow.'

Jonathan thanked me and said that would be reassuring.[1]

Sunday, 2 March, London

A very bitter and badly informed article from Andrew Adonis in the *Observer*. It is clear that Labour is briefing like mad. I am furious about this, since we played the game and succeeded in persuading the paper not to go ahead with something which was too beneficial to us. Meanwhile, Labour has briefed to make the whole thing into a triumph for them. Bob is very upset. Fed up with Andrew Adonis especially. He is going into one of his moods of deep depression.

Monday, 3 March, London

I had previously spoken to Bob Maclennan. He told me he stayed awake most of the night and that he had decided that the Adonis article – and the clear implications that Labour had been briefing against us – were just too much for him. He had rung Cook already and said that he wanted to stop the talks going ahead. He told Cook that he felt they would now end in failure. They had a meeting scheduled for Tuesday, but as far as Bob was concerned the talks were at an end unless Labour changed its view on PR for Europe. This is, of course, Bob being highly emotional. On the other hand, he is a brilliant player of brinkmanship in negotiations.

Tony rang me as agreed at 8 o'clock. He said it was all very difficult. He was facing a near rebellion in his Party. I said things were difficult my end, too. Bob wanted to end the talks as he felt there had been a breach of faith. It was up to Tony and me to sort this out tonight.

At 6.15, Becky drove me through rain and heavy traffic to Blair's house.

When I pressed the doorbell a female voice said, 'Who is it?' I felt a little exposed, since I could see some television cameras in there, so I just said, 'Paddy.' The buzzer went and the door opened.

---

1 I subsequently rang Will Hutton, the editor of the *Observer* and asked him not to run the story as a Lib Dem triumph.

I met Blair looking harassed coming up the stairs. He had had a day at home, apparently, filming a Party Political Broadcast.

He asked me what I would like to drink. I asked for a cup of coffee and we went downstairs to the kitchen to make it. He took a phone call while I was there, which protracted the coffee-making process, so I chatted to his daughter Kathryn. She was nine yesterday. A delightful little girl. I told her that I had had a birthday last week, too, which meant we were the same star sign. We had quite a discussion about astrology. I asked her whether she believed in it and she said no, but she had heard there was an eclipse or something this week and 'That's going to change both our lives for ever, it says.'

Tony and I then went up to the sitting room. He sat down with a sigh.

TB: Look, I've gone as far as I can go. Indeed, I will probably have to pull back a bit. I have had people hammering at my door all this weekend. Jack [Straw] and Ann Taylor have been saying to me, 'We have always trusted you. We assumed you knew what you were doing. But over this one, we haven't a clue. You are going too far. You are risking open rebellion in the Party. We don't understand why you have given in so much to the Lib Dems. They will not be worth anything to us after the next election. And we have gone far further in allowing PR than we should have done.' This by itself wouldn't be too bad. But Gordon has also been hammering down my door for much the same reasons. He believes I have taken a major step towards PR, which he is opposed to. And he thinks we've got nothing back from you. Then there is Ali telling me that the press will read the whole Cook/Maclennan outcome as a move on PR more than anything else. I am really nervous. It is exactly what I didn't want. No doubt it is what the *Independent* and the *Guardian* would like, but it's the influence of the Tory press I am really worried about. They will take me to the cleaners, saying I am a soft touch for you lot.

PA: Fine. That's how you feel. Now let me tell you how I feel. You and I made an agreement about what would happen at the end of these talks. I feel pretty aggrieved that you haven't been able to deliver on this. Over the weekend, as a result of a leak to the *Observer* (which we are certain came from your side), I rang Will Hutton to persuade him not to run the story in the terms that he was originally going to – i.e., as a triumph for the Lib Dems. So it was with some anger that I opened the paper on Sunday to discover your side had been briefing like hell that this was a 'victory' for you and that we had given in for nothing – witness the Andrew Adonis article. I regard that as an act of very bad faith.

Secondly, as I understand it – and this is confirmed by a brief conversation I had with Robin – there was a clear understanding in the Cook/Maclennan Committee that if we conceded on Scotland [that is, dilute our opposition there], then you in return would agree to go firm on PR for Europe in 1999. Our lot, at no small cost to Jim Wallace, backed off on the Scottish referendum only to open our newspapers and find that you are now saying there is no guarantee on Europe. Again, we feel very angry. We fulfilled our part of the bargain. But you now seem to be reneging on yours. We simply can't go on like this. I warned you from the start that PR for Europe is a break point for us.

We then got down to see if we could hammer this out.

I soon established that the real sticking point was PR for Westminster. He said he couldn't go further than he had already gone. Indeed, he would have to retreat to a position of mild hostility to recover the situation.

It was clear that I could not get him to go further on this than he had already agreed, so I said, 'OK. I accept that you have changed your mind on this. But if you must maintain a position of mild hostility tending to neutrality, you know what we will say. That it is a pretty bizarre position. That in the context of the General Election, those who wish to have PR in Britain will know who to vote for.'

TB: That would, frankly, be helpful to me. But I want to make it clear to you that I cannot go further than 'Not persuaded'.

PA: But what's going to happen if someone puts the very legitimate question to you, 'Mr Blair, how can you agree to a commission if you remain hostile to PR?' Will you then respond that you are not persuaded at the moment, but are ready to be persuaded – in other words, that your mind is open?

TB: Yes, I would be happy to do that, but I would prefer to do it after a decent interval, rather than straight away. Although I accept that if I am bowled the question I will have to respond along the lines you propose. But my plan is to make sure that the briefing we put out on Thursday [when the Cook/Maclennan is to be launched], in response to this heavily emphasizes that I remain unpersuaded, even hostile.

PA: Well, that's as far as we can get on that. Now let's talk about Europe. I will accept your position, even though it is a dilution of what we originally agreed, if, as I proposed to you before, you can confirm that it remains your intention to have PR for Europe before 1999. The very minimum we can accept in response to the question 'Will you have PR for 1999?' is something like 'That's our policy and that's our intention.'

TB: Well, if we have to do that, then we have to do it. Frankly I find it difficult to go that far, but I will. I want to make it clear, however, that I can't guarantee this. But if we say that it remains our intention, that's OK.

I summed up that:

1. We would, as far as possible, leave the working on PR for both Westminster and Europe on the table and not elucidate unless asked a specific question.

2. If he is asked about PR for Westminster he would admit the deficiencies of the present system, while saying that he remains 'not persuaded'. But, if asked, he would say he could be persuaded in the context of the commission outcome.

3. On PR for Europe, we would again leave the words in the document broadly as they are. If Robin were questioned about timing, he would say that to institute PR for Europe by 1999 was 'Labour's policy and our intention'. If asked whether or not this was a guarantee, Robin would say, 'Nothing can be a guarantee, of course. No one can tell what will happen to the legislative programme of a future government. But this remains our policy and intention.' I said, 'It is important that you authorize Robin to talk in precisely those terms.' He promised to do so.

At this stage, Jonathan came in. I was careful to reiterate the two formulae in front of him, reminding Tony that 'there is real tribal memory on this in my Party. We were stuffed by Callaghan in 1978. I just can't put the Party in the position where it could be treated in the same way by you. I, of course, trust you. We couldn't have got this far if I didn't. But you must realize that the Party at large has no reason to view commitments which you make on PR for Europe as in any way different from those of Callaghan. At least until we have a history of successful co-operation behind us. And the last three weeks have not helped with that.'

I was immensely relieved to have done the deal I hoped for with him and made to go. But just before I left he said, 'We must decide what to do after the election.'

I replied, 'I don't want to talk to you about Cabinet posts now. I want to be able to say that I have never discussed them with you.'

'No, I didn't mean that. We must decide how we continue with this relationship after the election. I have some thoughts on that. Have you?'

I replied that I had a few, but if there was something to talk about we should do so, perhaps after the election. We had established the groundwork for co-operation that ought to extend beyond the election. Then I said, 'I suspect this is the last time we will meet before the election, so best of luck.'

He wished me luck too, and I left.

Tuesday, 4 March, Westminster

In the evening, over to the Federal Policy Committee (FPC) meeting. I bleeped Bob to tell him that I would keep the FPC in session until he came back so he could explain the final outcome of the Cook/Maclennan talks.

During a short adjournment Bob came in and whispered to me, 'The deed is done. They have signed up and it was a splendid meeting.'

This is a really historic moment.

I gave Bob free rein for about fifteen minutes to explain the agreement. It was unanimously approved by the FPC, with everybody saying what a tremendous success it was for Bob. And so it is. Bob came to the office for a glass of champagne afterwards. He is delighted. We have done something really big.

I feel a huge sense of relief. I have been working at this for two and a half years. But we have now, it seems, finally pegged it down in a way they cannot get out of.

This is a major foundation block in building a new constitution for the country – and my trust in Blair, although it has been through rocky patches, has ultimately been proved reasonably well founded.

Wednesday, 5 March, Westminster

The Parliamentary Party Meeting at six. Widespread approval from all the Colleagues for the Cook/Maclennan agreement and warm congratulations for Bob. Cyril Smith even rang and said it was a wonderful agreement. Afterwards to the FE. I sat with them through the discussion on the constitutional talks. Even Donnachadh McCarthy[1] was in favour and Lembit Opik[2] quite warm, saying that this would encourage tactical voting,

1 Member of the Party's Federal Executive. Party activist who objected to my position of closer co-operation with Labour.
2 Member of the Party's Federal Executive. Member of Parliament for Montgomeryshire since 1997.

etc. Amazing. Tom McNally said that if all these people agreed he had better have a look at it again. Much laughter.

Tuesday, 11 March, London

I changed into my dinner jacket and went to the Guildhall for the celebration of the fiftieth anniversary of Indian independence. Blair not there.

Major came up and drew me away from some Labour MPs I was talking to. 'Do please tell Tony not to go for the primary purpose (immigration) rule.[1] I fear if they raise it, my Party will respond by playing the immigration and race card in the election. So, it is in the interest of all of us to keep it out of the front line. Can you please pass this message on?'

It was an extraordinary statement, not only because of its content but also because Major does not feel he can call Blair personally.

I said, 'I thought your answer the other day to Nick Budgen[2] [who had asked a deliberately provocative question on race and immigration] was magnificent. You were at your very best.'

He replied, 'That's very kind of you, but I am really serious about this. I do not want immigration to be an issue in the forthcoming election.'

I told him that I would do everything I could to ensure that it wasn't.

Thursday, 13 March, Westminster

I met Tom McNally this morning.

Among other things, I told him of my personal plans for the future. Something I have only discussed with Jane. I said that my intention was to try and deliver the Party a chance of power and then to leave the Party to make the decision whether to accept or not.

If we were successful, or if Blair came to us after the election, I anticipated that I would say to the Party, 'It has been my purpose as Leader to give you a chance to share in power. You have won that for yourselves. It is now up to you to decide whether to take it.'

I concluded, 'If, then, the Party rejects the possibility of sharing in

---

1 The Primary Purpose Rule made it necessary for foreign partners of British citizens to prove that their reason for marriage was not primarily to settle in the UK.
2 Member of Parliament (Conservative) for Wolverhampton South West 1974–97.

government, it will be time for someone else to take over and I shall leave without bitterness, having achieved most of the things I wanted to achieve.'

In those circumstances I might, if asked, try to play a part in finding peace in Northern Ireland.

However I did not tell Tom that, whatever happened, I would want to stand down as Leader some time during the next parliament, as this would have set hares running.

Monday, 17 March, London

Major went to the Palace this morning.

The General Election campaign has formally started. I received another death threat from Combat 18 in the post.

Tuesday, 18 March, London

Up at 5.15 to be picked up by Nick [South] for a succession of interviews. I met Peter Mandelson before we went into one of them and we chatted amiably about what was happening.

Gordon Brown came in while I was doing the *Today* programme. I could feel him shifting in his chair as I attacked Labour for its timidity on spending.

Afterwards back to my office to pre-record a *Newsnight* interview with Paxman.[1] He was indescribably rude. I have never had an interview like it. He started off by saying that I was old and past it. I ended up very angry with him, though I hope it didn't show on camera. It took great self-control.

None the less, I was convinced I had done terribly badly. The very worst start to the campaign. I also read this morning that we are down to 9.5 per cent in the polls. Single figures.

Watched Paxman at 10.30. Not as bad as I thought. I later heard that there had been more complaints to the BBC about this than about any interview Paxman had done for quite some time.

Sunday, 23 March, London

In the evening I started to wade through the manifesto, hopefully for the last time.

By arrangement with Anji Hunter I finally got through to Tony around six. We wished each other luck in the campaign and agreed that we should contact one another if there were any problems or difficulties. We agreed that Tom McNally, who has now completed his paper on our approach to a hung Parliament,[2] should make contact with Jonathan Powell before Easter with a view to giving them a bowdlerized copy for use in the week after the election.

Wednesday, 26 March, London

Breakfast at the National Liberal Club. A meeting of the HP Group to finalize our contingency plans for a hung Parliament. I had taken Richard aside the night before and told him that I wanted Tom McNally to take over on the day after the election in order to manage the post-election period if we got into serious discussions with Labour.

I told everyone else at the start of the breakfast. Afterwards, Tom went through the HP paper with me.

1 Jeremy Paxman, presenter of BBC TV's *Newsnight*.
2 See memo in Appendix I.

Philip Goldenberg has come up with an interesting proposition for a Cabinet Committee, which is worth looking at as a fallback position.

I made it clear that if, on the Friday after polling day, Blair asked to see me, I would go. But I would phone him first to make sure he wasn't proposing something we couldn't agree to. This shouldn't happen, as according to the agreement I made with Blair yesterday, Tom will see Jonathan Powell this week, and then again in the last week of the campaign to get some indication of what Labour has in mind. At all events we must avoid me going to Downing Street and failing to agree.

I also made it clear that, if they offered us Cabinet seats, these could only be in return for a negotiated agreement. Though realistically our demands would be very modest. What we couldn't accept, however – and what it must be made very clear to Labour we couldn't accept – was Lib Dem Cabinet ministers in a Labour Government administering a purely Labour programme. Tom was authorized to tell Jonathan Powell that now, so that there would be no future misunderstandings or intimations of betrayal.

I ended up by thanking them all for an excellent piece of work and saying that this was the moment I had led the Party for.

Jane Bonham-Carter rang at around seven to say that we had gone up substantially in the polls, to 14 per cent. (Too much. I don't believe it.)

Tuesday, 1 April, Westminster

Becky called while I was in the sauna. Gordon Brown wants to see me at 1.30pm to talk about Tatton.[1] Dashed back to the office to have a brief chat with Richard. He thinks the Party on the ground in Tatton are pretty hesitant. We must make that clear to Brown. Richard had spoken to Mandelson yesterday, who, much to our surprise, told him that he hadn't bothered to find anybody yet.

Brown came to my office and he, Richard and I had a long discussion on how we should play it and how to ensure that our hand was not visible in all this. He seemed in good form, saying that he believed the Tories were in a deep hole, but not irrecoverable. He is probably right, too.

---

1 With sleaze running as the major election issue, I had previously agreed with Blair that we ought to try to find an independent candidate for Tatton, where Neil Hamilton, the Tory MP who had been deeply embroiled in the cash-for-questions scandal, was re-standing.

Thursday, 3 April, London

We are having difficulties with our sitting candidate in Tatton, Roger Barlow. All the Northwest Lib Dems want him to stand, irrespective, and do not want to be seen to do anything which smells of co-operation with Labour. But Chris Rennard has managed to keep them on board. We are considering all sorts of options.

At Cowley Street everything now concentrated on tomorrow's manifesto launch. The tension is really building up. Labour's was launched today and has been a great success.

Friday, 4 April, London

Up at 5.45. A bath, then a read of the papers. Blair's coverage is absolutely stunning. Enormous acclaim from the *Sun* upwards. My fear is that this will unleash a pro-Labour bandwagon across the country that will encourage people to vote Labour rather than tactically.

I had a chat with Richard about the Tatton situation. Martin Bell has come forward. Magnificent news. But we will have God's own job getting our own Tatton people to agree to this.

Before leaving Somerset, I managed to speak to Roger Barlow. I said it was very important for the national campaign that he should stand down in favour of Martin Bell. Bell had come forward following an approach from the Labour Party, but I had known him from our time together in Sarajevo and he had been a young Liberal in his university days, etc.

Roger responded, 'I am here to serve the Party and I am happy to stand down. But I must tell you that it will be very difficult to persuade Tatton Lib Dems.'

At home I watched the 6 o'clock news, then the nine, ten and then *Newsnight*. Much, much better than I thought they would be. Our manifesto has gone down very well. All the hard work appears to have been worth it.

To bed about eleven.

Saturday, 5 April, Somerset

Up at seven, did some paperwork, then rang Roger Barlow in Tatton to thank him for standing down so selflessly.

There were policemen outside Vane Cottage yesterday in flak jackets and with automatic weapons. Very startling for the village. I asked them if they could please not carry weapons – it was completely unnecessary for me, and bad for the local kids, for whom they were proving an unhealthy attraction. Alastair Spalding, our excellent Special Branch man, backed me up. The weapons have disappeared today.

Sunday, 6 April, Somerset and London

Up at 7.30 and a chat with Martin Bell, who is being driven to Tatton by Tim Clement-Jones. There is still some resistance to him from the local party, but Chris is slowly overcoming this with a steady stream of phone calls.

To my relief, TCJ rang at about 4 o'clock to say that the constituency meeting had gone all right – five votes to six! I later learned that Martin Bell had had a much easier time with the Labour Party than with our lot. Why is our Party so difficult on these things? It comes from being liberals, I suppose.

Arrived at Cowley Street at about five for a campaign meeting at six. Although the opinion polls published in the papers are disappointing, Richard tells me that the private polling we have done in our target seats looks excellent.

Over to the office, briefly, to pick up some mail, then off with Richard for dinner at a Lebanese restaurant on the Edgware Road.

We talked about the final week's campaign. I said that I felt there was now a real danger that if the Tories thought they were going to lose they would turn their fire on us. Their aim would become not to win but to preserve as many heartland seats as possible and to try to prevent tactical voting in the West Country. Richard thinks I am pursuing a Liberal Democrat-centric view.

We also discussed how to respond to the public mood in the last week, should a Labour landslide seem likely. There might then be a sense in the country of not wanting Labour to have too big a majority.

We hatched up a rather daring plot: that in the last week I should reverse our position so that we went for leadership of the opposition. I could say, 'It is now clear that Labour will get a majority. What Britain needs, as the Tory Party fights for its soul and its new leader, is a decent constructive opposition. We intend to form that opposition. We will work with Labour where we agree with them and hold them to their promises. But we will work to prevent Labour from having its tail tweaked by its own left wing.'

This strategy has huge advantages. But high risks, too. We agreed to test out the idea with our focus groups.

Monday, 7 April, London

We are still at only around 10 per cent in the polls. I am getting seriously worried. We appear stuck there. The headline news is all about Martin Bell.

Richard took us through the private opinion polling. We have gone up 5 per cent in some of our target seats, which puts us ahead of Labour in these places. In February they were ahead of us. Good news. No sign of it being reflected in the national polls, though.

Tuesday, 8 April, London

Up at seven, gloriously late since I am excused the press conference. *Newsnight* last night was full of vox pops saying, 'We love the Lib Dems' manifesto but we are not going to vote for them because they will not have any power.'

How do we break out of this? I just have to keep plugging away at it and rely on the good sense of the voters.

A rally in the Horticultural Hall in Westminster. The place was full of smoke and balloons. I exploded all over the organizers, poor people. I had made it specifically clear that there was to be no razzmatazz of this sort. (I particularly didn't want smoke and balloons.)

Simon Hughes spoke first. Then Shirley. Both of them quite sombre. Then I was called in to a massive roar from the audience, which I reckoned numbered about nine hundred but the press reported as fifteen hundred. The speech (strongly attacking the Tories) went quite well.

Saturday, 12 April, Somerset

An absolutely perfect day. We went canvassing in my own constituency.

I am worried about the apathy on the doorstep. People from whom I would have got a ready commitment to vote for us in the past are now fed up with all politicians. A detectable rise in the Referendum Party vote. And one or two voting Labour because they think that is the best way to get rid of the Tories. In Yeovil!

I dread what is happening in other target seats. But we have gone up five points in a poll to be published in tomorrow's *Sunday Times*. Later in the evening we heard three other poll results showing us up one or two. This will give a huge boost to party morale.

Sunday, 13 April, Somerset

At about 10 o'clock Blair rang. We had agreed to have a chat halfway through the campaign.

Our polls now show the Tories lifting slightly, and we need to keep them down. 'This is a good time to co-ordinate, isn't it?'

He agreed. 'We have had a pretty rocky week. But I don't believe that should distract us. We are now going to shift to the positive. The more we can do to mount joint attacks on the Tories and not attack each other, the better.'

Then he quipped, 'Incidentally what's this about me not changing my tie without reference to the spin doctors?'

I said it was a joke that I had made nine months ago. 'Anyway, I have said enough good things about you, surely I am allowed to crack a joke here or there.'

Monday, 14 April, London and Scotland

Jane will join us on the campaign trail today. Up at 5.40 and off to the press conference. I had arranged for Jane to be picked up at 8.30. On the way I gave her a call. Had she spoken to Kate? Yes, she had started labour last night and the contractions were coming about every fifteen minutes. Jane said she sounded frightened. So am I.

I picked up Jane and we rang Kate again, who is waiting to go into hospital. Then off to London City Airport for a two-hour flight to Inverness. Jane and I talked throughout the whole flight about our hopes for an easy birth for Kate and for our grandchild. We are both terribly excited. I cannot think of anything else and it was with some difficulty that I dragged myself back to the election.

In the evening a rally in Aberdeen. My mind wholly on Kate, however. We now have the telephone number at her bedside and have rung her several times. She seems fine, but I can hear the fear in her voice. It must come tonight.

The rally itself was quite good. My speech went down well. We are up fantastically in the Scottish polls – it must be a rogue. From 10 to 16 per cent. This has cheered up the Scottish Party.

We flew back to London, leaving at about 9 o'clock. At my request, the pilot did a circle so that we could have a look at the Hale Bopp comet. Not as good a view, however, as we had on the ground, owing to the distortions of the windows.

We arrived back at Stansted at 11.15pm. Then into London, arriving around midnight. Jane absolutely shattered. And me quite tired as well. But happy that we have gone up in the polls. We are both worried for Kate.

Tuesday, 15 April, London, the South West, Hastings

Jane and I both had a very bad night. I left my mobile phone and my bleeper on, expecting to hear from Kate. But nothing. Up at 5.40am, having slept very little.

Then off at 8.40 for London City Airport and Exeter. I left Jane there on the tarmac and she went home. We hugged each other and the cameras took pictures, but they didn't know what was going on in our minds. It is difficult to keep our nervousness from them.

Jane promised to phone Kate when she got back and later in the day she rang to say she had spoken to Kate in the labour ward. The contractions have stopped. Oh, God! The doctors have said that they will let her go on until about Thursday, then induce if the baby hasn't come.

Off to Hatherleigh market to meet farmers, then on to Cornwall. Paul Tyler pretty confident that he can hold North Cornwall . . . John Burnett confident in Torridge, too. I am less so, but the posters look good.

An interview with Radio Five Live. I didn't do this very well. My mind still far too much on Kate and what the hell is happening.

At 3 o'clock we left Bude for Barnstaple. Nick Harvey and a crowd of about fifty or sixty there, but nothing like the last election when we had five or six hundred. No sense of excitement yet.

Back to Exeter Airport. I rang Jane. Still no news.

To London City Airport by 7.15.

Home to Methley Street, grabbed my jeans and sweater and piled into the Special Branch car at 9 o'clock and headed off for Hastings. Stopped off for dinner on the way down. We got into the Royal Victoria Hotel in Hastings at about 11.30. The Conservatives now seem in open civil war and the press is full of Clarke criticizing Howard and of Tory infighting. Fell asleep with the phone and the bleeper by my bed. Surely the child must come tonight. I prayed for her.

Wednesday, 16 April, Hastings and London

Nothing from Kate. Up at 4.30 and off at 5.15 for the harbour.[1] There we were met in the dim light of dawn by the crew, who loaded us on to a tiny fishing boat resting on the shingle beach. We were then pushed out to sea by a bulldozer to find our nets. These had been laid the day before. About four fleets of nets, five miles out from the coast. I took the helm on the way out. A lovely day. A bit of cloud to start with, but then bright sunshine; however a north-easterly wind made it bitterly cold. I tried not to think of Kate.

Once at sea we started lifting the nets. A few plaice here and there, but really very little. It was quite hard work. And made more difficult by the bucking deck of the fishing boat. Goodness knows what it is like to work on in a force 8. And during the winter months it must be freezing.

At 6.50am a boat came out bearing camera crews to take some photographs of us hauling in the last net. Then we headed back for the shore.

I finally got through to the hospital in Sens at 7.30, but couldn't get through to Kate. So I rang Jane, who will phone her as well. We try not to show our worry to each other in our voices.

---

1 We had agreed to try some *Beyond Westminster* style visits in our election campaign, allowing me to spend a little more time with people in their work environment.

Back by helicopter to Battersea. A beautiful morning flying over the South Downs, the whole of the South Coast laid out before us.

In the evening off to Kettners in Soho, where Maureen Thomas[1] had put together a fund-raising dinner. We must have raised about £40,000. I gave a small speech and told Maureen privately that I was terribly worried about Kate. She promptly announced to the dinner that I was awaiting the birth of my first grandchild.

At 11.30, dog tired, and now in a full-scale panic about Kate, from whom we have heard nothing since this morning. At midnight she rang Jane and told her she was going to be induced at 6.30 tomorrow morning. I went to bed, but I kept having nightmares about her. The ordeal she was going through, and the little child struggling from her womb.

Thursday, 17 April, London, Herefordshire, Wales

After the press conference I was taken by car to *The Times*, where I was interviewed by Peter Stothard,[2] Peter Riddell, Anatole Keletsky[3] and Polly Newton.[4] It was an hour's interview and I rather enjoyed it.

At the start of the interview I took a phone call from Jane. We had both been trying to get through to Kate, but without success. She must be in the labour ward now. Surely we will hear by midday? The journalists must have picked up some of the reverberations of the conversation, because they asked me if Kate was in labour. I denied it, of course.

Then off to City Airport for a flight to Cheltenham, then Hereford, where we did a walkabout which culminated in a large meeting in the City Square where I was presented with a soft toy in the shape of a Herefordshire bull for my grandchild.

Little did they know. Nothing from Kate. She has been in labour for seventy-two hours. I am now convinced something terrible has happened to both her and the baby.

Then back into the coach after an impromptu speech.

Brecon War Memorial Hospital next, where I met Richard Livsey. Paul

---

1 Friend and fund raiser for the Party. Dame Maureen organizes the annual Liberal Democrat Ball.
2 Editor of *The Times*.
3 Associate Editor of *The Times*.
4 Journalist on *The Times*; later joined the political staff of the *Daily Telegraph*.

Keetch is certain he will win Hereford. I think he might too. Richard less sure, though.

At any moment I expect my bleeper to go off. But nothing, nothing, nothing. It is now long after midday, when we thought we would hear.

After a visit during which I could hardly concentrate, we were driven to the local rugby club and taken by helicopter to Machynlleth. We flew over the Brecon Beacons – wonderful wild country and a reminder of training in my SBS days.

But I simply couldn't concentrate. As we took off, I thought of Kate and the tears started rolling down my face. I looked out of the helicopter window so nobody could see.

We arrived at Machynlleth to be met by Lembit Opik. I was taken round the nursery school, where I read a story to the kids. By now I was certain that some tragedy had befallen Kate and that she had lost her child. I don't think I have ever been through such torture as this.

Then back to the helicopter. By now my distress was showing to others. Mark Payne[1] and Ian Wright,[2] of course, knew why I was feeling like this, but the others only knew that I was upset.

Then the long flight down to Cardiff. Again waiting for the bleeper to go off, but also dreading it. Nothing.

As soon as we arrived, I rang Jane. It was now 4.15. They would have to do something serious if it didn't arrive by six. I said to Jane, 'When is this torture doing to end?'

I looked bleakly out of the window as we drove to the television studios in Cardiff. I sat down in front of the TV camera. Mike Steele[3] had just asked his first question when the door burst open and Mark came in beaming all over his face, a mobile phone in his hand. Kate had had a son!

I couldn't control myself and in front of the cameras the tears rolled down my face with relief.

Afterwards we explained what had happened. We also told the TV Wales people to keep it quiet as we wanted to release the news on our own terms.

Then back to the Moathouse Hotel and conversations with London about how the announcement would be done. They would release it with a news embargo for seven and I would mention it in my speech.

---

1 Mark had returned to my team for the duration of the election campaign.
2 Ian had come to work as my Press Officer for the 1997 General Election.
3 A lobby journalist for HTV.

The plan was for the birth to be announced by the television personality Barry Norman [who was chairing the rally for us] when he announced me. He would then give me a large bottle of champagne and I would make the speech, then leave.

He did as agreed, to a huge roar from the audience. I gave my speech and really felt it. I was emotionally exhausted. Left through cheering crowds, then outside for a series of interviews.

Then back to Vane Cottage. On the way I rang the hospital, who put me through to Kate. It was wonderful to speak to her. She says the baby is fine. But I later heard from Sebastien that he had come out terribly white and they had to put him in an incubator for an hour.

When I got back we opened a magnum of champagne and brought the Special Branch people in to share it. A moment of real joy.

To bed well after midnight, exhausted.

Saturday, 19 April, Somerset

Saturday. The day we have been looking forward to for so long. Up at 6.30. When I drew the curtains I saw a press cameraman already waiting outside.[1]

We set off to Westland to catch the plane to France, landing at the little airport just outside Auxerre at almost exactly 12 o'clock. There behind a picket fence were Lesley and Greg Jefferies. Many hugs, then we jumped into the car and drove to the hospital.

My heart was pounding in anticipation. It was lovely to see Kate, who met us at the door. More hugs and tears. We then had a look at my grandson, Matthias. He is absolutely wonderful. He had a small bruise on his forehead where they had to use forceps to pull him out of the birth canal. Big feet and hands. We opened a bottle of champagne, then sat around talking.

Many photographs taken of Matthias. I was so proud of him. As I held him in my arms I said a little prayer for him to have a happy, successful and peaceful life.

Then at seven o'clock back on the plane and home.

A great, great day.

---

1 We had asked for press privacy today.

Sunday, 20 April, London

The polls are quite good for us today. All three show us up, even if only by a little. After the press conference a quick telephone chat with Kate. Matthias is now fine.

At 6 o'clock into the campaign meeting. All is going really well. The opinion polls, particularly along the South Coast, show a massive swing from Labour to us. Labour are now well behind and we are squeezing very effectively in some of these seats. If we can keep this going for the next week it should be tremendous. But, as Richard reminded the campaign team, elections are won or lost in the last ten days. So everyone is on tenterhooks.

Wednesday, 23 April, Newbury

To Newbury, where we visited a school with David Rendel. We were met there by a large crowd of Newbury By-pass protesters and Green Party activists, many dressed in animal costumes, demonstrating outside the school gate.

When we came to leave, Special Branch said I was to jump into the car and drive out through the protesters, so they didn't block the bus. I said, no, I would go out and have a little debate with them.

The usual jeering when I went out, but I said, 'Let's go off into a corner, away from the road, and you can make your points to me.' So we did, surrounded by press and cameras.

I spotted somebody dressed up in what I thought was a badger's outfit. So I said, 'I would like to hear from this badger first.' The lady dressed as a badger complained, 'I am not a badger, I am a dormouse.'

I apologized profusely for the misunderstanding, but said I had been reliably informed that she was a badger; why was she masquerading as a dormouse? She said, 'No, I am a dormouse. And we dormice are feeling very sad and lonely, as are all our friends the rats, the voles, and the bats.'

'Well,' I said, 'I would like to hear from some more animals on this. Are there any other members of the animal kingdom who would like to join the debate?'

I spotted a cow. 'Now, this cow no doubt wishes to make a point.'

The two people in the cow costume waddled forward and said something to the cameras – to fits of hysteria from the press.

But the Greens took it all terribly seriously.

It all made for fine entertainment on the evening news.

On our way home late, Ian gave me the latest poll figures. We are up 4 per cent and the Tories are back down to 27. Excellent!

Spoke to Nick Speakman in Yeovil today. He told me everything was on track, but there was no particular certainty or enthusiasm in his voice. Some nasty leaflets circulating, threatening people who put up Lib Dem posters, which have had the effect of getting some to take them down. Apparently, anyone with a poster up gets a leaflet through the door saying I am a 'Paki lover' and voted for children's sex at sixteen. The police are doing their best to find out who it is. Probably the same people as before. The police have also heard some talk of another attack on our house in the near future.

Friday, 25 April, London

Today's papers are full of the Prime Minister calling Blair a liar,[1] which enables us to stay nicely above it all.

In the evening to see Richard, who has done absolutely brilliantly. He said he didn't dare tell me how well he thought we were doing. Just cross our fingers and hope we are right. He thinks the Tories are in a second-stage collapse and their attempts to win votes on Europe have failed. It's as though the nation has already made up its mind.

Sunday, 27 April, London

Tom McNally tells me he has been in touch with Jonathan Powell. The word is that Tony is upset by our attacks on them. They have angered him, and have no doubt been the cause of their attacks on us. Though I cannot understand why. We have stuck to the agreement religiously. We have taken votes off them, which no doubt bothers him. That he should worry, at 50 per cent!

However, the message from Tony was: 'He has decided what to do. This won't be altered by the result. He will speak to Paddy on Wednesday.'

---

1 There was an angry exchange between Major and Blair about their tax and spending plans, which resulted in Major calling Blair a barefaced liar.

At 5 o'clock the HP meeting, at which Tom was asked to go back to Jonathan and fix for me to speak to Blair on the phone next Thursday, polling day.

The general consensus (supported by hints made to Richard by Peter) is that he will offer something very small. Labour seem to think we are absolutely dying to be offered some part in government. They have consistently underestimated our position.

I have sent Blair enough messages to say (a) don't make us an offer we have to refuse and (b) please realize that if you are going to make a proposition it needs to be on an agreed programme, etc.

Richard is pretty sure they will just toss us some fairly junior positions, plus, he thinks, Northern Ireland for me. He believes this would be very dangerous and must be turned down. I agree.

I asked Tom to relay our views back to Jonathan. It is very important that Tony gets this message early, or our relationship could be damaged in the future.

We would stay on the opposition benches, I said, unless they offered something which contained the following:

1. A substantial offer on Cabinet positions (plural), with possibly one overseeing at Cabinet level the constitutional programme. (I could then argue to the Party that it was better for us to drive the constitutional programme from inside the Government, rather than as a supplicant, from outside.)

2. Some symbolic – but probably small – change to their agreed programme to accommodate the fact that it was a joint one, e.g. independence for the Bank of England.

We also agreed that Archy Kirkwood would send out a letter to candidates telling them:

1. To say nothing on Lib-Labbery after being elected.

2. To hold themselves ready for a meeting on Saturday (although this was unlikely).

3. Otherwise to meet on the following Wednesday.

Later in the evening I spoke to Roy Jenkins. He said the campaign was going exceptionally well. I told him of my fears that Tony would underestimate what we would accept and offer something small. I am even more worried that he will bounce us. There have been some echoes in today's press.

The aim must be to create a relationship which will last right through the next parliament. If they bounce us early and cause me to have to say no publicly, this prospect could be damaged. If Roy was speaking to anybody on their team, could he please pass this through to them?

I have been very worried about the *Observer* polls today. These seem to show that our vote is not as high as we think in some of our marginals. In some three-way marginals, Labour has overtaken us and leapt into pole position.

I spoke to Richard quietly about this before the campaign meeting. It was absolutely essential now that we encouraged tactical voting. I couldn't do this, but what about him suggesting to Peter, whom he is meeting later in the evening, that Tony should make an appeal for tactical voting on Wednesday? He could do it, but we couldn't. And if he did it we could then respond delphically. I told Richard that I thought we needed a bigger throw to ensure that we consolidated votes where we could win. The rise in the Labour vote is now seriously threatening some of our target seats and may well save Tory skins in some three-way marginals. Richard thinks it is the right throw, but he doubts whether Tony will do it. So do I, but it's worth a try.

At the campaign meeting we decided to keep plugging away at the twin messages that the Liberal Democrat vote helps remove the Tories and is also a vote for investment in education, etc. It was a good meeting. And Richard is very upbeat. He has run a brilliant campaign and morale is really high.

A letter from Shirley Williams today, saying that we shouldn't go in with Labour.

Tuesday, 29 April, London and Cheltenham

The penultimate day of campaigning. Up at 5.40. I am tired but still buoyed up. Tremendously looking forward to it all being over tomorrow night.

Then off to the press conference with Roy Jenkins and David Steel. Roy on wonderful form. And dismissive of Blair in a light-hearted way. He said he had been disappointed 'by Blair's timidity'.

Then off to Cheltenham, where, at the council offices, I met a 102-year-old lady, Mrs Gresham, who had voted Tory all her life but had now decided to vote Lib Dem. She said she thought John Major was a wimp. A great cheer from the crowd.

It was a superb image which ran through the day.

Wednesday, 30 April, London, South Coast

Into the helicopter again for the last full day of campaigning. Polls still looking good. We were being squeezed towards the end of the last election, but are rising at the end of this one.

A final press conference. At one stage somebody – Nick Clark from *The World At One*, I think – asked me what mistakes I had made during the election. I thought for a second and responded, 'None, of course. Any mistakes weren't mine, they were Richard's.' Everybody laughed and it took the tension out of the room.

By helicopter to Sutton, Eastleigh, Eastbourne, Christchurch, Poole, Bideford and Torpoint. And then finally Torbay. Here we arrived late, at 7 o'clock, the time the final rally was supposed to start.

Shirley spoke. She was brilliant. Gently caressing her audience with that wonderful voice of hers. And being really very moving about the Liberal Democrats and the role we had to play. I didn't do justice to my speech, the last of the campaign. But they gave me a dutiful send-off.

Then into the battle bus. I sat in the back talking with Jane. Delighted the campaign is over.

The light was fading as we left Torbay, leaving the Devon hills etched in stark black silhouette against a russet sky to the west of us. And a wonderful rim of orange and gold light over the hills. A glorious day. But what will happen tomorrow?

The bus took us to the Rose & Crown in Dinnington, where we ended the campaign with pieces done for the evening TV newses from the front of the pub.

Thursday, 1 May, Somerset

GENERAL ELECTION DAY

I couldn't sleep later than 6.30, so I got up and started prowling about.

A beautiful day. Sparkling sunshine and clear blue skies. Already the press has started to gather outside the cottage. Jane and I came out smack on 9.00 and went off to vote, holding hands, the dog in attendance. They took all the photographs they needed, including some nice ones under our apple tree (which is in full, glorious blossom).

Then back home, still with the press crowding around us.

In the meantime, Tom had come down by train. He had arranged with Jonathan for Tony to call me while I was at the Richard Huish College, in Jackie Ballard's Taunton constituency.

I was met by Jackie at the school gate. She looks confident. I think she is going to win.

I had hardly started the visit when Ian Wright sidled up to me and whispered that the call from Tony was coming through. I went to the phone in the Principal's office. The crews from ITN and Sky followed me and stood outside the door. They questioned Ian about what I was doing in there. Ian, who prides himself on never lying to the press, said, with as heavy irony as he could muster, 'Well, obviously he is in there talking to Blair about coalitions, isn't he?'

I was put through to Blair. I said that he was clearly going to win. He said, 'Yes, I suppose I accept that I will, now.' We exchanged compliments about each other's campaigns. He asked, 'How many will you get?'

I said our estimates were that we would get thirty at the low end and about thirty-eight tops. I then left a sufficient silence for him to come in.

TB: Look, I have more or less decided what to do. However, I want to speak to John Prescott and Robin Cook first. Then I will come back to you later. I am sorry I cannot speak to you in more detail now, but I do want you to know that I am absolutely determined to mend the schism that occurred in the progressive forces in British politics at the start of this century. It is just a question of finding a workable framework. But we are now in a position of strength and I intend to use that.

PA: Well, that is what we have always agreed. But I want to make three points to you. Firstly, please do not bounce us in the press. Don't put me in a position where you make me an offer in public which I have to refuse. I am perfectly happy to sit on the opposition benches. Under those circumstances I would want to see if we can open up a new salient of co-operative opposition, so we could support you when you needed it. And in my view, with a large majority, this may be your best opportunity.

TB (interrupting): No, curiously, with a large majority I can do things I couldn't otherwise have done. If you sit on opposite benches of the House then the natural process of politics will mean that the parties will move apart rather than together.

PA: I agree. But then you must understand my second point. We could not accept simply having Liberal Democrats administering a Labour programme. With a large majority you will want to implement your programme in full. But if we are to do something that is really a combination of both parties' ideas then you must be prepared to amend that. We don't need anything big; something relatively small and symbolic will do. Otherwise it simply will not work. When you make me the offer you intend, please remember that.

Lastly, please ensure that this is kept secret until you and I want to bring it out. I may have to put my whole political career on the line here. So it mustn't become public until after we have agreed a common position. We must not be seen to negotiate in public. And we mustn't be seen to disagree in public, either.

He said that was all fine and that after he had talked to Robin and John he would come back to me, perhaps this afternoon, perhaps tomorrow morning.

PA: Finally, I want you to consider one other option. On the basis that I still think is the most likely – that we sit on the opposition benches – there is a position we can adapt based on Parliamentary precedent. Perhaps Jonathan would look it up for you. It comes from the time of Baldwin. Then, opposition parties worked with the Government on a Cabinet Committee. If we were on the other side of the House there is no reason why we should not progress constitutional reform through such a committee. This would allow us, on the one hand, to stay on different sides of the House of Commons, but on the other to institutionalize the relationship, which, if it worked, would bring the two parties closer together in a gradualist way.

TB: That is very interesting and I will get someone to look it up for me.

The conversation lasted no more than five minutes.

I briefed Tom and Mark, who were with me. Tom said, 'Shit, this looks very big.'

I then returned to Yeovil and started my traditional round of committee rooms and polling stations. The Tories do not even have tellers at Chard or Yeovil. What is going on?

In the evening, round to Myles and Joan Raikes' for dinner. It was a lovely evening. We wandered round their garden, smelling the scents of the early summer flowers and feeling the slight chill of dusk at the end of a beautiful late-spring day. By the time we got back home, the camera lights were already shining outside Vane Cottage.

A huge gathering of press there, of course. I drew the curtains, then made some phone calls and went upstairs to try and get some sleep before the night started. I dozed for an hour or so. Then at ten o'clock, when the polls closed, we went out to the cameras and I said, 'The people have spoken etc.'

The exit poll at 10 o'clock gives us 17–18 per cent. They are predicting forty-five seats for us and a 159 seat majority for Labour.[1] Astonishing. The Tories down below 30 per cent. We were due to leave at 12.15am, but Nick Speakman said we should wait another twenty or thirty minutes. I was terribly nervous. Nick told me the result was OK though, so I relaxed a little. I hate this bit. One day I will lose and the result will take me completely by surprise.

We left at about 12.40am. A barrage of questions from the press, then into the counting hall. Everybody is confident I have done it, so I calmed down a bit. Across to watch the Somerton and Frome count (counted in the same hall). Very, very tight there. David Heath looking very glum. He thinks he has lost. Labour's vote too high.

I got my result at about 1.20am. Over 11,000 majority. Labour is pretty low and the Tories very disappointed. The Referendum Party did well, though. By now the scale of the Tory massacre was beginning to show. They are barely holding on to a seat. Government ministers going left, right and centre. We are beginning to win – and win substantially. All my Colleagues have been re-elected, which is wonderful. It looks as though the forty-five prediction is about right. I waited for the Somerton and Frome result, but it went to a recount with David 130 ahead. Too tight. But he will win. I left, shaking him warmly by the hand.

Then down to the Yeovil Liberal Club, where I received a royal welcome from a rather thin but enthusiastic crowd, watching the news and cheering every time a Tory defeat was announced – the greatest of all for Portillo. Labour is on track for a landslide. Probably the biggest election victory ever.

I left at 2.30am, having kissed Jane goodbye, and headed at high speed, under Special Branch escort, for London, arriving at the Pizza on the Park in Park Lane at 4.45am.

Dawn was just breaking. Huge cheers, and I gave a little speech which was broadcast live. The greatest breakthrough for sixty years. I am leading a party that is larger than Lloyd George's! I took Richard to one side, congratulated him and told him of my discussions with Blair.

I have been pondering on what the hell we will do all the way up. My view is that Blair's landslide is so big it would be somehow unseemly if we joined forces with him. There wouldn't be an effective opposition. I am plagued by the idea that it would be seen as an undemocratic, self-serving

---

1 The actual result was 46 seats for the Lib Dems and a 177-seat Labour majority. See Appendix J.

act. I was keen yesterday, but nervous. Now I think the scale of the Blair victory makes everything even more difficult.

We finished all the interviews and celebrations at around six and I tumbled into bed for an hour.

Friday, 2 May, London

The *Today* programme, then into the office for the first post-election meeting. Roy Jenkins came, as did Mark Payne, Ian Wright, Tom McNally and Richard Holme.

Roy said he thought the size of Labour's majority made it easier for us to work with them. But they would have to make us a substantial bid. Two Cabinet seats minimum, but we should go for three plus some changes in policy – what about independence for the Bank of England?

In other words, he suggested, a full coalition agreement. If they offered us something along those lines we should go for it, but if they didn't we had better not. Broadly, he was in favour.

Richard said he was broadly against.

Tom was equivocal.

We had a long discussion on this and I said that the only policy agreements I felt we could squeeze out of them, that would be reasonable, would be:

1. Tony making a personal commitment in favour of PR.

2. Dropping the second question [on tax-raising powers] on the Scottish Referendum.

3. Universal nursery education for all three- and four-year-olds.

4. Perhaps, as Roy had said, independence for the Bank of England.

If we got this plus Cabinet positions that gave us control of the constitutional reform programme, then it would be worth it. But it would really divide the Party. I would have to make a very difficult decision. I said I thought that sitting on the opposition benches might be better than combining with Labour formally.

Finally, there was the democratic question. Would it not seem odd, and somehow self-seeking, for us to add to Tony's huge majority?

Eventually I said we would have to let this earthquake settle. It was much bigger than we had originally imagined. We should play for time in order to think.

Shortly after the others left I started to make arrangements with Tom. It was at this stage that Jonathan rang and put me through to Tony.

His language has changed since yesterday. He explained that he was just about to go and see the Queen. He would want to speak to his main players this afternoon and put in place the major Cabinet appointments.

After which, perhaps in the early part of the afternoon, he would speak to me again. He said that what he had in mind now was a 'framework for co-operation'. I am glad of that, because I don't think we could go further. One of the points we Lib Dems had unanimously agreed on earlier was that none of us could be part of a Government in which Jack Straw was Home Secretary. I wished him luck and congratulated him. I said we would need time to consider whatever they wanted and that I thought it would now look much more difficult to do than previously.

TB: Yes, but I am absolutely determined to go ahead. I mean it when I say that I want to change politics with you and heal the schism. If we allow ourselves to get into a position where we play conventional opposition politics the schism will just reopen.

I had a chat with Tom about the implications of all this, as we walked across to Church House for our last press conference at 11.15. Then a glass of bubbly and a meeting of the workers in Cowley Street.

Afterwards, back to the office. I said to Bob that I thought Blair was taking the question of Cabinet Committees very seriously. Before Roy left the 9.30 meeting he had said, 'I think you would be hugely relieved if he didn't make you an offer.' I said I would indeed be relieved, but disappointed at the same time. Roy said, 'That's how I feel, too.'

Then home to the flat. Jonathan had rung Tom to tell him that everything was utter chaos and they were slipping behind schedule. He would ring at six or so.

So I returned to my office in the House. The HP team assembled and I left them downstairs waiting for Tony's call. Tom came with me to the office. Jonathan put Tony through at about 6.20.

At the start of our conversation I had called him 'Prime Minister', as I always had with Major. He giggled at the beginning, then at the end said, 'For God sake, don't call me Prime Minister. We have always known each other by our Christian names. Don't let's change that now.'

TB: Look, I am dog tired. But I wanted to call you now to tell you what is in my mind. I really do want to seize this opportunity, to demonstrate that we can follow a programme on which we can both work and which will bring us together. I want to put together the basis of co-operation in the future. I don't want you to hold me to this, but what I have in mind is the Cabinet Committee structure you suggested. We might have, for instance, two Cabinet Committees, with you on one and Ming on another. But I need you to know that I see this as a means of transition to an end position where you come into the show. Who knows what the ultimate destination for all this might be? It could be merger some way down the track. Or maybe not. We do not have to discuss that now. But we do not want to miss this opportunity and then end up squabbling with each other.

PA: If you ever mention merger it will be very damaging and cause immense ructions on both sides. If we are involved in a process, it should be an organic one.

I said that he had already taken too many decisions and that he was tired. He agreed. It seemed best, therefore, that we should leave this for a few days, after which Tom would speak to Jonathan to find out in more detail what they had in mind. Perhaps some time next week we could make some general warm announcement? I wasn't certain about the Cabinet Committees, but these were one way forward. He finished the conversation then.

All this absolves us of having to take any decisions immediately.

If he had made a serious proposition to me, I would have gone with it and risked splitting the Party. But since he hasn't, we have found an alternative way forward which will enable us to work together but will let the Party retain the 'responsible and radical' position we won for ourselves in the General Election. And place the idea of co-operative politics, which has been my dream ever since I came into politics, centre stage.

But I am equivocal. My concern remains that, in the long run, we will end up reverting to opposing each other again. The moment has been lost. But I cannot say, at present, that I am sorry.

Whatever bargaining position we have now will soon become stronger. And if we can win PR, which must now be our central aim for this parliament, then the whole process of converting politics to a more co-operative basis will have been established.

I went down to the HP Group and told them what had happened. I swore them to secrecy. We broke up the meeting shortly before seven.

Then it suddenly occurred to me what has happened. We are now represented in every region. Since Blair only got 43 per cent he must realize that the first past the post system may have worked for him this time, but could easily work against him next time. So we must get PR eventually.

And if we do, then the young and very talented MPs who have just been elected will, in time, be Government ministers and handle power in a way that the rest of us have never been able to do.

And we have laid the foundation for a great parliament of reform.

I tied up the loose ends at the office and told the team to have a long weekend and get as much rest as possible before the House reassembles.

The press is full of the Blair appointments. I saw Robin Cook appear on TV with the caption 'Foreign Secretary' under his name. And it looked absolutely right. And I was pleased. And the country feels better for it.

A great sigh of relief seems to have gone up across Britain at the removal of the Tories. Tony starts his Prime Ministership with a tidal wave of hope and good will behind him.

A new age.

Appendices

Appendix A, Extracts from Position Papers

Where We Are

We ended 1989 a long way from where I hoped we would be.

Nevertheless, we have achieved a number of important things.

1. The Party has been stabilized and the decline appears to have been stopped, if not yet reversed.

2. We are accepted as the 'third party', even if this is not established as clearly as I would like, either in the opinion polls or in the eyes of the commentators. I shall not be happy until this position is firmer.

3. We are listened to and reported when we are either quicker or clearer than the two main parties – but not as a matter of course. If we are to be 'in the game' we have to shoulder our way in.

4. The Party is beginning to rebuild its organization and morale is picking up, but slowly.

5. Our local government base has been largely maintained and is still our greatest physical asset. Our aims for May 1990 should be limited, but the resource we apply to them, concentrated.

Against these assets, we enter 1990 with a number of severe handicaps. These include lack of money, declining membership and an eroding local government base. But our chief handicap, from which all these stem, is that Britain is perceived to have returned to a two-party system. Our relevance is therefore diminished to that of a side-show. I think there are good rational arguments for believing that this will not persist. The crucial pillar sustaining the return to a two-party system is Labour's credibility and a belief that they can win on their own. It is vital to our Party that that credibility is broken. A successful by-election could do it for us overnight. An unsuccessful one for Labour would also help.

We will have to be patient, leaving the main attack on Labour to come from the Tories, but assisting where we can and waiting for the realities of the electoral situation to sink in.

We end 1989 with two crucial questions unanswered. What is our role in British politics; and what do we stand for?

The task in the first nine months of 1990 must be to provide a definitive and clear answer to these two questions.

What We Hope Will Happen Next

I think that 1990 will be seen, whether rightly or not, as a turning point. We should make use of this. Three points of change are especially relevant.

1. There is a perception that Thatcherism is running out of steam.
2. There is a new scepticism in the serious press about Labour.
3. There is a new understanding about the importance of Europe and about a more internationalist approach.

I believe that in the next few months, Labour's lead in the opinion polls is likely to become stuck at around 6–7 per cent, or even start to decline. If this happens (and even if it doesn't) we must hammer home the message 'Labour cannot do it on their own'.

The second condition necessary to get us back in the main game is to improve our own position. We need to be above 10 per cent in the opinion polls by the autumn.

The third condition is a rise in a anti-Thatcherism to the point where the desire to get rid of Mrs Thatcher is greater than the fear of Labour, making the prospect of a partnership Parliament a positive rather than negative electoral asset.

If these conditions are fulfilled, politics will move into a very fluid stage in the approach to the General Election.

We will have to be ready to move with events. This will require a good deal of flexibility.

It is vital that we clarify the Party's role, function and identity before this phase begins (i.e., before the autumn). It would be disastrous to try to take part in a more fluid process of politics without a clear idea of what we want and where we want to go. Establishing our identity is therefore another key aim of the first six months of 1990.

I stress that the above is not a prediction of what will happen, but a description of the best we can realistically hope for.

With Whom Should We Play?

It is vital that the Party realizes that we must be prepared to 'play' if and when politics gets more fluid. The bunker mentality we have had for the last two years has been natural and right for a party trying to find the space and freedom to rebuild itself. But this is a luxury we may not be able to afford for much longer. When the pre-eminent question being asked becomes 'How will we remove her?', we must be part of the answer, not separated from it.

But the crucial principle must be to 'play up', not to 'play down'. I see no point in 'playing' with the SDP (except in the three seats where there have been sitting MPs). Or with the Greens. Our game partners must be Labour. But this cannot happen until we are taken seriously. We have to be stronger first.

I do not believe, incidentally, that formal pacts are the way forward – we will have to find more imaginative, informal avenues. The key may lie in finding ways of giving an impetus to tactical voting.

Conclusion

We are still, I regret, in the first stage of a two-stage operation.

We have established a Party, but are not yet perceived to have a role.

We can react to the agenda, but we cannot yet set it.

We have a voice which is listened to by the 'chattering classes', but is not yet heard in Britain at large.

We have good local credentials, but not yet any national impact.

During 1990 we will have, at some point, to move to the second stage. But there is still ground to be prepared for this. We will need two qualities in 1990; the patience to wait for events to move our way and the daring to take advantage quickly and decisively when they do.

1990 shows every sign of being just as difficult as 1989, but perhaps a little more interesting.

POSITION PAPER, JANUARY 1991

Where We Are

1990 has been a good year for the Party. We have achieved almost all of the limited aims we set ourselves for the year.

During 1990:

1. *We have strengthened the Party*   Having stabilized in 1989, the Party has started to grow again in 1990. We will, for the first time since our foundation, end the year with a higher membership than we began it, even though the growth is modest and almost entirely confined to England. Our finances are stable. We are raising more than ever before. The most difficult judgement to be made this year is likely to be between the pull of the General Election and the need to preserve a capacity for continuing growth afterwards.

2. *We have improved our headquarters*   The problems of Cowley Street are now resolved and our Party headquarters, under Graham Elson, grows steadily more effective.

3. *We have begun to win in elections again*   We have done better than any of us dared hope. We got 18 per cent in the local elections in May and achieved consistently good results in local by-elections. The triumph at Eastbourne put us back on the political map.

4. *We have improved party morale*   Morale in the country is far better than perhaps it deserves to be – largely a result of the after-glow of Eastbourne. But morale is probably still very fragile.

5. *We have held our local government base*   Our local government base has continued to hold well and still represents by far the biggest asset of the Party. This will be severely tested in next May's elections. We have made some progress in rebuilding our shattered resource of 'second-tier' activists – but we are still crucially weak in this area.

6. *We have started planning the General Election*   A good start has been made here and, from a very low base, we are probably now better prepared than for many General Elections past. But money remains a serious worry, as do the number of candidates we have yet to find.

7. *We have made progress with our identity problem*   We have begun to establish a clearer identity.

8. *We have established ourselves as the only third party.*

Our Weaknesses

1. *Identity*   Lack of identity remains our crucial weakness.

2. *Two-party politics*   The press still see the country as having returned to two-party politics. If there is not a Gulf War, I find it difficult to see how (and on what subject) we are going to get in on the act.

3. *Labour's strength*   Labour's recent reversal is likely to be short lived. Their weaknesses were cruelly exposed at the time of Mrs Thatcher's departure. But how long will this last? And if it does, what will Labour do about it? We have more to fear from a Labour recovery than from almost anything else. If, on the other hand, Labour remains stuck at their present position, I expect them to do another raid on our policies, including, possibly, electoral reform.

4. *Weakness in Scotland*   Scotland is a major point of weakness for the Party.

What Happens Next?

1. *The Tories and Labour*   I expect the Tories' lead over Labour to even out or even go into reverse, particularly as the recession bites. The worst position for us is a narrow margin for one or the other, as this squeezes us badly.

2. *The economy*   In the absence of a Gulf War, the economy (the recession) will be the dominant issue in the run-up to the General Election.

3. *Europe*   Now that all the parties have scrambled on board for the rhetoric of Europe, I expect that this will be, in the short term, a less fertile area for us than it has been in the last year. Europe may (will?) re-emerge again after the middle of the year, as the decisions from the IGC[1] come to a head and start to be brought back for votes in the House. It is at this point that the Thatcherite wing of the Tory Party may start to get active, even destructive again.

4. *John Major*   The jury is still out on Major. But he has so far fallen short of my expectations of him.

---

1 Inter Governmental Conference – the start of Maastricht.

Conclusion

1990 was the year we established the Party. 1991 is the year we have to start building it again. With the possibility of a General Election, the probability of a Gulf War and the certainty of a recession, 1991 looks like being a turbulent and dangerous year. The risks and the potential rewards for all parties will be high. We are entitled to feel some confidence that we have established the right policy positions for the year ahead and are at least now strong enough to take part in the debate.

POSITION PAPER, 3 JANUARY 1992, FLAINE

The Lib Dems

Strengths

We have had a good year. My fears of being squeezed out of the action in 1991 proved to be groundless, chiefly because of:

1. The Gulf War, in which we scored a considerable success by planning ahead, mapping out a clear line and being constantly available.
2. The dominance of Europe, on which we had a clear line.
3. Our successes in campaigning, particularly at local and by-elections.
4. Our ability to spot issues before they came on the scene and map out a clear line on them.

This was the year when we have at last learned the lesson that having a clear line is vital to success.

Our biggest success is to have made people interested in us again, even if they are still far from being committed to us.

We end the year with the Party in good morale, with a reasonable standing in the public eye and with a good organizational and policy base. We cannot be complacent, but we are in a good position for the General Election and, barring accidents, ought to be able to make progress from any of the possible outcomes of this.

Weaknesses

Our biggest drawback still persists – *people still do not know what we stand for.* I think they now perceive us to be honest, straightforward and rational. But the message is still missing.

Secondly, the Parliamentary Party remains patchy in its performance. There are a few good performers, but they are still not taking nearly enough initiatives, or responding fast enough. There must also be considerable doubt of our ability to hold together as a Parliamentary Party under the strains of a hung Parliament.

Thirdly, while our finances are much better than they were (and are considerably sounder than those of the other two parties), we are, financially, weakly placed for a second election if one should result from an indecisive result in 1992.

Our Prospects in the General Election

Barring major disasters, I think we can reasonably expect to get between twenty and thirty-two seats at the election. In the case of a serious Tory collapse, this might be considerably increased. But our long-term prospects are still better served by a fourth Labour defeat.

If the present situation persists, I reckon that there is a 40 per cent chance of a Tory majority, a 35 per cent chance of a hung Parliament and a 25 per cent chance of a Labour majority.

We have almost completed our preparations for a hung Parliament. The final work (completing the HP document, consulting with the Palace, a final run through with the Parliamentary Party and negotiation training for key participants) must be completed by the end of the first week in February at the latest.

We should persist with our policy of not raising hung Parliaments, but letting them be raised by others. But we are getting interesting evidence that, this time, a hung Parliament may provide a boost, rather than a drag factor with voters. We should watch this carefully. If a hung Parliament looks a real possibility in the last few days of the election, we must be prepared to go for it flat out if that can enable us to dominate the last days of the campaign. The big danger with this issue is that our enemies will try to make us look as though we are indulging in ego-flattering pipe dreams. This must be avoided at all costs which is why the issue must be raised by others, not us.

POSITION PAPER, APRIL 1992: THE POST GENERAL ELECTION POSITION OF THE PARTIES

The Liberal Democrats

We are right to feel somewhat disappointed with the General Election result. We fought a good campaign, making, I believe, only one serious tactical mistake – allowing ourselves to be too deeply drawn into the hung Parliament scenarios over the last few days. It is doubtful, however, whether we could have resisted this, even if we had wanted to. Over the last two days the press were convinced that there was going to be a hung Parliament and were interested in exploring that and nothing else.

We were aware that the Tories would throw everything into hitching us up to Labour, but we were not aware just how effective this would be because we underestimated Labour's unpopularity, and we did not see the shift occurring on Monday, Tuesday and Wednesday. There are lessons to be drawn from this for the next campaign.

Nevertheless, the position we now find ourselves in is exactly the position which, a year ago, we had privately hoped for. Our disappointment arises, therefore, chiefly from the fact that we had allowed ourselves to believe our own more optimistic propaganda.

Moreover, our position now is stronger than it has been at any time since the Party was established.

We now have more MPs than in 1987, a united Party, sound finances, a rising membership and an established and respected body of policy.

We also have real opportunities to exploit from Labour's leadership contest and from their sense of failure arising out of a fourth electoral defeat.

Considering the progress we made in the 1987 parliament from dreadful beginnings, we have reason to be optimistic about what we should be able to achieve in this one.

Labour

Much will depend on the new Labour leadership. But two movements are now in train within the Labour Party which we should encourage.

1. *Proportional representation*   It must now be virtually certain that Labour will adopt PR. We want this to happen as soon as possible and in

terms which are acceptable to us (i.e., including Westminster and based on an electoral system we can agree with). We are almost certainly going to have to show flexibility on the question of systems. But we should not do this until the principle of PR for Westminster is accepted between the parties.

2. *Realignment of the left*   We must encourage this debate, whether we wish to participate in any realignment or not. The more this debate is heard within Labour the more their confidence will be sapped and the more their 'purists' will create trouble.

We should encourage the view that PR and realignment are linked. Without one there cannot be the other.

I do not believe that there is any scope for directly intervening in Labour's internal debate – indeed, this could be counter-productive. But we should be careful to cultivate the closest personal relationships with Labour and should refrain from attacking them openly or closing the door to dialogue (see below for more general realignment points).

If Labour gets its act together, we should expect them to move lock, stock and barrel on to our policy ground, especially in economic and constitutional terms.

The Conservatives

The prevailing wisdom is that the Conservatives are now in for ever and can't be beaten. I don't agree.

The election has dramatically shown up the bankruptcy of ideas within the Tory Party.

Major has his mandate, but I don't think he has the first idea what to do with it. There must be a real possibility that the Government will show signs of drift before very long. Michael Heseltine is the only one who appears to have ideas – but his are old ones and, as we have already seen, likely to stir up deep concern among the Thatcherite tendency.

Much will depend on the economic situation. There are those who say that the world economic situation is so dire that there are extremely tough times ahead; and those who say that we are out of the woods and it is all now plain sailing. We much reach a conclusion on which of these two scenarios is correct very early on.

If the economic situation does not improve there must be a real possibility that the Government's lack of direction, matched by an unenthusiastic public mood, will result in a very short 'honeymoon' period for Major.

With Labour distracted, we have a real opportunity to be leading the effective attack on the Government. We should not wait to give the Government the benefit of any new mandate, but should open our attack on them immediately, as though this was just the opening of a new session, not the start of a new parliament. But we need, as early as possible, to decide what our main lines of attack will be, especially on the economic and employment fronts.

Realignment

I anticipate a very strong public mood, reflected amongst our own members and those of Labour, that there must be some sort of formal realignment between us. This is a highly explosive issue, but it is one on which we have to have a clear line.

My view is as follows:

1. We must be seen to be at the centre of the realignment debate, not divorced from it. Those who wish to be rid of the Tories must see us as a vehicle for their wishes, not a barrier to them.
2. Over the last three years we have had to emphasize the distinctiveness of the Party in order to establish our identity. Over the next few years we are going to have to change from being exclusive about ourselves to being inclusive of a wider movement. There will be a tendency for the Party to get back in its pre-election trenches. This will have to be resisted.
3. But there must, for the moment, be no overt talk of, or welcome for, the notion of electoral pacts.
4. Proportional representation should be the issue around which all discussion should be centred. PR is at once the prerequisite for progress on any realignment and a lightning conductor to keep early discussion with Labour away from wider and more dangerous subjects.
5. Any development beyond PR should be around agreement on ideas and politics and NOT about mathematical arrangements, based on seats.

In order to do this, our strategy will have to be clear and understood.

Strategy

Up to now, our strategy has been threefold:

1. To emphasize the distinctiveness of the Party. This was essential in order to give us the space to rebuild the Party and establish our own policy agenda.
2. To stress the fact that we are equidistant from both Labour and Tory. This was necessary in order to maximize our appeal in seats where we challenged the Tories and to minimize the fear factor of Labour.
3. To accept that, in any hung Parliament, we could work with either Party and would respond to 'the wishes of the electorate', according to the mathematics of the election result.

We always knew that this strategy, necessary to the early years of the Party, would have to be reviewed after this election, particularly in our preferred outcome, a fourth defeat for Labour.

The moment for that review has now arrived. The facts we must now consider are:

1. Labour has now moved much closer to our agenda and can be expected to complete their transformation under any likely new leader.
2. We must now seriously contemplate the fact that we face the possibility of permanent Conservative Government on 42 per cent of the vote, unless the opposition parties co-operate.
3. The last election showed the difficulty of selling a post-election coalition made up of parties which the public could not predict. Britain is simply not educated to coalition Government and our hopes that we may be able to sell the concept to them foundered on the residual unpopularity of Labour and the fact that the Tories were able to play up the fear of the chaos which would result.
4. The need for us to be the gathering point for opposition forces over the next few years.

We need now rationally to consider an alternative strategy. This strategy could be outlined as follows:

1. That we work actively to establish around our agenda a broad intellectual front capable of producing an electable alternative to Conservatism. Wherever possible this development should be done in the widest possible forum, and not be confined just to Liberal Democrat bodies or members.

2. That we abandon the pretence of equidistance and revert to the position we adopted during Mrs Thatcher's time in office of being specifically an anti-Tory party committed, in the first place, to their removal at the next election.

3. That our long-term and, for the moment at least, undeclared aim should be to participate in a pre-election coalition to present to the electorate. This would, of course, mean a commitment to an agreed programme for government.

My own view is that a change of strategy along the lines outlined above is appropriate and in line with what we have always agreed might be necessary at this stage.

If we are to agree to this, however, we must do so soon, as it will be of considerable advantage to us to be seen to be leading in this debate, rather than merely responding to others.

Conclusion

We now embark on the second stage of the rebuilding of the Party. We have a strong base to build on.

And we are well placed to take advantage of what looks likely to be a very fluid period of politics on the left and the probability of a further swing against the Conservatives over the period of this parliament. But to do this, we are going to have to start strongly in order to continue the momentum established during the election and to take advantage of the current situation in the Labour Party.

If we are to respond effectively to the public mood and our own opportunities, we are going to have to be more flexible and open than in the first years of the Party. And, perhaps most crucial and difficult of all, we are going to have to reconsider our strategy.

POSITION PAPER, OCTOBER 1992

1 The Conservatives

1.1 The Conservatives seem to be in a damaged state. Their divisions on Europe have turned into open warfare and the events of Black Wednesday[1] have seriously – and perhaps permanently – damaged their strongest card, economic competence.

1.2 The Government's fundamental credibility has been significantly undermined. They now seem adrift. The Prime Minister's personal standing has been greatly reduced, possibly permanently.

1.3 It seems likely that Lamont will go before long. We should keep the pressure up, calling for his resignation and bracketing Major with him. Lamont currently protects Major. If (when?) he goes, the Prime Minister will be in the front line.

1.4 Given the above, I believe we should begin to work on the assumption that this may not be a full-term Government.

1.5 Despite the Government's difficulties, however, there is no sign as yet of any serious collapse of the Tory vote – they have had 43 per cent of the local government vote since the election and 38 per cent since Black Wednesday.

1.6 And we must never, never, underestimate the Conservative ability to recover – still less their ability to win General Elections.

2 Labour

2.1 It is clear that Smith has decided that his best tactic is to do as little as possible and wait for the Government to make his openings for him.

2.2 The Labour Conference was a purely holding operation. If anything they appear to be retreating on the Kinnock reforms, most notably on the Unions. Smith's style seems to be to re-associate Labour with its more traditional past.

2.3 I am told that Smith has decided that he doesn't want to make any policy decisions until 1995.

2.4 It was notable that Labour made no reference to us and little to the

---

1 Wednesday 16 September, when Britain dropped out of the ERM and the pound devalued by 20 per cent.

issue of PR. This could be a good sign, in the sense that Smith is leaving his door open on this issue. Whichever way they jump, Labour's decision on PR is of vital tactical and strategic importance to us.

2.5 At present Labour's 'one more heavers' and the traditionalists seem to be in the ascendant – perhaps because the modernizers have yet to put their point of view.

[...]

2.7 I think that Labour are going to fail to make themselves look modern – indeed they seem to look, if anything, more old-fashioned under Smith than they did under Kinnock.

2.8 Labour started very badly in local elections after the General Election – 33 per cent of the vote and losing seats predominantly to the Tories, but also to us. They have made better progress since Black Wednesday, getting 42 per cent of the vote.

3 The Liberal Democrats

3.1 We have stayed pleasingly high in the polls (up 3 to 16 per cent against static showings for Tory and Labour in the most recent polls) since the election. Normally, we drop back hard after General Elections – and after Labour Conferences.

3.2 But our local election score has been less impressive. We held our own in local by-elections up to Black Wednesday, getting 26 per cent of the vote, but have been getting some worrying results since then (23 per cent).

3.3 Our Conference was internally quite good. But I suspect the external image was less useful, though obscured by Black Wednesday. We inevitably looked a bit divided over strategy (as was only to be expected) and there was an impression that some of the silliness and unruliness of the old Liberal Party was re-emerging.

[...]

3.7 We should treat any hopeful by-election as an absolute priority – a by-election win in the current circumstances would give us a very considerable boost and could help generate a third-party bandwagon.

POSITION PAPER, JANUARY 1993

1 The Conservatives

1.1 The Government have probably come through the worst of their present crisis. They should be able to look forward to relatively calm water, at least in the near future.

1.2 The worst of the Maastricht process is now behind them.

1.3 The economy looks likely to turn up, if very slowly, in the next few months – a result of the stimulus given by the Government's recent actions. Growth will be below a respectable figure, but the low economic aspirations to which Britain has become conditioned probably means that anything which isn't a decline is regarded as satisfactory.

1.4 In the longer term there are real problems looming with inflation, but these are unlikely to be seriously felt until the end of the year at the earliest.

1.5 In the shorter term, the real problem is the twin deficits – how to restrain the level of Government borrowing, which is now set on an extremely dangerous upwards trend (£50 billion by next year), and how to deal with the trade deficit.

1.6 The Budget deficit may require an increase of taxation even as early as this Budget. We must establish a clear line on our attitude to increased taxation – particularly in view of our past policies.

1.7 Unemployment will continue to rise and will pass 3 million early in 1993. As we have seen in the past, this may increase Government unpopularity, but is unlikely directly to threaten the Government's survival.

1.8 The second problem is likely to be with the balance of payments, which will deteriorate very quickly if the recovery takes place.

[. . .]

1.12 The more serious problem for the Tories remains that they are without any clear vision of Britain's future and without any firm leadership from the top.

1.13 Our main point of attack should continue to concentrate on this deficiency; a Government exhausted of ideas, and condemned to drift, just at the moment when Britain needs new ideas and clear leadership.

2 Labour

2.1 Smith has had a really bad start. He has largely wasted his honeymoon period as a new Leader, both within his Party and at large. The recent split between modernizers and traditionalists is extremely significant and could do a lot more damage if Smith does not give a clear lead on it soon.

2.2 There is a strong impression that Labour is going backwards and has failed to face up to the changes necessary for the future. We should continue to point up Labour's failure to tackle the issues that matter.

2.3 With the Plant Commission[1] report coming up soon, it is very important to set PR up as a marker by which Labour's ability to face up to new challenges will be judged.

[...]

2.5 It is also clear that the Labour leadership are, for the moment at least, not interested in dialogue. Nor will they become interested in this until they have been brought to the realization that 'one more heave' will not work.

2.6 It is my view that the most fertile area for us in the next few months lies more in the vacuum left by Labour's failures than in the failures of the Government.

2.7 At best we could really begin to make progress at Labour's expense. At worst we could help Labour come to the realization that they cannot succeed without us.

2.8 This does not mean abandoning our strategy. It means reminding people that we are willing to work with others to oppose the Tories and bring the changes Britain needs, while continually pointing up Labour's failures. We have to be seen to be facing up to the questions Labour is seen to be ducking, giving a clear lead on those areas they are avoiding and adopting policy positions they should be adopting, but can't.

3 The Liberal Democrats

3.1 We appear to be doing most things about right, but not to be getting enough of the benefit.

3.2 I think that we can look back on the last few months with some satisfaction.

3.3 We have taken positions which have been clear and occasionally, as in Maastricht, courageous. Our predictions and positioning have been good. And we are getting some very satisfying local election results.

3.4 I sense that the Party is well positioned to make substantial progress.

3.5 But it seems to be obstinately slow in coming. Our opinion poll ratings

---

1 Labour's internal enquiry into PR.

have remained stable, which is good, especially after the worries people had expressed at the time of the Maastricht 'paving' vote. And our core vote is higher than for some years. But I had hoped for more.

3.6 More worryingly, commentators have continually referred to the 'failure of opposition', in which they include us.

3.7 Our biggest short-term failure remains our lack of a clear and understood economic policy.

3.8 In the long term, our problem remains what it always has been. People still do not know what we stand *for*, although there is evidence that we are constructing the building blocks for a sharper identity, especially in the areas of education, the environment and Europe.

3.9 I am concerned that we have started to drift. We have yet to define a strategy for the period up to the General Election and are resting on our laurels with the broad policy positions and approach which we constructed for the last election.

3.10 I identify four aims for 1993.

● To give the Party a new impetus.

● To make maximum use of the electoral opportunities which come our way.

● To define and start transmitting a single clear message of what we stand for.

● To start preparations for the next General Election.

[. . .]

10 Conclusion

10.1 We have real opportunities ahead of us, not just from the early unpopularity of the Government, but also and perhaps more significantly, from the perceived failures of Labour and their new Leader.

10.2 We must do everything we can to capitalize on this opportunity.

10.3 This means winning when we have the chance.

10.4 It means re-establishing a sense of impetus within the Party and clarifying the message we give outside it.

10.5 It means showing Labour up where we can and capturing territory from them where this is possible.

10.6 And it means beginning to prepare now for the General Election which we have already identified as the one by which we should be judged.

POSITION PAPER, JULY 1994

1.1 We are now halfway through this parliament. We have succeeded in securing an electoral base at European, Westminster and local level. In the face of 'Blairite' Labour resurgence and the stabilization of the Tory decline, *our next task is to communicate what the Liberal Democrats stand for and to mark out our own distinctive agenda.*

2.1 *The Tories*

2.1.1 They must be pleased that they appear to have stemmed the decline. They believe that they have 'seen off' the Liberal Democrat surge and can now look forward to a return to two-party politics, from which we are excluded.

2.1.2 They successfully convinced the press (with some help from our Party) that they were going to have a catastrophe in the Euros. So, when they only had a disaster, they were able to claim a success.

2.1.3 They are counting on the recovery continuing through to the General Election, so that by the time Major has to go (autumn 1996 or spring 1997 at the latest) he can point to four years of a continuously strengthening economy and continuously falling unemployment figures.

2.1.4 Despite the divisions within the Tory Party over Europe and the fragility of the recovery, we would be wise to plan for the probability of some recovery in the Tory vote.

2.2 *Labour*

2.2.1 Labour are enjoying a love-in with the Press.

2.2.2 Our failure to deliver beyond our target range in the Euros was due to the hardness of the Labour vote in our key areas and the rise of their vote in others.

2.2.3 They have handled both John Smith's death and Blair's coronation well (it is now clear that he will be elected) and can be expected to continue to gain from this into the autumn and the new session of Parliament.

2.2.4 Much depends on Blair's capacity to deliver for his Party what he stands for. Will he 'Blairize' the Party, or will the Party 'Labourize' him? Given Labour's hunger for power, the fear of the consequences of a fifth failure and the absence of anything else to say, Blair is likely to get his way to a larger extent than might have been expected at the beginning of this year.

2.2.5 Labour will attempt to steal our clothes from us, one by one, unless we are prepared to put them out of Labour's reach by radicalizing and clarifying our policies in ways which Labour cannot match. Among those in our Party who are most resistant to co-operating with Labour are also some who are most resistant to making our policies more distinctive from Labour. This paradox is becoming increasingly untenable and will have to be resolved.

2.2.6 Labour's message will be, 'If you want to get rid of the Tories, vote for the real thing since we are the only ones with the power to do it.' Our response should be: 'If you want *real* change, vote Liberal Democrat, since we are the only ones with the *policies* to do it.'

2.3 The Lib Dems

2.3.1 The aim we set for this year was to prove that the Liberal Democrats are distinctive, independent and growing as a force. The May and June elections have achieved the latter two. Our task now is to concentrate on distinctiveness.

2.3.2 We set ourselves three targets for the recent elections. To expand our local government base; to begin to win seats from Labour in the cities and to secure our first presence in the European Parliament. We have succeeded in all three.

2.3.3 In Scotland our results reflected our English ones, but at a lower level. But the rise of the Nationalists in Scotland gives cause for concern.

2.3.4 The situation in Wales is much more worrying. Our weakness here, unless stopped, could decline into obliteration in the long term.

2.3.5 Nevertheless, overall the Party is now stronger than it has ever been, with an electoral asset at every level, a European heartland in the South West peninsula, a key development 'box' for Westminster seats along the South Coast, from Sussex to Land's End and north to Berkshire and Wiltshire, and a local government asset which is now genuinely nationwide.

2.3.7 We therefore have good cause to feel pleased.

2.3.8 And yet, despite our expectation that this kind of success would have put us at the centre of the action, we seem to have been pushed out on to the periphery again [by Smith's death and Blair's advent]. Meanwhile, the rise and rise of Labour is disconcerting and there is concern that Blair will take possession of our ground.

2.3.9 So, instead of being in good heart, the Party is in a rather introspective, even nervous mood.

2.3.10 We also have a very big job to do to re-convince the serious press and opinion formers that we still have a role to play and a message to listen to [post Blair].

[. . .]

4 Relations with the Other Parties

4.1 The Tories

4.1.1 Wherever the Tories are under attack we must be seen to be part of the assault.

4.2 Labour

4.2.1 We will be under pressure from Labour and the *Guardian* 'Lib-Labbers' to abandon equidistance. There will be a moment when we will have to decide our future position vis-à-vis Labour in the context of the next election – and it would be better to do this well ahead of, rather than during, the election campaign. But we are not near that moment yet and must ensure that any decision we might take on this front is taken at a time and on grounds of our choosing. For the moment we should reject 'equidistance' as a concept ('Why should we be forced to define our position only in relation to the others?') in favour of independence and distinctiveness.

4.2.2 Our approach to Labour, therefore, should be to stress our differences while continuously setting them standards and benchmarks which they must achieve to be considered really modern. While Labour's press honeymoon lasts, our tone should be one more of sorrow than of anger.

4.2.3 Meanwhile, at local government level, our approach should continue to be 'twin track', encouraging partnership at local level where it is sensible, while continuing to build our local government base in Labour's areas. There is a real prospect of making substantial further inroads into their heartlands next May, when we are poised to make further progress in a number of Labour cities (e.g., Liverpool and Sheffield).

POSITION PAPER, FEBRUARY 1995

1 The Tories

1.1 The Conservatives appear hopelessly split and terminally mistrusted by the electorate. But we should not underestimate their capacity for recovery or for papering over their splits in the face of the ballot box.

1.2 The economic recovery seems set to continue. Although this is unlikely to deliver a 'feelgood factor' on the scale of previous elections, the Tories will be able to point to an impressive record of rising economic success and falling unemployment by the time of an election, say in late 1996. We should therefore continue to plan for the probability of a recovery in Tory fortunes. Much of this is likely to be at our expense in our target areas.

1.3 There is a view that we should consider the possibility of an earlier election, because the Tories 'just can't hold together much longer'. But this seems to me rather unlikely.

1.4 The Conservatives have everything to gain from letting this parliament run for as long as possible, consistent with having the election before the end of the IGC. They can delay the IGC, at least until the autumn of 1996 and probably until mid-1997 if they wished.

1.5 The main thrust of the Tories' election campaign is already clear. They will play on three basic themes. Stability, tax cuts and the flag.

2 Labour

2.1 Blair is doing extraordinarily well and will continue to do so.

2.2 The press are now wanting Labour to win, or, in the case of the anti-Major Tory press, prepared to use them to get rid of the Prime Minister.

2.3 Moreover, Labour is so desperate to win that they are prepared to give Blair whatever he wants. The extreme left will put up a token fight on Clause 4, but there is no serious prospect that they can win and the harder they fight, the more they enhance Blair's victory.

2.4 Blair will progressively take Labour on to our ground. He is genuinely keen on Europe and believes that he has to meet the Tories head-on on this agenda and win.

2.5 He is less keen on the principle of constitutional reform, but sees this as a talisman which marks Labour as a modern party.

2.6 He has no commitment, beyond the conventional skin-deep one, to the environmental agenda.

2.7 He knows that Labour's biggest enemy is complacency and their biggest task is to put together a coherent alternative message. For this reason I think he will, starting this year, fill out Labour's programme in surprising detail, especially on the economy.

2.8 By late 1996, Labour's programme will, in the main areas, be almost indistinguishable from ours, except probably on the environment and at the margins of the constitutional agenda. In all the things that make the majority of people vote, we will be saying virtually the same thing.

2.9 While Labour are likely to fall back from their present poll heights, they will probably maintain a position well ahead of the Tories through next year. Some of this will be at our expense, even in our target areas.

3 The Liberal Democrats

3.1 The Party at large feels cheated, fractious and uncertain. We hit all the targets we set for ourselves at the start of the year, but had the prize snatched from our hands by the change of Labour leadership. We damaged ourselves further at the Conference [by the drugs debate, etc.] and are now being increasingly ignored by the press because we are not seen as part of the story any longer.

3.2 With self-confidence so fragile, talk of strategy and positioning is unsettling. And yet, most people in the Party realize that we will have to clarify our position well before the next election. And, though many find it difficult to say so openly, most understand that there is no practical possibility that we could act to prolong the life of this Government. The 'strategy debate' which is now underway has a very great capacity to split the Party.

3.3 And yet our assets on the ground remain strong, especially in the 'Golden Box' in the South of England, which comprises our chief area of potential growth.

3.4 Our record in local government by-elections remains satisfactory, but no better.

3.5 Our opinion poll ratings are probably around 15 per cent, which may be a fairly solid base from which we are unlikely to fall much further. But I can't see any reason to believe that there is, at the moment, much scope for increase either. Our private polling shows Labour moving ahead of us, even in our target areas. This is normal at this stage in the parliament. What is unusual is that, for the first time anyone can remember, the prospect of any support for the Conservatives costs us dear electorally in our target seats, while 'sturdy independence', or co-operation with Labour both appear to produce net gains for us here.

3.6 There are worries about membership and finance in the longer term.

3.7 In this position, squeezed from left and right and with our ground being occupied by others, we *must* renew the Party's sense of mission and make clear what we stand *for*. This is not just a question of policy and message. Voters also want to know what the *effect* of a vote for us will be on who has power in Britain. If we cannot explain what it is people vote for when they vote for us, this next year is likely to be very uncomfortable.

POSITION PAPER, OCTOBER 1995

1 The Tories

1.1 They have had as good a Conference as they could have hoped for, given the disastrous way in which it started. Rows have been avoided; some new policies (but very few) have been unveiled and Major's position has been preserved, perhaps even strengthened. Barring unforeseen events, it now seems certain that the Tories will go into the next election under the leadership of John Major and looking relatively united on the surface.

1.2 However, the takeover of the Tory Party by the right, and particularly by the anti-Europeans, is now complete; Major is a prisoner of the right and has no alternative but to preside over their hijacking of the Party.

1.3 Portillo's speech[1] strikes me as a turning point. It was disgraceful, ugly and quite premeditated.

1.4 Meanwhile, that speech and the tone of the Conference will have sharpened the discomfort of the 'One-nation Tories'. The *Independent* reported that a number were very unhappy and mentioned us, rather than Labour, as a more likely home. I doubt if there will be more 'Howarths', but we should maintain close relations with likely candidates and keep close tabs on their feelings.

1.5 The one solid remaining Tory hope lies with substantial tax cuts. But,

---

1 A Euro-sceptic speech by Michael Portillo at the Conservative Party Conference in which he said: 'Around the world three letters send a chill down the spine of the enemy – SAS. And those letters spell out one clear message: Don't mess with Britain.' The speech became known as the SAS speech and was widely condemned.

given the underlying state of the economy, this will be difficult to achieve and could look irresponsible, except in very careful instalments.

1.6 There is a moment when a Government loses the next election. Labour lost the 1979 election in November 1978. I think this Government lost the next election in June/July this year. But they are not going to fall apart. What is more, any slight recovery will come disproportionately at our expense.

2 Labour

2.1 I had hoped that we had seen the high-water mark of Labour and that, in this sense, the next year would be easier than the last.

2.2 But Labour's Conference success means we must reassess this judgement. The tide is still coming in for them.

2.3 Whatever the rumblings of discontent during the summer (and they are no doubt still there under the surface), Labour will now unite for the election.

2.4 Labour has succeeded in making itself look like the coming force.
[. . .]

2.6 Having made a determined attempt to capture our physical territory last year (with more success than we like to admit), they will now move comprehensively on to our policy territory this year.

2.7 They made 1995 all about New Labour. They will try to make 1996 all about new (young) Britain.

3 The Liberal Democrats

3.1 We got through the last year magnificently, thanks to excellent campaigning, a lot of hard work and a good deal of luck.

3.2 Our local government asset is now very considerable. It comprises both an opportunity and a danger for us. How do we maximize the former and minimize the latter?

3.3 Our finances are stable and our membership, though slightly down on last year, is not at present a major cause for worry – though we will need a successful membership drive this year.

3.4 The Party is in good heart after a successful Conference. This is internally valuable, even if it has already been, externally, forgotten.

3.5 We now have a position which the Party feel happy with and a message which they feel enthusiastic about.

3.6 But our presumption that the worst was over, in terms of Labour invading our territory, is probably wrong, at least in the short term. Recent local government by-election results have been very worrying.

3.7 Past experience shows that the Party is always able to improve its position provided one of the other two parties is in decline. But it seems likely that, at least over the next few months, both Labour and the Tories may be on the rise. The squeeze on us could be painful.

Conclusions

If 1995 was the year of consolidation, 1996 is the year of communication. Take risks, look and sound different; use every opportunity to get our core message across.

Appendix B

Sensible politicians take time after a General Election result to reflect on its implications for their country and for their parties.

So I do not intend – and nor do I advise any Liberal Democrat – to rush to premature conclusions about our strategy and tactics for the next election, before we have all come to terms with the lessons of the last . . .

But this does not mean that we can absolve ourselves from a rational consideration of what happens next. Those who sit back in politics can quickly find that others have moved on.

As we move now into the second stage in the building of our Party, it would be foolish to compromise the long-term strategy which has served us so well.

But it would be equal folly to ignore the new opportunities which that strategy has now created.

Yes, we have made encouraging progress since the débâcle of 1988. But Britain still has a Conservative Government at Westminster.

Yes, we have won many of the arguments for change. But Britain still lacks a powerful movement to make change happen.

Yes, we have built an effective campaigning party of opposition. But Britain still lacks a credible, electable alternative Government to the Tories.

These three deficiencies mark our task in this parliament. It is this: to create the force powerful enough to remove the Tories; to assemble the policies capable of sustaining a different Government; and to draw together the forces in Britain which will bring change and reform.

Britain is in jeopardy of becoming entrenched in a system of almost permanent one-party Conservative government: elected by a minority but able to exercise the exclusive power of a majority.

What does this mean for those millions in Britain who are shut out from the Conservative view of how society should be? The poor, the unemployed, the homeless, those who have lost and will increasingly lose the small luxuries of hope as our public services continue to decline, our environment continues to get dirtier, and our pride in a compassionate and caring society withers away in the face of a continued Conservative assault on the things we took for granted as part of a civilized society only a few years ago.

As we now contemplate our strategy for the years ahead, let us never forget that these are the people who sit huddled outside, waiting for us to get it right.

And what would a near-permanent Conservative hegemony mean for the health of our democracy?

Many of the imperfections and injustices in our political system – the overweening power of the executive, the absence of proper protection for personal liberty, unfair voting, excessive secrecy, a Conservative-dominated press, the centralization of power – these were tolerated by many in Britain, precisely because, from time to time, power changed hands. Are they still to be tolerated if Britain is becoming a one-party state? Are we prepared to be witness to the slow death of pluralism within our democracy?

These are questions which will worry not just opposition politicians and the wider public.

Many thoughtful Conservatives will also be concerned about the implications of their victory for the health of our democratic system.

Mr Major is entitled to celebrate his victory. It was a considerable personal achievement. But a wise Prime Minister might also reflect for a moment on whether he won because of positive enthusiasm for what he promised, or because of fear of what Labour would do instead.

There was certainly little sign during the election of any positive vision of the Conservative future – nor is there now. Just the remnants of Thatcherism watered down with a spoonful of sugar.

Yet good government depends on the positive support of the people; on an effective opposition, and on the possibility of change . . .

So it is essential now that everyone in each of the parties, opposition and government, comes to terms with the significance of the political situation that we face.

And no party needs to do more to rethink than today's Labour Party . . .

They will blame the tabloid newspapers, or say that their policies were misunderstood. They will blame the professional campaign for which they were queuing up to take the credit only hours before the polls closed. They will even say that the voters didn't mean to vote the way they did.

But what really matters for Labour is not the excuses they find for the past, but what they do in the future.

For some in the Labour Party, the answer is 'one more heave'. But that is not a strategy, it is a pipe dream.

Labour can no longer win on their own. They are a drag factor on others who fight the Conservatives. They have now lost their historic role as the sole left-of-centre party capable of winning government and defeating the Conservatives.

If there is one hopeful sign in today's Labour Party it is that some, including perhaps some in leadership positions, are beginning to recognize that fact. If their recent careful and cautious words about consensus are meant to signify a coded recognition of the reality facing Labour then this is a shift of historic importance for the whole of British politics, and one which Liberal Democrats should welcome.

The question for Labour now is, can they come to terms with the reality of their position – and can they match the mood of the 1990s in order to become a force for change? Or will they cling to their old myths and old ideas, blocking progress and holding up the defeat of the Tories?

So what about we Liberal Democrats? How should we conduct ourselves in the months ahead?

I have little sympathy with those who say that, having won back our position in politics, we can now be satisfied with being no more than a party of local government, or a test-bed for new political ideas. And I have no sympathy for those who believe that politics is the art of waiting for something to turn up.

As a third party, these two options are simply not open to us. We have to maintain our momentum. And we have to take risks to shape and influence events in our favour, rather than allow others to shape them for us.

But we have to do something else as well.

We have to continue to win the argument for the values and policies for which we Liberal Democrats have been campaigning over the last three years.

In the 1970s, it was the new right which captured the intellectual initiative from the old left. And, more than anything else, it was the slothful self-satisfaction and indolence of the left's response which led to its downfall as an alternative force for government in Britain.

Now the left, in the shape of today's Labour Party, have abandoned socialism, because it made them unelectable. But they have found nothing to replace it and now drift dangerously unanchored in a period of change, without a convincing creed of their own to preach, or a firm set of ideas to cling to.

It is our task, as Liberal Democrats,

to set our sails to the new winds which will blow through the nineties;
to establish the new frontier between individual choice and collective responsibility;
to draw up the practical means to change our economic system in order to respond to the environmental challenge;
to liberate the political power of the individual within a practical system of government;
to build a powerfully competitive economy, based on individual enterprise and founded on a flexible labour market;
to create a taxation system whose purpose is not just to redistribute wealth, but also and perhaps chiefly, to redistribute opportunity;
to extend ownership as a means of spreading wealth and diffusing economic power;
to establish a network of individual rights which will fill the gap left by the death of collectivism;
to rediscover pride in being English, Scottish, Welsh and Northern Irish within a Britain that is big enough to allow different cultures and diffused government to flourish;
to respond to the decline of the nation state in Europe without recreating the nation state on a European scale;
to find practical means to strengthen global institutions so as to increase our capacity to action world peace and respond to global catastrophe.

These are some of the policy challenges which face Liberal Democrats in mapping out the new policies our country will need as we approach the turn of the century.

But will it be sufficient if we formulate these ideas just amongst ourselves? My answer is no.

Our contribution, if it is to be successful, must reach out beyond the limits of our own Party. Our role is to be the catalyst, the gathering point for a broader movement dedicated to winning the battle of ideas which will give Britain an electable alternative to Conservative government.

I do not believe that mathematically constructed pacts and alliances are the way forward, either for Liberal Democrats or for others. At best they would be a waste of precious time – at worst positively damaging.

What is, however, in both our interest and that of the country, is to work with others to assemble the ideas around which a non-socialist alternative to the Conservatives can be constructed, with Liberal Democrats at the centre of the process and a reformed voting system as the starting point.

What this means for Liberal Democrats is that we must be much less exclusive in our approach to politics, and much more inclusive to others.

We must look outward to the concerns of wider sections of our community. We must learn to work with others in a common cause. And we must have the self-confidence to risk our ideas in debate with others who seek the same basic aims.

Nothing more clearly showed Labour's failure to ditch their old arrogance and come to terms with their new realities than one recent suggestion that, as an example of Labour's new consensus approach, other parties might generously be allowed to give evidence to Labour's present committee on electoral reform and their future one on social justice.

There could be no surer way of blighting the birth of the new politics in Britain than requiring it to be delivered in a specially constructed bungalow annex in the grounds of Transport House!

So, as we enter this new parliament, here are the tasks which I believe lie ahead for us Liberal Democrats:

First, to continue to build our strength on the ground as an independent and distinctive force.

Second, to continue our energetic and courageous pursuit of new ideas and new policies.

And third, to be prepared to provide leadership for the wider debate about the construction of post-socialist, non-Conservative Britain, confident in our own ideas, clear about our objectives, but flexible in our approach to others.

It is time for us to begin the second stage in our development, in which we use our strength to lead the political debate on to ground where the Conservative Government can be defeated at the next election, and bring to our country the fundamental reforms and changes to which this Party has always been committed.

Appendix C

LETTER ABANDONING EQUIDISTANCE

25 May 1995
House of Commons
London SW1A 0AA

Confidential

Dear Colleague,

This Saturday we will be discussing the joint paper commissioned by the FE and FPC, and conducting a general review of the political situation in the light of the Local Election results.

As you know, over the last five months, I have been conducting an extensive listening and consultation exercise, during which I have visited each of the national and regional parties and spoken, in private, to a large number of our activists and key members.

In these sessions, we have been discussing the principal aims and positioning of the Party in the run-up to the General Election.

In the light of these discussions [this letter outlines] my judgement of where the broadest consensus of opinion in the Party now lies . . .

The Lessons of 4 May[1]

The voters gave us all a clear message [on 4 May]. Yes, they want to see an end to this discredited Conservative Government, which has gone on for too long, lurched

---

[1] Local Election Day, when Labour had a very good night (as did we) and the Tories lost heavily.

from crisis to crisis and has lost the confidence of the country. But Labour, while they won against the Tories, could not stop our growth. People voted for a strong, united and independent Liberal Democrat force to represent their interests against both of the other parties – Tory and Labour . . .

Our aim at the General Election will be to win as many Liberal Democrat seats and as many Liberal Democrat votes as possible . . .

Clear Policies

Our job now is to build upon our success and sharpen our identity – to campaign for our vision of a modern Britain, democratic and open in its government, competitive and enterprising in its economy, committed to long-term investment in education, justice in social policy, careful of the environment and certain about our future in Europe.

So we will oppose both Conservative and Labour parties at the next election. Britain needs the Liberal Democrats to provide the sort of change people want and Britain deserves. We will fight the election on a programme which is distinctive, sharp in its message, clear in its priorities and fully costed. ·

Clear Position

Just as we will be clear about our policies, so we must also be clear about our role.

Everyone knows that a vote for the Liberal Democrats is a vote to remove this Conservative Government. So it should surprise no one when we say that if the Conservatives lost their majority in Parliament and seek our support to continue in office, they will not receive it. People must know that if they kick the Tories out through the front door, we Liberal Democrats will not allow them to sneak in through the back.

But our opposition to the Conservatives does not mean cosying up to Labour. Britain's is not a two-party system, as Thursday's election showed – even if the press have still failed to notice it.

Labour may be changing. But they still fail the crucial tests to be trusted with the Government of Britain . . .

So our position could not be clearer. *No quarter for the Tories; no let up on Labour. The Liberal Democrats will continue to campaign and win for the principles and policies that WE believe in.*

Liberal Democrats are determined to promote a new style of politics in this country. But change must come from the ballot box, not from the smoke-filled room. So no pacts, no deals, no mergers. Liberal Democrats stand for a more co-operative approach to politics . . . We will work with others [where we] agree and if it is in the interests of those we represent to do so. And the more [we] agree, the more we can work together . . .

Yours

Paddy Ashdown MP

Appendix D

EMMA NICHOLSON'S LETTER
TO THE PRIME MINISTER

EMMA NICHOLSON MP
HOUSE OF COMMONS
LONDON SWIA OAA

29 December 1995

Dear John,

I felt that I should let you know in advance of the public statement that I am today leaving the Conservative Party and joining the Liberal Democrats.

As you know, I have supported the Government in every whipped vote, under Margaret Thatcher and yourself, and every unwhipped vote, when requested to do so, during my years as a Parliamentary Private Secretary.

However, my conviction now is that I would be wrong in terms of my principles, the interests of my constituents and the future of the country to continue that pattern of voting.

Rather than become a permanent rebel inside the Conservative Party, I deem it proper and honest to cast my votes, which will quite often be against the Government, from the Liberal Democrat benches. Their thrust is now mine.

I retain a high personal regard for yourself and many Conservative Ministers and Members.

Yours,

Emma

[Faxed to No. 10 Downing Street, 29 December 1995.]

Appendix E

THE LIB DEMS AND PARTNERSHIP POLITICS
[This is the minute I drafted as though from a Labour researcher, for Archy Kirkwood to give to Donald Dewar]

The Options

It is important that we know exactly what the options are so that there is no misunderstanding about the decisions which must soon be made.

The following is from close sources [in the Lib Dems] and represents the options as viewed by [them].

They believe there are two routes, either of which they are prepared to follow, depending on our response and especially TB's personal attitude to PR.

They describe these as the Little Thing and the Big Thing.

The Little Thing

They are perfectly happy with where they have now got to and will be quite content to fight the next election on the basis outlined in Ashdown's 'Bridge' speech of 22 January. They believe that we have done our worst and they have held their ground. There may be one or two seats where a rise in our vote could deny them victory over the Tories. But they believe these to be few and are confident that they can make considerable progress, whatever happens, at the next elections.

Meanwhile, they are also confident, both about their policy prospectus and about the role they can play in the likely battleground of the next election. They say their Party is united around the position of last May ('No quarter for the Tories, no let up on Labour, work with others where they agree with us'). Their policy positions are, they claim, clearer than ours and fully costed. On this basis they can fight the next election on a clear message based around their 'Guarantee' document[1] and on the role that a vote for them is a vote which makes change safer, because the public can't really trust us [Labour].

In short, they are quite content to fight a conventional election campaign, in which they target both other parties. They explain that, in these circumstances, they will have to attack us in order to differentiate themselves, and they will have to point up our deficiencies as they see them. Their tone will be different from the Tories – more in sadness than in anger. But, as one of them put it to me, 'We will nevertheless be snapping pretty aggressively at your heels – we will have to, that's what conventional campaigns are about.'

Ashdown thinks he is striking a chord with a disillusioned public with 'partnership' politics. But, in the context of the Little Thing, co-operation will be more about tone than substance and will be *ad hoc*, opportunistic and casual, rather than structured and substantial. They will be keen not to get too close to us because they feel this will diminish their distinctiveness, particularly on the constitutional agenda.

The Big Thing

The [Lib Dem] alternative under consideration is to do something which is genuinely groundbreaking, could open the way to an historic shift in politics and might, done in the right way, turn a Tory defeat into a rout.

They stand ready to consider the possibility of making a public declaration, jointly with us, that, in *whatever* circumstances the two parties find themselves after the next election, we would work in partnership on three, or possibly four key policy items, crucial to Britain's future. One of these would have to be constitutional change, where the model of the Scottish Convention is one they would like to follow. Another could be on Europe, where a common front to defend against Tory attacks makes good sense. The other one or two would have to be real 'bread-and-butter' issues, perhaps education and something on the economy and jobs.

In all other areas the two parties would pursue their own agendas and present different prospectuses. Indeed, they point out that it would still be necessary for them to maintain a healthy dynamic tension in other areas

1 A recent Lib Dem policy document outlining what a vote for the Lib Dems would 'guarantee'.

(e.g., the environment), in order to prevent being swallowed up. And, while an agreement on central issues would alter the whole nature and tone of the campaign and the relationships between the parties, they would still have to retain a role as the 'ratchet' to prevent what they would describe as backsliding from us or undue leverage from our 'old Labour' left.

Nevertheless, they believe that, consistent with their need to preserve what they describe as their distinctiveness, this would lead to a full partnership approach to the election and a whole new climate in politics, with, potentially, immense implications for the future.

Proportional Representation

This is their bottom line for the Big Thing. Without it Ashdown couldn't and wouldn't be prepared to try to carry his Party. This, they claim, is not just being partisan.

Ashdown believes that any dependable long-term relationship with us would be bound to come under strains and go through unpopular periods. Experience shows that in these it is the smaller party which suffers. Without PR this could destroy his Party and he is, not unreasonably, not prepared to ask his Party to swallow a suicide pill. As they see it PR is not only the price, but also the means to assure a durable relationship. Secondly, he sees PR as the guarantor of the pluralism which we are now talking about (see the recent Andrew Marr article in the *Independent* on this) and to which they are committed.

Finally, they see PR as the means to ensure that the Tories cannot get back 'on the bounce' at the election after next.

They are firmly wedded to STV. But in Scotland they have accepted a variant of AMS. They are strongly opposed to AV (used in many Labour internal elections). But the key thing for them is to establish the principle of electoral reform, rather than, at this stage, getting tangled up in the detail, which, anyway, might, in the end, be a matter for the referendum.

They are quite happy to take their chances in a referendum on PR, but could not do this in circumstances where electoral change was opposed by the Prime Minister. In other words, Blair's personal position on this is the crucial issue.

They believe that Blair cannot anyway adopt the Kinnock approach of saying nothing. And that it is very difficult to have a referendum and then ask people to vote against. So they take the view that he has to decide and it is almost certain that he has to decide to support change. If this can be done before the election, rather than after it, then the conditions are in place for the Big Thing to happen.

The choice, they say, is now ours.

Timing and Procedure

If we are to progress with the Big Thing, then, they believe that a decision in principle to try out this route has to be taken over the next two or three weeks because there is so much work to be done.

If such a decision was taken, confidentially and on the basis of an understanding about the end position on PR, then we could start immediately putting in hand the work on the constitutional agenda. This might be followed in due course by Europe and then the other agreed areas. We should not announce in advance the ultimate destination for all this, but arrive there, as it were, almost by accident in the autumn or at whatever other time it was felt electorally most useful.

Electoral Effect

They remain nervous about this. There is no point in going ahead if the result is a net loss of votes, rather than a net gain in their key seats and ours. They point out that this would not be in our interest either. So a final decision as to whether to proceed or not would depend on the outcome of polling work they will start in their target seats if and when a decision to proceed in principle is made.

We will no doubt wish to do parallel work in our seats, too.

30 January 1996

Appendix F

26 February 1996

Dear Prime Minister,

I promised that I would write to you setting out my intentions following our meeting on Monday.

I have now reflected on my position, and had the opportunity to canvass the views of many of my constituents in Bolton North-East. I have also considered carefully the points that you put to me.

After considerable thought, I have decided that I must, in good conscience, resign the Conservative Whip in the House of Commons on Monday 26 February, I will sit as an independent member of Parliament and you will not, I fear, be able to count on my vote in any future vote of no confidence.

You know from our discussions that I have been profoundly unhappy with the direction and performance of the Government for many months. Your Government has failed to offer the leadership the country needs. All too often, it has run away from problems, or simply given in to pressure groups on the Tory back benches. You know only too well that the Conservative Party is now a divided, unhappy and faction ridden party. I cannot in good faith remain a member of the Conservative Parliamentary Party.

I look forward to being able to represent my constituents and their interests as an independent MP, putting their views straightforwardly, without fear or favour, and fighting for my beliefs without regard to the Government's party interest.

This has not been an easy decision. I have been a Conservative MP for nearly thirteen years, and won three elections against the odds. All through that time, I have given loyal service to the Conservative Party and its leadership. I pay tribute to the enormous support and encouragement I have received from many wonderful people in the Bolton North-East Conservative Association, and those who helped to found and develop the Conservative Disability Group.

Loyalty cannot be blind, however. I now find that I can better represent the views of my constituents and pursue my commitments to high standards of public service, hard work, common sense and moderation from a new position in politics. I leave many good friends in the Conservative Party. But I no longer have confidence in the Conservative Party of today.

Yours

Peter

Appendix G

Britain must change, if Britain is to succeed again.

That applies to our politics, too. Respect for politicians and trust in the political system has fallen to dangerously low levels.

People are tired of watching the parties put political confrontation before the national interest.

So are we.

There needs to be new leadership and a new approach if we are to refresh and modernize our democracy.

We believe that partnership and pluralism are central to the new politics Britain needs, as we approach the new century.

We believe that political parties which are different and compete at the ballot box should still be able to work together where they agree and where it is in the national interest to do so.

We represent two different political traditions in Britain, with different origins, a different approach and many differences in policy. We relish these differences. They are essential to the richness, diversity and health of British politics and to the choice that people should have at the ballot box.

But there are also areas vital to Britain's future, where we agree and where we can co-operate as partners on the basis of shared policies, mutual respect and the national interest.

We therefore make a commitment to the British people that we will work together, whatever the outcome of the next election and wherever we sit in the new Parliament, to achieve the programme outlined below.

We intend this partnership for Britain's future to be a rock upon which to build a different future for our country.

1 Education

1.1 *Britain's education system is failing us.*

1.2 If we are to make this country successful again, we must make its education system the best in the world.

1.3 This means making education the nation's first priority in the years ahead.

1.4 We will work together to achieve that by

1.4.1 raising standards in our schools to world levels, by concentrating on core skills, constantly challenging pupils to higher achievement and continuously presenting them with new opportunities;

1.4.2 improving the quality of our teaching by establishing a National Teaching Council, charged with rigorously overseeing and policing professional standards;

1.4.3 making education funding the first call on the nation's financial resources;

1.4.4 giving every child in the country access to two years' free high-quality nursery provision before they enter school;

1.4.5 modernizing and restructuring Britain's higher- and further-education system to provide an efficient, flexible, credit-based system capable of providing a higher proportion of our young people with cost-effective, high-quality post-16 education and training to meet the needs of the next century.

2 Welfare

2.1 *Britain's welfare system has failed us.*

2.2 It traps people in poverty instead of freeing them. It makes them dependent instead of providing them with opportunities. It penalizes work instead of rewarding it.

2.3 It is wasteful, demeaning and extensively abused.

2.4 It is time to replace Beveridge's great scheme with something new which meets the new conditions of our time and can take Britain into the new century.

2.5 Recasting Britain's system of welfare and work will be best done through partnership across and beyond politics, if it is to succeed.

2.6 We will work together to establish the broadest base possible, including, we hope, those from the other political parties and from beyond politics, to renew and reconstruct Britain's welfare system.

2.7 our aim will be to create a system which

2.7.1 provides effective support for those who genuinely cannot support themselves; but

2.7.2 rewards those who can help themselves and do, above those who can help themselves and don't;

2.7.3 emphasizes the redistribution opportunities, rather than wealth;

2.7.4 encourages self-reliance and discourages dependence;

2.7.5 enlarges the support role of the community and reduces that of the state.

3 The Constitution

3.1 *Britain's political system has failed us.*

3.2 We will not solve Britain's problems unless we clean up the mess of our politics.

3.3 We reject the Tory notion that we cannot change Britain's constitution without endangering it. Quite the contrary. The strength of Britain's constitution has lain, precisely, in its ability to change and adapt down the years.

3.4 It is our job to do for our time what our forebears did for theirs – to modernize, update and democratize our system of government.

3.5 We will work together to

3.5.1 modernize and democratize our voting system at all levels within the next parliament;

3.5.2 reform the House of Commons and the House of Lords;

3.5.3 clean up the funding of the political parties;

3.5.4 protect our civil liberties, through a Bill of Rights;

3.5.5 bring in a Freedom of Information Act;

3.5.6 give Scotland and Wales the opportunity to elect their own assemblies;

3.5.7 re-enliven and strengthen local democracy and create the framework for a regional dimension to government which is locally accountable.

4 The Economy

4.1 *The British economy has been appallingly mismanaged by the Tories over the last sixteen years. And it is chiefly ordinary people who have paid the price for this.*

4.2 Creating a new future for Britain depends on maintaining a strong and secure economy and beginning to build for the long term

4.3 We will work together to ensure

4.3.1 a firm long-term low-inflation strategy with identifiable and publicized targets for inflation (at the moment 0–3 per cent);

4.3.2 a reduction in total public borrowing, expressed as a percentage of GDP (our aim is to bring this below 40 per cent over the next parliament);

4.3.3 a commitment to the 'golden rule' (i.e., that the level of the Government's borrowing should never exceed the level of the Government's capital investment);

4.3.4 the establishment of an Independent Central Reserve Bank, charged with maintaining price stability within a target range, set by Parliament;

4.3.5 Britain's adherence to the Maastricht criteria for entry into the European single currency;

4.3.6 tough action to strengthen competition in the British economy;

4.3.7 special assistance and encouragement for enterprise and small industry;

4.3.8 increased employment opportunities, especially for the young unemployed.

Signed

[Tony Blair]   [Paddy Ashdown]

Appendix H

PARTNERSHIP FOR BRITAIN'S FUTURE
[SECOND DRAFT]
Norton-Sub-Hamdon, Somerset   January 1997

The coming election is the last of this century and will decide the shape of our country for the next century.

We believe that Britain must change, if Britain is to succeed again.

That applies to our politics, too. Respect for politicians and trust in the political system have fallen to dangerously low levels.

People are tired of watching the parties put political confrontation before the national interest.

So are we.

There needs to be new leadership and a new approach if we are to refresh and modernize our democracy.

We believe that partnership and pluralism are central to the new politics that Britain needs for the future.

We believe that political parties which are different and compete at the ballot box, should still be able to work together where they agree and where it is in the national interest to do so.

We represent two different political traditions in Britain, with different origins, a different approach and many differences in policy. No doubt we shall continue to disagree, at times strongly, about these. That is as it should be. For these differences are essential to the richness, diversity and health of British politics and to the choice the people should have at the ballot box.

We have chosen these areas for action because we believe that our aims are common, not just to us, but shared by many in other political parties and even by some beyond them. We invite them to join us. This is not intended as an exclusive partnership, but as the cornerstone upon which we can build a different future for our country.

1 Cleaning up our Politics

1.1 *Our politics has become dangerously discredited.*

1.2 The funding of our political parties is murky and corrupting.

1.3 The rules governing the conduct of elected representatives, especially Members of Parliament, have proved to be inadequate.

1.4 Patronage has become endemic.

1.5 Far too much power and far too many decisions relating to public money are taken out of view of the public and outside the circle of public accountability.

1.6 We will work together to

> **1.6.1** clean up, and open up, the whole system of funding of political parties;
>
> **1.6.2** strengthen the rules governing the behaviour of MPs in the conduct of their public duties;
>
> **1.6.3** make the public appointments system subject to a system of check and scrutiny;
>
> **1.6.4** diminish the number of quangos and make those that remain more open and publicly accountable;
>
> **1.6.5** make those who sit on quangos subject to the same rules of declaration and interests as local government Councillors.

2 Modernizing our Constitution

2.1 *Britain's political system has failed us.*

2.2 We reject the notion that we cannot change Britain's constitution without endangering it. Quite the contrary. The strength of Britain's constitution has lain, precisely, in its ability to change and adapt down the years.

2.3 It is our job to do for our time, what our forebears did for theirs – to modernize, update and democratize our system of government.

2.4 We will work together to

> **2.4.1** modernize and democratize our voting system at all levels within the next parliament;
>
> **2.4.2** reform the House of Commons and the House of Lords;
>
> **2.4.3** protect our civil liberties, through a Bill of Rights;

2.4.4 bring in a Freedom of Information Act;

2.4.5 give Scotland and Wales the opportunity to elect their own assemblies;

2.4.6 re-enliven and strengthen local democracy and create the framework for a regional dimension to government which is locally accountable.

3 Reforming Our Welfare System

3.1 *Britain's welfare system has failed us.*

3.2 It traps people in poverty instead of freeing them. It makes them dependent instead of providing them with opportunities. It penalizes work instead of rewarding it.

3.3 It is wasteful, demeaning and extensively abused.

3.4 It is time to replace Beveridge's great scheme with something new which meets the new conditions of our time and can take Britain into the new century.

3.5 Recasting Britain's system of welfare and work will be best done through partnership across and beyond politics, if it is to succeed.

3.6 We will work together to establish the broadest base possible to review and reconstruct Britain's welfare system.

3.7 Our aim will be to create a system which

3.7.1 provides effective support for those who genuinely cannot support themselves; but

3.7.2 rewards those who can help themselves and do, above those who can help themselves and don't;

3.7.3 emphasizes the redistribution of opportunities, rather than wealth;

3.7.4 encourages self-reliance and discourages dependence;

3.7.5 enlarges the support role of the community and reduces that of the state.

4 Strengthening the Foundations of the Economy

4.1 *Creating a new future for Britain depends on building and maintaining a strong and secure economy based on skills, enterprise, and long-term investment.*

4.2 But, in these fundamentals, Britain's economy remains relatively weak.

4.3 Our education and skill levels are lower than nearly all our competitors. As is our level of industrial investment. Uncertainty about our future in

Europe and about our determination to resist inflation means higher interest rates for British businesses than nearly all our continental competitors. And the level of government debt remains dangerously high.

4.4 We will work together to ensure that

4.4.1 Britain's education and skills are raised to world levels;

4.4.2 we maintain a firm long-term low-inflation strategy with identifiable and publicized targets for inflation (at the moment 0–3 per cent);

4.4.3 total public borrowing, expressed as a percentage of GDP is reduced (our aim is to bring this below 40 per cent over the next parliament);

4.4.4 we adhere to the 'golden rule' (e.g., that the level of the Government's borrowing should never exceed the level of the Government's capital investment);

4.4.5 an independent Central Reserve Bank is established, charged with maintaining price stability within a target range, set by Parliament;

4.4.6 Britain adheres to the Maastricht criteria for entry into the European single currency;

4.4.7 tough action is taken to strengthen competition in the British economy;

4.4.8 special assistance and encouragement is given for enterprise and small businesses;

4.4.9 there are increased employment opportunities, especially for the young unemployed.

Signed

[Tony Blair]   [Paddy Ashdown]

Appendix I[1]

MEMORANDUM PREPARED BY TOM MCNALLY FOR
THE IMMEDIATE POST-ELECTION PERIOD

*Strictly Private and Confidential: Negotiating Participation in
Government; Overview Memorandum*

If it were done when 'tis done, then 'twere well it were done quickly.
Macbeth I.vii.1

Executive Summary

1. Before General Election

Section entitled 'The Negotiations' to be talked through with selected individuals, including Richard Holme and Jonathan Powell. (*NB Need, in the latter case, for two people to be present on each side, one taking a note.*)

Set up contact mechanisms between ourselves, and with Blair's office: during General Election: Holme/Mandelson; and post-GE: McNally/ Jonathan Powell.

Set up consultation systems involving potentially successful candidates and the Federal Executive.

William Wallace/Tom McNally/Phillip Goldenberg to draft mission statement.

2. After General Election

Choose whether seeking full coalition or alternative possibilities (see under 'Choices').

---

1 This memorandum was shown to the Cabinet Secretary before the 1997 General Election, and a minute based on it was left with Tony Blair's office at the beginning of the election campaign.

Arrange full support for steering group.
Archy Kirkwood and others to liaise with MPs.
Speedy arrangements for Special Conference and/or Members' ballot.

Assumptions

1. Labour offers negotiations in one of three situations:
    it has an overall majority, but decides that it wants to enter negotiations;
    it is the largest single party but without an overall majority; or
    it is not the largest single Party, but it and we are together the best combination available to form the Government.
2. PA decides to enter into these negotiations.
3. A prolonged period of negotiations is generally judged to be unviable.

Choices

1. If Labour has no overall majority, or an overall majority of no more than, say, twenty or thirty, then they will presumably be prepared to offer, and we would presumably seek, a full-blown coalition Government, in which we would share collective power in, and collective responsibility for, government.
2. If Labour has an overall majority of more than, say, twenty or thirty, then they are *unlikely* to offer this. We would not want, say, a couple of Cabinet Ministers, e.g. to oversee the constitutional reform programme, because we would end up with the 'reverse harlot' position of responsibility without power. In this situation, we should adopt a different approach (see the second part of first Blair/PA meeting).

The First Blair/PA Meeting

Either (full coalition)

1. Not just Lib Dem Ministers in Labour Government to implement Labour programme, must be proper coalition Government.
2. This entails a full structural coalition agreement relating to the machinery of *government* and including a mission statement.
3. Apart from the agreed constitutional reform programme (which should be strengthened), everything else *can* be left for the Queen's Speech (provided that, under the structural agreement, this has to be agreed between the

two parties); indeed, this is inevitable if the negotiations are to be speedy.

4. In making his Cabinet appointments, Blair must leave appropriate gaps.

5. Consider delaying the State Opening (can be done, but not by *less* than two weeks).

6. Civil Service support for Lib Dems in negotiations (separate unit, confidential from Ministers).

Or (alternative possibilities)

1. Happy to work with you but, if no full coalition, cannot take Cabinet posts.

2. Possibilities include:

(a) a Cabinet Committee, consisting of members of both parties, to oversee the constitutional reform programme (this is perfectly possible constitutionally, and there are precedents, *provided that* all members are Privy Counsellors – see separate note), perhaps with Robert Maclennan as Chair;

(b) a fast timetable for the agreed Commission on Electoral Reform, to include Lib Dem members (and perhaps with a Lib Dem Chair, such as Vernon Bogdanor);

(c) public agreed mission statement, and Blair's personal full commitment to campaign for PR for Westminster;

(d) a firm commitment to PR for the 1999 Euro-elections;

(e) a general consultative mechanism (which could be another Cabinet Committee as under (a) above);

(f) Chairs of some key Select Committees, with an agreement for full release of the relevant departmental papers;

(g) various external appointments (perhaps another two-party Cabinet Committee to deal with patronage generally);

(h) more 'short money' for opposition parties (with the formula changed to reflect responsibility of this sort of arrangement).

NB.

1. *There must be a prior personal Blair/PA telephone conversation so as to ensure that the meeting is not taking place on any false premise as to either Party's position.*

2. *This conversation should establish who will be present on each side. While it may well be appropriate for part of the meeting to be on a one-to-one basis, it should be appreciated that Blair will automatically be*

attended by his Principal Private Secretary and probably the Cabinet Secretary, and it is highly undesirable for PA not to be accompanied by an appropriate 'watching team'; it will be important to establish and maintain a 'marking' system.

The Negotiations

1. Duration

    1.1 If we were in a culture used to coalition negotiations, it would be possible to take the period (one week or more?) needed to reach (if appropriate) full agreement on a joint programme. However, the pressures of (a) the media and (b) the internal situations within both parties make this difficult.

    1.2 If this is to be a full coalition, it is *recommended* that, apart from the 'strengthened' constitutional reform programme and the mission statement, there be an 'agreement to agree' the contents of the Queen's speech. This will then give sufficient time for the necessary detailed discussions.

    1.3 If Labour has an overall majority, then the impact of any negotiations on international financial markets (if polling day is on 1 May, UK ones will be closed until the Tuesday morning, as Monday 5 May will be a Bank Holiday) will be nil. If the situation is uncertain, then it would be preferable to conclude the negotiations by the Sunday evening.

2. Content of the Deal

    2.1 There is no problem with the fallback position of judging each issue on its merits, with such degree of pre-consultation as a Labour Government wishes.

    2.2 What would be utterly unacceptable would be for a couple of Lib Dem MPs simply to accept Cabinet office in a Labour Government implementing a Labour *programme* (shades of Lloyd George!).

    2.3 It is accordingly *recommended* that the following are the *essential* components of any full Coalition deal:

        the agreed (and timetabled) constitutional reform programme;

        a full structural coalition agreement;

        an agreed mission statement; and

        an agreement to agree on the contents of the Queen's Speech, which should have full regard to both parties' election manifestos.

    2.4 On any deal for less than a full coalition, we should offer support for specific policies, and a consultative mechanism, against:

joint Cabinet Committees (see separate note);
cast-iron assurances on the timetable for electoral reform and Blair's support, and Lib Dem members of the Electoral Reform Commission;
an agreed mission statement;
a firm commitment for PR for the 1999 Euro Elections; and
other items

See generally the last paragraph of the first Blair/PA meeting.

NB. This section to be talked through pre-General Election with selected individuals.

The Parliamentary Parties

1. A full coalition agreement *must* constitute a binding agreement on all four Parliamentary parties, to the intent that, in each House, the two Parliamentary parties operate a joint Whip in support of the Government (this was the great fault of the Lib/Lab pact).
2. A full Coalition *must* be ratified by the Liberal Democrat Parliamentary Party in the *Commons*. They cannot be mandated by any other organ of the Party to do so. If it is thought appropriate to seek the opinion of a Special Conference, or of the generality of members by means of a ballot, the Lib Dem Parliamentary Party in the *Commons* must have so ratified the agreement, so that they are bound by collective responsibility before such ballot and/or Conference.[1] The agreement between Blair and PA and so ratified must, therefore, take immediate effect, but be subject to ratification by the appropriate procedures of both Parties.
3. Clearly Lib Dem MPs must be kept fully informed; equally clearly, undisciplined public *comments* would be unhelpful. It is *recommended* that:
Archy Kirkwood, as Chief Whip, have primary responsibility for liaising with Lib Dem MPs, with a support team: the division to be as follows:
Wales: Alex Carlile;

---

1 I had made it explictly clear that any proposal for a coalition agreed by the Parliamentary Party would nevertheless have to be subject to an affirmative resolution being passed by the Lib Dem Conference. I did not believe that this could be done by the Parliamentary Party alone. I also thought that entry into a coalition would, in the long run, be unsustainable unless backed by the conference resolution and a membership-wide ballot.

Scotland: Jim Wallace;

SW England: Paul Tyler;

NW England: Andrew Stunell;

and other: Archy Kirkwood

Candidates in all seats that might be won should receive, in their mailing at the last weekend before polling day, a categorical instruction to read an e-mail message that will be posted at 2100 hours on polling day before going to their respective counts; and

This e-mail message should give the place, date and time (1500 hours on the Saturday?) of a meeting of Lib Dem MPs which will take place (automatically, unless cancelled by subsequent e-mail message posted prior to 2200 hours on the Friday), and give a categorical instruction that no substantive public *comment* is to be made before then save as permitted by that message; it should also give details of the routine pre-session meeting of the Parliamentary Party.

The Party

1. The Constitution

1.1 The Parliamentary Party *cannot* be mandated (Article 2.5).

1.2 The Federal Executive or Federal Policy Committee may *summon* a Special Conference (Article 6.6).

1.3 The Federal Executive may order a members' ballot (Article 8.6).

2. Logistics

2.1 *Assuming* negotiations are concluded by the end of Bank Holiday Monday (5 May), the following is the shortest feasible timetable for consulting the Party:

(a) Thursday 8 May/Saturday 10 May: Ballot papers posted to members;

(b) Thursday 15 May (noon): Return date for ballot papers; and

(c) Saturday 17 May (at c1300 hours to allow for registration, possibly under secret ballot supervision): Special Conference.

2.2 The Federal Executive is scheduled to meet on Tuesday 6 May in any event.

2.3 It may be advisable, if negotiations occur, for the Federal Executive additionally to meet on Sunday 4 May (convened by telephone on Friday 2 May), so that it can take any formal decision to *summon* a Special Conference and/or order a members' ballot, thereby pre-empting any other requisition.

Appendix J

LIBERAL DEMOCRAT SEATS AFTER THE MAY 1997 GENERAL ELECTION

Name	Constituency	Result
ALLAN, Richard	Sheffield Hallam	LD majority 8,271
ASHDOWN, Paddy	Yeovil	LD majority 11,403
BAKER, Norman	Lewes	LD majority 1,300
BALLARD, Jackie	Taunton	LD majority 2,443
BEITH, Alan	Berwick-upon-Tweed	LD majority 8,042
BRAKE, Tom	Carshalton & Wallington	LD majority 2,267
BRAND, Peter	Isle of Wight	LD majority 6,406
BREED, Colin	South East Cornwall	LD majority 6,480
BRUCE, Malcolm	Gordon	LD majority 6,997
BURNETT, John	Torridge & West Devon	LD majority 1,957
BURSTOW, Paul	Sutton & Cheam	LD majority 2,097
CABLE, Vincent	Twickenham	LD majority 4,281
CAMPBELL, Menzies	North East Fife	LD majority 10,356
CHIDGEY, David	Eastleigh	LD majority 754
COTTER, Brian	Weston-super-Mare	LD majority 1,274
DAVEY, Edward	Kingston & Surbiton	LD majority 56
FEARN, Ronnie	Southport	LD majority 6,610
FOSTER, Don	Bath	LD majority 9,319
GEORGE, Andrew	St Ives	LD majority 7,170
GORRIE, Donald	Edinburgh West	LD majority 7,253
HANCOCK, Mike	Portsmouth South	LD majority 4,327
HARRIS, Evan	Oxford West & Abingdon	LD majority 6,285

HARVEY, Nick	North Devon	LD majority 6,181
HEATH, David	Somerton & Frome	LD majority 130
HUGHES, Simon	North Southwark & Bermondsey	LD majority 3,387
JONES, Nigel	Cheltenham	LD majority 6,645
KEETCH, Paul	Hereford	LD majority 6,648
KENNEDY, Charles	Ross, Skye & Inverness West	LD majority 4,019
KIRKWOOD, Archy	Roxburgh & Berwickshire	LD majority 7,906
LIVSEY, Richard	Brecon & Radnorshire	LD majority 5,097
MACLENNAN, Robert	Caithness, Sutherland & Easter Ross	LD majority 2,259
MICHIE, Ray	Argyll & Bute	LD majority 6,081
MOORE, Michael	Tweeddale, Ettrick & Lauderdale	LD majority 1,489
OATEN, Mark	Winchester	LD majority 21,556
ÖPIK, Lembit	Montgomeryshire	LD majority 6,303
RENDEL, David	Newbury	LD majority 8,517
RUSSELL, Bob	Colchester	LD majority 1,581
SANDERS, Adrian	Torbay	LD majority 12
SMITH, Robert	West Aberdeenshire & Kincardine	LD majority 2,662
STUNELL, Andrew	Hazel Grove	LD majority 11,814
TAYLOR, Matthew	Truro & St Austell	LD majority 12,501
TONGE, Jennifer	Richmond Park	LD majority 2,951
TYLER, Paul	North Cornwall	LD majority 13,847
WALLACE, James	Orkney & Shetland	LD majority 6,968
WEBB, Steve	Northavon	LD majority 2,137
WILLIS, Phil	Harrogate & Knaresborough	LD majority 6,236

Index

A1 Group 169

Adams, Gerry 240, 306, 309

Adie, Kate 302, 303

Adonis, Andrew 120, 364, 366, 532

Agnelli, Giovanni 43

Airlie, Countess of 429

Aitcheson, Jackie 215

Aitken, Ian 99

Aitken, Jonathan 285

Al Fayed, Mohamed 284–6, 289–90,
    291, 293

ALDC (Association of Liberal
    Democrat Councillors) 171, 194–5

Alderdyce, John 88

Allan, Alex 203, 257

Allason, Rupert 406

Allen, Graham 221

Allen, Ted 398, 408, 418

Alternative Member system *see* AMS

Alternative Vote *see* AV

Alton, David 10, 57, 72, 82, 224

Amiel, Barbara 122–3, 149–50, 168

AMS (Alternative Member System)
    381, 426, 482

Andrew, Prince 200

Annan, Kofi 305

Any Questions 308

Arafat, Yasser 435

Archer, Jeffrey 116

Archer, Mary 116

Ash, Timothy Garton 43

Ashdown, Jane (wife) 6, 12, 16, 18, 19,
    31, 49, 53, 56, 81, 82, 84, 138, 149,
    163, 168, 175, 177, 445, 454
  and Cherie Blair 360
  strength of 397
  and Tricia Howard affair 138, 139,
    140, 141, 142–3, 145, 155, 250,
    251, 252, 255–6
  upset by Amiel's article 150

Ashdown, Kate (daughter) 31, 48–9,
    85, 116, 126, 139, 141, 252
  and father's affair 143
  marriage 393
  pregnancy and birth of son 459,
    544–5, 546, 547, 548–9
  wedding day 454–5

Ashdown, Mark (brother) 133, 134

Ashdown, Paddy
  personal: and birth of grandson
    548–9; birthdays 31; car accident
    239–40; Christmas 125–6; and
    daughter's wedding day 454–5;
    and death of Aunt Joyce 171–2;
    death threats and hate mail
    398–9, 538; driving offence 86;
    fire bomb threats 408, 418,
    469–70; fire in car 389–91, 392,
    396; holidays and house in
    Burgundy 7, 84–5, 145, 181, 222,
    274–5, 340, 419; illegitimate child
    rumour 153, 160, 259; knife attack

Ashdown, Paddy – *cont.*
  incident and subsequent Mason
    case 362–3, 366, 367, 380, 388,
    399; marriage break-up rumours
    174–5; police protection 393, 408;
    serves in Royal Marines 176; sex
    scandal allegations 392–3, 394–5,
    397, 398, 400; SIS story 146–7;
    threatening phone calls 397, 398,
    402; and Tricia Howard affair
    132–5, 137–44, 145, 250–2, 255–6
  politics: article on in *Sunday Times*
    122–3, 149–50; *Beyond*
    Westminster 165, 215, 252, 253;
    and Bridge speech 379, 382–3,
    386; and Chard speech *see* Chard
    speech; *Citizens' Britain* 44, 50,
    51, 56, 486; constituency activities
    6; criticism of by press 50;
    decision to stand down after next
    election 463, 538; elected as leader
    of Liberal Democrats 5–6; and
    opinion polls 68, 143; Party
    Conference speeches 13–14, 67;
    proposal for 'A Programme for
    Britain' 38–9; position papers *see*
    position papers; problems
    inherited when elected leader 7;
    receives *Spectator* 'Party Leader
    of the Year' award 99–100;
    relationship with colleagues 166;
    sworn in as Privy Councillor
    25–6; theory of opposition
    politics 92; view of party politics
    419; visit to mine 215–18; visits to
    communities in Britain 165,
    215–18
Ashdown, Simon (son) 8, 126, 139,
    140, 141, 143, 379, 454
Ashton, Cathy 259
Ashton, Joe 230
Assinder, Nick 139

Association of Liberal Democrat
    Councillors *see* ALDC
Association of Social and Liberal
    Democrat Councillors (ASLDC)
    30, 56
Atkinson, Max 11, 55, 454, 455
Austin *see* Emma Nicholson
AV (Alternative Vote) 353, 370, 381,
    392, 387, 411, 412, 421, 422, 426,
    437, 453, 482, 524
Aziz, Tariq 105

Bailey, John 143, 418
Bailey, Stephanie 143, 164
Baker, James 105
Baker, John 97
Baker, Kenneth 94, 106, 156, 162
Bakewell, Cathy 133, 141
Baldwin, Stanley 448
Ballard, Jackie 114, 149, 157, 193, 462,
    555
Bank of England 498
Banks, Tony 53
Barker, Liz 194
Barlow, Roger 541, 542
Barnes, Rosie 41, 61
Barnett, Robert 269, 270–1
Beckett, Margaret 261, 385, 405, 480,
    508
beef
    BSE crisis 416–18, 430–1, 432–3,
      443, 475
    European ban on 430–4, 435–6, 439
Begin, Menachem 350
Beith, Alan 11, 13, 52, 70, 131, 161,
    196, 307, 431
    and committee on planning
      approach to hung Parliaments 71
    and Economic spokesmanship 10, 148
    and Gulf War 111
    and Lib/Lab co-operation issue 319,
      468

loses leadership contest 5
and name issue 57
Party Conference speech 462
Belfast Telegraph 15
Bell, Martin 327, 328
  candidate for Tatton 541, 542, 543
  in Sarajevo 206, 207, 270
Bell, Stuart 292
Bellotti, David 94, 158
Bentsen, Lloyd 43
Bevins, Tony 6, 293–4
Biffen, John 161
'Big Andy' 216–17
Bilderberg Conference (1989) 42–4
Black, Conrad 202
Blackstone, Tessa 7
Blair, Cherie (wife) 243, 274, 315, 358,
  360, 440–1, 443, 474
Blair, Euan (son), 383, 388
Blair, Kathryn (daughter) 275, 456, 533
Blair, Nicky (son) 286
Blair, Tony 98, 172, 220, 259, 261, 308,
  310, 407, 446
  Ashdown's view of 244, 265, 314
  and BSE crisis and beef ban 431,
    432, 435–6, 439
  and community concept 244
  discussions with Ashdown and
    feelings on Lib/Lab co-operation
    221, 228–9, 242–4, 275–8, 280,
    283–4, 286–9, 310–14, 323,
    324–6, 336–7, 341, 351–7, 383–8,
    410–11, 413, 414–15, 421, 424–9,
    436–8, 441–2, 449–54, 456–9,
    470–1, 474–5, 481–4, 500–3,
    505–12, 515–29, 532–6, 555–6,
    559–60
  and economy 385
  elected leader of Labour Party 268
  on electoral reform and
    proportional representation 276,
    278, 313, 336, 346, 347, 354,
    357–8, 360, 366, 379, 380, 384,
    386–7, 401, 412, 421, 424, 449,
    450–1, 453, 482, 500–1, 503, 504,
    506–8, 511, 515, 521–2, 527–8
  and Europe 276
  family background 358
  and Harman 383–4
  and Irvine 310
  and Jenkins 278, 346, 360, 366,
    379–80, 424, 439–40, 459, 477,
    508, 553
  Labour Party's attitude towards 308
  and Major 348, 384, 551
  and Mandelson 268
  Party Conference speech (1996) 463
  and Prescott 385
  and reform of Labour Party 243, 244
  relationship with Ashdown 277, 360,
    467
  relationship with Brown 243, 385,
    422, 436
  Shirley Williams' view of 446, 462
  and single currency 354
  speech on economics 267
  successor to Smith 262
  support of by 'Gang of Four' 272–3
Blaskic, General 338
Boizot, Peter 33
Bonham-Carter, Jane 256, 465, 466
Bonham-Carter, Mark 16–17
Bonsor, Nicholas 282
Boothroyd, Betty 161, 261, 445
Bootle by-election (1990) 82, 86
Borrie Commission 287, 289, 293, 427
Bosnia 181, 183, 211, 249, 258, 266, 283
  Ashdown's position over 225
  Ashdown's visit (1992) 175–80
  Ashdown's visits (1993) 231–8, 244–6
  Ashdown's visit (1994) 269–72
  Ashdown's visits (1995) 301–4,
    329–34
  and Hurd 254

Bosnia – *cont.*
  Major's policy over 124, 222–4, 249,
    321–2, 338
  and 'Map on the Menu' 315–16,
    337–8
  peace initiatives 241–2
  and safe havens 322
  and Soviet Union 255
  worsening of situation 321–2
  see also Sarajevo
Boutros-Ghali, Boutros 305, 306
Boycott, Rosie 530–1
Braine, Sir Bernard 91
Branson, Richard 279
Breakfast Time 40, 47, 121
Breakfast With Frost 252, 265, 499, 524
Bremner, Rory 304
Bridge speech 379, 382–3, 386
British Nationality Act 47
Brittan, Leon 78, 284–5
Brooke, Peter 161
Brown, Gordon 288, 388, 415, 540
  Ashdown's view of 488
  and Bruce 359, 413
  discussions with Ashdown 484–8,
    502
  and economy 487
  electoral reform and proportional
    representation 426, 436, 450, 488,
    533
  and Lib/Lab co-operation issue 385,
    428, 436, 450, 484, 485–8
  relationship with Blair 243, 385, 422,
    436
Brown, Nick 354
Bruce, Malcolm 60, 307, 319, 359, 413
Brunson, Michael 39
Bruton 350
BSE crisis 416–18, 430–1, 432–3, 443,
    475
Buckingham Palace
  Diplomatic Reception at 19–20

Budd, Dick 454
Budget (1992) 144, 147
Burnett, John 368, 545
Bush, George 111, 112
Butler, Sir Robin 123, 146, 219

Caine, Sir Michael 365, 371
Callaghan, Audrey 18
Campaigns and Communications
    Committee 45
Campbell, Alastair 81, 144, 256, 310,
    471
Campbell, Jack 264
Campbell, Menzies (Ming) 9, 10, 32,
    111, 112, 119, 131, 267, 276, 288,
    385, 402, 405, 446, 469, 515
Canterbury, Archbishop of 407
Carlile, Alex 32, 51, 161, 193, 198, 221,
    289, 292, 293, 319, 346, 385, 461
Carrington, Lord 42
Cartwright, John 10, 40–1, 58, 59, 61,
    62, 98
Carvel, John 10
Cash, Bill 439
cash for questions issue 285, 291–3
Ceremony of the Prorogation 71
Chalker, Lynda 266
Chaplin, Judith 219
Chapman, Deborah 204
Chapman, Jill 274, 275
Chard & Ilminster News 164
Chard speech (1992) 163–6, 168, 169,
    171, 192, 193, 195, 220, 590–4
Charles, Prince 18, 200, 203, 351, 448
Charriat, René and Jacqueline 274,
    275
Charter 88 38
Checkland, Michael 116
Chidgey, David 265
China
  Tiananmen Square massacre (1989)
    45–6, 47

Chirac, Jacques 354, 406, 407, 429
Chosic, President 183, 188
Christchurch by-election (1993) 229, 231
Clark, Nick 554
Clark, Sir William 70
Clarke, Charles 123, 145
Clarke, Kenneth 17, 25–6, 98, 419, 432
Cleese, Alyce Faye 170
Cleese, John 55, 170
Clement-Jones, Tim 12, 25, 31, 45, 542
Clinton, Bill 200, 224, 244, 263, 264, 303, 350, 351
Clinton, Hillary 263, 264
    The Agenda 354
Clist, Nigel 416
Clough, Gordon 12
Collins, Stan 363
Conference Day 14
Conference of European Liberals (1990) 88–9
Conservative Party 38, 144
    leadership contest (1990) 97–8
    and Liberal Democrats 123, 145, 279, 307
    see also Major, John
Contact Group 269, 270, 272
Conway, Clare 139, 168, 251
Cook, Colonel Mark 178–9, 180
Cook, Robin 171, 243, 263, 402, 403, 409, 424, 453, 515
    and Brown 422
    discussions with Ashdown 420–3
    as Foreign Secretary 561
    and Lib/Lab co-operation issue 171, 311, 312, 415, 420–3, 437
    speeches 405
    talks/commission/report with Maclennan 313–14, 325, 347, 353, 358, 359, 404, 421, 438, 444, 448–9, 451, 468, 470, 471, 472, 477–8, 481, 482, 506, 510, 512–13,
516, 520–1, 522, 530, 532, 533, 534, 536–7
Council of the Regions 221
Crewe, Ivor 218–19
Croatia 315, 337, 338
Cronkite, Walter 315
Crosland, Tony 34, 130
Cross Questions 24
Cryer, Bob 53
Cunningham, George 18
Cunningham, Jack 202, 243
curfews 434

Dacre, Paul 526
Dahrendorf Commission 287, 289, 427
Daily Express 136, 139
Daily Mail 256, 384
Daily Mirror 81, 139, 144, 256, 301, 436, 480, 513, 514, 529, 531
Daily Telegraph 374, 478, 509
Davey, Ed 196
Davies, Chris 335, 337, 446
de Burgh, Chris 116
de Klerk, President 78
de la Billière, General Sir Peter 110
De Mello, Sergio 269
decommissioning 309, 356
Dell, Edmund 8
Delors, Jacques 78
devolution 257, 310, 441–2
Dewar, Alison 415
Dewar, Donald 119, 263, 354, 385, 401, 413, 414, 495, 500, 522
Diabetic Society 11
Diana, Princess of Wales 18, 116, 120–1, 200, 203, 224
Dickie, John 364, 366
Dimbleby, David 114, 265
Dimbleby, Jonathan 30, 156
Divorce Bill 348
Dobson, Frank 70
Doherty, Wendy 142

Domestic Violence Bill 348
Don Giovanni 49–50, 144
Dorrell, Stephen 416
Downing, Alisoun 6
Downing Street 16
Drago, Stefan 301
Drljaca, Simo 190–1
drugs debate 281, 282
Duff, Andrew 468
Dykes, Hugh 430, 500, 501, 503

Eames, Archbishop Robert 280
Eastbourne by-election (1990) 92–3,
    93–4
Eastern Europe 43
Eastleigh by-election (1994) 253, 254,
    255, 265
Eatwell, John 7
Eberle, Admiral Sir James 101
economy 385, 428, 475, 486–7, 607–8,
    611–12
Eden, Anthony 448
Edinburgh, Duke of *see* Philip, Prince
education issue 427–8, 606
Edward, Prince 200
ELDR (European Liberals, Democrats
    and Radicals) 170–1
electoral reform 381–2, 421–2, 426,
    436, 450–1, 482–3, 504, 520–1,
    527–8
    see also AMS; AV; proportional
    representation; STV
Electoral Reform Society 5
Elizabeth, Queen 18, 26, 115–16, 144,
    445–6, 479, 480
Ellis, Andy 23, 39
Ellis, Mark 361, 390
Elson, Graham 66, 195, 226, 368, 369
Epping by-election (1989) 23
equidistance
    abandonment of 307, 311, 312,
    318–20, 321, 324, 595–7

ERM 172, 192, 196
European Commission 77–8
European elections 173
    (1989) 45, 48–9, 50, 51, 54
    (1994) 265–6
European Liberals, Democrats and
    Radicals *see* ELDR
European monetary union 43, 348, 476

Farewell Symphony 129
Farris, Les and Joan 400–1
FDP (Germany) 146
Fearn, Ronnie 158
Federal Executive (FE) 11
Federal Finance and Administration
    Committee *see* FFAC
Fellowes, Jane 224
Fellowes, Sir Robert 146, 200, 224, 252,
    407, 447–8
FFAC (Federal Finance and
    Administration Committee) 44, 59
Fidelio 445
Financial Times 188, 198, 436, 505,
    531
Fisher, Mark 100
Forbes, Bryan 282
Ford, David 48
Former Yugoslavia War Crimes
    Commission 360
Foster, Don 158, 172, 198, 221, 249,
    319, 468
Frazer, Peter 25
Freeman, Roger 405
Frost, David 12, 252

Ganic, Ejup 209, 237–8
Garnett, William 134
General Election (1992)
    budget 90
    campaigning by Ashdown 149, 151,
    153–4, 155–6, 157
    date announced 147–8

Labour's NHS election broadcast 152
manifesto 90, 148, 150, 151
opinion polls 151, 152, 153, 154, 156
polling day and results 157–9
seats lost 158, 159
and taxes 148
General Election (1997)
campaigning by Ashdown 538–9, 542–51, 553–4
manifesto 539, 541
manifesto costings 514
opinion polls 540, 543, 544, 550, 551, 553
polling day 554–8
results 557
Gibson, Anthony 416
Gladstone, William 345, 419, 424
Gladwyn, Lord 19
Glamorgan by-election (1989) 33, 37, 39–40
Goldenberg, Philip 194, 539–40
Goodhart, Willy 30, 56, 137
Gorbachev, Mikhail 36–7, 111, 121
Gore, Vice President Al 306
Gorman, Teresa 96–7
Gould, Bryan 70, 107
Gould, Philip 289
Goulding, Marrack 305
Gow, Ian 92
GQ magazine 146–7
Grafin Dohnoff, Marion 83
Granada 500 156
Greaves, Tony 194, 195
Green Party 48, 49, 50, 51, 53
Greer, Ian 290, 291, 292
Grender, Olly 109, 138, 158
Gresham, Mrs 553
Grimond, Jo 12, 261
Guardian 10, 23, 27, 30, 31–2, 101, 150, 182, 268, 272, 285, 286, 289, 291, 292, 335, 352, 440, 460, 531

Gulf War 101, 105, 107–13
Ashdown's position over 108, 110, 111
attack on civilians in Baghdad 110
beginnings of 97–8, 109
and Bush 111, 112
ending of 113–14
Gorbachev's peace proposals 111
ground assault 112–13
memorial service for those who served in 406–7
progression of 109–10
service of thanskgiving at end of 115–16
Gummer, John Selwyn 432

Habgood, John 116
Hague, William 28
Halmos, Tony 295
Hamilton, James Douglas 152
Hamilton, Neil 285, 289, 290, 291, 292–3, 540
Hannay, Sir David 78, 305, 306
Harman, Harriet 243, 381, 383–4, 388, 416, 440
Harris, John 16–17, 364
Harvey, Nick 200–1, 364–5, 477
Hattersley, Roy 85, 529
Havel, Vaclav 81, 82
Healey, Denis 38, 130, 259, 261
health policy 288
Heath, David 157, 557
Heath, Edward 85, 108, 115, 200, 304
Hemsworth by-election (1991) 123
Hennessy, Peter
    The Hidden Wiring 409
Heseltine, Michael 83, 84, 96, 98, 101, 466
Hewett, Gavin 269
Hicks, Bob 367, 368
Hinton, Nick 130
Hogg, Douglas 370, 416, 430, 445

Hollingsworth, Larry 176, 177, 207, 210, 211
Hollis, Patricia 202
Holme, Richard 12, 27, 30, 90, 137, 194, 265, 289, 416
    and Emma Nicholson's defection 365, 367–8, 369
    as General Election (1997) manager 228, 273, 304, 42?, 459
    and Lib/Lab co-operation issue 288, 438, 449, 468
    meeting with Mandelson 489
Hong Kong 53, 84
    Anglo-Chinese Agreement 46
    Ashdown's visit to (1989) 47–8
    right of abode for British citizens issue 46, 47, 49, 56–7, 85–6
Hooson, Emlyn 169
Hope and Homes for Children 180
Hopkins, Sir Brian 39
Hopkirk, Joyce 174
Howard, Michael 284, 285, 293
Howard, Sandra 81–2
Howard, Tricia 132–3, 134, 141, 155, 249–50, 250–1, 252–3, 255–6
Howarth, Alan 343
Howe, Geoffrey 47, 70, 72, 96, 100
Howell, David 83, 108
Howells, Geraint 33–4, 37, 52, 55, 57, 159
Hughes, Simon 23, 151, 164, 166, 319
    adoption as parliamentary candidate meeting story 129
    and Green Party 56
    and Gulf War 108
    and Maastricht Treaty 198–9
    and name debate 57, 62
Hume, John 240–1, 480
Hume–Adams initiative 240
Humphrys, John 403
hung Parliament issue 81, 107, 110, 120, 121–2, 123, 125, 129–31, 146, 448, 529, 539
Hunt, David 80, 81, 230
Hunter, Anji 276, 308
Hurd, Douglas 100, 181, 225, 231, 254, 266
Hussein, King of Jordan 350–1
Hussey, Marmaduke 20
Hussey, Susan 20
Hutcheson, Ian 145
Hutchinson, Juliet 9

immigration 537
Independent 6, 27, 50, 137, 163, 198, 268, 318, 328, 431, 467, 526, 531
Institute for Public Research (IPPR) 7
International Parliamentary Union 65
IRA 356
Iraq see Gulf War
Irvine, Derry 310, 313, 408–9
Israel 435
Izetbegovic, President 177, 181, 244, 271, 302, 317

Jackson, Gerald Vernon 321
Jacobovits, Lady 106
Jacobs, Anthony 63
Jacobs, Paul 24
Jefferies, Greg and Lesley 7, 454, 455, 549
Jenkins, Roy 27, 30, 88, 129–30, 169, 252, 395–6, 558
    and Blair 278, 346, 360, 366, 379–80, 424, 439–40, 459, 477, 508, 553
    Gladstone 345, 409, 419
    flat 129
    and Lib/Lab co-operation issue 509–10
    and Maastricht Treaty 199
    and name debate 62, 64
    and Owen 60–1

view on hung Parliament
contingencies 129–30
view of Shadow Cabinet members
(Labour) 440
Jenkins, Simon 202
Jessel, Toby 296
Jo Group 278, 288, 307, 345, 386, 404,
415, 448, 473, 513
Johnston, Russell 27, 54, 55, 161, 175,
181, 186, 188, 225
Johnstone, Ian 170
joint open selection see JOS
Jones, Nigel 447
Jones, Peter 209
JOS (joint open selection) 29, 30, 34–5
Joseph Rowntree Reform Trust 471
Joyce, Aunt 171–2

Kadic, Rasim 327
Karadzic, Radovan 181, 182, 184, 185,
186, 188, 232
Kasagic, Rajo 233–4
Kaufman, Gerald 107
Keetch, Paul 547–8
Keletsky, Anatole 547
Kellaway, Alex 264
Kellner, Peter 499
Kennedy, Charles 6, 27, 28, 32, 39, 60,
66, 129, 163, 198, 265, 276, 430
on abandoning equidistance 319
and Maastricht Treaty 199
and name issue 60
skill as a debater 32
speech at (1992) Party Conference
193
Kennedy, John 182, 232, 233
Kent, Duchess of 121
Kettle, Martin 351–2
KGB 125
Kilbrandon Commission 353
Kincardine & Deeside by-election
(1991) 123

King, Anthony 218–19
King, Tom 17, 112, 116, 230–1
Kinnock, Glenys 150
Kinnock, Neil 17, 18, 24, 40, 81, 98, 99,
115, 130, 145, 162, 529
and Gulf War 108
loses election 158
and Maastricht Treaty 168
and pact with Liberal Democrats 23
and press 100
singing voice 116
and Soviet Union 136–7
view of by Smith 107, 196–7
Kirkwood, Archy 16, 34, 37, 45, 52, 54,
86, 195, 225, 288, 290, 320, 372,
416, 495–7
Kissinger, Henry 43
Koenigswinter Conference (1990) 83–4
Kohl, Helmut 83, 84
Kolyevic, Nikolai 183, 209
Kosovo 223
Kozyrev, Andrei 283
Kuwait Policy Group 101

Labour Party
co-operation with Liberal
Democrats see Lib/Lab co-
operation
Glamorgan by-election success 40
leadership election 159
and Maastricht Treaty 197, 201–2
pact with Liberal Democrats 23
see also Blair, Tony
La Bohème 86
Lamont, Norman 25, 147, 227
Land, Tony 238
Lang, Ian 152
Langborough by-election (1991) 123
Lansbury, George 92
Lawley, Sue 156
Laws, David 514
Lawson, Nigel 69–70

Le Bretton Bill 194, 318
Leaman, Alan 9, 15, 31, 53, 65, 98, 134,
 162, 258, 288, 343
Lester, Anthony 219–20, 221, 228, 284,
 285, 289
Lester, Katya 228
Lewington, Charles 136
Lib/Lab co-operation 123, 531
 and Blair/Ashdown discussions 221,
  228–9, 242–4, 275–8, 280, 283–4,
  286–9, 310–14, 323, 324–6,
  336–7, 341, 351–7, 383–8,
  410–11, 413, 414–15, 421, 424–9,
  436–8, 441–2, 449–54, 456–9,
  470–1, 474–5, 481–4, 500–3,
  505–12, 515–29, 532–6, 555–6,
  559–60
 and proportional representation
  issue 278, 312–13, 336, 344, 353,
  356–7, 379, 386–7, 411–12,
  437–8, 469, 479, 481–3, 501, 506,
  507, 511–12, 515–18, 520–2, 525,
  526–8, 532, 534–5, 601
 areas worked together 287–8, 427–8
 Ashdown's policy and aims 7, 34–5,
  160, 161, 226–7, 283–4, 344–5,
  345–6, 471–2
 and Bridge speech 379, 382–3, 386
 Brown's view of 385, 428, 436, 450,
  484, 485–8
 colleagues carrying out
  departmental responsibilities if
  partnership Parliament 131
 and Cook/Maclennan talks/
  commission/report 313–14, 325,
  347, 353, 358, 359, 404, 421, 438,
  444, 448–9, 451, 468, 470, 471,
  472, 477–8, 481, 482, 506, 510,
  512–13, 516, 520–1, 522, 530, 532,
  533, 534, 536–7
 and General Election 552–3, 555–6,
  558

 and Jenkins 509–10
 and local government 311, 359
 opinion polls on 470–1, 474, 499
 and Partnership Agreement 495, 496,
  502, 513, 605–12
 Partnership Politics paper 599–602
 reaction to by colleagues and
  councillors 295–6, 343–5, 446–7,
  467–9, 479, 489–90, 495–8
 Shadow Cabinet's view of 436–7
 Smith on 171, 172, 196–7, 243, 258
 view of by Scottish Lib Dems 294–5
Liberal Democrats
 and Conservative Party 123, 145,
  279, 307
 co-operation with Labour Party see
  Lib/Lab co-operation
 deep divisions within 39
 finances 253–4, 328
 financial problems 8, 14–15, 16, 44,
  59, 60, 62, 63
 and Green Party 50, 51
 logo 86
 low morale 37, 39, 50, 51
 membership 328
 name debate 11–12, 13, 32, 33–4,
  41, 51, 52, 53, 54–5, 56, 57, 59, 60,
  62–4, 68
 and opinion polls 57, 68, 73, 167,
  228, 256, 366, 478, 499, 509
 organization of 7
 pact with Labour Party 23
 and press 40, 64
 and SDP 29, 30, 31, 33, 35, 38, 58–9,
  60–1
Liddle, Roger 170, 171, 295, 364, 409
Lidija (interpreter) 179
Lindley, Clive 45, 67
Lithgow, Adrian 367
Littleborough & Saddleworth by-
  election (195) 322–3, 325–6, 327,
  334–5, 336–7

Livsey, Richard 30, 52, 54, 55, 62
Lloyd George, David 456
lobby system 136
local elections
    (1989) 37, 39–40
    (1990) 82, 86
    (1991) 114–15
    (1992) 163
    (1993) 222, 225–6
    (1994) 253
    (1995) 314
    (1996) 423, 424, 425
Lockerbie air crash (1988) 20
Lorin, Jocelyne 419
Luff, Caroline 170
Luff, Peter 170
Lyell, Nicholas 402
Lynne, Liz 11, 164, 166, 167, 194, 195,
    224, 319, 504

MI6 218
Maastricht Treaty
    Ashdown's position over 173, 197,
        198–200, 225, 229
    Danes' 'no' vote 167, 168
    and Labour Party 197
    and Major 168, 173–4, 200, 202–3,
        220, 230
    and press 202
    rebellion within Tory Party 220
    and Social Chapter 220–1, 225,
        229–30
    vote on paving bill 200–2
McCarthy, Donnachadh 536
McColl, Colin 218
McDonald, Angus 215
Macedonia 223
McGivan, Alec 25, 72
Macintyre, Don 135, 172
MacKenzie, Kelvin 173
Mackenzie, Major General Lewis 176
McKie, Dave 31–2

Maclennan, Robert 6, 11, 100, 130,
    148, 347, 515
    criticism of Des Wilson 117
    and Lib/Lab co-operation issue
        161–2, 295–6
    and name debate 62
    and Owen 60, 61
    talks/commission/report with Cook
        313–14, 325, 347, 353, 358, 359,
        404, 421, 438, 444, 448–9, 451,
        468, 470, 472, 477–8, 481, 482,
        506, 510, 512–13, 516, 520–1, 522,
        530, 532, 533, 534, 536–7
    trip to Hong Kong 46, 47, 48
    work on hung Parliament
        contingencies 110
McNally, Tom 2, 9, 25, 31, 44–5, 66,
    199, 272, 273, 288, 307, 488–9
    memo on hung Parliament 539,
        613–18
McNamara, Kevin 131
Maddock, Diana 231, 318
Maginnis, Ken 406
Mail On Sunday 56, 174, 367, 466
Major, John 65, 100, 115, 165, 266,
    348, 384, 499
    and Al Fayed 293
    Ashdown's view of 106, 162, 173,
        258
    and Blair 348, 551
    and Bosnia 124, 222–4, 249, 321–2,
        338
    and BSE crisis 417–18, 430–1, 433
    depressed 439
    and devolution 257
    discussions and meetings with
        Ashdown 256–8, 309
    and goldfish story 338–9, 340
    and Gulf War 108, 109–10, 111, 112
    and immigration 537
    and Lamont's resignation speech 227
    and leadership election (1995) 327

Major, John – *cont*
  and Maastricht Treaty 168, 173–4,
    200, 202–3, 220, 230
  and monetary union 348
  and Murdoch 279
  and Northern Ireland 309
  and Queen 480
  at Rabin's funeral 350
  relationship with Ashdown 140, 231
  and Sarajevo 203, 229
Major, Norma 106, 430
'Making Change Our Ally' (pamphlet)
  277
Malaysia, King of 241
Mandela, Nelson
  first state visit to Britain (1996)
    444–6
  release of (1990) 78
Mandelson, Peter 170, 171, 267–8, 288,
    304, 308, 323, 422, 429–30, 489,
    515, 517–18
  The Blair Revolution 409
Manjaca prison camp (Yugoslavia)
  188–90, 360–1
'Map on the Menu' 315–16, 337
Marquand, David 38
Marr, Andrew 162–3, 318, 439, 441,
    453, 467, 526
  Ruling Britannia 409
Marron, Sallyann 268, 269, 270
Marsh Arabs 369
Marshall, Penny 190, 191
Martin, Pat 362
Mason, Chris 362, 363, 366, 367, 380,
    388, 391, 394, 398, 399
Mawhinney, Brian 440
Meacher, Michael 24, 243, 308
Mellor, David 173
Messiah, The 85
MI5 124–5
Michie, Ray 135, 159
Midgely, Jim 380

Miller, Fiona 255, 256
Milliband, David 288
Milligan, Stephen 253, 255
Milosevic, Slobodan 183, 317
minimum wage 278, 281
Mitchell, Andrew 162
Mitchell, Austin 81
Mitterrand, François 263–4
Mladic, Ratko 185, 234
Moberly, John 101
Molyneaux, Jim 91
Moncrieff, Chris 404
monetary union *see* European
  monetary union
Monktonhall Colliery 215–18
Montgomery, David 94, 95, 301,
    513–14
Moore, Charles, 202
Moore, Sir Jeremy 101
Morris, Michael 406
Mosey, Roger 374
Mowlam, Mo 258, 279
Mubarak, President Hosni Said 120,
    121
Mull of Kintyre helicopter disaster
  memorial service 279–80
Murdoch, Rupert 94–5, 202, 279, 301

Nakas, Dr 245–6
name debate 11–12, 13, 32, 33–4, 41,
    51, 52, 53, 54–5, 56, 57, 59, 60,
    62–4, 68
'named organizations'
  in party constitution debate 58
National Health Service *see* NHS
NATO 58, 66–7, 254, 303
Neil, Andrew 94, 95, 144
'NERDS' 166, 259
New Agenda debate 193
Newbury by-election (1993) 219, 222,
    225–6
Newby, Dick 45, 262

Newham North-East by-election
   (1994) 264
News International 94
News of the World 132, 133, 134, 135,
   136, 137, 139, 155, 391, 392, 393,
   400
Newsnight 10, 14, 29, 63, 66, 80, 86,
   98, 109, 141, 261, 291, 335, 539,
   541, 543
News Statesman 448–9
Newton, Polly 547
Newton, Tony 24
NFU (National Farmers' Union) 416,
   417
NHS (National Health Service)
   review 25–6
Nicholson, Emma
   defection from Conservative Party
      364–5, 366–7, 367–72, 373,
      374–6, 379
   letter to Major telling him of her
      departure from Conservative
      Party 598
Nolan Committee 294, 309
North Korea 266
Northern Ireland 16–17, 240–1, 309,
   355–6, 356, 439, 480
nuclear weapons 37, 43

Oakley, Robin 155, 375
Observer 56, 57, 284, 293, 499, 531–2,
   533, 553
O'Connell, Daniel 367
O'Driscoll, Cornelius Martin 239–40
O'Kane, Maggie 182, 186
O'Malley, Des 88
Omarska prison camp 189, 190, 191
OMOV (One Member One Vote) 239
On The Record 30, 45, 57, 156, 167,
   169
Opik, Lembit 536–7, 548
Owen, David 17, 252

and Bosnia 241–2, 246, 249, 283, 303
   discussions with Ashdown 34–6,
      60–2
   and folding of SDP 44, 88
   and JOS proposals 34–5
   and Labour Party 41
   and SDP Conference (1988) 8, 10
   and SDP's relationship with Liberal
      Democrats 29, 30, 31, 33, 35, 60–1
   working with Kinnock suggestion 40
Owen, Debbie 283
Owen, Matthew 356

Paisley by-election (1990) 99
Paisley, Ian 262
Palmer, Monro 5
Parker-Bowles, Camilla 351
Parkinson, Cecil 42, 43
Partnership Agreement 495, 496, 502,
   513, 605–12
Party Conferences
   (1988) 8, 12–14
   (1989) 32, 66–9
   (1992) 172, 192–6
   (1994) 281–2
   (1995) 341–2
   (1996) 460, 461–2
Party Political Broadcasts 8, 14, 55
Patten, Chris 65, 66, 130, 158
Paxman, Jeremy 539
Payne, Mark 24, 29, 79, 87, 109, 134,
   140, 160, 548
Pearce, Barbara 24
Perez, Shimon 351
Philip, Prince 18, 241, 480
Phillips, Andrew 132, 133–5, 147, 218,
   227, 256, 391, 392, 404
Phillips, Jo 276
Phillips, Penelope 218
Pienaar, John 373
Pimlott, Ben 38
Plant Commission 153, 313

Poll Tax
    demonstrations against 79–81
Pontypridd by-election (1989) 28
Porritt, Jonathon 38, 53
Portillo, Michael 407, 557
position papers 77
    (1990) 82, 565–7
    (1991) 568–70
    (1992) 570–8
    (1993) 579–81
    (1994) 582–4
    (1995) 304, 585–9
Powell, Charles 109
Powell, Jonathan 276, 409, 416, 531
Prescott, John 261, 288, 354, 384, 385,
    388, 415, 437
Preston, Peter 31–2, 101, 285, 289,
    291
Price, Fred 270
Primary Purpose Rule 537
Privacy Bill 348
Privy Council 25, 26
'Programme for Britain, A' 38
proportional representation (PR)
    560–1
    and Blair 276, 278, 313, 336, 346,
        347, 354, 357–8, 360, 366, 379,
        380, 384, 386–7, 401, 412, 421,
        424, 449, 450–1, 453, 482, 500–1,
        503, 504, 507–8, 511, 515, 521–2,
        527–8
    and Brown 436, 488
    and Europe 520, 522, 527, 530
    importance of to Lib/Lab co-
        operation issue 278, 312–13, 336,
        344, 353, 356–7, 379, 386–7,
        411–12, 437–8, 469, 479, 481–3,
        501, 506, 507, 511–12, 515–18,
        520–2, 525, 526–8, 532, 534–5,
        601
    and Kinnock 153, 156
    and Major 153, 173–4

and referendum 276, 382, 437
    and Smith 196

Queen Mother 91, 348
Queen's Speech (1992) 162–3
Question Time 14, 24, 50, 420

Rabin, Yitzhak 347
    funeral 349–51
Radley, Steve 390, 418
Raikes, Myles and Joan 19, 556
Rapid Reaction Force 327
Rathbone, Major 264
Rawnsley, Andrew 284
Razzall, Tim 18, 117, 448
Referendum Party 544, 557
Regan, Bob 204
Reinventing Government 244
Remembrance Sunday (1988) 17–18
Rendel, David 219, 226, 318, 462
Rennard, Chris 63, 92–3, 94, 171, 231,
    396
Renton, Tim 230
Ribble Valley by-election (1991) 113,
    114
Richmond by-election (1989) 18, 23,
    24, 26, 28–9, 32
Riddell, Peter 150, 267, 352, 376
Ridgeway, Rosanne 43
Rifkind, Malcolm 242, 322, 328
Robertson, George 231, 441, 442
Rodgers, Bill 169, 272, 446
Rogaly, Joe 172
Rooker, Geoff 122
Roper, John 18
Rose, General Sir Michael 255, 272,
    283, 302, 303, 333
Ross, Robin 315
Rowe, Tina 395
Rowland, Tiny 284, 285
Royal Commissions 427
Runcie, Archbishop Robert 106

Russell, Conrad 169
Ryder, Richard 173, 296

Sacks, Jonathan 347, 348, 349, 351
Saddam Hussein 110, 112
Sainsbury, David 33, 34, 35
St Paul's Cathedral 317
Salkic, Hasib 327, 329–33
Sarajevo 181, 203, 229, 234, 251, 254,
    255, 327
  Ashdown's trip (1992) 175–8, 181,
    184–91, 206–11
  Ashdown's trip (1993) 235, 237–8,
    244–6
  Ashdown's trip (1994) 269–72
  Ashdown's trip (1995) 301–4, 327,
    328, 330–4
  tunnel 302, 331–2
Savill, Annika 147
Scotland 353, 441–2, 449–50
Scotsman 139
Scott Report 257, 402, 403, 405
Scottish convention 119, 122, 353
SDP 7, 41, 87
  Conference (1988) 8, 10
  folding of 44, 87, 88
  and local council elections (1989) 40
  and Pontypridd by-election 28
  problems 41
  relations with Liberal Democrats 29,
    30, 31, 33, 35, 38, 58–9, 60–1
  and Richmond by-election 24, 26,
    28
  see also Owen, David
Seear, Nancy 32, 193
Serbs 183, 206–7, 209, 211, 223, 232,
    234, 254, 283, 302, 322
Sergeant, John 282
She magazine 255, 256
She Stoops to Conquer 250
Sherwell, Alan 172, 193–4
Short, Clare 100

Silajdzic, Haris 271, 303–4, 306, 334
Simple Truth concert (1991) 116
Sinden, Donald 250
single currency 354, 406–7
Single Transferable Vote see STV
Sinn Fein
  banning from access to BBC 15
SIS (Special Intelligence Service) 146,
    402–3
Sissons, Peter 168
Sissons, Sylvia 168
Skidelsky, Professor Robert 38
Skinner, Dennis 53, 168, 293
Slade, Adrian 66
Smith, Chris 427
Smith, Cyril 358, 536
Smith, Elizabeth 263, 267
Smith, Harriet 9, 12
Smith, John 42, 159, 165, 227–8, 239,
    241, 259–60
  Ashdown's view of 107
  death 260–1
  funeral and memorial service 262–3,
    267
  on Lib/Lab co-operation 171, 172,
    196–7, 243, 258
  and Maastricht Treaty 197, 200, 230
  relationship with Ashdown 197
  view of Kinnock 107, 196–7
Smith, General Sir Rupert 333
Smith, Tim 285, 289
Snow, Peter 265
Soames, Nicholas 280
Social Chapter 220–1, 225, 229–30
Soley, Clive 80–1
Sommer, Teo 43
South Africa 78
South, Nick 204, 232, 288, 289, 464,
    467, 468, 538
Soviet Union 43, 255
  see also Gorbachev, Mikhail
Spalding, Alastair 542

Speakman, Nick 138, 157, 551
Special Intelligence Service *see* SIS
Spectator 99
Srebrenica 254
Steel, David 12, 27, 28, 53, 61, 88, 108,
    115, 123, 261, 514
    defeated on defence policy in 1986
        Party Conference 194
    and Gulf War 111
    and hung Parliament contingencies
        131
    leaving politics 267
    and Lib/Lab co-operation issue 344,
        469, 490
    and name debate 53
    and Wilson 118
Stephen, David 123, 130, 145
Stephen, Nicol 158, 462
Stewart, Colonel Bob 205, 206
Stewart, Ian 25
Stothard, Peter 547
Straw, Jack 243, 255, 313, 381–2, 385,
    422, 434, 440, 559
Stunell, Andrew 194, 318
STV (Single Transferable Vote) 353,
    370, 381, 411, 482, 483
Suarez, Mario 224
Sun 154, 362, 363, 380, 393, 541
Sunday Correspondent 95
Sunday Express 174–5, 249, 250–2, 474
Sunday Mirror 392
Sunday People 267
Sunday Telegraph 56, 466
Sunday Times 94, 122–3, 135–6, 137,
    149–50, 166, 317, 318, 391, 392,
    393, 473, 544
Sutherland, Peter 43

Tang, Mark and Heidi 48
Tatton by-election (1997) 540, 541, 542
Taverne, Dick 31
taxation issue 312, 354, 358, 486, 502

Taylor, Ann 480
Taylor, Matthew 27, 56, 62, 86, 161–2
Tebbit, Norman 86
Teverson, Robin 265
Thatcher, Margaret 18, 37, 82, 83, 106,
    115, 439
    appearance 72, 93, 430
    Ashdown's view of 71, 91, 121
    and Europe 43, 73
    handshake 16
    and Hong Kong passport issue 49,
        53
    and Howe's resignation speech 96
    and leadership contest (1990) 96–7,
        98
    resignation 99
    speech at Koenigswinter Conference
        83–4
Theurel, Marie 455
Theurel, Sebastien 85, 393, 455, 549
Thomas, Maureen 547
Thomas, Susan 196
Thompson, Major-General Julian 101
Thurnham, Peter
    defection of from Tories 343, 347,
        363, 366, 368, 379, 380, 388, 389,
        396, 404, 464–7
    letter to Major resigning
        Conservative Whip 603–4
Tiananmen Square massacre (1989)
    45–6, 47
Tickell, Sir Crispin 252
The Times 10, 41, 155, 267, 272, 375,
    403, 431, 519, 547
Today (newspaper) 94
Today (programme) 11, 13, 31, 40,
    121, 163, 372, 373, 376, 390, 403,
    500, 538, 558
Tower Hamlets 382
Trefgarne, Lord 25
Trimble, David 355, 405, 406, 407, 425,
    439, 476, 480

Trimmingham, Karina 253
Tudjman, Franjo 315–17, 334, 337, 338
Turnbull, Andrew 123
TV AM 12, 13, 121
Tyler, Paul 290–1, 317, 367, 469, 545

unemployment 288
Unionists 425
United Nations 305
United States 43, 223, 254
UNPROFOR 185, 270

Vale of Glamorgan by-election *see*
    Glamorgan by-election
VAT
    on fuel 296–7
Vauxhall by-election (1989) 50
VE Day thanksgiving service 317
Vigar, David 245, 256
VJ Day parade 338
Vye, Becky 260–1

Waddington, David 85
Wade, Virginia 170
Wakeham, John 25, 26
Waldegrave, Caroline 82
Waldegrave, William 402, 403
Walden 156
Walden, Brian 156
Wales, Prince of *see* Charles, Prince
Wales, Princess of *see* Diana, Princess
    of Wales
Walker, Sir Patrick 124–5
Wallace, Jim 6, 10, 18, 27, 37, 52, 55,
    99, 111, 162, 442, 468
Wallace, William 9, 119
Warsaw Pact 43
Watson, Graham 265
Weatherall, Jack 161
Weatherill, Bernard 91
Week in Politics, A 317
Weinstock, Arnie 279

Weizman, President 349, 351
welfare issue 427, 498, 606–7, 611
Welsh Grand Committee 37
West Lothian question 353
Western Daily Press 394, 395, 396, 398,
    400
Western Morning News 374–5
Wheeler, Sir John 480
Whitmore, Keith 490
Whittam Smith, Andreas 163
Williams, Shirley 13, 27, 71, 88, 199,
    446, 462, 554
Williamson, David 78
Wilson, Brian 100
Wilson, Des 5, 25, 31, 89, 135, 154
    book 165
    criticism of by Party 117, 118
    as General Election manager 72, 77,
        79, 89–90, 105, 117, 118, 129, 148,
        151, 156
    relationship with Ashdown 5, 95,
        105, 118
Wilson, Harold 252
Wilson, Mary 18
Wintour, Patrick 30
Wolseley *see* Thurnham, Peter
Worcester, Bob 89, 478–9
World At One, The 8, 554
World This Weekend, The 12, 30
World Tonight, The 153
Worsthorne, Sir Peregrine 202
Wrigglesworth, Ian 5, 9, 25, 30, 54
Wright, Ian 87, 548
Wyatt, Woodrow 279

Yeltsin, Boris 121, 283
Yeovil
    attacks against ethnic restaurants
        361–2
York, Duchess of 121
Young, Hugo 363, 405
Younger, George 36

Yugoslavia 117, 124, 172, 315–16
  Ashdown's trips (1992) 175–80, 181,
    182–92, 204–11
  Ashdown's trip (1993) 231–8

Ashdown's trip (1994) 268–72
Ashdown's trips (1995) 301–4, 327,
  328, 330–4
see also Bosnia; Sarajevo